Street by Stree

C000283333

HERTFORDSHIRE

Enlarged areas HARLOW, HEMEL HEMPSTEAD, LUTON, ST ALBANS, STEVENAGE, WATFORD

Plus Amersham, Barnet, Bishop's Stortford, Chalfont St Peter, Chesham, Dunstable, Hertford, Hitchin, Stanmore, Stansted Airport, Waltham Abbey

3rd edition September 2008
© Automobile Association Developments Limited 2008

Original edition printed May 2001

 This product includes map data licensed from Ordnance Survey® with the permission of the Controller of Her Majesty's Stationery Office. © Crown copyright 2008. All rights reserved. Licence number 100021153.

The copyright in all PAF is owned by Royal Mail Group plc.

 Information on fixed speed camera locations provided by RoadPilot © 2008 RoadPilot® Driving Technology.

Published by AA Publishing (a trading name of Automobile Association Developments Limited, whose registered office is Fanum House, Basing View, Basingstoke, Hampshire RG21 4EA. Registered number 1878835).

Produced by the Mapping Services Department of The Automobile Association. (A03730)

A CIP Catalogue record for this book is available from the British Library.

Printed by Oriental Press in Dubai

The contents of this atlas are believed to be correct at the time of the latest revision. However, the publishers cannot be held responsible or liable for any loss or damage occasioned to any person acting or refraining from action as a result of any use or reliance on any material in this atlas, nor for any errors, omissions or changes in such material. This does not affect your statutory rights. The publishers would welcome information to correct any errors or omissions and to keep this atlas up to date. Please write to Publishing, The Automobile Association, Fanum House (FH12), Basing View, Basingstoke, Hampshire, RG21 4EA. E-mail: streetbystreet@theaa.com

Ref: ML117y

Key to map pages	ii–iii
Key to map symbols	iv–1
Enlarged map pages	2–13
Main map pages	14–173
Index - towns & villages	174–176
Index - streets	176–210
Index - featured places	211–217
Acknowledgements	217

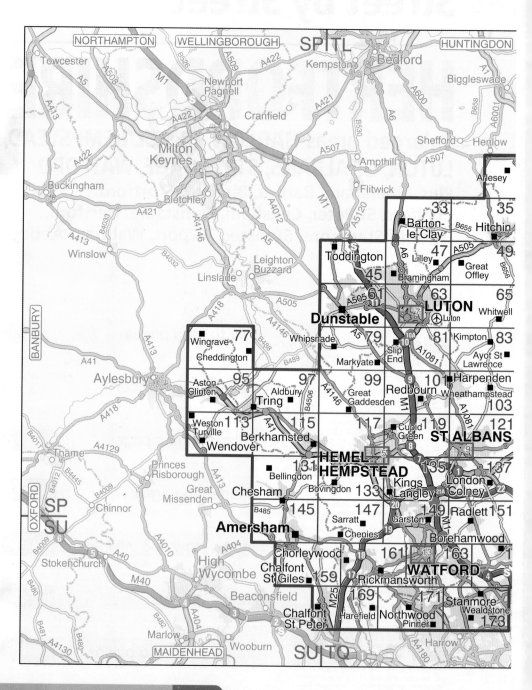

Street by Street

NORTHAMPTON WELLINGBOROUGH SPITL HUNTINGDON

Towcester
Kempston Bedford
Biggleswade

Newport
Pagnell
Cranfield
Shefford Henlow

Milton
Keynes
Ampthill
Arlesey

Buckingham
Bletchley
Flitwick
33   35
Barton-
le-Clay Hitchin

Winslow
Leighton
Buzzard
Toddington
Lilley 47   49
Great
Offley
45 Bramingham

BANBURY
Linslade
61 63   65
Dunstable LUTON Whitwell
Luton

Wingrave 77
Whipsnade 79 81 Kimpton 83
Cheddington
Aylesbury
Markyate Slip
End Ayot St
Lawrence

Aston
Clinton 95 97 99 101 Harpenden
Aldbury Great
Gaddesden Redbourn Wheathampstead
Tring 103

Weston
Turville 113 115 117 119 121
Berkhamsted Cupid
Green ST ALBANS
Wendover

Thame
HEMEL
HEMPSTEAD 131 135 137
Princes
Risborough Bellingdon London
Colney
Great
Missenden Chesham Bovingdon 133 Kings
Langley

OXFORD Chinnor 145 147 149 Radlett 151
SP Sarratt
SU Amersham Garston
Chenies Borehamwood

Stokenchurch Chorleywood 161 163
High
Wycombe Chalfont
St Giles 159 Rickmansworth WATFORD

Beaconsfield 169 171 Stanmore
Wealdstone
Chalfont
St Peter Harefield Northwood 173
Marlow Pinner
Wooburn Harrow
MAIDENHEAD SUTO

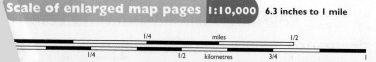

Scale of enlarged map pages 1:10,000 6.3 inches to 1 mile

1/4 miles 1/2
1/4 1/2 kilometres 3/4 1

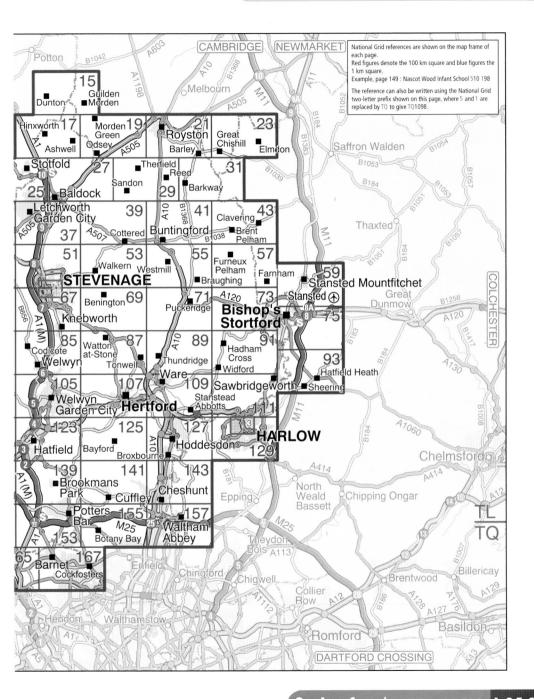

National Grid references are shown on the map frame of each page.
Red figures denote the 100 km square and blue figures the 1 km square.
Example, page 149 : Nascot Wood Infant School 510 198

The reference can also be written using the National Grid two-letter prefix shown on this page, where 5 and 1 are replaced by TQ to give TQ1098.

2.5 inches to 1 mile **Scale of main map pages** **1:25,000**

0   1/2   miles   1   1 1/2

0   1/2   kilometres   1   1 1/2   2

Junction 9 Motorway & junction

Motorway service area

Primary road single/dual carriageway

Primary road service area

A road single/dual carriageway

B road single/dual carriageway

Other road single/dual carriageway

Minor/private road, access may be restricted

One-way street

Pedestrian area

Track or footpath

Road under construction

Road tunnel

30 Speed camera site (fixed location) with speed limit in mph

V Speed camera site (fixed location) with variable speed limit

40 Section of road with two or more fixed camera sites; speed limit in mph or variable

50 → ← 50 Average speed (SPECS™) camera system with speed limit in mph

P Parking

P+ Park & Ride

Bus/coach station

Railway & main railway station

Railway & minor railway station

Underground station

Light railway & station

Preserved private railway

LC Level crossing

Tramway

Ferry route

Airport runway

County, administrative boundary

Mounds

17 Page continuation 1:25,000

3 Page continuation to enlarged scale 1:10,000

River/canal, lake, pier

Aqueduct, lock, weir

465
▲
Winter Hill
Peak (with height in metres)

Beach

Woodland

Park

Cemetery

Built-up area

Map Symbols

Industrial/business building		Abbey, cathedral or priory	
Leisure building		Castle	
Retail building		Historic house or building	
Other building		National Trust property (Wakehurst Place NT)	
City wall		Museum or art gallery	
Hospital with 24-hour A&E department		Roman antiquity	
Post Office		Ancient site, battlefield or monument	
Public library		Industrial interest	
Tourist Information Centre		Garden	
Seasonal Tourist Information Centre		Garden Centre, Garden Centre Association Member	
Petrol station, 24 hour, Major suppliers only		Garden Centre, Wyevale Garden Centre	
Church/chapel		Arboretum	
Public toilet, with facilities for the less able		Farm or animal centre	
Public house, AA recommended		Zoological or wildlife collection	
Restaurant, AA inspected		Bird collection	
Hotel, AA inspected (Madeira Hotel)		Nature reserve	
Theatre or performing arts centre		Aquarium	
Cinema		Visitor or heritage centre	
Golf course		Country park	
Camping, AA inspected		Cave	
Caravan site, AA inspected		Windmill	
Camping & caravan site, AA inspected		Distillery, brewery or vineyard	
Theme park		Other place of interest	

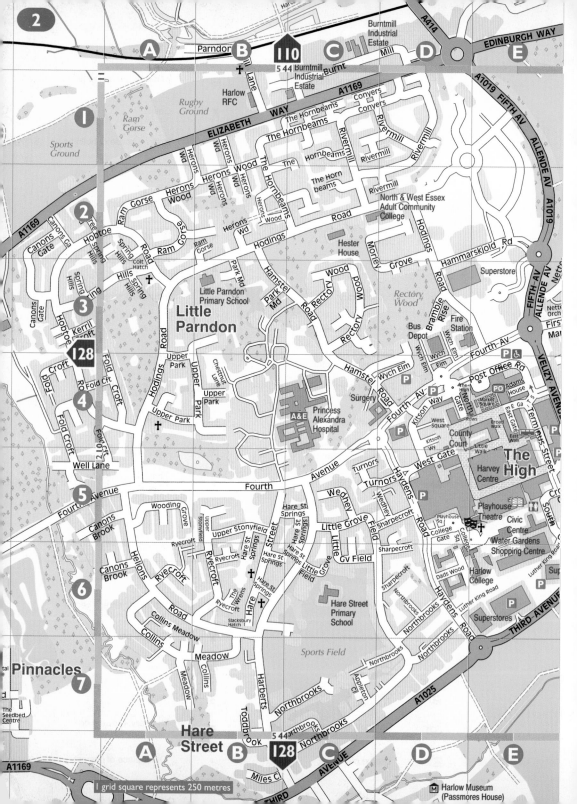

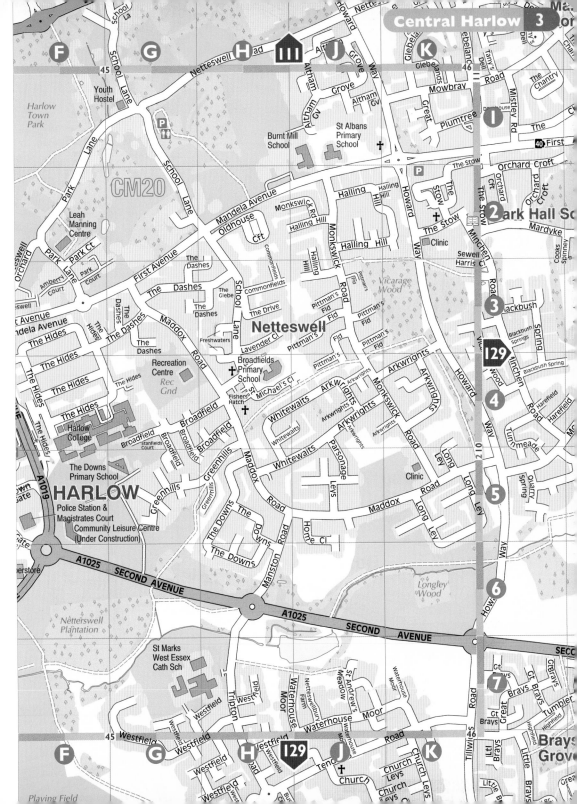

Ma.

F   G   H   J   K

45   School La   46

Netteswell

Netteswell Hd

Youth Hostel

School Lane

Harlow Town Park

CM20

Leah Manning Centre

Park Lane

Park Ct

Park Court

Ambery Court

First Avenue

Mandela Avenue

The Dashes

The Glebe

The Dashes

The Drive

Commonfields

Oldhouse Crft

Mandela Avenue

The Hides

The Dashes

Maddox Road

Recreation Centre

Rec Gnd

Freshwaters

Lavender Cl

Broadfields Primary School

Michael's Cl

Fishers Hatch

The Hides

Harlow College

Broadfield

Stanfields Court

Broadfield

Greenhills

The Downs Primary School

HARLOW

Police Station & Magistrates Court

Community Leisure Centre (Under Construction)

Greenhills

The Downs

The Downs

A1019

Town Gate

Gate

erstore

A1025 SECOND AVENUE

Netteswell Plantation

Maddox Road

Manston Road

Whitewaits

Whitewaits

Parsonage Leys

Home Cl

Maddox Road

Long Ley

A1025 SECOND AVENUE

Longley Wood

St Marks West Essex Cath Sch

Westfield

Westfield

Westfield

Tripton Road

Westfield

Westfield

Waterhouse Moor

Netteswellbury Farm

St Andrew's Meadow

Waterhouse Moor

Waterhouse Moor

Church Leys

Church

Church Leys

Church Leys

Burnt Mill School

St Albans Primary School

Mandela Avenue

Monkswick Rd

Halling Hill

Halling Hill

Halling Hill

Halling Hill

Monkswick Road

Halling Hill

Commonfields

Pittman's Fld

Pittman's Fld

Pittman's Fld

Pittman's Fld

Pittman's Fld

Pittman's Fld

Arkwrights

Arkwrights

Arkwrights

Arkwrights

Arkwrights

Monkswick Road

Clinic

Vicarage Wood

Altham Gv

Altham Grove

Grove

Altham Gv

Howard Way

Grove Way

Glebelands

Glebelands

The Stow

Howard Way

The Stow

The Stow

Clinic

Sewell Harris Cl

Howard Way

Long Ley

Long Ley

Mowbray

Great Plumtree

Great Plumtree

The Chantry

Mistley Rd

Denehouse

40 First

Orchard Croft

Orchard Crft

Orchard Croft

The Stow

2 ark Hall Sc

Mardyke

Cooks Spinney

Minchen Road

Victoria Wood

3 lackbush

I29

4

Blackbush Springs

Blackbush Spring

Harefield

Harefield

Tunmeade

Quarry Spring

5

Howard Way

6

Brays Grove

SECC

Gt Brays

Great Brays

Gt Brays

Gt Brays

Tumbler

Highfield

Ltl Brays

Little Brays

Tillwicks

Church Road

45   Westfield   46

Westfield

I29

Westfield

F   G   H   J   K

Playing Field

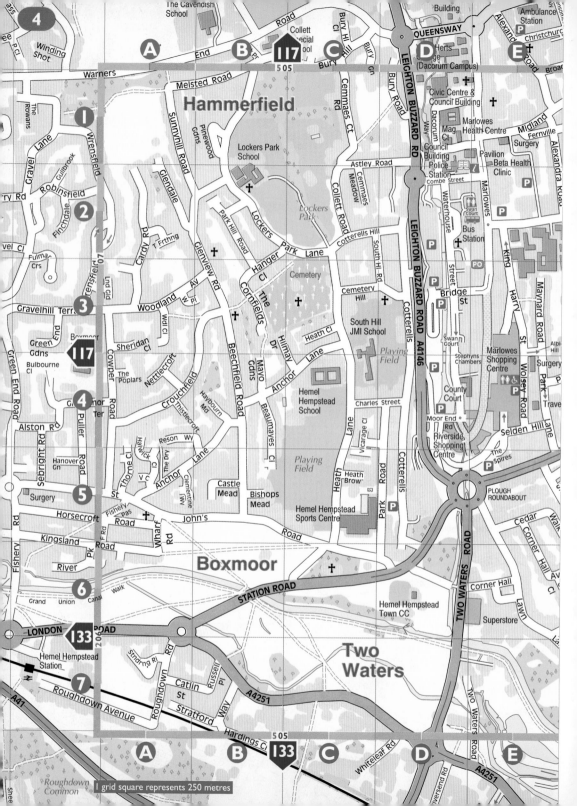

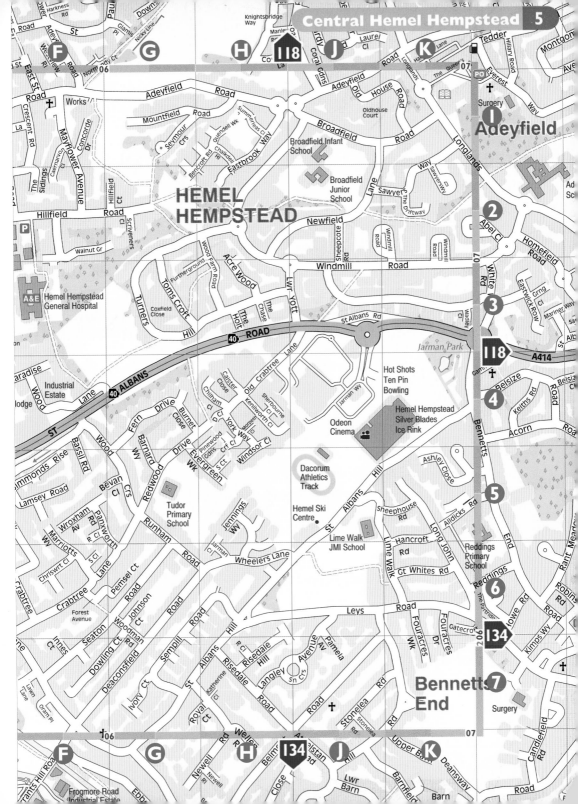

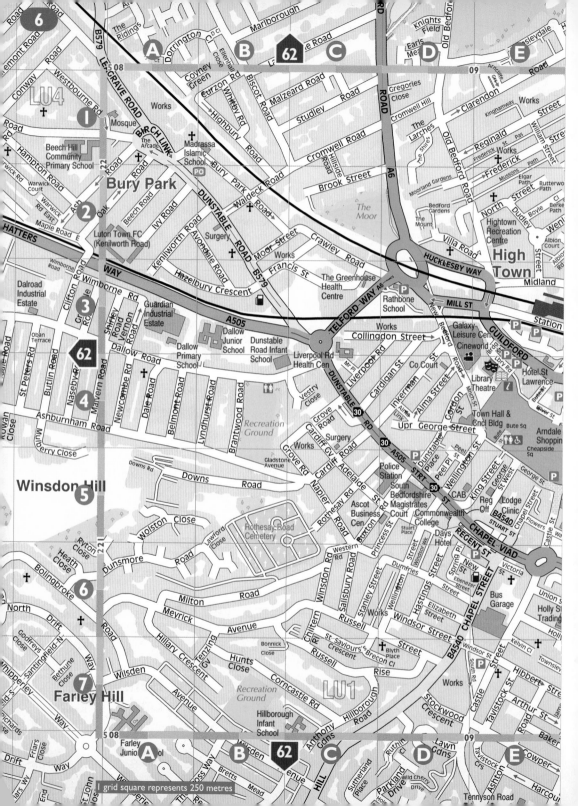

I grid square represents 250 metres

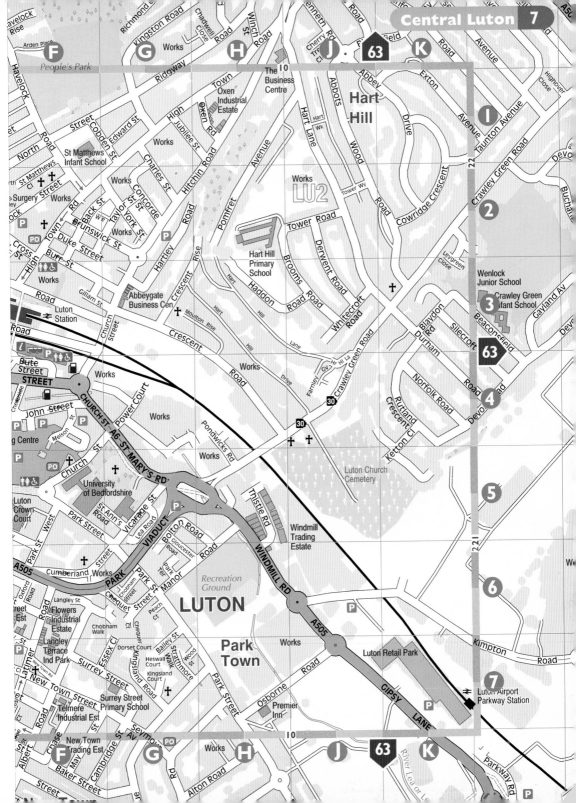

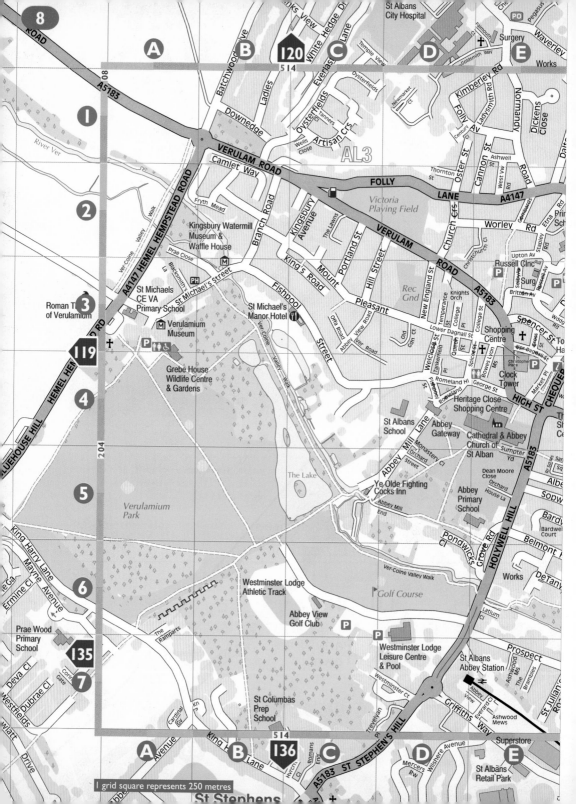

8
ROAD
A5183

A   B   120   C   D   E
              514

St Albans
City Hospital

PO

Pegasus

Che

Surgery
Waverley
Works

Normandy

Dickens
Close

I

River Ver

White Hedge Dr
Banks View
Ladies
Oysterfields

Temple view
Oysterfields
Tanners
Wells Close
Artisan Crs

Newmarket Ct.
Century

Goldsmith Way

Kimberley Rd
Ladysmith Rd
Folly Av

Oster St
Cannon St

Downedge

Everlast

AL3

Thornton
St

Ashwell
Road

VERULAM ROAD

FOLLY

Worley Rd
Prin
Sch

2

Camlet Way

Branch Road

Fryth Mead

Kingsbury Watermill
Museum &
Waffle House

Prae Close

M

Kingsbury Avenue

The Lawns

Portland St
Hill Street

LANE

A4147

Victoria
Playing Field

VERULAM

ROAD
A5183

Church Crs
ChristChurch

Erna St
Stapley
Rd

Worley
Rd

Upton Av
Russell Clnc
P
Surg

Britton Av

A4147 HEMEL HEMPSTEAD ROAD

Blacksmith's La

St Michael's Street

PH

St Michaels
CE VA
Primary School

King's Road

Mount
Pleasant

Rec
Gnd

New England St
Temperance
Lower Dagnall St

Knights
Orch

College Pl
College St

Spicer St
Queen

St

Shopping
Centre

Spencer St
Vpr Dagnall St

Market Pl

Tho
Hal

P

3

Roman T
of Verulamium

St Michael's
Manor Hotel

Offa Road

Abbey View Road
Old
Verr Road

Old
Gan Ct

Welclose St
Tankerfield

Bowes Lyon
Ms

Christopher
Place

Clock
Tower

119

Verulamium
Museum

P

Grebe House
Wildlife Centre
& Gardens

Fishpool Street

Ver-Colne

Valley Walk

Frederick
Romeland Hl
George St

Romeland

Heritage Close
Shopping Centre

HIGH ST

CHEQUER

4

HEMEL HEM   RD

204

St Albans
School

Abbey
Gateway

Abbey Mill Lane

Monastery Cl

Orchard
Street

Cathedral & Abbey
Church of
St Alban

Sumpter
Yd

Th
Sh
Ar

Dean Moore
Close

A5183

Albe

Sopw

Bardw

5

Verulamium
Park

The Lake

Abbey

Ye Olde Fighting
Cocks Inn

Abbey Mill
End

Abbey Primary
School

Orchard
House La

HOLYWELL HILL

Bardwell
Court

Belmont
DeTany

6

King Harry Lane
Mayne Avenue
Ermine Cl
le Ga

Ver-Coine Valley Walk

Golf Course

Westminster Lodge
Athletic Track

Abbey View
Golf Club

P

Pondwicks
Cl

Grove Rd

Latium

Works

7

Prae Wood
Primary
School

135

Deva Cl
Dubrae Cl
Nestfields

Corn
Gate

The Ramparts
Cardinal Gv

Kn

Westminster Lodge
Leisure Centre
& Pool

Westminster Ct.

St Columbas
Prep
School

P

St Albans
Abbey Station

Griffiths Way

Trevelyan

Prospect

Ashwood
Ms
The
Brambles

St Julians Rd

A   Avenue   B   136   C   St Stephen's Hill   D   E
King St   514   A5183   Superstore

Lane   Romans

Hrch
Cl

Mercers
Rw

Wilstone Avenue

St Albans
Retail Park

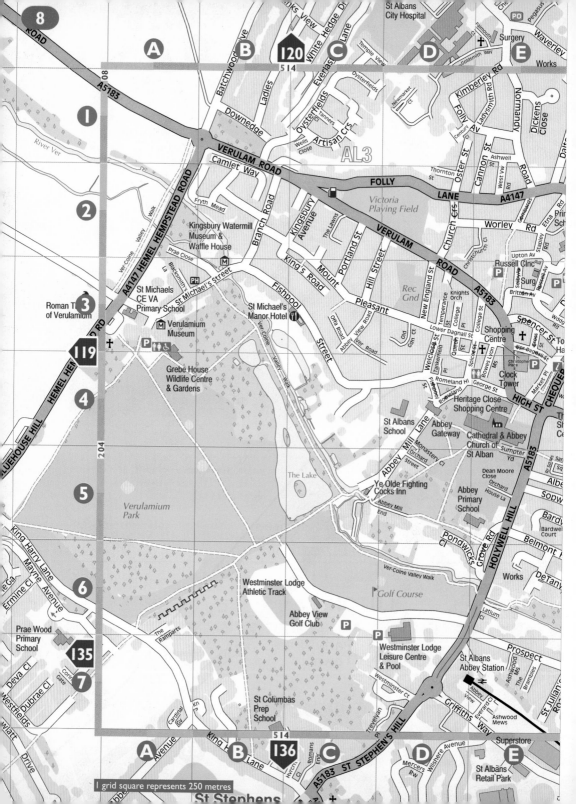

1 grid square represents 250 metres

St Stephens

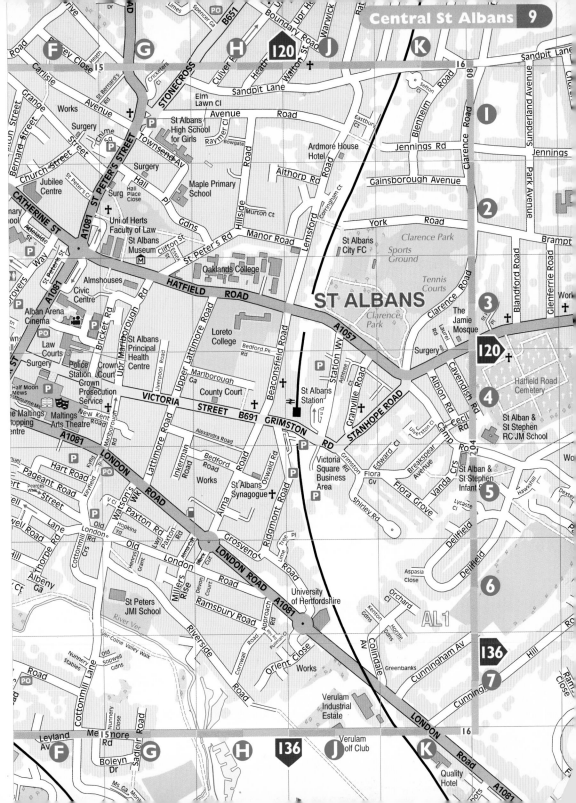

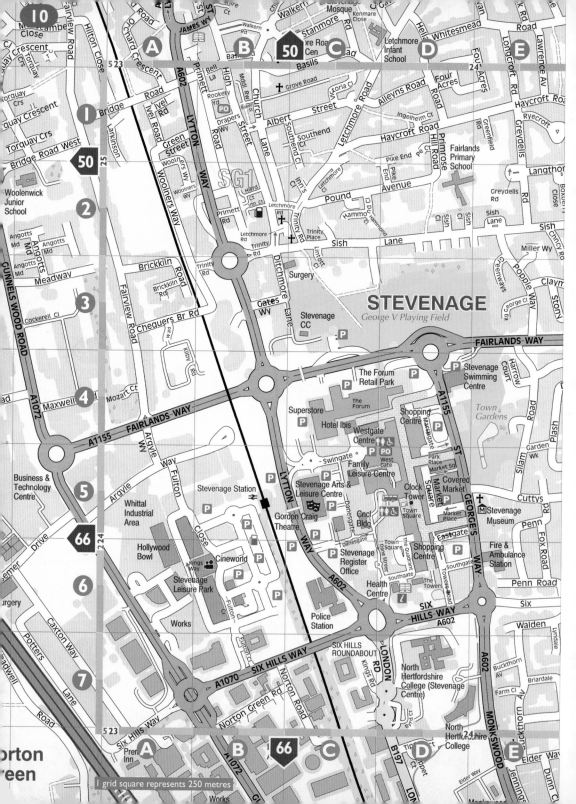

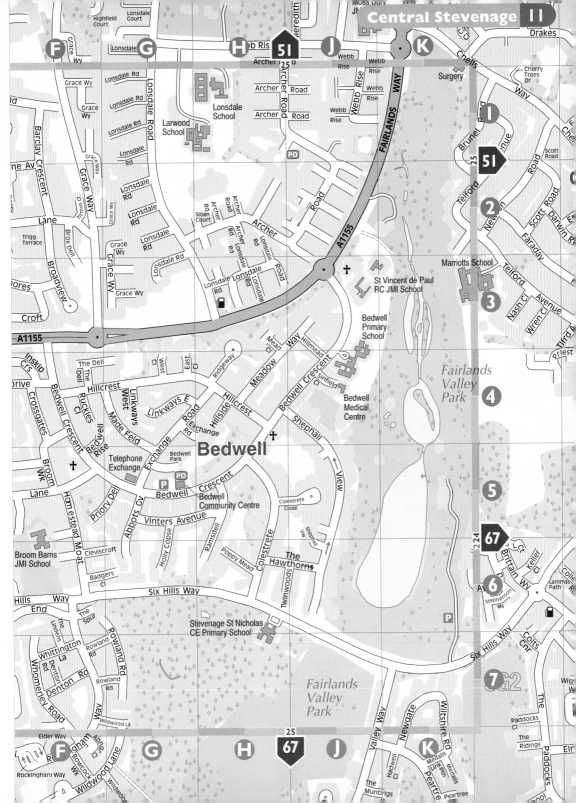

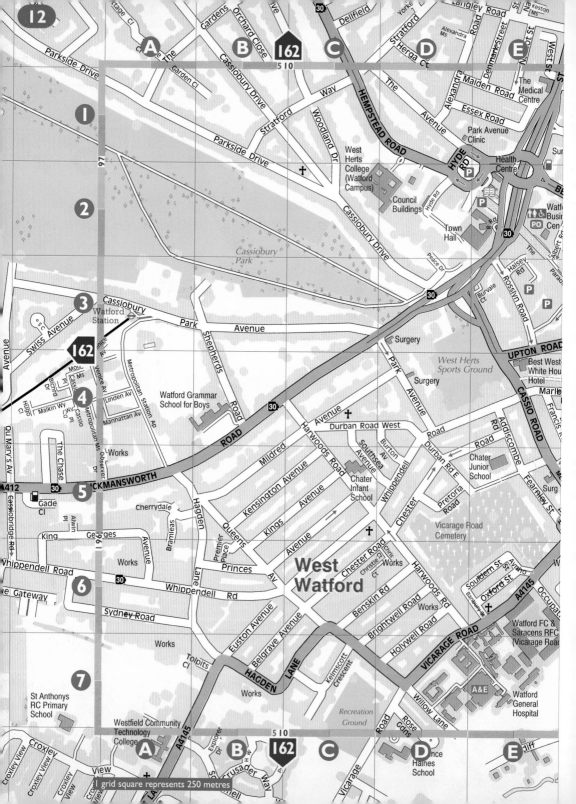

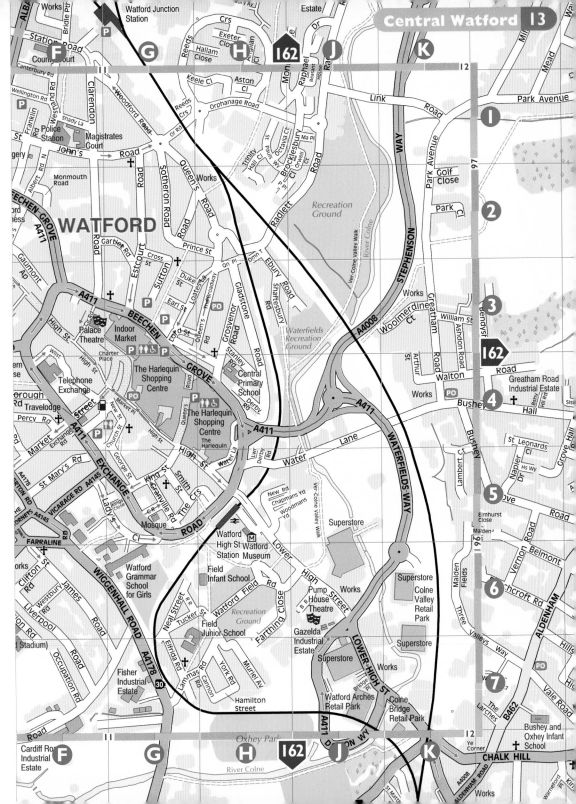

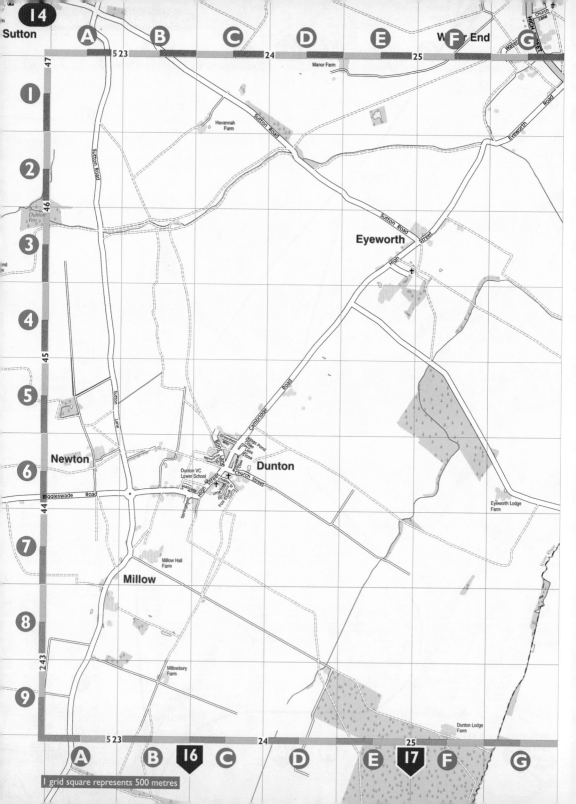

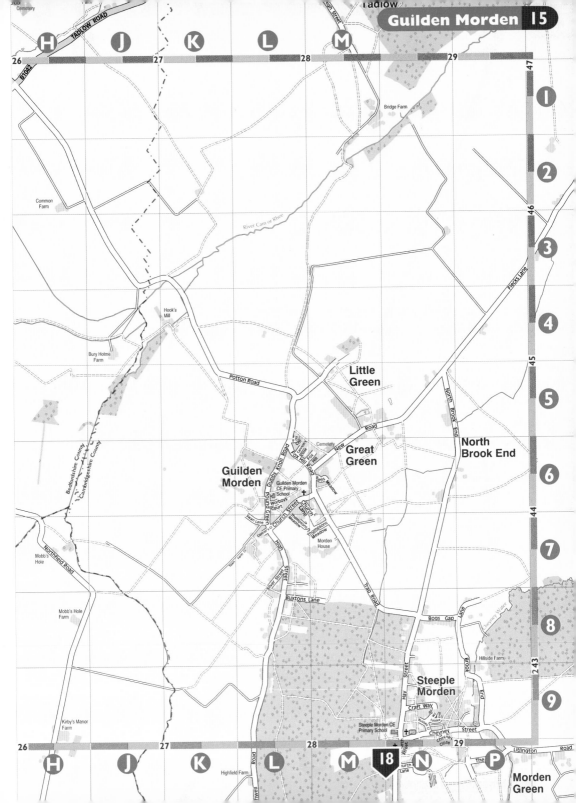

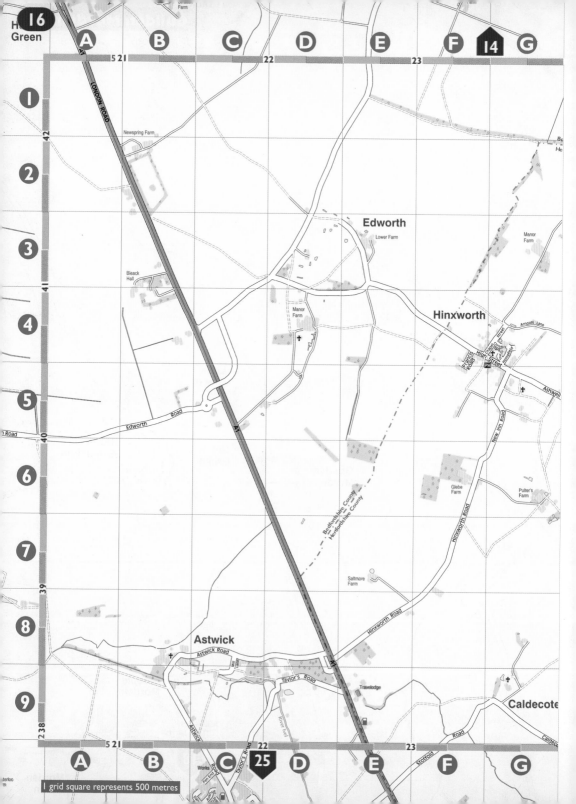

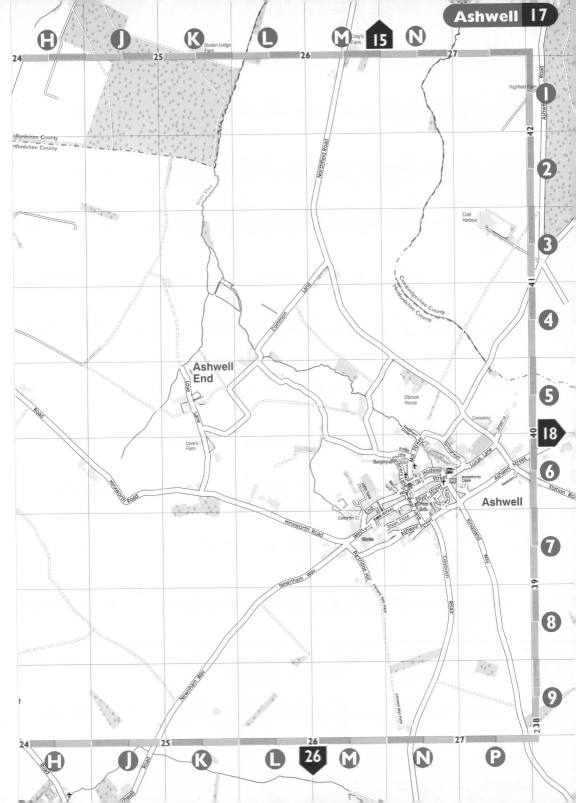

H **J** **K** **L** **M** **N**

15

24 25 26 27

Dunton Lodge
Farm

Highfield Farm

1

42

Bedfordshire County
Hertfordshire County

2

River Rhee

Cold
Harbour

3

41

Cambridgeshire County
Hertfordshire County

4

Northfield Road

Common Lane

Elbrook
House

5

Ashwell
End

Cemetery

Green La

Lucas Lane

Love Lane

40

18

Love's
Farm

Mill Street

Springhead

Ashwell Street

6

Hodwell
Street

Woodforde
Close

Hinxworth Road

Surgery

Gardiners Lane

High Street

Silver Street

Walkden St

Station Rd

Ashwell

Colbron Cl

West End

Bear Lane

Kingsland Way

7

Hinxworth Road

Works

Ashwell Street

Claybush Road

39

Newnham Way

Partridge Hill

8

Icknield Way Path

238

9

Newnham Way

Icknield Way Path

24 25 26 27

H **J** **K** **L** **M** **N** **P**

26

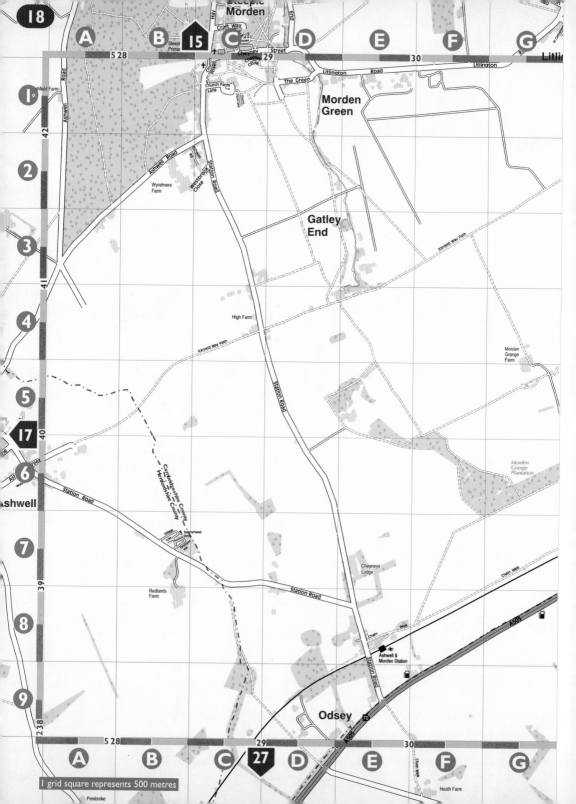

18

A B **15** C D E F G

Steeple Morden

Craft Way
Hay
Steeple Prima
Cheyney Street
Church Street
Cheyneys Close
29
Litlington Road
30
Litli

1 Highfield Farm
Church Farm Lane
The Green
Morden Green

2 Wyndmere Farm
Ashwell Road
Westbrook Close
Station Road

3

Gatley End

4 High Farm
Icknield Way Path
Icknield Way Path
Morden Grange Farm

5

17
Station Road
Morden Grange Plantation

6 Station Road
Cambridgeshire County
Hertfordshire County
Ashwell

7 Cheyneys Lodge
Chain Walk
Redlands Farm
Station Road
Sunnymead
Village

8 A505
Chain Walk
Ashwell & Morden Station

9 Chain Walk

Odsey
A505
27
Heath Farm

A B C **27** D E F G
5 28 **29** **30**

Pembroke

1 grid square represents 500 metres

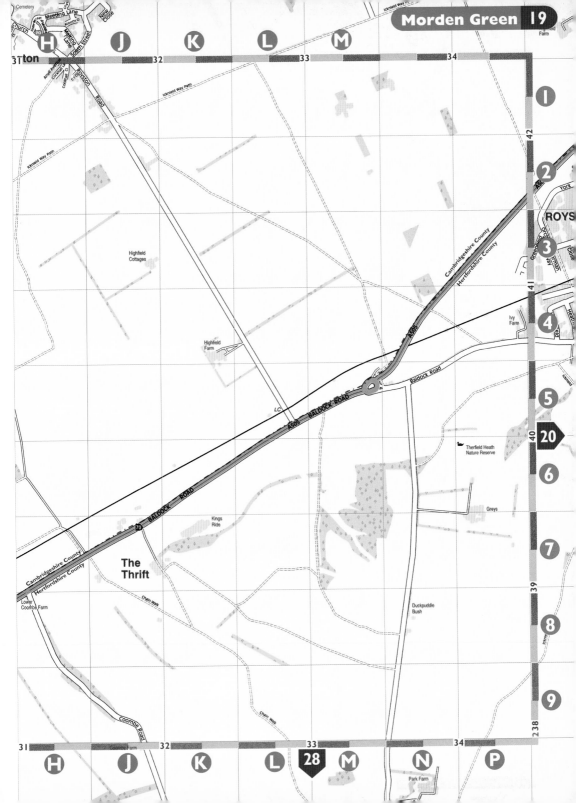

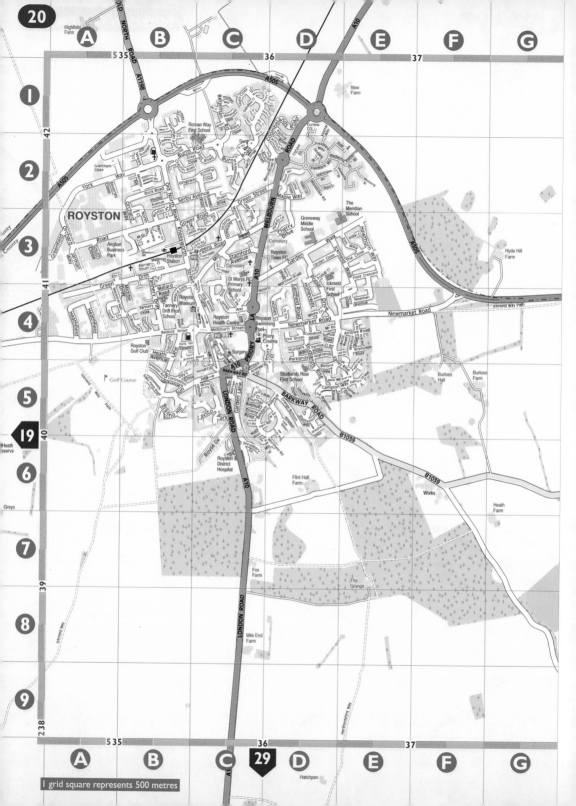

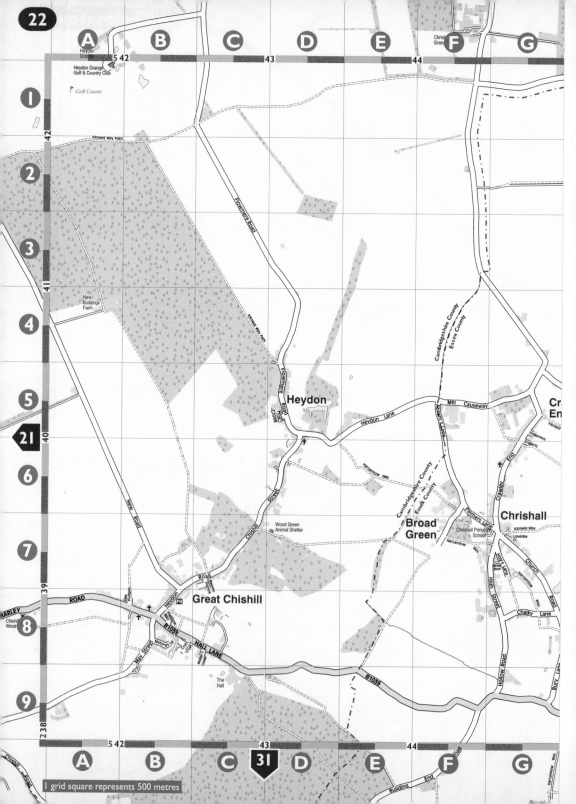

H J K L M

45 46 47 48

I

Rectory Farm

Ickleton Granges

Grange Road

Redlands

Royston Lane

42

Valance Farm

2

Cambridgeshire County
Essex County

3

41

Lodge Farm

The Poplars

4

Quickset Road

New Jersey Farm

5

40

Hertford Lane

awley d

Elmondbury

Strethall

6

Way Path

Elmdon

Ickleton

Elm Court

Horseshoe Close

Hollow Road

Icknield Way

Heydon Lane

Hertford Lane

Essex Hill

Way

Freewood Lane

Freewood Farm

7

Park Wood

Lofts Hall

39

8

Essex Hill

9

2 38

45 46 47 48

H J K L M N P

B1039

Hope Farm

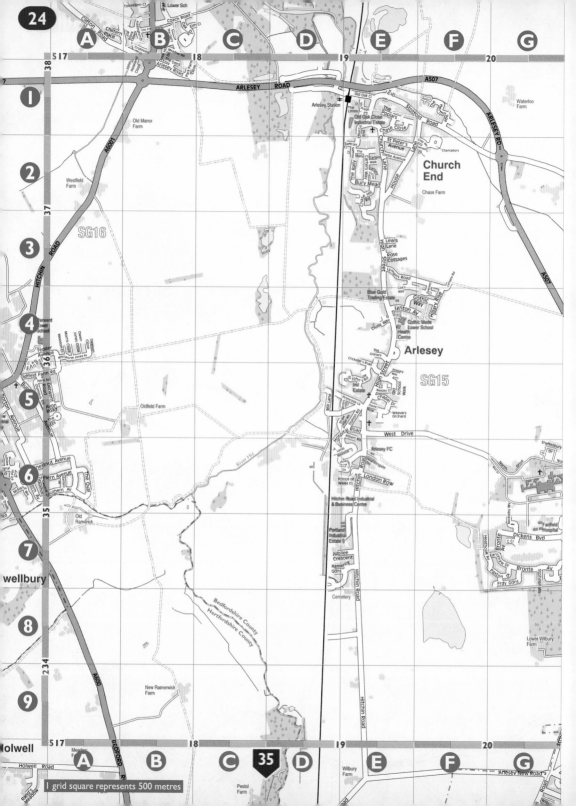

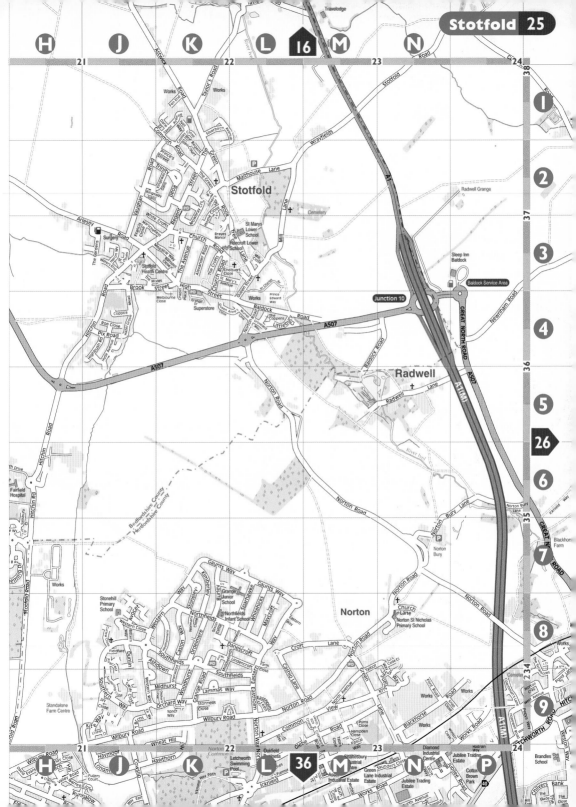

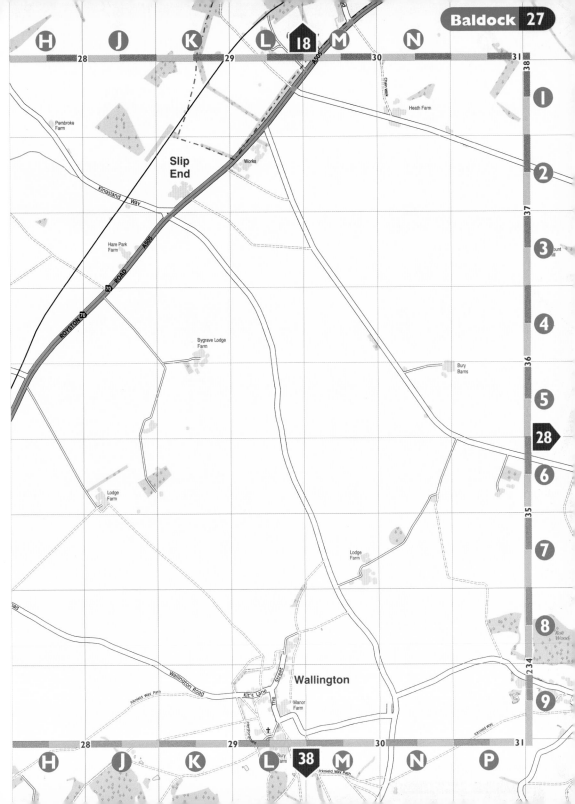

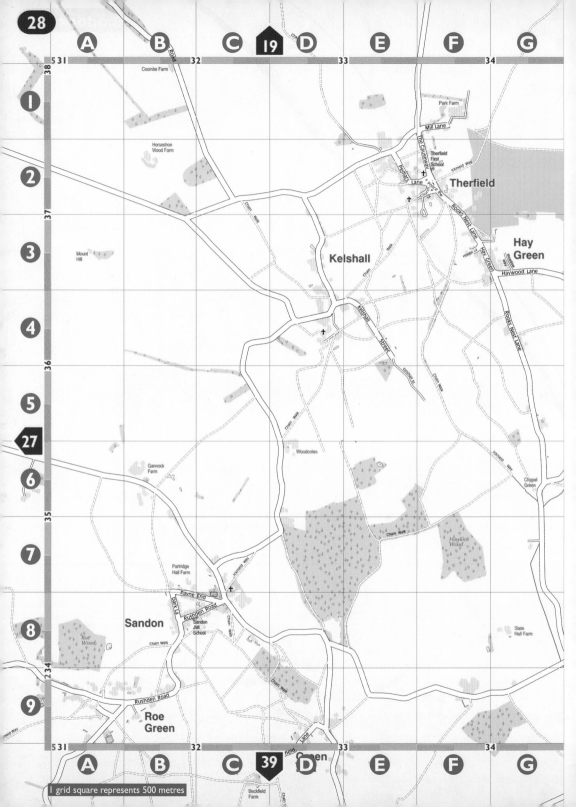

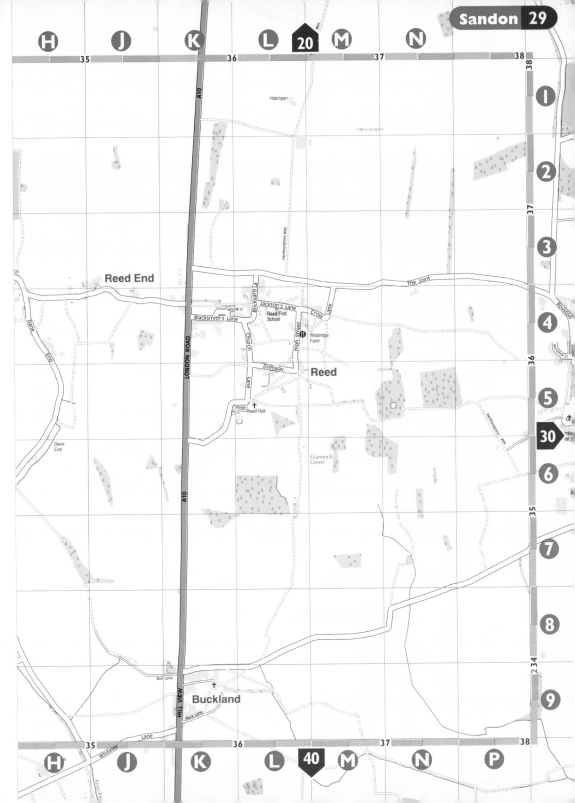

H J K L 20 M N

35 36 37 38

I

2

3

Reed End

The Joint

Dane End

Brickyard La

Jackson's Lane

Reed First School

Crow Lane

Hertfordshire Way

Hatchpen

Royston

Willow Cl

Blacksmith's Lane

Church Lane

High Street

Wisbridge Farm

4

Driftway

Reed

36

Church Lane

Reed Hall

Hertfordshire Way

5

30

Dane End

Grannock Green

6

35

7

8

2 34

Bull Lane

HILL VIEW

Back Lane

Buckland

9

LONDON ROAD

A10

Whiteley

Lane

35 36 37 38

River Rib

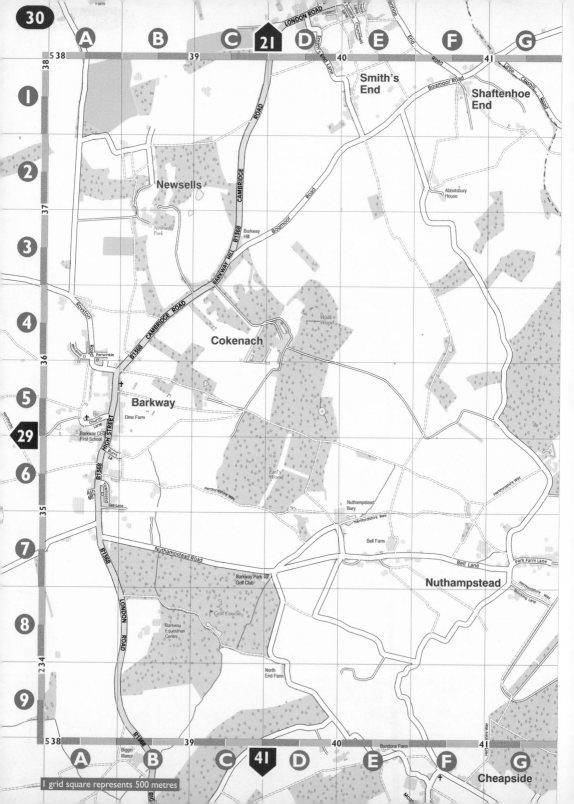

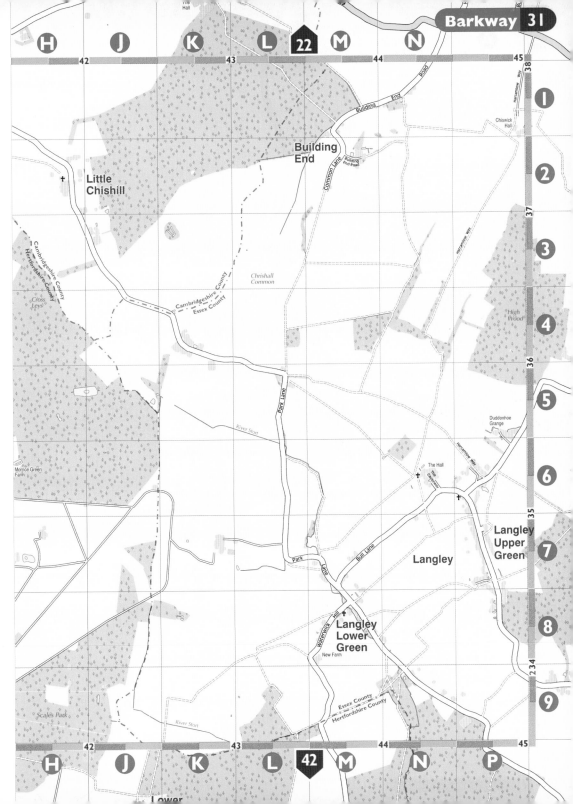

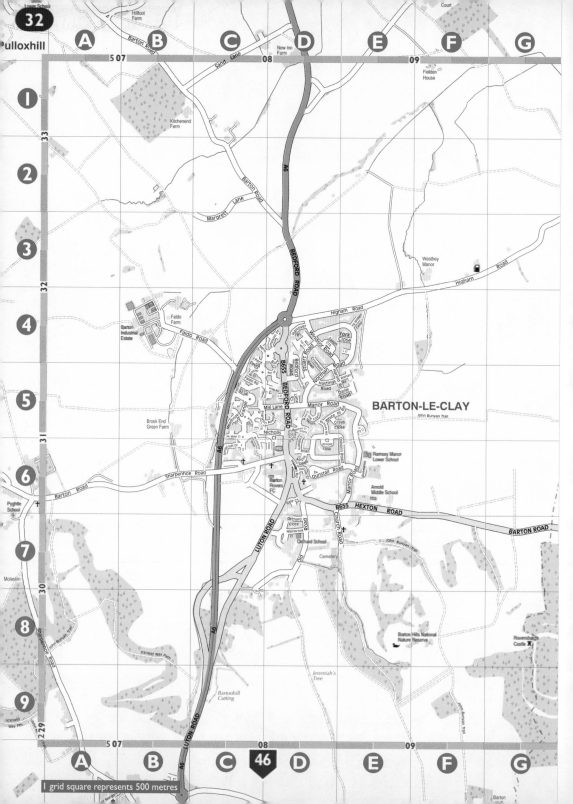

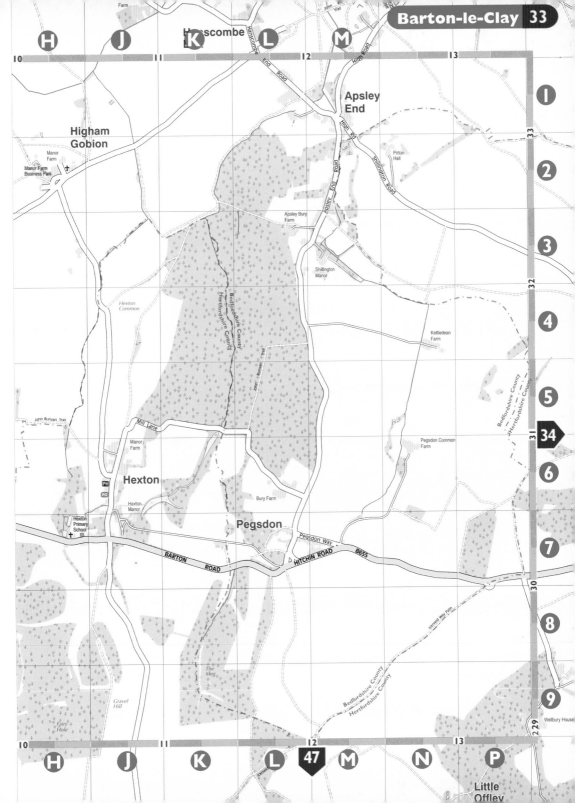

Hanscombe

Apsley
End

Higham
Gobion

Manor
Farm

Manor Farm
Business Park

Pirton
Hall

Apsley Bury
Farm

Shillington
Manor

Hexton
Common

Bedfordshire County
Hertfordshire County

Bunyan Trail

Kettledean
Farm

John Bunyan Trail

Mill Lane

Manor
Farm

Pegsdon Common
Farm

Bedfordshire County
Hertfordshire County

34

Hexton

Hexton
Manor

Bury Farm

Hexton
Primary
School

Pegsdon

Pegsdon Way

BARTON   ROAD

HITCHIN ROAD   B655

The
Meg

Named Way Path

Gravel
Hill

Fairy
Hole

Bedfordshire County
Hertfordshire County

Wellbury House

Little
Offley

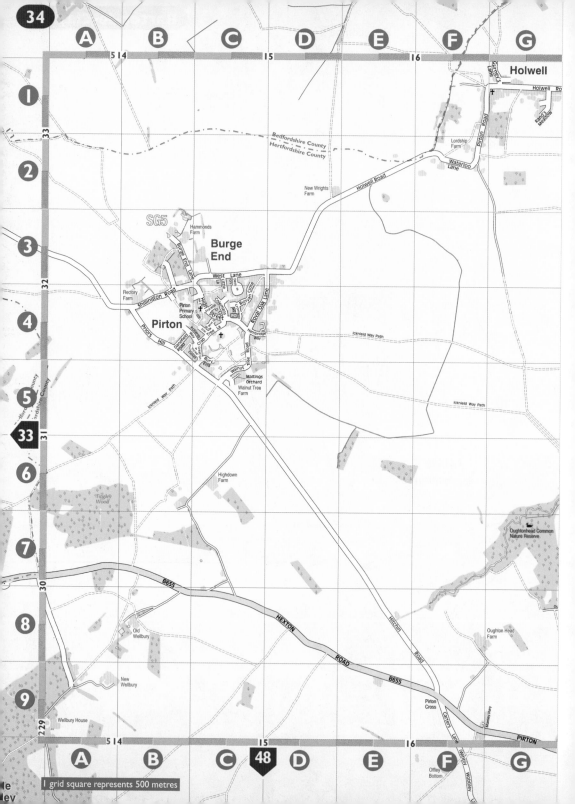

A B C D E F G

514 15 16

I

33

2

3

32

4

5

33 31

6

7

30

8

9

229

A B C 48 D E F G

514 15 16

Holwell

Gurney's Lane

Holwell Ro

Rans's Meadow

Lordship Farm

Pirton Road

Waterloo Lane

New Wrights Farm

Holwell Road

SG5

Hammonds Farm

Burge End

West Lane

Burge End Lane

Rectory Farm

Shillington Road

Pirton Primary School

High Street

Burvyn Close

Royal Oak Lane

Brambridge Way

Pirton

Priors Hill

Danefield Road

Crab Tree Lane

Bury End

Walnut Tree Road

Icknield Way Path

Maltings Orchard Walnut Tree Farm

Icknield Way Path

Highdown Farm

Oughtonhead Common Nature Reserve

Tingley Wood

B655

HEXTON

ROAD

Hitchin

Road

B655

Old Welbury

New Welbury

Pirton Cross

Oughton Head Farm

Carters Lane

Nanny Way

Wobby Way

PIRTON

Wellbury House

Offley Bottom

Bedfordshire County
Hertfordshire County

le
ey

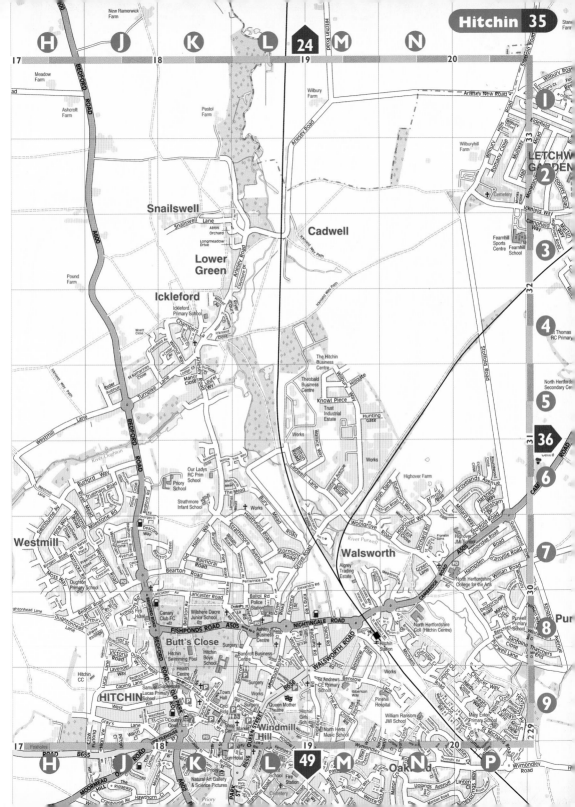

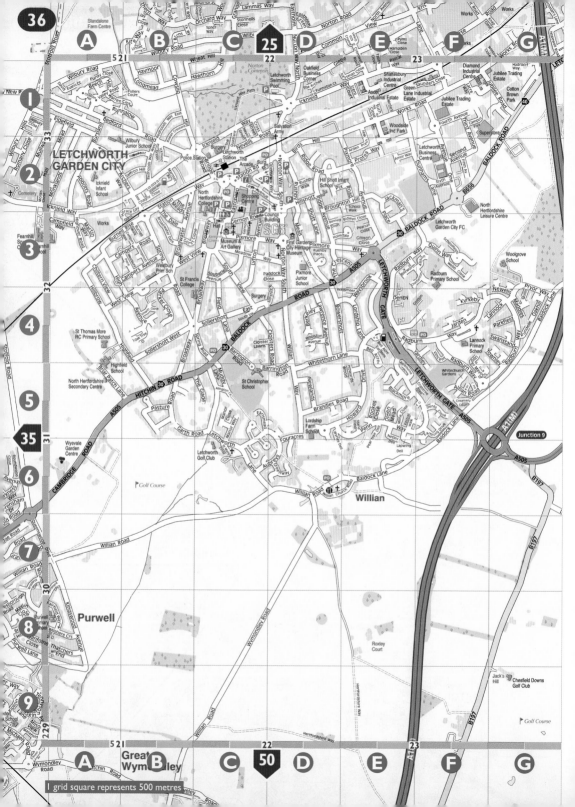

Baldock

Clothall
Common

Clothall

Green End

Weston

Weston
Bury

Weston
Park

Damask
Green

Warren's
Green

Hall's
Green

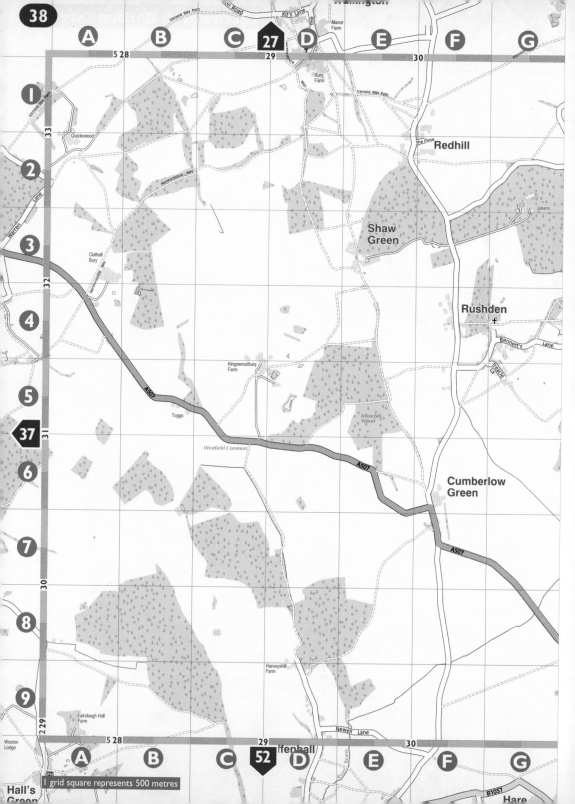

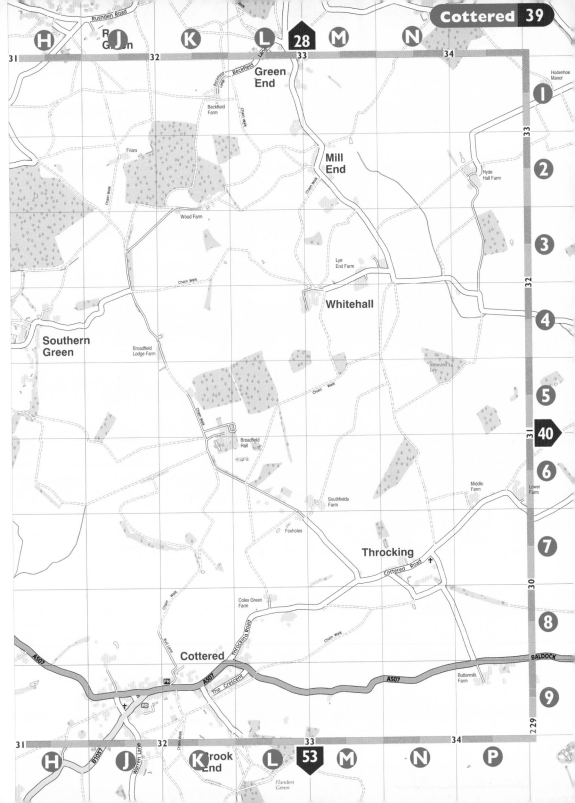

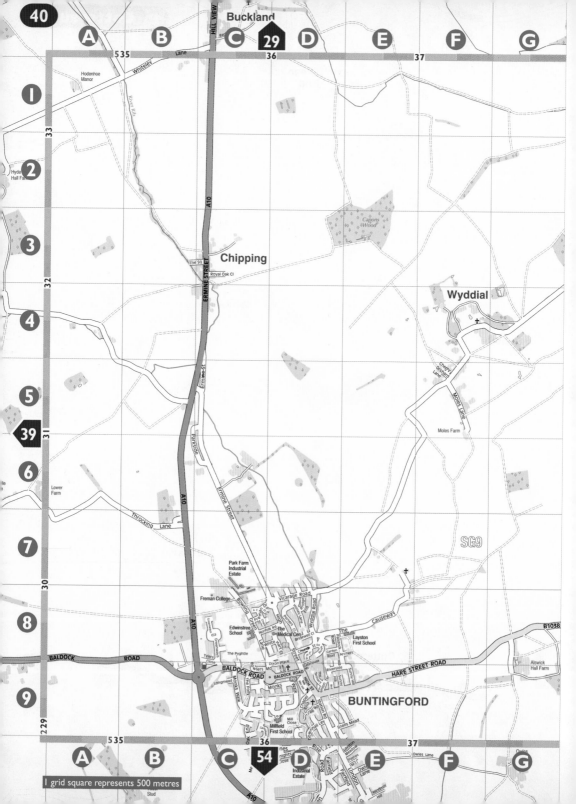

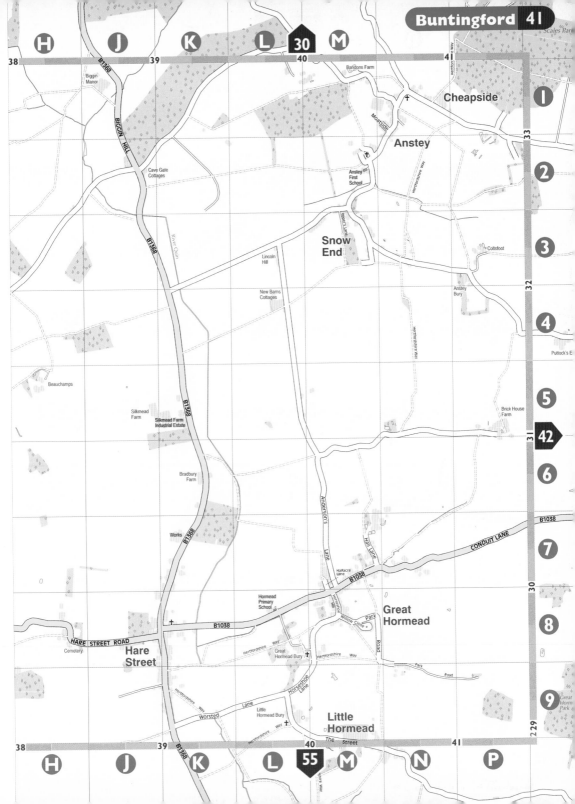

Scales Park

H J K L **30** M

38 39 40 41

B1368

Biggin Manor

BIGGIN HILL

Bandons Farm

Cheapside **1**

Montside

Anstey

33

Cave Gate Cottages

Hertfordshire Way

2

32

River Quin

Lincoln Hill

Snow End

Anstey First School

Stan's Lane

Coltsfoot

3

New Barns Cottages

Anstey Bury

Hertfordshire Way

4

Puttock's E

Beauchamps

B1368

Silkmead Farm

Silkmead Farm Industrial Estate

Brick House Farm

5

31 **42**

Bradbury Farm

6

B1038

Works

B1368

Anderson's Lane

Hall Lane

CONDUIT LANE

7

30

Halfacre Lane

B1038

Great Hormead

Hormead Primary School

Willow Close

8

Hormead Hill

Park Road

9

Hare Street Road

B1038

Cemetery

Hertfordshire Way

Great Hormead Bury

Hertfordshire Way

Park Road

Great Horm Park

Hare Street

Horsehoe Lane

Hertfordshire Way

Worsted Lane

Little Hormead Bury

Little Hormead

The Street

229

38 39 40 41

H J K **55** L M N P

B1368

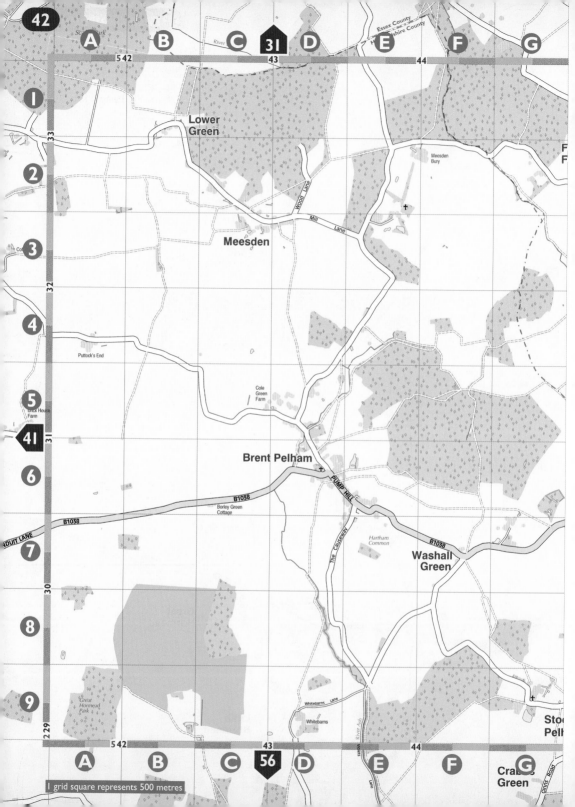

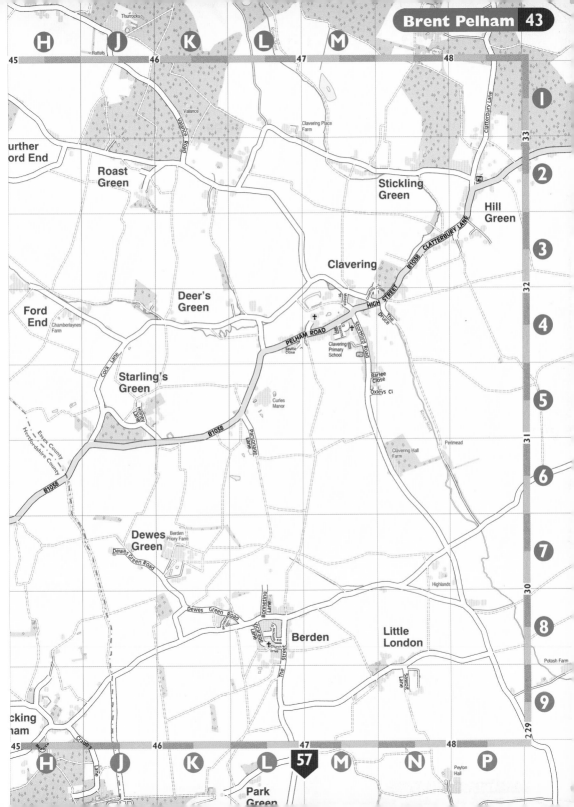

Thurrocks

Ruttels

H J K L M

45 46 47 48

I

33

Further
Ford End

Roast
Green

Valance

Clavering Place
Farm

Stickling
Green

PH

Hill
Green

2

Clavering

CLATTERBURY LANE

B1058

Clatterbury Lane

3

32

Ford
End

Chamberlaynes
Farm

Deer's
Green

HIGH STREET

The Drive

4

Starling's
Green

Cock Lane

PELHAM ROAD

Saville
Close

Stortford Road

Clavering Primary
School

PO

Bariee
Close

Oxleys Cl

River Stort

5

31

Horley Lane

B1058

Curles
Manor

Parsonage Lane

Clavering Hall
Farm

Perimead

6

Dewes
Green

Dewes Green Road

Berden
Priory Farm

7

30

Highlands

Dewes Green Road

Bonnetting Lane

Vicarage Lane

Church Drive

Berden

Little
London

Savall Lane

8

Potash Farm

Mead

Cramb's Lane

9

29

45 46 47 48

H J K

Peyton
Hall

Park
Green

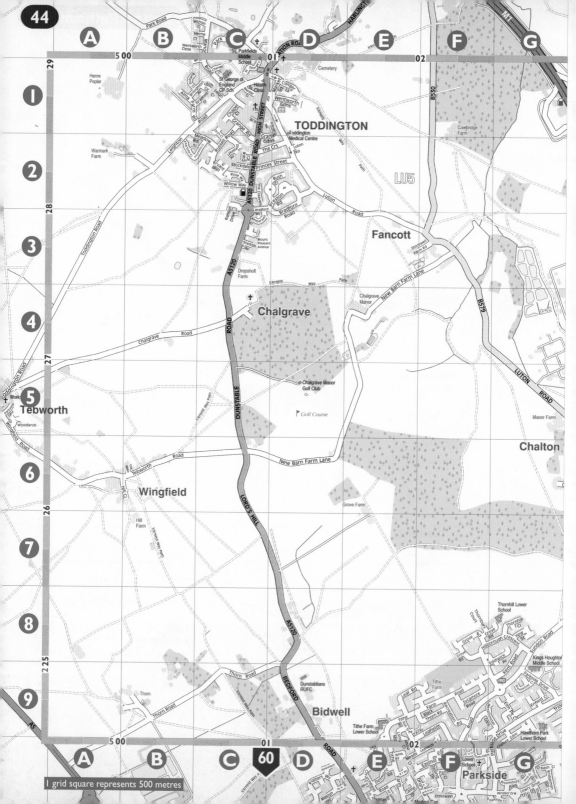

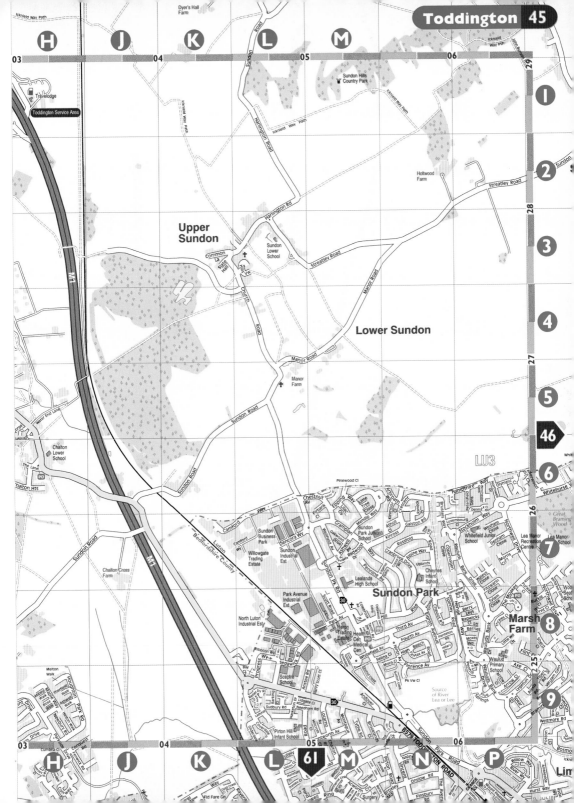

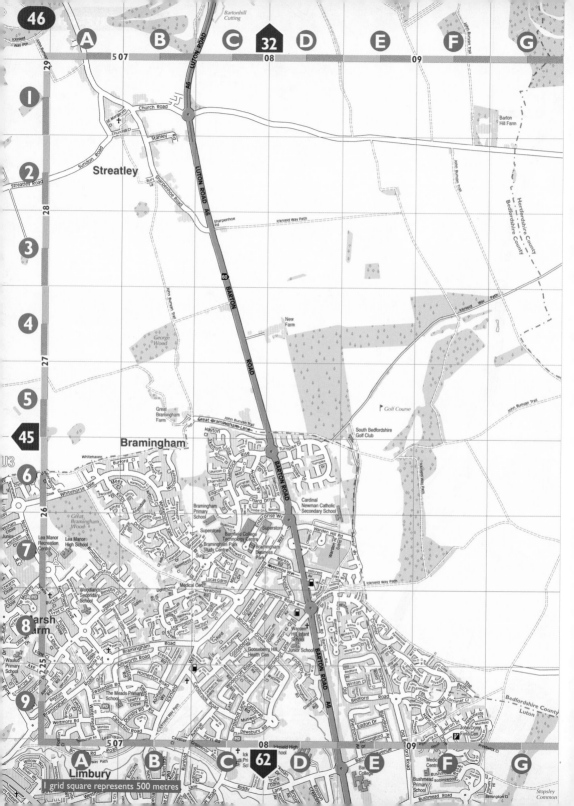

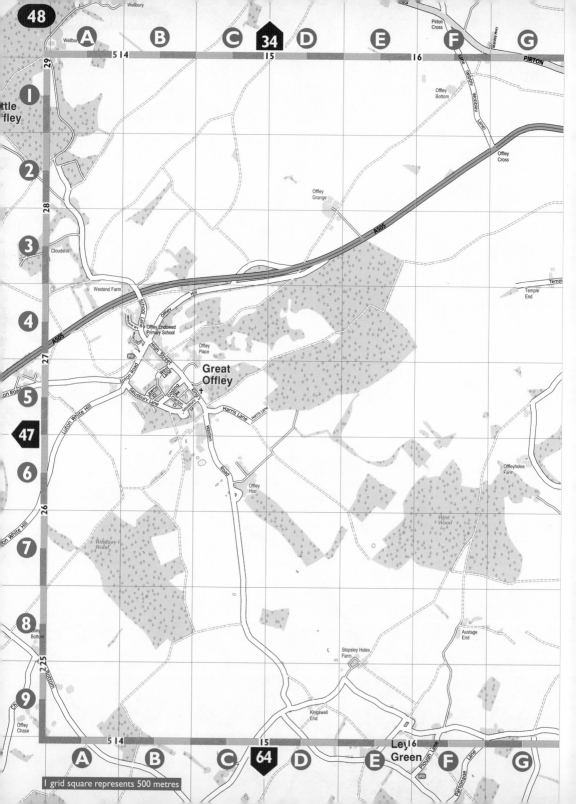

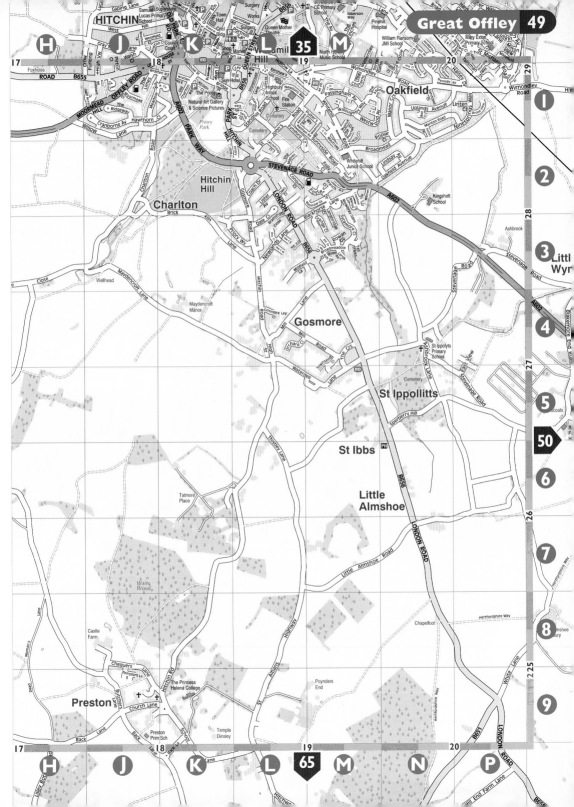

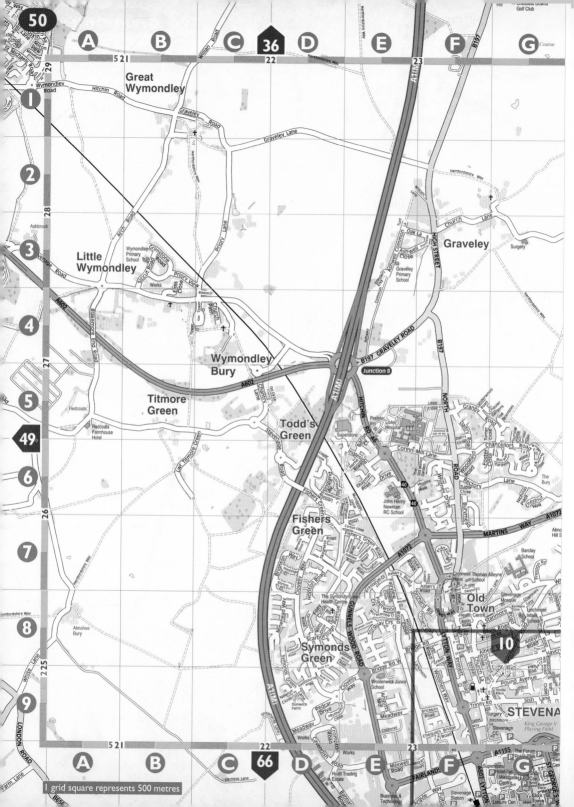

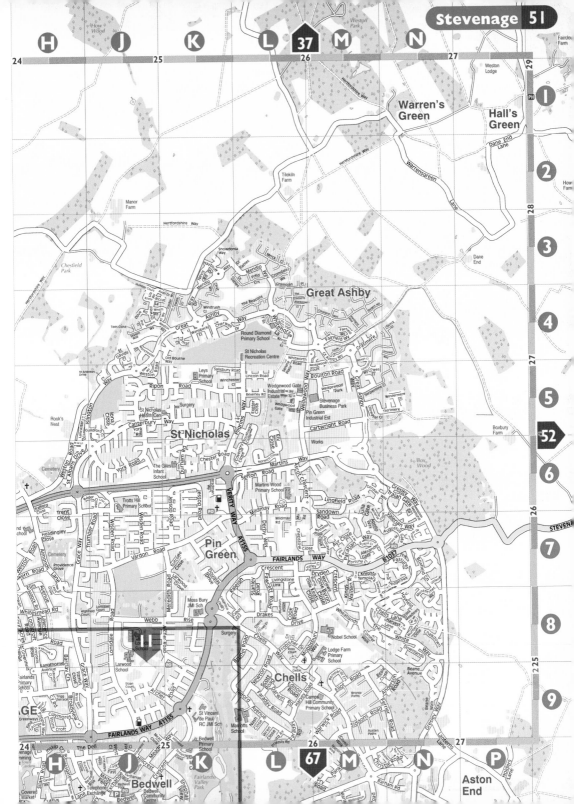

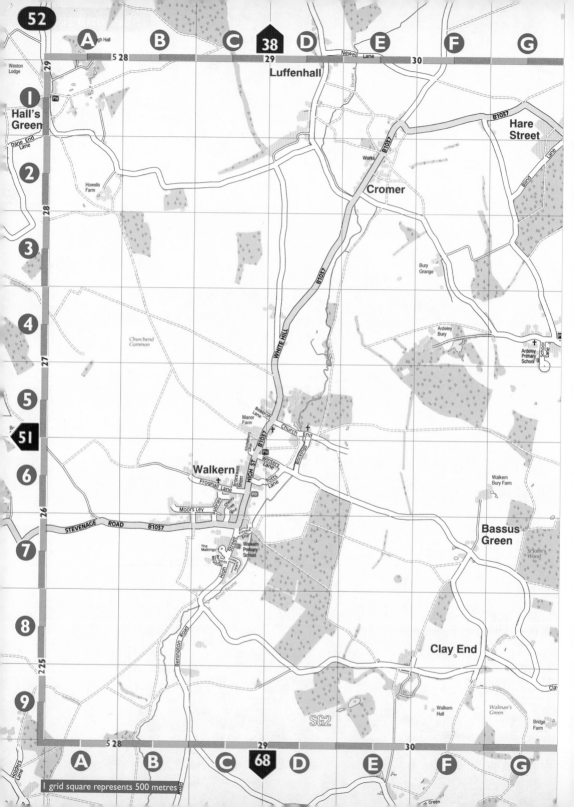

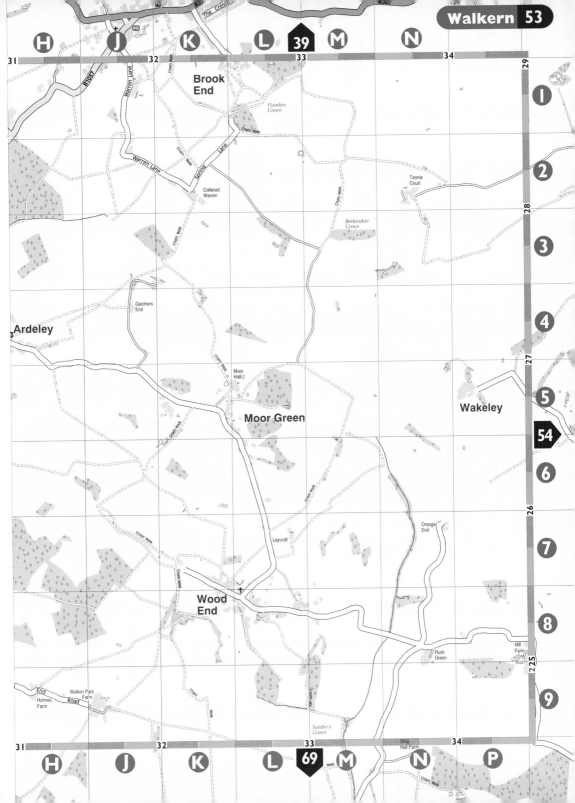

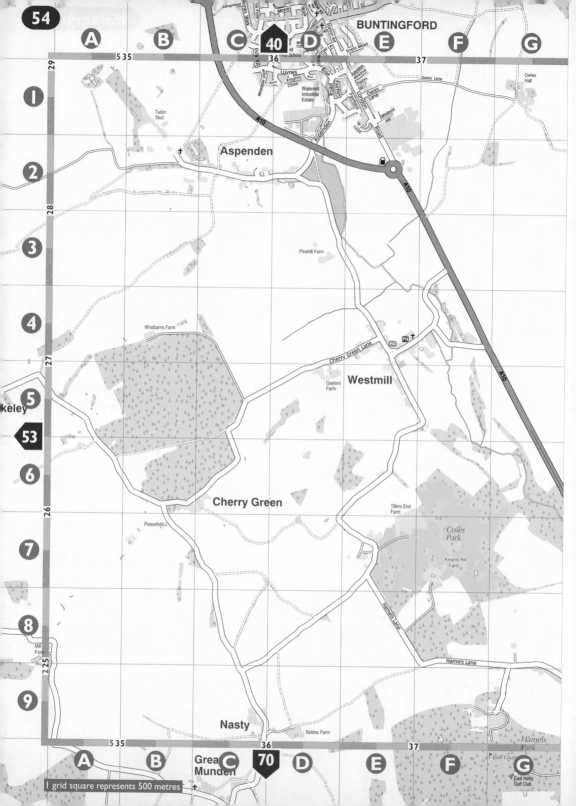

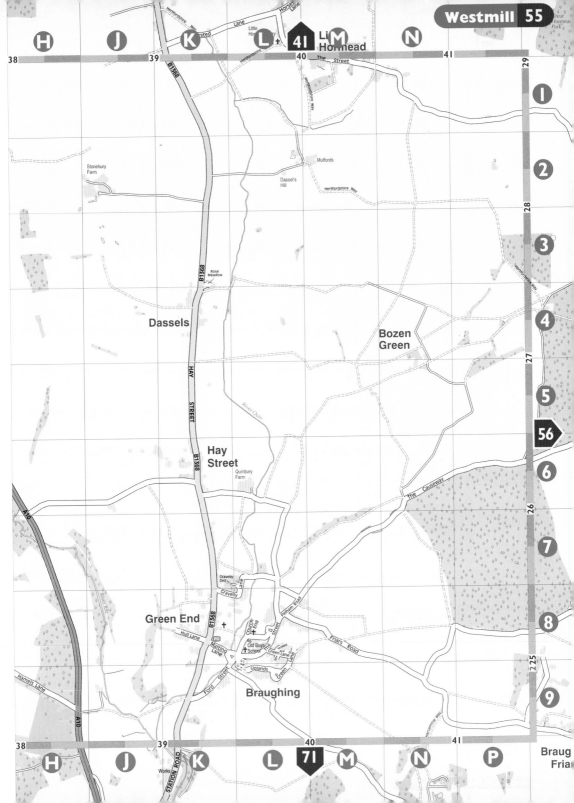

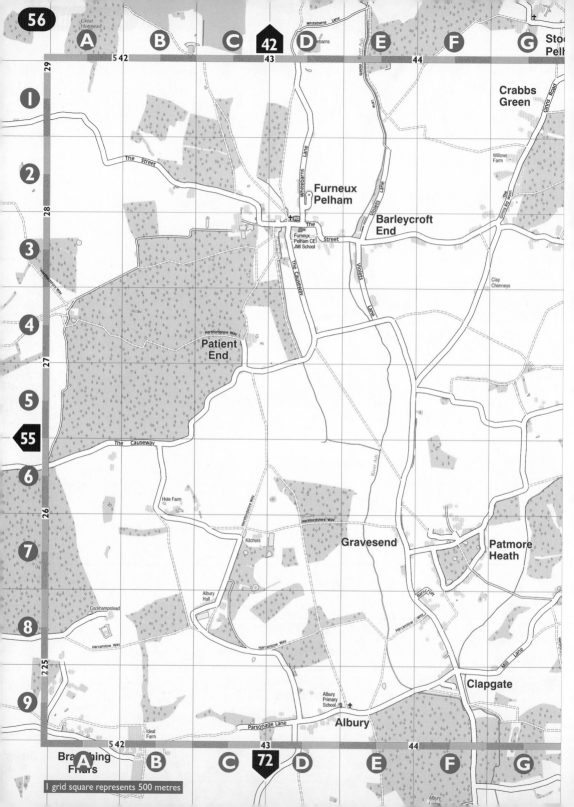

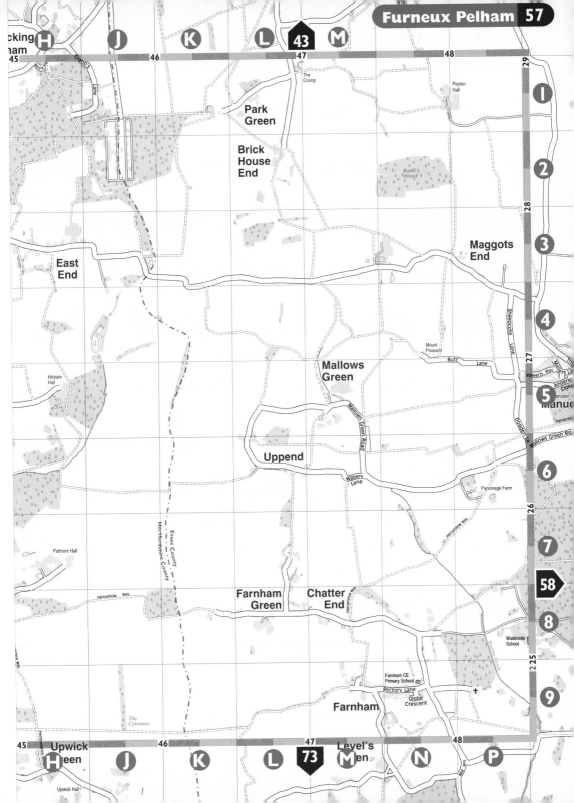

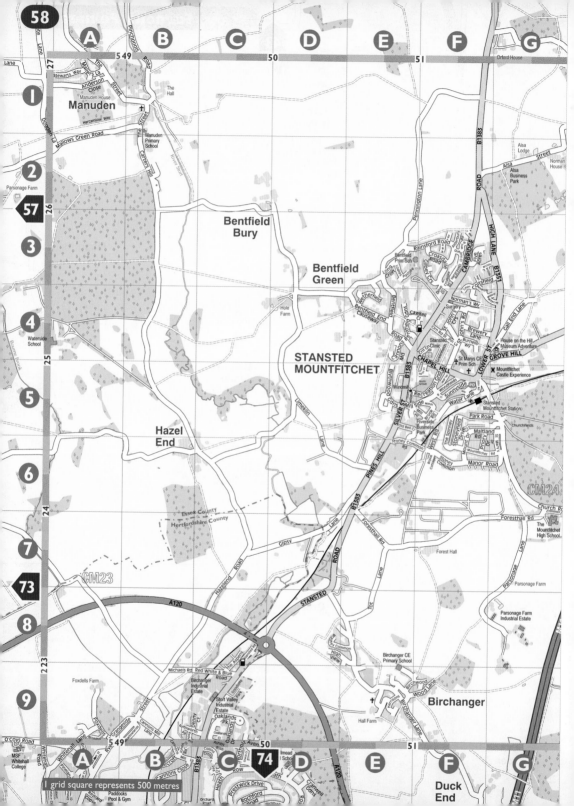

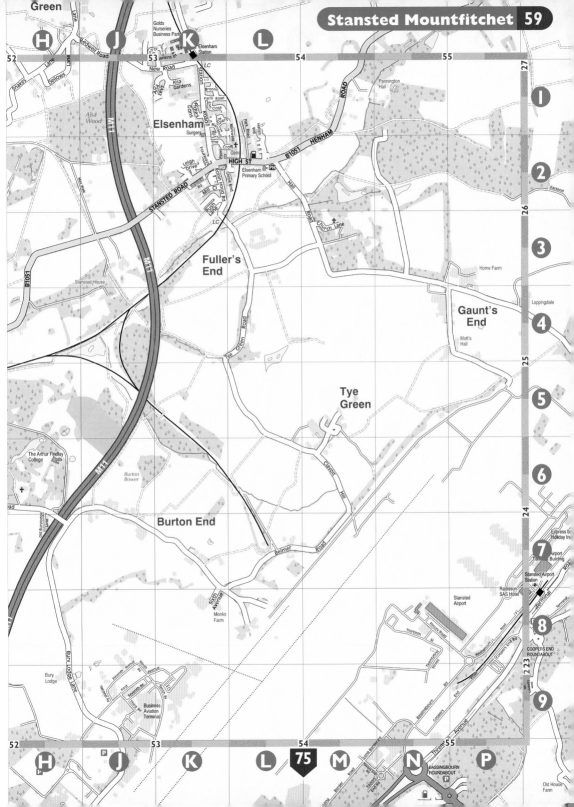

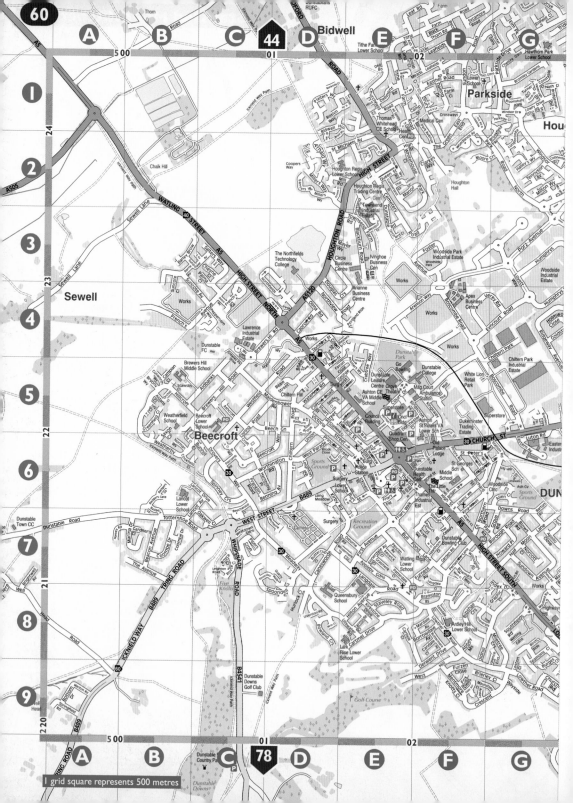

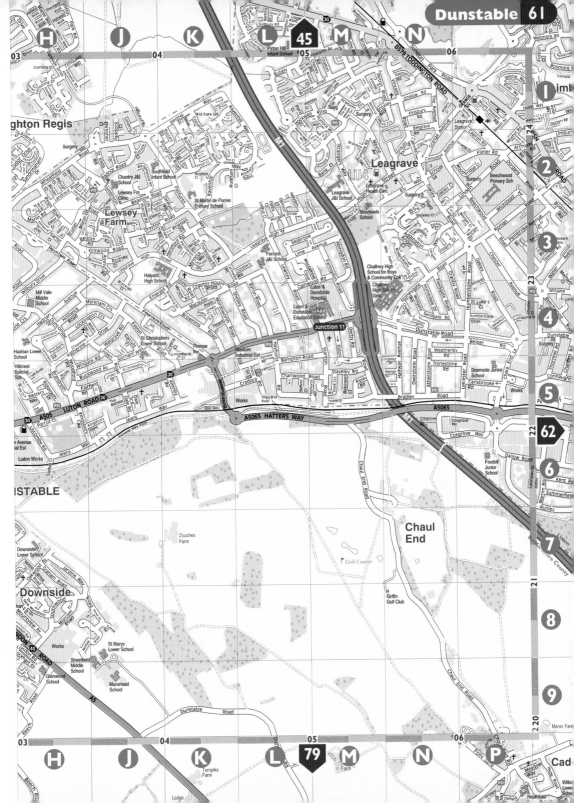

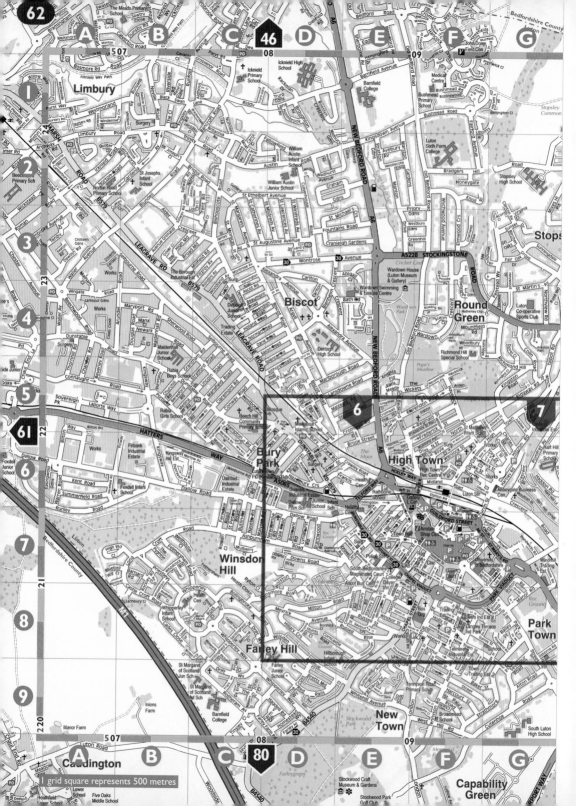

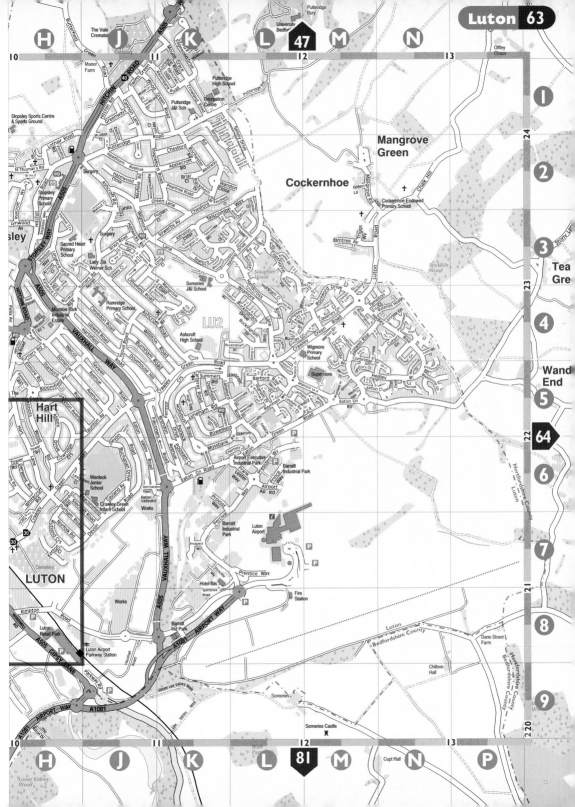

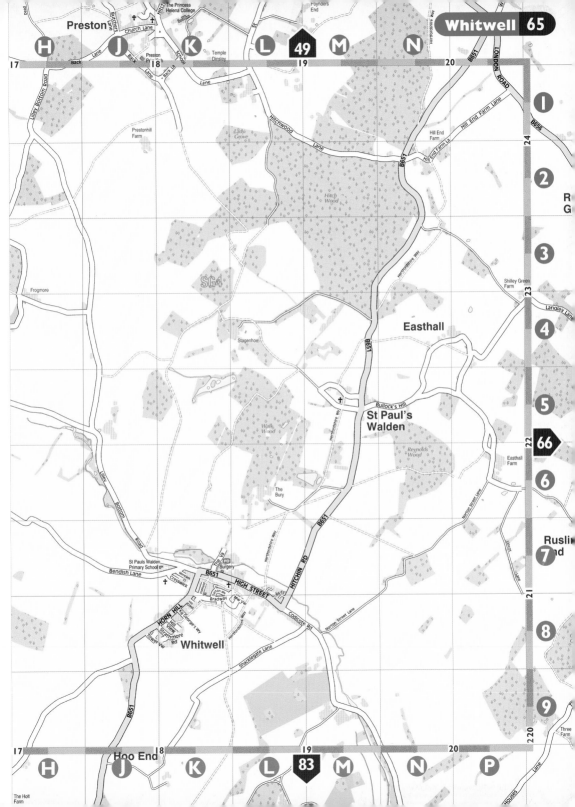

Preston

H · J · K · L · 49 · M · N

17 · 18 · 19 · 20

I · 24 · 2 · 3 · 23 · 4 · 5 · 22 · 66 · 6 · 21 · 7 · 8 · 20 · 9

The Princess Helena College

Church Lane

Butchers Lane

Back Lane

Lilley Bottom Road

School Lane

Temple Dinsley

Preston

Prestonhill Farm

Lady Grove

Hitchwood Lane

Hitch Wood

Hill End Farm

Hill End Farm La

Hill End Farm Lane

London Road

B656

R G

SG4

Frogmore

Hertfordshire Way

Shilley Green Farm

Langley Lane

Easthall

B651

Stagenhoe

Bullock's Hill

St Paul's Walden

Hertfordshire Way

Walk Wood

Reynolds Wood

Easthall Farm

Rusli nd

Norton Street Lane

Lincoln Lane

Lilley Bottom Road

The Bury

B651

St Pauls Walden Primary School

Bendish Lane

Cresswick

High Street

Hitchin Rd

Surgery

Codicote Rd

Norton Street Lane

Horn Hill

St George's Wy

Strathmore Rd

Tower Vw

Whitwell

Hertfordshire Way

Shackgate Lane

B651

Three Farm

Houses Lane

The Holt Farm

Hoo End

H · J · K · L · 83 · M · N · P

17 · 18 · 19 · 20

2 20

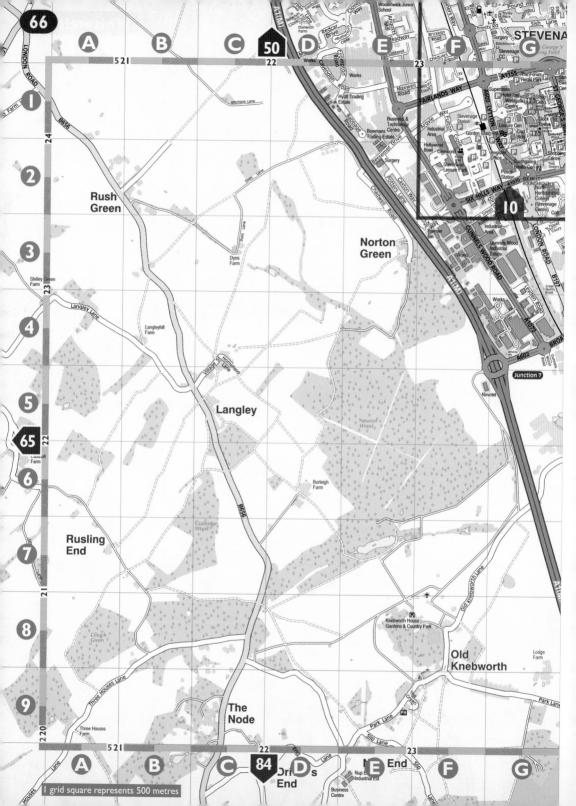

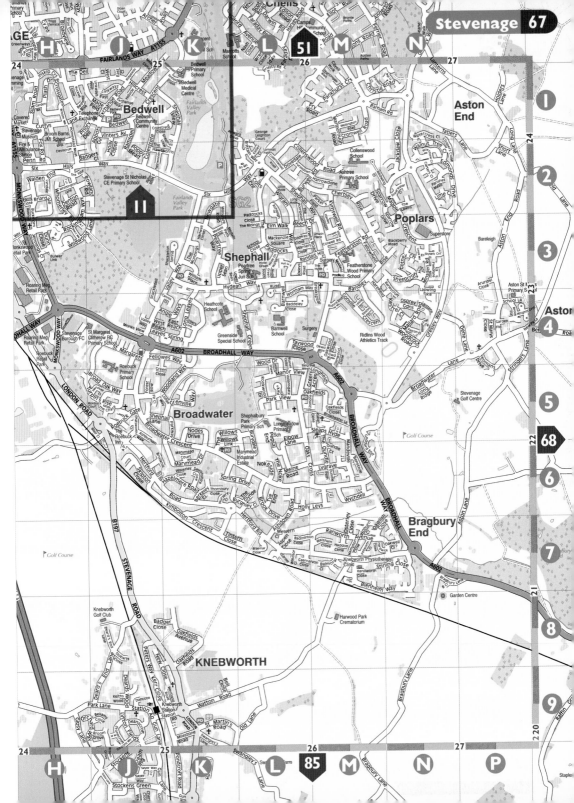

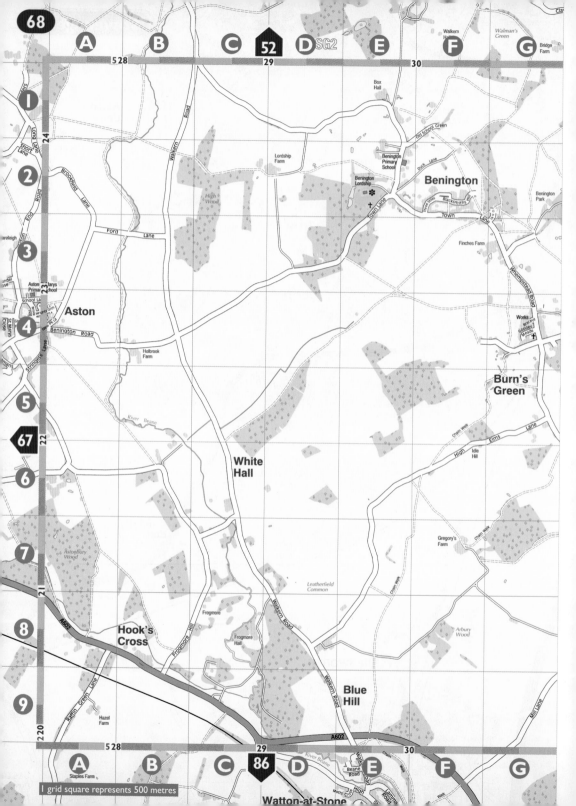

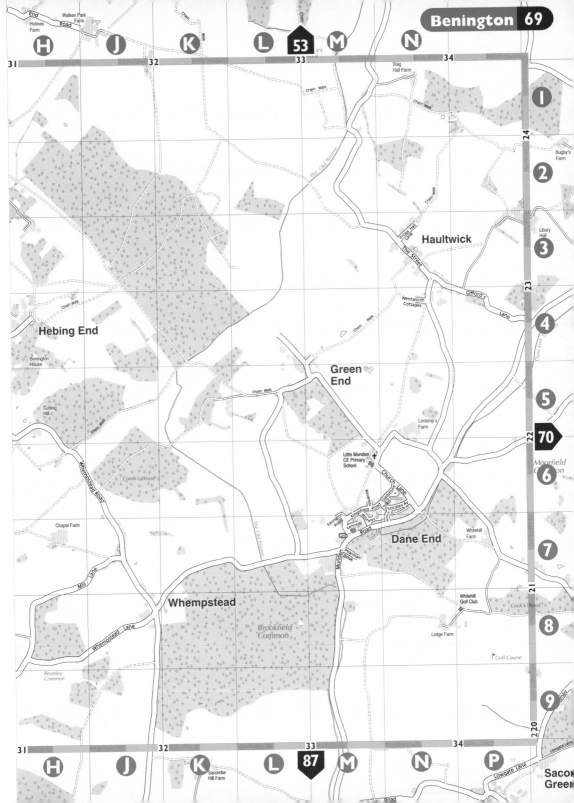

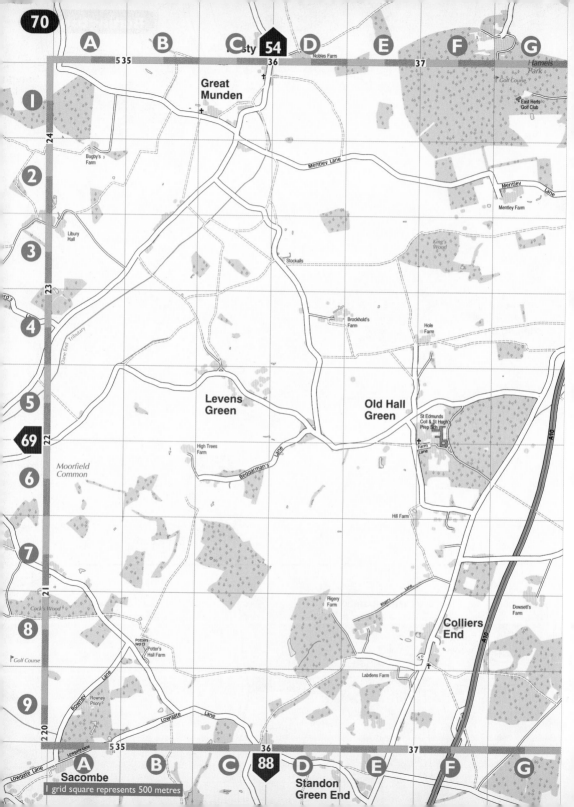

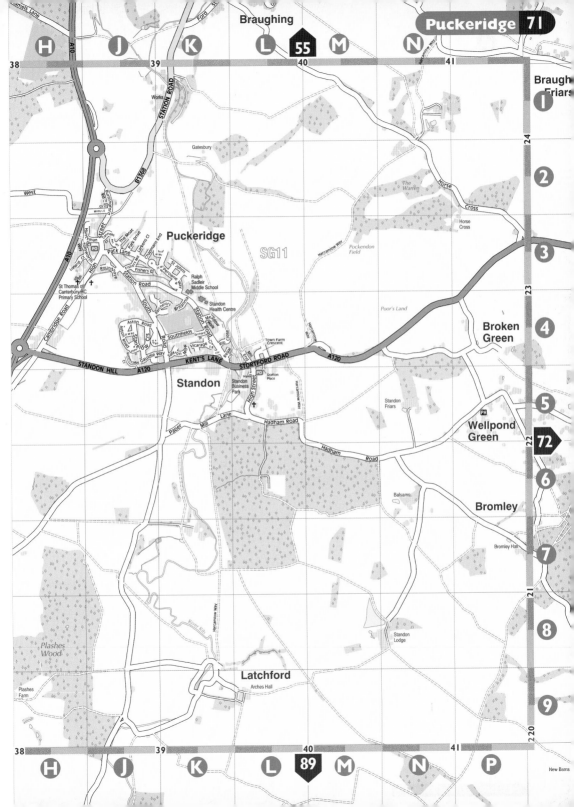

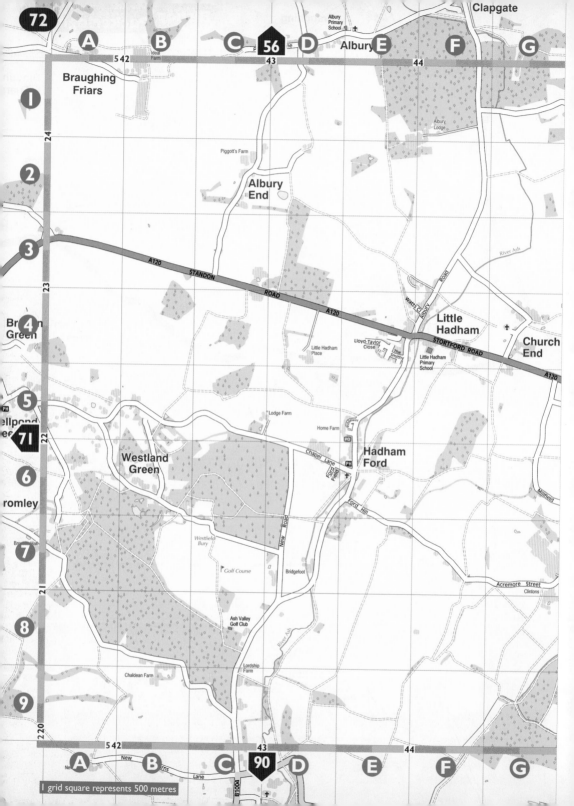

72

A B C **56** D E F G

Braughing
Friars

Albury
Primary
School

Albury

Ideal
Farm

I

24

2

Albury
End

Piggott's Farm

Albury
Lodge

River Ash

3

A120 STANDON ROAD A120

23

Br___n
Green

4

Little Hadham
Place

Lloyd-Taylor
Close

The
Smithy

Watts Cl

Albury Road

STORTFORD ROAD

Little
Hadham

Church
End

Little Hadham
Primary
School

A120

ellpond

PH

5

Lodge Farm

Home Farm

PO

71

22

Westland
Green

Chapel Lane

Ford Field

PH

Hadham
Ford

Millfield

romley

6

Westfield
Bury

New Road

Ford Hill

7

Bro___ Hall

Golf Course

Bridgefoot

Acremore Street

Clintons

21

8

Ash Valley
Golf Club

River Ash

Chaldean Farm

Lordship
Farm

9

20

A B rns C **90** D E F G

New   New   Lane

B1004

I grid square represents 500 metres

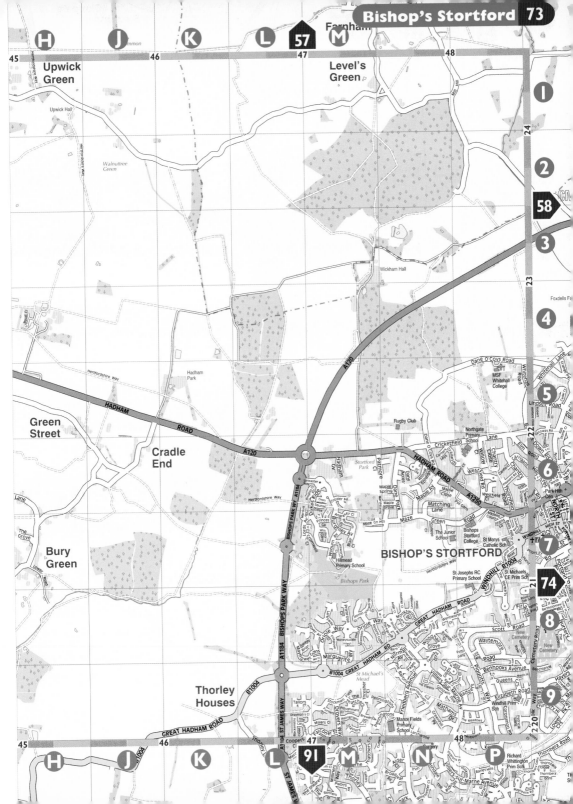

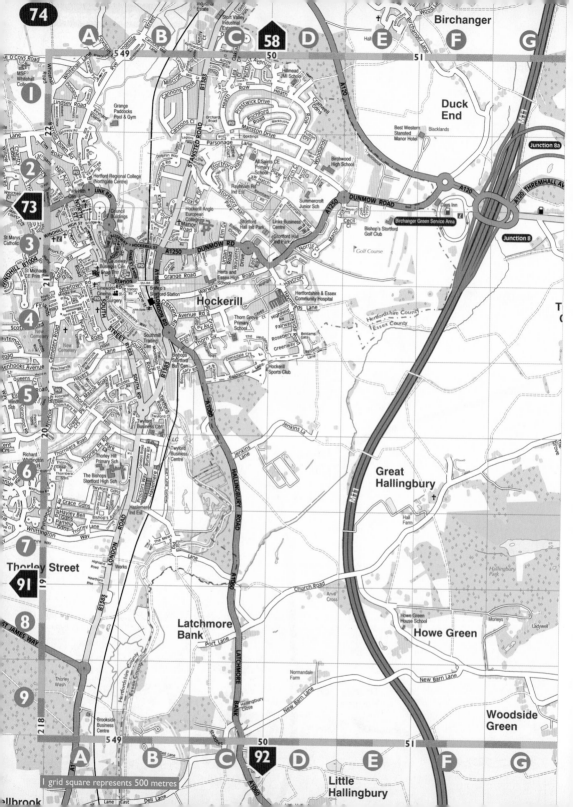

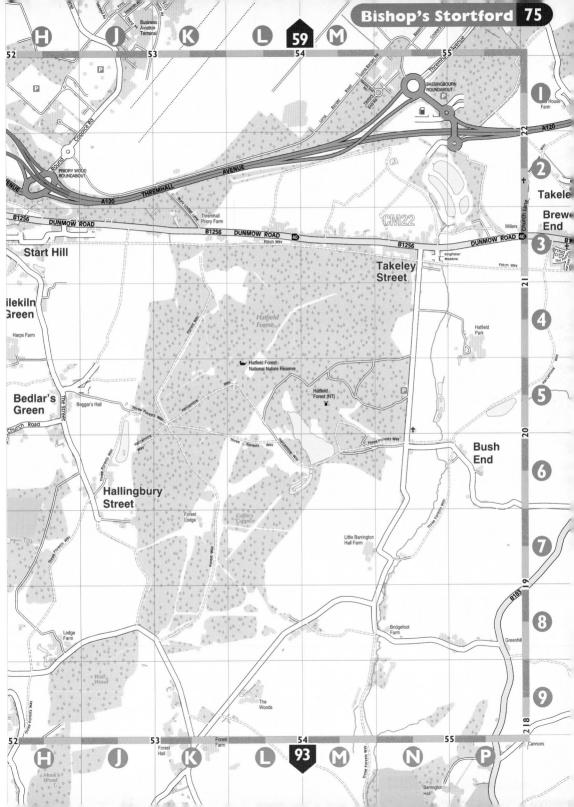

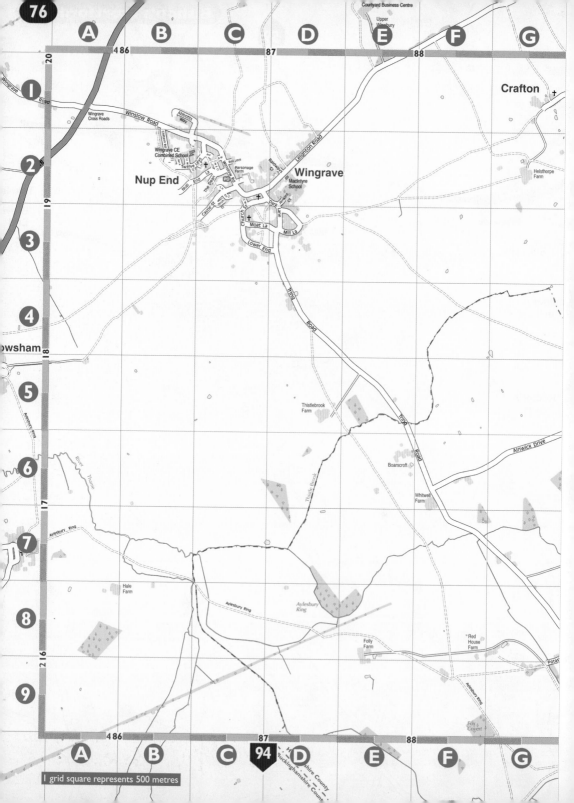

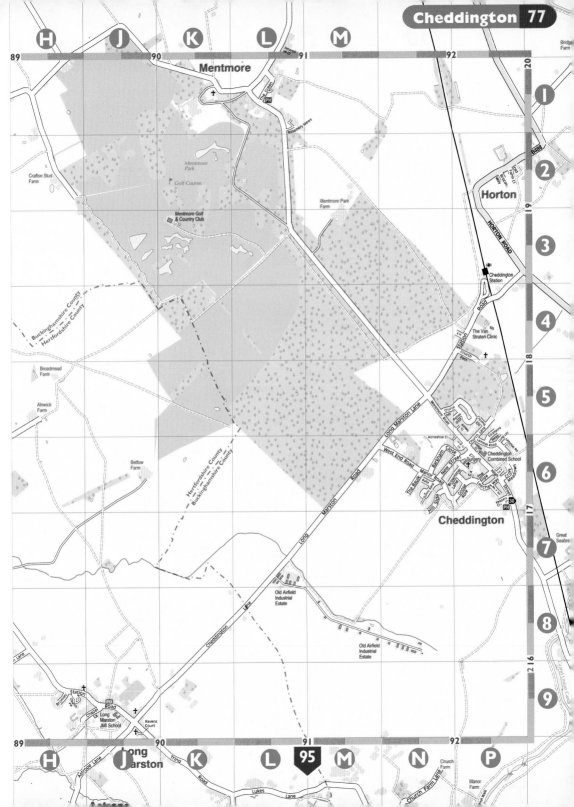

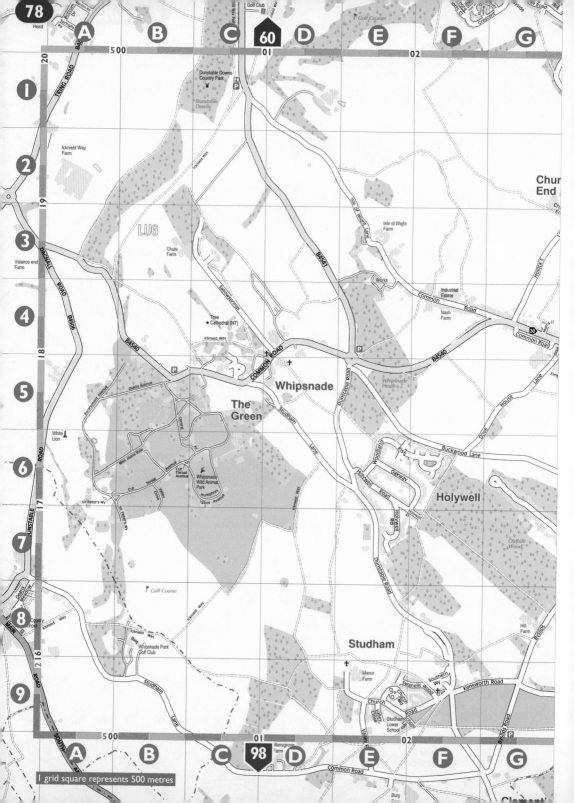

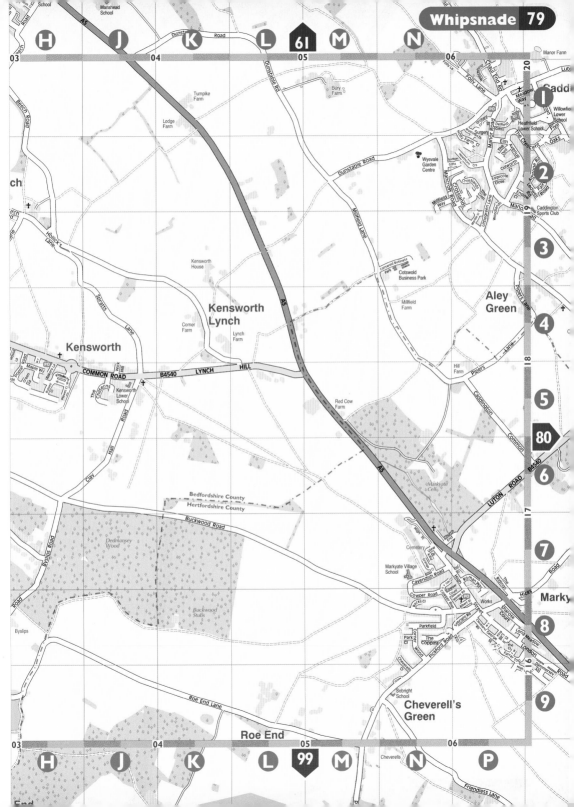

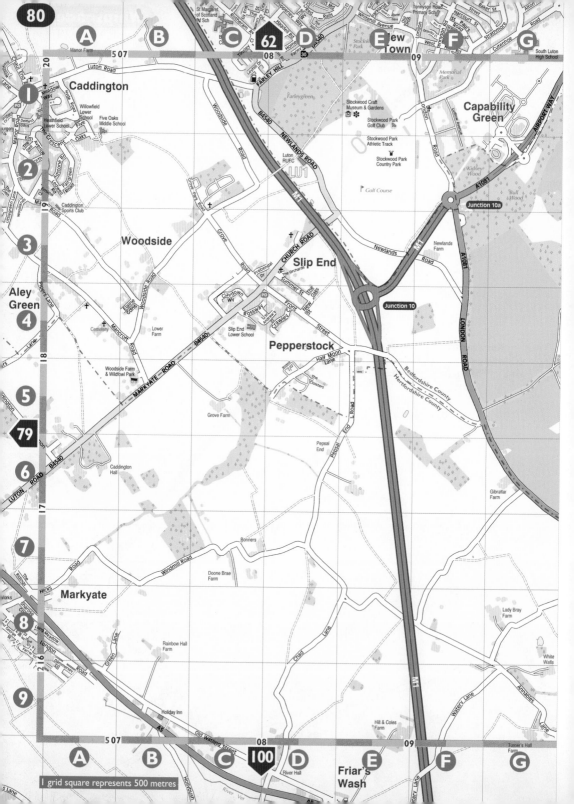

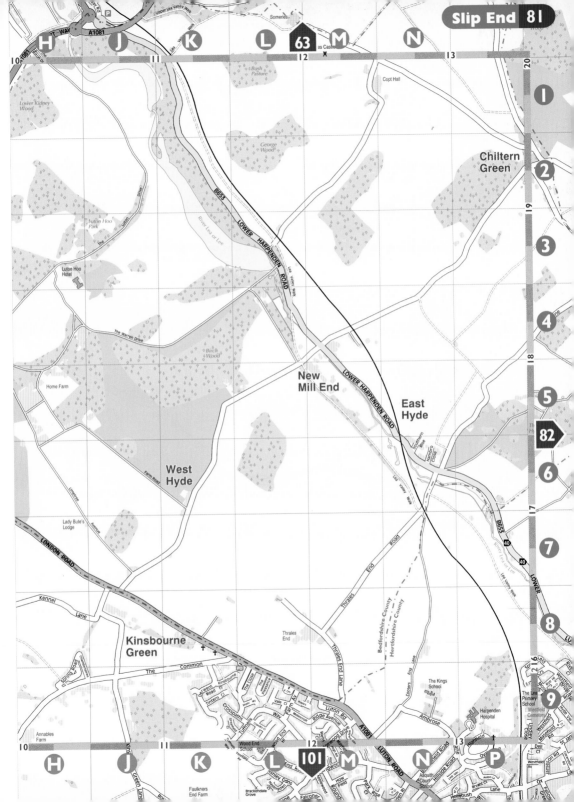

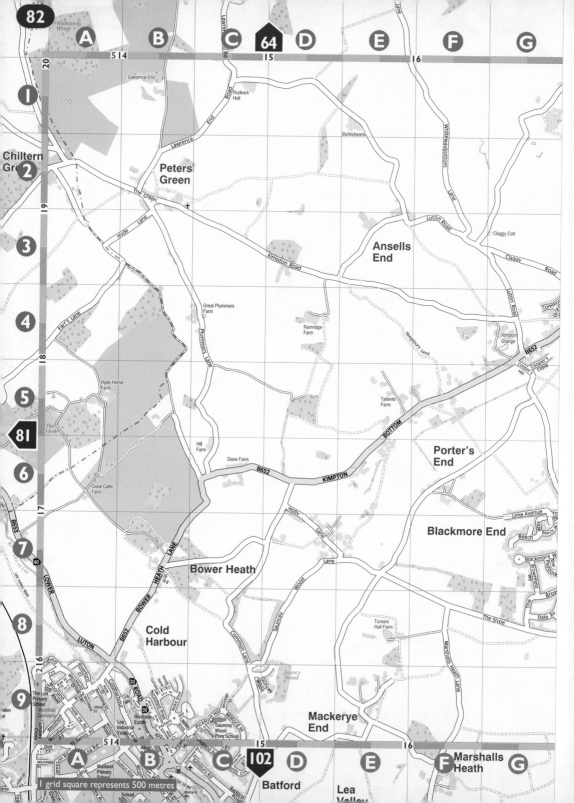

Map grid references and labels:

82

A **B** **C** **64** **D** **E** **F** **G**

514 15 16

20

Withstocks Wood

Lawrence End

I

Rudwick Hall

Peco End

Chiltern Green

2

Peters Green

Barleybeans

The Green

Whitewaybottom Lane

Lawrence Lane

3

Hyde Lane

Kimpton Road

Ansells End

Luton Road

Claggy Cott

Claggy Road

19

4

Farr's Lane

Great Plummers Farm

Ramridge Farm

Stagbury Lane

Kimpton Grange

B652

18

Plummer's Lane

Common

Cooper's Close

5

Hyde Home Farm

Tallents Farm

81

The Hyde

BOTTOM

Porter's End

6

Hill Farm

Dane Farm

B652

KIMPTON

17

Great Cutts Farm

B653

Holly Lane

Lime Avenue

Beech

7

River of Lea

LOWER

40

HEATH LANE

Bower Heath

Lane

Blackmore End

Blackmore W

Brownfield

The Dale Av

The Slype

8

LUTON

BOWER

B652

Cold Harbour

Saucey Wood

Common Lane

Turners Hall Farm

Marshalls Heath Lane

16

The Lea Primary School

ROAD

30

30

Saucey Wood

Sauncey Wood Prim School

Saucey Wood

Mackerye End

9

Westfield Cemetery

Riverside Estate

Pickford Hill

Mitford Hill

Westfield Primary School

514

A **B** **C** **102** **D** **E** **F** **G**

Batford

Lea Valley

Marshalls Heath

1 grid square represents 500 metres

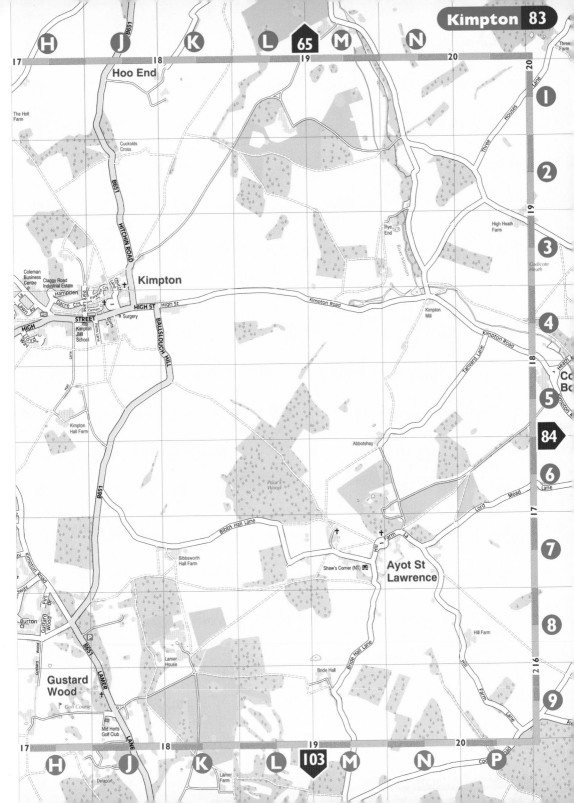

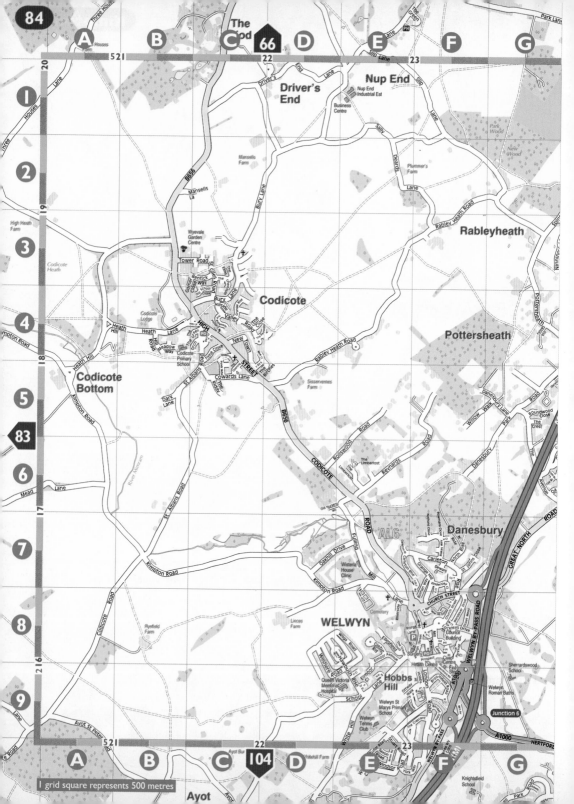

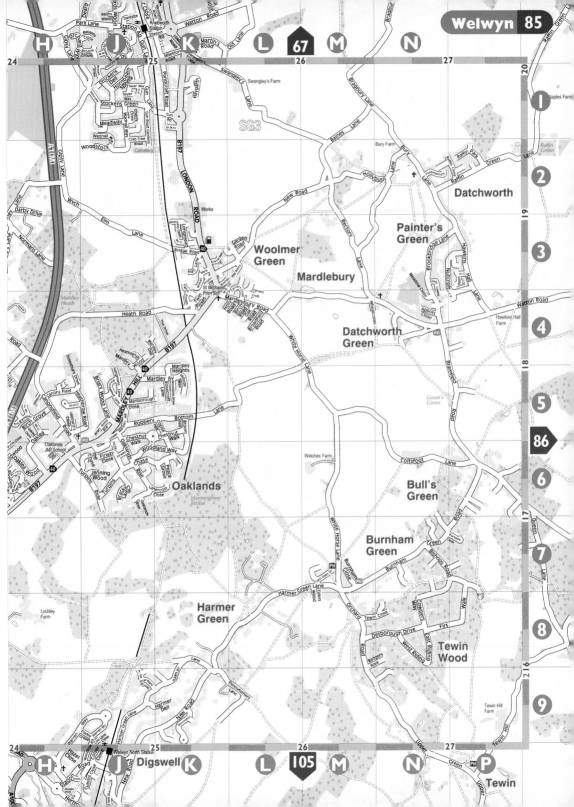

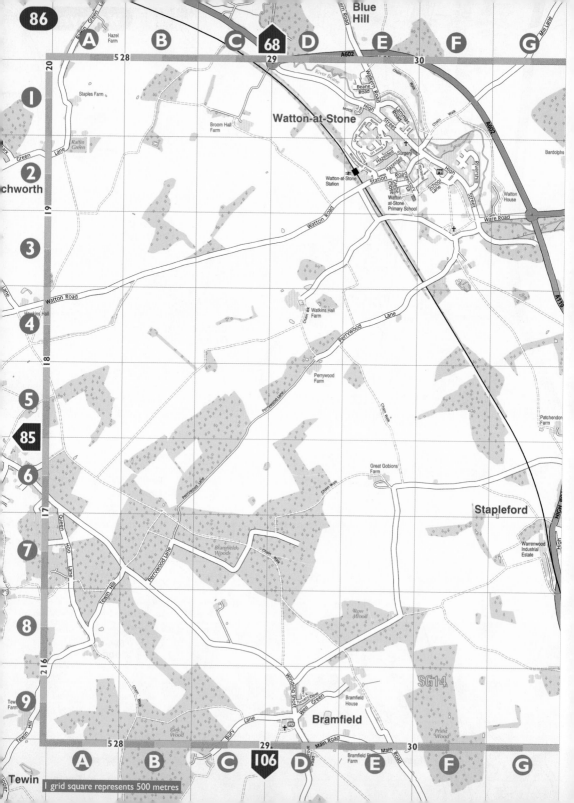

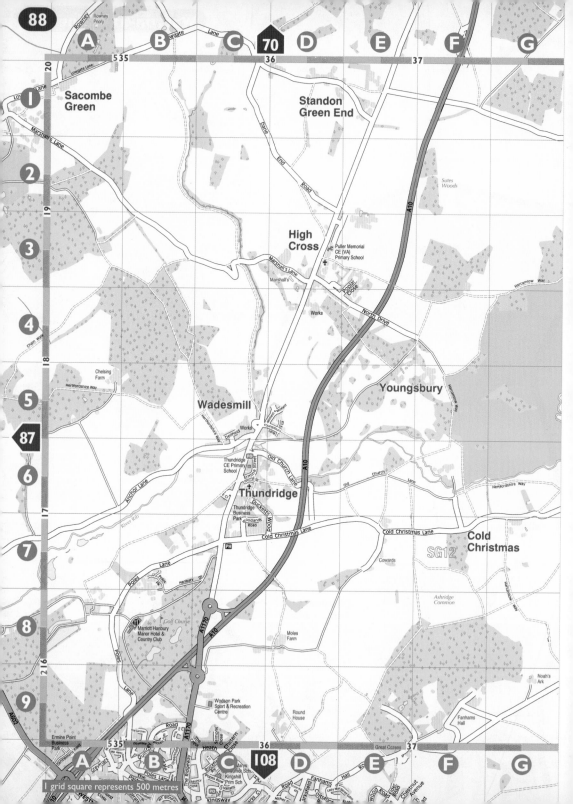

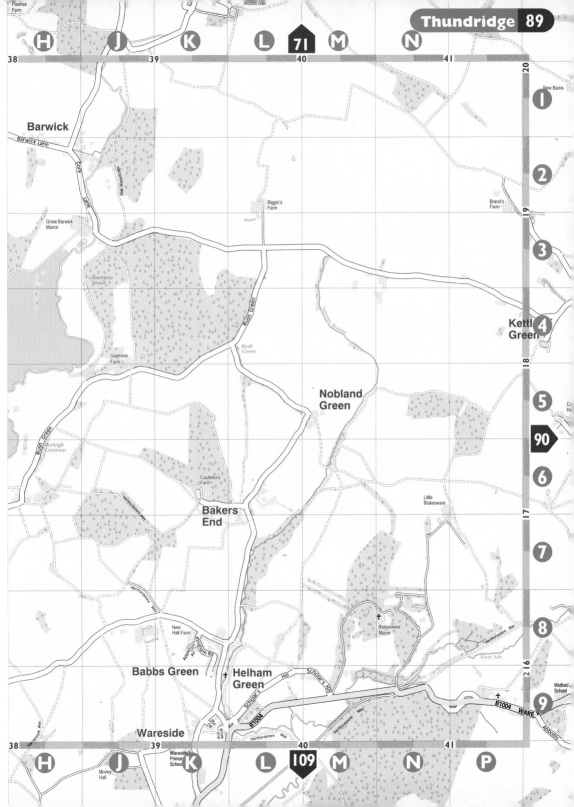

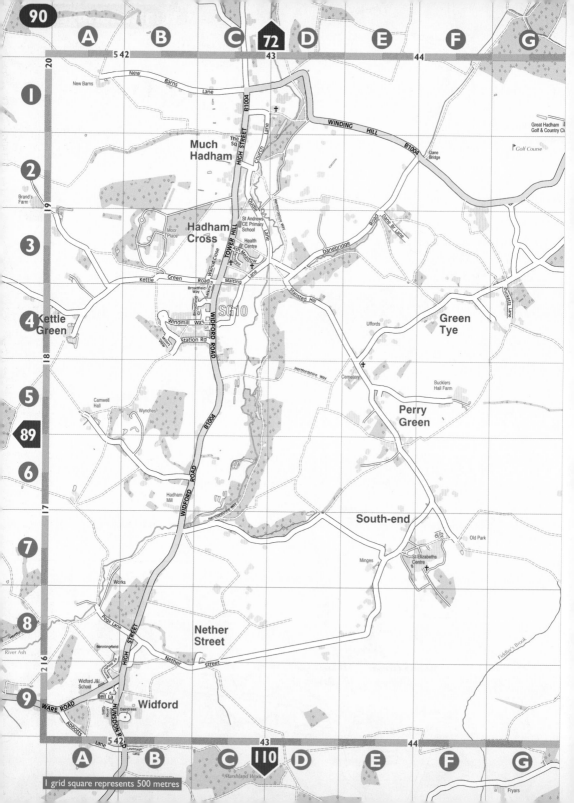

A B C 72 D E F G

5 42 43 44

New Barns
New Barns Lane
B1004

I

Much
Hadham

Winding Hill
B1004

Great Hadham
Golf & Country Club

The Sq
Church Lane
HIGH STREET

Golf Course

Dane
Bridge

2
Brand's
Farm

19

Hertfordshire Way

St Andrews
CE Primary
School

Hadham
Cross

Dane Br Lane

Dane

3

TOWER HILL

Walnut Close
Maltings Lane

Health
Centre

ASH Meadow

Danebridge

Kettle Green Road

Stansted Hill

Uffords

Green
Tye

Ducketts Lane

4 Kettle
Green

Moor
Place

Broadfield
Way

Windmill Way
Broadfield Lane

SG10

WIDFORD ROAD

Station Rd

Mill Way

18

5

Camwell
Hall

Wynches

Hertfordshire Way

Cemetery

Perry
Green

Bucklers
Hall Farm

89

6

B1004

WIDFORD ROAD

Hadham
Mill

Hertfordshire Way

17

South-end

Old Park

7

St Elizabeths
Centre

Minges

Works

8

HIGH STREET

Pegs Lane

Benningfield

Fiddler's Brook

Hertford

2 16

River Ash

Nether
Street

Nether Street

Widford J&I
School

Bell La

9

Ware Road

HUNSDON ROAD

Widford

Daintrees

Abbotts

Lane

Leventage
Lane

5 42

A B C 110 D E F G

43 44

Marshland Wood

Fryars

I grid square represents 500 metres

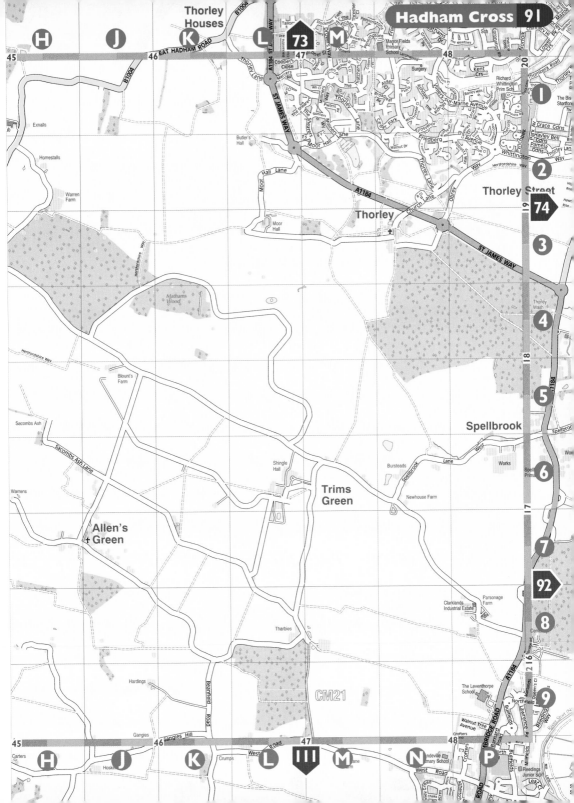

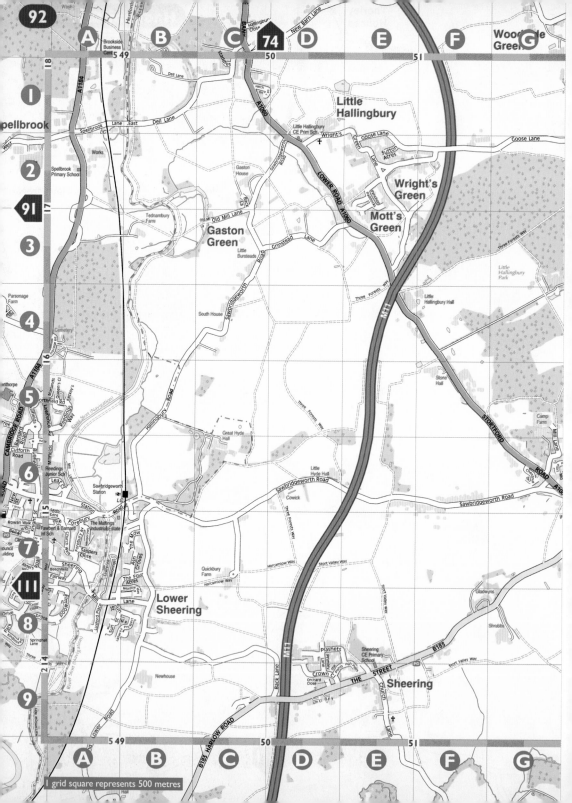

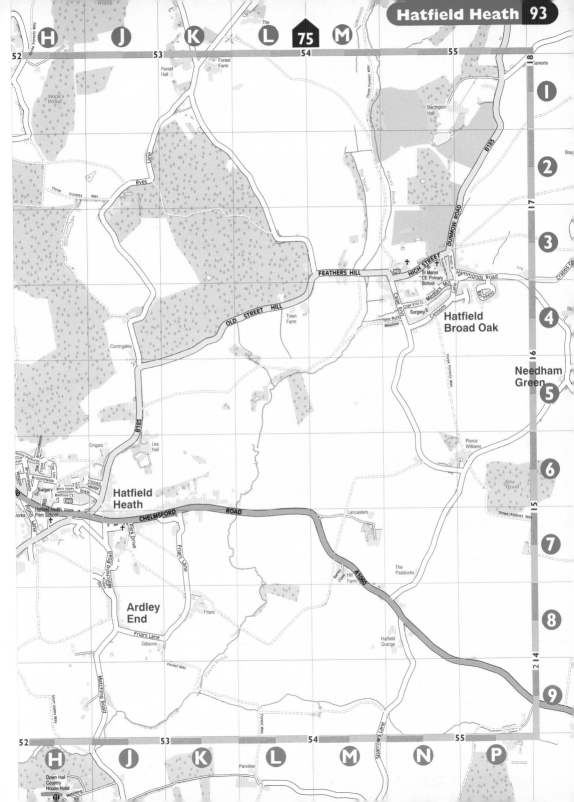

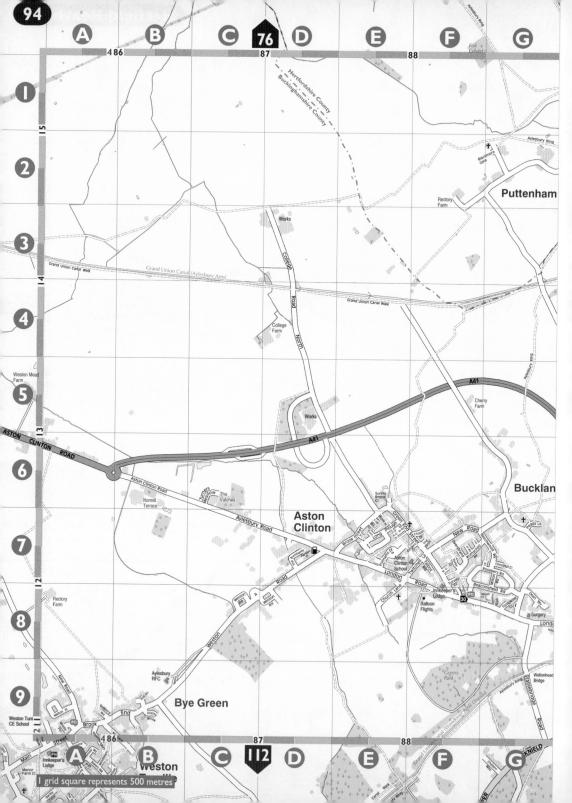

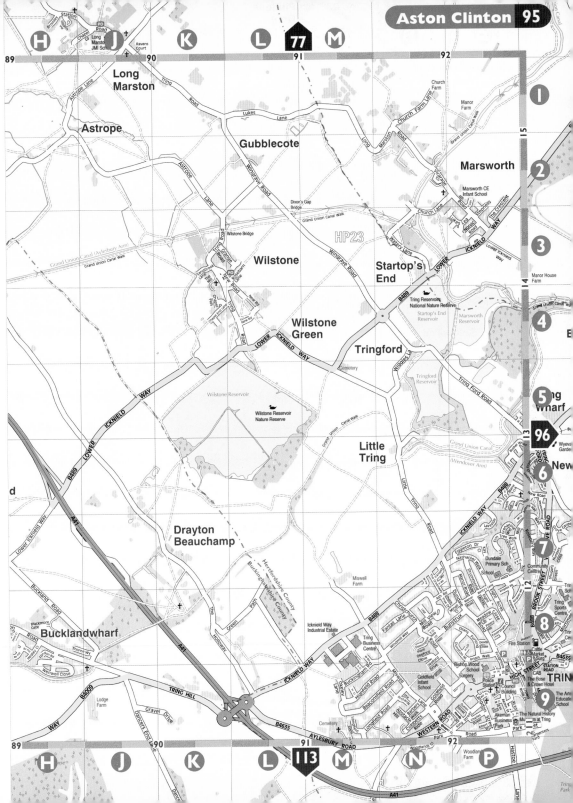

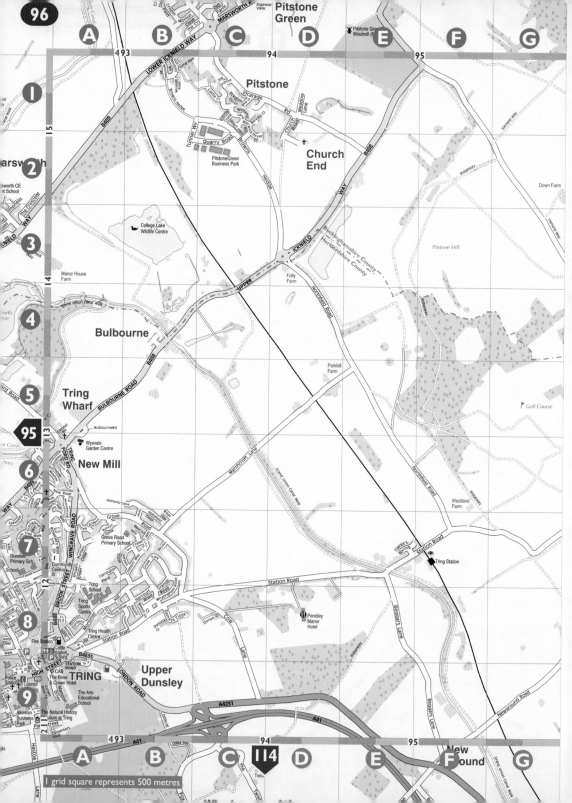

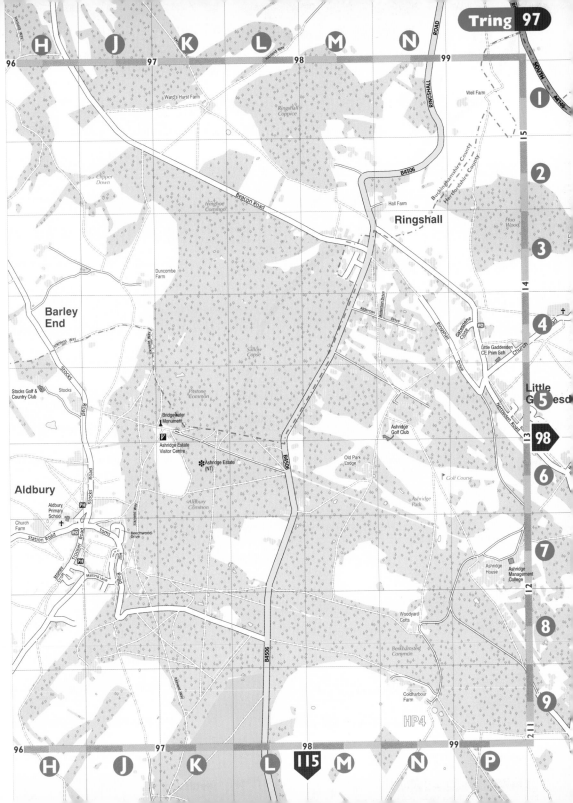

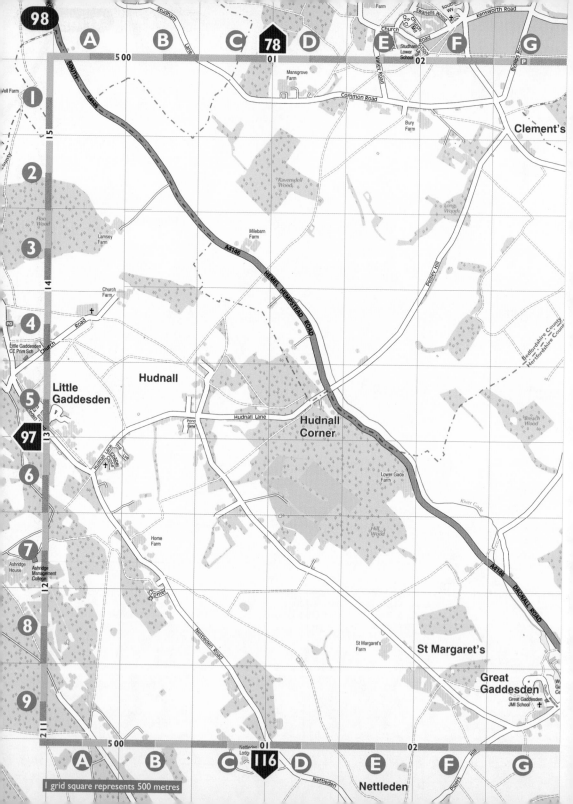

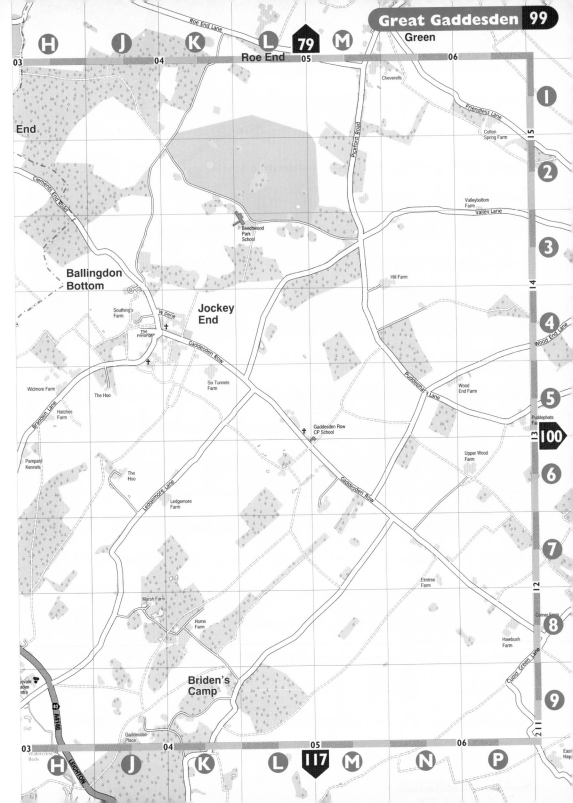

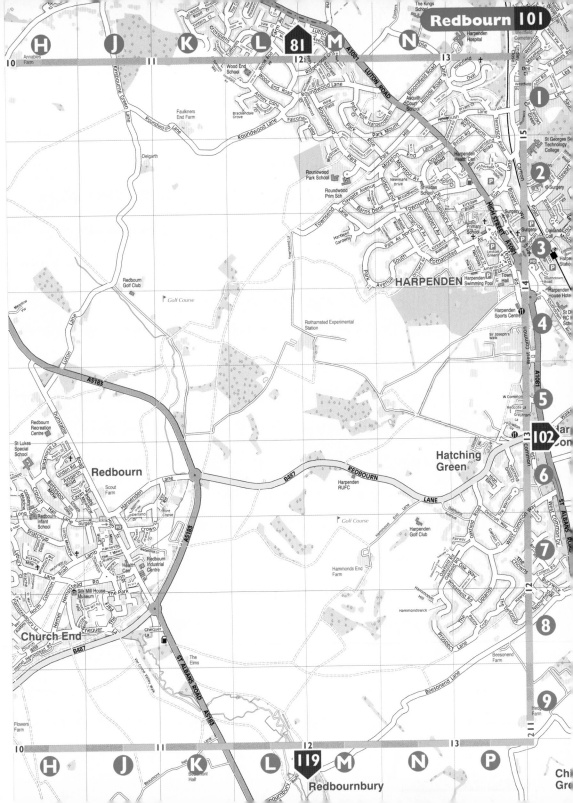

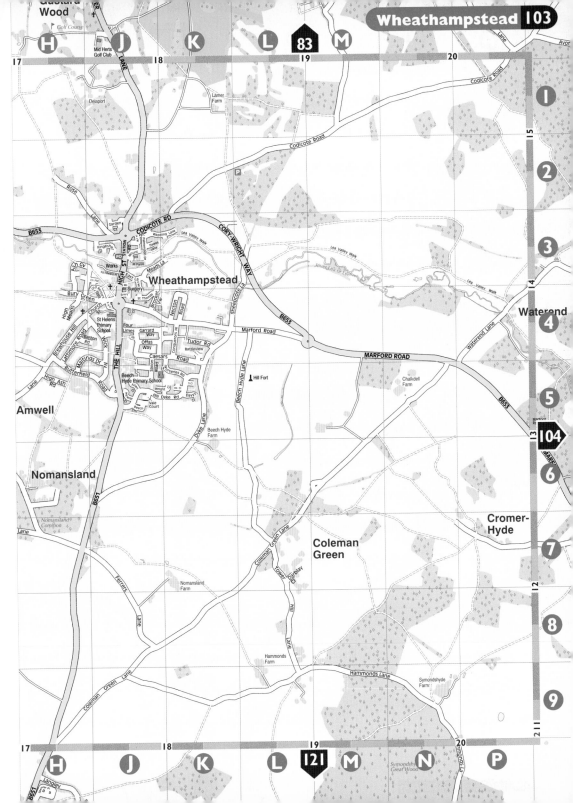

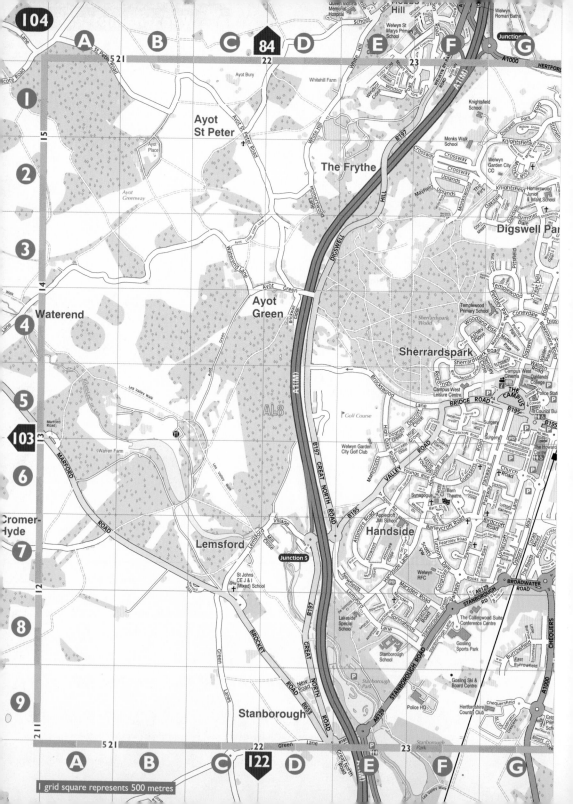

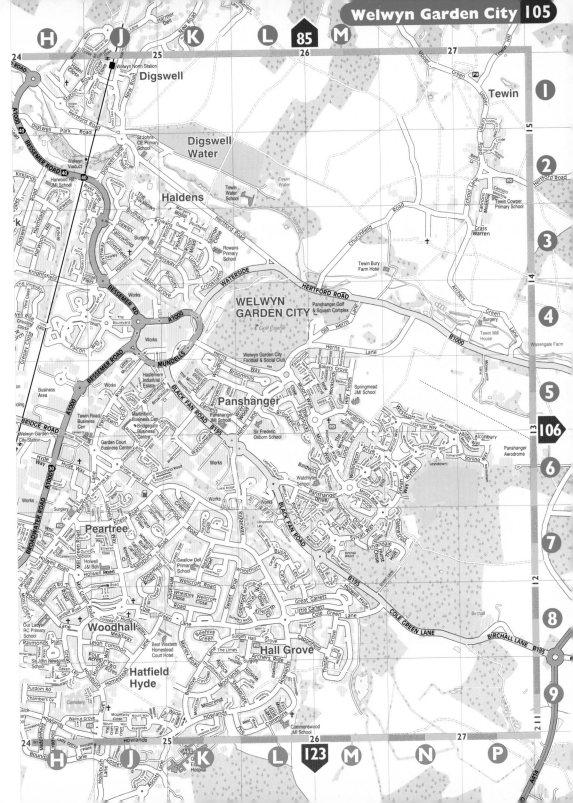

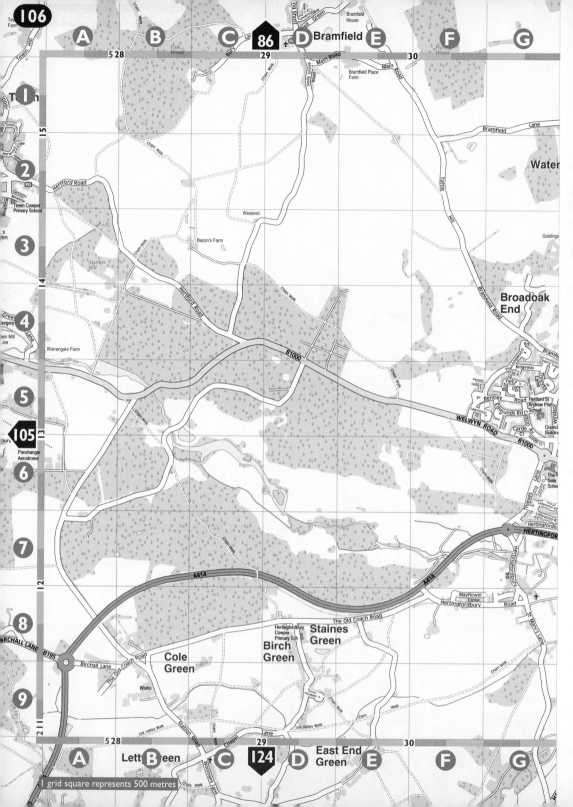

A   **B**   **C**   **D** Bramfield   **E**   **F**   **G**

86

5 28   29   30

I   T

15

2

Tewin Cowper
Primary School

3

Marden Hill

14

Bacon's Farm

Westend

Hertford Road

4

Warrengate Farm

Hertford Road

Chain Walk

B1000

5

13

WELWYN ROAD

B1000

105

Panshanger
Aerodrome

6

7

12

A414

HERTINGFOR

8

RCHALL LANE   B195   Birchall Lane

The Old Coach Road

The Old Coach Road

Hertingfordbury
Cowper
Primary Sch

Staines
Green

Mayflower
Close
HERTINGFORDBURY

**Cole
Green**

Works

**Birch
Green**

9

2 11

5 28   29   30

Chapel Lane

Lea Valley Walk

Lea Valley Walk

A   Lett**B**een   **C**   124   **D** East End
Green   **E**   **F**   **G**

Bramfield House

Bramfield Place
Farm

Main Road

Main Road

Bramfield Lane

Tattle Hill

Water

Goldings

Broadoak
End

Bramfield Road

Ridgeway
Bentley Road   Hertford St Andrew Prim School
Lawrence
Edmunds Rd
Carde
Windsor
Council
Building

Thieves Lane

The Sele School

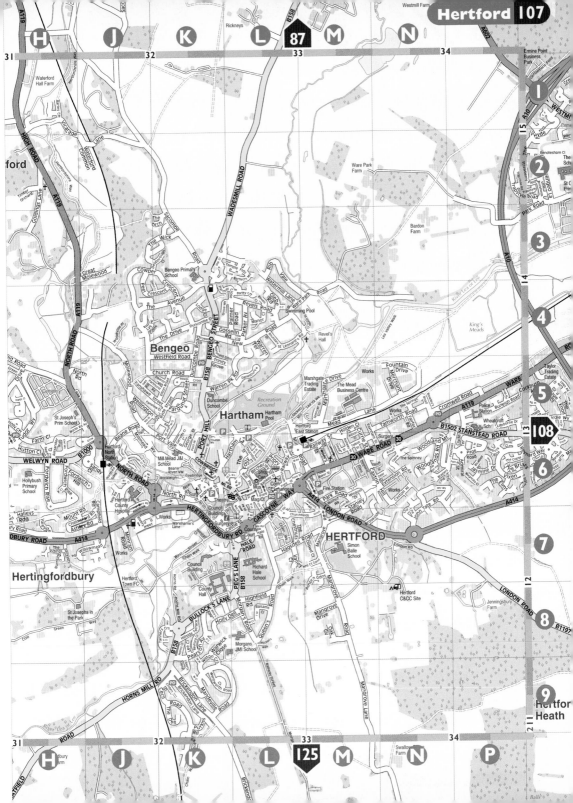

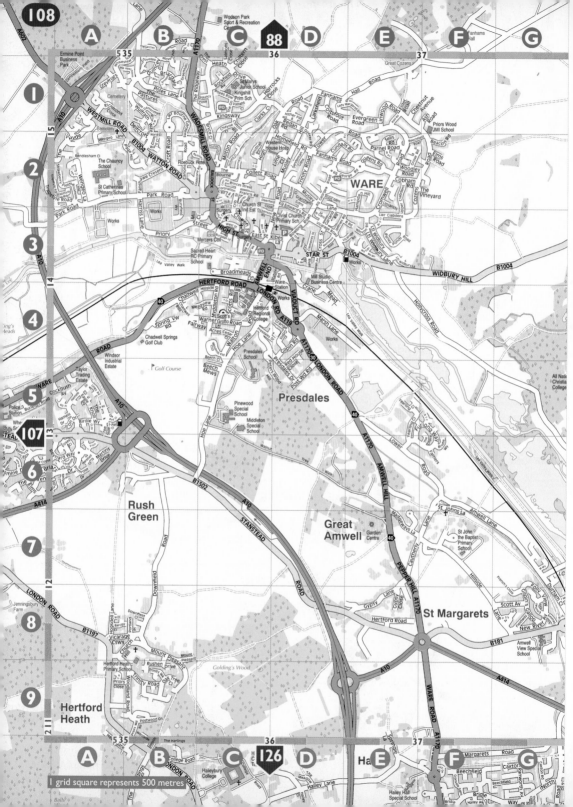

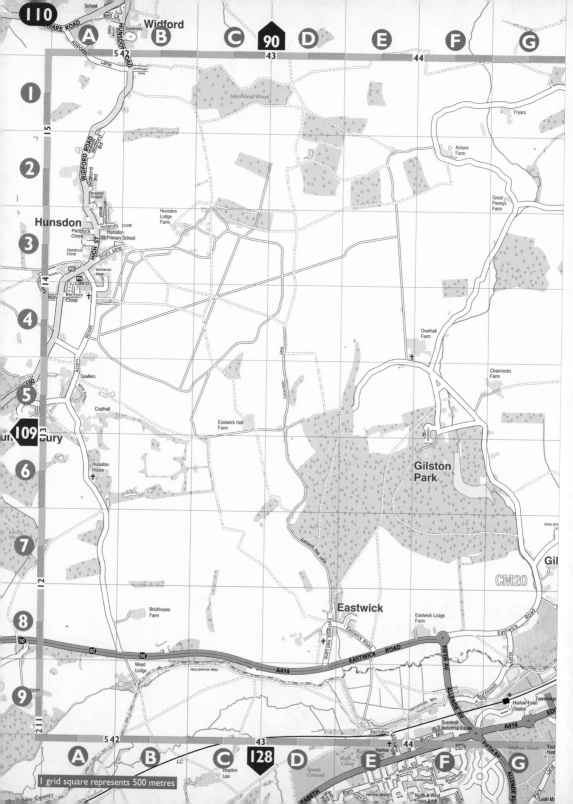

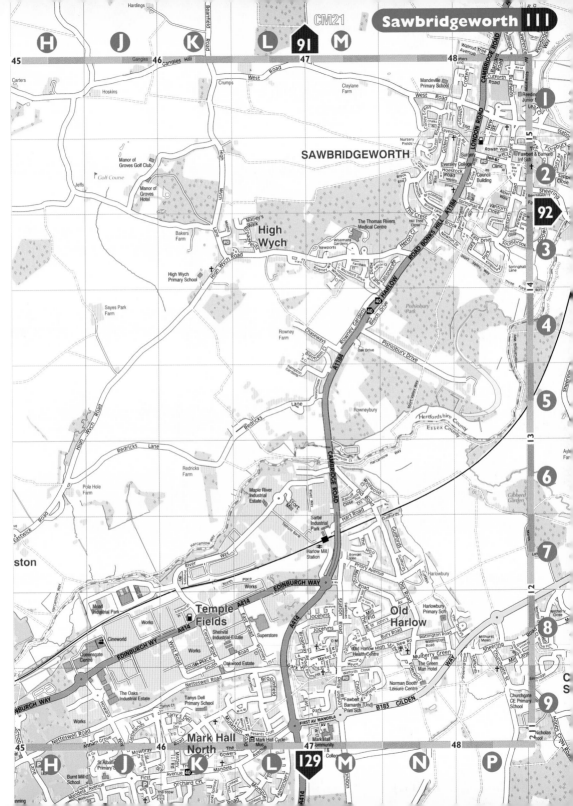

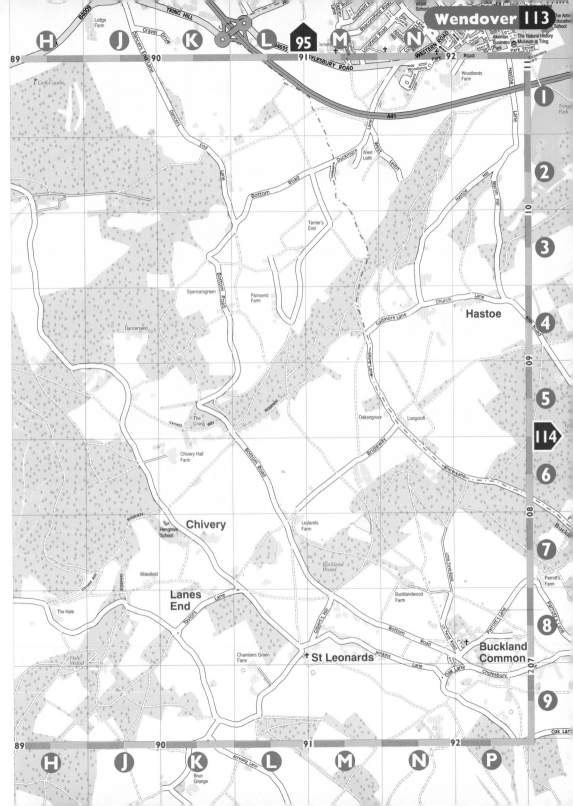

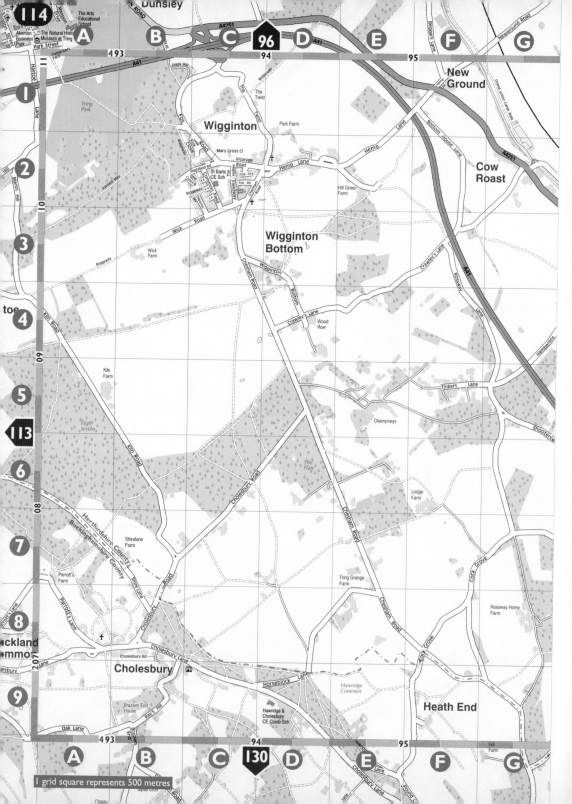

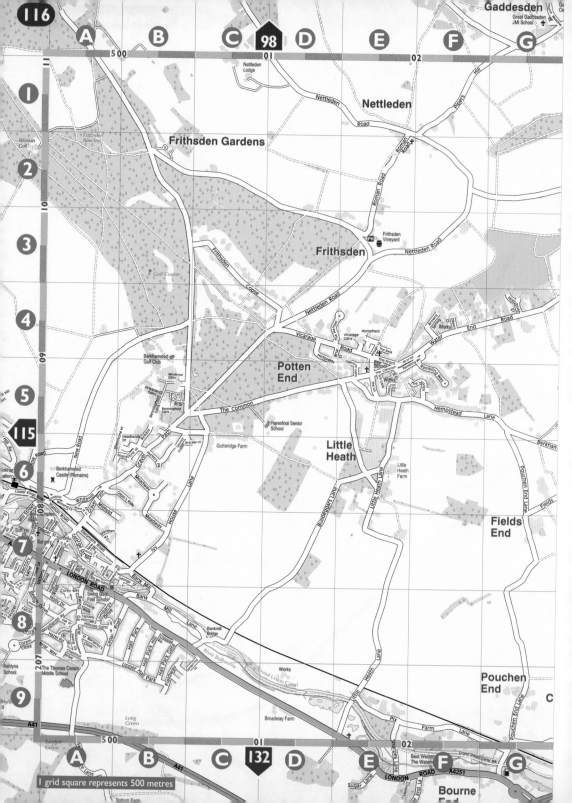

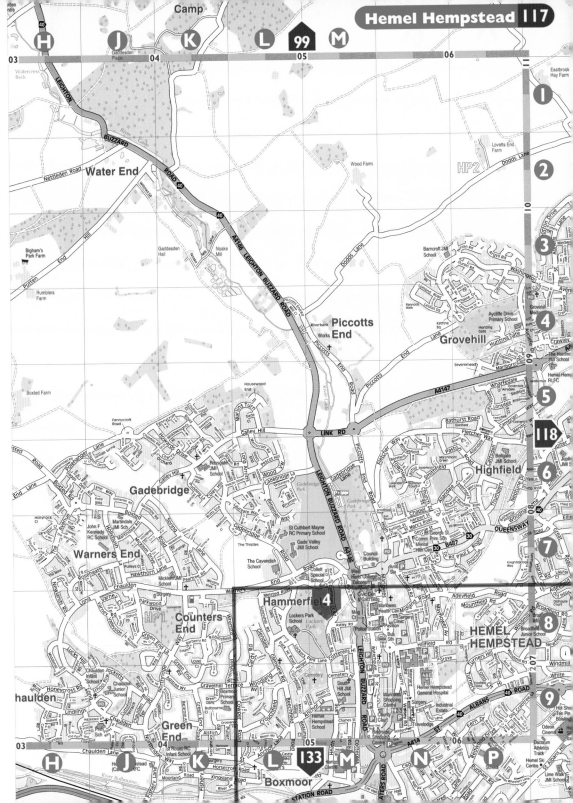

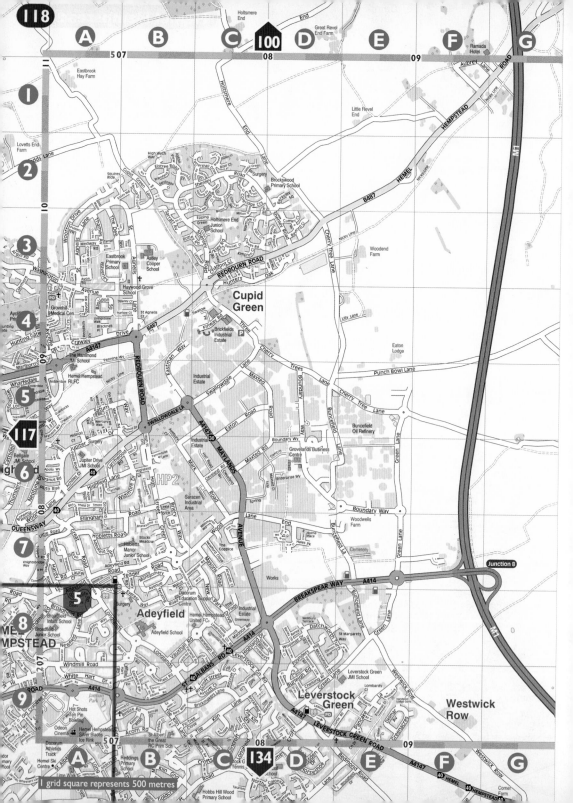

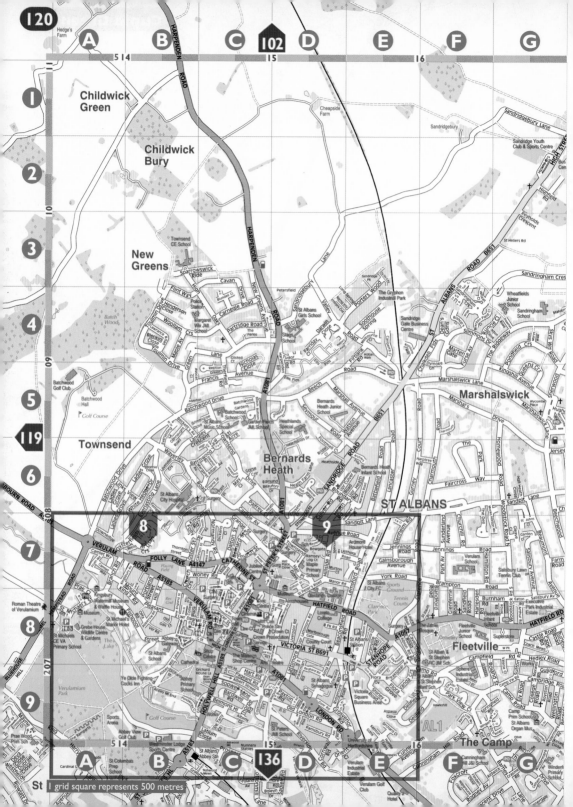

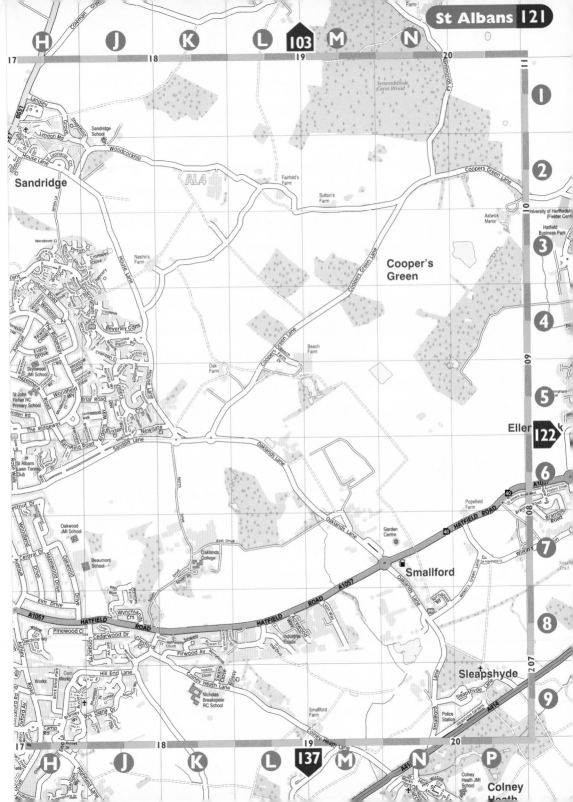

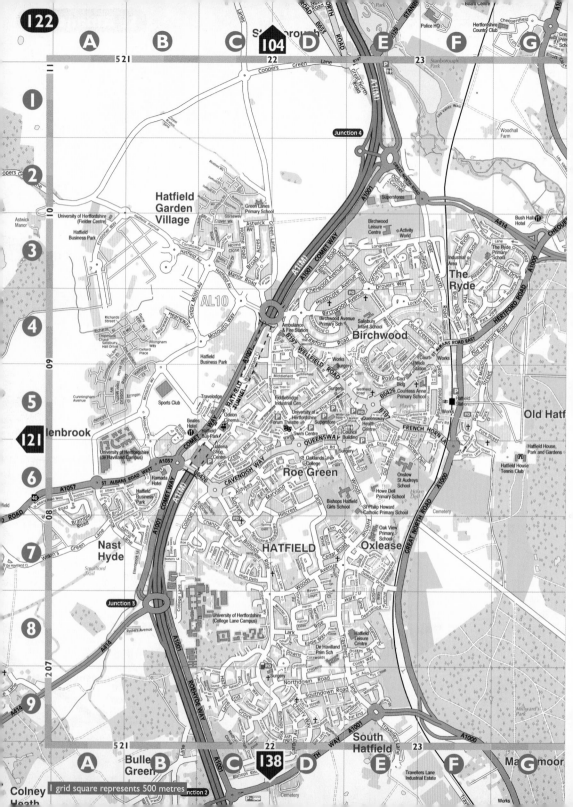

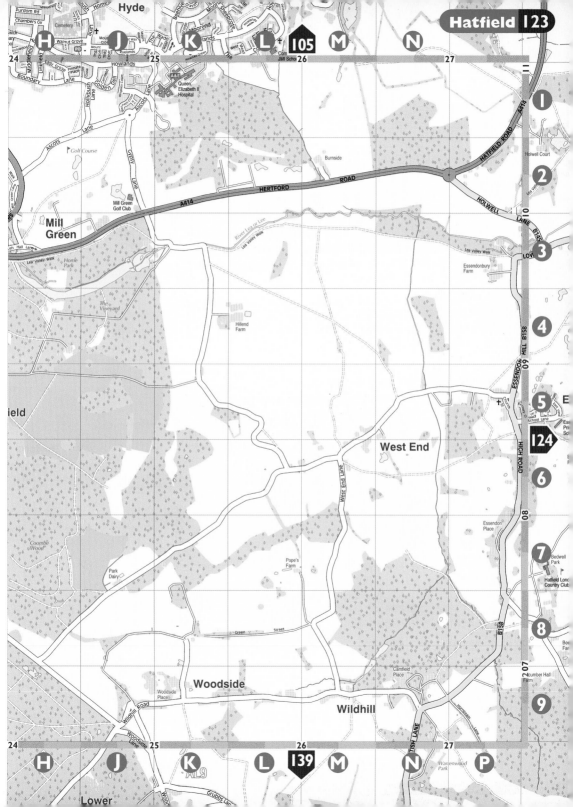

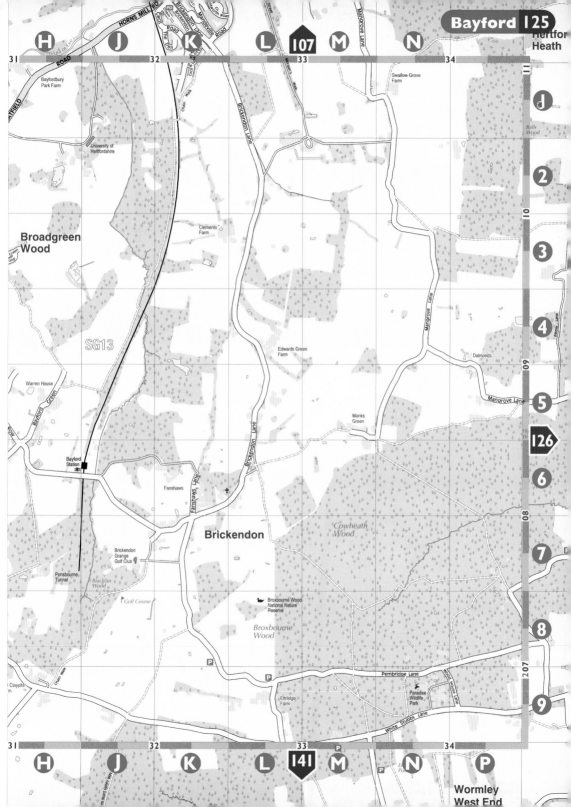

H   J   K   L   107   M   N

31   32   33   34

Bayfordbury
Park Farm

Swallow Grove
Farm

J

Balls
Wood

2

University of
Hertfordshire

Clements
Farm

Broadgreen
Wood

3

4

SG13

Edwards Green
Farm

Dalmonds

Warren House

Mangrove Lane

5

Bayford Green

Monks
Green

126

Bayford
Station

6

Fanshaws

Fanshaws Lane

Brickendon Lane

Cowheath
Wood

7

Brickendon

Ponsbourne
Tunnel

Brickendon
Grange
Golf Club

Blackfan
Wood

8

Golf Course

Broxbourne Wood
National Nature
Reserve

Broxbourne
Wood

Claypits

Chain Walk

Pembridge Lane

Paradise
Wildlife
Park

Wood House Lane

207

9

Ettridge
Farm

White Stubbs Lane

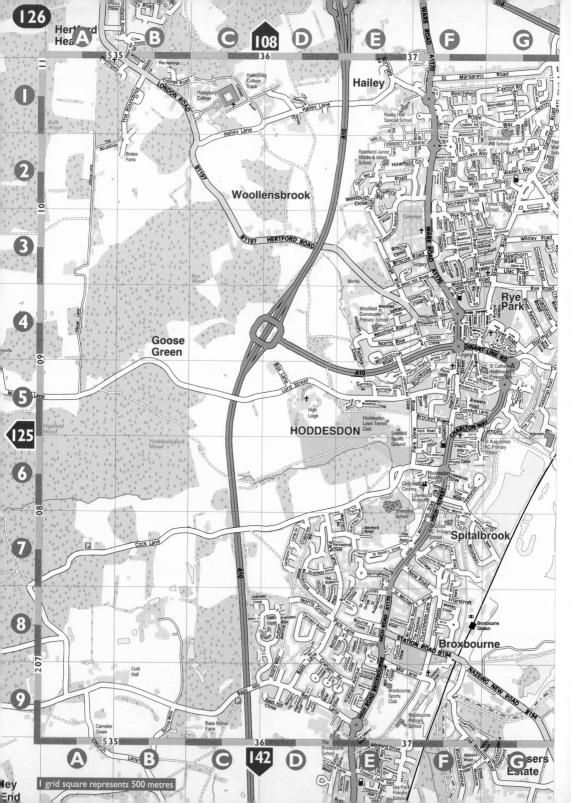

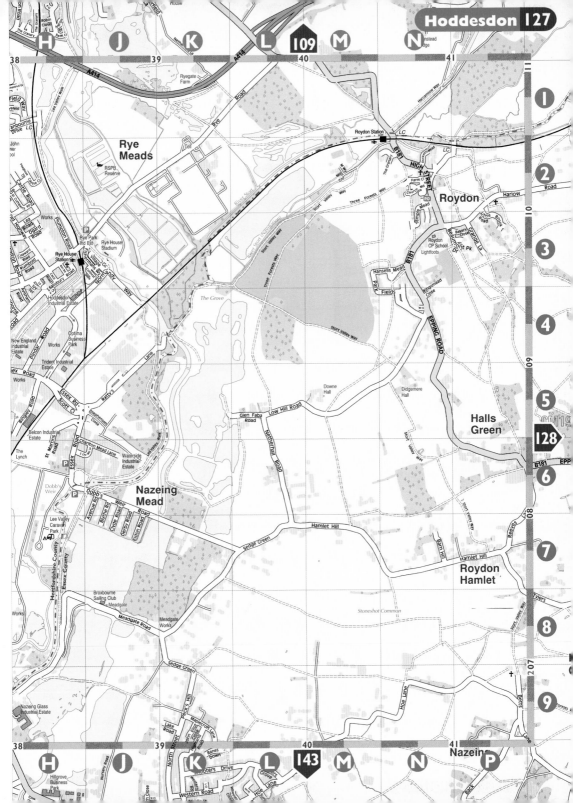

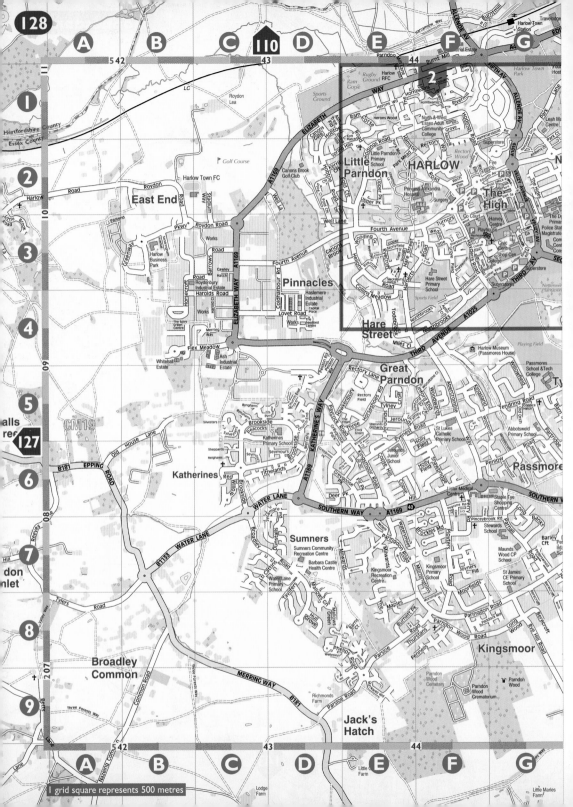

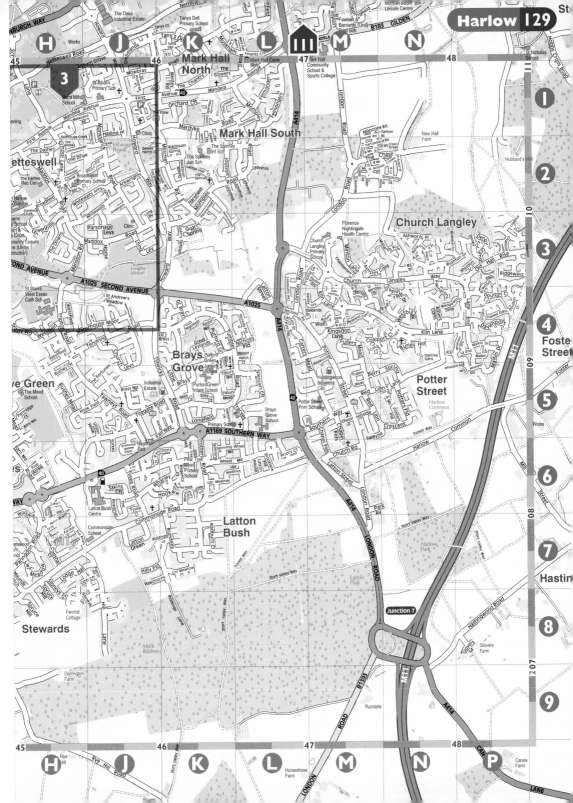

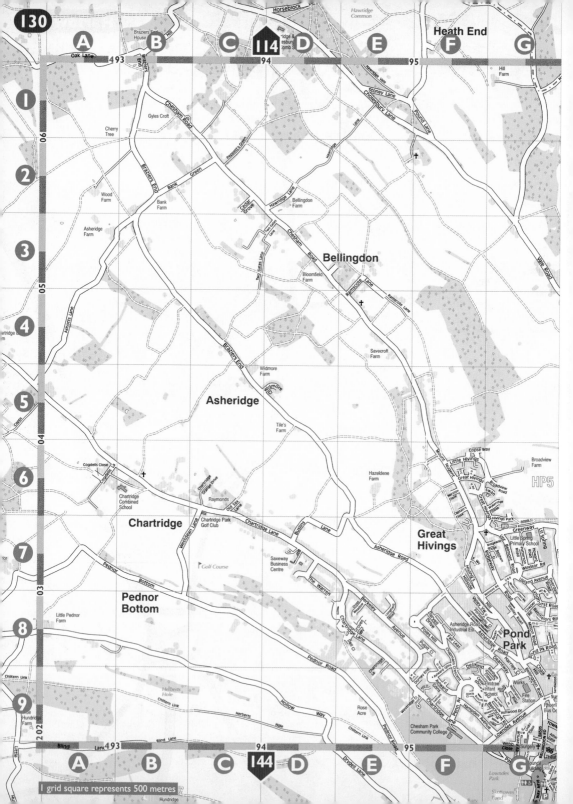

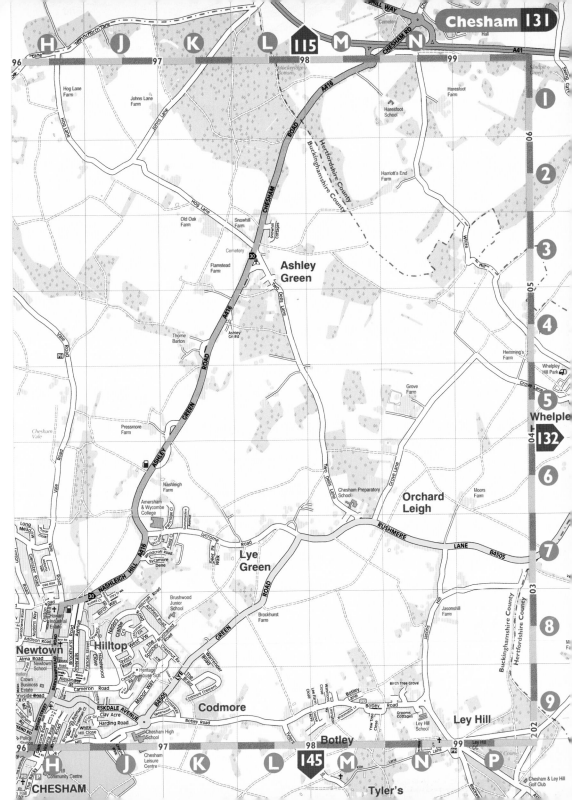

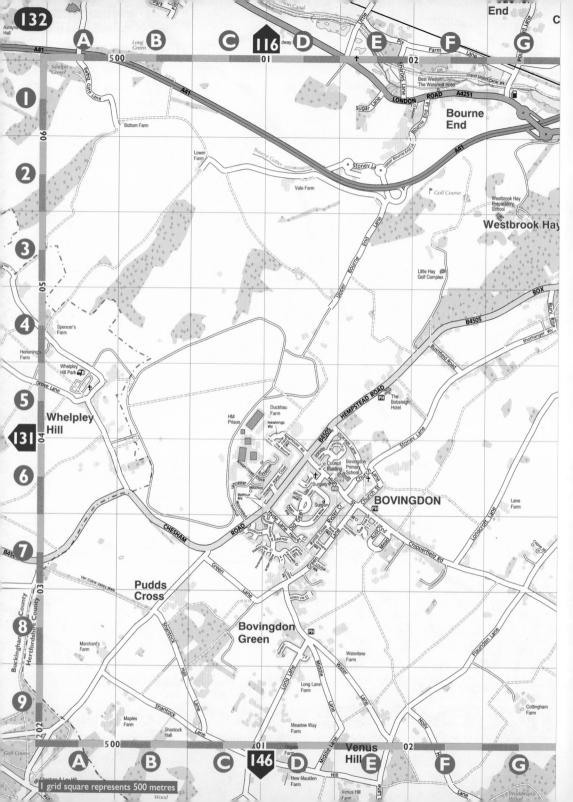

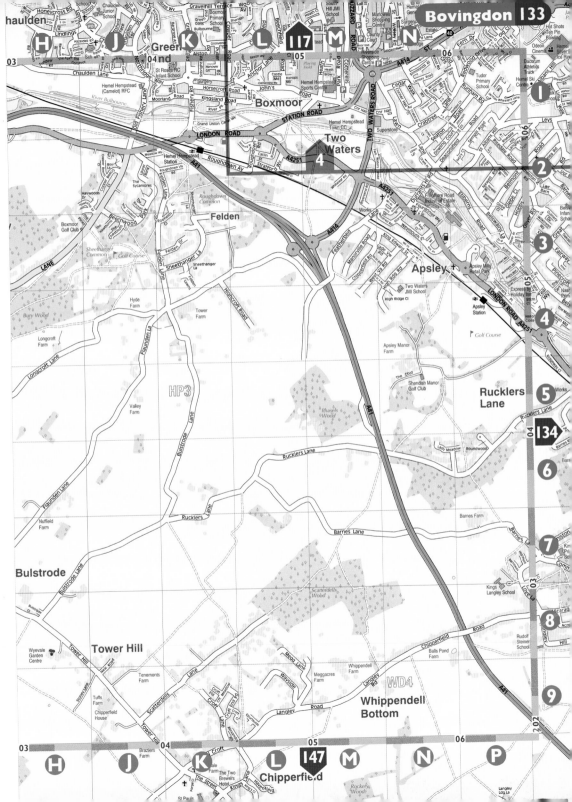

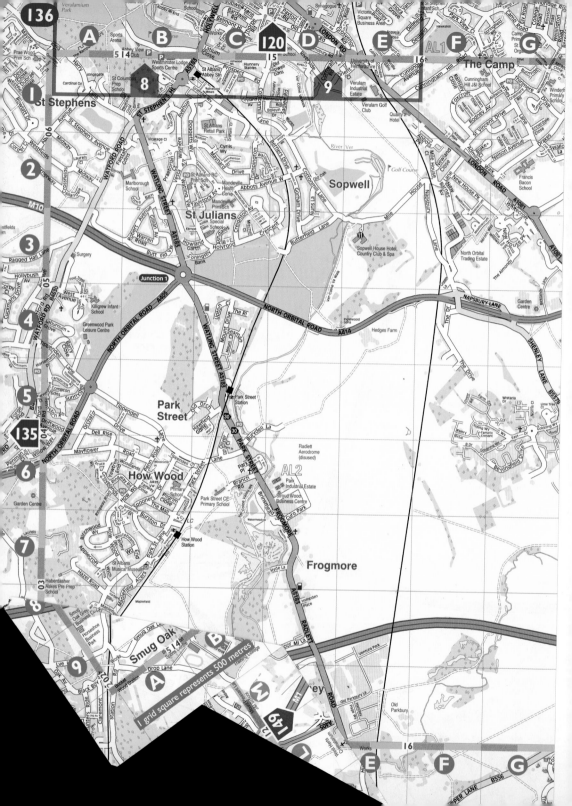

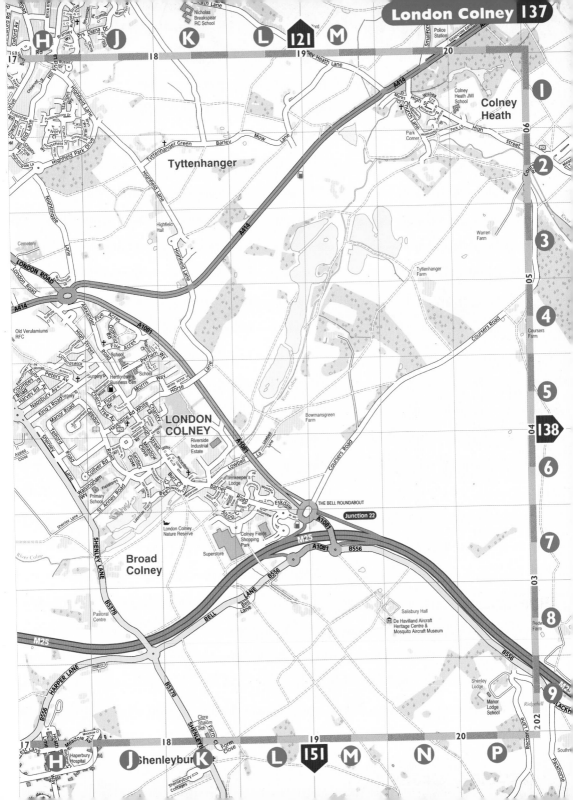

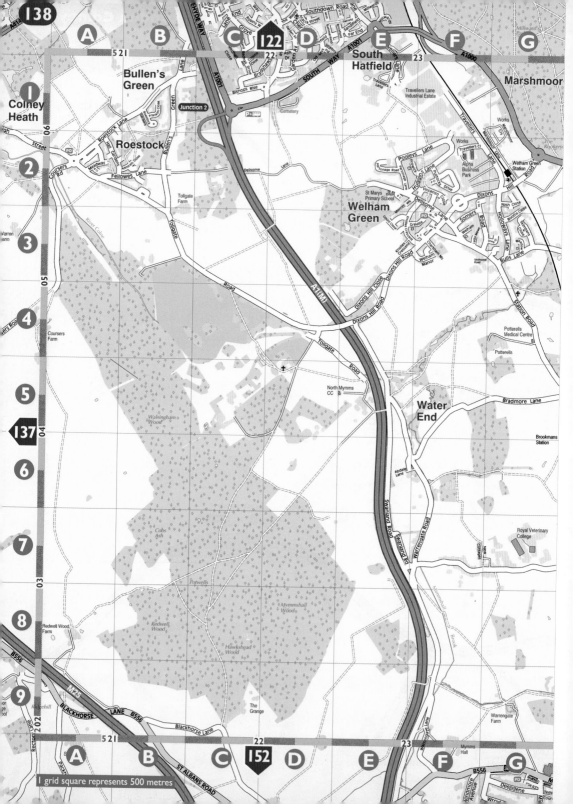

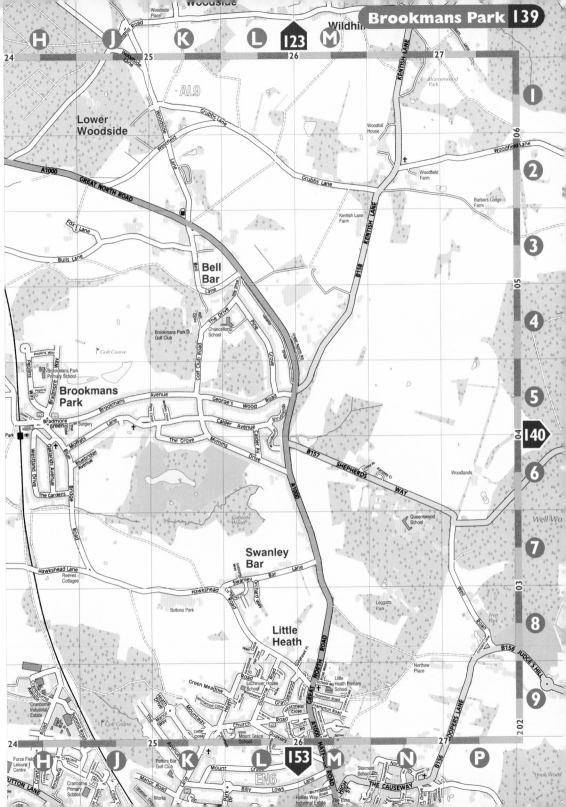

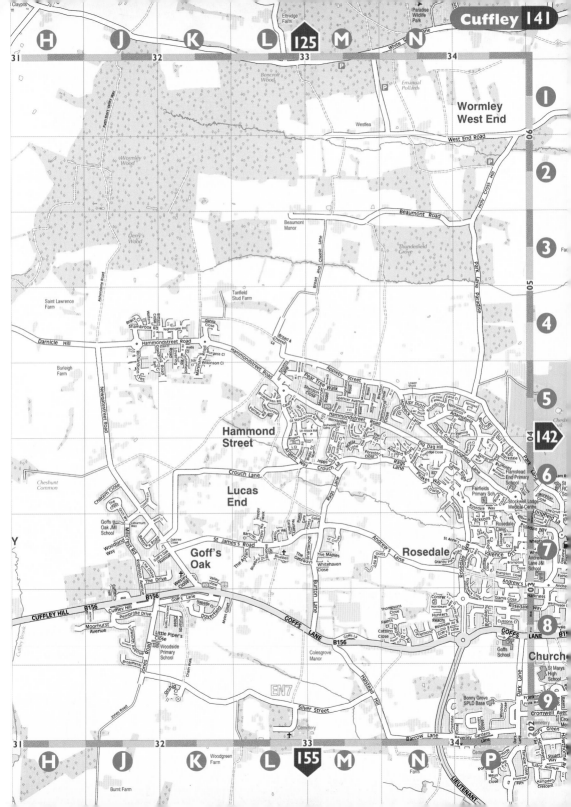

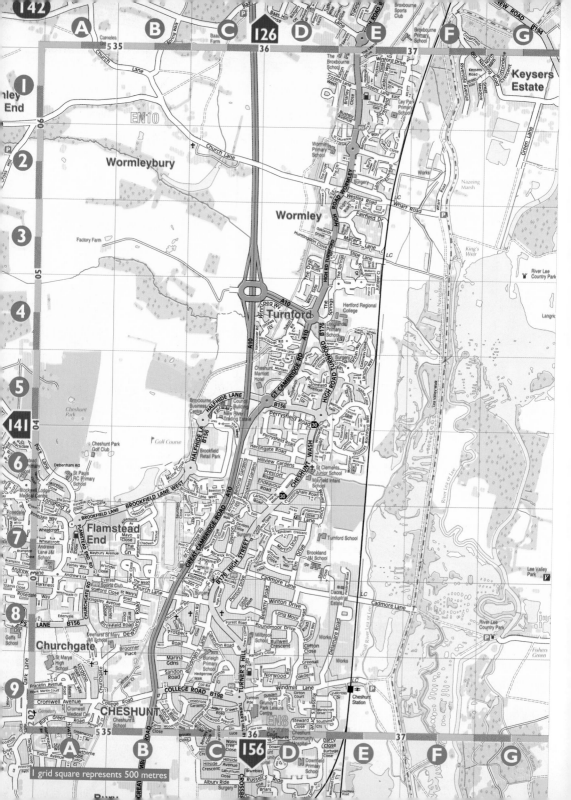

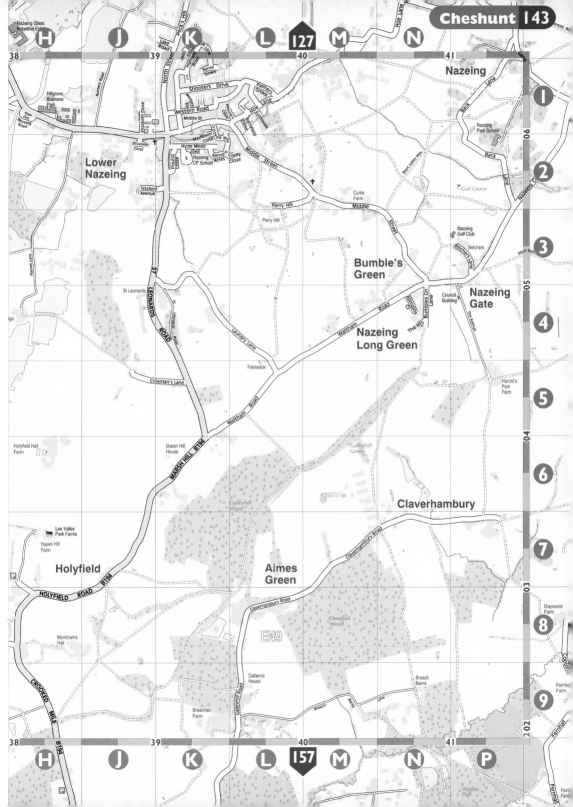

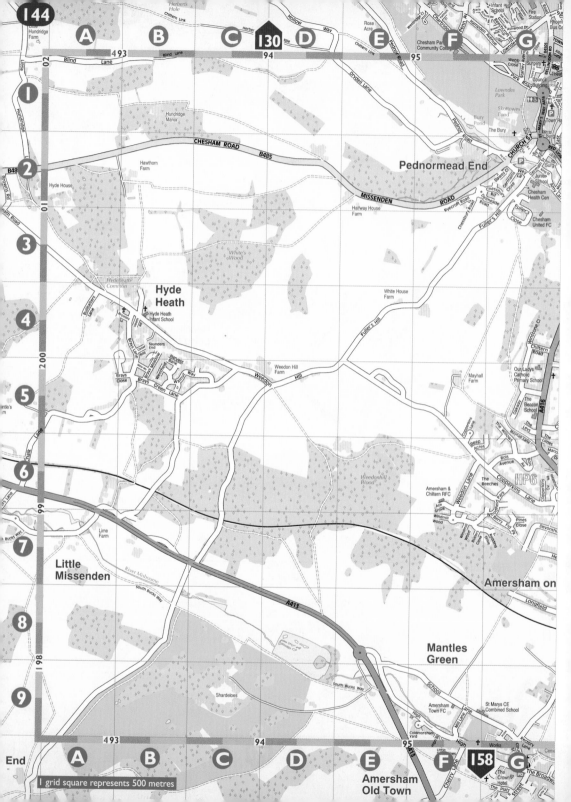

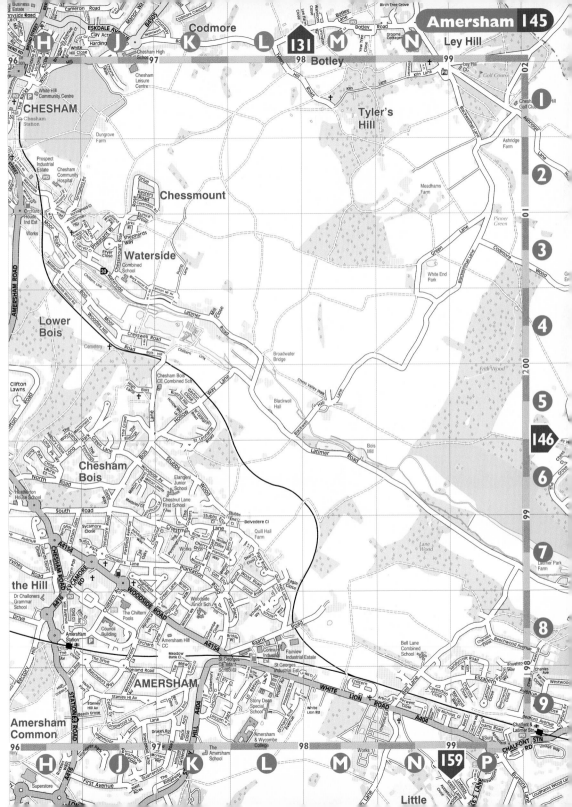

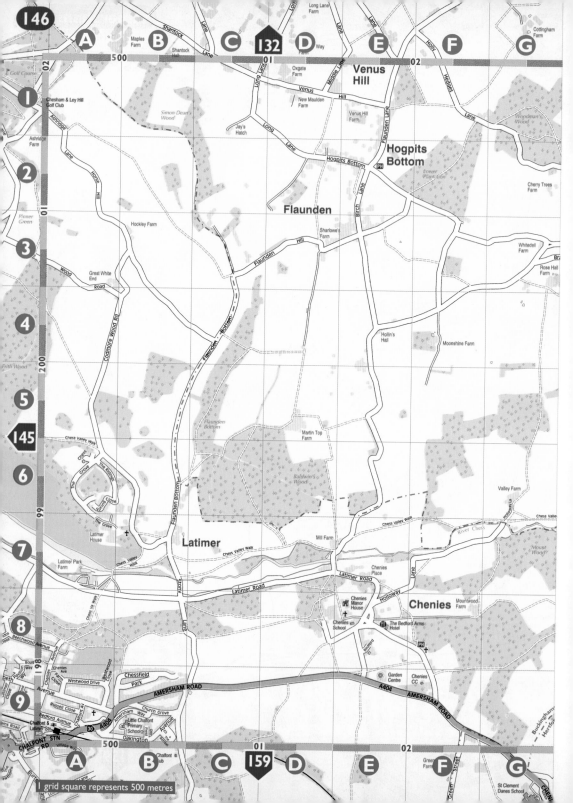

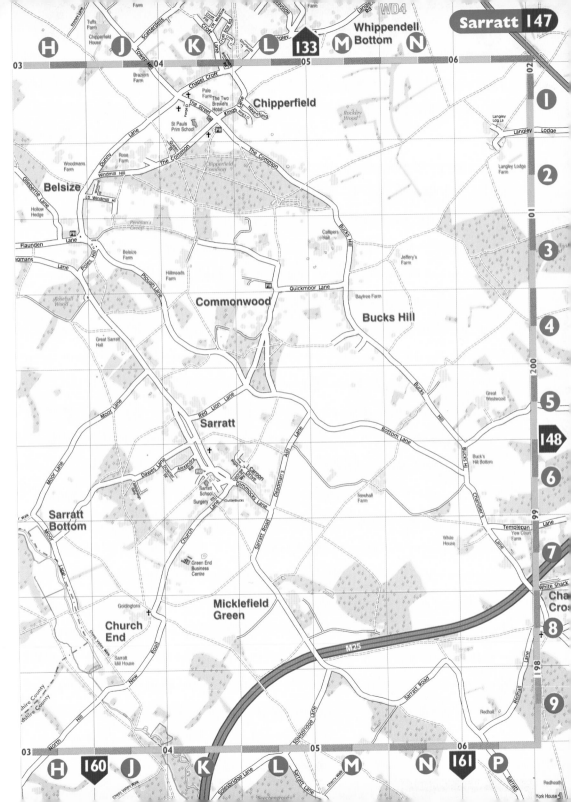

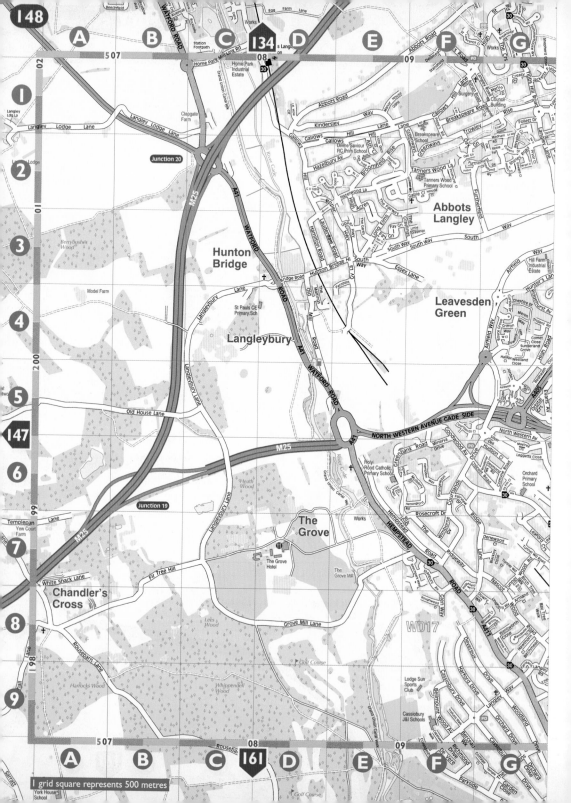

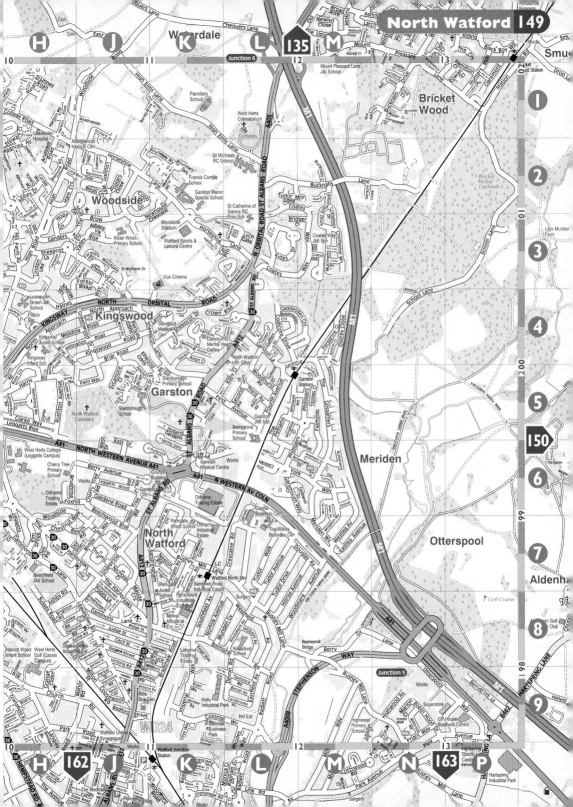

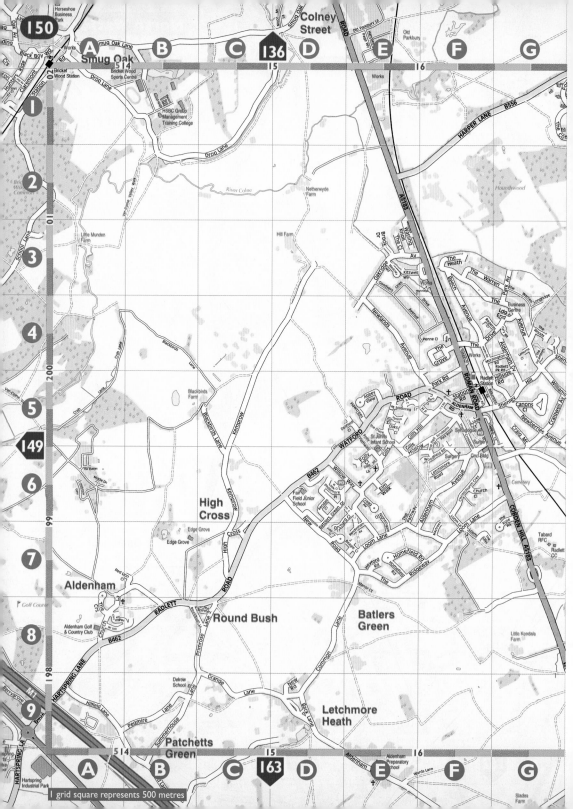

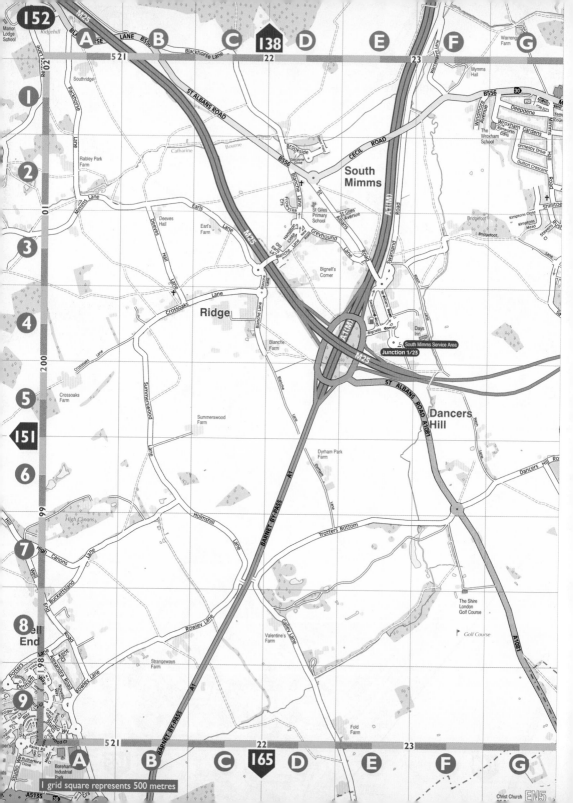

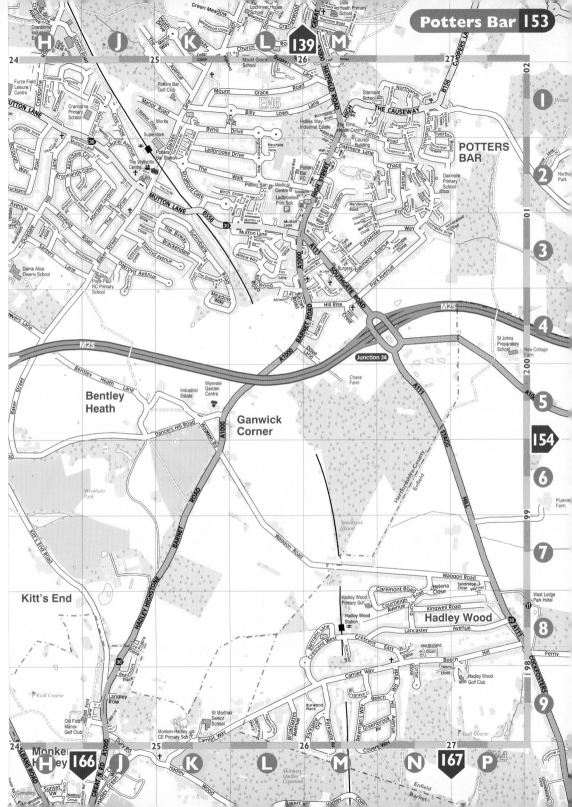

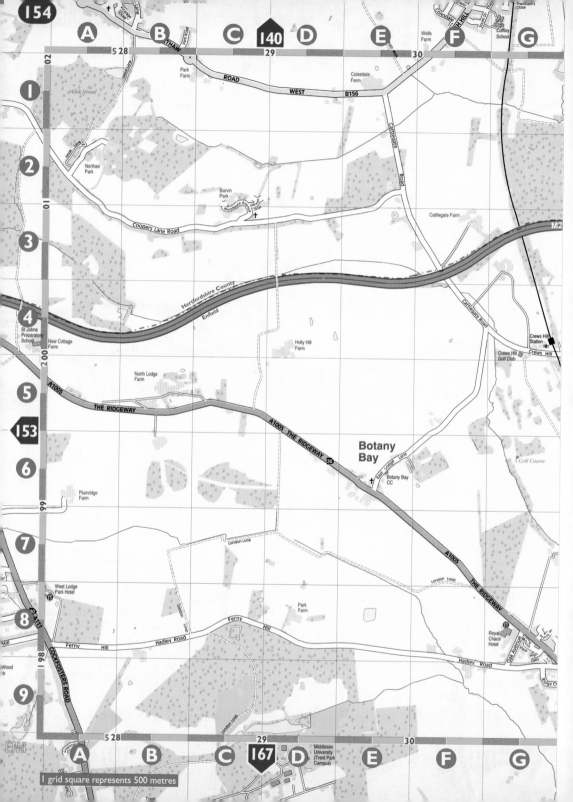

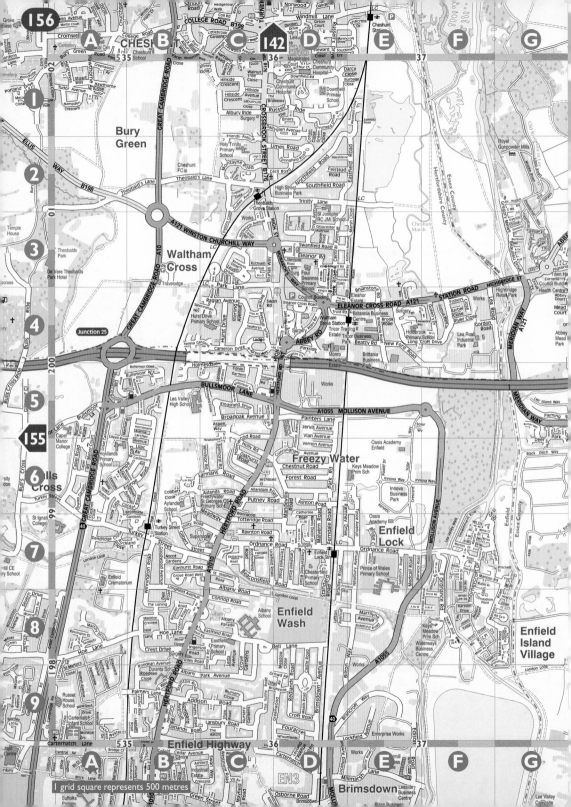

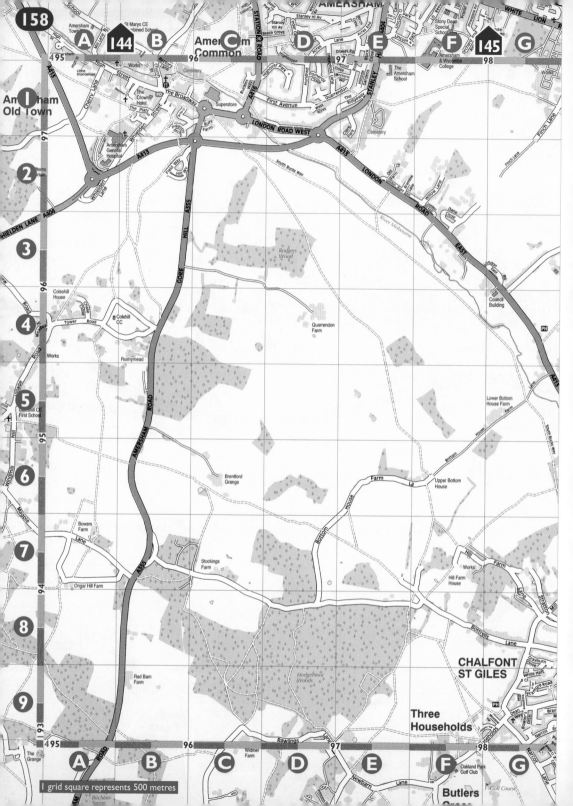

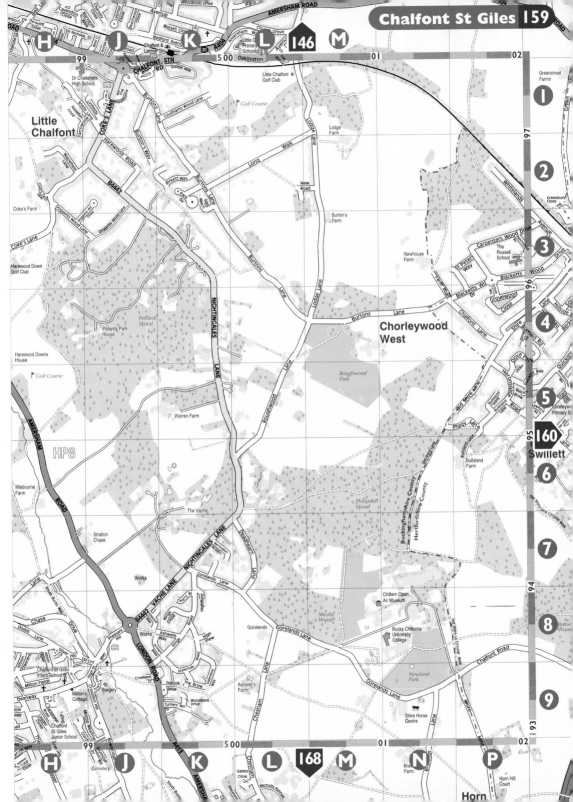

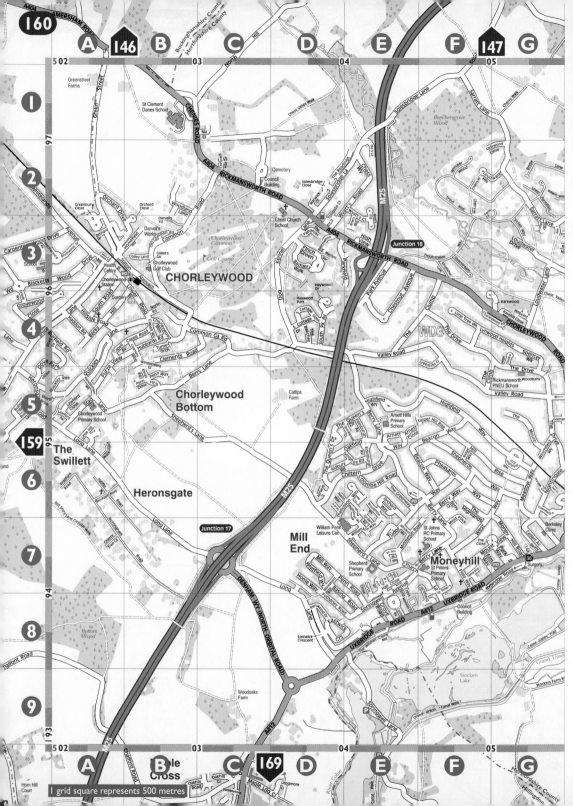

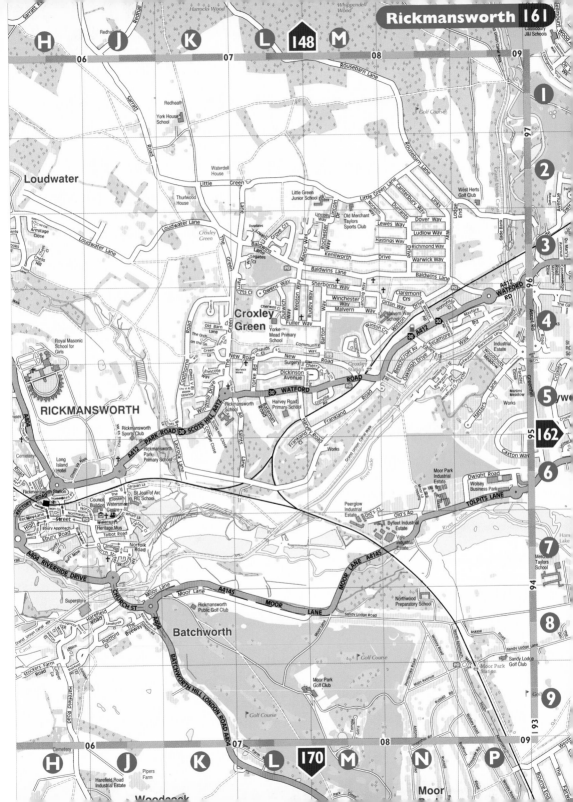

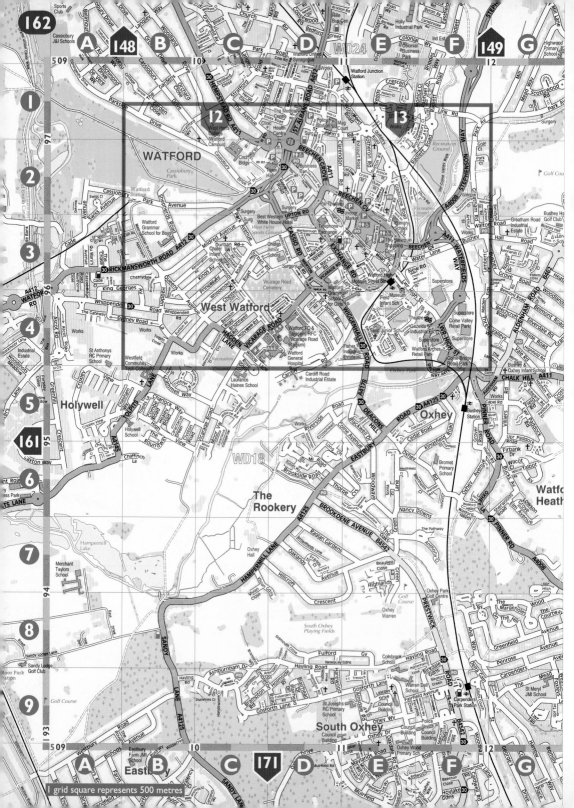

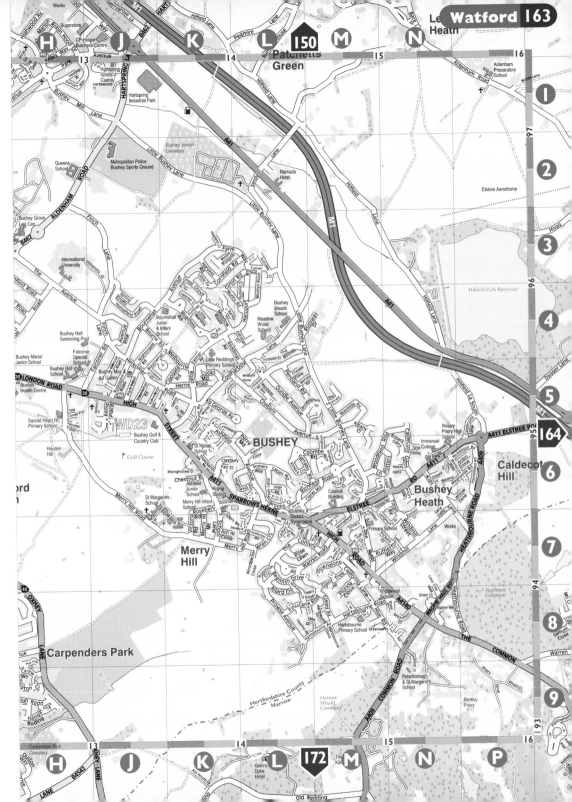

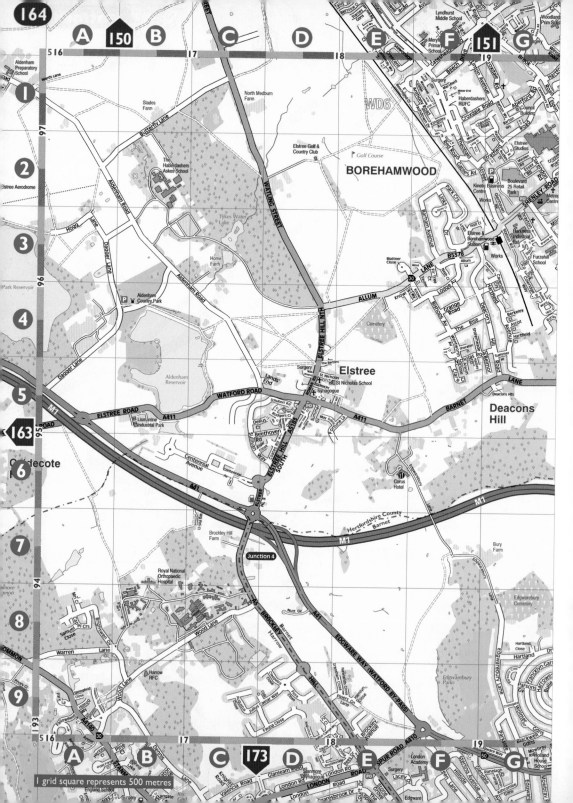

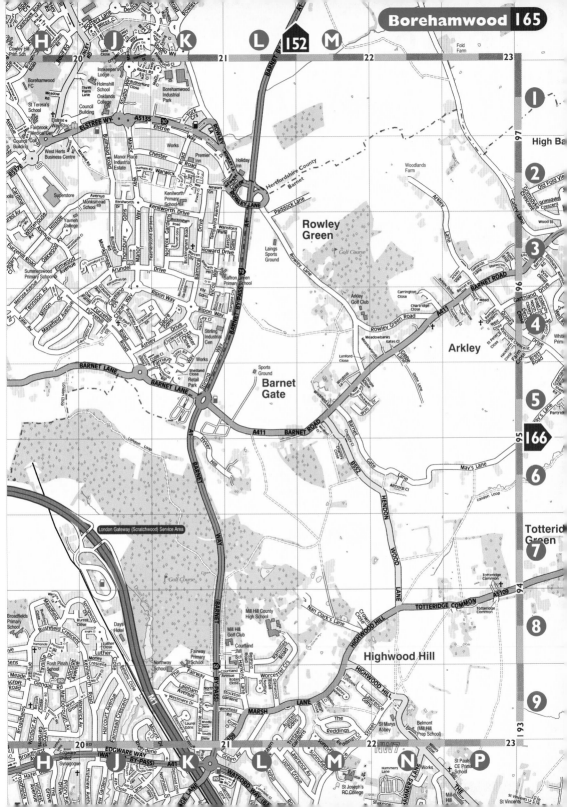

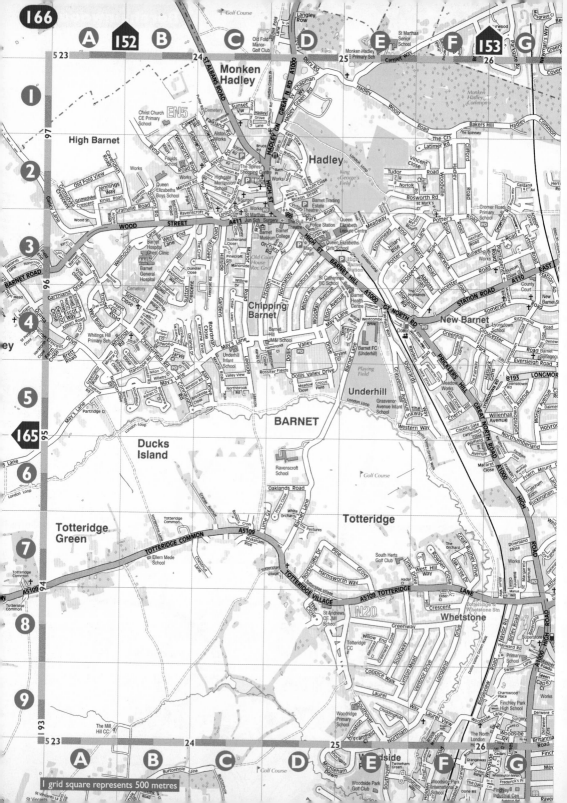

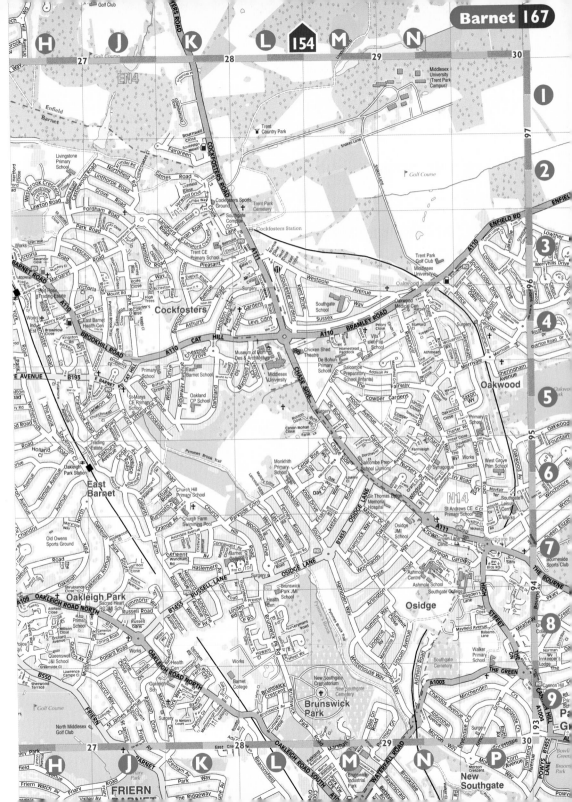

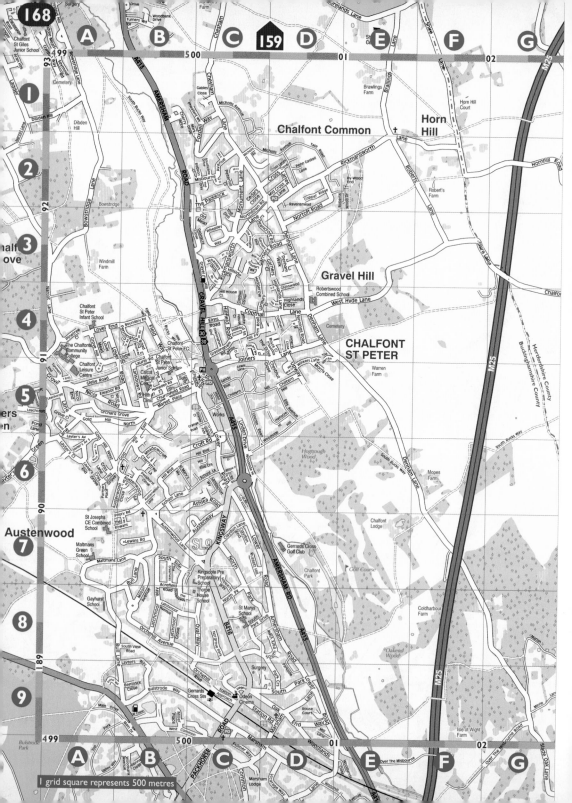

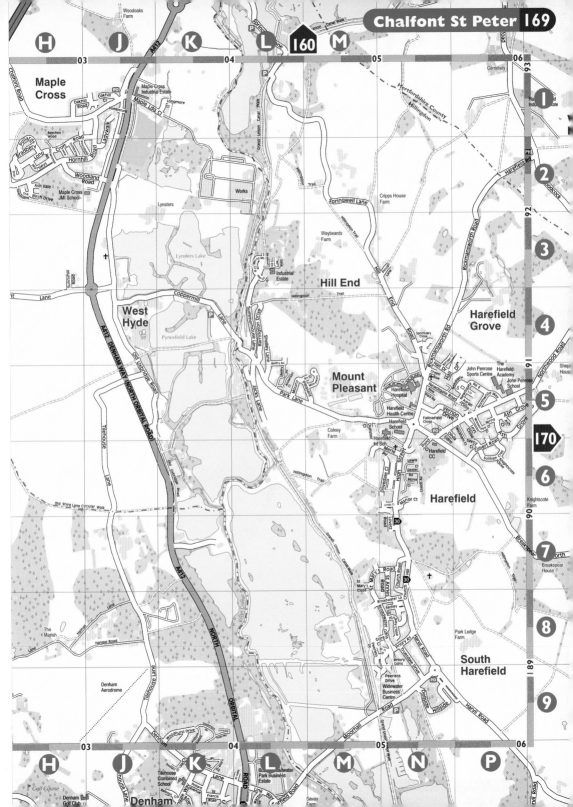

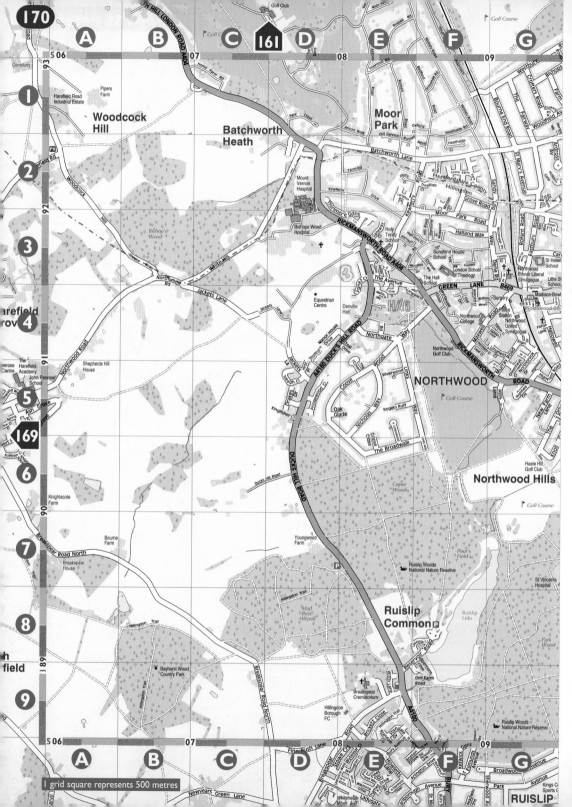

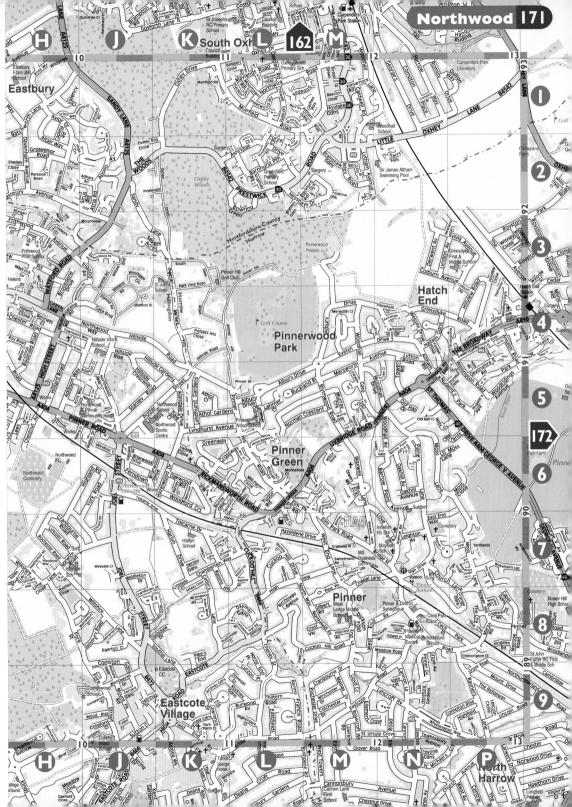

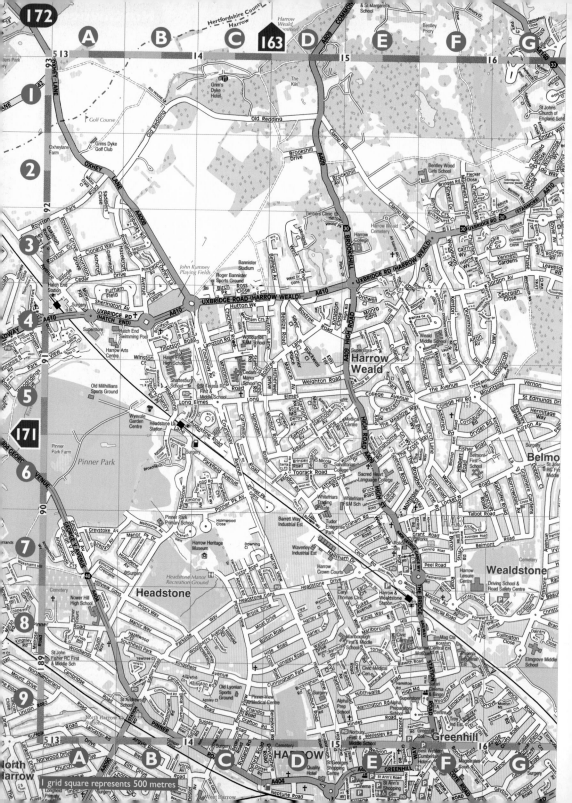

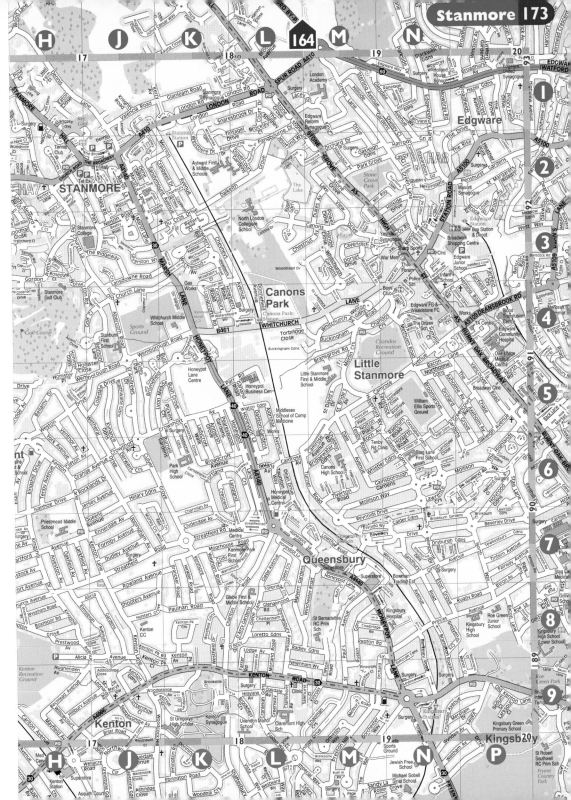

Abbots Langley....148 F2
Adeyfield....118 B8
Aimes Green....143 L7
Albury....56 D9
Albury End....72 C2
Aldbury....97 H6
Aldenham....150 A7
Aley Green....79 P4
Allen's Green....91 J7
Amersham....145 J9
Amersham Common....145 H9
Amersham on the Hill....144 G7
Amwell....103 H5
Ansells End....82 E5
Anstey....41 N2
Apsley....133 N3
Apsley End....53 M1
Ardeley....53 H4
Ardley End....93 J8
Arkley....165 P4
Arlesey....24 E4
Asheridge....130 C5
Ashley Green....131 L3
Ashwell....17 L3
Ashwell End....17 K5
Aspenden....54 C2
Aston....68 A4
Aston Clinton....67 P7
Aston End....67 N2
Astrope....95 J1
Astwick....16 C8
Ayot Green....104 C4
Ayot St Lawrence....83 N7
Ayot St Peter....104 C1
Ayres End....102 E7
Babbs Green....89 J9
Bakers End....89 K6
Baldock....26 B9
Ballingdon Bottom....99 H3
Barkway....30 B5
Barley....21 M8
Barleycroft End....56 E3
Barley End....97 H4
Barnet....166 D5
Barnet Gate....165 L5
Barton-le-Clay....32 E5
Barwick....89 H1
Bassus Green....52 F7
Batchworth....71 K8
Batchworth Heath....170 C1
Batford....102 D1
Batlers Green....150 E8
Bayford....124 G6
Bedlar's Green....75 H5
Bedmond....134 F6
Bedwell....11 H5
Beecroft....60 B6
Bell Bar....139 K3
Bellingdon....130 D3
Belmont....172 G6
Belsize....147 H2
Bendish....64 F7
Bengeo....107 J4
Bennington....68 F2
Bennetts End....5 K7
Bentfield Bury....58 C3
Bentfield Green....58 D3
Bentley Heath....153 J5
Berden....43 L8
Berkhamsted....115 M7
Bernards Heath....120 C6
Bidwell....44 D9
Birchanger....58 F9
Birch Green....106 D8
Birchwood....122 E4
Biscot....29 J3
Bishop's Stortford....73 M7
Blackmore End....82 F7
Blue Hill....68 E9
Borehamwood....164 E2
Botany Bay....165 J8
Botley....145 M1
Bourne End....132 F1
Bovingdon....132 E6
Bovingdon Green....132 C8
Bower Heath....82 C7
Boxmoor....4 B6
Bozen Green....55 M4
Bragbury End....67 N7
Bramfield....86 D9
Bramingham....46 B6
Braughing....55 L9
Braughing Friars....72 A1
Brays Grove....129 K4
Breachwood Green....64 D6
Brent Pelham....42 C6
Brickendon....125 K7
Bricket Wood....149 N1
Brick House End....57 L2
Briden's Camp....99 K3
Broad Colney....137 J7
Broad Green....22 E7
Broadgreen Wood....125 H3
Broadley Common....128 A8
Broadoak End....106 C4
Broadwater....42 C7
Broken Green....71 P4
Bromley....71 P6
Brook End....53 K1
Brookmans Park....139 H5
Broxbourne....126 F8
Brunswick Park....167 L9
Buckland....94 C6
Buckland Common....29 K9
Buckland Common....113 P8
Bucklandwharf....95 H8
Bucks Hill....147 N4
Building End....31 L2
Bulbourne....96 A4
Bullen's Green....138 C5
Bull's Cross....155 P6
Bull's Green....105 J8
Bulstrode....133 H7
Bumble's Green....143 M3
Buntingford....40 E9
Burge End....34 C3
Burnham Green....85 N8
Burn's Green....68 C5
Burton End....59 K7
Bury Green....73 H7

Bury Green....156 A1
Bury Park....62 C6
Bush End....75 P6
Bushey....163 L6
Bushey Heath....163 N6
Butt's Close....35 K8
Bye Green....94 B9
Bygrave....26 E4
Caddington....80 A4
Cadwell....35 M3
Caldecote....16 C9
Caldecote Hill....163 P6
The Camp....136 F1
Canons Park....173 L4
Capability Green....80 F1
Carpenders Park....163 H8
Chalfont Common....168 D3
Chalfont St Giles....158 F8
Chalfont St Peter....168 E4
Chalgrave....44 C4
Chalton....44 G6
Chandler's Cross....148 A8
Chapmore End....87 K8
Charlton....49 J2
Chartridge....130 B7
Chatter End....57 L8
Chaulden....116 C9
Chaul End....61 N7
Cheapside....41 N1
Cheddington....79 K3
Chells....51 L9
Chenies....146 F8
Cherry Green....54 C6
Chesham....145 H6
Chesham Bois....145 H6
Cheshunt....142 A9
Chessmount....145 K2
Cheverell's Green....81 J8
Childwick Bury....120 B2
Childwick Green....120 A1
Chiltern Green....81 P2
Chipperfield....147 L1
Chipping....40 C3
Chipping Barnet....166 C4
Chiswick Green....135 N4
Chivery....113 K7
Cholesbury....114 B9
Chorleywood....160 B5
Chorleywood Bottom....160 B5
Chorleywood West....159 N4
Chrishall....22 C7
Church End....24 F2
Church End....78 G2
Church End....96 D2
Church End....101 H8
Church End....147 J8
Churchgate....142 A8
Church Langley....129 N3
Clapgate....56 F9
Claverambury....143 N6
Clavering....43 M5
Clay End....52 F8
Clay Hill....155 K7
Clement's End....98 G1
Clothall....37 N4
Clothall Common....26 D9
Cockernhoe....63 L2
Cockfosters....167 J4
Codicote....84 C4
Codicote Bottom....84 A5
Codmore....131 K9
Cokenach....30 C4
Cold Christmas....88 F7
Cold Harbour....82 B8
Cole Green....106 B8
Coleman Green....103 M7
Colliers End....70 F8
Colney Heath....137 P1
Colney Street....136 D9
Commonwood....147 K4
Cooper's Green....121 N3
Cottered....39 K8
Counters End....117 K8
Cow Roast....114 F2
Crabbs Green....56 G1
Cradle End....73 J6
Crafton....75 J6
Crawley End....22 G5
Crews Hill....155 J5
Cromer....52 E2
Cromer-Hyde....103 P7
Croxley Green....161 L4
Cuffley....140 G7
Cumberlow Green....38 F6
Cupid Green....118 C4
Damask Green....37 L8
Dancers Hill....152 F4
Dane End....69 N7
Danesbury....84 F7
Darleyhall....64 B5
Dassels....55 J4
Datchworth....85 J4
Datchworth Green....85 M4
Deacons Hill....164 G5
Deer's Green....43 K4
Dewes Green....43 J7
Digswell....105 J1
Digswell Park....104 G3
Digswell Water....105 K2
Downside....61 H8
Drayton Beauchamp....95 K7
Driver's End....84 D1
Duck End....74 F1
Ducks Island....166 B6
Dudswell....115 J3
Dunstable....60 G6
Dunton....14 C6
East Barnet....167 H6
Eastbury....171 H1
Eastcote Village....171 K9
East End....128 B2
East End....57 H5
East End Green....124 D1
Easthall....22 D5
East Hyde....81 N5
Eastwick....110 E8
Edgware....173 P1
Edworth....16 E5
Ellenbrook....121 P7

Elmdon....23 K6
Elsenham....59 J1
Elstree....164 E5
Enfield Island Village....156 E7
Enfield Lock....156 E7
Enfield Wash....156 D8
Epping Green....140 E1
Essendon....124 A5
Eyeworth....14 A1
Fancott....44 E3
Farley Hill....62 C8
Farnham....57 M9
Farnham Green....57 L8
Felden....133 K5
Fields End....116 G7
Fishers Green....50 D7
Flamstead....100 D2
Flamstead End....142 A7
Flaunden....146 D2
Fleetville....120 F6
The Folly....102 G2
Ford End....43 H4
Forty Hill....155 N9
Freezy Water....156 D6
Friar's Wash....100 E1
Frithsden....116 B2
Frithsden Gardens....116 B2
Frogmore....136 D7
The Frythe....104 D2
Fuller's Park....59 K3
Furneux Pelham....56 D7
Further Ford End....42 G2
Gadebridge....117 J6
Ganwick Corner....153 L5
Garston....149 K5
Gaston Green....92 C3
Gatley End....18 D3
Gaunt's End....59 P4
Gilston....110 C7
Gilston Park....110 F6
Goff's Oak....141 K7
Goose Green....126 D4
Gorhambury....119 K7
Gosmore....49 L4
Graveley....50 F5
Gravel Hill....168 C6
Gravesend....56 D7
Great Amwell....108 D7
Great Ashby....51 L4
Great Chishill....22 B8
Great Gaddesden....98 F9
Great Green....15 M6
Great Hallingbury....74 E6
Great Hivings....130 F7
Great Hormead....41 N8
Great Munden....70 C1
Great Offley....48 C5
Great Parndon....128 E5
Great Wymondley....50 B1
Green End....37 M6
Green End....39 L1
Green End....55 J8
Green End....69 M5
Green End....117 J9
Greenhill....172 F9
Green Street....73 H5
Green Street....151 M7
The Green....78 C5
Green Tye....90 F4
Grovehill....117 N4
The Grove....148 D7
Gubblecote....95 L2
Guilden Morden....15 K6
Gustard Wood....83 H9
Haddington Hill....112 F4
Hadham Cross....90 B3
Hadham Ford....72 E6
Hadley....166 D2
Hadley Wood....153 N8
Hailey....126 E1
Haldens....105 K2
Hall Grove....105 L8
Hallingbury Street....91 P7
Hall's Green....51 P1
Halls Green....127 P5
Halton....112 E2
Hammerfield....4 A1
Hammond Street....141 K5
Handside....104 E7
Harefield....169 N6
Harefield Grove....169 P4
Hare Green....41 J8
Hare Street....57 L9
Hare Street....128 E4
Harlow....3 F5
Harmer Green....85 K8
Harpenden....101 N3
Harpenden Common....81 H7
Harrow Weald....172 E4
Hartham....107 K5
Hart Hill....7 J1
Hastoe....111 P4
Hatch End....171 N4
Hatching Green....101 N6
Hatfield....122 C7
Hatfield Broad Oak....93 N4
Hatfield Garden Village....122 B2
Hatfield Heath....93 J6
Hatfield Hyde....105 J9
Haultwick....69 L6
Hay Green....28 G3
Hay Street....55 K6
Hazel End....58 B5
Headstone....172 D8
Heath End....114 P9
Hebing End....69 H4
Helham Green....89 L9
Hemel Hempstead....5 G2
Hertford....107 M7
Hertford Heath....108 A9
Hertingfordbury....107 H7
Hexton....33 J6
Heydon....22 D5
Higham Gobion....33 H1
High Barnet....166 A2
High Beach....157 N9
High Cross....88 D3
High Cross....150 C6
Highfield....117 P6

The High....2 E5
High Town....6 E2
Highwood Hill....165 M8
High Wych....111 L3
Hill End....169 M3
Hill Green....43 P2
Hilltop....131 J8
Hinxworth....16 F4
Hitchin....35 J9
Hitchin Hill....49 K2
Hobbs Hill....49 K2
Hockerill....74 C4
Hoddesdon....126 D5
Hogpits Bottom....146 E2
Holwell....34 G1
Holyfield....143 H7
Holywell....162 A5
Holywell....78 F6
Hoo End....83 J1
Hook's Cross....68 B8
Horn Hill....168 F1
Horton....77 P2
Houghton Regis....60 C1
Howe Green....74 F8
How Wood....136 B6
Hudnall....98 B5
Hudnall Corner....98 D5
Hunsdon....109 P3
Hunsdonbury....109 P6
Hunton Bridge....148 C3
Hyde Heath....134 B4
Ickleford....35 J4
Jack's Hatch....128 E9
Jockey End....99 K3
Katherines....128 B6
Kelshall....28 D3
Kensworth....79 K4
Kensworth Lynch....79 K4
Kenton....173 J7
Kettle Green....89 P4
Keysers Estate....142 G1
Kimpton....83 J2
Kings Langley....134 B7
Kingsmoor....128 F8
King's Walden....64 E3
Kinsbourne Green....149 J4
Kitt's End....153 H8
Knebworth....67 K3
Lanes End....113 K8
Langley....66 C5
Langleybury....148 C4
Langley Lower Green....31 N8
Langley Upper Green....31 P7
Latchford....71 L9
Latchmore Bank....91 J2
Latchmore Bank....146 B7
Latton Bush....129 K7
Leagrave....61 M2
Leasey Bridge....102 E3
Lea Valley....102 E1
Leavesden Green....149 H4
Lemsford....104 C7
Letchmore Heath....150 D9
Letchworth Garden City....36 A2
Letty Green....124 B1
Levens Green....73 M1
Leverstock Green....118 D9
Lewsey Farm....61 J3
Ley Green....64 E1
Ley Hill....131 N9
Lilley....62 A1
Limbury....62 A1
Little Almshoe....49 M6
Little Berkhamsted....124 B7
Little Chalfont....159 L2
Little Chishill....31 J2
Little Gaddesden....98 A5
Little Green....15 M5
Little Hadham....72 F4
Little Hallingbury....92 D1
Little Heath....139 L8
Little Hormead....41 M9
Little London....43 N8
Little Missenden....144 A7
Little Offley....47 P1
Little Parndon....2 A3
Little Stanmore....173 M5
Little Tring....95 M6
Little Wymondley....50 A3
London Colney....137 K5
Long Marston....95 J1
Loudwater....161 P2
Lower Bois....145 H4
Lower Green....35 K3
Lower Green....142 F4
Lower Nazeing....143 J2
Lower Sheering....92 B8
Lower Sundon....45 M4
Lower Woodside....139 J1
Lucas End....141 K6
Luffenhall....53 J3
Luton....7 G6
Lye Green....131 L7
Mackerye End....82 D9
Magpots End....57 P3
Mallows Green....57 J6
Mangrove Green....63 N2
Mantles Green....144 F8
Manuden....58 A1
Maple Cross....169 L7
Mardlebury....85 L3
Mark Hall North....111 K9
Mark Hall South....129 K1
Markyate....80 A8
Marshalls Heath....82 D9
Marshalswick....121 K4
Marsh Farm....45 P8
Marshmoor....138 C1
Marsworth....95 P2
Meesden....42 D3
Mentmore....79 K1
Meriden....148 M6
Merry Hill....163 K7
Micklefield Green....147 K8
Mill End....39 M2
Mill End....160 D7

Mill Green....123 H3
Millow....14 B7
Moneyhill....160 F7
Monken Hadley....166 C1
Moor Green....53 L5
Moor Park....170 E1
Morden Green....14 F1
Mott's Green....92 E3
Mount Pleasant....169 M6
Much Hadham....90 B2
Nash Mills....134 B4
Nasty....122 A7
Nast Hyde....54 C9
Nazeing....143 N1
Nazeing Gate....143 P4
Nazeing Long Green....143 M4
Nazeing Mead....143 M3
Needham Green....19 P5
Nether Street....90 C8
Netteswell....3 F1
Newbarnet....116 E1
New Barnet....166 F4
Newgate Street....140 F3
New Greens....120 B3
New Ground....114 F1
New Mill....96 A6
New Mill End....81 L5
Newnham....30 B2
Newsells....14 A6
Newton....62 E9
New Town....131 H8
Newtown....69 N8
Nobland Green....89 M5
The Node....66 C9
Nomansland....103 H6
Northaw....140 B9
North Brook End....15 J6
Northchurch....115 J5
North Watford....149 J7
Northwood....170 E5
Northwood Hills....171 G5
Norton....25 M8
Norton Green....66 B8
Nup End....76 B2
Nup End....84 E1
Nuthampstead....30 F7
Oakfield....49 N1
Oaklands....35 K6
Oakleigh Park....167 H8
Oakwood....167 P5
Odsey....18 D9
Old Hall Green....70 E5
Old Harlow....111 M8
Old Hatfield....122 C5
Old Knebworth....66 F8
Old Town....50 F8
Orchard Leigh....131 H8
Osidge....167 N8
Otterpool....149 N7
Oxhey....162 F5
Oxlease....122 E7
Painter's Green....85 N3
Panshanger....105 K5
Park Green....57 L1
Parkside....28 A1
Park Street....136 B5
Park Town....7 H7
Passmores....128 G4
Patchetts Green....150 B9
Patient End....56 C4
Patmore Heath....56 G7
Peartree....105 J5
Pednor Bottom....130 B8
Pednormead End....144 E2
Pegsdon....33 K7
Pepperstock....80 D4
Perry Green....91 K5
Peters Green....82 B2
Piccotts End....117 M4
Pimlico....134 F3
Pin Green....51 K7
Pinner....171 M8
Pinnacles....128 D3
Pinner Green....171 L6
Pinnerwood Park....171 L4
Pirton....34 B4
Pitstone....96 C1
Pond Park....130 C8
Poplars....167 N3
Porter's End....82 F6
Potten End....116 D5
Potters Bar....153 P2
Potters Crouch....135 L3
Pottersheath....84 F4
Potter Street....128 G9
Pouchen End....116 C9
Presdales....126 C8
Preston....49 H9
Puckeridge....71 K3
Pudds Cross....133 B7
Purwell....36 A8
Puttenham....94 C2
Queensbury....173 L7
Radlett....151 H5
Radwell....25 N5
Redbourn....101 J6
Redbournbury....119 M1
Redhill....38 E2
Reed....29 M5
Reed End....29 N3
Rickmansworth....161 H5
Ridge....152 C4
The Ridgeway....140 C6
Ringshall....97 N3
Roast Green....43 H6
Roe End....99 J3
Roe Green....28 B9
Roe Green....122 D6
Roestock....138 A2
The Rookery....116 D7
Rosedale....141 H7
Round Bush....150 C8
Round Green....7 L3
Rowley Green....165 M3
Roydon....127 N2
Roydon Hamlet....143 L5
Royston....20 A3
Rucklers Lane....133 P5
Ruislip Common....170 E8

Rushden	38 F4	Snow End	41 M3	Tewin Wood	85 N8	Walkern	52 C6	Whempstead	69 K8
Rush Green	66 A2	Sopwell	136 D2	Therfield	28 F7	Wallington	27 L9	Whetstone	166 F8
Rush Green	108 B6	South-end	90 E7	Thorley	91 M3	Walsworth	35 M7	Whippendell Bottom	133 M9
Rusling End	66 A7	Southern Green	39 H4	Thorley Houses	73 K9	Waltham Abbey	157 J2	Whipsnade	78 D5
The Ryde	122 F3	South Harefield	169 P8	Thorley Street	91 P2	Waltham Cross	156 B3	White Hall	68 C6
Rye Meads	127 J2	South Hatfield	122 E9	Three Households	158 F9	Wandon End	64 A5	Whitehall	39 M4
Rye Park	126 G4	South Mimms	152 E2	The Thrift	19 J7	Ware	108 E2	Whitwell	65 K8
Sacombe	87 M2	South Oxhey	162 D9	Throcking	39 M7	Wareside	89 J9	Widford	90 B9
Sacombe Green	88 A1	Spellbrook	91 P5	Thundridge	88 C6	Warners End	117 H7	Wigginton	114 C1
St Albans	9 J3	Spitalbrook	126 F7	Tilekiln Green	74 G4	Warren's Green	51 N1	Wigginton Bottom	114 D3
St Ibbs	49 M6	Staines Green	106 D8	Titmore Green	50 B5	Washall Green	42 E7	Wildhill	123 M9
St Ippolitts	49 M5	Stanborough	104 C9	Toddington	44 D1	Waterdale	135 K9	Willian	36 C6
St Julians	136 B3	Standon	71 K5	Todd's Green	50 D5	Water End	117 J2	Wilstone	95 L3
St Leonards	113 M8	Standon Green End	88 D1	Tolmers	140 F5	Water End	103 P4	Wilstone Green	95 L4
St Margaret's	37 H7	Stanmore	173 H2	Tonwell	87 N6	Waterend	103 P4	Windmill Hill	35 L9
St Margarets	108 F8	Stanstead Abbotts	109 K8	Totteridge	166 E7	Waterford	106 G2	Wingfield	44 B6
St Nicholas	51 K5	Stansted Mountfitchet	58 D4	Totteridge Green	166 A7	Waterside	145 J3	Wingrave	76 D2
St Paul's Walden	65 M5	Stapleford	86 F6	Tower Hill	133 J8	Watford	13 F2	Winsdon Hill	62 C7
St Stephens	135 P1	Starling's Green	43 J5	Townsend	120 A6	Watford Heath	162 G6	Woodcock Hill	170 A1
Sandon	28 B8	Start Hill	75 H5	Trims Green	91 M6	Watton-at-Stone	86 D1	Wood End	53 K8
Sandridge	121 H2	Startop's End	95 N3	Tring	96 A9	Wealdstone	172 C7	Wood Green	157 P4
Sarratt	147 K5	Steeple Morden	15 N9	Tringford	95 M4	Welham Green	138 E2	Woodhall	105 H8
Sarratt Bottom	147 H6	Stevenage	10 C3	Tring Wharf	96 A5	Well End	151 P8	Woodside	80 B3
Sawbridgeworth	111 L2	Stewards	129 H8	Trowley Bottom	100 C4	Welham Green	71 P5	Woodside	123 K9
Sewell	60 A4	Stickling Green	43 N2	Turnford	142 D4	Welwyn	84 D8	Woodside	149 J2
Shaftenhoe End	30 F1	Stocking Pelham	42 G9	Two Waters	4 C7	Welwyn Garden City	105 L4	Woodside Green	74 G9
Shaw Green	38 E3	Stopsley	62 G3	Tye Green	128 G5	Wendover	112 D7	Woollensbrook	126 C2
Sheering	92 E9	Stotfold	25 L2	Tye Green	59 M5	Westbrook Hay	132 F3	Woolmer Green	85 L3
Shenley	151 L4	Streatley	43 J5	Tyler's Causeway	140 C1	West End	123 N6	World's End	112 A4
Shenleybury	151 J1	Strethall	23 P6	Tyler's Hill	145 M1	West Hyde	81 K6	Wormley	142 D3
Shephall	67 K3	Studham	78 E8	Tyttenhanger	137 K2	West Hyde	169 J4	Wormleybury	142 A2
Sherrardspark	104 E4	Sumners	128 D7	Underhill	166 E5	Westland Green	72 B6	Wormley West End	141 P1
Shootersway	115 K7	Sundon Park	45 M8	Uppend	57 L6	Westmill	35 H7	Wright's Green	92 E2
Sleapshyde	121 P9	Swanley Bar	139 L7	Upper Dunsley	96 B9	Westmill	54 E5	Wyddial	40 F4
Slip End	27 K2	The Swillett	160 A6	Upper Sundon	45 K5	Weston	37 M7	Wymondley Bury	50 C4
Slip End	121 N7	Symonds Green	50 D8	Upshire	157 P2	Weston Turvill	112 B1	Youngsbury	88 E5
Smallford	121 N7	Takeley Street	75 N3	Upwick Green	73 H1	West Watford	12 C6	
Smith's End	30 E1	Tea Green	64 A3	Venus Hill	146 E1	Westwick Row	118 F9	
Smug Oak	136 A9	Temple Fields	111 K8	Wadesmill	88 C5	Wheathampstead	103 J3	
Snailswell	35 J2	Tewin	105 P1	Wakeley	53 P5	Whelpley Hill	132 A5	

USING THE STREET INDEX

Street names are listed alphabetically. Each street name is followed by its Postcode District, the page number, and the reference to the square in which the name is found.

Standard index entries are shown as follows:

Abbey Av *STALW/RED* AL3 .... **135** P2

Street names and selected addresses not shown on the map due to scale restrictions are shown in the index with an asterisk:

Abbots HI *HHS/BOV* HP3 * **134** C4

GENERAL ABBREVIATIONS

ACC	ACCESS	CTYD	COURTYARD	HLS	HILLS	MWY	MOTORWAY	SE	SOUTH EAST
ALY	ALLEY	CUTT	CUTTINGS	HO	HOUSE	N	NORTH	SER	SERVICE AREA
AP	APPROACH	CV	COVE	HOL	HOLLOW	NE	NORTH EAST	SH	SHORE
AR	ARCADE	CYN	CANYON	HOSP	HOSPITAL	NW	NORTH WEST	SHOP	SHOPPING
ASS	ASSOCIATION	DEPT	DEPARTMENT	HRB	HARBOUR	O/P	OVERPASS	SKWY	SKYWAY
AV	AVENUE	DL	DALE	HTH	HEATH	OFF	OFFICE	SMT	SUMMIT
BCH	BEACH	DM	DAM	HTS	HEIGHTS	ORCH	ORCHARD	SOC	SOCIETY
BLDS	BUILDINGS	DR	DRIVE	HVN	HAVEN	OV	OVAL	SP	SPUR
BND	BEND	DRO	DROVE	HWY	HIGHWAY	PAL	PALACE	SPR	SPRING
BNK	BANK	DRY	DRIVEWAY	IMP	IMPERIAL	PAS	PASSAGE	SQ	SQUARE
BR	BRIDGE	DWGS	DWELLINGS	IN	INLET	PAV	PAVILION	ST	STREET
BRK	BROOK	E	EAST	IND EST	INDUSTRIAL ESTATE	PDE	PARADE	STN	STATION
BTM	BOTTOM	EMB	EMBANKMENT	INF	INFIRMARY	PH	PUBLIC HOUSE	STR	STREAM
BUS	BUSINESS	EMBY	EMBASSY	INFO	INFORMATION	PK	PARK	STRD	STRAND
BVD	BOULEVARD	ESP	ESPLANADE	INT	INTERCHANGE	PKWY	PARKWAY	SW	SOUTH WEST
BY	BYPASS	EST	ESTATE	IS	ISLAND	PL	PLACE	TDG	TRADING
CATH	CATHEDRAL	EX	EXCHANGE	JCT	JUNCTION	PLN	PLAIN	TER	TERRACE
CEM	CEMETERY	EXPY	EXPRESSWAY	JTY	JETTY	PLNS	PLAINS	THWY	THROUGHWAY
CEN	CENTRE	EXT	EXTENSION	KG	KING	PLZ	PLAZA	TNL	TUNNEL
CFT	CROFT	F/O	FLYOVER	KNL	KNOLL	POL	POLICE STATION	TOLL	TOLLWAY
CH	CHURCH	FC	FOOTBALL CLUB	L	LAKE	PR	PRINCE	TPK	TURNPIKE
CHA	CHASE	FK	FORK	LA	LANE	PREC	PRECINCT	TR	TRACK
CHYD	CHURCHYARD	FLD	FIELD	LDG	LODGE	PREP	PREPARATORY	TRL	TRAIL
CIR	CIRCLE	FLDS	FIELDS	LGT	LIGHT	PRIM	PRIMARY	TWR	TOWER
CIRC	CIRCUS	FLS	FALLS	LK	LOCK	PROM	PROMENADE	U/P	UNDERPASS
CL	CLOSE	FM	FARM	LKS	LAKES	PRS	PRINCESS	UNI	UNIVERSITY
CLFS	CLIFFS	FT	FORT	LNDG	LANDING	PRT	PORT	UPR	UPPER
CMP	CAMP	FTS	FLATS	LTL	LITTLE	PT	POINT	V	VALE
CNR	CORNER	FWY	FREEWAY	LWR	LOWER	PTH	PATH	VA	VALLEY
CO	COUNTY	FY	FERRY	MAG	MAGISTRATE	PZ	PIAZZA	VIAD	VIADUCT
COLL	COLLEGE	GA	GATE	MAN	MANSIONS	QD	QUADRANT	VIL	VILLA
COM	COMMON	GAL	GALLERY	MD	MEAD	QU	QUEEN	VIS	VISTA
COMM	COMMISSION	GDN	GARDEN	MDW	MEADOWS	QY	QUAY	VLG	VILLAGE
CON	CONVENT	GDNS	GARDENS	MEM	MEMORIAL	R	RIVER	VLS	VILLAS
COT	COTTAGE	GLD	GLADE	MI	MILL	RBT	ROUNDABOUT	VW	VIEW
COTS	COTTAGES	GLN	GLEN	MKT	MARKET	RD	ROAD	W	WEST
CP	CAPE	GN	GREEN	MKTS	MARKETS	RDG	RIDGE	WD	WOOD
CPS	COPSE	GND	GROUND	ML	MALL	REP	REPUBLIC	WHF	WHARF
CR	CREEK	GRA	GRANGE	MNR	MANOR	RES	RESERVOIR	WK	WALK
CREM	CREMATORIUM	GRG	GARAGE	MS	MEWS	RFC	RUGBY FOOTBALL CLUB	WKS	WALKS
CRS	CRESCENT	GT	GREAT	MSN	MISSION	RI	RISE	WLS	WELLS
CSWY	CAUSEWAY	GTWY	GATEWAY	MT	MOUNT	RP	RAMP	WY	WAY
CT	COURT	GV	GROVE	MTN	MOUNTAIN	RW	ROW	YD	YARD
CTRL	CENTRAL	HGR	HIGHER	MTS	MOUNTAINS	S	SOUTH	YHA	YOUTH HOSTEL
CTS	COURTS	HL	HILL	MUS	MUSEUM	SCH	SCHOOL		

POSTCODE TOWNS AND AREA ABBREVIATIONS

ABLGY	Abbots Langley	BROX	Broxbourne	DEN/HRF	Denham/Harefield	GSTN	Garston	HHW	Hemel Hempstead
AMP/FLIT/BLC	Ampthill/Flitwick/	BSF	Bishop's Stortford	DUN/HR/TOD	Dunstable/	GTDUN	Great Dunmow		west
	Barton-le-Clay	BUNT	Buntingford		Houghton Regis/	GTMIS/PWD	Great Missenden/	HLW	Harlow
AMS	Amersham south	BUSH	Bushey		Toddington		Prestwood	HLWE	Harlow east
AMSS	Amersham south	CDALE/KGS	Colindale/Kingsbury	DUN/WHIP	Dunstable/	HADM	Haddenham	HLWS	Harlow south
ARL/CHE	Arlesey/	CFSP/GDCR	Chalfont St Peter/		Whipsnade	HARP	Harpenden	HLWW/ROY	Harlow west/
	Church End		Gerrards Cross	EBAR	East Barnet	HAT	Hatfield		Roydon
BAR	Barnet	CHES/WCR	Cheshunt/	EDGW	Edgware	HERT/BAY	Hertford/Bayford	HNLW	Henlow
BEAC	Beaconsfield		Waltham Cross	EN	Enfield	HERT/WAT	Hertford/	HOD	Hoddesdon
BERK	Berkhamsted	CHESW	Cheshunt west	ENC/FH	Enfield Chase/		Watton at Stone	HRW	Harrow
BGSW	Biggleswade	CHING	Chingford		Forty Hill	HHNE	Hemel Hempstead	HTCH/STOT	Hitchin/Stotfold
BLDK	Baldock	CSHM	Chesham	EPP	Epping		northeast	HTCHE/RSTV	Hitchin east/
BORE	Borehamwood	CSTG	Chalfont St Giles	FBAR/BDGN	Friern Barnet/	HHS/BOV	Hemel Hempstead south/		Rural Stevenage
BRKMPK	Brookmans Park	DEN/HRF	Denham/Harefield		Bounds Green		Bovingdon	KGLGY	Kings Langley

KNEB..........Knebworth
KTN/HRWW/WS..........Kenton/Harrow Weald/Wealdstone
LBUZ..........Leighton Buzzard
LCOL/BKTW..........London Colney/Bricket Wood
LOU..........Loughton
LTN..........Luton
LTNE..........Luton east
LTNN/LIM..........Luton north/Limbury
LTNW/LEA..........Luton west/Leagrave
LWTH..........Letchworth

MHAD..........Much Hadham
MLHL..........Mill Hill
NFNCH/WDSPK..........North Finchley/Woodside Park
NTHWD..........Northwood
OXHEY..........Oxhey
PEND..........Ponders End
PIN..........Pinner
POTB/CUF..........Potters Bar/Cuffley
RAD..........Radlett
RAYLNE/WEN..........Rural Aylesbury north & east/Wendover

RBSF..........Rural Bishop's Stortford
RKW/CH/CXG..........Rickmansworth/Chorleywood/Croxley Green
ROY..........Royston
RSLP..........Ruislip
RYLN/HDSTN..........Rayners Lane/Headstone
SAFWN..........Saffron Walden north
SAFWS..........Saffron Walden south
SBW..........Sawbridgeworth
SDY/GAM/POT..........Sandy/Gamlingay/Potton

STAL..........St Albans
STALE/WH..........St Albans east/Wheathampstead
STALW/RED..........St Albans west/Redbourn
STAN..........Stanmore
STDN..........Standon
STHGT/OAK..........Southgate/Oakwood
STSD..........Stansted
STVG..........Stevenage
STVGE..........Stevenage east
TRDG/WHET..........Totteridge/Whetstone

TRING..........Tring
WAB..........Waltham Abbey
WARE..........Ware
WAT..........Watford
WATN..........Watford north
WATW..........Watford west
WGCE..........Welwyn Garden City east
WGCW..........Welwyn Garden City west
WLYN..........Welwyn

Index - streets

Abb - Ard

A

Abbey Av STALW/RED AL3 .... 135 P2
Abbey Cl PIN HA5 .... 7 J7
Abbey Ct WAB EN9 .... 156 G4
Abbey Dale Cl HLWE CM17 .... 129 M4
Abbey Dr ABGLY WD5 .... 149 H2
  LTNE LU1 * 7 J1
Abbey Ms DUN/WHIP LU6 .... 60 F8
Abbey Mill End
  STALW/RED AL3 .... 8 C5
Abbey Mill La STALW/RED AL3 .... 8 D5
Abbey Rd CHES/WCR EN8 .... 156 D4
Abbey Vw MLHL NW7 .... 165 M9
  RAD WD7 .... 150 E5
  STAL AL1 .... 8 E7
Abbeyview WAB EN9 .... 156 G3
Abbey View Rd
  STALW/RED AL3 .... 8 C5
Abbey Wk DUN/HR/TOD LU5 .... 45 H9
Abbis Orch HTCH/STOT SG5 .... 35 K3
Abbot John Ms
  STALE/WH AL4 .... 103 J3
Abbots Av STAL AL1 .... 135 H2
Abbots Av West STAL AL1 .... 136 C2
Abbots Cl KNEB SG3 .... 85 N4
Abbots Gv STVG SG1 .... 11 O5
Abbotshall Av
  STHGT/OAK N14 .... 167 N9
Abbots Hi HHS/BOV HP3 * 154 C4
Abbots Pk STAL AL1 .... 136 C3
Abbots Pl BORE WD6 .... 151 N8
Abbots Ri KGLGY WD4 .... 134 A6
Abbots Rd ABLGY WD5 .... 148 D1
Abbots Vw KGLGY WD4 .... 134 A5
Abbotsweld HLWS CM18 .... 128 C6
Abbotswood Pde LTNE LU2 * 7 J1
Abbots Wood Rd LTNE LU2 * 7 J1
Abbots Ct WARE SG12 .... 109 J8
Abbots Dr WAB EN9 .... 157 M8
Abbots La WARE SG12 .... 90 A9
Abbots Ri WARE SG12 .... 109 J8
Abbots Rd BAR EN5 .... 166 F5
  LWTH SG6 .... 36 A2
Abbots V CSHM HP5 .... 131 H7
Abbots Wy BSF CM23 .... 91 P2
  RAYLNE/WEN HP22 .... 76 B1
  WARE SG12 .... 109 J8
Abdale La BRKMPK AL9 .... 138 E6
Abel Cl HHNE HP2 .... 9 H8
Abercorn Gv RSLP HA4 .... 170 F8
Abercot Rd LTNW/LEA LU4 .... 61 J3
  STAN HA7 .... 172 J3
Abercrombie Dr EN EN1 .... 155 P9
Aberdale Wy
  HLWW/ROY CM19 .... 128 F5
Aberdale Gdns
  POTB/CUF EN6 .... 153 J2
Aberdeen Cots STAN HA7 * 173 J4
Aberdeen Rd
  KTN/HRWW/WS HA3 .... 172 F6
Aberford Rd BORE WD6 .... 164 G1
Abigail Cl HHNE HP2 .... 9 H8
Abingdon Cl LTNW/LEA LU4 .... 61 M3
Abingdon Pl POTB/CUF EN6 .... 153 L2
Abingdon Rd LTNW/LEA LU4 .... 61 M3
Abraham Cl OXHEY WD19 .... 171 K1
Abram's La ROY SG8 .... 22 F5
Abridge Cl CHES/WCR EN8 .... 156 C1
Abstacle Hi TRING HP23 .... 95 N9
Acacia Cl CHESW EN7 .... 141 M6
  CSHM HP5 .... 130 F9
  STAN HA7 .... 172 E3
Acacia Gv BERK HP4 .... 115 N8
Acacia Rd ENC/FH EN2 .... 155 L9
Acacia Wk HARP AL5 .... 122 D9
Acers LCOL/BKTW AL2 .... 136 E7
Achilles Cl HHNE HP2 .... 118 A6
Ackroyd Rd ROY SG8 .... 20 D2
Acme Rd WATN WD24 .... 148 G8
Acorn Cl ENC/FH EN2 .... 155 H9
  CSHM HP5 .... 145 K9
  STAN HA7 .... 172 E3
Acorn Gld WLYN AL6 .... 85 J9
Acorn La POTB/CUF EN6 .... 140 F8
Acorn Rd HHW HP1 .... 116 B6
The Acorns STALE/WH AL4 * 121 J8
Acorn St WARE SG12 .... 110 A5
Acrefield Rd CFSP/GDCR SL9 .... 168 B8
Acremore St STDN SG11 .... 72 D2
Acre Piece HTCHE/RSTV SG4 .... 49 M1
Acres End AMSS HP7 .... 145 K9
Acre Wy NTHWD HA6 .... 171 H5
Acre Wd HHNE HP2 .... 5 H2
Acrewood Wy
  STALE/WH AL4 .... 121 L8
Acton Cl CHES/WCR EN8 .... 156 D1
Acworth Crs LTNW/LEA LU4 .... 61 M1
Ada Cl FBAR/BDGN N11 .... 166 G2
Adamsfield CHESW EN7 .... 141 N5
Adams House HLW CM20 .... 2 E4
Adams Wy TRING HP23 .... 96 A7

Adderley Rd BSF CM23 .... 74 A3
  KTN/HRWW/WS HA3 * 172 F7
Addington Wy LTNW/LEA LU4 .... 61 N3
Addis Cl PEND EN3 .... 156 C9
Addiscombe Cl
  KTN/HRWW/WS HA3 .... 173 J9
Addiscombe Wk WAT WD18 .... 12 E4
Addison Av STHGT/OAK N14 .... 167 M5
Addison Cl NTHWD HA6 .... 171 J5
  PEND EN3 .... 156 B9
Addison Rd CSHM HP5 .... 131 H8
  PEND EN3 .... 156 B9
Addison Wy NTHWD HA6 .... 171 H5
Adelaide Cl EN EN1 .... 155 M8
  STAN HA7 .... 172 C1
Adelaide St LTN LU1 .... 6 C5
  STALW/RED AL3 .... 9 F2
Adele Av WLYN AL6 .... 105 J1
Adeyfield Gdns HHNE HP2 .... 118 A7
Adeyfield Rd HHNE HP2 .... 5 C1
Adhara Rd NTHWD HA6 .... 171 J2
Adinger Cl STVG SG1 .... 67 H3
Admirals Cl STALE/WH AL4 .... 138 B2
Admiral St HERT/BAY SG13 .... 107 P6
  STAL AL1 .... 136 F1
Admiral Wk HOD EN11 .... 126 F7
  STAL AL1 .... 136 F1
Admiral Wy BERK HP4 .... 115 L5
Adlington Cl BAR EN5 .... 166 B5
  DEN/HRF UB9 .... 169 P5
Adrian Rd ABLGY WD5 .... 148 F1
Adstock Ms CFSP/GDCR SL9 * 168 B5
Adstone Rd LTN LU1 .... 80 A2
Aidans Cl DUN/WHIP LU6 .... 60 B5
Aisworth Rd LTNN/LIM LU3 .... 46 B9
Ainsdale Crs PIN HA5 .... 172 A7
Ainsdale Rd OXHEY WD19 .... 162 E9
Aintree Rd ROY SG8 .... 20 E4
Aintree Wy STVG SG1 .... 51 M7
Airedale HHNE HP2 .... 117 P5
Airfield Wy GSTN WD25 .... 148 G4
Airport Approach Rd
  LTNE LU2 .... 63 L6
  LTNE LU2 .... 63 J8
Aitken Rd BAR EN5 .... 166 B5
Akeman Cl STALW/RED AL3 * 135 N1
Akeman St TRING HP23 .... 95 P9
Alamein Cl BROX EN10 .... 126 C8
Alandale Dr PIN HA5 .... 171 K5
Alan Dr BAR EN5 .... 166 C5
Alban Av STALW/RED AL3 .... 120 C6
Alban Crs BORE WD6 .... 151 N9
Alban Pk STALE/WH AL4 * 121 L8
Albany Cl BUSH WD23 .... 165 M5
Albany Ct EDGW HA8 .... 173 N4
Albany Ga CSHM HP5 .... 130 C9
Albany Ms LCOL/BKTW AL2 * 135 P6
  WARE SG12 .... 108 D3
Albany Pde PEND EN3 .... 156 C8
Albany Pk PEND EN3 * 156 C8
Albany Park Av PEND EN3 .... 156 B9
Albany Rd PEND EN3 .... 156 C7
  WGCE AL7 * 96 A6
Albany Ter TRING HP23 * 96 A6
Albemarle Av CHES/WCR EN8 .... 142 B7
  POTB/CUF EN6 .... 153 L3
Albemarle Pk STAN HA7 * 173 J2
Albemarle Rd EBAR EN4 .... 167 J6
Albert Cl LTNW/LEA LU4 .... 61 J3
Albert Ct DUN/WHIP LU6 .... 60 F7
Albert Gdns HLWE CM17 .... 129 N4
Albert Rd ARL/CHE SG15 .... 24 E5
  CSHM HP5 .... 145 H1
  EBAR EN4 .... 166 G3
  LTN LU1 .... 62 F9
  RYLN/HDSTN HA2 * 172 C7
Albert Rd North WAT WD17 .... 13 F2
Albert Rd South WAT WD17 .... 12 E2
Albert St STAL AL1 .... 8 E5
  STALW/RED AL3 .... 79 F8
  STVG SG1 .... 10 B1
  TRING HP23 .... 95 P9
Albion Cl HERT/BAY SG13 .... 107 M6
Albion Crt LTNE LU2 * 6 E2
  STAN HA7 .... 173 H4
Albion Crs CSTG HP8 .... 159 H9
Albion Hi HHNE HP2 .... 5 G1
Albion Rd CSTG HP8 .... 159 H8
  LTNE LU2 .... 6 E3
Albion St DUN/WHIP LU6 .... 60 E6
Albuhera Cl ENC/FH EN2 .... 155 H9
Albury Cl LTNN/LIM LU3 .... 46 B9
Albury Crs HHS/BOV HP3 * 171 L5
Albury Grove Rd
  CHES/WCR EN8 .... 142 C9
Albury Ride CHES/WCR EN8 .... 156 C1
Albury Rd STDN SG11 .... 72 F4
Albury Wk CHES/WCR EN8 .... 142 B9
Alconbury BSF CM23 .... 74 D1
  WGCE AL7 * 105 P6
Alconbury Cl BORE WD6 .... 151 L9
Aldbanks DUN/WHIP LU6 .... 60 C5
Aldbury Cl GSTN WD25 .... 149 L6
  STALE/WH AL4 .... 121 H3
Aldbury Gdns TRING HP23 * 96 A6

Aldbury Gv WGCE AL7 .... 105 L6
Aldbury Rd
  RKW/CH/CXG WD3 .... 160 D6
Aldeburgh Cl HARP AL5 .... 50 D6
Aldenham Av RAD WD7 .... 150 F7
Aldenham Cl LTNW/LEA LU4 .... 61 J3
Aldenham Gv RAD WD7 .... 150 G4
Aldenham Rd BORE WD6 .... 150 F5
  BUSH WD23 .... 163 H8
Aldenham Rd OXHEY WD19 .... 162 B5
Alderbury Rd STSD CM24 .... 58 B1
Alder Cl BLDK SG7 .... 37 H1
  BSF CM23 .... 91 N1
  HOD EN11 .... 126 C3
  LCOL/BKTW AL2 .... 136 A7
Alder Crs LTNN/LIM LU3 .... 62 B3
Alderley Ct BERK HP4 .... 115 N8
Alderman Cl BRKMPK AL9 .... 138 C3
Alders End La HARP AL5 .... 101 N2
Alders Wk SBW CM21 .... 111 P2
Alderton Cl LTNE LU2 .... 63 L5
Alderton Dr BERK HP4 .... 97 M4
Alder Wk GSTN WD25 .... 149 J8
Alderwood Ms EBAR EN4 .... 153 M8
Aldhous Cl LTNN/LIM LU3 .... 62 C1
Aldis Ms PEND EN3 .... 156 F7
Aldock WGCE AL7 .... 105 K8
Aldock Rd STVG SG1 .... 51 N7
Aldridge Av EDGW HA8 .... 165 H9
  PEND EN3 .... 156 F8
  STAN HA7 .... 173 L5
Aldridge Ct LTNW/LIM LU3 .... 62 A1
Aldwick STAL AL1 .... 136 C1
Aldwickbury Crs HARP AL5 .... 102 C3
Aldwick Rd HARP AL5 .... 102 D4
Aldwyke Ri HARP AL5 .... 101 P8
Aldykes HAT AL10 .... 122 C6
Alesia Rd LTNN/LIM LU3 .... 45 P9
Alexander Cl EBAR EN4 .... 167 H3
Alexander Ct BLDK SG7 * 26 A9
Alexander Ga STVG SG1 .... 51 M7
Alexander Ms HLWE CM17 .... 129 N5
Alexander Rd
  HERT/WAT SG14 .... 107 H6
  HTCH/STOT SG5 .... 25 K3
  LCOL/BKTW AL2 .... 137 H4
Alexandra Av LTNN/LIM LU3 .... 62 C3
Alexandra St HTCH/STOT SG5 .... 25 L3
Alexandra Ct STHGT/OAK N14 .... 167 C1
Alexandra Rd BORE WD6 .... 152 A8
  HHNE HP2 .... 4 E1
  HLWE CM17 .... 129 M2
  HTCH/STOT SG5 .... 25 L3
  KGLGY WD4 .... 133 K9
  RKW/CH/CXG WD3 .... 147 K6
  STAL AL1 .... 9 H4
  STAL AL1 .... 12 D1
Alexandra Wy
  CHES/WCR EN8 .... 156 E4
Aleyn Wy BLDK SG7 .... 26 D8
Alfred St DUN/WHIP LU6 .... 60 F6
Alfriston Cl LTNE LU2 .... 63 K3
Algar Cl STAN HA7 .... 172 F2
Alguin Ct STAN HA7 * 173 J5
Alicia Av KTN/HRWW/WS HA3 .... 173 H8
Alicia Cl KTN/HRWW/WS HA3 .... 173 J8
Alicia Gdns
  KTN/HRWW/WS HA3 .... 173 H8
Alington La LWTH SG6 .... 36 C5
Allandale HHNE HP2 .... 117 N6
  STALW/RED AL3 .... 136 A2
Allandale Crs POTB/CUF EN6 .... 153 H2
Allandale Rd PEND EN3 .... 156 D9
Allard Crs BUSH WD23 .... 163 J8
Allard Wy BROX EN10 .... 126 D9
Alldicks Rd HHNE HP2 .... 5 K5
Allenby Av DUN/HR/TOD LU5 .... 61 K5
Allen Cl DUN/HR/TOD LU5 .... 60 G6
  RAD WD7 .... 151 H3
Allen Ct HAT AL10 * 122 E8
Allendale LTNN/LIM LU3 .... 46 A9
Allenford Ct HRW HA1 .... 172 B9
Allerton Cl BORE WD6 .... 151 K8
Allerton Rd BORE WD6 .... 151 K8
Alleyns Rd STVG SG1 .... 50 C1
Allington Rd
  RYLN/HDSTN HA2 .... 172 C9
Allis Ms HLWE CM17 .... 129 N5
Allison LWTH SG6 .... 36 F3
Allison Cl WAB EN9 .... 157 M3
Allmains Cl WAB EN9 .... 143 N4
All Saints Cl BSF CM23 .... 74 B2
Allsaints Crs GSTN WD25 .... 148 G1
All Saints La
  RKW/CH/CXG WD3 .... 161 L5
All Saints Ms STAN HA7 .... 172 E3
All Saints Rd
  DUN/HR/TOD LU5 .... 44 B1
Allum La BORE WD6 .... 164 E4
Allum Wy TRDG/WHET N20 .... 166 C7
Allwood Rd CHESW EN7 .... 141 N6
Alma Cut STAL AL1 .... 9 G6
Alma Farm Rd
  DUN/HR/TOD LU5 .... 44 B1
Alma Link LTN LU1 .... 6 D4

Alma Rd BERK HP4 .... 115 K5
  CSHM HP5 .... 131 H8
  STAL AL1 .... 9 H5
Alma Rw
  KTN/HRWW/WS HA3 * 172 D5
Alma St LTN LU1 .... 6 C3
Almonds La STVG SG1 .... 51 H7
The Almonds STAL AL1 .... 136 C3
Almond Wy BORE WD6 .... 165 H3
  RYLN/HDSTN HA2 .... 172 B6
Almshouse La EN EN1 .... 156 A7
Alms La BLDK SG7 .... 17 N6
Alnwick Dr TRING HP23 .... 76 C6
Alpha Pl BSF CM23 .... 74 A2
Alpine Cl HTCHE/RSTV SG4 .... 49 M2
Alpine Wk BUSH WD23 .... 163 N8
Alpine Wy LTNN/LIM LU3 .... 45 N7
Alsa Gdns RBSF CM22 .... 59 K1
Alsa Leys RBSF CM22 .... 59 K1
Alsa St STSD CM24 .... 58 G2
Alsop Cl DUN/HR/TOD LU5 .... 44 E3
  LCOL/BKTW AL2 .... 137 K7
Alston Rd BAR EN5 .... 166 A5
  HHW HP1 .... 117 K9
Altair Wy NTHWD HA6 .... 171 H2
Altham Ct
  RYLN/HDSTN HA2 * 172 B5
Altham Gv HLW CM20 .... 3 J1
Altham Rd PIN HA5 .... 171 N4
Althorp Cl BAR EN5 .... 165 N6
Althorpe Rd HARP AL5 .... 172 C9
Alton Av STAN HA7 .... 172 F4
Alton Rd LTN LU1 .... 62 D9
Altwood HARP AL5 .... 102 C3
Alva Wy OXHEY WD19 .... 162 F8
Alverstone Av EBAR EN4 .... 167 H6
Alverton STALW/RED AL3 .... 120 B5
Alveston Av
  KTN/HRWW/WS HA3 .... 173 H7
Alwin Pl WATW WD18 .... 162 A3
Alwoodley Cl BORE WD6 .... 164 F5
  LTNE LU2 .... 62 F4
Alyngton BERK HP4 .... 115 K4
Alzey Gdns HARP AL5 .... 102 C4
Amberleigh Gdns
  CFSP/GDCR WD3 .... 147 J6
Amberley Cl HARP AL5 .... 102 A2
  LTNE LU2 .... 62 E4
  PIN HA5 .... 171 P7
Amberley Gv WARE SG12 .... 88 B9
Amberry Ct HLW CM20 .... 3 F5
Ambleside HARP AL5 * 102 C2
  LTNN/LIM LU3 .... 62 A1
Ambrose La HARP AL5 .... 81 N9
Amenbury La HARP AL5 .... 101 N9
Amersham Rd
  CFSP/GDCR SL9 .... 168 B1
Amersham Wy AMS HP6 .... 146 B9
Amesbury WAB EN9 .... 157 M2
Ames Cl LTNN/LIM LU3 .... 46 A6
Amethyst Wk WGCW AL8 .... 104 B8
Amhurst Rd LTNW/LEA LU4 .... 61 H3
Amor Wy LWTH SG6 .... 36 E2
Amwell Cl GSTN WD25 .... 149 M5
Amwell Common WGCE AL7 .... 106 C4
  WAB EN9 .... 157 K3
Amwell End WARE SG12 .... 108 C4
Amwell Hl WARE SG12 .... 108 C6
Amwell La STALE/WH AL4 .... 102 C5
  WARE SG12 .... 108 C6
Amwell St HOD EN11 .... 126 E6
  LTN LU1 .... 6 C3
Ana Cl CSHM HP5 .... 144 C2
Anchor Cl CHES/WCR EN8 .... 142 C7
Anchor La HHW HP1 .... 4 A5
Anchor Rd BLDK SG7 .... 87 H7
Anchor St BSF CM23 .... 74 A4
Anderson Cl HARP AL5 .... 81 H1
  DEN/HRF UB9 .... 169 L5
Anderson Rd RAD WD7 .... 151 M3
Anderson's La BUNT SG9 .... 40 E8
Andover Cl LTNW/LEA LU4 .... 45 M9
Andrew Cl RAD WD7 .... 151 L3
Andrews Cl HHNE HP2 .... 117 N6
Andrewsfield WGCE AL7 .... 105 M6
Andrew's La CHESW EN7 .... 141 M7
Anelle Ri HHS/BOV HP3 .... 154 B4
Anershall RAYLNE/WEN HP22 .... 76 C2
Angel Cl LTNW/LEA LU4 .... 61 K3
Angel's Meadow BLDK SG7 .... 17 N6
Angels La DUN/HR/TOD LU5 .... 44 E4
Anglefield Rd BERK HP4 .... 115 M7
Anglesey Cl BSF CM23 .... 73 M7
Anglesey Rd OXHEY WD19 .... 171 L2
Anglesmede Crs PIN HA5 .... 172 A7
Anglesmede Wy PIN HA5 .... 172 A7
Anglian Cl WAT WD24 .... 162 E1
Angotts Md STVG SG1 .... 50 E9
Angus Cl LTNW/LEA LU4 .... 61 K3
Anmer Gdns LTNW/LEA LU4 .... 61 J2

Anmersh Gv STAN HA7 .... 173 K5
Annables La HARP AL5 .... 80 C9
Annette Cl
  KTN/HRWW/WS HA3 .... 172 E6
Anns Cl TRING HP23 .... 95 M9
Anselm Rd PIN HA5 .... 171 P4
Anson Cl HHS/BOV HP3 .... 154 C1
  STAL AL1 .... 136 C3
  STALE/WH AL4 .... 121 H2
Anson Wk NTHWD HA6 .... 170 E1
Anstee Rd LTNW/LEA LU4 .... 45 L9
Anstey Brook
  RAYLNE/WEN HP22 .... 94 B9
Anthony Cl NTHWD WD19 .... 162 F7
Anthony Gdns LTN LU1 .... 62 E9
Anthony Rd BORE WD6 .... 164 E1
Anthony Cl POTB/CUF EN6 .... 153 L1
Anthus Ms NTHWD HA6 .... 170 F4
Antoinette Ct ABLGY WD5 * 134 G8
Antoneys Cl PIN HA5 .... 171 M6
Antonine Ga STALW/RED AL3 .... 119 P9
Anvil Av STAN HA7 .... 19 H1
Anvil Cl HHS/BOV HP3 .... 132 C7
Anvil Ct LCOL/BKTW AL2 * 135 P5
Apex Point BRKMPK AL9 * 138 F1
Aplins Cl HARP AL5 .... 101 N2
Apollo Av NTHWD HA6 .... 171 J2
Apollo Cl DUN/HR/TOD LU5 .... 60 C7
Apollo Wy HHNE HP2 .... 117 P6
  STVGE SG2 .... 51 M7
Appleby Gdns DUN/WHIP LU6 .... 60 E7
Appleby St CHESW EN7 .... 141 M5
Apple Cots HHS/BOV HP3 .... 132 D6
Applecroft BERK HP4 .... 115 L2
  LCOL/BKTW AL2 .... 136 A7
  WCCW AL8 .... 104 E6
Appledore Cl EDGW HA8 .... 173 N5
Appledore Gdns
  AMP/FLIT/BLC MK45 .... 32 D6
The Apple Orch HHNE HP2 .... 118 A6
Appleton Av WARE SG12 .... 89 K8
Appleton Cl AMSS HP7 .... 146 F9
  HLWW/ROY CM19 .... 2 C7
Appleton Flds BSF CM23 .... 91 P1
Appletree Dell
  RKW/CH/CXG WD3 .... 160 D3
Appletree Gdns EBAR EN4 .... 167 J3
Appletree Gv STALW/RED AL3 .... 101 J6
Appletrees HTCH/STOT SG5 .... 49 J1
Appletree Wk CSHM HP5 .... 145 J4
  GSTN WD25 .... 149 J5
Applewood Cl HARP AL5 .... 101 M1
  TRDG/WHET N20 .... 167 J7
Appleyard Ter PEND EN3 * 156 B7
Approach Rd EBAR EN4 .... 166 G3
  STAL AL1 .... 9 H6
The Approach
  POTB/CUF EN6 .... 153 J2
Appspond La LCOL/BKTW AL2 .... 135 K3
Apsley Cl BSF CM23 .... 91 P1
  HRW HA1 .... 172 C9
Apsley End Rd
  HTCH/STOT SG5 .... 33 M3
Apton Cl BSF CM23 .... 74 A3
Apton Flds BSF CM23 .... 74 A4
Apton Rd BSF CM23 .... 74 A3
Aquarius Wy NTHWD HA6 .... 170 F1
Aragon Cl ENC/FH EN2 .... 154 C8
  HHNE HP2 .... 118 D3
Aran Cl HARP AL5 .... 102 C6
Aran Hts CSTG HP8 .... 159 H9
Arbour Wy AMSS HP7 .... 145 N9
Arbroath Gn OXHEY WD19 .... 162 C9
Arbroath Rd LTNW/LIM LU3 .... 45 N6
The Arcade LTNW/LEA LU4 .... 6 A1
Archer Cl KGLGY WD4 .... 134 A8
Archer Rd STVG SG1 .... 11 H1
  STVG SG1 .... 11 H2
Archers BUNT SG9 .... 40 E8
  HLWW/ROY CM19 .... 128 D8
Archers Ct HERT/WAT SG14 .... 106 C9
Archers Flds STAL AL1 * 120 E6
Archers Green La WLYN AL6 .... 105 N4
Archers Ride WGCE AL7 .... 105 L8
Archers Wy LWTH SG6 .... 36 E1
Archery Cl
  KTN/HRWW/WS HA3 .... 172 F7
The Arches LWTH SG6 .... 36 D1
Archfield Ct BSF CM23 * 91 H3
Archibald Cl PEND EN3 .... 156 D6
Archive Ct
  RAYLNE/WEN HP22 .... 94 E7
Archive Rd
  RAYLNE/WEN HP22 .... 94 E7
Arch Rd HTCHE/RSTV SG4 .... 50 A3
Archway Rd LTNN/LIM LU3 .... 62 A2
Arden Cl BUSH WD23 .... 163 P6
  HHS/BOV HP3 .... 132 D7
Arden Gv
Arden Mhor PIN HA5 .... 171 K8
Arden Pl LTNE LU2 .... 62 F5

Arden Press Wy LWTH SG6 * 36 E2
Ardens Marsh STALE/WH HA4 * 121 K6
Ardens Wy STALE/WH AL4 ...... 121 J6
Ardleigh Gn LTNE LU2 ...... 63 M5
Ardley Cl DUN/WHIP LU6 ...... 60 F9
Ardley Crs RBSF CM22 ...... 95 J7
Ardross Av NTHWD HA6 ...... 170 C2
Arenson Wy DUN/HR/TOD LU5 ...... 60 E4
Argent Wy CHESW EN7 ...... 141 L6
Argyle Cl WATW WD18 * 12 A5
Argyle Rd BAR EN5 ...... 166 A3
Argyle Wy STVG SG1 ...... 10 A4
Argyll Av LTNN/LIM LU3 ...... 62 D4
Argyll Gdns EDGW HA8 ...... 173 P6
Argyll Rd HHNE HP2 ...... 117 P3
Arkley Cl BAR EN5 ...... 165 N3
Arkley La BAR EN5 ...... 165 N2
Arkley Rd HHNE HP2 ...... 118 C3
Arkley Vw BAR EN5 ...... 165 P3
Arkwrights HLW CM20 * J4
Arlesey New Rd LWTH SG6 ...... 35 P1
Arlesey Rd LTNN/LIM LU3 ...... 35 K4
Arlington NFNCH/WDSPK N12 ...... 166 E9
Arlington Crs CHES/WCR EN8 ...... 7 L2
Arlington Rd STVG SG1 ...... 8 D7
  STHGT/OAK N14 ...... 167 M8
Armand Cl WAT WD17 ...... 168 B8
Armfield Rd ENC/FH EN2 ...... 155 L9
Armitage Cl RKW/CH/CXG WD3 ...... 161 N3
Armitage Gdns LTNW/LEA LU4 ...... 61 N5
Armourers Cl BSF CM23 ...... 91 L1
Armour Ri HTCHE/RSTV SG4 ...... 35 N6
Armstrong Cl BORE WD6 ...... 165 J2
  LCOL/BKTW AL2 ...... 167 H2
Armstrong Crs EBAR EN4 ...... 167 H2
Armstrong Gdns RAD WD7 ...... 151 K2
Armstrong Pl HHW HP1 ...... 117 M6
Arnald Wy DUN/HR/TOD LU5 ...... 60 D2
Arnett Cl RKW/CH/CXG WD3 ...... 160 E5
Arnett Wy RKW/CH/CXG WD3 ...... 160 E5
Arnold Av East PEND EN3 ...... 156 F8
Arnold Av West PEND EN3 ...... 156 E8
Arnold Cl
  AMP/FLIT/BLC MK45 ...... 32 C6
  HTCHE/RSTV SG4 ...... 35 N8
  LTNE LU2 ...... 63 H3
  STVG SG2 ...... 50 C6
Arnold Rd WAB EN9 ...... 157 H5
Arnolds La BLDK SG7 ...... 16 C4
Arnold Ter STAN HA7 * 172 F2
Arran Cl HHS/BOV HP3 ...... 134 D1
Arran Dr STAN HA7 ...... 173 J1
Arran Gn OXHEY WD19 * 171 M1
Arranmore Ct BUSH WD23 * 162 G3
Arretine Cl STALW/RED AL3 ...... 135 N1
Arrow Cl LTNN/LIM LU3 ...... 45 P9
Artesian Gv BAR EN5 ...... 166 C3
Arthur Gibbons Ct STVG SG1 * 51 K3
Arthur Cl PIN HA5 * 171 J4
Arthur St STAL AL1 ...... 120 C8
Arthur St BUSH WD23 ...... 13 K4
  ...... 6 E7
Artichoke Dell RKW/CH/CXG WD3 * 160 C3
Artisan Crs STALW/RED AL3 ...... 8 C1
Arundel Cl CHES/WCR EN8 ...... 142 A7
  HHNE HP2 ...... 118 C2
  STVG SG2 ...... J8
Arundel Dr BORE WD6 ...... 165 J3
Arundel Gv STALW/RED AL3 ...... 120 C4
Arundell Rd ABLGY WD5 ...... 149 H2
Arundel Rd EBAR EN4 ...... 167 J3
  LTNW/LEA LU4 ...... 62 B4
Ascot Cl RKW/CH/CXG WD3 * 161 M5
  BSF CM23 ...... 74 D2
Ascot Gdns PEND EN5 ...... 156 B7
Ascot Rd LTNN/LIM LU3 ...... 62 C4
  ROY SG8 ...... 20 E4
  WATW WD18 ...... 162 A4
Ascots La BRKMPK AL9 ...... 123 H2
Ascott Ct PIN HA5 * 171 H1
Ashanger La BLDK SG7 ...... 17 N4
Ashbourne Sq NTHWD HA6 ...... 170 D3
Ashbourne Cl TRDG/WHET N20 ...... 167 N8
Ashbourne Ct LWTH SG6 ...... 36 C4
Ashbourne Ct STALE/WH AL4 ...... 137 H1
Ashbourne Gdns HERT/BAY SG13 ...... 107 M8
Ashbourne Rd BROX EN10 ...... 126 E8
Ashbrook Edgw HA8 * 173 M5
Ashbrook La HTCHE/RSTV SG4 ...... 49 N4
Ashburnam Wk STVGE SG2 ...... 67 J3
Ashburnham Cl OXHEY WD19 * 162 C9
Ashburnham Dr OXHEY WD19 * 162 C9
Ashburnham Rd LTN LU1 ...... 62 C7
Ashbury Cl HAT AL10 ...... 122 H6
Ashby Ct HHNE HP2 ...... 118 C2
Ashby Dr AMP/FLIT/BLC MK45 ...... 32 D5
Ashby Gdns STAL AL1 ...... 136 C5
Ashby Rd BSF CM23 ...... 74 C1
Ashby Rd BERK HP4 ...... 115 J4
  WATN WD24 ...... 148 E2
Ash Cl ABLGY WD5 ...... 139 K4
  BRKMPK AL9 ...... 123 M2
  DEN/HRF UB9 ...... 169 J5
  GSTN WD25 ...... 149 J5
Ashcombe BRKMPK AL9 ...... 123 M2
Ashcombe Gdns EDGW HA8 ...... 173 H3
Ash Copse LCOL/BKTW AL2 ...... 149 N6
Ashcroft DUN/WHIP LU6 ...... 60 C5
Ashcroft Cl HARP AL5 ...... 102 D4
Ashcroft Rd LTNE LU2 ...... 63 K3
Ashdale STAL AL1 ...... 136 C5
Ashdene PIN HA5 ...... 171 H1
Ashdon Rd BUSH WD23 ...... 13 K3
Ashdown LWTH SG6 ...... 25 J8

Ashdown Crs CHES/WCR EN8 ...... 142 D7
Ashdown Dr BORE WD6 ...... 164 F1
Ashdown Rd LTNE LU2 ...... 63 L4
Ashdown Wy AMS HP6 ...... 145 J7
Ash Dr HAT AL10 ...... 122 G8
  HTCHE/RSTV SG4 ...... 49 M3
  HTCHE/RSTV SG4 * 82 E5
Ashendene Rd CSHM HP5 ...... 141 J4
  HERT/BAY SG13 ...... 124 G6
Ashfield Av BUSH WD23 ...... 150 E7
Ashfield Rd BUSH WD23 ...... 163 K5
Ashfield Rd CSHM HP5 ...... 131 J8
  STHGT/OAK N14 ...... 167 N9
Ashfields LWTH SG6 ...... 36 C4
Ashfield Wy LTNN/LIM LU3 ...... 45 N7
Ashford Gn OXHEY WD19 ...... 171 M2
Ash Gv AMS HP6 ...... 144 F6
  DEN/HRF UB9 ...... 169 P5
  DUN/HR/TOD LU5 ...... 60 C6
  HHS/BOV HP3 ...... 134 A3
  STALE/WH AL4 ...... 103 H5
Ash Groves SBW CM21 ...... 92 B7
Ash Hill Cl BUSH WD23 ...... 163 K7
Ash Hill Dr PIN HA5 ...... 171 H1
Ashlea Rd CFSP/GDCR SL9 ...... 168 D7
Ashley Cl STVGE SG2 ...... 67 L2
Ashley Cl HHNE HP2 ...... 5 L5
  LBUZ LU7 ...... 77 P5
  PIN HA5 ...... 171 K6
  WCCW AL8 ...... 104 F4
Ashley Dr BORE WD6 ...... 165 J4
Ashley Gdns HARP AL5 ...... 101 L1
Ashley Green Rd CSHM HP5 ...... 131 J6
  STAL AL1 ...... 121 H8
Ashleys RKW/CH/CXG WD3 ...... 160 D6
Ashlyn Cl BUSH WD23 ...... 163 P5
Ashlyns Ct BERK HP4 ...... 115 N8
Ashlyns Rd BERK HP4 ...... 115 N8
Ashmead STHGT/OAK N14 ...... 167 N4
Ash Mi ROY SG8 ...... 30 A6
Ashmore Gdns HHS/BOV HP3 ...... 118 C9
Ashotts La CSHM HP5 ...... 130 A4
Ash Ride ENC/FH EN2 ...... 155 H5
Ashridge Cl BORE WD6 ...... 132 D7
Ashridge Dr LCOL/BKTW AL2 ...... 135 M9
  OXHEY WD19 ...... 171 N8
Ashridge Gdns PIN HA5 ...... 171 N8
Ashridge La CSHM HP5 ...... 129 N4
Ashridge Ri BERK HP4 ...... 115 J6
Ashridge Rd LTNW/LEA LU4 ...... 62 C6
  TRING SG23 ...... 95 N8
  WARE SG12 ...... 108 F1
Ashton Rd DUN/WHIP LU6 ...... 60 E5
  LTN LU1 ...... 62 E6
  PEND EN3 ...... 156 D6
Ashton's La BLDK SG7 ...... 37 J2
Ashton Sq DUN/WHIP LU6 ...... 60 E6
Ashtree Ct STAL AL1 ...... 120 F5
Ash Tree Fld HLW CM20 ...... 128 D1
Ash Tree Rd DUN/HR/TOD LU5 ...... 44 E9
  WATN WD24 ...... 149 K6
Ashtree Wy HHW HP1 ...... 117 K9
Ashurst Cl NTHWD HA6 ...... 170 G4
Ash V RKW/CH/CXG WD3 ...... 169 H2
Ashville Wy BLDK SG7 ...... 26 C8
Ashwell Av LTNW/LEA LU4 ...... 45 M7
Ashwell Common STVG SG1 ...... 50 E5
Ashwell Pk HARP AL5 ...... 102 C3
Ashwell Rd WATN WD24 ...... 149 N7
Ashwells Wy CSTG HH9 ...... 159 J8
Ashwell Wk DUN/HR/TOD LU5 ...... 45 H9
Ashwood Dr CSHM HP5 ...... 130 C9
Ashwood Ms STAL AL1 ...... 4 B1
Ashworth Pl HLWE CM17 ...... 129 N5
Askew Rd NTHWD HA6 ...... 161 P8
Aspasia Cl STAL AL1 ...... 9 K6
Aspen Cl LCOL/BKTW AL2 ...... 135 M9
  STVGE SG2 ...... 67 L7
Aspenden Rd BUNT SG9 ...... 171 H7
Aspen Gv PIN HA5 ...... 171 H1
Aspen Park Dr GSTN WD25 ...... 149 J5
Aspen Pl STVGE SG2 ...... 67 J6
Aspens WAB EN9 ...... 157 P5
Aspens Pl HHW HP1 ...... 133 J2
The Aspens BSF CM23 ...... 58 C9
Aspfield Rw HHW HP1 * 117 L6
Aspley Cl LTNW/LEA LU4 ...... 61 N3
Ass House La KTN/HRWW/WS HA3 ...... 172 N1
Astall Cl KTN/HRWW/WS HA3 ...... 172 D5
Aster Cl BSF CM23 ...... 73 N8
The Asters CHESW EN7 ...... 141 L7
Astley Gn LTNE LU2 ...... 63 L4
Astley Rd HHW HP1 ...... 4 C2
Aston Clinton Rd RYLN/HDSTN HA2 ...... 94 B6
Aston Cl BUSH WD23 ...... 163 L1
  STVG SG2 ...... 13 H1
Aston End Rd STVGE SG2 ...... 67 P3
Aston Gra HERT/WAT SG14 ...... 107 L4
Aston La STVGE SG2 ...... 67 N1
Aston Ri HTCHE/RSTV SG4 ...... 49 N1
Aston Rd STVG SG11 ...... 71 J4
Astons Ri NTHWD HA6 ...... 161 N9
Aston Wy POTB/CUF EN6 ...... 153 N2
Astrope La TRING WD23 ...... 122 C3
Astwick Rd HTCH/STOT SG5 ...... 16 B9
Athelstan Rd HHS/BOV HP3 ...... 133 P2
Athelstan Wk North WCCE AL7 ...... 105 H7
Athelstan Wk South WCCE AL7 ...... 104 G7
Athelstone Rd KTN/HRWW/WS HA3 ...... 172 D6

Athenaeum Rd TRDG/WHET N20 ...... 166 G7
Athena Pl NTHWD HA6 ...... 171 H5
Athenia Cl CHESW EN7 ...... 141 J8
Atherstone Rd LTNW/LEA LU4 ...... 61 N5
Atherton End SBW CM21 ...... 111 P1
Atherton Pl RYLN/HDSTN HA2 ...... 172 C7
Athlone Cl RAD WD7 * 150 E6
Athol Cl PIN HA5 ...... 171 K5
Athol Gdns PIN HA5 ...... 171 K5
Atholl Cl LTNN/LIM LU3 ...... 45 N7
Atria Rd NTHWD HA6 ...... 171 J2
Attenborough Cl OXHEY WD19 ...... 162 C9
Attfield Cl TRDG/WHET N20 ...... 167 H8
Attimore Cl WGCW AL8 ...... 104 C7
Attimore Rd WGCW AL8 ...... 104 C7
Auber Cl HOD EN11 ...... 126 E2
Aubrey Av LCOL/BKTW AL2 ...... 137 H5
Aubrey Gdns LTNW/LEA LU4 ...... 45 L9
Aubrey La STALW/RED AL3 ...... 118 F1
Aubreys LWTH SG6 ...... 36 C6
Aubreys Rd HARP AL5 ...... 117 H9
Aubries STVGE SG2 ...... 52 C7
Auckland Cl EN EN1 ...... 156 A9
Auden Dr BORE WD6 ...... 164 G4
Audley Cl BORE WD6 ...... 164 G3
Audley Ct PIN HA5 ...... 171 J4
Audley Gdns LTNE LU2 ...... 63 M5
Audley Pl LTNE LU2 * 63 M5
Audrey Gdns BSF CM23 ...... 74 A7
Audwick Cl CHES/WCR EN8 ...... 142 C7
Augustine Cl SLW SG8 ...... 156 C3
Augustine Rd KTN/HRWW/WS HA3 ...... 172 B5
Augustus Cl STALW/RED AL3 ...... 135 P1
Augustus Ga STVGE SG2 ...... 51 M7
Austell Gdns MLHL NW7 ...... 165 L9
Austen Paths STVGE SG2 ...... 51 M7
Austenway CFSP/GDCR SL9 ...... 168 C7
Austen Wd CFSP/GDCR SL9 ...... 168 C7
Austin Rd LTNN/LIM LU3 ...... 62 C7
Austin Canons CFSP/GDCR SL9 ...... 168 A6
Austin Rd LTNN/LIM LU3 ...... 132 C7
Austins Pl HHNE HP2 ...... 5 G2
Austin Vis CSTN WD25 ...... 149 J1
Autumn Glades HHS/BOV HP3 ...... 134 D1
Autumn Gv WCCE AL7 ...... 105 L8
Avalon Cl GSTN WD25 ...... 149 M2
Avebury Av LTNE LU2 ...... 62 E2
Avebury Ct HHNE HP2 ...... 118 B5
Avenue Ap STHGT/OAK N14 ...... 85 H6
Avenue Cl STHGT/OAK N14 ...... 85 H6
Avenue One LWTH SG6 ...... 36 F7
Avenue Ri BUSH WD23 ...... 163 J4
Avenue Rd BSF CM23 ...... 74 B4
  HOD EN11 ...... 127 J7
  PIN HA5 ...... 171 K5
  STAL AL1 ...... 9 I
  STHGT/OAK N14 ...... 85 H6
Avenue St Nicholas HARP AL5 ...... 101 P3
Avenue Ter OXHEY WD19 * 162 C5
The Avenue AMSS HP7 ...... 145 H4
  BAR EN5 ...... 165 H3
  BUSH WD23 ...... 163 H5
  BSF CM23 ...... 60 D7
  DUN/WHIP LU6 ...... 60 D7
  HERT/WAT SG14 ...... 107 H7
  HHW HP1 ...... 117 H7
  HOD EN11 ...... 127 J7
  HTCH/STOT SG5 ...... 25 K3
  HTCHE/RSTV SG4 ...... 35 W9
  KTN/HRWW/WS HA3 ...... 172 B5
  LTNW/LEA LU4 ...... 61 N1
  NTHWD HA6 ...... 170 E3
  PIN HA5 ...... 171 P3
  POTB/CUF EN6 ...... 139 J9
  RAD WD7 ...... 150 F6
  WAB EN9 ...... 143 P4
  WAT WD17 ...... 147 P9
  WLYN AL6 ...... 84 G6
Avia La LG IC10 * 157 M8
Avior Rd NTHWD HA6 ...... 171 J1
Avocet LWTH SG6 ...... 36 C7
Avocet Cl STALW/RED AL3 ...... 120 B5
Avon Cl GSTN WD25 ...... 149 K4
Avon Ct PIN HA5 * 172 A4
Avondale Av EBAR EN4 ...... 167 K7
Avondale Rd KTN/HRWW/WS HA3 ...... 172 D5
  LTN LU1 ...... 4 A5
Avon Dr STVG SG1 ...... 51 J4
Avon Ms PIN HA5 ...... 171 P1
Avon Sq HHNE HP2 ...... 118 A5
Awberry Ct WATW WD18 * 147 P5
Axe Cl LTNN/LIM LU3 ...... 45 P9
Axenholm Av EDGW HA8 ...... 173 N5
Axholme Rd EDGW HA8 ...... 117 P4
Aycliffe Dr HHNE HP2 ...... 117 P4
Aycliffe Rd BORE WD6 ...... 163 P1
Aydon Rd LTNN/LIM LU3 ...... 46 C9
Aylands Rd PEND EN3 ...... 156 C6
Aylesbury Ring RAYLNE/WEN HP22 ...... 112 A7
  TRING SG23 ...... 94 G2
Aylesbury Rd RAYLNE/WEN HP22 ...... 94 C7
  TRING WD23 ...... 112 A7
Aylets Fld HLWS CM18 ...... 129 N6
Aylmer Cl STAN HA7 ...... 172 C1
Aylmer Dr STAN HA7 ...... 172 C1
Aylotts Cl BUNT SG9 ...... 40 C8
Aylsham Rd HOD EN11 ...... 127 H6
Aylward Gdns CSHM HP5 ...... 130 F5
Aylwards Ri STAN HA7 ...... 172 C1
Aynho Wk WATW WD18 ...... 12 E6

Aynscombe Cl DUN/WHIP LU6 ...... 60 C5
Aynsley Gdns HLWE CM17 ...... 129 M5
Aynsworth Av BSF CM23 ...... 58 B9
Ayot Gn WLYN AL6 ...... 104 C3
Ayot Little Green La WLYN AL6 ...... 104 C3
Ayot St Peter Rd WLYN AL6 ...... 84 E1
Ayr Ct STVG SG1 ...... 51 M7
Ayres End La HARP AL5 ...... 102 C8
Aysgarth Cl HARP AL5 ...... 102 A4
Aysgarth Rd STALW/RED AL3 ...... 101 H6
Azalea Cl LCOL/BKTW AL2 ...... 137 H6

B

Baas Hl BROX EN10 ...... 126 C9
Baas Hill Cl BROX EN10 ...... 126 D9
Baas La BROX EN10 ...... 126 D9
Babbage Rd STVG SG1 ...... 8 A5
Babington Rd RAYLNE/WEN HP22 ...... 112 E5
Back La BUNT SG9 ...... 29 K9
  GSTN WD25 ...... 150 C2
  HTCHE/RSTV SG4 ...... 49 H9
  RBSF CM22 ...... 143 P1
  WAB EN9 ...... 143 K6
  WLYN AL6 ...... 105 P2
The Backs CSHM HP5 ...... 145 H1
Back St BLDK SG7 ...... 17 M7
  LTNE LU2 ...... 7 F2
  RAYLNE/WEN HP22 ...... 112 C7
The Back La HARP HP4 ...... 116 E4
Bacombe La RAYLNE/WEN HP22 ...... 112 B8
Bacon La EDGW HA8 ...... 173 N5
Bacons Dr POTB/CUF EN6 ...... 140 F7
Bacon's Yd BLDK SG7 ...... 17 N6
Badbury Ct WAB EN9 ...... 157 L3
Baddeley Cl PEND EN3 ...... 156 F7
Bader Cl STVG SG1 ...... 51 M6
  WCCE AL7 ...... 105 M6
Badgers Cl BORE WD6 ...... 67 J8
Badgers BSF CM23 ...... 73 P9
Badger Wy HAT AL10 ...... 122 C8
Badgers Cl BROX EN10 ...... 126 D9
  HHNE HP2 ...... 118 C9
  TRDG/WHET N20 ...... 166 C6
Badgers Ga DUN/WHIP LU6 ...... 60 B6
Badgers Meadow RAYLNE/WEN HP22 ...... 112 D6
Badgers Wk RKW/CH/CXG WD3 ...... 160 D3
  WLYN AL6 ...... 85 M8
Baird Cl BUSH WD23 ...... 163 K5
Baines La KNEB SG3 ...... 85 M2
Baird Memorial Cots STDN SG11 * 167 H8
Bairstow Ct BORE WD6 ...... 151 K9
Bakers Cl STAL AL1 ...... 120 F9
Bakers La DUN/WHIP LU6 ...... 79 H5
Bakerscroft CHES/WCR EN8 ...... 142 C7
Bakers Hill BAR EN5 ...... 166 F1
Bakers La DUN/WHIP LU6 ...... 84 C4
Bakers La ROY SG8 ...... 21 L7
Baker St BAR EN5 ...... 153 H5
  EN EN1 ...... 155 N6
  HERT/BAY SG13 ...... 107 M8
  LTN LU1 ...... 62 F9
  POTB/CUF EN6 ...... 153 J3
  STVG SG1 ...... 10 B1
Bakers Wk RAYLNE/WEN HP22 ...... 112 A1
Bakery Cl HLWW/ROY CM19 ...... 127 D5
Bakewell Cl LTNW/LEA LU4 ...... 61 M5
Balams La STHGT/OAK N14 ...... 167 P9
Balcary Gdns BERK HP4 ...... 115 K8
Balcombe Cl LTNE LU2 ...... 63 K2
Balcon Wy BORE WD6 ...... 151 P5
Baldock Cl LTNW/LEA LU4 ...... 61 L3
Baldock La BUNT SG9 * 40 C9
Baldock Rd BUNT SG9 ...... 40 E9
  HTCH/STOT SG5 ...... 16 D5
  LWTH SG6 ...... 36 E3
  ROY SG8 ...... 19 J7
Baldock St BORE WD6 ...... 108 C2
  WARE SG12 ...... 108 C2
Baldways Cl RAYLNE/WEN HP22 ...... 76 C2
Baldwins WGCE AL7 ...... 105 J5
Baldwins La RKW/CH/CXG WD3 ...... 161 L3
Balfour Cl HARP AL5 ...... 102 B1
Balfour Gv TRDG/WHET N20 ...... 166 F1
Balfour Ms HHS/BOV HP3 ...... 134 A2
Balfour St HERT/BAY SG13 ...... 172 D6
Baliol Rd HTCH/STOT SG5 ...... 35 L8
Ballards Rd NTHWD HA6 ...... 173 H5
Ballards Rw RAYLNE/WEN HP22 * 94 E6
Balater Cl OXHEY WD19 ...... 171 H5
Ballinger Ct BERK HP4 ...... 115 M8
Ballslough Hl HTCHE/RSTV SG4 ...... 50 D6
Balmoral Dr BORE WD6 ...... 164 G4
Balmoral Rd ABLGY WD5 ...... 149 H2
  HTCH/STOT SG5 ...... 25 L1
  PEND EN3 ...... 156 C6
  WATN WD24 ...... 149 K8

Balmore Crs EBAR EN4 ...... 167 L4
Balmore Wd LTNN/LIM LU3 ...... 46 C6
Balsams Cl HERT/BAY SG13 ...... 107 L8
Bampton Rd LTNW/LEA LU4 ...... 61 L5
Bamville Wd HARP AL5 ...... 102 B7
Banbury Cl ENC/FH EN2 ...... 155 J9
  LTNW/LEA LU4 ...... 62 A2
Bancroft HTCH/STOT SG5 ...... 35 C3
Bancroft Gdns KTN/HRWW/WS HA3 ...... 172 C5
Bancroft Rd KTN/HRWW/WS HA3 ...... 172 C6
  LTNN/LIM LU3 ...... 62 C2
Bandley Ri STVGE SG2 ...... 67 M3
Banes Down WAB EN9 ...... 143 K1
Bank Cl LTNW/LEA LU4 ...... 61 M2
Bank Ct HHNE HP2 ...... 5 F3
Bank Ms BERK HP4 ...... 116 C8
Bankmill Br BERK HP4 ...... 116 C8
Bank Mill La BERK HP4 ...... 116 C8
Bankside ENC/FH EN2 ...... 155 J9
  RAYLNE/WEN HP22 ...... 112 C7
Bank Side ROY SG8 ...... 21 L7
Bankside Cl DEN/HRF UB9 ...... 169 L3
  DUN/HR/TOD LU5 ...... 60 D1
Bankside Down RKW/CH/CXG WD3 * 161 H5
Bankstock Ed EDGW HA8 ...... 165 L1
Barbaraville Camp BRKMPK AL9 * 123 J3
Barbel Cl CHES/WCR EN8 ...... 156 F4
Barberry Rd HHW HP1 ...... 117 K8
Barbers Wk TRING HA5 ...... 135 M9
Barchester Rd KTN/HRWW/WS HA3 ...... 172 D5
Barclay Cl HERT/BAY SG13 ...... 108 A8
  WATW WD18 ...... 162 C5
Barclay Ct HOD EN11 ...... 126 F6
Barclay Crs STVG SG1 ...... 51 P1
Barden Cl DEN/HRF UB9 ...... 169 N5
Bards Cnr HHW HP1 * 117 L7
Bardwell Ct STAL AL1 ...... 8 E5
Barfield Av TRDG/WHET N20 ...... 167 L8
Barford Ri LTNE LU2 ...... 63 L5
Bargrove Av HHW HP1 ...... 117 K9
Barham Av BORE WD6 ...... 164 F2
Barham Rd STVG SG1 ...... 67 M1
Baring Rd EBAR EN4 ...... 166 G3
Barker Cl NTHWD HA6 ...... 171 H4
Barkham Cl LBUZ LU7 ...... 77 N6
Barking Cl LTNW/LEA LU4 ...... 61 N3
Barkway Cl LTNW/LEA LU4 ...... 30 C5
Barkway Rd ROY SG8 ...... 20 G5
Barlee Cl SAFWS CB11 ...... 43 M5
Barley Brow DUN/WHIP LU6 ...... 60 B3
Barley Cl BUSH WD23 ...... 163 K4
  RAYLNE/WEN HP22 ...... 112 A1
  RBSF CM22 * 93 M7
The Barleycorn LTNN/LIM LU3 * 6 C2
Barleycroft STVG SG2 ...... 67 J3
Barley Crt HERT/WAT SG14 ...... 107 H1
  HLWS CM18 ...... 128 C7
  KNEB SG3 ...... 85 K3
Barleycroft STVGE SG2 ...... 67 J3
Barleycroft Gn WGCW AL8 ...... 104 F6
Barleycroft Rd WGCW AL8 ...... 104 F6
Barleyfield Wy DUN/HR/TOD LU5 ...... 60 D1
Barley Hills BSF CM23 ...... 91 H1
Barley Ley LTNW/LEA LU4 ...... 61 M1
Barley Mow La STALE/WH AL4 ...... 137 K2
Barley Ponds Cl WARE SG12 ...... 108 E3
Barley Ponds Rd WARE SG12 ...... 108 E3
  HARP AL5 * 82 B9
Barley Rd ROY SG8 ...... 21 M7
Barleyvale LTNN/LIM LU3 ...... 46 B8
Barlings Rd HARP AL5 ...... 102 A7
Barlow Rd RAYLNE/WEN HP22 ...... 112 D6
Barmor Cl RYLN/HDSTN HA2 ...... 172 B6
Barnack Gv ROY SG8 ...... 20 B3
Barnacres Rd HHS/BOV HP3 ...... 134 B5
Barnard Acres WAB EN9 ...... 143 K2
Barnard Gn WGCE AL7 ...... 105 J7
Barnard La HTCH/STOT SG5 ...... 16 B9
Barnard Rd LTN LU1 ...... 62 B7
  SBW CM21 ...... 111 J1
Barnard Wy HHNE HP2 ...... 134 A2
Barn Cl HARP AL5 ...... 119 H8
  HHS/BOV HP3 ...... 150 F5
  RAD WD7 ...... 150 F5
  WCCW AL8 ...... 104 F6
Barn Crs STAN HA7 ...... 173 J3
Barncroft Rd BERK HP4 ...... 115 L8
Barncroft Wy STAL AL1 ...... 120 F9
Barndell Cl HTCH/STOT SG5 ...... 25 L3
Barndicott WGCE AL7 ...... 105 M6
Barnes Av CSHM HP5 ...... 131 M7
Barnes La RKGLY WD4 ...... 134 A6
Barnes Rn RKGLY WD4 ...... 134 A6
Barnet By-Pass BORE WD6 ...... 165 L4
Barnet La BORE WD6 ...... 165 M5
Barnet Ga BAR EN5 ...... 165 M5
Barnet Rd BAR EN5 ...... 153 K7
  LCOL/BKTW AL2 ...... 137 K6
Barnet Way (Barnet By-Pass) MLHL NW7 ...... 165 K6
Barnfield HHS/BOV HP3 ...... 134 A2
  RBSF CM23 * 93 P4
Barnfield Av LTNE LU2 ...... 62 E1
Barnfield Cl HOD EN11 ...... 126 F3
  WAB EN9 ...... 143 L1
Barnfield Ct HARP AL5 ...... 102 B8
Barnfield Rd BAR EN5 ...... 102 A4
  STALE/WH AL4 ...... 121 H6
  WCCE AL7 ...... 105 K6
Barn Hl HLWW/ROY CM19 ...... 127 N7
Barnhill Pth HHW HP1 ...... 171 L6
Barn La RKW/CH/CXG WD19 ...... 160 E2
Barn Lea RKW/CH/CXG WD3 ...... 160 E2
Barn Md HLWS CM18 ...... 128 G5

Barns Ct HLWW/ROY CM19........ 128 E8
Barnsdale Cl BORE WD6............. 151 L9
Barns Dene HARP AL5................ 101 M2
Barnside Ct WAT WD24.............. 16 E3
The Barns BGSW SG18 *............. 16 E5
Barnston Cl LTNE LU2................ 63 L5
Barnsway KGLGY WD4................ 133 P7
Barnwell STVGE SG2.................. 67 L4
Baron Ct STVG SG1................... 50 E6
Barons Ga EBAR EN4.................. 167 J5
Barons Md HEN HA5 *................ 172 E8
Baronsmere Ct BAR EN5 *........... 166 C3
The Barons BSF CM23................ 73 N9
Barr Rd HLS/BOV HP3................ 134 C2
Barrass Ct PEND EN3 *............... 161 J1
Barratt Wy
    KTN/HRWW/WS HA3............. 172 D7
Barrells Down Rd BSF CM23........ 73 P5
Barrett La BSF CM23.................. 74 A3
Barrie Av DUN/WHIP LU6............ 60 B5
Barrington Dr DEN/HRF UB9........ 169 L4
Barrington Park Gdns
    CSTG HP8........................... 159 K7
Barrons Rw LWTH SG6................ 36 C4
Barrowby Cl LTNE LU2............... 102 C5
Barrow La CHESW EN7............... 155 N1
Barrowdene Cl PIN HA5.............. 171 N6
Barrow La CHESW EN7............... 155 N1
Barrow Point Av PIN HA5............ 171 N6
Barrow Point La PIN HA5............ 171 N6
Barrows Rd
    HLWW/ROY CM19................ 128 C3
Barr Rd POTB/CUF EN6.............. 153 M3
Barry Cl LCOL/BKTW AL2............ 136 A4
Bartel Cl HHS/BOV HP3............. 135 J6
Bartholomew Gn
    STALW/RED AL3................... 79 P8
Bartholomew Rd BSF CM23......... 74 A4
Bartletts Md HERT/WAT SG14...... 107 L3
Barton Av DUN/HR/TOD LU5...... 60 C6
Barton Cl HARP AL5.................. 102 B1
Barton Rd
    AMP/FLIT/BLC MK45............ 32 A6
    HTCH/STOT SG5.................. 32 C7
    LTNN/LIM LU3.................... 46 C4
    STALW/WH AL4................... 63 L5
The Bartons BORE WD6.............. 164 D5
Barton Wy BORE WD6................ 164 C1
Bartrams La EBAR EN4................ 153 M8
Bartrop Cl CHESW EN7 *............ 141 L7
Barwick La STVG SG11............... 89 K2
Basbow La BSF CM23................. 74 A2
Basildon Cl WATW WD18............ 161 N5
Basildon Sq HHNE HP2............... 118 A4
Basil Ms HLWE CM17................. 129 M2
Basils Rd STVG SG1.................. 10 C1
Basing Rd RKW/CH/CXG WD3..... 160 D3
Baslow Cl
    KTN/HRWW/WS HA3............. 172 D5
Bassett Cl STALW/RED AL3.......... 101 J7
Bassil Rd HHW HP2 *................. 5 F4
Bassingbourn Rd CBROX EN10.... 126 E8
Bassingbourn Rd STSD CM24...... 59 N9
Bassingbourn Rbt
    STSD CM24......................... 75 N1
Bassingham Wk WCCE AL7......... 89 P9
Batchelors STDN SG11.............. 91 M4
Batchelors Wy AMSS HP6........... 145 J9
Batchworth HP5...................... 130 C8
Batchworth Dr
    STALW/RED AL3................... 8 B1
Batchworth Gdns
    STALW/RED AL3................... 120 C5
Batchworth Vw
    STALW/RED AL3................... 120 B6
Batchworth Hl
    RKW/CH/CXG WD3.............. 161 J8
Batchworth Hill London Rd
    RKW/CH/CXG WD3.............. 161 J8
Batchworth La NTHWD HA6....... 170 E2
Bateman Rd
    RKW/CH/CXG WD3.............. 161 L5
Bates La RAYLNE/WEN HP22....... 112 A1
Batford Cl WGCE AL7................ 105 L7
Batford Mi HARP AL5 *.............. 102 C1
Bath Pl BAR EN5...................... 166 C6
Bath Rd LTNN/LIM LU3.............. 62 E4
Bathurst Rd HHNE HP2.............. 117 N5
Batley Rd ENC/FH EN2............... 155 K9
Battlefield Rd STAL AL1.............. 120 D4
Battlers Green Dr WAT WD7........ 150 D7
Battleview STALW/WH AL4.......... 103 K4
Baud Cl STDN SG11.................. 73 H4
The Baulk LBUZ LU7.................. 77 N6
Bawdsey Av ILFN/IG................. 47 L5
Bawtry Rd TRDG/WHET N20...... 167 K9
Baxendale TRDG/WHET N20...... 166 G8
Bay Cl LTNN/LIM LU3................ 45 L9
Baycroft Cl PIN HA5.................. 171 L7
Bayford Cl HERT/BAY SG13........ 125 K9
    HHNE HP2.......................... 5 J9
Bayford Ct HERT/BAY SG13 *...... 36 E5
Bayford La HART/BAY SG13........ 124 G3
Bayford Ln NTHWD HA6............ 171 H3
Baylam Dell LTNE LU2............... 63 M5
Bayley Hall Ms
    HERT/WAT SG14.................. 107 L2
Bayley Md HHW HP1 *............... 4 B5
Baylie Cl HHNE HP2................. 117 P7
Baylie La HHNE HP2................. 117 P7
Baynes Cl EN EN1.................... 155 P9
Bay Tree Cl CHESW EN7............ 141 N6
    LCOL/BKTW AL2.................. 136 A6
Bay Tree Wk WAT WD17............ 148 G8
Bayworth LWTH SG6................. 36 E5
Beacon Av DUN/WHIP LU6......... 60 B7
Beacon Cl CFSP/GDCR SL9........ 168 C4
Beacon Ct HERT/BAY SG13 *...... 108 B9
Beacon Rd BERK HP4................ 97 L2
Beacon St STVGE SG2................ 108 F2
Beaconsfield Cots
    TRDG/WHET N20 *.............. 166 F9
Beaconsfield Ct HAT AL10 *........ 122 F4
Beaconsfield Rd HAT AL10......... 122 F5
    PEND EN3.......................... 156 C7
    RAYLNE/WEN HP22............. 94 F7

    STAL AL1............................ 9 H4
    TRDG/WHET N20................ 167 K9
The Beacons STVG SG1.............. 51 L4
Beacon Wy
    RKW/CH/CXG WD3.............. 160 E6
    TRING HP23........................ 135 H8
The Beadles RBSF CM22............. 92 C1
Beadlow Rd LTNW/LEA LU4........ 62 A7
Beagle Cl RAD WD7.................. 150 E7
Beale Cl STVGE SG2.................. 51 M9
Beale St DUN/WHIP LU6............ 60 D4
Beamish Dr BUSH WD23............ 163 L7
Beane Av STVGE SG2................ 51 N9
Beane River Vw
    HERT/WAT SG14.................. 107 K6
Beane Rd HERT/WAT SG14......... 86 E1
    HERT/WAT SG14................... 107 J6
The Beanside
    HERT/WAT SG14.................. 86 E1
Beane Wk STVGE SG2............... 51 N9
Beanfield Rd SBW CM21........... 91 K9
Beanley Cl LTNE LU2................. 63 M4
Beardow Gv
    STHGT/OAK N14 *............... 167 N5
Bear La BLDK SG7.................... 17 N6
Bearton Av HTCH/STOT SG5...... 35 J7
Bearton Gn HTCH/STOT SG5...... 35 J7
Bearton Rd HTCH/STOT SG5...... 35 J8
Bearwood Cl POTB/CUF EN6...... 153 N1
Besant House WATN WD24........ 13 J1
Beatham Ct WARE SG12 *.......... 87 M9
Beatrice Cl PIN HA5.................. 171 H4
Beatty Rd CHES/WCR EN8.......... 156 E4
    STAN HA7.......................... 173 J3
Beauchamp Gdns
    RKW/CH/CXG WD3.............. 160 E7
Beauchamps WCCE AL7 *.......... 105 L7
Beaufort Av
    KTN/HRWW/WS HA3............. 172 G8
Beaulieu Cl OXHEY WD19.......... 162 E7
Beaulieu Dr WAB EN9............... 156 C2
Beaumayes Cl HHW HP1 *......... 4 B4
Beaumonts STAL AL1 *.............. 9 G3
Beaumont La BSF CM23............. 120 C7
Beaumont Ga WAD WD7............ 150 F5
Beaumont Hall La
    STALW/RED AL3................... 119 J1
Beaumont Ms PIN HA5 *............ 171 N7
Beaumont Park Dr
    HLWW/ROY CM19................ 127 N3
Beaumont Pl BAR EN5............... 153 J9
Beaumont Rd BRON EN10......... 141 N5
    LTNN/LIM LU3.................... 62 C4
Beaumont Vw CHESW EN7......... 141 L5
Beazley Cl WARE SG12.............. 108 D2
Beckbury Cl LTNE LU2............... 63 M4
Becket Fold HAY HA1 *............. 172 F9
Becket Gdns WLYN AL6............. 84 F9
Beckets Sq BERK HP4 *............. 115 M5
Beckets Wk WARE SG12 *.......... 108 C3
Beckett's Av STALW/RED AL3...... 120 B5
Beckfield La BUNT SG9.............. 39 K1
Beckham Cl LTNE LU2............... 63 M4
Becks Cl STALW/RED AL3.......... 79 N8
Becmead Av
    KTN/HRWW/WS HA3............. 173 H9
Bede Cl PIN HA5..................... 171 M5
Bedford Av AMS HP6................ 145 P9
    BAR EN5............................ 166 D4
Bedford Cl
    RKW/CH/CXG WD3.............. 146 E8
Bedford Crs PEND EN3.............. 156 D5
Bedford Gdns LTNN/LIM LU3..... 6 A2
Bedford Park Rd STAL AL1.......... 9 H3
Bedford Rd
    AMP/FLIT/BLC MK45............ 32 C4
    DUN/HR/TOD LU5................ 44 D9
    HTCH/STOT SG5.................. 35 H1
    MLHL NW7......................... 165 L8
    NTHWD HA6....................... 170 F1
    STAL AL1........................... 9 H5
Bedford St BERK HP4................ 116 A7
    HTCH/STOT SG5.................. 35 J9
    WATN WD24....................... 149 J9
Bedmond La ABLGY WD5.......... 135 H5
Bedmond Rd HHS/BOV HP3....... 134 E2
Bedwell Av HERT/BAY SG13...... 124 E5
Bedwell Cl WGCE AL7............... 105 H7
Bedwell Crs STVG SG1.............. 11 F4
Bedwell Pk STVG SG1............... 11 G5
Beech Av ENC/FH EN2.............. 155 L1
    RAD WD7.......................... 150 F5
    TRDG/WHET N20................ 167 J7

Beechfield Cl HHW HP1.............. 4 B3
    WARE SG12......................... 108 E2
    WGCE AL7.......................... 105 H8
Beechfield Wk WAB EN9............ 157 J5
Beech Dr DUN/WHIP LU6.......... 60 C5
Beech Gn AMSS HP6................. 145 P9
    TRING HP23....................... 96 B8
Beech Hl EBAR EN4.................. 153 N8
    LTNE LU2........................... 47 K8
Beech Hl Av EBAR EN4.............. 153 M9
Beech Hill Ct BERK HP4............. 116 A6
Beech Hill Gdns WAB EN9.......... 157 N7
Beech Hyde La
    STALW/WH AL4................... 103 L5
Beeching Cl HARP AL5.............. 82 A9
Beechlands BSF CM23............... 108 C5
Beech Ms STVGE SG2............... 108 D6
Beechpark Wy WAT WD17......... 148 F7
Beech Pl STALW/RED AL3 *......... 120 C5
Beech Ridge HARP AL5 *............ 81 J8
Beech Rd DUN/WHIP LU6.......... 61 H9
Beech Tree Cl STAN HA7........... 173 J2
Beechtree La STALW/RED AL3..... 135 J1
Beech Tree Wy
    DUN/HR/TOD LU5................ 60 E1
Beech Wk STALW/WH AL4......... 82 G7
    RKW/CH/CXG WD3.............. 153 L3
    POTB/CUF EN6.................... 153 L3
    RKW/CH/CXG WD3.............. 159 P3
Beech Wy STALW/RED AL3........ 80 A8
Beechwood Cl AMS HP6............ 145 P9
    KTN/HRWW/WS HA3............. 172 A4
Beechwood Ct
    DUN/WHIP LU6................... 60 C7
Beechwood Dr TRING HP23....... 97 J7
Beechwood La
    RAYLNE/WEN HP22.............. 112 E6
Beechwood Pk
    HHS/BOV HP3..................... 133 J3
    RKW/CH/CXG WD3.............. 160 D3
Beechwood Ri WATN WD24........ 149 H1
Beechwood Rd
    LTNW/LEA LU4.................... 62 A4
Beechwood Wy
    RAYLNE/WEN HP22.............. 94 F7
Beecroft La STVGE SG2.............. 52 C5
Beecroft Wy DUN/WHIP LU6...... 60 D8
Beehive Cl BORE WD6.............. 164 D5
Beehive Gn WGCE AL7.............. 105 K9
Beehive Gn WGCE AL7.............. 105 K9
Beehive La WGCE AL7.............. 105 K9
Beehive Rd CHES/WCR EN8....... 141 J7
Beel Cl AMSS HP7................... 145 P9
Beesonend La HARP AL5............ 101 N9
    STALW/RED AL3................... 119 L1
Beeston Cl OXHEY WD19........... 171 M1
Beeston Dr CHES/WCR EN8........ 142 C6
Beeston Rd EBAR EN4.............. 167 H5
Beethoven Rd BORE WD6.......... 164 A4
Beeton Rd HAS HA5 *............... 172 A4
Beggarman's La STDN SG11....... 70 C6
Beggars Bush La
    WATW WD18....................... 161 K6
Beggars La TRING HP23............. 96 E8
Beken Ct GSTN WD25............... 149 K5
Belcher Rd HOD EN11............... 153 J6
Belchers La WAB EN9................ 143 P5
Beldam Av ROY SG8................. 20 C5
Beldams Ga BSF CM23.............. 74 B4
Beldams Gn OXHEY WD19......... 171 M2
Belfairs Gn OXHEY WD19 *........ 171 M2
Belford Rd BORE WD6.............. 151 L8
Belfry Av RKW/CH/CXG WD3..... 160 C7
The Belfry LTNE LU2................. 63 M4
Belfry La RKW/CH/CXG WD3...... 160 C7
Belgrave Av WATW WD18.......... 12 B7
Belgrave Cl STALW/WH AL4........ 121 H4
    STHGT/OAK N14................. 167 N4
Belgrave Rd LTNW/LEA LU4....... 61 N1
Belgravia Cl BAR EN5................ 166 C3
Belgrave Ms STVGE SG2............ 67 L4
Belgrave Rd LTNW/LEA LU4........ 61 N1
Bell Acre LTNE LU2.................. 36 E4
Bell Acre Gdns LWTH SG6.......... 36 E4
Bellamy Cl EDGW HA8.............. 173 H5
    WATW WD18....................... 161 K6
Bellamy Dr STAN HA7............... 173 H5
Bellamy Rd CHES/WCR EN8....... 142 D8
Bellchambers Cl
    LCOL/BKTW AL2.................. 137 H5
Bell Cl ABLGY WD5.................. 134 C6
    HTCHE/RSTV SG4................ 49 N1
    KNEB SG3.......................... 69 H7
    PIN HA5............................ 171 L7
Bellerby Ri LTNW/LEA LU4......... 45 L9
Belle Vue La BUSH WD23........... 163 M7
Belle Vue Rd HART/BAY SG13..... 108 D3
Belle Vue Ter DEN/HRF UB9 *..... 169 H7
Bellfield Av
    KTN/HRWW/WS HA3............. 172 D3
Bellfield Gdns HLWE CM17........ 129 M3
Bellgate HHNE HP2 *............... 117 P5
Bell La BERK HP4 *.................. 115 M5
Bellingdon Rd CSHM HP5.......... 130 C7
Bell La ABLGY WD5.................. 135 H6
    AMSS HP7.......................... 115 K6
    BRKMPK AL9..................... 139 H6
    BROX EN10........................ 126 B3
    HERT/WAT SG14.................. 107 L6
    HOD EN11.......................... 153 H1
    LCOL/BKTW AL2.................. 137 K8
    PEND EN3.......................... 156 C7
    ROY SG8............................ 30 F7
    STVG SG1.......................... 10 E1
    WARE SG12......................... 90 A9
Bell Leys RAYLNE/WEN HP22...... 76 C2

Bell Mead SBW CM21............... 111 P2
Bellmount Wood Av
    WAT WD17......................... 148 F9
Bell Rd EN EN1....................... 155 L9
The Bell Rbt LCOL/BKTW AL2..... 137 H6
Bell Rw BLDK SG7................... 26 A9
Bells Hl BAR EN5.................... 166 B4
    BSF CM23.......................... 75 P7
Bells Meadow ROY SG8............ 15 M6
Bell St SBW CM21................... 111 P2
Bell Vw STALW/WH AL4............ 121 J8
Bell Wk RAYLNE/WEN HP22....... 76 C2
Belmer Rd STVG SG12.............. 59 L7
Belmers Rd TRING HP23........... 114 C2
Belmont Av WAT WD17............. 167 K4
Belmont Cir
    KTN/HRWW/WS HA3............. 173 H5
Belmont Cl EBAR EN4............... 167 K3
    TRDG/WHET N20................ 166 F7
Belmont Hl STAL AL1................ 8 E5
Belmont Rd BUSH WD23........... 162 G5
    CSHM HP5.......................... 130 C7
    HHS/BOV HP3..................... 133 P2
    KTN/HRWW/WS HA3............. 173 H5
    LTN LU1............................ 6 A4
Belmor BORE WD6.................. 164 B5
Belper Rd LTNW/LEA LU4.......... 61 P4
Belsham Cl CSHM HP5.............. 150 C7
Belsham Pl LTNE LU2............... 63 M4
Belsize Cl HHNE HP2............... 118 B9
    POTB/CUF EN6.................... 153 L3
    RKW/CH/CXG WD3.............. 159 P3
Belsize Cl HHNE HP2................ 118 B9
    STALW/WH AL4................... 121 H3
Belsize Rd
    HHNE HP2.......................... 118 B9
    KTN/HRWW/WS HA3............. 172 D4
    STALW/WH AL4................... 121 H3
Belswains La HHS/BOV HP3....... 61 H3
Beltona Gdns CHES/WCR EN8.... 142 C6
Belton Rd BERK HP4................ 116 C6
Belvedere Av OXHEY WD19....... 162 F7
Belvedere Gdns
    LCOL/BKTW AL2.................. 135 N6
Belvedere Gdns
    LCOL/BKTW AL2.................. 135 N6
Belvedere Rd
    LCOL/BKTW AL2.................. 135 N6
Bembridge Gdns
    LTNN/LIM LU3.................... 46 A8
Bembridge Pl GSTN WD25 *....... 149 H3
Bemboro Cl STALW/RED AL3...... 101 H8
Benbow Cl STAL AL1................. 137 N2
Benchley Hl HTCHE/RSTV SG4.... 35 M9
Benchleys Rd HHW HP1............ 116 F5
Bench Manor Crs
    CFSP/GDCR SL9................... 168 A6
Bencroft CHESW EN7............... 141 J9
Bencroft La HOD EN11.............. 152 G1
Bendish La HTCHE/RSTV SG4..... 65 M4
Bendysh Rd BUSH WD23.......... 162 G2
Benedictine Ga
    CHES/WCR EN8................... 142 D6
Benfleet Wy FBAR/BDGN N11... 153 F4
Benford Rd HOD EN11.............. 152 B4
Bengarth Dr
    KTN/HRWW/WS HA3............. 172 D6
Bengeo Ms HERT/WAT SG14 *.... 107 K3
Bengeo St HERT/WAT SG14........ 107 K3
Bengeo St HERT/WAT SG14........ 107 K3
Ben Hale Cl STAN HA7.............. 173 H2
Benham Cl CSHM HP5.............. 130 C8
Benhooks Av BSF CM23............ 73 P9
Benington Ct HHNE HP2 *......... 5 K5
Benington Rd STVGE SG2.......... 52 D2
Benningfield Gdns BERK HP4..... 116 B5
Benningfield Rd WARE SG12...... 90 A9
Bennington Dr BORE WD6......... 151 L9
Benskins Cl BSF CM23.............. 45 H8
Benslow La HTCHE/RSTV SG4..... 35 M9
Benslow Ri HTCHE/RSTV SG4..... 35 M9
Benson Cl LTNN/LIM LU3.......... 46 A8
Bentsede STVGE SG2................ 67 M6
Bentfield End Cswy
    STSD CM24......................... 58 E4
Bentfield Gdns STSD CM24......... 58 E4
Bentfield Rd STSD CM24........... 58 E4
Bentick Wy HTCH/STOT SG5...... 84 C3
Bentinck Cl CFSP/GDCR SL9...... 168 B9
Bentley Cl BSF CM23................ 74 A4
Bentley Dr HLWE CM17............ 129 M4
Bentley Heath La BAR EN5......... 153 H5
Bentley Rd HERT/WAT SG14....... 106 F5
Benton Rd OXHEY WD19........... 172 C2
Bentons Wk BAR EN9............... 143 P5
Bentsley Cl STALW/WH AL4........ 121 J8
Berceau Wk WAT WD17............ 148 F9
Beresford Cl CFSP/GDCR SL9..... 168 A9
Beresford Av
    TRDG/WHET N20................ 167 K8
Beresford Rd HRW HA1............ 172 G7
    LTNE LU2........................... 47 H3
    RKW/CH/CXG WD3.............. 160 D7
    STAL AL1........................... 121 H9
Bericot Wy WGCE AL7............. 105 M6
Berkeley Cl ABLGY WD5............ 135 H5
    BORE WD6.......................... 164 C4
    CSHM HP5.......................... 130 C8
    HTCH/STOT SG5.................. 35 J8
    POTB/CUF EN6.................... 153 H2
    STVG SG1.......................... 67 K6
    WARE SG12......................... 108 D2
Berkeley Ct
    RKW/CH/CXG WD3.............. 161 P4

Berkeley Crs EBAR EN4.............. 167 H4
Berkeley Pl LTNE LU2............... 6 E2
Berkeley Rd CDALE/KGS NW9... 173 N8
Berkeley Sq HHNE HP2.............. 118 D2
Berkhampstead Rd
    CSHM HP5.......................... 131 H9
Berkhamsted Rd HHW HP1........ 116 C6
Berkley Av CHES/WCR EN8......... 156 C4
Berkley Cl LBUZ LU7................ 96 C1
    STALW/WH AL4................... 121 H4
Berkley Pl CHES/WCR EN8......... 156 C4
Berks Hl RKW/CH/CXG WD3...... 160 A4
Bermer Rd WATN WD24............ 149 K9
Bernard Cl DUN/HR/TOD LU5..... 60 E5
Bernard Gv WAB EN9............... 156 C3
Bernard St STALW/RED AL3........ 9 F2
Bernays Ct STAN HA7............... 173 J3
Berners Dr STAL AL1................. 135 J1
Berners Wy BROX EN10............ 142 E2
Bernhardt Crs STVGE SG2.......... 51 M9
Berridge Gn EDGW HA8............ 173 H4
The Berries STALW/WH AL4........ 120 F4
Berrow Cl LTNE LU2................. 63 M4
Berry Av WATN WD24............... 13 J1
Berry Cl RKW/CH/CXG WD3...... 160 F6
Berryfield LBUZ LU7................. 77 N6
Berry Field Pk AMS HP6............ 144 G7
Berry Grove La GSTN WD25....... 149 N8
Berrygrove La CSTN WD25......... 149 N8
Berry Grove La WATN WD24...... 149 M8
Berry Hl STAN HA7.................. 173 L1
Berrylands LTNN/LIM LU3.......... 45 P8
Berry La RKW/CH/CXG WD3...... 160 F6
Berrymead HHNE HP2 *............ 5 K5
Berthold Ms WAB EN9.............. 156 C3
Berwick Cl STAN HA7............... 172 F3
Berwick Rd BORE WD6............. 151 L8
Besford Cl LTNE LU2................ 63 L4
Bessemer Cl HTCH/STOT SG5..... 35 K5
Bessemer Ct STVGE SG2........... 66 E2
Bethecar Rd HAY HA1.............. 172 E9
Bethune Cl LTN LU1................. 62 C8
Betjeman Cl CHESW EN7........... 141 P7
    HARP AL5.......................... 102 B3
Betjeman Rd ROY SG8.............. 172 A8
Betjeman Wy HHW HP1............ 20 C1
Betony V ROY SG8.................. 20 D5
Bettespol Mdw
    STALW/RED AL3................... 101 H6
Betts La WAB EN9.................... 157 J5
Betty's La TRING HP23.............. 95 P8
Betula Ter CHES/WCR EN8 *....... 156 D2
Beulah Cl EDGW HA8............... 165 H9
Beverley Cl CHESW EN7 *.......... 5 F5
Bevan Hl CSHM HP5................. 130 C7
Bevan Rd EBAR EN4................. 167 K3
Beverley Cl ROY SG8................ 20 A2
Beverley Dr EDGW HA8............ 173 M7
Beverley Gdns CHESW EN7........ 155 N1
    STALW/WH AL4................... 121 J4
    STAN HA7.......................... 172 F5
    WCCE AL7.......................... 105 M6
Beverley Rd LTNW/LEA LU4........ 62 A5
    STVG SG5........................... 51 L5
Beverly Cl BROX EN10.............. 126 D9
Bewdley Cl HARP AL5............... 102 D2
Bewley Cl CHES/WCR EN8......... 156 C1
Bexhill Rd LTNE LU2 *............... 63 L4
Beyers Gdns HOD EN11............ 126 F2
Beyers Prospect HOD EN11....... 126 F2
Beyers Ride HOD EN11............. 126 F2
Bibbs Hall La
    HTCHE/RSTV SG4................ 83 K7
Bibshall Crs DUN/WHIP LU6...... 60 B8
Bicknoller Rd EN EN1............... 155 P8
Biddenham Turn GSTN WD25.... 137 H6
Bideford Cl EDGW HA8............. 173 M5
Bideford Rd PEND EN3.............. 156 E8
Bidwell Cl LWTH SG6............... 36 E5
Biggin Hl BUNT SG9................. 60 D1
Biggin La HTCH/STOT SG5......... 35 K9
Biggs Grove Rd CHESW EN7...... 141 M6
Bignells Cmr POTB/CUF EN6...... 152 E4
Bignell's Cmr POTB/CUF EN6...... 152 E4
Billet La BERK HP4.................. 115 M5
Billy Lows La POTB/CUF EN6...... 153 L1
Bilton Rd HTCHE/RSTV SG4....... 35 L6
Bilton Wy LTN LU1................... 62 G5
    PEND EN3.......................... 156 E9
Binder Cl LTNW/LEA LU4........... 61 H2
Bingen Rd HTCH/STOT SG5....... 35 H7
Bingham Cl HHW HP1.............. 117 H6
Bingley Rd HOD EN11.............. 127 H5
Binyon Crs STAN HA7............... 172 F2
Birchall Cl HERT/WAT SG14....... 105 P8
Birchall Wd WCCE AL7............. 105 M7
Birchanger La BSF CM23........... 58 F3
Birch Cl AMS HP6................... 145 K7
Birch Copse LCOL/BKTW AL2..... 135 M9
Birch Ct HHW HP1 *................. 118 C3
    RKW/CH/CXG WD3.............. 169 H2
Birch Dr HAS HA5 *.................. 62 G3
Birchen Gv LTN LU2................. 63 K1
Birches Cl PIN HA5.................. 171 N9
The Birches BUSH WD23........... 163 J4
    HHS/BOV HP3..................... 133 J6
    HTCHE/RSTV SG4................ 84 C5
    LWTH SG6.......................... 25 J9
    WAB EN9........................... 157 H4
Birchfield Rd CHES/WCR EN8..... 142 A4
Birch Gdns HLWE CM17............ 129 M4
Birch Gn HHW HP1 *................ 117 K9
    HERT/WAT SG14.................. 106 A1
Birch Gv POTB/CUF EN6............ 153 K2
    WLYN AL6.......................... 83 H8
Birch Leys HHNE HP2 *............. 118 D3
Birch Link LTNW/LEA LU4.......... 6 A1
Birchmead WAT WD17.............. 148 G8

Birchmead Av PIN HA5 ... 171 L8
Birchmead Cl
  STALW/RED AL3 * ... 120 C5
Birch Rd BERK HP4 ... 115 J4
  KNEB SG3 ... 85 L4
Birch Side DUN/WHIP LU6 ... 60 C8
Birch Tree Cl CSHM HP5 ... 131 N9
Birch Tree Wk WAT WD17 ... 148 C7
Birch Wk BORE WD6 * ... 151 M9
Birchway HAT AL10 ... 122 D4
Birchway Wy LCOL/BKTW AL2 ... 137 J6
Birchwood BSF CM23 ... 58 E9
  RAD WD7 ... 151 M4
Birchwood Av HAT AL10 ... 122 D4
Birchwood Cl HAT AL10 ... 122 D5
Birchwood Wy
  LCOL/BKTW AL2 ... 136 A7
Birdcroft Rd WGCW AL8 ... 104 C7
Birdie Wy HERT/BAY SG13 ... 108 A5
Birds Cl WCCE AL7 ... 105 L8
Birdsfoot La LTNE/LIM LU3 ... 46 C4
Birds Hl LWTH SG6 ... 36 D2
Birkbeck Rd ENC/FH EN2 ... 155 L8
Birkdale Av PIN HA5 ... 172 A7
Birkdale Gdns OXHEY WD19 ... 162 F9
Birkett Wy CSTG HP8 ... 159 K2
Birklands La LCOL/BKTW AL2 ... 136 C4
Birklands Pk STAL AL1 ... 136 C5
Birley Rd TRDG/WHET N20 ... 166 C8
Birling Dr LTNE LU2 ... 63 K1
Birstal Gn OXHEY WD19 ... 161 P3
Birtley Cft LTNE LU2 ... 63 M5
Biscot Rd LTNN/LIM LU3 ... 6 B1
Bishop Cl ABLGY WD5 ... 148 C1
Bishop Ken Rd
  KTN/HRWW/WS HA3 ... 172 F6
Bishops Av BORE WD6 ... 164 F4
Bishop's Av BSF CM23 ... 74 A7
Bishop's Cl BAR EN5 ... 165 J6
Bishops Cl STALE/WH AL4 ... 120 F4
Bishopscote Rd
  LTNN/LIM LU3 ... 62 C3
Bishops Ct CHES/WCR EN8 * ... 142 A9
Bishopsfield HLWS CM18 ... 129 H6
Bishops Fld
  RAYLNE/WEN HP22 ... 95 H8
Bishops Md HHW HP1 ... 4 B5
Bishops Park Wy BSF CM23 ... 122 B5
Bishops Ri HAT AL10 ... 138 C1
Bishops Rd HAYES HA5 ... 85 N7
Biskra WAT WD17 ... 149 H9
Bisley Cl CHES/WCR EN8 ... 156 C3
Bittern Cl CHESW EN7 ... 141 J5
  HHS/BOV HP3 ... 134 A4
  STVGE SG1 ... 67 N4
Bittern Wy STVGE SG2 ... 67 N7
The Bit TRING HP23 ... 114 C2
Black Acre Cl AMSM HP7 ... 145 N9
Blackberry Md STVGE SG2 ... 67 N3
Blackbirds La GSTN WD25 ... 150 B4

Blackdale CHESW EN7 ... 141 P6
Black Ditch Rd HHW HP1 ... 157 H6
Black Ditch Wy WAB EN9 ... 156 C6
Blackdown Cl STVG SG1 ... 51 L4
Blackett-ord St ROY SG8 ... 20 C3
Blacketts Wood Dr
  RKW/CH/CXG WD3 ... 159 P3
Black Fan Cl ENC/FH EN2 ... 155 K9
Black Fan Rd HAT AL10 ... 105 J5
Blackford Rd OXHEY WD19 ... 171 N2
Black Green Wood Cl
  LCOL/BKTW AL2 ... 136 A8
Black Horse Av CSHM HP5 ... 145 J3
Blackhorse Cl
  HTCHE/RSTV SG4 ... 49 M2
  POTB/CUF EN6 ... 138 A9
  STALW/RED AL3 ... 101 H6
Black Horse Rd PIN HA5 * ... 171 K9
Blackhorse Rd LWTH SG6 ... 25 P5
Blackley Cl WAT WD17 ... 148 C7
Black Lion Cl HLWE CM17 * ... 111 M8
Black Lion Hl RAD WD7 ... 151 K2
Blackmoor La WAT WD18 ... 161 P4
Blackmore Cl LWTH SG6 ... 36 E5
Blackmore Ct WAB EN9 ... 157 M3
Blackmore Ga
  RAYLNE/WEN HP22 ... 95 H8
  TRING HP23 ... 82 G7
Blackmore Wy STALW/RED AL3 * ... 102 G1
Blacksmith Cl HTCH/STOT SG5 ... 25 K2
Blacksmiths Cl BSF CM23 ... 58 E1
Black Smiths Cl WARE SG12 ... 108 F5
Blacksmiths Hl STALE/WH AL4 ... 68 F2
Blacksmith's La ROY SG8 ... 29 K4
  STALW/RED AL3 ... 11 N2
Blacksmiths Rw
  STALW/RED AL3 * ... 79 P8
Blacksmiths Wy SBW CM21 ... 111 L3
Black Swan Ct WARE SG12 * ... 108 D3
Black Swan La LTNN/LIM LU3 ... 62 B1
Blackthorn Cl GSTN WD25 ... 121 H5
  STALE/WH AL4 ... 121 H5
Black Thorn Rd
  DUN/HR/TOD LU5 ... 44 F9
Blackthorn Rd WGCE AL7 ... 105 K7
Blackwater La HHS/BOV HP3 ... 134 F2
Blackwell Cl
  KTN/HRWW/WS HA3 ... 172 D4
Blackwell Dr OXHEY WD19 ... 162 E5
Blackwell Gdns EDGW HA8 ... 173 N1

Blackwell Hall La CSHM HP5 ... 145 L5
Blackwellhall La CSHM HP5 ... 145 P3
Blackwell Rd KGLGY WD4 ... 134 B8
Bladon Cl HTCHE/RSTV SG4 ... 50 C4
Blagden's La
  STHGT/OAK N14 ... 167 P8
Blaine Cl TRING HP23 ... 95 P6
Blair Cl BSF CM23 ... 73 M7
  HHNE HP2 ... 118 C2
  STVGE SG2 ... 67 J5
Blairhead Dr OXHEY WD19 ... 162 D9
Blake Cl ROY SG8 ... 20 C1
  STAL AL1 ... 136 F2
Blakelands
  AMP/FLIT/BLC MK45 ... 32 E6
Blakemore End Rd
  HTCHE/RSTV SG4 ... 50 A4
Blakeney Cl LTNE LU2 ... 46 D8
Blakeney Dr LTNE LU2 ... 46 D8
Blakeney Rd STVG SG1 ... 50 E8
Blakes Wy WLYN AL6 ... 84 F7
Blanchard Dr WATW WD18 ... 162 A3
Blanchard Gv PEND EN3 ... 156 F8
Blanche La POTB/CUF EN6 ... 152 C4
Blandford Av LTNE LU2 ... 46 E9
Blandford Rd STAL AL1 ... 120 F7
The Blanes WARE SG12 ... 108 B1
Blattner Cl BORE WD6 ... 164 E3
Blawith Rd HRW HA1 ... 172 E8
Blaydon Rd LTNE LU2 ... 7 K3
Blegberry Gdns BERK HP4 ... 115 K8
Blenheim Cl OXHEY WD19 ... 162 E6
  STVGE SG1 ... 67 N1
  WARE SG12 ... 111 L4
Blenheim Ct EDGW HA8 ... 173 M7
  WGCE AL7 ... 123 J8
Blenheim Crs LTNN/LIM LU3 ... 62 D4
Blenheim Rd BAR EN5 ... 166 B2
  STAL AL1 ... 9 K1
Blenheim Wy STVGE SG2 ... 67 N7
Blenheim Rd ABLGY WD5 ... 148 B3
Blenkin Cl STALW/RED AL3 ... 120 B4
Blind La BUNT SG9 ... 52 C2
  GTMIS/PWD HP16 ... 144 A1
Blindman's La
  CHES/WCR EN8 ... 142 C9
Bloomfield Av LTNE LU2 ... 63 H5
Bloomfield Rd CHESW EN7 ... 141 K4
  HARP AL5 ... 101 N1

Bloomsbury Gdns
  DUN/HR/TOD LU5 ... 60 G1
Blossom La ENC/FH EN2 ... 155 K9
Blows Rd DUN/HR/TOD LU5 ... 60 G7
Blucher St CSHM HP5 ... 131 J8
Bluebell Cl HERT/BAY SG13 ... 107 P6
  HHW HP1 * ... 117 H9
Bluebell Dr ABLGY WD5 ... 134 C6
  CHESW EN7 ... 141 L7
Bluebells WLYN AL6 ... 85 H6
Bluebell Wy HAT AL10 ... 122 C2
Bluebell Wood Cl LTN LU1 ... 62 A7
Blueberry Cl STALW/RED AL3 ... 120 C4
Bluebird Wy LCOL/BKTW AL2 ... 135 N9
Bluebridge Av BRKMPK AL9 ... 139 H6
Blue Bridge Rd BRKMPK AL9 ... 139 H6
Bluecoats Av HERT/WAT SG14 ... 107 L6
Bluecoat Yd WARE SG12 ... 108 C3
Bluehouse Hill
  Hemel Hempstead Rd ... 119 P9
Bluett Rd LCOL/BKTW AL2 ... 137 J6
Blundell Cl STALW/RED AL3 ... 120 C4
Blundell Rd LTNW/LEA LU4 ... 62 B3
Blunesfield POTB/CUF EN6 ... 153 N1
Blunts La LCOL/BKTW AL2 ... 135 L5
Blyth Cl BORE WD6 ... 151 L9
  STVG SG1 ... 50 D8
Blythe Rd HOD EN11 ... 127 J7
Blyth Pl LTN LU1 ... 62 A6
Blythway WGCE AL7 ... 105 J5
Blythwood Gdns
  STSD CM24 ... 58 E5
Blythwood Rd PIN HA5 ... 171 M5
Boardman Cl BAR EN5 ... 166 C4
Bockings STVGE SG2 ... 52 D6
Boddington Rd
  RAYLNE/WEN HP22 ... 112 D7
Bodmin Rd LTNW/LEA LU4 ... 62 A2
Bodwell Cl HHW HP1 ... 117 K7
Bogmoor Rd ROY SG8 ... 30 D3
Bognor Gdns OXHEY WD19 * ... 171 L2
Bogs Gap La ROY SG8 ... 15 N8
Bohemia HHW HP1 ... 117 P7
Bohun Gv EBAR EN4 ... 167 J5
Bois Av AMS HP6 ... 144 G6
Bois Hl AMS HP6 ... 145 J5
Bois Mi CSHM HP5 ... 145 M6
Bois Moor Rd CSHM HP5 ... 145 K4
Boissy Cl STALE/WH AL4 ... 121 K9
Boleyn Av EN EN1 ... 156 B6
Boleyn Cl LTN LU1 ... 118 D3
Boleyn Ct BROX EN10 ... 126 D9
Boleyn Dr STAL AL1 ... 136 C1
Boleyn Wy BAR EN5 ... 166 G2
Bolingbroke Rd LTN LU1 ... 62 C8
Bolingbrook STALE/WH AL4 ... 121 H5
Bolney Gn LTNE LU2 ... 63 L3
Bolton Rd HRW HA1 ... 172 C8
  LTN LU1 ... 7 G5
Bonham Carter Rd
  RAYLNE/WEN HP22 ... 112 E4
Bonham Ct
  RAYLNE/WEN HP22 ... 94 E7
Boniface Gdns
  KTN/HRWW/WS HA3 ... 172 B4
Boniface Wk
  KTN/HRWW/WS HA3 ... 172 B4
Bonks Hi SBW CM21 ... 111 N3
Bonneting La BSF CM23 ... 43 L8
Bonney Gv CHESW EN7 ... 141 P9
Bonnick Cl LTN LU1 ... 8 D1
Booths Cl BRKMPK AL9 ... 138 C3
Boot La BCSW SG18 ... 14 C6
Boot Pde EDGW HA8 * ... 173 L6
Boreham Ms HOD EN11 ... 126 F7
Bornedene POTB/CUF EN6 ... 153 H1
Borough Rd
  DUN/HR/TOD LU5 ... 60 D7
Borough Wy POTB/CUF EN6 ... 153 H2
Borrell Cl BROX EN10 ... 126 D8

Borrowdale Av
  KTN/HRWW/WS HA3 ... 172 C6
Borrowdale Cl HHNE HP2 ... 117 P5
Bosanquet Rd HOD EN11 ... 127 H3
Boscombe Cl STALW/RED SG6 * ... 36 E5
Boscombe Rd
  DUN/HR/TOD LU5 ... 60 C5
Bosmore Rd LTNN/LIM LU3 ... 62 A1
Boswell Cl RAD WD7 ... 151 K2
Boswell Ct HTCH/STOT SG5 ... 35 K4
Boswell Gdns STVG SG1 ... 50 G6
Boswell Rd LTNE LU2 ... 46 E9
Bosworth Cl BAR EN5 ... 166 C2
Bosworth Rd BAR EN5 ... 166 C2
Botany Cl EBAR EN4 ... 167 J3
Botley La CSHM HP5 ... 131 M9
Botley Rd CSHM HP5 ... 131 K9
  HHNE HP2 ... 118 B3
Bottom Dr DUN/WHIP LU6 ... 60 A9
Bottom House Farm La
  CSTG HP8 ... 158 D7
Bottom House La
  TRING HP23 ... 114 F1
Bottom La KGLGY WD4 ... 147 M5
Bottom Rd TRING HP23 ... 113 K3
Bottrells La CSTG HP8 ... 158 C6
Boughton Wy AMS HP6 ... 145 P9
Boulevard WATW WD18 ... 161 N4
The Boulevard WATW WD18 ... 161 P4
  WGCE AL7 ... 105 J4
Boulton Rd STVG SG1 ... 50 G6
Boundary La HHNE HP2 ... 117 N6
Boundary Cl BAR EN5 ... 166 C2
Boundary Dr HERT/WAT SG14 ... 107 L4
Boundary La WGCE AL7 ... 123 H1
Boundary Pk HHNE HP2 ... 2 E4
Boundary Rd BSF CM23 ... 74 B5
  CFSP/GDCR SL9 ... 168 B4
  STAL AL1 ... 120 D6
The Boundary
  HERT/BAY SG13 ... 124 D7
Boundary Wy CSTN WD25 ... 149 J2
  HHNE HP2 ... 118 C5
Bourne Av BEAR EN4 ... 167 H4
Bourne Cl BROX EN10 ... 126 E8
  WARE SG12 ... 108 C2
Bourne End La HHNE HP2 ... 117 J1
Bourne End Rd HHNE HP2 ... 170 C1
Bournehall Av BUSH WD23 ... 163 J5
Bournehall La BUSH WD23 ... 163 J5
Bournehall Rd BUSH WD23 ... 163 J5
Bourne Honour WARE SG12 ... 87 M6
Bournemead BUSH WD23 ... 163 J5
Bournemouth Rd STVG SG1 ... 50 F7
Bourne Rd BERK HP4 ... 115 L6
  BUSH WD23 ... 163 J4
Bournside Crs
  STHGT/OAK N14 ... 167 P7
The Bourne BSF CM23 ... 74 B2
  HARP AL5 ... 101 N2
  HHS/BOV HP3 ... 132 D6
  WARE SG12 ... 108 C2
Bouvier Rd PEND EN3 ... 156 F7
Bovingdon Crs GSTN WD25 ... 149 L4
Bow Br STALW/RED AL3 ... 119 M5
Bowbrook V LTNE LU2 ... 63 N5
Bowbrook Wk STVG SG1 ... 67 H3
Bower Heath La HARP AL5 ... 82 B8
Bowershott LWTH SG6 ... 36 D4
Bower's Pde HARP AL5 ... 101 P2
Bowers Wy HARP AL5 ... 101 P2
Bowes Lyon Ms
  STALW/RED AL3 ... 8 E4
Bowgate STAL AL1 ... 120 D6
Bowland Crs DUN/WHIP LU6 ... 60 D8
Bowlers Md BUNT SG9 ... 38 C9
Bowlers Orch CSTG HP8 ... 158 C6
Bowles Gdn EN EN1 ... 156 A6
Bowling Cl HARP AL5 ... 102 A5
Bowling Gn STVG SG1 ... 50 F8
Bowling Green La BUNT SG9 ... 50 F8
Bowls Cl STAN HA7 ... 173 H2
Bowmans Av
  HTCHE/RSTV SG4 ... 35 N9
Bowmans Cl DUN/WHIP LU6 ... 60 F2
  POTB/CUF EN6 ... 153 N2
  WLYN AL6 ... 84 F6
Bowmans Gn HHNE HP2 ... 117 N6
Bowmans Gn GSTN WD25 ... 149 L6
Bowmans Wy
  DUN/WHIP LU6 ... 60 F2
Bowring Gn OXHEY WD19 ... 171 L2
Bowstridge La CSTG HP8 ... 168 A3
Bowyers HHNE HP2 ... 117 N6
Bowyer's Cl
  HTCH/STOT SG5 ... 35 J7
Boxberry Cl STVG SG1 ... 51 N7
Boxfield WGCE AL7 ... 123 J5
Boxfield Gn STVGE SG2 ... 51 N7
Boxgrove Cl LTNE LU2 ... 46 F9
Boxhill HHNE HP2 ... 117 N6
Box La HHS/BOV HP3 ... 132 C4
  HOD EN11 ... 132 G4
Boxmoor Rd
  KTN/HRWW/WS HA3 ... 173 H8
Boxted Cl LTNW/LEA LU4 ... 61 M1
Boxted Rd HHW HP1 ... 117 H6
Box Tree Cl CSHM HP5 ... 145 J3
Boxtree La
  KTN/HRWW/WS HA3 ... 172 C5
Boxtree Rd
  KTN/HRWW/WS HA3 ... 172 C4
Boxwell Rd BERK HP4 ... 115 N9
Boyce Cl BORE WD6 ... 151 K9
Boyd Cl BSF CM23 ... 74 C2
Boyes Crs LCOL/BKTW AL2 ... 136 C5
Boyle Cl LTNE LU2 ... 63 M5
Braceby Cl LTNN/LIM LU3 ... 46 A9
Brace Cl CHESW EN7 ... 141 J4
Bracey's Rd STALW/RED AL3 ... 101 H2
Bracken Cl EDGW HA8 * ... 173 N9
Brackendale POTB/CUF EN6 ... 153 K3
Brackendale Gv HARP AL5 ... 101 J1

Brackendene
  LCOL/BKTW AL2 ... 135 N9
Bracken Hl BERK HP4 ... 116 B6
Bracken La WLYN AL6 ... 84 B8
Bracklesham Gdns LTNE LU4 ... 63 L3
Bracknell Cl LTNW/LEA LU4 ... 61 J3
Bracknell Pl HHNE HP2 ... 118 A4
Bradbury RKW/CH/CXG WD3 ... 169 H2
Bradbury Cl BORE WD6 ... 151 N9
Bradden La HHNE HP2 ... 99 H5
Braden Av BAR EN5 * ... 166 C2
Bradenham Rd
  KTN/HRWW/WS HA3 ... 173 H8
Bradford Cl
  DUN/HR/TOD LU5 ... 44 D3
  RKW/CH/CXG WD3 ... 160 A6
Bradford Wy
  DUN/HR/TOD LU5 ... 44 D3
Bradgate POTB/CUF EN6 ... 140 E6
Bradgate POTB/CUF EN6 ... 154 E1
Bradgers Hill Rd LTNE LU2 ... 62 F2
Bradley Common BSF CM23 ... 58 D8
Bradley Rd LTNW/LEA LU4 ... 61 N5
  PEND EN3 ... 156 D8
Bradleys Cnr
  HTCHE/RSTV SG4 ... 35 P8
Bradman Wy STVG SG1 ... 51 K6
Bradmore Gn BRKMPK AL9 ... 139 H5
Bradmore La BRKMPK AL9 ... 138 G5
Bradmore Wy BRKMPK AL9 ... 139 H5
Bradshaw Rd STVGE SG2 ... 67 L3
Bradshaw Rd WATN WD24 ... 149 K9
Bradshaws Cl WGCE AL7 ... 123 K4
Braeburn Cl
  AMP/FLIT/BLC MK45 ... 32 C5
Bradway HTCHE/RSTV SG4 ... 65 K8
Braeburn Wk ROY SG8 ... 20 B3
Braemar Gdns STVG SG1 ... 67 L2
Braemar Turn HHNE HP2 ... 118 C2
Braeside Cl PIN HA5 ... 172 A4
Bragbury Cl STVGE SG2 ... 88 M1
Bragbury La KNEB SG3 ... 67 N7
  STVGE SG2 ... 67 N7
Bragmans La
  RKW/CH/CXG WD3 ... 146 C3
The Braid CSHM HP5 ... 122 E5
Brain Cl HAT AL10 ... 122 E5
Braintree Ct LTNW/LEA LU4 ... 61 J3
Braithwaite Gdns STAN HA7 ... 173 J5
Brakynbery BERK HP4 ... 115 K4
Brallings La CFSP/GDCR SL9 ... 168 C5
Bramble Cl CFSP/GDCR SL9 ... 168 C5
  GSTN WD25 ... 149 H4
  HARP AL5 ... 101 N1
  LTNW/LEA LU4 ... 61 M2
  STAN HA7 ... 173 K4
Bramble La AMSS HP7 ... 158 C9
Bramble Ri HLW CM20 ... 2 D3
Bramble Rd HAT AL10 ... 121 P7
  LTNW/LEA LU4 ... 61 M2
The Brambles BSF CM23 ... 73 M8
  CHES/WCR EN8 ... 156 C5
  ROY SG8 ... 20 D5
  STAL AL1 ... 50 C5
  STVG SG1 ... 50 C5
Brambling Cl BUSH WD23 ... 162 C3
Brambling Ri HHNE HP2 ... 117 P5
Bramfield GSTN WD25 ... 149 M4
Bramfield La HERT/WAT SG14 ... 106 F1
Bramfield Pl HHNE HP2 ... 118 B2
Bramfield Rd
  HERT/WAT SG14 ... 106 F4
  KNEB SG3 ... 85 N4
Bramingham Ct NTHWD HA6 * ... 170 C2
Bramingham Rd
  LTNN/LIM LU3 ... 45 N8
Bramley Cl BORE WD6 * ... 12 A6
Bramley Cl STHGT/OAK N14 ... 167 H1
  PIN HA5 ... 171 H7
Bramley Ct DUN/HR/TOD LU5 ... 44 C3
  GSTN WD25 ... 149 J2
Bramley Gdns OXHEY WD19 ... 171 L1
Bramley House Ct
  ENC/FH EN2 * ... 155 L7
Bramley Pde STHGT/OAK N14 ... 154 C5
Bramley Rd STHGT/OAK N14 ... 154 C5
Bramley Shaw WAB EN9 ... 143 P1
Bramley Wy STALE/WH AL4 ... 121 H9
Brampton Cl CHESW EN7 ... 141 P7
  HARP AL5 ... 118 A1
Brampton Gv
  KTN/HRWW/WS HA3 ... 172 G3
Brampton Park Rd
  HTCH/STOT SG5 ... 35 K7
Brampton Ri DUN/WHIP LU6 ... 60 F8
Brampton Rd
  CDALE/KGS NW9 ... 173 P1
  OXHEY WD19 ... 162 C9
  ROY SG8 ... 20 E4
  STAL AL1 ... 120 F5
Brampton Ter BORE WD6 * ... 151 M8
Bramshaw Gdns
  OXHEY WD19 ... 171 M2
Bramshott Cl
  HTCHE/RSTV SG4 ... 162 C8
Bramshot Av OXHEY WD19 ... 162 C8
Branch Cl HAT AL10 ... 136 C6
Branch Rd LCOL/BKTW AL2 ... 136 C6
Brancker Rd
  KTN/HRWW/WS HA3 ... 173 K7
Brancroft Wy PEND EN3 ... 156 G8
Brandles Rd LWTH SG6 ... 41 N7
Brandon Cl CHESW EN7 ... 141 N5
Brandreth Av
  DUN/HR/TOD LU5 ... 61 N9
Brand St HTCH/STOT SG5 ... 35 K7
Branksome Cl HHNE HP2 ... 118 A3
Bransgrove Rd EDGW HA8 ... 173 M5
Branton Cl LTNE LU2 ... 63 M4
Brantwood Rd LTN LU1 ... 63 M4
Bray Cl BORE WD6 ... 151 K9
Bray Dr STVG SG1 ... 51 K4

Brayes Mnr HTCH/STOT SG5 ... 25 K3
Bray Ldg CHES/WCR EN8 * ... 142 D6
Brays Cl AMS HP6 ... 144 A5
Brays Green La AMS HP6 ... 144 B4
Brays La AMS HP6 ... 144 B4
Brays Md HLWS CM18 ... 128 G3
Brays Meadow AMS HP6 ... 144 B5
Brays Rd LTNE LU2 ... 63 M4
Brayton Gdns ENC/FH EN2 ... 167 P3
Brazier Cl
  AMP/FLIT/BLC MK45 ... 32 C5
Braziers End CSHM HP5 ... 130 B2
Braziers Fld HERT/BAY SG13 ... 107 N6
Braziers Quay BSF CM23 ... 74 B4
Breach Barns La WAB EN9 ... 143 N9
Breachwell Pl LBUZ LU7 ... 77 P4
Bread & Cheese La
  CHESW EN7 ... 141 L4
Breadcroft La HARP AL5 ... 102 A2
Breadmead WGCE AL7 ... 105 L8
Breakspear STVGE SG2 ... 67 M3
Breakspear Av STAL AL1 ... 9 K5
Breakspear Ct ABLGY WD5 ... 148 J8
Breakspear Rd ABLGY WD5 ... 148 T4
Breakspear Rd North
  DEN/HRF UB9 ... 169 P7
Breakspear Wy HHNE HP2 ... 118 D6
Breaks Rd HAT AL10 ... 122 E6
Brecon Cl LTN LU1 ... 6 C7
Brecon Cl LTN LU1 ... 6 C7
Brendon Av LTNE LU2 ... 63 K5
Brendon Ct RAD WD7 ... 150 C4
Brent Pl BAR EN5 ... 166 E4
Brentwood Cl
  DUN/HR/TOD LU5 ... 44 C9
Bressey Av EN EN1 ... 155 C9
Brett Pl WATN WD24 ... 149 H7
Brett Rd BAR EN5 ... 166 A4
Bretts Md LTN LU1 ... 62 C3
Brewers Cl BSF CM23 ... 73 M9
Brewers Hill Rd
  DUN/WHIP LU6 ... 60 C4
Brewery La BLDK SG7 ... 26 A8
Brewery Rd HOD EN11 ... 126 F5
Brewhouse Hl STALE/WH AL4 ... 103 H4
Brewhouse La
  HERT/WAT SG14 ... 107 K6
Briants Cl PIN HA5 ... 171 P8
Briants Hill HHW HP1 ... 117 H7
Briar Cl BERK HP4 ... 116 C4
  CHES/WCR EN8 ... 63 K2
  LTNE LU2 ... 50 B1
Briardale STVG SG1 ... 50 B1
Briarley Cl BROX EN10 ... 142 E1
Briar Patch La LWTH SG6 ... 41 H5
  KTN/HRWW/WS HA3 ... 173 J4
  STALE/WH AL4 ... 122 C6
Briar Rd HAT AL10 ... 122 C6
Briars La HAT AL10 ... 122 C6
The Briars CHES/WCR EN8 ... 156 D1
  HERT/WAT SG14 ... 106 C7
  HLWS CM18 ... 129 H6
  RKW/CH/CXG WD3 ... 147 K6
Briarswood Crescent ... 141 M7
Briars Wd HAT AL10 ... 122 C6
Briar Wy BERK HP4 ... 115 P8
Briarwood Dr NTHWD HA6 ... 173 H6
Briary La EDGW HA8 ... 20 B5
Brick Kiln Cl OXHEY WD19 ... 171 N2
Brickcroft BROX EN10 ... 142 D5
Brickenden Ct WAB EN9 ... 157 L3
Brickenden La
  HERT/BAY SG13 ... 125 L7
Bricket Rd STAL AL1 ... 9 F3
Brickfield HAT AL10 ... 122 D9
Brickfield Av HHS/BOV HP3 ... 118 C9
Brickfield La BAR EN5 ... 165 M5
The Brickfields WARE SG12 ... 108 A2
Brickhill La LTN LU1 ... 80 D5
Brick Kiln Cl OXHEY WD19 ... 49 K2
Brick Knoll Pk STAL AL1 ... 121 H9
Brickly La STAN HA7 ... 173 K4
Brickley Rd LTNW/LEA LU4 ... 61 L1
Brickmakers La
  HHS/BOV HP3 ... 118 C9
Brick Rw RKW/CH/CXG WD3 ... 160 C4
Brickwall Cl WLYN AL6 ... 104 C7
Brickyard La ROY SG8 ... 29 J2
Bride Hall La WLYN AL6 ... 83 M9
Bridge End BUNT SG9 ... 40 B8
Bridge End Rd WGCE AL7 ... 150 C5
Bridgefields WGCE AL7 ... 105 J5
Bridgefoot BUNT SG9 ... 40 D9
Bridge Foot WARE SG12 ... 108 E7
Bridgefoot La
  POTB/CUF EN6 ... 152 F5
Bridgeman Dr
  DUN/HR/TOD LU5 ... 60 C1
Bridgend Rd EN EN1 ... 156 B5
Bridgenhall Rd EN EN1 ... 155 N9
Bridge Pl AMS HP6 ... 145 K8
  WAT WD17 ... 13 J7
Bridger Cl GSTN WD25 ... 149 L3
Bridge Rd KGLGY WD4 ... 146 D8
  KNEB SG3 ... 85 K3
  LWTH SG6 ... 36 C2
  STVG SG1 ... 50 E8
  WGCW AL8 ... 104 B5
Bridge Rd East WGCE AL7 ... 105 H5
Bridge Rd West STVG SG1 ... 50 E9
Bridges Ct HERT/BAY SG13 ... 107 K6
Bridge St STAN HA7 ... 172 H2
  HHNE HP2 ... 2 D4
  HTCH/STOT SG5 ... 74 B1
  HTCHE/RSTV SG4 ... 49 K1
  LTN LU1 ... 171 M7
  PIN HA5 ... 171 M7
The Bridge
  KTN/HRWW/WS HA3 ... 172 F7

Bridgewater Gdns
EDGW HA8 173 M6
Bridgewater Hl BERK HP4 115 L4
Bridgewater Rd BERK HP4 115 N5
Bridgewater Wy BUSH WD23 163 K5
Bridgeways HOD EN11 126 G5
Bridle Cl HOD EN11 126 F1
PEND EN3 156 E7
STALW/RED AL3 120 D6
Bridle La RKW/CH/CXG WD3 160 G2
Bridle Pth WAT WD17 162 D1
Bridle Wy BERK HP4 115 M5
HOD EN11 126 F2
Bridleway
RAYLNE/WEN HP22 112 A1
TRING HP23 113 M6
Bridle Wy TRING HP23 * 113 N6
WARE SG12 108 F6
Bridle Way (North)
HOD EN11 126 F1
Bridleways
RAYLNE/WEN HP22 112 B6
Bridle Way (South)
HOD EN11 126 F2
Bridlington Rd OXHEY WD19 162 F9
Brierley Cl DUN/WHIP LU6 60 F9
LTNE LU2 63 L4
Briery Fld RKW/CH/CXG WD3 160 E2
Briery Wy AMS HP6 145 K7
HHNE HP2 118 B6
Brigadier Av ENC/FH EN2 155 K9
Brigadier Hl ENC/FH EN2 155 K8
Brighton Rd WATN WD24 149 H8
Brighton Wy STVG SG1 50 D7
The Brightside PEND EN3 156 C9
Brightview Cl
LCOL/BKTW AL2 135 M8
Brightwell Rd WATW WD18 12 C7
Brightwen Gv STAN HA7 164 A8
Brill Cl LTNE LU2 63 L4
Brimfield Cl LTNE LU2 63 L4
Brimsdown Av PEND EN3 156 D9
Brimstone Wy BERK HP4 115 L5
Brinkburn Cl EDGW HA8 173 P7
Brinkburn Gdns EDGW HA8 173 N7
Brinklow Ct STALW/RED AL3 136 A2
Brinley Cl CHES/WCR EN8 156 C1
Brinsley Rd
KTN/HRWW/WS HA3 172 D6
Brinsmead LCOL/BKTW AL2 136 C6
Briscoe Cl HOD EN11 126 E3
Briscoe Rd HOD EN11 126 E3
Bristol Rd LTNN/LIM LU3 62 B2
Britain St DUN/WHIP LU6 60 F6
Britannia STDN SG11 71 K4
Britannia Av LTNN/LIM LU3 62 C1
Britannia Pl BSF CM23 73 P9
Britannia Rd CHES/WCR EN8 156 E4
CSHM HP5 131 H8
NFNCH/WDSPK N12 166 G9
Brittain Wy STVGE SG2 67 L1
Britten Cl BORE WD6 164 D5
Britton Av STALW/RED AL3 8 E3
Britwell Dr BERK HP4 116 B5
Brive Rd DUN/HR/TOD LU5 61 H7
Brixham Cl STVG SG1 50 E8
Brixton Rd WATN WD24 149 J9
Broad Acre LCOL/BKTW AL2 135 M9
Broad Acres HAT AL10 122 C5
Broadacres LTNE LU2 46 E9
Broad Ct WGCE AL7 105 H6
Broadcroft HHNE HP2 117 N6
LWTH SG6 36 C6
Broadcroft Av STAN HA7 173 K6
Broadfield BSF CM23 58 A9
HLW CM20 3 G4
Broadfield Cl MHAD SG10 90 C4
Broadfield Ct BUSH WD23 163 N8
Broadfield Pde EDGW HA8 * 165 H9
Broadfield Pl WGCW AL8 104 E7
Broadfield Rd HHNE HP2 5 J1
KNEB SG3 85 L4
Broadfields CHESW EN7 141 J8
HARP AL5 101 N2
RYLN/HDSTN HA2 172 B6
SBW CM21 111 L3
Broadfields Av EDGW HA8 165 H9
Broadfields Hts EDGW HA8 173 P1
Broadfields La OXHEY WD19 162 D7
Broadfield Wy MHAD SG10 90 B4
Broadgate WAB EN9 157 L3
Broadgates Av EBAR EN4 153 L9
Broad Gn HERT/BAY SG13 124 G3
Broadgreen Rd CHESW EN7 141 L5
Broad Green Wd
HERT/BAY SG13 124 G3
Broadhall Wy STVG SG1 66 G4
Broadhurst Av EDGW HA8 173 P1
Broadlake Cl LCOL/BKTW AL2 137 J6
Broadlands Av CSHM HP5 131 H9
Broadlawns Ct
KTN/HRWW/WS HA3 172 F5
Broadleaf Av BSF CM23 91 M1
Broadley Rd
HLWW/ROY CM19 128 C7
Broadmead HTCHE/RSTV SG4 49 M2
Broad Md LTNN/LIM LU3 62 B3
Broadmead Cl PIN HA5 * 171 N4
Broadmeadow Ride
HTCHE/RSTV SG4 49 M3
Broadmeads WARE SG12 108 C3
Broadoak Av PEND EN3 156 C5
Broadoak End
HERT/WAT SG14 * 106 G3
Broad Oak Wy STVGE SG2 67 J5
Broadstone Rd HARP AL5 102 B6
Broad St CSHM HP5 131 H9
HHNE HP2 4 E1
RBSF CM22 93 N3
Broadview STVG SG1 11 F3
Broadview Rd CSHM HP5 130 G6
Broadwalk
DUN/HR/TOD LU5 * 60 E6
Broad Wk HLW CM20 2 E4
Broadwalk
RYLN/HDSTN HA2 * 172 B9
The Broadwalk NTHWD HA6 170 E6
Broadwater BERK HP4 115 P6
POTB/CUF EN6 139 L9
Broadwater Av LWTH SG6 36 B3
Broadwater Crs STVGE SG2 67 J5
WGCE AL7 104 G7
Broadwater Dl LWTH SG6 36 B3
Broadwater Gdns
DEN/HRF UB9 169 M8
Broadwater La DEN/HRF UB9 169 M8
STVGE SG2 67 M5
Broadwater Rd WGCW AL8 104 G7
Broadway LWTH SG6 36 B5
Broadway Av HLWE CM17 111 L8
Broadway Cl AMSS HP7 158 B1
Broadway Pde
RYLN/HDSTN HA2 * 172 B9
The Broadway AMSS HP7 158 B1
BRKMPK AL9 122 F6
CFSP/GDCR SL9 * 168 C5
CSHM HP5 144 G1
KTN/HRWW/WS HA3 172 E6
PIN HA5 171 P4
POTB/CUF EN6 * 153 J2
STAL AL1 * 9 F3
STALE/WH AL4 82 G8
STAN HA7 173 J2
WAT WD17 13 H3
Brocas Wy LBUZ LU7 77 P2
Brocket Rd HOD EN11 126 F5
WGCW AL8 104 C8
Brockett Cl WGCW AL8 104 E6
Brocket Vw STALE/WH AL4 103 J4
Brockhurst Cl STAN HA7 172 F3
Brockhurst Rd CSHM HP5 131 H8
Brocklesbury Cl WATN WD24 13 H2
Brockles Md
HLWW/ROY CM19 128 F7
Brockley Av STAN HA7 164 E9
Brockley Cl STAN HA7 173 L1
Brockley Hl STAN HA7 164 D8
Brockleyside STAN HA7 173 K1
Brockswood La WGCW AL8 104 E5
Brockton Cl LTN LU1 62 B7
Brockwell Shott STVGE SG2 52 C6
Brodewater Rd BORE WD6 165 H1
Brodie Rd ENC/FH EN2 155 K8
Bromborough Gn
OXHEY WD19 171 L2
Bromefield STAN HA7 173 J5
Bromefield Ct WAB EN9 157 M3
Bromet Cl WAT WD17 148 G8
Bromleigh Cl CHES/WCR EN8 142 D7
Bromley TRING HP23 77 H9
Bromley Cl HLW CM20 111 L8
Bromley Gdns
DUN/HR/TOD LU5 60 G1
Bromley La AMS HP6 144 A4
Brompton Cl LTNN/LIM LU3 46 A7
Bronte Av HTCH/STOT SG5 24 G7
Bronte Crs HHNE HP2 118 C2
Bronte Paths STVGE SG2 51 M9
Brook Av EDGW HA8 173 P3
Brookbridge La KNEB SG3 85 N3
Brook Cl BORE WD6 165 H2
DUN/WHIP LU6 60 D5
RAYLNE/WEN HP22 94 E7
Brook Cots STSD CM24 58 F6
Brook Ct RAD WD7 * 150 F3
Brookdene Av OXHEY WD19 162 D6
Brookdene Dr NTHWD HA6 171 H4
Brook Dr HRW HA1 172 C8
RAD WD7 150 E3
STVGE SG2 67 L6
Brooke Cl BUSH WD23 163 L6
Brooke End STALW/RED AL3 101 H8
Brooke Gdns BSF CM23 74 D3
Brook End
RAYLNE/WEN HP22 94 A9
ROY SG8 15 P8
SBW CM21 111 N2
WARE SG12 89 K9
Brookend Dr
AMP/FLIT/BLC MK45 32 C5
Brooke Rd ROY SG8 20 C2
Brooker Rd WAB EN9 157 H4
Brooke Wy BUSH WD23 163 L6
Brook Farm Cl BSF CM23 91 M2
Brook Fld STVGE SG2 67 P4
Brookfield Av
DUN/HR/TOD LU5 60 F2
Brookfield Cl TRING HP23 96 A8
Brookfield Crs
KTN/HRWW/WS HA3 173 L9
Brookfield Gdns
CHES/WCR EN8 142 C6
Brookfield La CHES/WCR EN8 142 A7
STVGE SG2 68 A2
Brookfield La East
CHES/WCR EN8 142 C6
Brookfield La West
CHES/WCR EN8 142 B6
Brookfields SBW CM21 111 N2
Brookhill STVGE SG2 67 J6
Brookhill Cl EBAR EN4 167 J4
Brookhill Rd EBAR EN4 167 H4
Brooklands Cl LTNW/LEA LU4 45 M9
Brooklands Ct STAL AL1 * 9 G3
Brooklands Gdns
POTB/CUF EN6 153 H2
Brook La BERK HP4 115 N6
SBW CM21 111 N2
Brooklane Fld HLWS CM18 129 L6
Brookmans Av BRKMPK AL9 139 J5
Brookmill Cl OXHEY WD19 * 162 D6
Brook Pl BAR EN5 166 E4
Brook Rd BORE WD6 151 M9
CHES/WCR EN8 156 E4
SBW CM21 111 N3
STSD CM24 58 F5
Brooks Ct HERT/WAT SG14 * 106 G5
Brooksfield WGCE AL7 105 L5
Brookshill
KTN/HRWW/WS HA3 172 E3
Brookshill Av
KTN/HRWW/WS HA3 172 D2
Brookshill Dr
KTN/HRWW/WS HA3 172 D2
Brookside EBAR EN4 167 J5
HAT AL10 122 A6
HERT/BAY SG13 107 M7
HLWW/ROY CM19 128 C5
HOD EN11 126 F5
LWTH SG6 * 36 C3
POTB/CUF EN6 152 D2
RAYLNE/WEN HP22 112 A1
WAB EN9 157 K2
WATN WD24 * 149 L6
Brookside Cl BAR EN5 166 B5
KTN/HRWW/WS HA3 173 K9
Brookside Crs POTB/CUF EN6 140 F6
Brookside Gdns EN EN1 156 A7
Brookside Rd OXHEY WD19 162 D6
Brookside South EBAR EN4 167 L6
Brook St HTCH/STOT SG5 25 J3
LTNN/LIM LU3 6 C2
RAYLNE/WEN HP22 94 E7
TRING HP23 96 A8
Brook Vw HTCHE/RSTV SG4 49 P1
Broom Cl CHESW EN7 141 P6
HAT AL10 122 C9
Broom Cnr HARP AL5 * 102 B4
Broomer Pl CHES/WCR EN8 142 B8
Broom Farm Rd RBSF CM22 59 K1
Broomfield HLW CM20 111 L9
LCOL/BKTW AL2 136 B6
Broomfield Av BROX EN10 142 D5
Broomfield Cl WLYN AL6 84 F9
Broomfield Ri ABLGY WD5 148 E2
Broomfield Rd WLYN AL6 84 F9
Broomfields RBSF CM22 93 H6
Broom Gv KNEB SG3 67 J9
WAT WD17 149 H8
Broomgrove Gdns
EDGW HA8 173 N5
Broom Hl HHW HP1 117 H9
WLYN AL6 85 K5
Broomhills WGCE AL7 105 K5
Broomleys STALE/WH AL4 121 H5
Brooms Cl WGCW AL8 104 G3
Brooms Rd LTNE LU2 7 H2
Broomstick Hall Rd WAB EN9 157 K3
Broomstick La CSHM HP5 131 M9
Broom Wk STVG SG1 11 F5
Broughinge Rd BORE WD6 165 H1
Broughton Av
DUN/HR/TOD LU5 44 B1
LTNN/LIM LU3 62 D1
Broughton Hl LWTH SG6 36 D2
Broughton Wy
RKW/CH/CXG WD3 160 E6
Brownfields WGCE AL7 105 J5
Brownfields Ct WGCE AL7 105 J5
Brownfield Wy
STALE/WH AL4 82 G7
Browning Dr
HTCHE/RSTV SG4 35 N8
Browning Rd ENC/FH EN2 155 L8
HARP AL5 102 B2
LTNW/LEA LU4 61 K4
Brownings La
HTCHE/RSTV SG4 64 C5
Brownlow Cl EBAR EN4 167 H4
Brownlow La LBUZ LU7 77 N6
Brownlow Rd BERK HP4 115 P6
BORE WD6 164 G3
Browns Cl LTNW/LEA LU4 61 N1
Browns Hedge LBUZ LU7 96 B1
Brown's Ri TRING HP23 113 N8
Browns Spring BERK HP4 116 F4
The Brow CSTG HP8 159 K9
GSTN WD25 149 J3
Brox Dell STVG SG1 11 F2
Broxley Md LTNW/LEA LU4 61 M1
Bruce Gdns TRDG/WHET N20 167 K9
Bruce Gv WATN WD24 149 J8
Bruce Rd BAR EN5 166 C2
KTN/HRWW/WS HA3 172 E6
Bruce Wy CHES/WCR EN8 156 C3
Brunel Ct LTNW/LEA LU4 61 H3
Brunel Rd LTNW/LEA LU4 61 H3
STVGE SG2 11 K1
Brunswick Av
FBAR/BDGN N11 167 L9
Brunswick Crs
FBAR/BDGN N11 167 L9
Brunswick Gv
FBAR/BDGN N11 167 L9
Brunswick Park Gdns
FBAR/BDGN N11 167 L8
Brunswick Park Rd
FBAR/BDGN N11 167 L9
Brunswick Rd PEND EN3 156 F8
Brunswick St LTNE LU2 7 F2
Brushmakers Ct CSHM HP5 131 H9
Brushrise WATN WD24 149 H6
Brushwood Dr
RKW/CH/CXG WD3 160 A3
Brushwood Rd CSHM HP5 131 J8
Brussels Wy LTNN/LIM LU3 45 N6
Bryan Rd BSF CM23 74 A2
Bryanstone Rd
CHES/WCR EN8 156 E4
Bryant Cl BAR EN5 166 D4
Bryant Ct HARP AL5 101 P1
Bryants Acre
RAYLNE/WEN HP22 112 C6
Bryant Wy DUN/HR/TOD LU5 44 C2
Bryce Cl WARE SG12 108 C1
Bryn Wy STALE/WH AL4 137 J1
Bryony Wy DUN/WHIP LU6 60 B5
Buchanan Ct BORE WD6 * 165 J1
Buchanan Dr LTNE LU2 63 J6
Buckettsland La BORE WD6 152 A8
Buckingham Av
TRDG/WHET N20 166 G6
Buckingham Dr LTNE LU2 63 K4
Buckingham Gdns STAN HA7 173 L4
Buckingham Pde
CFSP/GDCR SL9 * 168 C5
STAN HA7 * 173 J2
Buckingham Rd BORE WD6 165 K3
EDGW HA8 173 M4
HRW HA1 172 D9
TRING HP23 95 M9
WATN WD24 149 K7
Buckland Ri PIN HA5 171 L5
Buckland Rd
RAYLNE/WEN HP22 95 H7
Bucklands OXHEY WD19 * 162 F9
Buckle Cl LTNN/LIM LU3 46 A8
Bucklersbury
HTCH/STOT SG5 49 K1
Bucklers Cl BROX EN10 142 E1
Bucknalls Cl GSTN WD25 149 M2
Bucknalls Dr LCOL/BKTW AL2 149 N1
Bucknalls La GSTN WD25 149 M2
Bucks Aly HERT/BAY SG13 124 E7
Bucks Av OXHEY WD19 162 G6
Bucks Hl KGLGY WD4 147 M3
Buckthorn Av STVG SG1 10 E7
Buckton Rd BORE WD6 151 L8
Buckwood Av
DUN/HR/TOD LU5 61 H5
Buckwood La DUN/WHIP LU6 78 F6
Buckwood Rd
DUN/WHIP LU6 79 K7
Buddcroft WGCE AL7 105 L5
Bude Crs STVG SG1 50 D9
Building End Rd ROY SG8 31 M1
Bulbourne Cl BERK HP4 115 L5
HHW HP1 117 K9
Bulbourne Ct TRING HP23 95 P5
Bulbourne Rd TRING HP23 96 A5
Bullace Cl HHW HP1 117 J7
Bullbaiters La AMS HP6 144 A4
Bullbeggars La BERK HP4 116 D7
Bullen's Green La
STALE/WH AL4 138 B2
Bullescroft Rd EDGW HA8 164 G9
Bullfields SBW CM21 91 P9
Bullhead Rd BORE WD6 165 J3
Bull La BUNT SG9 39 K8
CFSP/GDCR SL9 168 B7
SAFWS CB11 31 M7
STALE/WH AL4 102 F6
Bullock's Hl HTCHE/RSTV SG4 65 M5
Bullock's La HERT/BAY SG13 107 K8
Bull Pln HERT/WAT SG14 107 L6
Bull Pond La DUN/WHIP LU6 60 E7
Bull Rd HARP AL5 102 A4
Bullrush Cl HAT AL10 122 E7
Bull's Cross EN EN1 155 P6
Bulls Cross Ride ENC/FH EN2 155 P5
Bullsland Gdns
RKW/CH/CXG WD3 159 P5
Bullsland La
RKW/CH/CXG WD3 159 P5
Bulls La BRKMPK AL9 138 G3
Bullsmoor Cl CHES/WCR EN8 156 B5
Bullsmoor Gdns
CHES/WCR EN8 156 A5
Bullsmoor La ENC/FH EN2 155 P5
Bullsmoor Ride
CHES/WCR EN8 156 B5
Bullsmoor Wy
CHES/WCR EN8 156 A5
Bull Stag Gn BRKMPK AL9 122 F4
Bullwell Crs CHES/WCR EN8 142 D8
Bulstrode Cl KGLGY WD4 133 H8
Bulstrode La KGLGY WD4 133 H8
Bulstrode Wy
CFSP/GDCR SL9 168 B9
Bulwer Gdns BAR EN5 166 G3
Bulwer Link STVG SG1 67 H3
Bulwer Rd BAR EN5 166 F3
Bumbles Green La WAB EN9 143 N4
Buncefield La HHNE HP2 118 D7
Buncefield Terminal
HHNE HP2 * 118 E6
The Bungalows HARP AL5 102 B1
Bunhill Cl DUN/WHIP LU6 60 C6
Bunkers La HHS/BOV HP3 134 B4
Bunnsfield WGCE AL7 105 M5
Bunstrux TRING HP23 95 N8
Buntingford Rd STDN SG11 71 J2
Bunting Rd LTNW/LEA LU4 61 K2
Bunyan Cl HTCH/STOT SG5 34 C4
TRING HP23 96 A7
Bunyan Rd HTCH/STOT SG5 35 K8
Bunyans Cl LTNN/LIM LU3 62 B1
Burbage Cl CHES/WCR EN8 156 D1
Burchell Ct BUSH WD23 163 L6
Burfield Cl HAT AL10 122 D4
Burfield Rd
RKW/CH/CXG WD3 159 P4
Burford Cl LTNN/LIM LU3 46 A6
Burford Gdns HOD EN11 126 G4
Burford St HOD EN11 126 F4
Burford Wy HTCH/STOT SG5 35 H6
Burgage Ct WARE SG12 * 108 C3
Burgage La WARE SG12 108 C3
Burge End La
HTCH/STOT SG5 34 B3
Burges Cl DUN/WHIP LU6 60 G9
Burgess Cl CHESW EN7 141 K4
Burghley Av BORE WD6 165 J4
BSF CM23 73 M7
Burghley Cl STVGE SG2 67 K6
Burgundy Cft WGCE AL7 105 J8
Burhill Gv PIN HA5 171 N6
Burke Rd RAYLNE/WEN HP22 112 D6
Burleigh Ct BUSH WD23 * 162 G3
Burleigh Gdns
STHGT/OAK N14 167 N7
Burleigh Md BRKMPK AL9 122 F4
Burleigh Pde
STHGT/OAK N14 * 167 P7
Burleigh Rd CHES/WCR EN8 * 156 D2
HERT/BAY SG13 107 P5
HHNE HP2 118 D9
STAL AL1 120 G8
Burleigh Wy POTB/CUF EN6 140 F9
Burley LWTH SG6 25 K8
Burley Hl HLWE CM17 129 N4
Burley Rd BSF CM23 74 B6
Burlington Cl PIN HA5 171 K7
Burlington Ri EBAR EN4 167 J7
Burlington Rd ENC/FH EN2 155 L9
Burn Cl GSTN WD25 * 163 M3
Burnell Gdns STAN HA7 173 K6
Burnell Ri LWTH SG6 36 A3
Burnells Wy STSD CM24 58 F4
Burnell Wk LWTH SG6 36 B3
Burnet Cl HHNE HP2 5 G4
Burnett Pk HLWW/ROY CM19 128 E8
Burnett Sq HERT/WAT SG14 106 G5
Burnham Cl EN EN1 155 M8
KTN/HRWW/WS HA3 172 G8
WLYN AL6 85 M7
Burnham Green Rd
WLYN AL6 85 N7
Burnham Rd LTNE LU2 63 J4
STAL AL1 120 F8
The Burnhams
RAYLNE/WEN HP22 94 D7
Burnley Cl OXHEY WD19 171 L2
Burnsall Pl HARP AL5 102 B6
Burns Cl HTCHE/RSTV SG4 35 N8
STVGE SG2 51 L7
Burns Dr HHNE HP2 118 C3
Burnside HERT/WAT SG14 107 H7
HOD EN11 126 E5
SBW CM21 111 N2
STAL AL1 136 G1
Burnside Cl BAR EN5 166 E2
Burns Rd ROY SG8 20 B2
Burnt Cl LTNN/LIM LU3 46 A8
Burntfarm Ride ENC/FH EN2 155 J4
Burnt Mi HLW CM20 2 C1
Burntmill Cl HLW CM20 110 F9
Burntmill La HLW CM20 110 F9
Burnt Oak Broadway
EDGW HA8 173 P4
Burr Cl AMP/FLIT/BLC MK45 32 D4
LCOL/BKTW AL2 137 K6
Burrell Cl EDGW HA8 165 H8
The Burren AMS HP6 * 145 J7
Burrowfield WGCE AL7 104 G8
Burrows Cha WAB EN9 157 J6
Burrs La ROY SG8 30 A6
Burr St DUN/WHIP LU6 60 E6
LTNE LU2 7 F2
Bursland LWTH SG6 36 A2
Burston Dr LCOL/BKTW AL2 136 B7
Burton Av WATW WD18 12 D4
Burton Cl STALE/WH AL4 83 H8
Burton Dr PEND EN3 156 F7
Burton La CHESW EN7 141 M7
Burtons La CSTG HP8 159 J1
Burton's Wy CSTG HP8 159 J1
Burvale Ct WATW WD18 12 E3
Burwell Rd STVGE SG2 67 L2
Burwood Av PIN HA5 171 L9
Burwood Pl EBAR EN4 153 M9
Burycroft WGCW AL8 105 H3
Burydale STVGE SG2 67 L5
Burydell La LCOL/BKTW AL2 136 C6
Bury End HTCH/STOT SG5 34 C4
Bury Farm AMSS HP7 158 C1
Buryfield Wy WARE SG12 108 B2
Bury Gn HHW HP1 117 M7
STALE/WH AL4 103 H4
Bury Green Rd CHESW EN7 155 P2
Bury Hl HHW HP1 117 M7
Bury Hill Cl HHW HP1 117 M7
Bury Holme BROX EN10 142 E2
Bury La CSHM HP5 144 G1
HERT/WAT SG14 86 C9
HTCHE/RSTV SG4 84 C4
KNEB SG3 85 N2
LTNN/LIM LU3 46 B2
RKW/CH/CXG WD3 161 H7
ROY SG8 22 G9
Bury Lodge La STSD CM24 75 K2
Bury Md ARL/CHE SG15 24 E2
Burymead STVG SG1 50 F6
Bury Mdw
RKW/CH/CXG WD3 161 H7
Bury Mead Rd
HTCH/STOT SG5 35 L6
Bury Park Rd LTN LU1 6 B1
Bury Ri HHS/BOV HP3 132 G4
Bury Rd HAT AL10 122 F5
HHW HP1 4 D1
HLWE CM17 111 M8
The Bury CSHM HP5 * 144 G2
Burywick HARP AL5 102 A7
Bushbarns CHESW EN7 141 P8
Bushby Av BROX EN10 142 E1
Bush Cl DUN/HR/TOD LU5 44 D2
Bushell Gn BUSH WD23 163 M8
Bushel Whf TRING HP23 95 P6
Bushey Cl WGCE AL7 105 L7
Bushey Cft HLWS CM18 129 H5
Bushey Gn WGCE AL7 105 L7
Bushey Grove Rd
BUSH WD23 13 K4
Bushey Hall Dr BUSH WD23 162 G3
Bushey Hall Pk BUSH WD23 * 162 G3
Bushey Hall Rd BUSH WD23 13 K4
Bushey Ley WGCE AL7 105 L7
Busheymill Br WATN WD24 149 M8
Bushey Mill Crs WATN WD24 149 K6
Bushey Mill La BUSH WD23 163 H1
WATN WD24 149 K7
Bushfield Cl EDGW HA8 165 H8
Bushfield Crs EDGW HA8 165 H8
Bushfield Rd HHS/BOV HP3 132 F4
Bush Gv STAN HA7 173 K4
Bush Hall La BRKMPK AL9 122 G3
Bushmead Rd LTNE LU2 62 F1
Bush Spring BLDK SG7 26 C8
Bushwood Cl BRKMPK AL9 138 E2
Buslins La CSHM HP5 130 D7
Butchers La HTCHE/RSTV SG4 49 J9
Butely Rd LTNW/LEA LU4 61 L1
Bute Sq LTN LU1 6 E4
Bute St LTN LU1 6 E4
Butler Cl EDGW HA8 173 P6
Butlers Cl AMS HP6 144 F7
Butlers Dr CHING E4 157 H8
Butlers Yd BLDK SG7 26 A8
Butlin Rd LTN LU1 62 C7
Buttercup Cl DUN/WHIP LU6 60 D7
HAT AL10 122 C2
Butterfield Green Rd
LTNE LU2 47 H9
Butterfield La STAL AL1 136 D3
Butterfield Rd STALE/WH AL4 103 H5
Butterfly La BORE WD6 164 B2
Buttermere Av
DUN/WHIP LU6 60 F8
Buttermere Cl STAL AL1 120 G9
Buttermere Pl GSTN WD25 * 149 N4
Buttersweet Ri SBW CM21 111 P3
Butterwick GSTN WD25 149 M6
Butterworth Pth LTNE LU2 * 6 E2
Butt Field Vw STAL AL1 136 B3
Butt La BSF CM23 57 N5
Buttlehide
RKW/CH/CXG WD3 169 H2
Buttondene Crs BROX EN10 142 G1
Butts End HHW HP1 117 K7

Butts Gn HTCHE/RSTV SG4 * ... 37 M7
Buttsmead NTHWD HA6 ... 170 E4
The Butts BROX EN10 ... 142 D3
Buxton Cl STALE/WH AL4 ... 121 J5
Buxton Pth OXHEY WD19 * ... 162 E9
Buxton Rd LTN LU1 ...
WAB EN9 ... 157 M2
Buxtons La TRDG/WHET N20 ... 15 L8
Buzzard Rd LTNW/LEA LU4 ... 61 K1
Byde St HERT/WAT SG14 ... 107 K5
Bye Gn RAYLNE/WEN HP22 ... 98 B9
Byers Cl POTB/CUF EN6 ... 153 M4
Byewaters WATW WD18 ... 161 N5
The Bye Wy
KTN/HRWW/WS HA3 ... 172 E5
The Byeway
RKW/CH/CXG WD3 ... 161 J8
Byfield WGCW AL8 ... 105 H3
Byfield Cl DUN/HR/TOD LU5 ... 44 B1
LTNW/LEA LU4 ... 61 L5
Bygrave Rd BLDK SG7 ... 28 N8
Byng Dr POTB/CUF EN6 ... 153 K1
Bynghams HLWW/ROY CM19 ... 128 C5
Byng Rd BAR EN5 ... 26 A6
Byrd St STVG SG1 ... 10 D7
Byrd Wk BLDK SG7 ... 22 D7
Byre Rd STHGT/OAK N14 ... 167 L5
Byron Av BORE WD6 ... 164 G4
CDALE/KGS NW9 ... 173 P8
WATN WD24 ... 149 L9
Byron Cl HHNE HP2 ... 2 C6
HTCHE/RSTV SG4 ... 35 N8
Byron Pl HHNE HP2 ... 118 C2
Byron Rd HARP AL5 ... 101 P2
KTN/HRWW/WS HA3 ... 172 F6
LTNW/LEA LU4 ... 61 L4
ROY SG8 ... 20 C2
Byslips Rd DUN/WHIP LU6 ... 98 C1
By The Wd OXHEY WD19 ... 162 A6
Byways BERK HP4 ... 116 B6
The Byway POTB/CUF EN6 ... 153 K3
By-wood End
CFSP/GDCR SL9 ... 168 E2

C

Cabot Cl STVGE SG2 ... 51 K8
Caddington Cl EBAR EN4 ... 167 J4
Caddington Common
STALW/RED AL3 ... 79 P5
Caddis Cl STAN HA7 * ... 172 F4
Cade Cl LTN LU1 ... 25 N8
Cades La LTN LU1 ... 62 B8
Cadmore La CHES/WCR EN8 ... 142 D7
Cadwell La HTCHE/RSTV SG4 ... 35 L6
Caernarvon Cl HHNE HP2 ... 2 C6
STVGE SG2 ... 67 L7
Caesars Rd STALW/WH AL4 ... 103 J4
Cage End HHNE HP2 ... 93 M4
Cage End Cl RBSF CM22 ... 93 N4
Cage Pond Rd RAD WD7 ... 151 M3
Cairns Cl STALE/WH AL4 ... 121 J9
Cairn Wy STAN HA7 ... 172 F3
Caishowe Rd BORE WD6 ... 151 N9
Caister Cl HHNE HP2 * ... 5 H4
Caizac La CHESW EN7 ... 141 L5
Calbury Cl STAL AL1 ... 120 C9
Calcutt Cl DUN/HR/TOD LU5 ... 61 J4
Caldbeck WAB EN9 ... 157 J4
Caldecote Av CHESW EN7 ... 141 N8
Caldecote Gdns BUSH WD23 ... 163 N5
Caldecote La BUSH WD23 ... 163 P6
Caldecot Wy BROX EN10 ... 142 E1
Calder Av BRKMPK AL9 ... 139 K5
Calder Gdns EDGW HA8 ... 173 L7
Calder Wy STVG SG2 ... 51 K4
Calderwood Pl EBAR EN4 ... 153 L9
Caldwell Rd OXHEY WD19 ... 171 M1
Caleb Cl LTNW/LEA LU4 ... 62 A4
Caledon Rd LCOL/BKTW AL2 ... 137 H5
California BLDK SG7 ... 16 D8
California La BUSH WD23 ... 163 M7
The Callanders BUSH WD23 * ... 163 N7
Callowland Pl WATN WD24 ... 149 J8
Calnwood Rd LTNW/LEA LU4 ... 61 L4
Calthorpe Gdns EDGW HA8 ... 173 M2
Calton Av HERT/WAT SG14 ... 106 C5
Calverley Cl BSF CM23 ... 91 P2
Calverton Rd LTNN/LIM LU3 ... 46 G7
Calvert Rd BAR EN5 ... 166 B1
Camberley Pl HARP AL5 ... 102 C6
Cambrian Wy HHNE HP2 ... 117 P4
Cambridge Cl CHES/WCR EN8 ... 142 C7
EBAR EN4 ... 167 L7
Cambridge Dr POTB/CUF EN6 ... 153 H1
Cambridge Rd BGSW SG18 ... 14 C5
HLW CM20 ... 111 M6
HTCHE/RSTV SG4 ... 35 B4
STDN SG11 ... 54 B9
STVGE SG2 ... 80 B4
RYLN/HDSTN HA2 ... 172 A9
STAL AL1 ... 120 C9
STDN SG11 ... 71 H4
STSD CM24 ... 58 C5
WATN WD24 ... 12 B1
Cambridge St LTN LU1 ... 62 C9
Cambridge Ter BERK HP4 ... 116 B4
Camden Rw PIN HA5 ... 171 L7
Cameron Cl STVGE SG2 ... 51 L8
TRDG/WHET N20 ... 167 J8
Cameron Ct WARE SG12 ... 108 C4
Cameron Dr CSHM HP5 ... 131 H9
Camfield WGCE AL7 ... 125 J4
Camford Wy LTNW/LEA LU4 ... 45 K7
Camlet Wy EBAR EN4 ... 8 L1
STALW/RED AL3 ... 8 L1
Campania Gv LTNN/LIM LU3 ... 46 D2
Campbell Cl BUNT SG9 ... 40 C9

HLWE CM17 ... 129 L4
HTCHE/RSTV SG4 ... 35 N8
Campbell Cft EDGW HA8 ... 173 N2
Camp Dr DUN/HR/TOD LU5 ... 60 E1
Campers Av LWTH SG6 ... 36 B5
Campers Rd LWTH SG6 ... 36 A5
Campers Wk LWTH SG6 ... 36 B3
Campfield Rd
HERT/WAT SG14 ... 107 J6
STAL AL1 ... 5 L3
Campfield Wy LWTH SG6 ... 36 A5
Campian Cl DUN/WHIP LU6 ... 60 B5
Campine Cl CHES/WCR EN8 ... 142 C7
Campion Cl GSTN SG2 ... 149 H3
Campion Rd HAT AL10 ... 122 C2
Campions Cl BERK HP4 ... 117 H9
Campions Cl BERK HP4 ... 115 M8
The Campions BORE WD6 ... 151 L8
STSD CM24 ... 58 F4
Campion Wy ROY SG8 ... 20 D5
Camplin Md STVG SG2 ... 67 N5
Camp Rd
KTN/HRWW/WS HA3 ... 173 L9
Camp St STAL AL1 ... 9 A4
Campus Five LWTH SG6 ... 36 F1
The Campus HHNE HP2 ... 118 C6
WGCW AL8 ... 104 C5
Camp View Rd STAL AL1 ... 120 G9
Camrose Av STAN HA7 ... 173 L6
Cam Sq HTCHE/RSTV SG4 * ... 35 M5
Canada La BROX EN10 ... 142 D4
Canada Park Pde
EDGW HA8 * ... 173 P5
The Canadas BROX EN10 ... 142 D5
Canalside BERK HP4 ... 115 L5
Canal Wy DEN/HRF UB9 ... 169 L3
Canberra Cl STALE/WH AL4 ... 120 E4
Canberra Gdns LTNN/LIM LU3 ... 46 C9
Candale Cl DUN/WHIP LU6 ... 60 F8
Candlefield Rd HHS/BOV HP3 ... 138 A5
Canesworde Rd
DUN/WHIP LU6 ... 60 D7
Canfield BSF CM23 ... 73 P6
Cangels Cl HHW HP1 ... 133 K1
Canham Cl HTCHE/RSTV SG4 ... 83 M4
Canning Rd
KTN/HRWW/WS HA3 ... 172 E7
Cannix Cl STVG SG2 ... 67 P4
Cannon Hi STHGT/OAK N14 ... 167 P9
Cannon La LTNE LU2 ... 63 J1
PIN HA5 ... 171 N9
Cannon Ms WAB EN9 ... 156 C5
Cannon Mill Av CSHM HP5 ... 145 J5
Cannon Rd WATW WD18 ... 13 C7
Cannons Cl BSF CM23 ... 74 B1
Cannons Cl STDN SG11 ... 71 J3
Cannons Md STSD CM24 ... 58 E4
Cannons Meadow KLBA AL6 ... 105 P2
Cannons Mill La BSF CM23 ... 58 B9
Cannon St STALW/RED AL3 ... 8 B7
Canonbury Rd EN EN1 ... 155 M9
Canon Mohan Cl
STHGT/OAK N14 ... 167 L5
Canons Brook
HLWW/ROY CM19 ... 128 C3
Canons Cl EDGW HA8 ... 173 M3
RAD WD7 ... 150 C5
Canons Cots EDGW HA8 * ... 173 M3
Canons Dr EDGW HA8 ... 173 L3
Canons Fld STALE/WH AL4 ... 103 J3
WLYN AL6 ... 85 H5
Canonsfield Rd WLYN AL6 ... 105 P2
Canons Ga CHES/WCR EN8 ... 142 C5
Canons Md HLW CM20 ... 128 D3
Canopus Wy NTHWD HA6 ... 171 J1
Canopy La HLWE CM17 ... 129 M2
Canterbury Cl AMSS HP7 ... 145 K9
LTNN/LIM LU3 ... 45 M7
NTHWD HA6 ... 171 H1
Canterbury Rd BORE WD6 ... 164 G1
HRW HA1 ... 172 B9
Canterbury Wy
RKW/CH/CXG WD3 ... 161 N2
STVG SG1 ... 51 J5
Capel Cl TRDG/WHET N20 ... 166 C9
Capel Crs STAN HA7 ... 164 A8
Capella Rd NTHWD HA6 ... 171 H1
Capell Av RKW/CH/CXG WD3 ... 160 A4
Capell Rd RKW/CH/CXG WD3 ... 160 B5
Capel Rd EBAR EN4 ... 167 J3
EN EN1 ... 155 P4
OXHEY WD19 ... 162 F5
Capelvere Wk WAT WD17 ... 148 F9
Cape Rd STAL AL1 ... 120 G8
Capital Pl HLWW/ROY CM19 ... 128 D4
Caponfields WGCE AL7 ... 105 L8
Cappell La WARE SG12 ... 109 H7
Capron Rd DUN/HR/TOD LU5 ... 61 P2
Captain's Cl CSHM HP5 ... 130 F6
Captains Wk BERK HP4 ... 116 A8
Capuchin Cl STAN HA7 ... 173 H3
Caractacus Cottage Vw
WATW WD18 ... 162 C6
Caractacus Gn WATW WD18 ... 162 B5
Caravan La
RKW/CH/CXG WD3 ... 161 J6
Carbone Hl POTB/CUF EN6 ... 140 C9
Cardiff Cl STVG SG2 * ... 67 L7
Cardiff Gv LTN LU1 ... 6 C4
Cardiff Rd LTN LU1 ... 6 C5
WATW WD18 ... 162 D5
Cardigan Cl LTN LU1 * ... 6 C5
Cardigan Gv LTN LU1 ... 62 E9
Cardigan St LTN LU1 ... 4 C7
Cardinal Av BORE WD6 ... 165 H2
Cardinal Cl STALW/RED AL3 ... 8 A7
Cardinal Wy
KTN/HRWW/WS HA3 ... 172 E7
Cardy Rd HHW HP1 ... 4 A3
Carew Rd NTHWD HA6 ... 170 H1
Carew Wy OXHEY WD19 ... 163 H9

Careys Cft BERK HP4 ... 115 L4
Carfax Cl LTNW/LEA LU4 ... 61 H3
Carisbrook Cl EN EN1 ... 155 N9
Carisbrooke Av WATN WD24 ... 149 L9
Carisbrooke Cl STAN HA7 ... 173 K6
Carisbrooke Rd HARP AL5 ... 102 B2
LTNW/LEA LU4 ... 61 P5
Carisbrook Rd
LCOL/BKTW AL2 ... 136 A5
Carleton Rd CHES/WCR EN8 ... 142 C6
Carlisle Av STALE/WH AL4 ... 120 C6
Carlisle Cl DUN/WHIP LU6 ... 60 E8
Carlton Av
KTN/HRWW/WS HA3 ... 173 H9
STHGT/OAK N14 ... 167 H4
Carlton Bank HARP AL5 * ... 102 A3
Carlton Cl BORE WD6 ... 165 K3
Carlton Ct EDGW HA8 ... 173 N2
Carlton Crs LTNN/LIM LU3 ... 62 D3
Carlton Rd HARP AL5 ... 101 P2
Carman Cl TRING HP23 ... 95 N9
Carmelite Rd
KTN/HRWW/WS HA3 ... 172 C5
LTNW/LEA LU4 ... 61 K3
Carnaby Rd BROX EN10 ... 126 D6
Carnarvon Rd BAR EN5 ... 166 C2
Carnegie Cl PEND EN3 ... 156 D3
Carnegie Rd STALE/WH AL4 ... 120 C4
Caro La HHS/BOV HP3 ... 134 B1
Carol Cl LTNN/LIM LU3 ... 62 C2
Caroline Ct STAN HA7 ... 172 C3
Caroline Dr RKW/CH/CXG WD3 ... 161 M6
Carpenders Av OXHEY WD19 ... 162 C9
Carpenters Cl HARP AL5 ... 81 J9
Carpenters Cl BAR EN5 ... 166 F5
Carpenters Rd EN EN1 ... 156 B6
The Carpenters BSF CM23 ... 73 L9
Carpenters Wood Dr
RKW/CH/CXG WD3 ... 159 P5
Carpenters Yd TRING HP23 ... 114 A1
Carpenter Wy POTB/CUF EN6 ... 153 M3
Carr Cl STAN HA7 ... 172 C5
Carrigans BSF CM23 ... 78 G1
Carrington Av BORE WD6 ... 165 H4
Carrington Cl BORE WD6 ... 165 N4
Carrington Crs
RAYLNE/WEN HP22 ... 112 B4
Carrington Pl TRING HP23 ... 96 A7
Carrington Sq
KTN/HRWW/WS HA3 ... 172 C4
Carsdale Cl LTNN/LIM LU3 ... 46 B9
Carson Rd EBAR EN4 ... 167 K3
Carteret Rd LTNE LU2 ... 63 N3
Cartehatch La EN EN1 ... 155 N9
Carters Cl ARL/CHE SG15 ... 24 C7
STVG SG2 ... 67 N2
Cartersfield Rd WAB EN9 ... 157 H4
Carters La
(Wibbly Wobbley Lane)
HTCH/STOT SG5 ... 34 F9
Carters Leys BSF CM23 ... 73 N6
Carters Md HLWE CM17 ... 129 L4
Carters Wk ARL/CHE SG15 ... 24 C2
Carters Wy ARL/CHE SG15 ... 24 C3
Carter Wy STAL AL1 * ... 10 D3
Carterways
HOD EN11 ... 61 J9
Carmel Dr DUN/WHIP LU6 ... 60 E8
Cart Pth GSTN SG2 ... 149 K3
The Cart Tr HHS/BOV HP3 ... 134 H4
Cartwright Rd ROY SG8 ... 20 C5
STVG SG1 ... 2 A1
Carve Leyd WGCE AL7 ... 105 L7
Carvers Cft KNEB SG3 ... 85 L4
Cary Wk RAD WD7 ... 150 G4
Cashio La LWTH SG6 ... 25 K8
Casion Wy LWTH SG6 ... 25 K8
Cassandra Ga CHES/WCR EN8 ... 142 B3
Cassiobridge Rd WATW WD18 ... 162 A3
Cassiobury Ter
RKW/CH/CXG WD3 * ... 161 P4
Cassiobury Dr WAT WD17 ... 12 C2
Cassiobury Park Av
WATW WD18 ... 162 A2
Cassio Pl WATW WD18 ... 12 E4
Cassio Whf WATW WD18 * ... 161 P4
Castellane Cl STAN HA7 ... 172 C4
Castle Gdns KGLGY WD4 ... 134 A3
Castle Cl BUSH WD23 ... 163 K5
HOD EN11 ... 127 H2
LBUZ LU7 ... 95 C7
Castle Ct HTCH/STOT SG5 ... 13 N5
Castle Croft Rd LTN LU1 ... 62 E8
Castleford Cl BORE WD6 ... 151 N6
Castle Ga STALE/WH AL4 ... 107 K7
Castle Gate Wy BERK HP4 ... 115 L5
Castle Hi BERK HP4 ... 115 L5
Castle Hill Cl BERK HP4 ... 115 P5
Castle Hill Ct BERK HP4 ... 115 P5
Castle Hill Rd BERK HP4 ... 115 P5
Castle Md HHW HP1 ... 5 H1
RAYLNE/WEN HP22 ... 112 B6
Castle Mead Gdns
HERT/WAT SG14 * ... 107 K6
Castle Ms BERK HP4 * ... 115 L5
Castle Park Rd
RAYLNE/WEN HP22 ... 112 B5
Castle Ri STALE/WH AL4 ... 102 C6
Castle Rd HOD EN11 ... 126 G2
STAL AL1 ... 120 G8
Castles Cl HTCH/STOT SG5 ... 13 P7
Castle St BERK HP4 ... 115 P7
HERT/WAT SG14 ... 74 A4
HTCH/STOT SG5 ... 13 P7
LTN LU1 ... 4 D5
RAYLNE/WEN HP22 ... 76 C3
Castle Vw BSF CM23 ... 74 B3
Castlewood Rd EBAR EN4 ... 154 C9
Catchacre DUN/WHIP LU6 ... 60 C5
Caterham Rd WAB EN9 ... 157 L4
Catesby Gn LTNN/LIM LU3 ... 46 B6
Catham St WAB EN9 * ... 157 J4
Catherall Rd LTNN/LIM LU3 ... 46 G7
Catherine Cl HHNE HP2 ... 118 D3

Catherine Ct STHGT/OAK N14 ... 167 N4
Catherine Pl HRW HA1 ... 172 F9
Catherine Rd PEND EN3 ... 156 D7
Catherine St STALW/RED AL3 ... 9 F2
Cat Hi EBAR EN4 ... 167 J3
Cathrow Ms HOD EN11 ... 117 L7
Catisfield Rd PEND EN3 ... 156 E1
Catkin Cl HHW HP1 ... 117 L7
Catlin's La PIN HA5 ... 171 J1
Catlin St HHS/BOV HP3 ... 133 L2
Catsbrook Rd LTNN/LIM LU3 ... 46 C9
Catsdell Bottom
HHS/BOV HP3 ... 138 D7
Catsey La BUSH WD23 ... 163 L6
Catsey Wd BUSH WD23 ... 163 L6
Catterick Wy BORE WD6 ... 151 L9
Cattlegate Rd ENC/FH EN2 ... 154 E1
Cattle Cl BAR EN5 ... 166 C3
Cattley Cl BAR EN5 ... 166 C3
Cattlins Cl CHESW EN7 ... 141 M8
Cattsdell HHNE HP2 ... 117 P6
Causeway Cl POTB/CUF EN6 ... 153 N4
The Causeway BSF CM23 ... 74 A3
STVG SG1 ... 40 D8
BUNT SG9 ... 66 C6
POTB/CUF EN6 ... 153 M1
ROY SG8 ... 21 J3
SAFWS SG11 ... 31 N6
STDN SG11 ... 53 N6
Cautherly La WARE SG12 ... 108 E2
Cavalier Cl LTNE LU2 ... 48 B9
Cavalier Ct BERK HP4 ... 115 P7
Cavan Dr STALW/RED AL3 ... 79 H7
Cavan Pl PIN HA5 ... 171 P5
Cavan Rd STALW/RED AL3 ... 101 H6
Cavell Cl BSF CM23 ... 74 C4
Cavell Rd CHESW EN7 ... 141 N6
Cavell Wk STVG SG2 ... 67 P3
Cavendish Cl AMS HP6 ... 145 N9
RAYLNE/WEN HP22 ... 112 C5
Cavendish Ct
RKW/CH/CXG WD3 * ... 161 P4
Cavendish Crs BORE WD6 ... 164 C3
Cavendish Dr EDGW HA8 ... 173 M3
Cavendish Rd BAR EN5 ... 166 A2
CSHM HP5 ... 145 J2
LTNN/LIM LU3 ... 62 C4
STALW/RED AL3 ... 79 H7
STAL AL1 ... 120 D7
STVG SG1 ... 50 D9
Cavendish Wy HAT AL10 ... 122 C6
Cawkell Ct STSD CM24 ... 58 E4
Cawley Hatch
HLWW/ROY CM19 ... 128 C3
Caxton Ga STVG SG1 * ... 66 E2
Caxton Hi HERT/BAY SG13 ... 107 M6
Caxton Pl STVG SG1 ... 66 E2
Caxton Rd HOD EN11 ... 126 C1
Caxton Wy STVG SG1 ... 66 E2
WATW WD18 ... 161 P6
Cecil Cl BSF CM23 ... 74 E3
Cecil Ct BAR EN5 ... 166 B2
HLWS CM18 ... 128 F6
Cecil Crs HAT AL10 ... 122 F4
Cecil Pk PIN HA5 ... 171 N1
Cecil Rd CHES/WCR EN8 ... 156 C1
ENC/FH EN2 ... 155 L5
HERT/BAY SG13 ... 125 L1
HOD EN11 ... 127 H3
KTN/HRWW/WS HA3 * ... 172 F2
POTB/CUF EN6 ... 153 P2
STAL AL1 ... 9 K4
WATN WD24 ... 167 M7
Cedar Av BAR EN5 ... 166 C4
ENC/FH EN2 ... 156 C7
Cedar Cl BORE WD6 ... 164 C2
BSF CM23 ... 91 N1
STALW/RED AL3 ... 121 J8
Cedar Crs ROY SG8 ... 30 F9
Cedars Av CHES/WCR EN8 ... 142 A3
CSHM HP5 ... 145 J9
Cedar Gn HOD EN11 ... 126 F6
Cedar Gv AMSS HP7 ... 145 J9
Cedar Lawn Av BAR EN5 ... 166 C4
Cedar Pk BSF CM23 ... 91 N1
Cedar Park Rd ENC/FH EN2 ... 155 K8
Cedar Rdg AMS HP6 ... 144 D4
Cedar Rd STHGT/OAK N14 ... 167 H6
ENC/FH EN2 ... 155 J8
HAT AL10 ... 122 D7
OXHEY WD19 ... 162 E5
The Cedars BERK HP4 ... 116 B2
HHW HP1 ... 117 H9
HARP AL5 * ... 102 A3
RAYLNE/WEN HP22 ... 112 B6
Cedar Wy BERK HP4 ... 116 B2
Cedar Wood Dr GSTN SG2 ... 149 J5
Cedarwood Dr
STALE/WH AL4 ... 121 J8
Ceders Dell HTCHE/RSTV SG4 ... 49 L1
Celandine Dr LTNN/LIM LU3 ... 46 B7
Celandine Rd
STHGT/OAK N14 ... 167 N4
Cell Barnes Cl STAL AL1 ... 136 G1
Cell Barnes La STAL AL1 ... 136 G2
Cemetery Hl HHW HP1 ... 4 C3
Cemetery Rd BSF CM23 ... 74 A3
LTN LU1 ... 62 C5
RAYLNE/WEN HP22 ... 76 C3
Cemmaes Court Rd HHW HP1 * ... 5 F3
Cemmaes Meadow HHW HP1 ... 5 F3
Centenary Rd ENC/FH EN2 ... 156 C6
Centenary Pk LTNN/LIM LU3 ... 46 C6
Centenary Wk LOU IG10 ... 157 P9
Centennial Av BORE WD6 ... 164 D6
Centennial Pk BORE WD6 * ... 164 D6
Central Av CHES/WCR EN8 ... 156 C5

DUN/WHIP LU6 ... 78 B5
Central Dr STAL AL1 ... 121 H7
WGCE AL7 ... 105 J4
Central Pde HRW HA1 ... 172 F9
Central Rd HLW CM20 ... 111 K8
Central Wy NTHWD HA6 ... 170 C4
Centre Wy WAB EN9 ... 157 P2
Centro HHNE HP2 ... 118 D6
Century Cl STALW/RED AL3 ... 8 D1
Century Ct WATW WD18 * ... 161 N6
Century Pk WAT WD17 * ... 13 H7
Century Rd HOD EN11 ... 126 G2
WARE SG12 ... 108 C2
Cervantes Ct NTHWD HA6 * ... 171 H4
Cestreham Crs CSHM HP5 ... 131 J8
Chace Av POTB/CUF EN6 ... 153 N2
The Chace STVG SG2 ... 67 J5
Chad La STALW/RED AL3 ... 100 B3
Chadwell WARE SG12 ... 108 B4
Chadwell Av CHES/WCR EN8 ... 142 B7
Chadwell Cl LTNE LU2 ... 48 B9
Chadwell Ri WARE SG12 ... 108 B4
Chadwell Rd STVG SG1 ... 66 E2
Chadwick Cl DUN/WHIP LU6 ... 60 D5
Chaffinches Gn
HHS/BOV HP3 ... 134 B3
Chaffinch La WATW WD18 ... 162 B2
Chagny Cl LWTH SG6 ... 36 B2
Chalk Wk BUNT SG9 * ... 53 K2
HERT/BAY SG13 ... 140 D1
HERT/WAT SG14 ... 68 E7
ROY SG8 ... 86 B9
Chalet Cl BERK HP4 ... 115 L7
Chalfont Av AMS HP6 ... 146 A9
Chalfont Cl HHNE HP2 ... 118 C3
Chalfont La
RKW/CH/CXG WD3 ... 159 P4
RKW/CH/CXG WD3 ... 168 C4
Chalfont Pl STAL AL1 * ... 9 G3
Chalfont Rd CSTG HP8 ... 168 C3
Chalfont Station Rd
AMSS HP7 ... 159 J1
Chalfont Wk PIN HA5 * ... 171 L6
Chalfont Wy LTNE LU2 ... 63 K4
Chalgrave Rd
DUN/HR/TOD LU5 ... 44 B4
Chalgrove WGCE AL7 ... 105 N5
Chalk Acres
DUN/HR/TOD LU5 ... 105 L5
Chalk Cl WGCE AL7 ... 105 L5
Chalkdell Flds STALE/WH AL4 ... 5 H1
Chalkdown LTNE LU2 ... 48 E8
Chalk Fld LWTH SG6 ... 36 F5
Chalk Hl CSHM HP5 ... 130 G8
OXHEY WD19 ... 162 G5
Chalk Hills BLDK SG7 ... 37 J3
Chalk La EBAR EN4 ... 167 K2
Chalks Av SBW CM21 ... 111 N1
Chalky La ROY SG8 ... 22 G8
Challney Cl LTNW/LEA LU4 ... 129 F9
Chalton Hts LTNW/LEA LU4 ... 44 G6
Chalton Rd LTNW/LEA LU4 ... 61 M1
Chamberlain Cl HLWE CM17 ... 129 K1
Chamberlaines HARP AL5 ... 81 H8
Chamberlain Pl LTNN/LIM LU3 ... 46 B8
Chamberlain Wy PIN HA5 ... 171 K7
Chambersbury La
HHS/BOV HP3 ... 134 B4
Chambers Ga STVG SG1 * ... 50 D8
Chambers Gv WGCE AL7 ... 105 H9
Chambers La HTCH/STOT SG5 ... 35 K4
Chambers' St
HERT/WAT SG14 ... 107 K6
Champions Cl BORE WD6 ... 151 N7
Champions Wd HOD EN11 ... 126 F2
Champneys OXHEY WD19 ... 162 C8
Chancellors ARL/CHE SG15 ... 24 C4
Chancellors Cl STVG SG1 ... 50 F6
Chancery Cl STALW/WH AL4 ... 121 J8
Chandlers Cft BSF CM23 ... 91 M1
Chandler's La
RKW/CH/CXG WD3 ... 147 P5
Chandlers Rd STALE/WH AL4 ... 121 H5
Chandlers Wy
HERT/WAT SG14 ... 107 H6
Chandos Cl BSF CM23 ... 91 H1
Chandos Cl AMS HP6 ... 145 J9
Chandos Ct STAN HA7 ... 173 H5
Chandos Crs EDGW HA8 ... 173 L3
Chandos Rd BORE WD6 ... 164 F1
HRW HA1 ... 172 C9
LTNW/LEA LU4 ... 61 K3
Chanfield Cl LTNN/LEA LU4 ... 61 J3
Chantry Cl BAR EN5 ... 165 M5
ENC/FH EN2 ... 155 K8
KGLGY WD4 ... 173 M9
MLHL NW7 ... 165 M5
Chantry La HAT AL10 ... 122 C7
LCOL/BKTW AL2 ... 137 J5
STVG SG1 ... 50 C8
Chantry Pl
KTN/HRWW/WS HA3 ... 172 B5
The Chantry HLW CM20 ... 129 K1
KTN/HRWW/WS HA3 ... 172 B5
Chaomans LWTH SG6 ... 36 F5
Chapel Cl BERK HP4 ... 116 B2
DUN/HR/TOD LU5 ... 44 C1
WGCE AL7 ... 148 C4
Chapel Cots HHNE HP2 ... 2 A7
STAL AL1 ... 136 C2
Chapel Crofts BERK HP4 ... 115 K5
Chapel Dr ARL/CHE SG15 ... 24 C5
RAYLNE/WEN HP22 ... 94 F7
Chapel End BUNT SG9 ... 40 B4
CFSP/GDCR SL9 ... 168 B6
Chapel End La HHNE HP2 ... 126 F6
Chapel Flds HLWE CM17 ... 129 M5
TRING HP23 ... 95 K4

Chapelfields WARE SG12 ... 109 J7
Chapel Hl STSD CM24 ... 58 E4
Chapel La HERT/WAT SG14 ... 124 C1
HLWE CM17 ... 129 M5
PIN HA5 ... 171 M7
RAYLNE/WEN HP22 ... 112 C8
STDN SG11 ... 72 D6
TRING HP23 ... 77 J9
Chapel Pl HTCH/STOT SG5 ... 25 K4
STAL AL1 * ... 136 C2
Chapel Rd HTCHE/RSTV SG4 ... 64 D5
STALW/RED AL3 ... 100 C2
Chapel Rw DEN/HRF UB9 ... 169 N5
HTCH/STOT SG5 * ... 35 L8
Chapel St BERK HP4 ... 115 P7
BGSW SG18 ... 14 C6
BLDK SG7 ... 16 F4
HHNE HP2 ... 117 N7
LTN LU1 ... 6 D6
TRING HP23 ... 95 N9
Chapel Viad LTN LU1 ... 6 D5
Chapel Wy ABLGY WD5 ... 134 G6
Chapman Crs
KTN/HRWW/WS HA3 ... 173 L9
Chapman Rd STVG SG1 ... 50 E6
Chapmans Crs CSHM HP5 ... 130 F8
Chapmans End STDN SG11 ... 71 J3
The Chapmans
HTCH/STOT SG5 * ... 49 K1
Chapmans Yd WAT WD17 ... 13 H5
Chappell Ct WARE SG12 ... 87 M6
Chappel Meadow TRING HP23 ... 96 A6
Chapter House Rd
LTNW/LEA LU4 ... 61 K4
Chard Dr LTNN/LIM LU3 ... 46 C6
Chardia Ter CHES/WCR EN8 * ... 142 C9
Charding Crs ROY SG8 ... 20 B3
Chardins Cl HHW HP1 ... 117 J7
Charkham Ms BRKMPK AL9 ... 138 F3
Charlbury Av STAN HA7 ... 173 K2
Charles St BERK HP4 ... 115 N7
HHW HP1 ... 4 C4
LTNE LU2 ... 7 G1
TRING HP23 ... 95 P9
Charlesworth Cl
HHS/BOV HP3 ... 5 F6
Charlock Wy WATW WD18 ... 162 B5
Charlotte Cl STALE/WH AL4 ... 121 K8
Charlton Cl HOD EN11 ... 126 F5
Charlton Mead La HOD EN11 ... 127 H6
Charlton Rd HTCH/STOT SG5 ... 49 J2
KTN/HRWW/WS HA3 ... 173 K8
Charlton Wy HOD EN11 ... 126 F6
Charlwood Cl
KTN/HRWW/WS HA3 ... 172 E3
Charlwood Rd LTNW/LEA LU4 ... 61 L5
Charmbury Ri LTNE LU2 ... 63 H2
Charmian Av STAN HA7 ... 173 K7
Charmouth Ct STAL AL1 ... 120 F5
Charmouth Rd STAL AL1 ... 120 F6
Charndon Cl LTNN/LIM LU3 ... 46 C6
Charnwood Pl
TRDG/WHET N20 ... 166 G9
Charnwood Rd EN EN1 ... 156 A6
Charsley Cl AMS HP6 ... 145 P9
Charter Pl WAT WD17 ... 13 F3
Charters Cross HLWS CM18 ... 128 G6
Charter Wy STHGT/OAK N14 ... 167 N5
Chartley Av STAN HA7 ... 172 F3
Chartridge OXHEY WD19 * ... 162 F8
Chartridge Cl BAR EN5 ... 165 N4
BUSH WD23 ... 163 L5
Chartridge Grange Dr
CSHM HP5 ... 130 C6
Chartridge La CSHM HP5 ... 130 C7
Chartridge Wy HHNE HP2 ... 118 D8
Chartwell Cl WAB EN9 ... 157 K3
Chartwell Dr LTNE LU2 ... 62 F3
Chartwell Rd NTHWD HA6 ... 171 H3
Charwood Cl RAD WD7 ... 151 K3
Chasden Rd HHW HP1 ... 117 J5
Chase Cl AMSS HP7 ... 158 A4
ARL/CHE SG15 ... 24 E1
Chase Hill Rd ARL/CHE SG15 ... 24 E2
Chase Side STHGT/OAK N14 ... 167 L5
Chaseside Cl LBUZ LU7 ... 77 P6
Chase Side Crs ENC/FH EN2 ... 155 L9
Chase St LTN LU1 ... 62 F9
The Chase BSF CM23 ... 74 A4
CHESW EN7 ... 141 J7
CSHM HP5 ... 130 G8
EDGW HA8 ... 173 P5
HERT/BAY SG13 ... 107 N7
HHNE HP2 ... 5 H3
HLWE CM17 ... 129 M2
PIN HA5 ... 171 P8
RAD WD7 ... 150 E5
WARE SG12 ... 108 F6
WLYN AL6 ... 85 J6
Chase Wy STHGT/OAK N14 ... 167 M7
Chaseways SBW CM21 ... 111 L4
Chasten Hl LWTH SG6 ... 36 A1
Chatsworth Cl BORE WD6 ... 164 G2
BSF CM23 ... 73 M7
Chatsworth Ct STVGE SG2 ... 67 J5
Chatsworth Rd
LTNW/LEA LU4 ... 62 C5
Chatteris Cl LTNW/LEA LU4 ... 61 N2
Chatterton LWTH SG6 ... 36 E3
Chatton Cl LTNE LU2 ... 63 M4
Chaucer Cl BERK HP4 ... 115 L6
Chaucer Rd LTNN/LIM LU3 ... 62 D4
ROY SG8 ... 20 B2
Chaucer Wk HHNE HP2 ... 118 C2
Chaucer Wy HOD EN11 ... 126 F1
HTCHE/RSTV SG4 ... 35 P9
Chaulden House Gdns
HHW HP1 ... 133 J1
Chaulden La HHW HP1 ... 133 H1
Chaulden Ter HHW HP1 ... 117 J9
Chaul End Rd LTNW/LEA LU4 ... 61 L5
Chauncy Av POTB/CUF EN6 ... 153 M3
Chauncy Cl WARE SG12 ... 108 B1
Chauncy Gdns BLDK SG7 ... 26 D8
Chauncy Rd STVG SG1 ... 10 E2
Chaworth Gn LTNW/LEA LU4 ... 61 M1
Cheapside LTN LU1 ... 7 F4
Cheapside Sq LTN LU1 ... 6 E4
Chedburgh WGCE AL7 ... 105 N5
Cheddington La TRING HP23 ... 77 K8
Cheffins Rd HOD EN11 ... 126 E2
Chells La STVGE SG2 ... 51 M7
Chells Wy STVGE SG2 ... 51 L8
Chelmsford Rd
HERT/WAT SG14 ... 107 H7
RBSF CM22 ... 93 J7
STHGT/OAK N14 ... 167 N6
Chelsea Cl EDGW HA8 ... 173 N6
Chelsea Flds HOD EN11 ... 126 G1
Chelsea Gdns
DUN/HR/TOD LU5 ... 60 G1
HLWE CM17 ... 129 P4
Chelsing Ri HHNE HP2 ... 118 D9
Chelsworth Cl LTNE LU2 ... 63 L5
Cheltenham Pl
KTN/HRWW/WS HA3 ... 173 L8
Chelveston WGCE AL7 ... 105 N5
Chelwood Av HAT AL10 ... 122 D4
Chelwood Cl NTHWD HA6 ... 170 E4
Chenduit Wy STAN HA7 ... 172 F2
Chene Dr STALW/RED AL3 ... 120 C6
Cheney Cl DUN/HR/TOD LU5 ... 44 C1
Cheney Rd LTNW/LEA LU4 ... 61 M1
Cheney St PIN HA5 ... 171 L8
Chenies Av AMS HP6 ... 146 A9
Chenies Ct HHNE HP2 ... 118 C3
Chenies Pde AMSS HP7 * ... 159 J1
Chenies Rd
RKW/CH/CXG WD3 ... 160 B1
Chenies Wy WATW WD18 ... 162 A6
Chennells HAT AL10 ... 122 C7
Chennells Cl HTCHE/RSTV SG4 ... 35 N6
The Chennies HARP AL5 * ... 102 B5
Chepstow Cl STVG SG1 ... 51 L7
Chequer Ct LTN LU1 ... 7 G6
Chequer La STALW/RED AL3 ... 101 H8
Chequers BRKMPK AL9 ... 122 G3
BSF CM23 ... 73 M6
WGCE AL7 ... 104 G8
Chequers Bridge Rd
STVG SG1 ... 10 A3
Chequers Cl BUNT SG9 ... 40 C8
HTCH/STOT SG5 ... 25 K3
STDN SG11 ... 71 J2
Chequersfield WGCE AL7 ... 104 G9
Chequers Hl STALW/RED AL3 ... 100 D2
Chequers La GSTN WD25 ... 135 J9
HTCHE/RSTV SG4 ... 49 J8
The Chequers PIN HA5 * ... 171 M7
Chequer St LTN LU1 ... 7 F6
STAL AL1 ... 8 E4
Cheriton Cl EBAR EN4 ... 167 K2
STALE/WH AL4 ... 121 J4
Cherry Acre CFSP/GDCR SL9 ... 168 B1
Cherry Bank HHNE HP2 * ... 117 N6
Cherry Blossom Cl
HLWE CM17 ... 111 M8
Cherry Cl KNEB SG3 ... 85 J1
Cherry Ct PIN HA5 ... 171 M5
Cherry Cft RKW/CH/CXG WD3 ... 161 L5
WGCW AL8 ... 104 G2
Cherry Croft Gdns PIN HA5 * ... 171 P4
Cherrydale WATW WD18 ... 12 A5
Cherry Dr ROY SG8 ... 20 D3
Cherry Gdns BSF CM23 ... 74 B2
TRING HP23 * ... 95 N9
Cherry Green La BUNT SG9 ... 54 D4
Cherry Hl BAR EN5 ... 166 F5
KTN/HRWW/WS HA3 ... 172 E3
LCOL/BKTW AL2 ... 135 P4
RKW/CH/CXG WD3 ... 160 F2
Cherry Hills OXHEY WD19 ... 171 N2
Cherry Hollow ABLGY WD5 ... 148 G1
Cherry La AMSS HP7 ... 158 A1
Cherry Orch AMS HP6 ... 145 K7
HHW HP1 ... 117 J6
Cherry Orchard La BUNT SG9 ... 40 F5
Cherry Ri CSTG HP8 ... 159 K8
Cherry Rd PEND EN3 ... 156 B8
Cherry Tree Av
LCOL/BKTW AL2 ... 137 J5
Cherry Tree Cl LTNE LU2 ... 63 H5
ROY SG8 ... 19 H1
Cherry Tree Dr STVG SG1 * ... 66 G3
Cherry Tree Gn
HERT/WAT SG14 ... 106 G4
Cherrytree La
CFSP/GDCR SL9 ... 168 B6
HHNE HP2 ... 118 D3
Cherry Tree La HHNE HP2 ... 118 E5
RKW/CH/CXG WD3 ... 160 A7
STALE/WH AL4 ... 102 F2
TRING HP23 ... 113 P8
Cherry Tree Ri STVGE SG2 ... 52 C6
Cherry Tree Rd HOD EN11 ... 126 F4
WATN WD24 ... 149 J6
Cherry Trees Dr STVGE SG2 ... 51 L8
Cherry Tree Wk CSHM HP5 ... 131 J8
Cherry Tree Wy STAN HA7 ... 173 H3
Cherry Wk
RKW/CH/CXG WD3 ... 160 G1
Cherry Wy HAT AL10 ... 122 D9
Chertsey Cl LTNE LU2 ... 63 K6
Chertsey Ri STVGE SG2 ... 67 M2
Cherwell Cl
RKW/CH/CXG WD3 ... 161 L4
Cherwell Dr STVG SG1 ... 51 K4
Chesfield Cl BSF CM23 ... 74 A5
Chesford Rd LTNE LU2 ... 63 K3
Chesham La CFSP/GDCR SL9 ... 159 L9
Chesham Rd CSHM HP5 ... 130 B1
GTMIS/PWD HP16 ... 144 C2
TRING HP23 ... 114 C3
Chesham Wy WATW WD18 ... 162 A5
Cheshire Dr GSTN WD25 ... 148 G4
Cheshunt Wash
CHES/WCR EN8 ... 142 D6
Cheslyn Cl LTNE LU2 ... 63 M4
Chessbury Rd CSHM HP5 ... 144 F2
Chess Cl CSHM HP5 ... 146 A6
RKW/CH/CXG WD3 ... 161 H3
Chessfield Pk AMS HP6 ... 146 B9
Chess Hl RKW/CH/CXG WD3 ... 161 H3
Chessington Ct PIN HA5 ... 171 P8
Chess La RKW/CH/CXG WD3 ... 161 H3
Chessmount Ri CSHM HP5 ... 145 J3
Chess Vale Ri
RKW/CH/CXG WD3 ... 161 K5
Chess Valley Wk CSHM HP5 ... 145 L5
Chess Wy RKW/CH/CXG WD3 ... 160 E2
Chesswood Ct
RKW/CH/CXG WD3 * ... 161 H7
Chesswood Wy PIN HA5 ... 171 M6
Chester Av LTNW/LEA LU4 ... 61 P3
Chester Cl LTNW/LEA LU4 ... 62 A4
Chesterfield Rd BAR EN5 ... 166 B4
PEND EN3 ... 156 D7
Chester Gibbons Gn
LCOL/BKTW AL2 ... 137 J5
Chester Pl NTHWD HA6 * ... 170 G4
Chester Rd BORE WD6 ... 165 J2
NTHWD HA6 ... 171 H4
STVG SG1 ... 51 K6
WATW WD18 ... 12 C6
Chesterton Av HARP AL5 ... 102 B3
Chesterton Cl CSHM HP5 ... 130 G8
Chestnut Av CSHM HP5 ... 131 J8
EDGW HA8 ... 173 L3
LTNN/LIM LU3 ... 45 L6
NTHWD HA6 ... 171 H6
RAYLNE/WEN HP22 ... 112 D3
RKW/CH/CXG WD3 ... 160 E4
WARE SG12 ... 108 E1
Chestnut Cl AMS HP6 ... 145 J7
BERK HP4 ... 116 E5
CFSP/GDCR SL9 ... 168 D5
RAYLNE/WEN HP22 ... 94 G7
STHGT/OAK N14 ... 167 N4
WARE SG12 ... 110 A3
Chestnut Cots
TRDG/WHET N20 * ... 166 C7
Chestnut Ct HTCH/STOT SG5 ... 35 J8
Chestnut Dr BERK HP4 ... 116 A8
KTN/HRWW/WS HA3 ... 172 F4
RBSF CM22 ... 92 G6
STAL AL1 ... 120 G6
Chestnut End
RAYLNE/WEN HP22 ... 112 D2
Chestnut Gv EBAR EN4 ... 167 K4
HOD EN11 ... 126 G1
Chestnut La AMS HP6 ... 145 K7
HLW CM20 ... 2 B4
TRDG/WHET N20 ... 166 C7
Chestnut Ri BUSH WD23 ... 163 K6
Chestnut Rd PEND EN3 ... 156 D6
The Chestnuts
HERT/BAY SG13 ... 107 L7
HHS/BOV HP3 ... 133 J3
HTCHE/RSTV SG4 ... 84 C3
PIN HA5 * ... 171 P4
Chestnut Wk
CFSP/GDCR SL9 * ... 168 C4
HTCHE/RSTV SG4 ... 49 M3
WATN WD24 ... 149 H7
WLYN AL6 ... 85 J5
Chetwynd Av EBAR EN4 ... 167 K7
Chevalier Cl STAN HA7 ... 164 D9
The Cheveralls
DUN/WHIP LU6 ... 60 F8
Cheverells Cl STALW/RED AL3 ... 79 N8
Cheviot Cl BUSH WD23 ... 163 L5
Cheviot Rd LTNN/LIM LU3 ... 45 N8
Cheviots HAT AL10 ... 122 D9
HHNE HP2 ... 118 A5
Cheviot Wy STVG SG1 ... 51 K3
Cheyne Cl DUN/WHIP LU6 ... 60 C3
WARE SG12 ... 108 C1
Cheyne Ct BUSH WD23 * ... 162 G3
Cheyne Wk CSHM HP5 ... 145 J1
Cheyney Cl ROY SG8 ... 18 C1
Cheyneys Av EDGW HA8 ... 173 K3
Cheyney St ROY SG8 ... 15 N9
Chicheley Rd
KTN/HRWW/WS HA3 ... 172 C4
Chichester Cl
DUN/HR/TOD LU5 ... 60 G7
Chichester Ct STAN HA7 ... 173 L7
Chichester Wy GSTN WD25 ... 149 M3
Chicken La LCOL/BKTW AL2 * ... 137 J6
Chiddingfold
NFNCH/WDSPK N12 ... 166 E9
Chilcote La AMSS HP7 ... 145 N9
Chilcott Rd WATN WD24 ... 148 F6
Chilcourt ROY SG8 ... 20 B4
Childs Av DEN/HRF UB9 ... 169 N6
Childwick Ct HHS/BOV HP3 ... 134 C2
Childwick Wy LWTH SG6 ... 25 J9
Chilham Cl HHNE HP2 ... 5 H4
Chiltern Av AMS HP6 ... 145 J8
BUSH WD23 ... 163 L5
Chiltern Cl BERK HP4 ... 115 M6
BORE WD6 ... 164 F1
BUSH WD23 ... 163 K5
CHESW EN7 ... 141 J6
WARE SG12 ... 108 C1
Chiltern Dr
RKW/CH/CXG WD3 ... 160 D6
Chiltern Est WATN WD24 * ... 149 K9
Chiltern Gdns LTNW/LEA LU4 ... 62 A3
Chiltern Hts AMSS HP7 ... 145 M9
Chiltern Hl CFSP/GDCR SL9 ... 168 C5
Chiltern Link CSHM HP5 ... 130 B9
Chiltern Pde AMS HP6 ... 145 H7
Chiltern Pk DUN/HR/TOD LU5 ... 60 G4
Chiltern Park Av BERK HP4 ... 115 M5
Chiltern Ri LTN LU1 ... 6 C7
Chiltern Rd
AMP/FLIT/BLC MK45 ... 32 D5
AMS HP6 ... 144 G4
BLDK SG7 ... 37 J2
DUN/WHIP LU6 ... 60 D6
HTCHE/RSTV SG4 ... 35 M9
PIN HA5 ... 171 L9
RAYLNE/WEN HP22 ... 76 B2
RAYLNE/WEN HP22 ... 112 B6
STALE/WH AL4 ... 121 H3
Chilterns HAT AL10 ... 122 D9
HHNE HP2 ... 117 P5
The Chilterns DUN/WHIP LU6 ... 79 J5
HTCHE/RSTV SG4 ... 49 M1
STVG SG1 ... 51 L4
Chiltern Vw LWTH SG6 ... 36 A3
Chiltern Wy
RAYLNE/WEN HP22 ... 112 G1
TRING HP23 ... 96 B7
Chilton Gn WGCE AL7 ... 105 M6
Chilton Rd CSHM HP5 ... 131 H8
EDGW HA8 ... 173 N3
Chilvers Bank BLDK SG7 ... 37 H1
Chilwell Gdns OXHEY WD19 ... 171 L1
Chilworth Ga BROX EN10 ... 142 E1
Chime Sq STALW/RED AL3 ... 9 F1
Chindit Cl BROX EN10 ... 126 C8
Chinnery Cl EN EN1 ... 155 N8
Chinnery Hl BSF CM23 ... 74 A5
Chipmunk Cha HAT AL10 ... 122 A4
Chippenham Cl PIN HA5 * ... 171 H8
Chipperfield Rd
HHS/BOV HP3 ... 132 E7
Chipping Cl BAR EN5 ... 166 C2
Chippingfield HLWE CM17 ... 111 M9
Chipstead CFSP/GDCR SL9 ... 168 A5
Chishill Rd ROY SG8 ... 21 M8
Chishill St ROY SG8 ... 22 C7
Chiswell Ct WATN WD24 ... 149 K8
Chiswell Green La
LCOL/BKTW AL2 ... 135 L4
Chittenden Cl HOD EN11 ... 126 G2
Chivenor Pl STALE/WH AL4 ... 137 H1
Chobham St LTN LU1 ... 7 G6
Chobham Wk LTN LU1 ... 7 F6
Cholesbury La CSHM HP5 ... 130 E1
TRING HP23 ... 113 P9
Chorleywood Bottom
RKW/CH/CXG WD3 ... 160 B4
Chorleywood Cl
RKW/CH/CXG WD3 ... 161 H6
Chorleywood House Dr
RKW/CH/CXG WD3 ... 160 C2
Chorleywood Rd
RKW/CH/CXG WD3 ... 160 F4
Chouler Gdns STVG SG1 ... 50 G5
The Chowns HARP AL5 ... 101 P7
Christchurch Av
KTN/HRWW/WS HA3 ... 172 F8
Christchurch Cl
STALW/RED AL3 ... 8 D3
Christchurch Crs RAD WD7 ... 150 F6
Christchurch Gdns
KTN/HRWW/WS HA3 ... 172 G8
Christ Church La BAR EN5 ... 166 C1
Christchurch Ldg EBAR EN4 * ... 167 K3
Christchurch Rd HHNE HP2 ... 117 N7
TRING HP23 ... 95 N8
Christie Cl BROX EN10 ... 126 E9
Christie Ct WATW WD18 ... 12 C6
Christie Rd STVGE SG2 ... 67 M1
WAB EN9 ... 156 G5
Christopher Ct WARE SG12 * ... 108 C3
Christopher Pl
STALW/RED AL3 ... 8 E4
Christy's Yd BLDK SG7 ... 16 G4
Churchbury La EN EN1 ... 155 M9
Church Cl DUN/HR/TOD LU5 ... 60 F6
DUN/WHIP LU6 ... 78 E9
HTCHE/RSTV SG4 ... 84 C3
NTHWD HA6 ... 171 H4
POTB/CUF EN6 ... 140 F8
RAD WD7 ... 150 F6
ROY SG8 ... 29 L5
TRDG/WHET N20 ... 167 J9
Church Ct BROX EN10 * ... 126 F8
Church Crs STALW/RED AL3 ... 8 D2
TRDG/WHET N20 ... 167 J9
Church Cft STALE/WH AL4 ... 137 H1
Church Dr BSF CM23 ... 43 L8
Church End ARL/CHE SG15 ... 24 E2
DUN/HR/TOD LU5 ... 60 D1
DUN/WHIP LU6 ... 78 G2
HLWW/ROY CM19 ... 128 D5
ROY SG8 ... 21 M9
STALE/WH AL4 ... 121 H1
STALW/RED AL3 ... 79 N7
STALW/RED AL3 ... 101 H8
STDN SG11 ... 55 L8
STVGE SG2 ... 52 D5
Church Farm EBAR EN4 * ... 167 K6
Church Farm La ROY SG8 ... 18 C1
TRING HP23 ... 95 N1
Church Farm Wy GSTN WD25 ... 150 A8
Churchfield HARP AL5 ... 102 B4
HLW CM20 ... 129 K1
ROY SG8 ... 21 M9
Church Fld WARE SG12 ... 108 A1
Churchfield Cl
RYLN/HDSTN HA2 ... 172 C8
Church Field Pth
CHES/WCR EN8 ... 142 B8
Churchfield Rd
CFSP/GDCR SL9 ... 168 B5
DUN/HR/TOD LU5 ... 60 E1
WLYN AL6 ... 105 M3
Churchfields BROX EN10 ... 126 F8
HERT/BAY SG13 ... 107 L7
Church Flds RAD WD7 * ... 150 F6
Churchfields STDN SG11 ... 71 K4
STSD CM24 ... 58 G5
Churchfields La BROX EN10 ... 126 F8
Churchgate CHES/WCR EN8 ... 142 A9
Churchgate Rd
CHES/WCR EN8 ... 142 A8
Churchgate St HLWE CM17 ... 111 P8
Church Gn HARP AL5 ... 101 P3
Church Green Ms HARP AL5 * ... 101 P3
Church Green Rw HARP AL5 * ... 101 P3
Church Gv AMS HP6 ... 146 B9
Church Hl ABLGY WD5 ... 134 G5
DEN/HRF UB9 ... 169 N8
HERT/BAY SG13 ... 108 A8
LBUZ LU7 ... 77 N5
Church Hill Rd EBAR EN4 ... 167 J5
Churchill Cl LTNN/LIM LU3 ... 46 A2
Churchill Rd
AMP/FLIT/BLC MK45 ... 32 D5
DUN/WHIP LU6 ... 60 G9
EDGW HA8 ... 173 M3
LTNW/LEA LU4 ... 62 B5
STAL AL1 ... 120 F6
Church La ARL/CHE SG15 ... 24 E1
BERK HP4 ... 115 P7
BLDK SG7 ... 17 N6
BRKMPK AL9 ... 122 F6
BROX EN10 ... 142 A1
BSF CM23 ... 91 N3
CFSP/GDCR SL9 ... 168 B5
CHES/WCR EN8 ... 142 B8
GSTN WD25 ... 150 A8
HERT/WAT SG14 ... 87 H7
HHS/BOV HP3 ... 132 E6
HTCHE/RSTV SG4 ... 37 N7
HTCHE/RSTV SG4 ... 49 J9
HTCHE/RSTV SG4 ... 50 F3
HTCHE/RSTV SG4 ... 83 J3
KGLGY WD4 ... 134 B9
KTN/HRWW/WS HA3 ... 172 F5
LBUZ LU7 ... 77 P6
LOU IG10 ... 157 N9
LWTH SG6 ... 25 N8
MHAD SG10 ... 90 C2
PIN HA5 ... 171 N7
POTB/CUF EN6 ... 140 A9
RAYLNE/WEN HP22 ... 112 A2
RBSF CM22 ... 59 M3
RBSF CM22 ... 92 E9
RKW/CH/CXG WD3 ... 147 K7
RKW/CH/CXG WD3 ... 160 E7
ROY SG8 ... 15 L6
ROY SG8 ... 28 F2
STALE/WH AL4 ... 137 N1
STVG SG1 ... 10 B1
TRING HP23 ... 95 N3
TRING HP23 ... 113 N4
WARE SG12 ... 69 N6
Church Langley Wy
HLWE CM17 ... 129 M3
Church Leys HLWS CM18 ... 129 J4
Church Md DUN/WHIP LU6 ... 78 E9
HLWW/ROY CM19 ... 127 N2
Churchmead WAB EN9 * ... 143 H1
Churchmead Cl EBAR EN4 ... 167 J5
Church Meadow HHW HP1 ... 98 G9
Church Pas BAR EN5 * ... 166 D2
Church Pth HTCHE/RSTV SG4 ... 50 C4
LBUZ LU7 ... 77 P4
Church Pl WLYN AL6 ... 84 F8
Church Rd
AMP/FLIT/BLC MK45 ... 32 D6
BERK HP4 ... 97 P4
DEN/HRF UB9 ... 169 N7
DUN/WHIP LU6 ... 78 E9
HERT/BAY SG13 ... 124 D7
HERT/WAT SG14 ... 107 J5
HHS/BOV HP3 * ... 134 D1
HLWE CM17 ... 129 M6
HTCH/STOT SG5 ... 25 K3
HTCHE/RSTV SG4 ... 64 E3
LBUZ LU7 ... 96 D2
LTN LU1 ... 80 D3
LTNN/LIM LU3 ... 45 L4
NTHWD HA6 ... 171 H4
POTB/CUF EN6 ... 139 L9
RBSF CM22 ... 74 D8
ROY SG8 ... 22 G7
STALW/RED AL3 ... 100 C2
STAN HA7 ... 173 H2
STSD CM24 ... 58 G6
WAT WD17 ... 149 H9
WGCW AL8 ... 104 F6
Church Sq DUN/HR/TOD LU5 ... 44 C1
Church St AMSS HP7 ... 158 B1
BGSW SG18 ... 14 C6
BLDK SG7 ... 26 A9
BRKMPK AL9 ... 122 F5
BRKMPK AL9 ... 123 P5
BSF CM23 ... 74 A3
BUNT SG9 ... 40 D8
CSHM HP5 ... 144 G1
DUN/HR/TOD LU5 ... 60 F6
HERT/WAT SG14 ... 107 L6
HHNE HP2 ... 117 N6
HHS/BOV HP3 ... 132 E6
LTN LU1 ... 7 F4
RAYLNE/WEN HP22 ... 76 C3
RKW/CH/CXG WD3 ... 161 J7
ROY SG8 ... 18 C1
SBW CM21 ... 111 P2
STALE/WH AL4 ... 103 J4
STALW/RED AL3 ... 9 F2
WAB EN9 ... 157 H3
WARE SG12 ... 108 C3
WATW WD18 ... 13 G4
WLYN AL6 ... 84 F8
Church Vw BROX EN10 ... 126 E8
RAYLNE/WEN HP22 ... 112 D2
STALE/WH AL4 * ... 103 J4
TRING HP23 ... 77 H9
Church Wk BUSH WD23 ... 163 J5
DUN/HR/TOD LU5 ... 60 E6
RAYLNE/WEN HP22 ... 112 A2
SBW CM21 ... 92 A7
Church Wy TRDG/WHET N20 ... 167 J9
Church Yd TRING HP23 ... 95 P8
The Chyne CFSP/GDCR SL9 ... 168 D9
Cicero Dr LTNN/LIM LU3 ... 46 B7
Cillocks Cl HOD EN11 ... 126 F4
Cinema Pde EDGW HA8 * ... 173 N3
The Circuits PIN HA5 ... 171 L8
City Pk WGCE AL7 * ... 105 K5
Claggy Rd HTCHE/RSTV SG4 ... 82 G3
Claire Ct NFNCH/WDSPK N12 ... 166 G9
Claire Gdns STAN HA7 ... 173 J2
Clamp Hl STAN HA7 ... 172 D1
Clapgate Rd BUSH WD23 ... 163 K5
Clare Cl BORE WD6 ... 164 F5
Clare Ct NTHWD HA6 ... 170 G2
Clare Crs BLDK SG7 ... 37 H2
Claremont CHESW EN7 ... 141 N8
LCOL/BKTW AL2 ... 149 P1
Claremont Av
KTN/HRWW/WS HA3 ... 173 L9
Claremont Crs
RKW/CH/CXG WD3 ... 161 N4
Claremont House
WATW WD18 * ... 161 P5
Claremont Rd EBAR EN4 ... 153 M8
KTN/HRWW/WS HA3 ... 172 E6
LTNW/LEA LU4 ... 62 C5
Clarence Cl BUSH WD23 ... 163 P6
EBAR EN4 ... 167 H4
Clarence Rd BERK HP4 ... 115 L7
HARP AL5 ... 101 P2
STAL AL1 ... 9 K3
STSD CM24 ... 58 F4
Clarenden Flds
RKW/CH/CXG WD3 ... 148 A8
Clarendon Ms BORE WD6 * ... 164 G2
Clarendon Rd BORE WD6 ... 164 G2
CHES/WCR EN8 ... 142 C8
HARP AL5 ... 102 A1
LTNE LU2 ... 6 D1

WAT WD17	**13**	F2
Clare Pk *AMSS* HP7	**158**	E1
Clarion Cl *HTCH/STOT* SG5	**48**	B5
Clarke Grn *GSTN* WD25	**149**	H5

Clarkes Pightle
AMP/FLIT/BLC MK45 *	**32**	D6
Clarke's Rd *HAT* AL10	**122**	E4
Clarke's Spring *TRING* HP23	**96**	E7
Clarke Wy *DUN/HR/TOD* LU5	**60**	C2
Clarke Wy *STVG* SG1	**51**	M4
Clarkfield *RKW/CH/CXG* WD3	**160**	E7
Clarkhill *HLWS* CM18	**129**	H6
Clark Rd *ROY* SG8	**20**	C3
Clarks Cl *WARE* SG12	**108**	C1
Clarks Md *BUSH* WD23	**163**	L6
Clatterbury La *SAFWS* CB11	**43**	N3
Claudian Pl *STALW/RED* AL3	**119**	P9
Claudius Cl *STAN* HA7	**164**	D9
Claverhambury Rd *WAB* EN9	**143**	L8
Claverley Gn *STAN* LU2	**63**	H4
Claverton Cl *HHS/BOV* HP3	**132**	D7
Clay Acre *CSHM* HP5	**131**	J9
Claybury *BUSH* WD23	**163**	K6
Claycroft *WGCE* AL7	**105**	L5
Claydon Cl *LTNW/LIM* LU3	**46**	D8
Claydon End *CFSP/GDCR* SL9	**148**	C7
Claydon La *CFSP/GDCR* SL9	**168**	C7
Clay End Rd *STVGE* SG2	**52**	G9

Clayfield Rd
RAYLNE/WEN HP22	**112**	D3
Claygate Av *HARP* AL5	**101**	M2
Clay Hall Rd *DUN/WHIP* LU6	**79**	J6
Clay Hl *ENC/FH* EN2	**155**	P8
Clay La *BUSH* WD23	**163**	N6

RAYLNE/WEN HP22	**117**	P4
Claymore *HHNE* HP2	**8**	B3
Claymore Dr *HTCH/STOT* SG5	**35**	L3
Claymore *STVG* SG1	**2**	E3
Claypit Hl *HERT/BAY* SG13	**59**	M6
WAB EN9	**157**	P6
Clayponds *BSF* CM23	**74**	B3
Clayton Dr *HHS/BOV* HP3	**134**	E1

Clayton Pde
CHES/WCR EN8 *	**142**	C9
Clayton Wk *AMSS* HP7	**146**	F9
Cleall Av *WAB* EN9	**157**	H4

The Cleavers
DUN/HR/TOD LU5	**44**	C2
The Cleave *HARP* AL5	**102**	C3
Clementine Wy *HHW* HP1	**4**	A5
Clement Rd *CHES/WCR* EN8	**142**	D6

Clements End Rd
HHW HP1	**99**	H2

Clements Rd
RKW/CH/CXG WD3	**160**	D5
Clements St *WARE* SG12	**108**	D3
Cleopatra Cl *STAN* HA7	**164**	D9
Cleveland End *LTNE* LU2	**63**	J4
Cleveland Crs *BORE* WD6	**165**	J4
Cleveland Rd *HHNE* HP2	**118**	C6
STALW/RED AL3	**79**	P8
STVG SG1	**51**	M4
Cleveland Wy *HHNE* HP2	**8**	C1
Cleviscroft *STVG* SG1	**11**	F6

Clewer Crs
KTN/HRWW/WS HA3	**172**	D5
Clifford Crs *LTNW/LEA* LU4	**61**	M1
Clifford Rd *BAR* EN5	**166**	F2

Clifton Av
KTN/HRWW/WS HA3	**173**	H6
Clifton Av *LTNE* LU2	**62**	D0
Clifton Hatch *HLWS* CM18	**129**	K6
Clifton La *AMS* HP6	**145**	H5
Clifton Rd *AMS* HP6	**144**	C5
DUN/WHIP LU6	**60**	D5
KTN/HRWW/WS HA3	**173**	M9
LTN LU1	**62**	C6
WATW WD18	**13**	F6
Clifton St *STAL* AL1	**9**	G2
Clifton Wy *BORE* WD6	**151**	M9
WARE SG12	**108**	C2
The Climb *RKW/CH/CXG* WD3	**160**	F5
Clinton Av *LTNE* LU2	**62**	D0
Clinton Cl *WAT* WD17	**12**	D3
Clipped Hedge *RBSF* CM22	**93**	H6
Clitheroe Gdns *OXHEY* WD19	**162**	F3
Clive Cl *POTB/CUF* EN6	**153**	J1
Clive Wy *WATN* WD24	**149**	K9

Clockhouse Ms
RKW/CH/CXG WD3 *	**160**	C2
Cloister Garth *BERK* HP4	**115**	P7
STAL AL1	**136**	D3
Cloister Lawns *LWTH* SG6	**36**	C4
Cloisters *HARP* AL5	**101**	L3
Cloisters Rd *LTNW/LEA* LU4	**61**	L5
LWTH SG6	**36**	C1

The Cloisters
DUN/HR/TOD LU5 *	**60**	F6
HHS/BOV HP3	**134**	B2
HTCH/STOT SG5	**35**	M8
LTN LU1	**80**	D5
RKW/CH/CXG WD3	**161**	J6
WGCW AL8	**104**	C6
Cloister Wk *HHNE* HP2	**117**	N6
Clonard Wy *PIN* HA5	**172**	A3
Closemead Cl *NTHWD* HA6	**170**	E5
The Close *BLDK* SG7	**16**	C4
BLDK SG7	**37**	H1
BRKMPK AL9	**122**	C5
BRKMPK AL9	**139**	H5
BUNT SG9	**38**	E2
BUSH WD23 *	**163**	J5
EBAR EN4	**167**	K5
HARP AL5	**81**	J9
HHS/BOV HP3 *	**132**	F7
HTCHE/RSTV SG4	**84**	C4
LTNW/LIM LU3	**62**	B1
POTB/CUF EN6	**153**	K2
RAD WD7	**150**	D3
RSF CM22	**93**	H3
RKW/CH/CXG WD3	**160**	F7
ROY SG8	**20**	C3
ROY SG8	**28**	F1
STAL AL1	**136**	B2
STALW/RED AL3	**79**	P6
STHGT/OAK N14	**167**	P8
STVG SG1 *	**50**	F6

TRDG/WHET N20	**166**	D8
WARE SG12	**108**	D3
Clothall Rd *BLDK* SG7	**37**	L2
Clovelly Cl *PIN* HA5	**171**	K7
Clovelly Wy *STVG* SG1	**50**	D8
Clover Av *BSF* CM23	**73**	L8
Clover Cl *LTNW/LEA* LU4	**61**	J3
Clover Fld *HLWS* CM18	**129**	X6
Cloverfield *WGCE* AL7	**105**	J5
The Clover Fld *BUSH* WD23	**163**	H5
Cloverland *HAT* AL10	**122**	C9
Clover Wk *HAT* AL10	**122**	C3
Clover Wy *HHW* HP1	**117**	L7
Cloyster Wd *EDGW* HA8	**175**	K4

The Clump
RKW/CH/CXG WD3	**160**	E4
Cluny Wy *ARL/CHG* SG15	**24**	E4
Clusterbots *HERT/WAT* SG14	**87**	H7

Clutterbucks
RKW/CH/CXG WD3	**147**	K6
Clyde Pk *HOD* EN11	**127**	J7
Clydesdale Av *HAT* AL10	**173**	K7
Clydesdale Cl *BORE* WD6	**165**	K4
Clydesdale Pth *BORE* WD6 *	**165**	K4

Clydesdale Rd
LTNW/LEA LU4	**61**	K3
ROY SG8	**20**	D4
Clyde Sq *HHNE* HP2	**118**	A3
Clyde Ter *HERT/BAY* SG13	**107**	P6
Clyfton Cl *BROX* EN10	**142**	D2
Clyston Rd *WATW* WD18	**162**	B5
Coach Dr *HTCHE/RSTV* SG4	**49**	L2

Coachhouse Ms
WAT WD17 *	**107**	K5

The Coach House
AMP/FLIT/BLC MK45	**32**	D5
Coachman's La *BLDK* SG7	**25**	P9
Coach Ms *STAL* AL1	**120**	C8
Coalport Cl *HLW* CM17	**129**	M4
Coates Dell *GSTN* WD25	**149**	M3
Coates Rd *BORE* WD6	**164**	D6
Coates Wy *GSTN* WD25	**149**	L2
Cobb Cl *BORE* WD6	**165**	J4
Cobbets Rd *GSTN* WD25	**156**	D6
Cobbetts Ride *TRING* HP23	**95**	N3
Cobb Gn *GSTN* WD25	**149**	J2
Cobbinsbank *WAB* EN9 *	**157**	J3
The Cobbins *WAB* EN9	**157**	K2
Cobbins Wy *HLWE* CM17	**111**	P8

Cobblers Wck
RAYLNE/WEN HP22	**76**	C2
Cobb Rd *BERK* HP4	**115**	L7
Cobden Hl *RAD* WD7	**150**	D6
Cobden St *LTNE* LU2	**7**	J1
Cobden Cl *EDGW* HA8	**175**	H6
Cobham Rd *WARE* SG12	**108**	E2
Cob Lane Cl *WLYN* AL6	**85**	H9
Cobmead *HAT* AL10	**122**	A4
Cockburn Av *HERT/BAY* SG13	**107**	P5
Cockerell Cl *STVG* SG1	**26**	X6
Cocker Rd *EN EN1	**156**	A6
Cockfosters Pde *EBAR* EN4 *	**167**	L3
Cockfosters Rd *EBAR* EN4	**154**	A8
Cock Gn *HLWW/ROY* CM19	**128**	A5
Cock Gv *BERK* HP4	**115**	L6
Cockhall Cl *ROY* SG8	**19**	H1
Cockhall La *ROY* SG8	**18**	D6
Cock La *BROX* EN10	**126**	B7
SAFWS CB11	**43**	J5
Cockle Wy *RAD* WD7	**151**	K3
Cockrobin La *HLW* CM20	**110**	D5
Codicote Dr *GSTN* WD25	**149**	L4

Codicote Rd
HTCHE/RSTV SG4	**65**	L8
STALW AL4	**103**	P1
WLYN AL6	**103**	H5
Codicote Rw *HHNE* HP2	**118**	B3
Codmore Cl *CSHM* HP5	**131**	K9

Codmore Wood Rd
CSHM HP5	**145**	P3
Cody Cl *KTN/HRWW/WS* HA3	**173**	J3
Coe's Aly *BAR* EN5	**166**	C3
Cogdells Cl *CSHM* HP5	**130**	A6
Cogdells La *CSHM* HP5	**130**	A6
Coke's Farm La *CSTG* HP8	**159**	H2
Coke's La *CSTG* HP8	**159**	K3
Colbron Cl *BLDK* SG7	**17**	M7
Colburn Av *PIN* HA5	**171**	N9
Colchester Dr *PIN* HA5	**171**	M9
Colchester Rd *NTHWD* HA6	**170**	E8

Cold Christmas La
WARE SG12	**88**	C7
Coldham Gv *PEND* EN3	**156**	D2
Coldharbour La *BUSH* WD23	**163**	K5
HARP AL5	**82**	A9

Coldharbour Rd
HLWW/ROY CM19	**128**	D3
Coldmoreham Yd *AMSS* HP7 *	**144**	F9
Colebrook Av *LTNN/LIM* LU3	**45**	M8
Coledale Dr *STAN* HA7	**173**	J5
Cole Green La *WGCE* AL7	**105**	J8
Cole Green Wy		
HERT/WAT SG14	**107**	H6
Colehills Cl *SAFWS* CB11	**43**	M4

Coleman Green La
STALW/WH AL4	**103**	H9
Coleman's Cl *HTCH/STOT* SG5	**34**	C4
Coleman's La *WAB* EN9	**143**	J5

Colemans Rd
HTCHE/RSTV SG4	**64**	C5
Coleridge Cl *CHESW* EN7	**141**	N6
STVG SG1	**35**	M8
Coleridge Crs *HHNE* HP2	**118**	C2
Coleridge Wy *BORE* WD6	**164**	D3
Cole Rd *WAT* WD17	**149**	J9
Colesdale *POTB/CUF* EN6	**153**	L7
Coles Hl *HHW* HP1	**117**	K6
Colestrete *STVG* SG1	**11**	H5
Colestrete Cl *STVG* SG1 *	**11**	H6
Colet Rd *RAYLNE/WEN* HP22	**76**	A2
Coleswood Rd *HARP* AL5	**102**	B5
Colgate Pl *PEND* EN3	**156**	F7
Colgrove *WGCW* AL8	**104**	C7
Colindale Av *STAL* AL1	**122**	E4
Colin Rd *LTNE* LU2	**62**	G4

College Av
KTN/HRWW/WS HA3	**172**	E5
College Cl *BSF* CM23	**73**	N7

KTN/HRWW/WS HA3	**172**	E4
College Ct *CHES/WCR* EN8	**142**	B9
College Gdns *ENC/FH* EN2	**155**	L9
College Ga *HLW* CM20	**2**	D5

College Hill Rd
KTN/HRWW/WS HA3	**172**	E4
College La *HAT* AL10	**122**	B8
College Pl *STALW/RED* AL3	**8**	D3
College Rd *ABLGY* WD5	**149**	H1
CHES/WCR EN8	**142**	A9
HERT/BAY SG13	**35**	L8
HTCH/STOT SG5	**35**	L8
STALW/RED AL3	**172**	E5
STAL AL1	**120**	C9

College Rd North
RAYLNE/WEN HP22	**94**	D3
College Sq *HLW* CM20	**2**	D5
College St *STALW/RED* AL3	**8**	E3
Colley Land		
RKW/CH/CXG WD3	**160**	B3
Collier Dr *EDGW* HA8	**175**	N6
Collingdon St *LTN* LU1	**6**	C3
Collingtree *LTNE* LU2	**63**	J2
Collingwood Dr		
LTNW/LEA LU4	**61**	N3
Collingwood Rd *STALW/RED* AL3	**137**	J4
Collins Av *STAN* HA7	**173**	L6
Collins Cross *BSF* CM23	**74**	C1

Collins Meadow
HLWW/ROY CM19	**2**	A6
Collins Wd *LTN* LU1 *	**79**	P1
Collison Cl *HTCHE/RSTV* SG4	**35**	P6
Collyer Rd *LCOL/BKTW* AL2	**137**	J6

Colmer Pl
KTN/HRWW/WS HA3	**172**	D4
Colnbrook Cl *LCOL/BKTW* AL2	**137**	K6
Colne Av *RKW/CH/CXG* WD3	**162**	D5
Colne Gdns *LCOL/BKTW* AL2	**137**	K6
Colne Ldg *BUSH* WD23 *	**13**	K4
Colne Md *RKW/CH/CXG* WD3	**160**	E8

Colne Valley Trail
STALE/WH AL4	**160**	G2
Colne Wy *HHNE* HP2	**118**	A3
Colne Way Ct *WATN* WD24 *	**149**	L7
Colney Heath La		
STALE/WH AL4	**121**	K9
Colonial Wy *WATN* WD24	**149**	K9
The Colonnades *HAT* AL10 *	**122**	F4

The Colonnade
CHES/WCR EN8	**142**	C7
STALW/RED AL3	**8**	E3
Colonsay *HHS/BOV* HP3	**134**	D1
Colston Crs *CHESW* EN7	**141**	J6
Colt Hatch *HLW* CM20	**2**	A3
Colthurst Gdns *HOD* EN11	**127**	J5
Colton Rd *HHW* HP1	**172**	E9
Colts Cnr *STVGE* SG2	**67**	L2
Colts Cft *ROY* SG8	**22**	B8
Coltsfield *STSD* CM24	**58**	F4
Coltsfoot *WGCE* AL7	**123**	H2
Coltsfoot Ct *ROY* SG8	**20**	D4
Coltsfoot Gn *LTNW/LEA* LU4	**61**	K1
Coltsfoot La *KNEB* SG3	**85**	N6
Coltsfoot Rd *WARE* SG12	**108**	D1
The Coltsfoot *HHW* HP1	**117**	L7
Columbia Av *EDGW* HA8	**175**	P5
Columbia Rd *BROX* EN10	**142**	D5
Columbus Ct *STVGE* SG2	**51**	K8
Columbus Gdns *NTHWD* HA6	**170**	F7
Colvin Gdns *CHES/WCR* EN8	**156**	C5
Colwell Ri *LTNE* LU2	**63**	M4
Colwell Rd *STVGE* SG2	**67**	M3
Colwyn Cl *STVG* SG1	**50**	E7
Colyer Cl *WLYN* AL6	**105**	J1
Combe Rd *WATW* WD18	**162**	B5
Combe St *HHNE* HP2	**8**	A1
Comet Cl *GSTN* WD25	**148**	C4
Comet Rd *HAT* AL10	**122**	C6
Comet Wy *HAT* AL10	**122**	A9
Common Fld *TRING* HP23	**114**	C2
Commonfields *HLW* CM20	**3**	H2
Common Gdns *BERK* HP4	**116**	E5

Common Gate Rd
RKW/CH/CXG WD3	**160**	B4
Common La *BLDK* SG7	**17**	L4
GSTN WD25	**150**	D8
HARP AL5	**82**	C8
KGLCY WD4	**134**	A7
LTNN/LIM LU3	**45**	K8
ROY SG8	**31**	M2
Common Rd *HTCHE/RSTV* SG4	**35**	N9
Common Rd *BUSH* WD23	**163**	M5
HTCH/STOT SG5	**25**	L4
RKW/CH/CXG WD3	**160**	B3
STAN HA7	**164**	B9
WAB EN9	**128**	B9
Commonside Rd *HLWS* CM18	**129**	M4
Commons La *HHNE* HP2	**117**	N7
The Commons *WGCE* AL7	**105**	K9
The Common *BERK* HP4	**116**	C5
HARP AL5	**81**	J5
HAT AL10	**122**	D9
KGLCY WD4	**150**	D1
RKW/CH/CXG WD3	**160**	C4
STAN HA7	**163**	P8
Common Vw *LWTH* SG6	**25**	L9
Common Whf *WARE* SG12	**108**	D3

Community Wy
RKW/CH/CXG WD3	**161**	L4
Compania Vw *LTNN/LIM* LU3	**46**	B7
Compass Cl *EDGW* HA8	**173**	N1
Compton Av *LTNW/LEA* LU4	**61**	N1

Compton Gdns
LCOL/BKTW AL2	**136**	A5
Compton Pl *OXHEY* WD19	**171**	N1
Compton Ri *PIN* HA5	**171**	N9

Compton Rd		
RAYLNE/WEN HP22	**112**	D6
Comredcy Cl *ENC/FH* EN2	**155**	J9
Comyne Rd *WATN* WD24	**148**	C6
The Comyns *BUSH* WD23	**163**	J7
Concorde Dr *HHNE* HP2	**5**	F1
Concorde St *LTNE* LU2	**7**	H1
Conduit La *BUNT* SG9	**41**	P7

Conduit La East
HOD EN11	**126**	F5
Conduit La East *HOD* EN11	**126**	E6
Coney Cl *HAT* AL10	**122**	E8
Coneydale *WGCW* AL8	**104**	A4
Coney Gn *STAN* LU1	**111**	N1
Conger La *DUN/HR/TOD* LU5	**44**	C1
Congreve Rd *WAB* EN9	**143**	K8
Conifer Cl *CHESW* EN7	**141**	N8
Conifer Cl *CHESW* EN7	**141**	K8
HERT/BAY SG13	**107**	K3
Conifers Wy *STVG* SG2	**133**	J2
The Conifers *GSTN* WD25	**148**	B3

Conifer Wk
STVG SG2	**51**	M8
Coningesby Dr *WAT* WD17	**148**	F9
Coningsby Bank *STAL* AL1	**136**	B3
Coningsby Cl *BRKMPK* AL9	**138**	F5
Coningsby Ct *RAD* WD7	**150**	D5
Coningsby Dr *POTB/CUF* EN6	**153**	N3
Conisbee Ct *STHGT/OAK* N14	**167**	N4
Coniston Cl *HHS/BOV* HP3	**118**	D9
Coniston Gdns *PIN* HA5	**170**	E2
Coniston Rd *KGLCY* WD4	**134**	B8
LTNN/LIM LU3	**62**	A1
Connaught Av *EBAR* EN4	**167**	K7
Connaught Cl *HHNE* HP2	**118**	B6
Connaught Gdns *BERK* HP4	**115**	L4
Connaught Rd *BAR* EN5	**166**	B5
HARP AL5	**102**	A2
KTN/HRWW/WS HA3	**172**	D5
LTNW/LEA LU4	**62**	A5
STALW/RED AL3	**8**	B2
Connemara Cl *BORE* WD6 *	**165**	J5
Connop Rd *PEND* EN3	**156**	D8
Conquerors Hl *STALE/WH* AL4	**103**	K4
Conquest Cl *HTCHE/RSTV* SG4	**49**	L2

Conquest Rd
DUN/HR/TOD LU5	**61**	H1

Constable Cl
DUN/HR/TOD LU5	**60**	G1
Constable Gdns *HLWS* HA8	**173**	N5
Constantine Cl *STVG* SG1	**51**	J6
Constantine Pl *BLDK* SG7	**17**	K8
Convent Cl *HTCH/STOT* SG5	**35**	L8
Conway Cl *DUN/HR/TOD* LU5	**61**	H1
STAN HA7	**163**	L9
Conway Gdns *ENC/FH* EN2	**155**	M8
Conway Rd *LTNW/LEA* LU4	**62**	A5
Conybury Cl *WAB* EN9	**157**	M2
Conyers Cl *CHESW* EN7	**141**	M6
Conyers *HLW* CM20	**3**	L2
Cookfield Cl *DUN/WHIP* LU6	**60**	B6
Cook Rd *STVGE* SG2	**76**	E1
Cooks Hole Rd *ENC/FH* EN2	**155**	J8
Cooks Md *BUSH* WD23	**163**	J6
Cooks Spinney *HLW* CM20	**129**	K1
Cooks Vennel *HHW* HP1	**117**	K6
Cook's Wy *HTCHE/RSTV* SG4	**35**	M7

Coombe Av
RAYLNE/WEN HP22	**112**	D6
Coombe Cl *EDGW* HA8	**173**	M6
Coombe Dr *DUN/WHIP* LU6	**60**	B7
Coombe Gdns *BERK* HP4	**115**	L6

Coombe Hill Rd
RKW/CH/CXG WD3	**160**	G7
Coombehurst Cl *EBAR* EN4	**167**	K1
Coombelands Rd *ROY* SG8	**20**	D2
Coombe Rd *BUSH* WD23	**163**	J9
The Coltsfoot *HHW* HP1	**19**	J9
Coombes Rd *LCOL/BKTW* AL2	**173**	P5
Cooms Wk *EDGW* HA8	**175**	P5
Coopers Cl *BSF* CM23	**91**	L1
Coopers Ct *HTCHE/RSTV* SG4	**52**	N2
Coopers Cl *STVGE* SG2	**52**	N2
Coopers Crs *BORE* WD6	**151**	P9
Coopers Ga *STALE/WH* AL4	**137**	N1

Coopers Lane Rd
POTB/CUF EN6	**155**	J1

Coopers Meadow
STALW/RED AL3	**101**	H6
Cooper Rd *POTB/CUF* EN6	**139**	M9

Coopers Wy
POTB/CUF EN6	**153**	J1
Cooper Wy *BERK* HP4	**116**	A7
Cooters End La *HARP* AL5	**81**	N9

Cope La
STALE/WH AL4	**121**	L5
Cooper's Hl *HTCHE/RSTV* SG4	**82**	G4
Cope La *POTB/CUF* EN6	**153**	P1

Copenhagen Cl
LTNN/LIM LU3	**45**	N7
Copley Rd *STAN* HA7	**163**	L8

Copmans Wick
RKW/CH/CXG WD3	**160**	B4
The Coppens *HTCH/STOT* SG5	**25**	L4

Copper Beech Cl
HHS/BOV HP3	**133**	J2
Copper Beeches *HARP* AL5	**102**	A3
WLYN AL6	**102**	G4

Copperfield Cl
HTCH/STOT SG5	**24**	C7
Copperfields *LTNW/LEA* LU4	**61**	L4
ROY SG8	**20**	B4
WGCE AL7	**105**	M7

Copperfields
DUN/HR/TOD LU5	**60**	C2
Copperfield Wy *PIN* HA5	**171**	N9
Copperkins La *AMS* HP6	**144**	D5

Coppermill La
RKW/CH/CXG WD3	**159**	K4
Copper Ridg *CFSP/GDCR* SL9	**168**	A5
Copperwood *HERT/BAY* SG13	**107**	N6
Coppice Cl *HAT* AL10	**138**	C1
Coppice Hatch *HLWS* CM18	**128**	C5
Coppice Mead *HTCH/STOT* SG5	**25**	J4
The Coppice *BAR* EN5 *	**166**	F5

BSF CM23	**73**	N9
HHW HP1	**118**	C7
OXHEY WD19	**162**	E5
TRING HP23	**114**	C2
Coppice Wk *TRDG/WHET* N20	**166**	E9
The Coppings *HOD* EN11	**126**	F2
Coppins Cl *BERK* HP4	**115**	K7

The Coppins
KTN/HRWW/WS HA3	**172**	E3
Copse Cl *NTHWD* HA6	**170**	G5
Copse Hl *HLWW/ROY* CM19	**128**	E6
Copse Hill Cl *HHS/BOV* HP3	**132**	C7
The Copse *AMSS* HP7	**145**	H8
BLDK SG7	**37**	J1
BSF CM23	**73**	P6
HERT/BAY SG13	**85**	K5
HHW HP1	**117**	H6
Copse Wy *CSHM* HP5	**130**	F6
LTNE LU2	**45**	N7
Copsewood Rd *WATN* WD24	**149**	J9
Copse Wood Wy *NTHWD* HA6	**170**	C7
Copshall Cl *HLWS* CM18	**129**	H7
Copthall Cl *CFSP/GDCR* SL9	**168**	C4
Copthall La *CFSP/GDCR* SL9	**168**	C4
Copthorne *LTNE* LU2	**63**	L3
Copthorne Av *BROX* EN10	**126**	E8

Copthorne Cl
RKW/CH/CXG WD3	**161**	K4

Copthorne Rd
RKW/CH/CXG WD3	**161**	K5
Corals Md *WGCE* AL7	**104**	G7
Coram Cl *BERK* HP4	**115**	P8
Corbar Cl *EBAR* EN4	**153**	N8
Corbridge Dr *LTNE* LU2	**63**	M4
Cordell Cl *CHES/WCR* EN8	**135**	P4
Cordell Cl *CHES/WCR* EN8	**142**	A9
Cordell Cl *STALW/RED* AL3	**135**	P2
Coreys Mill La *STVG* SG1	**50**	E6
Corfe Cl *BORE* WD6	**165**	K2
HHNE HP2	**5**	H5
Corinium Gdns *LTNN/LIM* LU3	**46**	B7
Corinium St *STALW/RED* AL3	**8**	B7
Cornbury Rd *EDGW* HA8	**173**	K4
Corncastle Rd *LTN* LU1	**6**	B7
Corncrake Cl *LTNE* LU2	**63**	K1
Corncroft *HAT* AL10	**122**	C4
Cornel Cl *LTN* LU1	**80**	C4
Cornerfield *HAT* AL10	**122**	E3
Corner Hall *HHNE* HP2	**4**	E6
Corner Hall Av *HHNE* HP2	**4**	E5
Corner Meadow *HLWS* CM18	**129**	K7
Corners *WGCE* AL7	**105**	K5
Corner Wd *STALW/RED* AL3	**79**	N8
Cornfield Crs *BERK* HP4	**115**	J4
Cornfield Rd *BUSH* WD23	**163**	K3
The Cornfields *HHW* HP1 *	**4**	B3
Cornflower Wy *HAT* AL10	**122**	B3
Cornhill Dr *PEND* EN3	**156**	D7
Corn Md *WCCW* AL8	**104**	F3
Cornmill *WAB* EN9	**156**	G3
Cornmill *CHES/WCR* EN8	**142**	A3
Cornwall Rd *HARP* AL5	**102**	A2
PIN HA5	**171**	P4
STAL AL1	**9**	H7

Coronation Av
ROY SG8	**20**	B5
Coronation Rd *BSF* CM23	**73**	P9
WARE SG12	**108**	C2
Coronation Rw *ROY* SG8 *	**29**	L4
Corringham Ct *STAL* AL1	**9**	G5
Corton Cl *STVG* SG1	**50**	B8
Corvus Cl *ROY* SG8	**20**	D2
Cory-wright Wy		
STALE/WH AL4	**103**	K3
Cosgrove Wy *LTN* LU1	**6**	A3
Cosne Ms *HARP* AL5	**102**	B5
Cotefield *LTNW/LEA* LU4	**61**	M3
Coteford Cl *PIN* HA5	**171**	J9
Cotesmore Rd *HHW* HP1	**117**	H9

Cotlandswick
LCOL/BKTW AL2	**137**	H4
Cotney Cft *STVGE* SG2	**67**	N3
Cotswold *LTNE* LU2	**62**	G4
Cotswold Av *BUSH* WD23	**163**	L5

Cotswold Business Pk
LTN LU1	**79**	N3
Cotswold Cl *STALE/WH* AL4	**121**	H5

Cotswold Gdns
LTNN/LIM LU3	**45**	M8
Cotswolds *HAT* AL10	**122**	D8

Cottage Cl
RKW/CH/CXG WD3	**161**	K5
WAT WD17	**162**	B1

Cottage Gdns
CHES/WCR EN8	**142**	C8
The Cottages *EDGW* HA8 *	**175**	P4
Cottered Rd *BUNT* SG9	**39**	N7
Cotterells *HHW* HP1 *	**4**	D3
Cotterells Hl *HHW* HP1	**4**	C2
Cotton Dr *HERT/BAY* SG13	**107**	M3
Cotton Fld *HAT* AL10	**122**	E4
Cottonmill Crs *STAL* AL1	**9**	J6
Cottonmill La *STAL* AL1	**136**	D1
Cotton Rd *POTB/CUF* EN6	**153**	M1
Coulser Cl *HHW* HP1	**117**	K5
Coulter Cl *POTB/CUF* EN6	**140**	E6
Counters Cl *HHW* HP1	**117**	K8
Countess Cl *DEN/HRF* UB9	**168**	N1
County Ga *BAR* EN5	**166**	F5
Coursers Rd *LCOL/BKTW* AL2	**137**	M6
STALE/WH AL4	**137**	N4
Courtaulds *KGLCY* WD4	**133**	L9
Court Cl *KTN/HRWW/WS* HA3	**173**	K7
Courtenay Av *KTN/HRWW/WS* HA3	**172**	B4
Courten Ms *STAN* HA7	**173**	J4
Courtfield Av *HRW* HA1 *	**172**	F8
Courtfield Cl *BROX* EN10	**126**	F8
Courtfield Crs *HRW* HA1	**172**	F8
Courtfields *HARP* AL5	**81**	P9
Courtland Av *MLHL* NW7	**165**	H8
Courtlands Cl *WATN* WD24	**148**	G9
Courtlands Dr *WAT* WD17	**148**	F6
Courtleigh Av *EBAR* EN4	**153**	N4

Court Ldg RAD WD7 * 151 M4
Courtside STALW/RED AL3 * 120 B6
The Courtway OXHEY WD19 .... 162 G8
Courtyard CI AMS HP6 .... 145 H8
The Courtyards
  WATW WD18 * 161 P6
The Courtyard HHS/BOV HP3 .... 133 N5
  STALE/WH AL4 .... 121 L8
Covent Garden CI
  LTNW/LEA LU4 .... 62 A3
Coventry CI STVG SG1 .... 51 L6
Coverack CI STHGT/OAK N14 .... 167 N5
Coverdale HHW HP2 .... 117 P5
  LTNW/LEA LU4 ....
Covert CI BERK HP4 .... 115 J5
Covert Rd BERK HP4 .... 115 J4
The Covert NTHWD HA6 .... 176 B4
Covert Wy EBAR EN4 .... 166 C1
Cowards La HTCHE/RSTV SG4 .... 84 C5
Cowbridge Rd
  KTN/HRWW/WS HA3 .... 173 M8
Cowdray CI LTNE LU2 .... 63 K3
Cow La BUSH WD23 * 163 J5
  GSTN WD25 .... 149 K6
  TRING HP23 .... 96 C8
Cowles CHESW EN7 .... 141 N6
Cowley HI BORE WD6 .... 151 M7
Cowlins HLWE CM17 .... 111 N8
Cowper Ct STALW/RED AL3 .... 79 N8
  WATN WD24 .... 149 N7
Cowper Crs HERT/WAT SG14 .... 107 J7
Cowper Gdns
  STHGT/OAK N14 .... 167 M5
Cowper Ri STALW/RED AL3 .... 79 N8
Cowper Rd BERK HP4 .... 115 N7
  CSHM HP5 .... 130 C8
  HARP AL5 .... 102 A3
  HHW HP1 .... 4 A5
  STALW/RED AL3 .... 79 N8
  STHGT/OAK N14 .... 167 M7
  WATW WD18 * 105 J8
Cowper St LTN LU1 .... 62 F9
Cowpers Wy WLYN AL6 .... 85 N8
Cowridge Crs LTNE LU2 .... 7 K2
Cowslip HI LWTH SG6 .... 36 B1
Cox CI RAD WD7 .... 151 K2
Coxe PI KTN/HRWW/WS HA3 .... 172 G8
Cox Ley CBSF CM22 .... 93 H6
Coxs Gdns BSF CM23 .... 73 P9
Cox's Wy ARL/CHE SG15 .... 24 E4
Coyney Gn LTNW/LIM LU3 .... 6 A1
Cozens La East BROX EN10 .... 142 E1
Cozens La West BROX EN10 .... 142 D1
Cozens Rd WARE SG12 .... 127 J5
Crabbe Crs CSHM HP5 .... 145 M6
Crabbs CI HTCH/STOT SG5 * 35 K9
Crabbs La GSTN WD25 .... 43 H9
Crab La GSTN WD25 .... 150 A4
Crabtree CI BUSH WD23 .... 163 K4
  HHS/BOV HP3 ....
Crabtree Dell LWTH SG6 .... 36 F5
Crabtree La HARP AL5 .... 102 A4
  HHS/BOV HP3 .... 5 F6
Crab Tree La HTCH/STOT SG5 .... 34 C4
Crab Tree Rd KNEB SG3 .... 69 H2
Crabtree Wk BROX EN10 .... 126 D7
Crabtree Wy DUN/WHIP LU6 .... 60 A6
Crackley Meadow HHNE HP2 .... 116 C3
Cracknell CI EN * 156 A7
Cradock Rd LTNW/LEA LU4 .... 6 A5
Crafton Gn STSD CM24 .... 58 F4
Craft Wy ROY SG8 .... 15 N9
Crags Av RAD WD7 .... 150 E6
Cragside STVG SG1 .... 67 M7
Craigavon Rd LTNE LU2 .... 118 A4
Craiglands STALE/WH AL4 .... 121 J4
Craig Mt RAD WD7 .... 150 C5
Craigside Wk CSHM HP5 .... 142 C7
Craigweil Av RAD WD7 .... 150 C5
Craigweil CI STAN HA7 .... 173 K2
Craigweil Dr STAN HA7 .... 173 K2
Crakers Md WATW WD18 * 12 E3
Cranborne Av
  HTCH/STOT SG5 .... 49 J1
Cranborne CI HERT/BAY SG13 .... 107 K9
  POTB/CUF EN6 .... 153 H1
Cranborne Crs
  POTB/CUF EN6 .... 153 H1
Cranborne Gdns WCCE AL7 .... 105 J7
Cranborne Pde
  POTB/CUF EN6 .... 152 G2
Cranborne Rd
  CHES/WCR EN8 .... 156 C2
  HAT AL10 .... 122 E5
  HOD EN11 .... 116 C6
  POTB/CUF EN6 .... 153 H1
Cranbourne Av
  POTB/CUF EN6 .... 139 H9
Cranbourne Dr HHS/BOV HP3 .... 102 B6
  HOD EN11 .... 126 C1
  PIN HA5 .... 171 M9
Cranbourne Rd NTHWD HA6 .... 171 H7
Cranbrook CI WARE SG12 .... 108 C1
Cranbrook Dr LTNW/LIM LU3 .... 45 N7
  STALE/WH AL4 .... 121 K8
Cranbrook Rd EBAR EN4 .... 167 H5
Cranefield Dr GSTN WD25 .... 149 M2
Crane Md WARE SG12 .... 108 D4
Cranfield Crs POTB/CUF EN6 .... 140 F8
Cranleigh CI CHESW EN7 .... 141 P7
Cranleigh Gdns
  KTN/HRWW/WS HA3 .... 173 L9
  LTNW/LIM LU3 .... 62 D3
Cranmer CI POTB/CUF EN6 .... 139 M9
Cranmer CI STAN HA7 .... 173 J4
Cranmer Rd EDGW HA8 .... 165 H9
Cranmore CI AMS HP6 .... 145 K1
Cravells Rd HARP AL5 .... 102 B6
Crawford Rd HAT AL10 .... 122 D4
Crawley CI LTN LU1 .... 80 D4
Crawley Dr HHNE HP2 .... 118 A4
Crawley Green Rd LTNE LU2 .... 7 J4
Crawley Rd LTN LU1 .... 6 C2
Crawley's La TRING HP23 .... 114 D4
Creamery Ct LWTH SG6 .... 36 F5

Creasey Park Dr
  DUN/WHIP LU6 .... 60 C4
Creasy CI ABLGY WD5 .... 148 G1
Crecy Gdns STALW/RED AL3 .... 101 H6
Creighton Av STAL AL1 .... 136 C3
Crescent East EBAR EN4 .... 153 M8
Crescent NI EBAR EN4 .... 167 J4
Crescent Rd
  LTNE LU2 .... 7 G3
Crescent Rd BSF CM23 .... 74 B4
  EBAR EN4 .... 167 H3
  HHNE HP2 .... 5 F1
  LTNE LU2 .... 7 G3
The Crescent ABLGY WD5 .... 134 G9
  BAR EN5 .... 166 F2
  BUNT SG9 .... 39 K9
  DUN/HR/TOD LU5 .... 44 C2
  GSTN WD25 .... 150 A8
  HAT AL10 .... 111 M6
  HTCH/STOT SG5 .... 35 J7
  HTCHE/RSTV SG4 .... 49 M4
  LCOL/BKTW AL2 .... 135 P9
  LTN LU1 .... 79 P1
  LTNE LU2 .... 7 G3
  RKW/CH/CXG WD3 .... 161 M5
  TRING HP23 .... 95 P3
  WATW WD17 .... 13 G5
  WLYN AL6 .... 84 F9
Crescent West EBAR EN4 .... 153 M8
Cress End RKW/CH/CXG WD3 .... 160 E7
Cresset CI WARE SG12 .... 109 H9
Cresswell Rd CSHM HP5 .... 145 J4
Cresswick WCCE AL7 * 65 K7
Cresta CI DUN/HR/TOD LU5 .... 61 M4
Crest Dr PEND EN5 .... 156 B8
Crest Pk HHNE HP2 .... 118 D7
The Crest CHESW EN7 .... 141 J6
  DUN/HR/TOD LU5 .... 61 H5
  POTB/CUF EN6 * 153 M1
  SBW CM21 .... 111 N2
  WARE SG12 .... 88 C9
  WLYN AL6 .... 84 G5
Crest Vw PIN HA5 .... 171 M8
Creswick Ct WCCE AL7 * 104 G7
Crew Curve BERK HP4 .... 115 L4
Crib St WARE SG12 .... 108 C2
Cricketers CI STALW/RED AL3 ....
  STHGT/OAK N14 .... 167 N6
Cricketers Rd ARL/CHE SG15 .... 24 E4
Cricketfield La BSF CM23 .... 73 N6
Crispin Ter HTCH/STOT SG5 .... 35 J9
Criss Gv CFSP/GDCR SL9 .... 168 A6
Criss La CFSP/GDCR SL9 .... 168 A6
Croasdale Rd STSD CM24 .... 58 F5
Croasdale Ct STSD CM24 .... 58 F5
Crocus Fld BAR EN5 .... 166 D5
Croft CI KGLGY WD4 .... 133 K4
  MLHL NW7 .... 165 L1
Croft Ct BORE WD6 .... 165 K2
  HARP AL5 * ....
Croft End Rd KGLGY WD4 .... 133 K9
Crofters SBW CM21 .... 111 P1
Crofters End SBW CM21 .... 91 P9
Crofters Rd NTHWD HA6 .... 170 C1
Croft Fld HAT AL10 .... 111 J5
  KGLGY WD4 .... 133 K9
Croft Gn DUN/WHIP LU6 .... 60 C6
Croft La KGLGY WD4 .... 133 K9
Croft Meadow KGLGY WD4 .... 133 K9
Croft Mdw LBUZ LU7 .... 76 D4
Crofton Wy BAR EN5 * 166 F5
Croft Rd CFSP/GDCR SL9 .... 168 C6
  LTNE LU2 .... 63 J5
  PEND EN5 .... 156 D9
  WARE SG12 .... 108 B2
Crofts Pth HHS/BOV HP3 .... 134 C1
The Crofts HHS/BOV HP3 .... 118 C9
  HTCH/STOT SG5 .... 25 K3
The Croft BAR EN5 .... 166 C3
  BROX EN10 .... 142 D2
  LCOL/BKTW AL2 .... 135 P4
  LTNN/LIM LU3 .... 45 N7
  RBSF CM22 .... 99 M2
  WARE SG12 .... 89 K9
  WCCE AL7 .... 105 J9
Croftwell HARP AL5 .... 102 A4
Cromarty Rd EDGW HA8 .... 165 H8
Cromdale Wk STVG SG1 .... 51 L3
Cromer CI BERK HP4 .... 98 B8
Cromer Rd BAR EN5 .... 166 C3
  WATN WD24 .... 149 K8
Cromer Wy LTNE LU2 .... 46 E8
Crompton PI PEND EN5 .... 156 A8
Crompton Rd STVG SG1 .... 50 D9
Cromwell Av CHESW EN7 .... 142 A9
Cromwell CI BSF CM23 .... 73 L7
  CSTG HP8 .... 159 J9
  STALE/WH AL4 .... 121 J3
Cromwell Gn LWTH SG6 .... 25 M9
Cromwell HI LTNN/LIM LU3 .... 6 C1
Cromwell Rd
  AMP/FLIT/BLC MK45 .... 32 C4
  BORE WD6 .... 151 K9
  CHESW EN7 .... 142 A9
  HERT/BAY SG13 .... 107 N5
  LTNN/LIM LU3 .... 6 C1
  LWTH SG6 .... 25 M9
  STVG SG1 .... 67 M1
  WARE SG12 .... 108 E3
Cromwell Wy
  HTCH/STOT SG5 .... 34 C4
Crooked Mile WAB EN9 .... 157 H5
Crooked Wy WAB EN9 .... 143 K1
Crookhams WCCE AL7 .... 105 H9
Crop Common HAT AL10 .... 122 E4
Crosby CI DUN/WHIP LU6 .... 60 F8
  LTNW/LEA LU4 .... 62 BA
  STALE/WH AL4 .... 137 H2
Crossbrook St
  CHES/WCR EN8 .... 156 C1
Crossett End HHS/BOV HP3 .... 134 D1
Crossfell Rd HHS/BOV HP3 .... 134 C1
Crossfield Rd HOD EN11 .... 126 C3
Crossfields STALW/RED AL3 .... 136 A2
Crossfields CI BERK HP4 .... 115 L7
Crossgate EDGW HA8 .... 164 G9

Crossgates STVG SG1 .... 11 F4
Cross Gn BUNT SG9 * 39 K9
Crossways LTN LU1 .... 79 P2
Cross La HARP AL5 .... 102 B7
  HERT/WAT SG14 .... 107 J6
Cross Lanes CFSP/GDCR SL9 .... 168 D2
Cross Lanes CI
  CFSP/GDCR SL9 .... 168 D2
Crossleys CSTG HP8 .... 168 A1
Crossmead LU5 .... 25 K7
Crossleys HI CSTG HP8 .... 159 J9
Crossmead OXHEY WD19 .... 162 D5
Cross Meadow CSHM HP5 .... 130 E8
Cross Oak Rd BERK HP4 .... 115 M8
Crossoaks La BORE WD6 .... 152 A4
Crosspaths HARP AL5 .... 81 K9
The Crosspath HAT AL10 .... 150 F5
Cross Rd CHES/WCR EN8 .... 156 E5
  HARP AL5 .... 107 K5
  WATN WD24 .... 172 D8
Cross St LTNE LU2 .... 162 G5
  LWTH SG6 .... 36 C1
  STALW/RED AL3 .... 8 E3
  WARE SG12 .... 108 D3
  WAT WD17 .... 13 G2
Cross St North
  DUN/WHIP LU6 * 60 D5
Crossway CSHM HP5 .... 131 K9
Cross Wy HARP AL5 .... 102 B1
Crossway HLWE CM17 .... 129 N2
  PIN HA5 .... 171 K6
  WGCW AL8 .... 104 E2
Crossways BERK HP4 .... 115 L8
  DUN/HR/TOD LU5 .... 60 F1
  HHS/BOV HP3 .... 118 C8
  ROY SG8 .... 21 K8
The Cross Wy
  KTN/HRWW/WS HA3 .... 172 E6
  LTN LU1 .... 62 D9
Crouchfield HERT/WAT SG14 .... 107 K3
  HHW HP1 .... 4 A4
Crouchfield La WARE SG12 .... 87 M9
Crouch Hall Gdns
  STALW/RED AL3 .... 101 H6
Crouch Hall La
  STALW/RED AL3 .... 101 H6
Crouch La CHESW EN7 .... 141 K6
Crowborough Pth
  OXHEY WD19 * 171 M1
Crow Furlong
  HTCH/STOT SG5 .... 49 J1
Crowland Rd LTNE LU2 .... 63 K1
Crow La ROY SG8 .... 29 M4
Crowni CI MLHL NW7 .... 165 M4
  RBSF CM22 .... 92 D9
Crownfield BROX EN10 .... 126 F9
Crown Ga HLW CM20 .... 2 E5
Crown La STHGT/OAK N14 .... 167 N7
Crown Pde STHGT/OAK N14 * 167 N7
Crown RI GSTN WD25 .... 149 K4
Crown Rd BORE WD6 .... 151 M9
Crown Rose Ct TRING HP23 .... 95 P9
Crown St STALW/RED AL3 .... 101 J7
Crown Ter BSF CM23 .... 74 B5
  STHGT/OAK N14 .... 167 P7
Crown Wk HHS/BOV HP3 .... 133 P3
Crowshott Av STAN HA7 .... 173 J5
Croxdale Rd BORE WD6 .... 164 F1
Croxden CI EDGW HA8 .... 173 K7
Croxley Vw WATW WD18 .... 162 A5
Croxton CI LTNW/LIM LU3 .... 46 E8
Crozier Av BSF CM23 .... 73 M6
Crundale Av CDALE/KGS NW9 .... 173 N9
Crusader Wy WATW WD18 .... 162 B5
Crystal Wy HRW HA1 .... 173 P8
Cubbington CI LTNN/LIM LU3 .... 46 E8
Cubitt CI HTCHE/RSTV SG4 .... 35 P9
Cubitts CI WLYN AL6 .... 105 J1
Cublands HERT/BAY SG13 .... 108 A6
Cuckmans Dr
  LCOL/BKTW AL2 .... 135 P4
Cuckoo HI PIN HA5 .... 171 L7
Cuckoo Hill Dr PIN HA5 .... 171 L7
Cuckoo Hill Rd PIN HA5 .... 171 M8
Cucumber La BRKMPK AL9 .... 124 A4
Cuffley Av GSTN WD25 .... 149 L4
Cuffley CI LTNN/LIM LU3 .... 62 E3
Cuffley Ct HHNE HP2 .... 118 D3
Cuffley HI CHESW EN7 .... 141 H6
Cullera CI NTHWD HA6 .... 170 D5
Cullings Ct WAB EN9 .... 157 L5
Cullington CI
  KTN/HRWW/WS HA3 .... 172 G8
Culrose Ct STVGE SG2 .... 77 J8
Culverden Rd OXHEY WD19 .... 162 D9
Culver Cr STAN HA7 .... 173 J6
Culverhouse Rd
  LTNN/LIM LU3 .... 62 D3
Culverlands CI STAN HA7 .... 173 H1
Culver Rd STAL AL1 .... 9 H1
Culworth Ct LTN LU1 .... 79 P7
Cumberland CI AMSS HP7 .... 145 N9
  HERT/WAT SG14 .... 107 J6
  HHS/BOV HP3 .... 134 F3
Cumberland Dr
  STALW/RED AL3 .... 101 P5
Cumberland Rd HRW HA1 .... 172 D9
  STAN HA7 .... 173 M7
Cumberland St
  DUN/HR/TOD LU5 .... 60 E2
  LTN LU1 .... 6 B5
Cumberlow PI HHNE HP2 .... 118 D9
Cumbria CI DUN/HR/TOD LU5 .... 61 H1
Cundalls Rd WARE SG12 .... 108 D2
Cunningham Av HAT AL10 .... 122 E4
Cunningham Hill Rd STAL AL1 .... 9 K7
Cunningham Pk HRW HA1 .... 172 D9
Cupid Green La HHNE HP2 .... 117 K6
Curlew CI BERK HP4 .... 115 P8
  LWTH SG6 .... 25 J8
Curlew Ct BROX EN10 * 142 B1
Curlew Crs ROY SG8 .... 20 D1
Curlew Rd LCOL/BKTW AL2 .... 63 K1
Curo Pk LCOL/BKTW AL2 .... 156 D7
Currie St HERT/BAY SG13 .... 107 M5

Curteys HLWE CM17 .... 111 N7
Curthwaite Gdns
  ENC/FH EN2 .... 155 P3
Curtis CI RKW/CH/CXG WD3 .... 160 E7
Curtis Rd HHS/BOV HP3 .... 118 E9
Curtiss Dr GSTN WD25 .... 148 G4
Curtis Wy BERK HP4 .... 116 A8
Curzon Av STAN HA7 .... 173 G5
Curzon PI PIN HA5 .... 171 J9
Curzon Rd LTNN/LIM LU3 .... 45 N8
Cussen PI LTNN/LIM LU3 * 45 N8
Cussons CI CHESW EN7 .... 142 A8
Cusworth Wy DUN/HR/TOD LU5 .... 60 B5
Cutenhoe Rd LTN LU1 .... 62 D9
Cutforth Rd SBW CM21 .... 111 P1
Cuthbert CI EN7 .... 141 N8
Cutlers CI BSF CM23 .... 91 M1
Cutlers Gn LTNE LU2 .... 63 N4
Cutmore Dr STALE/WH AL4 .... 137 N1
Cut Throat Av BERK HP4 .... 78 B6
Cuttsfield Ter HHW HP1 .... 117 J9
Cutts La HTCHE/RSTV SG4 .... 84 B8
Cuttys La STVG SG1 .... 10 E5
Cuxton La LTNW/LIM LU3 .... 118 A4
Cygnet CI BORE WD6 .... 151 P9
  NTHWD HA6 .... 170 E4
Cygnet Ct BSF CM23 .... 91 N3
Cylers Thicket WLYN AL6 .... 84 F7
Cypress Av ENC/FH EN2 .... 155 H5
  WGCE AL7 .... 148 C7
Cypress CI WAB EN9 .... 157 J4
Cypress Rd
  KTN/HRWW/WS HA3 .... 172 D6
Cypress Wk STALW/RED AL3 * 149 J5
Cyrils Wy STAL AL1 .... 136 C2

D

Dacorum Wy HHNE HP2 .... 4 D1
Dacre Crs HTCHE/RSTV SG4 .... 83 H4
Dacre Gdns BORE WD6 .... 165 K4
Dacre Gn ROY SG8 .... 20 E4
Dacre Rd HTCH/STOT SG5 .... 35 M8
  RAYLNE/WEN HP22 .... 112 F4
Dads Wd HLW CM20 .... 2 E4
Daffodil CI HAT AL10 .... 122 C2
Dagger La BORE WD6 .... 164 A5
Daggs Dell Rd HHW HP1 .... 117 H6
Dagnall Rd HHW HP1 .... 98 C7
Dagnalls LWTH SG6 .... 36 D5
Dahlia CI CHESW EN7 .... 141 K4
  LTNE LU2 .... 63 J3
Daintrees The WARE SG12 .... 89 J2
Daintry CI
  KTN/HRWW/WS HA3 .... 172 D6
Dairyglen Av CHES/WCR EN8 .... 156 C1
Dairy Wy ABLGY WD5 .... 134 B9
Daisy Ct LWTH SG6 .... 25 L9
Daisy Dr HAT AL10 .... 122 C3
Dalby CI LTNW/LEA LU4 .... 61 L2
Dale Av EDGW HA8 .... 173 M5
  STALE/WH AL4 .... 121 J3
Dale CI EBAR EN5 .... 166 F5
  DUN/HR/TOD LU5 .... 61 J3
  DUN/HR/TOD LU5 .... 61 J3
  HTCHE/RSTV SG4 * 49 M4
  PIN HA5 .... 171 K5
Dale Ct GSTN WD25 * 149 H3
  SBW CM21 .... 111 N3
Dale Green Rd
  FBAR/BDGN N11 .... 167 M9
  DUN/HR/TOD LU5 .... 61 J3
Daleside LTN LU2 .... 7 J4
Dales Pth BORE WD6 .... 165 K4
Dales Rd BORE WD6 .... 165 K4
The Dale HHS/BOV HP3 .... 134 B1
  WAB EN9 .... 156 G3
Dale Vw BAR EN5 * 166 D2
Dalewood HARP AL5 .... 102 C3
  WCCE AL7 .... 148 C4
Dalkeith Gv STAN HA7 .... 173 K2
Deakin CI WATW WD18 .... 162 A6
Deanacre CI CFSP/GDCR SL9 .... 168 B3
Dean CI CFSP/GDCR SL9 .... 168 C3
Deancroft Rd CFSP/GDCR SL9 .... 168 C2
Dean Dr STAN HA7 .... 173 L6
Deane Ct NTHWD HA6 * 170 C5
Dean Fld HHS/BOV HP3 .... 132 D6
Dean Moore CI STAL AL1 .... 8 B6
Deansbrook Rd EDGW HA8 .... 173 P4
  AMS HP6 .... 145 L7
  TRING HP23 .... 95 P8
Deans Furlong TRING HP23 .... 95 P8
Deansgate CHES/WCR EN8 .... 156 E6
Deansway CSHM HP5 .... 130 G8
  STVG SG1 .... 134 A2
The Dean RAYLNE/WEN HP22 .... 158 G9
Deanway CSTG HP8 .... 159 H9
Dean Wy RAYLNE/WEN HP22 .... 94 G8
Deard's End La KNEB SG3 .... 67 J9
Deards Wd KNEB SG3 .... 67 K9
Dearne CI STAN HA7 .... 172 G2
Debenham Rd CHESW EN7 .... 142 A6
De Bohun Av STHGT/OAK N14 .... 167 M5
Deep Acres AMS HP6 .... 144 F6
Deepdene POTB/CUF EN6 .... 152 C1
Deep Denes LTNE LU2 .... 63 H4
Deeping CI KNEB SG3 .... 85 J1
Deer CI HERT/BAY SG13 .... 107 N6
Deerfield CI WARE SG12 .... 108 C2
Deerings The RBSF CM22 .... 3 G3
The Deerings HARP AL5 .... 101 P8
Deer Pk HLWW/ROY CM19 .... 128 D6
Deer Park Wk HHNE HP5 .... 131 K7
Deer Park Wy WAB EN9 .... 156 G6
Deerswood Av HAT AL10 .... 122 E8
The Dee HHNE HP2 .... 118 A3

WLYN AL6 .... 84 G5
Danesbury Park Rd
  WLYN AL6 .... 84 F6
Danescourt LWTH SG6 .... 25 K8
Danes Ga HRW HA1 .... 172 E7
Danesgate STVG SG1 .... 10 C5
The Danes LCOL/BKTW AL2 .... 136 B7
Dane St BSF CM23 .... 74 B3
  STVG SG1 .... 51 J2
Daniells WGCE AL7 .... 105 K5
Danvers Cft TRING HP23 .... 96 B3
Danvers Dr LTNN/LIM LU3 .... 46 D6
Danziger Wy BORE WD6 .... 151 P9
Darby CI STALE/WH AL4 .... 137 H3
Darby Dr WAB EN9 .... 157 H3
  WLYN AL6 .... 85 H2
D'Arcy CI CHES/WCR EN8 .... 156 D1
  TRDG/WHET N20 .... 167 H8
D'Arcy Dr
  KTN/HRWW/WS HA3 .... 173 K8
D'Arcy Gdns
  KTN/HRWW/WS HA3 .... 173 L8
Darkes La POTB/CUF EN6 .... 153 K2
Dark La BUNT SG9 .... 28 B8
  CHESW EN7 .... 141 P9
  HARP AL5 .... 102 C5
  HTCHE/RSTV SG4 .... 84 B5
  RAYLNE/WEN HP22 .... 76 C2
Darlands Dr BAR EN5 .... 166 B5
Darley Cft LCOL/BKTW AL2 * 136 A7
Darley Rd LTNE LU2 .... 64 A5
Darnicle HI CHESW EN7 .... 141 H4
Darrington Rd BORE WD6 .... 151 K9
Darr's La BERK HP4 .... 115 J6
The Dart HHNE HP2 .... 118 A3
Darvell Dr CSHM HP5 .... 130 F8
Darvells Yd
  RKW/CH/CXG WD3 .... 160 B3
Darwin CI FBAR/BDGN N11 .... 167 M9
  HHNE HP2 .... 118 A3
  STALW/RED AL3 .... 120 D4
Darwin Gdns OXHEY WD19 .... 171 L2
Darwin Rd STVGE SG2 .... 51 L9
The Dashes HLWE CM17 .... 3 G3
Datchet CI HHNE HP2 .... 118 D8
Datchworth Turn HHNE HP2 .... 118 D8
Davenham Av NTHWD HA6 .... 171 H1
Davenport HLWE CM17 .... 129 P4
Daventer Dr STAN HA7 .... 172 F4
David Evans Ct LWTH SG6 .... 36 A1
David Dr STVG SG1 .... 107 M6
Davis Ct STAL AL1 * 7 J4
Davison CI CHES/WCR EN8 .... 142 C7
Davison Dr CHES/WCR EN8 .... 142 C7
Davis' Rw ARL/CHE SG15 .... 24 A2
Davys CI STALE/WH AL4 .... 103 K5
Dawes CI CSHM HP5 .... 144 G2
Dawes La RKW/CH/CXG WD3 .... 147 J3
  STALE/WH AL4 .... 103 J3
Dawley CI HHW HP2 * 118 A4
Dawlish CI STVGE SG2 .... 67 M7
Dawlish Rd LTNW/LEA LU4 .... 62 A3
Dawlish Wk STVGE SG2 .... 67 M7
Dayemead WCCE AL7 * 105 L9
Daymer Gdns PIN HA5 .... 171 L8
Days CI HAT AL10 .... 122 C6
Day's Cft ROY SG8 .... 20 B5
Deacon CI STAL AL1 .... 136 C3
Deacons CI BORE WD6 .... 164 G3
  PIN HA5 .... 171 K6
Deaconsfield Rd
  HHS/BOV HP3 .... 5 F7
Deacons Hts BORE WD6 .... 164 G5
Deacons HI OXHEY WD19 .... 162 E5
Deacon's Hill Rd BORE WD6 .... 164 F4
Deacons Wy HTCH/STOT SG5 .... 35 J7
Deadmans La CI ENC/FH EN2 * 159 L7
Deadman's An La
  RKW/CH/CXG WD3 .... 147 L6
Dead Woman's La
  HTCHE/RSTV SG4 .... 49 H9

De Havilland Wy ABLGY WD5 ... 148 G2
Deimos Dr HHNE HP2 .... 118 B5
Delahay Ri BERK HP4 .... 115 N5
Delamere Rd CHES/WCR EN8 .. 142 E8
Delamere Rd BORE WD6 ..... 151 N9
Delco Wy DUN/WHIP LU6 ..... 108 B1
Delfcroft WARE SG12 .... 108 B1
Delfield Gdns LTN LU1 .... 79 F1
Delius Cl BORE WD6 .... 164 C5
Dell Cl CSHM HP5 .... 130 E8
　HARP AL5 .... 102 A1
Delicot Cl LTNE LU2 .... 63 J1
Dellcott Cl WGCW AL8 .... 104 C5
Dellcroft Wy HARP AL5 ...... 101 P6
Dellcut Rd HHNE HP2 .... 118 C4
Dell Farm Rd RSLP HA4 ..... 170 F9
Dellfield CSHM HP5 .... 130 F8
　STAL AL1 .... 9 K6
　WARE SG12 .... 88 C5
Dellfield Av BERK HP4 ...... 115 N5
Dellfield Cl BERK HP4 ...... 115 N5
　RAD WD7 .... 162 E4
　WAT WD17 .... 162 C1
Dellfield Rd HAT AL10 ...... 122 D6
Dell La BSF CM23 .... 78 B5
　RBSF CM22 .... 92 B1
Dellmeadow ABLGY WD5 ..... 148 C2
Dell Meadow HHS/BOV HP3 . 133 P3
Dellmont Rd
　DUN/HR/TOD LU5.......... 60 C6
Dellors Cl BAR EN5 .... 166 B4
Dellows La HERT/WAT SG14 . 59 H1
Dell Ri LCOL/BKTW AL2 ..... 136 A5
Dell Rd BERK HP4 .... 115 J4
　PEND EN3 .... 156 E8
　WATN WD24 .... 12 A5
Dellside DEN/HRF UB9 ...... 169 N9
Dell Side WATN WD24 ...... 12 A4
Dellsome La STALW/WH AL4 . 138 C2
Dell Springs BUNT SG9 ..... 40 D8
The Dells HHS/BOV HP3 ..... 118 C9
Dellswood Cl HERT/BAY SG13 . 107 M7
Dells Wood Cl HOD EN11 .... 126 E2
The Dell BLDK SG7 .... 37 H2
　CFSP/GDCR SL9 .... 168 C3
　HERT/BAY SG13 .... 107 K9
　LTN LU1 .... 79 F2
　LTNE LU2 .... 63 N5
　NTHWD HA6 .... 162 A8
　PIN HA5 .... 171 M6
　RAD WD7 .... 150 F6
　ROY SG8 .... 20 B5
　STAL AL1 .... 120 F6
　STVG SG1 .... 11 F4
　WAB EN9 .... 157 H6
Dellwood RKW/CH/CXG WD3 . 160 F7
Delmar Av HHNE HP2 .... 118 C9
Delmeade Rd CSHM HP5 .... 144 F2
Delmerend La
　STALW/RED AL3 .... 100 D3
Delphine Cl LTN LU1 .... 62 B8
Delta Gain OXHEY WD19 .... 162 F8
De Mandeville Rd RBSF CM22 . 59 K1
Demontfort Ri WARE SG12 .. 108 D3
Denbigh Cl HHNE HP2 ...... 5 H4
Denby Rd LTNN/LIM LU3 .... 62 C4
Denby LWTH SG6 .... 25 J4
Denby Gra HLWE CM17 ..... 129 P3
Dencora Wy LTNN/LIM LU3 .. 45 L7
Dendridge Cl LTN LU1 ...... 156 A7
Dene Gdns STAN HA7 ...... 173 J2
Dene La STVGE SG2 .... 67 N4
Dene Rd NTHWD HA6 ...... 170 E3
　TRDG/WHET N20 .... 167 K7
Denewood BAR EN5 .... 166 C4
Denewood Cl WAT WD17 ... 148 C7
Denham Cl HHNE HP2 ...... 118 B5
　LTNN/LIM LU3 .... 45 P7
Denham Green La
　DEN/HRF UB9 .... 169 H9
Denham La CFSP/GDCR SL9 . 168 D4
Denham Rd TRDG/WHET N20. 167 K8
Denham Wy CFSP/GDCR SL9 . 168 D2
　BORE WD6 .... 151 P9
Denham Way
　(North Orbital Road)
　RKW/CH/CXG WD3....... 169 J4
Denmark Cl LTNN/LIM LU3.... 45 P6
Denmark St WAT WD17 ..... 12 E1
Dennis Cl RAYLNE/WEN HP22. 94 G8
Dennis La STAN HA7 .... 173 H1
Dennis Pde STHGT/OAK N14 * 167 J4
Denny Av WAB EN9 .... 157 J4
Denny Ct BSF CM23 .... 58 C9
Denny Ga CHES/WCR EN8.... 142 E6
Denny Gro HLWE CM17 ..... 104 H4
Densley Cl WGCW AL8 ...... 104 C4
Denton Cl BAR EN5 .... 166 A4
　LTNN/LEA LU4 .... 61 L2
Denton Rd STVG SG1 .... 11 F7
Dents Cl LWTH SG6 .... 26 A1
Deodora Cl TRDG/WHET N20. 167 J9
Derby Av
　KTN/HRWW/WS HA3 ..... 172 D5
Derby Rd HOD EN11 .... 127 J7
　LTNN/LIM LU3 .... 61 H4
　WAT WD17 .... 12 A3
Derby Wy STVG SG1 .... 51 F4
Derry Leys HAT AL10 .... 122 B4
Derwent Av EBAR EN4 ..... 167 K4
　LTNN/LIM LU3 .... 46 C8
　PIN HA5 .... 171 N3
Derwent Cl AMSS HP7 ..... 145 N9
　GSTN WD25 .... 149 K3
Derwent Crs
　NFNCH/WDSPK N12 ..... 166 G9
　STAN HA7 .... 173 J6
Derwent Dr DUN/WHIP LU6 . 81 K9
Derwent Rd HARP AL5 ..... 118 D9
　HHS/BOV HP3 .... 118 D9
　LTN LU1 .... 7 J2
Desborough Cl
　HERT/WAT SG14 .... 107 K3
　WGCE AL7 .... 105 L9
Desborough Rd
　HTCHE/RSTV SG4 .... 35 P8
Desmond Rd WATN WD24 .. 148 G6

De Soissons Cl WGCW AL8 .. 104 E8
De Tany Ct STAL AL1 .... 8 E6
Deva Cl STALW/RED AL3 .... 135 P1
Devereux Dr WAT WD17 .... 148 F8
De Vere Wk WAT WD17 ..... 162 A1
Devon Ct STAL AL1 .... 9 H6
Devon Man
　KTN/HRWW/WS HA3 *.... 173 J9
Devon Rd STAL AL1 .... 122 A4
Devon Rd LTNE LU2 .... 63 J7
　WATN WD24 .... 149 L9
Devonshire Av AMS HP6 .... 144 C7
Devonshire Cl STVGE SG2 ... 67 K6
Devonshire Rd HARP AL5 ... 102 A2
　PIN HA5 .... 84 F7
Dewars Cl WLYN AL6 .... 84 F7
Dewes Green Rd BSF CM23 . 43 J7
Dewgrass Gv CHES/WCR EN8. 156 C5
Dewhurst Rd CHES/WCR EN8 . 142 D8
Dewpond Cl STVG SG1 ...... 51 M7
Dewsbury Rd LTNN/LIM LU3 . 46 C9
　STAL AL1 .... 120 F7
Dexter Cl LTN LU1 .... 120 F7
Dexter Rd BAR EN5 .... 166 B5
　STHGT/OAK N14 .... 169 N6
Dharam Marg GSTN WD25 * . 150 D9
Diamond Rd WATN WD24 ... 149 H8
Dianne Rd EBAR EN4 .... 167 J3
Dickens Bvd LTNN/LIM LU3 . 46 E8
Dickens Cl STALW/RED AL3 . 135 N8
Dickens Ct HHNE HP2 ...... 118 C2
Dickenson Wy WARE SG12 .. 108 C3
Dicket Mi HERT/BAY SG13 ... 107 L5
Dicket Md WLYN AL6 .... 84 F8
Dickins Cl CHESW EN7 ..... 141 P6
Dickinson Av
　RKW/CH/CXG WD3 .... 161 L5
Dickinson Quay
　HHS/BOV HP3 .... 133 P4
Dickinsons Fld HARP AL5 ... 102 B5
Dickinson Sq
　RKW/CH/CXG WD3 .... 161 L5
Dickson CHESW EN7 .... 141 N6
Dickson Fold PIN HA5 ...... 171 M8
Dig Dag Hi CHESW EN7 .... 141 N4
Digswell Cl BORE WD6 ..... 151 M8
Digswell Ms WGCE AL7 ..... 104 D5
Digswell La WGCE AL7 ..... 105 J2
Digswell Park Rd WGCW AL8 . 104 C4
Digswell Ri WGCW AL8 ..... 104 C4
Digswell Rd WGCE AL7 ..... 105 H3
Dimmocks La
　RKW/CH/CXG WD3 .... 147 K6
Dimsdale Crs BSF CM23 .... 74 C5
Dimsdale St HERT/WAT SG14. 107 L8
Dinant Link Rd HOD EN11 .. 126 F4
Dingle Cl BAR EN5 .... 165 M5
Dinmore HHS/BOV HP3 ..... 132 C7
Dione Rd HHNE HP2 .... 118 A5
Dison Cl PEND EN3 .... 156 C8
Ditchfield Rd HOD EN11 .... 126 F2
Ditchling Cl LTNE LU2 ...... 63 K3
Ditton Gn LTNE LU2 .... 63 L4
Divewell Rd HERT/BAY SG13 . 108 A5
Dixies Cl BLDK SG7 .... 13 P7
Dixon Pl BUNT SG9 .... 40 D9
Dixons Ct WARE SG12 * 108 B1
Dixons Gap Br TRING HP23 .. 95 L2
Dixons Hill Rd BRKMPK AL9 . 138 E4
Dixons Hill Cl BRKMPK AL9 . 138 E4
Dobbin Cl
　KTN/HRWW/WS HA3 ..... 172 G6
Dobbins La
　RAYLNE/WEN HP22 ...... 112 B6
Dobb's Weir Rd HOD EN11 .. 127 J6
Docklands HTCH/STOT SG5 .. 34 C4
Doctor's Commons Rd
　BERK HP4 .... 115 N8
Dodds La CSTG SG9 .... 159 H8
Dodford HHNE HP2 .... 117 M3
Dodwood WGCE AL7 .... 105 K7
Dogden La BSF CM23 .... 57 P5
Doggetts Ct EBAR EN4 ..... 167 J4
Doggetts Wy STAL AL1 ..... 136 B1
Doggetts Wood Cl CSTG SG9 . 159 H2
Dog Kennel La HAT AL10 ... 122 D5
Dognell Gn WGCW AL8 ..... 104 E5
Dolesbury Dr WGCE AL7 .... 85 H4
Dollimore Cl
　HTCHE/RSTV SG4 .... 84 C4
Dollis Valley Dr BAR EN5 ... 166 A4
Dollis Valley Green Wk
　TRDG/WHET N20 .... 166 F9
Dollis Valley Wy BAR EN5 .. 165 P4
Dolmans Pl DUN/WHIP LU6 . 60 H3
Dolphin Dr DUN/HR/TOD LU5. 60 F1
Dolphin Sq TRING HP23 .... 95 P9
Dolphin Yd STAL AL1 .... 8 E4
　WARE SG12 * 108 C3
Dominic Cl WAB EN9 .... 156 C3
Dominion Pde HRW HA1 * .. 172 F9
Domino Cl TRDG/WHET N20. 167 H8
Doncaster Cl STVG SG1 .... 51 M7
Doncaster Gn OXHEY WD19 . 171 L2
Donkey La TRING HP23 ..... 95 M9
Donne Cl ROY SG8 .... 20 B2
Dorchester Av EDGW HA8 .. 173 L3
Dorchester Rd HOD EN11 ... 126 F3
Dorchester Cl
　DUN/HR/TOD LU5 .... 60 E5
Dorchester Wy
　KTN/HRWW/WS HA3 ..... 173 N1
Dordans Rd LTNN/LEA LU4... 61 J2
Dorel Cl LTN LU1 .... 62 G4
Dorian Ct TRING HP23 ..... 95 N8
Dormans Cl NTHWD HA6 ... 170 H4
Dormer Ct BAR EN5 .... 166 A4
Dormers HHS/BOV HP3 ..... 133 M6
Dormie Cl STALW/RED AL3 . 135 J2
Dormywood RSLP HA4 ..... 171 N9
Dorney End CSHM HP5 ..... 130 F9

Dorrien's Cft BERK HP4 ..... 115 L4
Dorrington Cl LTNN/LIM LU3. 45 P7
Dorrofield Cl
　RKW/CH/CXG WD3 .... 161 N4
Dorset Cl BERK HP4 .... 115 L6
　LTN LU1 .... 7 G7
Dorset Rd BAR EN5 .... 165 N3
Dorset St LTNE LU2 .... 63 P3
Dove Cl BSF CM23 .... 59 P1
　STAN HA7 .... 172 G2
Dovecot Cl PIN HA5 .... 171 L9
Dove Ct HAT AL10 .... 122 D8
Dovedale La
　DUN/HR/TOD LU5 .... 46 F9
Dovedale St DEN/HRF UB9 .. 169 N6
Dovehouse Cft HAT AL10 ... 122 D6
Dovehouse Cl DEN/HRF UB9. 129 K1
Dovehouse Hi LTNE LU2 .... 63 J4
Dove House La
　DUN/WHIP LU6 .... 78 F6
Dove La HHS/BOV HP3 ..... 133 M6
Dove Pk PIN HA5 .... 171 P4
Dovehouse Rd WGCE AL7 *.. 85 M4
Dover Cl LTNN/LIM LU3 ..... 62 B8
Dovercourt Gdns STAN HA7. 173 L2
Doverfield CHESW EN7 ..... 141 K8
Dove Rd STVG SG1 .... 51 J4
Dover Wy RKW/CH/CXG WD3 . 161 N5
Dowding Cft HARP AL5 ..... 102 B6
Dowding Pl STAN HA7 ...... 173 H3
Dowding Wy GSTN WD25 ... 148 G4
Dowley Wd WGCE AL7 ..... 105 L6
Dowling Ct HHS/BOV HP3 .. 5 F7
Downalong BUSH WD23 .... 163 M7
Downedge STALW/RED AL3 . 100 A3
Downer Dr
　RKW/CH/CXG WD3 .... 147 J6
Downes Rd STALE/WH AL4 .. 120 C4
Downfield Cl HARP AL5 ..... 102 B8
Downfield Rd
　CHES/WCR EN8 .... 156 D1
　HERT/BAY SG13 .... 108 B8
Downfields WGCW AL8 ..... 104 C5
Down Green La
　STALE/WH AL4 .... 102 G5
Downhall Ley BUNT SG9 .... 54 D1
Downing Cl
　RYLN/HDSTN HA2 .... 172 C7
Downings Wd
　RKW/CH/CXG WD3 .... 169 J7
Downland Cl
　TRDG/WHET N20 .... 166 G7
Downlands BLDK SG7 ...... 26 C8
　LTNN/LIM LU3 .... 45 M8
　ROY SG8 .... 20 B4
　STVGE SG2 .... 51 N8
　WAB EN9 .... 157 K4
Downside HHNE HP2 .... 117 P7
Downsfield HAT AL10 ...... 122 D9
Downs La HAT AL10 .... 122 D8
Downs Rd DUN/HR/TOD LU5. 60 C6
　LTN LU1 .... 6 A5
The Downs HAT AL10 ...... 122 D8
　STVG SG1 .... 3 H5
Downs Vw
　POTB/CUF EN6 .... 140 G8
Dowry Wk WAT WD17 ...... 11 G1
Dragon Rd HAT AL10 ...... 122 A5
Drakes Cl CHES/WCR EN8 .. 142 D8
Drakes Dr NTHWD HA6 .... 170 D5
　STAL AL1 .... 136 C2
　STVGE SG2 .... 51 L8
Drakes Rd AMSS HP7 ...... 145 H3
Drakes St ENC/FH EN2 ..... 155 L3
Drakes Wy HAT AL10 ...... 122 E8
Drapers Ms LTNN/LIM LU3 *. 62 D5
Drapers Wy STVG SG1 ...... 50 H1
Drayman's Cl BSF CM23 .... 73 L9
Drayton Av POTB/CUF EN6 . 153 N2
Drayton Rd BORE WD6 ..... 164 C3
　LTNN/LEA LU4 .... 61 J3
The Drey POTB/CUF EN6 ... 168 C2
Driftway ROY SG8 .... 29 L5
The Driftway HHNE HP2 .... 5 K2
Driftwood Av
　LCOL/BKTW AL2 .... 135 P5
Drive Ct EDGW HA8 * 173 N2
Driver's End La
　STVGE SG2 .... 84 C1
The Drive AMSS HP7 ...... 145 J8
　BAR EN5 .... 166 C2
　CFSP/GDCR SL9 .... 168 C4
　EBAR EN4 .... 167 J6
　EDGW HA8 .... 173 N2
　ENC/FH EN2 .... 155 L9
　HARP AL5 .... 101 P3
　HERT/BAY SG13 .... 140 F3
　HERT/WAT SG14 .... 107 K4
　HOD EN11 .... 3 H5
　LCOL/BKTW AL2 .... 136 F4
　NTHWD HA6 .... 170 C6
　POTB/CUF EN6 .... 153 P4
　ROY SG8 .... 21 H3
　RSLP HA4 .... 171 H9
　SBW CM21 .... 111 P2
　STALE/WH AL4 .... 82 G6
　WAT WD17 .... 148 E7
　WLYN AL6 .... 85 H4
Drovers Wy BSF CM23 ..... 73 M9

　DUN/WHIP LU6 .... 60 C6
　STAL AL10 .... 8 E8
　STAL AL1 .... 8 E8
The Druce SAFWS CB11 .... 43 N4
Drummond Dr STAN HA7 .. 172 F4
Drury Cl DUN/HR/TOD LU5 . 60 F1
Drury La DUN/HR/TOD LU5 . 60 F1
　WARE SG12 .... 110 A3
Dryburgh Gdns
　CDALE/KGS NW9 .... 173 N7
Drycroft WGCE AL7 .... 123 H1
Drydell La CSHM HP5 ...... 144 E1
Dryden Crs STVGE SG2 ..... 57 N7
Dryden Rd
　KTN/HRWW/WS HA3 ..... 172 F5
Drysdale Cl NTHWD HA6 ... 170 E7
Dubbs Knoll Rd ROY SG8 ... 15 L6
Dubrae Cl STALW/RED AL3 . 135 P1
Duchess Cl BSF CM23 ...... 73 L7
Duchy Rd EBAR EN4 .... 153 P9
Duck Aly CSHM HP5 .... 143 M8
Ducketts La MHAD SG10 ... 90 G4
Ducketts Md
　HLWW/ROY CM19 .... 127 N2
Duck La STVGE SG2 .... 88 C6
Duckling La SBW CM21 .... 111 P2
Ducks Hill Rd NTHWD HA6 . 170 C6
Du Cros Dr STAN HA7 ..... 173 K3
Dudley Av CHES/WCR EN8 . 143 J7
Dudley Hill Cl WLYN AL6 ... 83 H5
Dudswell La BERK HP4 ..... 115 J3
Dudswell Mi BERK HP4 * ... 115 J3
Duffield Cl HRW HA1 ...... 172 F9
Dugdale Hill La
　POTB/CUF EN6 .... 153 H3
Dugdales RKW/CH/CXG WD3 . 161 J3
Dukes Av DUN/WHIP LU6 ... 78 B7
　EDGW HA8 .... 173 M3
　HRW HA1 .... 172 E8
Duke's La HTCH/STOT SG5 . 35 N7
Dukes Orch RBSF CM22 .... 93 K3
Dukes Ride BSF CM23 ..... 79 M3
Duke St HOD EN11 .... 126 F4
　LTNE LU2 .... 13 G5
　WAT WD17 .... 13 F3
Dulwich Wy
　CHES/WCR EN8 .... 156 C4
Dumbarton Av
　CHES/WCR EN8 .... 156 C4
Dumbleton Cl
　RKW/CH/CXG WD3 ...... 162 C9
Dumfries Cl OXHEY WD19 .. 161 J1
Dumfries St LTN LU1 ...... 166 C3
Duncan Cl BAR EN5 .... 166 C3
Duncan Wy BUSH WD23 ... 149 K8
Duncombe Cl AMS HP6 .... 145 K8
　HERT/WAT SG14 .... 107 K4
　LTNN/LIM LU3 .... 46 D9
Duncombe Dr
　DUN/HR/TOD LU5 .... 60 C6
Duncombe Rd BERK HP4 ... 115 K5
　HERT/WAT SG14 .... 107 J4
Duncots Cl HTCH/STOT SG5 . 35 K5
Dundale Rd TRING HP23 ... 95 P8
Dundas Ms PEND EN3 ..... 156 F7
Dunhams Ct LWTH SG6 .... 25 J8
Dunhams La LWTH SG6 .... 25 J8
Dunlin LWTH SG6 .... 25 J3
Dunlin Rd HHNE HP2 ...... 117 P7
Dunmow Rd BSF CM23 .... 74 C3
　STVGE SG2 .... 67 H3
Dunnock Cl BORE WD6 .... 163 P8
Dunny La CHES/WCR EN8 .. 147 J3
Dunraven Av LTN LU1 ..... 62 B6
Dunsany Rd LTNN/LIM LU3 . 61 J8
Dunsley Pl TRING HP23 .... 96 A9
Dunsmore OXHEY WD19 * . 161 J1
Dunsmore Rd LTN LU1 ..... 6 A5
Dunsmore Wy BUSH WD23.. 163 M5
Dunstable Cl LTNN/LEA LU4. 61 K5
Dunstable Rd
　DUN/HR/TOD LU5 .... 44 C5
　DUN/HR/TOD LU5 .... 60 D1
　LTN LU1 .... 61 K9
　LTN LU1 .... 61 K9
Dunstall Rd
　AMP/FLIT/BLC MK45 ..... 32 D6
Dunstalls HLWW/ROY CM19 . 128 D7
Dunster Cl BAR EN5 .... 166 B3
　DEN/HRF UB9 .... 169 H8
Dunster Rd HHNE HP2 .... 118 B8
Dunsters Md WGCE AL7 ... 105 K8
Dunston Hl TRING HP23 ... 95 P8
Dunwich Farm STVG SG1 .. 50 D9
Durban Rd East WATW WD18. 12 D4
Durban Rd West
　WATW WD18 .... 12 C4
Durbar Rd LTN LU1 .... 62 C4
Durham Rd BORE WD6 .... 172 B9
　HRW HA1 .... 172 B9
　LTN LU1 .... 7 K3
　STVG SG1 .... 51 L9
Durler Gdns LTN LU1 ...... 62 E9
Durrants Dr
　RKW/CH/CXG WD3 ...... 161 N2
Durrants Hill Rd
　HHS/BOV HP3 .... 5 F8
Durrants La BERK HP4 ..... 115 J5
Durrants Rd BERK HP4 .... 115 H5
Durrant Wy ROY SG8 ..... 21 H4
Duxford Cl LTNN/LIM LU3 .. 153 J9
Duxons Turn HHNE HP2 ... 5 H3
Dwight Rd WATW WD18 ... 161 N6
Dyes La LTNN/LIM LU3 .... 46 E6
Dyke La STALE/WH AL4 ... 103 K5
Dylan Cl BORE WD6 .... 164 C6

Dymoke Gn STALE/WH AL4.. 120 F5
Dymoke Ms STVG SG1 * 50 F8
Dymokes Wy HOD EN11 ... 126 F2
Dyrham La BAR EN5 .... 152 D6
Dysons Cl CHES/WCR EN8... 156 C3

E

Eagle Centre Wy
　LTNW/LEA LU4 .... 45 L8
Eagle Cl AMS HP6 .... 145 L7
　LTNW/LEA LU4 .... 61 K2
　WAB EN9 .... 157 M4
Eagle Ct POTB/CUF EN6 * .. 152 D3
Eagle Wy HAT AL10 .... 122 D8
Ealing Cl BORE WD6 ...... 164 D1
Earls Cl BSF CM23 .... 73 N8
Earls Cnr POTB/CUF EN6 * . 152 D3
Earls Crs HRW HA1 .... 172 E8
Earls Hill Gdns ROY SG8 ... 20 B4
Earls Meade LTNE LU2 .... 62 E5
Earl St WAT WD17 .... 13 H3
Earnshaw Dr HTCHE/STOT SG5. 24 C7
Easedale Cl DUN/WHIP LU6.. 60 F8
Easington Rd WARE SG12 .. 69 M7
Easingwold Gdns LTN LU1 . 62 A6
Eastbrook Av DUN/WHIP LU6. 60 G6
Eastbrook Wy HHNE HP2 .. 5 L2
East Burrowfield WGCE AL7. 104 G8
Eastbury Av EN EN1 ...... 155 M9
　NTHWD HA6 .... 170 C2
Eastbury Ct OXHEY WD19 * . 162 E6
　　　　　　　　　　　　　　J1
Eastbury Rd NTHWD HA6 .. 170 C3
　OXHEY WD19 .... 162 E6
Eastcheap LWTH SG6 ..... 36 C3
East Cl BAR EN5 .... 167 J1
　HARP AL5 .... 35 N7
　LCOL/BKTW AL2 .... 136 A4
　RSLP HA4 .... 11 G4
Eastcote Dr HARP AL5 .... 102 G4
Eastcote Rd PIN HA5 ..... 171 M9
Eastcott Cl LTNE LU2 ..... 171 L8
Eastcroft Cl LTNE LU2 .... 63 K4
East Dr GSTN WD25 ...... 149 J6
　LCOL/BKTW AL2 .... 136 C5
　NTHWD HA6 .... 162 A8
　SBW CM21 .... 111 P3
East End Rd
　DUN/HR/TOD LU5 .... 60 C5
East End Wy PIN HA5 ..... 171 N1
Eastern Cl LTNE LU2 ...... 156 C5
　DUN/HR/TOD LU5 .... 60 D5
　HNLW SG16 .... 10 C5
Eastern Wy LWTH SG6 .... 25 L9
Eastfield Av WATN WD24 .. 149 L9
Eastfield Cl LTNE LU2 ..... 63 L8
Eastfield Ct STALE/WH AL4. 121 J3
Eastfield Rd PEND EN3 .... 156 C8
　ROY SG8 .... 20 C3
Eastfields PIN HA5 .... 171 L9
East Flint HLW CM20 ..... 117 H7
East Ga HLW CM20 .... 2 E4
East Hill LTNN/LIM LU3 .... 170 G2
Eastham Cl BAR EN5 ..... 166 C4
Easthall Rd DUN/HR/TOD LU5. 60 F1
Eastholm LWTH SG6 ...... 25 L9
Eastholm Gn LWTH SG6 ... 25 L9
East La ABLGY WD5 ...... 135 M8
　STALE/WH AL4 .... 103 J3
Eastlea Av GSTN WD25 ... 149 M7
East Lodge La ENC/FH EN2. 154 E6
Eastman Wy HHNE HP2 ... 118 B5
East Md WGCE AL7 .... 105 H8
East Mimms HHNE HP2 ... 117 P7
Eastmoor Pk HARP AL5 ... 102 B6
East Pk HLWE CM17 ...... 111 L9
Eastor WGCE AL7 .... 105 K3
East Pk Cl HLWE CM17 ... 111 L9
East Pole Cots
　STHGT/OAK N14 * 167 P3
East Reach STVGE SG2 ... 85 N6
East Ridgeway
　POTB/CUF EN6 .... 140 G9
East Riding BSF CM23 .... 74 C3
　EDGW HA8 .... 173 M6
　HLW CM20 .... 111 L8
　STVG SG1 .... 156 B8
East St CSHM HP5 .... 144 C2
　LTNE LU2 .... 7 H1
　WARE SG12 .... 108 C1
East Vw BAR EN5 .... 166 D1
　BRKMPK AL9 .... 124 A5
　HTCHE/RSTV SG4 .... 49 P5
East Wy WAB EN9 .... 157 H6
Eastwick Crs
　RKW/CH/CXG WD3 ...... 160 D8
Eastwick Hall La HLW CM20. 110 D8
Eastwick Rd HLW CM20 ... 110 E8
　WARE SG12 .... 109 N9
Eastwick Rw HHNE HP2 ... 118 D9
Eaton Cl BROX EN10 ..... 153 H2
Eaton Ga NTHWD HA6 .... 170 D6
Eaton Green Rd LTNE LU2 . 63 L5
Eaton Pl LTNE LU2 .... 63 L5
Eaton Rd HHNE HP2 ..... 118 C5
　LTNE LU2 .... 63 L5
　STAL AL1 .... 136 E3
Eaton Valley Rd LTNE LU2 . 63 J6
Eaton Wy BORE WD6 ..... 151 L9
Ebberns Rd HHS/BOV HP3 . 133 P2
Ebberston Ct LTN LU1 * ... 63 F2
Ebury Ap
　RKW/CH/CXG WD3 ...... 161 H7

Ebury Cl NTHWD HA6 170 E2
Ebury Rd WAT WD17 13 H2
Eccleston Cl EBAR EN4 167 J4
Echo Hl ROY SG8 20 B5
Eddington Crs WGCE AL7 104 G9
Eddiwick Av
DUN/HR/TOD LU5 44 G8
Eddy St BERK HP4 115 M6
Eden Cl PEND EN3 156 F8
Edenhall Cl HHNE HP2 118 E9
Edens Cl BSF CM23 74 C3
Edenvale CHESW EN7 142 A8
Edgars Ct WGCE AL7 105 H7
Edgbaston Dr RAD WD7 151 K2
Edgcott Cl LTNN/LIM LU3 46 C6
Edgecote Cl LTN LU1 79 P2
Edgehill Gdns
LTNN/LIM LU3 45 M7
Edgewood Dr LTNE LU2 47 K9
Edgeworth Cl STVGE SG2 67 M5
Edgeworth Rd EBAR EN4 167 J3
Edgwarebury Gdns
EDGW HA8 173 N2
Edgwarebury La BORE WD6 164 F6
EDGW HA8 173 N1
Edgware Road High St
EDGW HA8 173 N3
Edgware Way
(Watford By-Pass)
EDGW HA8 173 N1
Edinburgh Av
RKW/CH/CXG WD3 160 E5
Edinburgh Crs
CHES/WCR EN8 156 D3
Edinburgh Dr ABLGY WD5 149 H2
Edinburgh Pl HLW CM20 111 K8
Edinburgh Wy HLW CM20 110 G9
Edingburgh Gdns BSF CM23 73 N8
Edison Cl STALE/WH AL4 121 H9
Edison Rd PEND EN3 156 E9
STVGE SG2 51 L9
Edkins Cl LTNE LU2 62 F1
Edlyn Cl BERK HP4 115 L6
Edmonds Dr STVGE SG2 67 N2
Edmund Beaufort Dr
STALW/RED AL3 120 C6
Edmund Ms KGLGY WD4 134 B8
Edmunds Rd
HERT/WAT SG14 106 G5
Edridge Cl BUSH WD23 163 L4
Edson Cl GSTN WD25 148 G3
Edulf Rd BORE WD6 165 H1
Edward Amey Cl
GSTN WD25 149 K6
Edward Cl ABLGY WD5 148 G2
STAL AL1 9 J5
Edward Ct HHS/BOV HP3 133 N3
WAB EN9 157 L3
Edward Gv EBAR EN4 167 H4
Edward Rd EBAR EN4 167 H4
RYLN/HDSTN HA2 172 C7
Edward St DUN/WHIP LU6 60 D5
LTNE LU2 7 G1
Edwin Ware Ct PIN HA5 * 171 L6
Edworth Rd BGSW SG18 16 B5
Edwyn Cl BAR EN5 166 A5
Egdon Dr LTNE LU2 46 E9
Egerton Cl PIN HA5 171 J8
Egerton Rd BERK HP4 115 M5
Egg Farm La KGLGY WD4 134 D9
Egglesfield Cl BERK HP4 115 K5
Eggleton Dr TRING HP23 95 P7
Eight Acres TRING HP23 95 P8
Eighth Av LTNN/LIM LU3 45 N8
Eisenberg Cl BLDK SG7 26 C8
Elaine Gdns LTN LU1 80 B4
Elbow La HOD EN11 126 A4
STVGE SG2 67 L5
Eldefield LWTH SG6 36 A1
Elderbeck Cl CHESW EN7 141 P7
Elderberry Cl LTNE LU2 63 J2
Elderberry Dr
HTCHE/RSTV SG4 49 M3
Elderberry Wy GSTN WD25 149 J5
Elder Cl TRDG/WHET N20 166 F8
Elder Ct BUSH WD23 163 N8
Elderfield HLWE CM17 111 N8
WGCE AL7 105 L6
Elder Rd WARE SG12 108 E1
Elder Wy STVG SG1 66 G3
Eldon Av BORE WD6 164 G1
Eldon Rd HOD EN11 127 J7
LTNW/LEA LU4 61 M4
Eleanor Av STALW/RED AL3 120 C6
Eleanor Cross Rd
CHES/WCR EN8 156 D4
Eleanor Gdns BAR EN5 166 B4
Eleanor Rd CFSP/GDCR SL9 168 D3
CHES/WCR EN8 156 D3
HERT/WAT SG14 107 K5
Eleanors Cl WARE SG12 88 C6
Eleanor's Cross
DUN/WHIP LU6 60 E6
Eleanor Wy CHES/WCR EN8 156 E4
Eleventh Av STSD CM24 59 J9
Elfrida Rd WATW WD18 13 G7
Elgar Cl BORE WD6 164 C6
Elgar Pth LTNE LU2 6 E2
Elgin Av
KTN/HRWW/WS HA3 173 H6
Elgin Dr NTHWD HA6 170 G4
Elgin Rd CHES/WCR EN8 142 B9
Elgiva La CSHM HP5 144 G1
Elgood Av NTHWD HA6 171 J3
Eliot Rd ROY SG8 20 C2
STVGE SG2 51 M9
Elizabeth Av AMS HP6 145 P9
Elizabeth Cl BAR EN5 166 B2
HERT/WAT SG14 106 G5
WAB EN9 143 J1
WGCE AL7 105 M6
Elizabeth Ct STALE/WH AL4 121 J5
Elizabeth Dr TRING HP23 95 A6
Elizabeth Gdns STAN HA7 173 J3
Elizabeth Rd BSF CM23 73 P9
Elizabeth St LTN LU1 6 D6
Elizabeth Wy HLW CM20 2 B1
HLWW/ROY CM19 128 C4
Elkanette Ms
TRDG/WHET N20 166 G8
Ellement Cl PIN HA5 171 M9
Ellenborough Cl BSF CM23 73 N9
Ellenbrook Cl
WATN WD24 * 149 K9
Ellenbrook Crs HAT AL10 122 A6
Ellenbrook La HAT AL10 122 A6
Ellen Cl HHNE HP2 118 A7
Ellenhall Cl LTNN/LIM LU3 62 D5
Ellen Webb Dr
KTN/HRWW/WS HA3 172 E7
Ellerdine Cl LTNN/LIM LU3 62 C2
Ellesborough Cl
OXHEY WD19 171 L2
Ellesborough Rd
RAYLNE/WEN HP22 112 A8
Ellesfield WLYN AL6 84 E8
Ellesmere Av MLHL NW7 165 K9
Ellesmere Gv BAR EN5 166 D4
Ellesmere Rd BERK HP4 116 A7
Ellingham Cl HHNE HP2 118 B6
Ellingham Rd HHNE HP2 118 A7
Elliott Cl WGCE AL7 104 G9
Elliott Rd STAN HA7 172 G3
Ellis Av CFSP/GDCR SL9 168 D5
STVG SG1 51 H7
Ellis Cl HOD EN11 126 E1
Ellis Flds STALW/RED AL3 120 D4
Elliswick Rd HARP AL5 102 A2
Ellwood Gdns GSTN WD25 149 J4
Ellwood Ri CSTG HP8 159 J8
Elm Av LTN LU1 79 P2
OXHEY WD19 162 G6
Elmbank Av BAR EN5 166 A3
Elmbrook Dr BSF CM23 91 P2
Elm Cl AMS HP6 145 H8
RAYLNE/WEN HP22 112 A1
RBSF CM22 59 K1
WAB EN9 157 J4
Elmcote Wy
RKW/CH/CXG WD3 161 K5
Elm Ct SAFWS CB11 23 L6
WAT WD17 * 13 F2
Elmcroft Crs
RYLN/HDSTN HA2 172 A7
Elmcroft Gdns
CDALE/KGS NW9 173 N9
Elm Dr CHES/WCR EN8 142 D7
HAT AL10 122 D7
STALE/WH AL4 121 H8
Elmer Gdns EDGW HA8 173 P4
Elmfield Cl POTB/CUF EN6 153 H3
Elmfield Rd POTB/CUF EN6 153 H3
Elm Gdns ENC/FH EN2 155 L8
WGCW AL8 104 E6
Elm Gn HHW HP1 117 H6
Elm Gv BERK HP4 115 N7
BSF CM23 74 C3
DUN/HR/TOD LU5 44 C1
WATN WD24 149 H7
Elmgrove Crs HRW HA1 172 F9
Elmgrove Gdns HRW HA1 172 G9
Elmgrove Rd HRW HA1 172 F9
Elm Hatch PIN HA5 171 P4
Elmhurst Cl BUSH WD23 162 G3
Elmhurst Rd PEND EN3 156 B7
Elm Lawn Cl STAL AL1 9 H1
Elmoor Av WLYN AL6 84 E8
Elmoor Cl WLYN AL6 84 E9
Elmore Rd LTNE LU2 63 H5
PEND EN3 156 C9
Elm Pk BLDK SG7 26 B9
STAN HA7 173 H2
Elm Park Cl
DUN/HR/TOD LU5 44 G9
Elm Park Rd PIN HA5 171 L6
Elm Rd BAR EN5 166 D3
BSF CM23 73 P6
Elmroyd Av POTB/CUF EN6 153 J3
Elmroyd Cl POTB/CUF EN6 153 J3
Elms WAB EN9 157 P5
Elms Cl HTCHE/RSTV SG4 50 B4
Elmscroft Gdns
POTB/CUF EN6 153 J2
Elmside DUN/WHIP LU6 78 G5
Elmside Wk HTCH/STOT SG5 35 K9
Elmsleigh Av
KTN/HRWW/WS HA3 173 H8
Elms Rd CFSP/GDCR SL9 168 C4
KTN/HRWW/WS HA3 172 E4
WARE SG12 108 F2
Elmstead Cl
TRDG/WHET N20 166 E8
The Elms BORE WD6 * 151 M9
HERT/BAY SG13 107 P6
HTCHE/RSTV SG4 84 C3
Elm Ter KTN/HRWW/WS HA3 172 D6
Elmtree Av LTNE LU2 63 M3
Elmtree Hl CSHM HP5 130 G9
Elm Tree Wk
RKW/CH/CXG WD3 * 160 D3
TRING HP23 95 P7
Elm Wk RAD WD7 150 E6
ROY SG8 20 E3
STVGE SG2 67 L3
Elm Wy RKW/CH/CXG WD3 160 F7
Elmwood SBW CM21 92 A8
WGCW AL8 104 E7
Elmwood Av BLDK SG7 37 J1
BORE WD6 165 H3
KTN/HRWW/WS HA3 172 G9
Elmwood Ct BLDK SG7 * 26 B9
Elmwood Crs LTNE LU2 62 F3
Elsinge Rd EN EN1 156 A6
Elstree Ga BORE WD6 * 165 K1
Elstree Hl North BORE WD6 164 D4
Elstree Hl South BORE WD6 164 C6
Elstree Pk BORE WD6 * 165 K5
Elstree Rd BUSH WD23 163 M7
HHNE HP2 118 B2
Elstree Wy BORE WD6 165 J1
Elton Av BAR EN5 166 D4
Elton Pk WAT WD17 162 C1
Elton Rd HERT/WAT SG14 107 K5
Elveden Cl LTNE LU2 46 F9
Elvington Gdns
LTNN/LIM LU3 46 C6
Elwood HLWE CM17 129 P4
Ely Cl AMSS HP7 145 K9
HAT AL10 122 C5
STVG SG1 51 L5
Ely Gdns BORE WD6 165 K4
Ely Rd STAL AL1 120 G9
Ely Wy LTNW/LEA LU4 61 N2
Embleton Rd OXHEY WD19 162 C9
Embry Cl STAN HA7 172 G1
Embry Dr STAN HA7 172 G3
Embry Wy STAN HA7 172 G2
Emerald Rd LTNW/LEA LU4 61 J4
Emerton Ct BERK HP4 115 K4
Emerton Garth BERK HP4 115 K4
Emily Ct HARP AL5 102 B5
Emmanuel Rd NTHWD HA6 171 H4
Emma Rothschild Ct
TRING HP23 95 P7
Emmas Crs WARE SG12 108 G8
Emmer Gn LTNE LU2 63 N4
Emmitt Cl RAD WD7 151 K3
Emperor Cl BERK HP4 115 L4
Emperors Ga STVG SG1 51 N7
Empress Rd LTNN/LIM LU3 61 P2
Endeavour Rd
CHES/WCR EN8 142 D6
Enderby Rd LTNN/LIM LU3 46 D8
Enderley Rd
KTN/HRWW/WS HA3 172 D5
Endersby Rd BAR EN5 166 A4
Endymion Ct HAT AL10 122 F5
Endymion Ms HAT AL10 122 F5
Endymion Rd HAT AL10 122 F5
Enfield Cl DUN/HR/TOD LU5 44 G9
Enfield Rd ENC/FH EN2 167 P3
England Av DUN/WHIP LU6 60 B3
Englands La
DUN/HR/TOD LU5 60 F6
Englehurst HARP AL5 102 C3
Engleric ROY SG8 22 G6
Enid Cl LCOL/BKTW AL2 149 N1
Ennerdale Av
DUN/WHIP LU6 60 E7
STAN HA7 173 J7
Ennerdale Cl STAL AL1 136 G1
Ennis Cl HARP AL5 102 C6
Ennismore Cl LWTH SG6 36 F5
Ennismore Gn LTNE LU2 63 N5
Enslow Cl LTN LU1 79 P2
Enterprise Wy HHNE HP2 118 D6
LTNN/LIM LU3 46 C7
Epping Gn HHNE HP2 118 C3
Epping Rd
HLWW/ROY CM19 127 N4
Epping Wy LTNN/LIM LU3 45 M6
Ereswell Rd LTNN/LIM LU3 46 B8
Erin Cl LTNW/LEA LU4 62 B4
Ermine Cl CHESW EN7 156 A1
ROY SG8 20 C2
STALW/RED AL3 119 P9
Ermine Ct BUNT SG9 40 D8
Ermine St BUNT SG9 40 C6
WARE SG12 88 C6
Errington Cl HAT AL10 122 B5
Escarpment Av
DUN/WHIP LU6 78 A5
Escot Wy BAR EN5 166 A4
Esdaile La HOD EN11 126 F6
Eskdale LCOL/BKTW AL2 137 L6
LTNW/LEA LU4 61 M1
Eskdale Av CSHM HP5 131 J9
Eskdale Ct HHNE HP2 117 P5
Essendon Gdns WGCE AL7 105 J6
Essendon Hl BRKMPK AL9 123 P5
Essex Cl LTN LU1 7 F7
Essex Hl SAFWS CB11 23 K7
Essex La KGLGY WD4 148 E3
Essex Md HHNE HP2 118 A2
Essex Rd BORE WD6 164 G2
CSHM HP5 131 H8
HOD EN11 126 G4
STVG SG1 50 E7
WAT WD17 12 D1
Essex St STAL AL1 9 G2
Essoldo Wy EDGW HA8 173 M7
Estcourt Rd WAT WD17 13 G3
Ethelred Cl WGCE AL7 105 J7
Ethorpe Crs CFSP/GDCR SL9 168 C9
Etna Rd STALW/RED AL3 8 E2
Eton Av EBAR EN4 167 J5
Eton Gv CDALE/KGS NW9 173 N7
Eunice Gv CSHM HP5 145 J3
Europa Rd HHNE HP2 118 A5
Euston Av WATW WD18 12 B7
Evans Av GSTN WD25 148 G5
Evans Cl DUN/HR/TOD LU5 60 G2
Evan's Cl RKW/CH/CXG WD3 161 L4
Evans Cl ROY SG8 20 C3
Evans Gv STALE/WH AL4 121 H4
Evans Wy TRING HP23 96 A8
Evans Whf HHS/BOV HP3 133 P3
Evedon Cl LTNN/LIM LU3 46 A9
Evelyn Dr PIN HA5 171 M4
Evelyn Rd DUN/HR/TOD LU5 61 J4
EBAR EN4 167 K3
Evensyde WATW WD18 161 N5
Everard Cl STAL AL1 8 E7
Everest Cl ARL/CHE SG15 24 F4
Everest Gdns BSF CM23 73 N8
Everest Wy HHNE HP2 118 B8
Everett Cl BUSH WD23 163 N7
CHESW EN7 141 K4
PIN HA5 171 H7
Evergreen Cl KNEB SG3 85 K3
Evergreen Rd WARE SG12 108 E1
Evergreen Wk HHNE HP2 5 G5
Evergreen Wy LTNN/LIM LU3 46 B7
Everlasting La
STALW/RED AL3 8 C1
Eversleigh Rd BAR EN5 166 G4
Everton Dr STAN HA7 173 L7
Exchange Rd STVG SG1 11 G4
WATW WD18 13 F4
Executive Pk STAL AL1 * 120 G8
Exeter Cl STVG SG1 51 L5
WATN WD24 162 E1
Exeter Rd STHGT/OAK N14 167 M7
Explorer Dr WATW WD18 162 B5
Extension Rd HERT/BAY SG13 107 N6
Exton Av LTNE LU2 7 K1
Eyeworth Rd
SDY/GAM/POT SG19 14 G2
Eyncourt Rd
DUN/HR/TOD LU5 60 F4
Eynsford Ct HTCHE/RSTV SG4 49 L1
Eynsford Rd LTNW/LEA LU4 61 N3

F

Faggots Cl RAD WD7 151 H5
Faints Cl CHESW EN7 141 N8
Fairacre HHS/BOV HP3 134 A3
Fairacres Cl POTB/CUF EN6 153 J3
Fairburn Cl BORE WD6 151 M9
Fair Cl BUSH WD23 163 K6
Faircross Wy STAL AL1 120 F6
Fairfax Av LTNN/LIM LU3 45 N8
Fairfax Rd HERT/BAY SG13 107 N5
Fairfield BUNT SG9 54 D1
Fairfield Av EDGW HA8 173 P3
OXHEY WD19 162 E9
Fairfield Cl DUN/HR/TOD LU5 61 J5
HARP AL5 102 C3
RAD WD7 150 D7
Fairfield Crs EDGW HA8 173 P3
STVG SG1 51 L3
Fairfield Dr BROX EN10 142 E3
RYLN/HDSTN HA2 172 C7
Fairfield Rd
DUN/HR/TOD LU5 61 H5
HOD EN11 126 F3
Fairfield Wy BAR EN5 166 E4
HTCHE/RSTV SG4 35 P8
STVG SG1 51 M4
Fairfolds GSTN WD25 149 M5
Fairford Av LTNE LU2 62 F1
Fairgreen EBAR EN4 167 K2
Fairgreen Ct EBAR EN4 * 167 K2
Fairgreen Rd LTN LU1 80 A2
Fairhaven LCOL/BKTW AL2 * 136 C6
Fairhaven Crs OXHEY WD19 162 C9
Fairhill HHS/BOV HP3 134 A3
Fairholme Ct PIN HA5 * 172 A3
Fairholme Rd HRW HA1 172 E9
Fairlands Wy STVG SG1 10 A4
Fairlawn Cl STHGT/OAK N14 167 P5
Fairlawns PIN HA5 171 L6
WAT WD17 148 G9
Fair Leas CSHM HP5 130 F8
Fairley Wy CHESW EN7 142 A7
Fairmead Av HARP AL5 102 B4
Fair Oak Dr LTNE LU2 62 G3
Fairoaks Gv PEND EN3 156 C7
Fairseat Cl BUSH WD23 163 N8
Fairthorn Cl TRING HP23 95 M9
Fair Vw POTB/CUF EN6 139 L9
Fairview Dr WAT WD17 148 F6
Fairview Rd ENC/FH EN2 155 H9
STVG SG1 10 A3
STVG SG1 50 E7
Fairview Wy EDGW HA8 173 N1
Fairway BSF CM23 74 D4
HHS/BOV HP3 134 A3
SBW CM21 92 A7
WARE SG12 108 B4
Fairway Av BORE WD6 165 H1
CDALE/KGS NW9 173 P7
Fairway Cl HARP AL5 101 P7
LCOL/BKTW AL2 136 B6
Fairway Ct MLHL NW7 * 165 K9
Fairways CHES/WCR EN8 142 C5
STAN HA7 173 L6
The Fairways
CHES/WCR EN8 * 142 C5
The Fairway ABLGY WD5 148 E2
BAR EN5 166 F5
HLWS CM18 129 J6
MLHL NW7 165 K9
NTHWD HA6 170 G1
STHGT/OAK N14 167 M5
Faithfield BUSH WD23 * 162 G5
Faithorn Cl CSHM HP5 130 F9
Falcon Cl DUN/WHIP LU6 60 D5
HAT AL10 122 D8
NTHWD HA6 170 G4
SBW CM21 111 M3
STVGE SG2 67 N4
Falconer Rd BUSH WD23 163 J5
Falconers Fld HARP AL5 101 L1
Falconers Pk SBW CM21 111 N3
Falconers Rd LTNE LU2 63 J5
Falconer St BSF CM23 73 M9
Falcon Rdg BERK HP4 115 P8
Falcon Wy GSTN WD25 149 M4
KTN/HRWW/WS HA3 173 L9
WGCE AL7 105 H4
Faldo Rd
AMP/FLIT/BLC MK45 32 B4
Falkirk Gdns OXHEY WD19 171 M2
Falkland Rd BAR EN5 166 C1
Fallow End WLYN AL6 84 G4
Fallowfield LTNN/LIM LU3 62 C2
STAN HA7 164 A9
STVGE SG2 67 M3
WGCE AL7 105 J3
Fallowfield Cl DEN/HRF UB9 169 N5
Fallowfield Ct STAN HA7 164 A9
Fallow Ri HERT/BAY SG13 107 M6
Fallows Gn HARP AL5 102 A1
Falmouth Ct STALW/RED AL3 120 C6
Falstaff Gdns STAL AL1 136 A2
Falstone Gn LTNE LU2 63 M4
Fanhams Gra WARE SG12 * 88 F9
Fanhams Hall Rd WARE SG12 108 D1
Fanhams Rd WARE SG12 108 D2
Fanshaw Ct HERT/WAT SG14 107 J5
Fanshawe Crs WARE SG12 108 B2
Fanshawe St HERT/WAT SG14 107 J5
Fanshaws La HERT/BAY SG13 125 K6
Fantail La TRING HP23 95 N8
Faraday Cl LTNW/LEA LU4 61 M5
WATW WD18 161 P5
Faraday Gdns
HTCH/STOT SG5 24 G7
Faraday Rd STVGE SG2 51 L9
Far End HAT AL10 122 E9
Faringdon Rd LTNW/LEA LU4 61 M3
Faringford Cl POTB/CUF EN6 153 N1
Farland Rd HHNE HP2 118 B8
Farley Farm Rd LTN LU1 62 C9
Farley Hl LTN LU1 80 C1
Farman Ter
KTN/HRWW/WS HA3 * 173 K8
Farm Av HARP AL5 81 L9
Farmbrook LTNE LU2 46 E8
Farm Cl AMS HP6 146 A9
BAR EN5 165 P4
BORE WD6 151 K8
CHES/WCR EN8 142 B9
DUN/HR/TOD LU5 60 F1
HERT/WAT SG14 107 H6
HLWW/ROY CM19 127 N2
LWTH SG6 25 L8
POTB/CUF EN6 140 F6
RAD WD7 137 K9
STVG SG1 10 E7
WGCW AL8 104 F6
Farm Crs LCOL/BKTW AL2 136 F5
Farmer Ct WAB EN9 157 M3
Farmers Cl GSTN WD25 149 J3
Farmers Pl CFSP/GDCR SL9 168 A6
Farm Gn LTN LU1 62 D9
Farm Hill Rd WAB EN9 157 J4
Farmhouse Cl BROX EN10 * 142 E4
Farmhouse La HHNE HP2 118 B6
Farmlands ENC/FH EN2 155 H9
PIN HA5 171 J8
Farm La HOD EN11 127 H3
RKW/CH/CXG WD3 160 F2
STDN SG11 70 F6
STHGT/OAK N14 167 L5
Farmleigh STHGT/OAK N14 167 N6
Farm Pl BERK HP4 115 L6
Farm Rd LTN LU1 81 J6
NTHWD HA6 170 E2
RKW/CH/CXG WD3 159 N3
STAL AL1 120 G7
Farmstead Rd
KTN/HRWW/WS HA3 172 D5
Farm Wy BUSH WD23 163 K3
NTHWD HA6 170 G1
Farnham Cl HHS/BOV HP3 132 D7
SBW CM21 111 M3
TRDG/WHET N20 166 G6
Farnley Gv LTNE LU2 7 J4
Farorna Wk ENC/FH EN2 155 H9
Farquhar St HERT/WAT SG14 107 K5
Farraline Rd WATW WD18 13 F5
Farrant Wy BORE WD6 151 K9
Farrer Rd
KTN/HRWW/WS HA3 173 L9
Farrer Top STALW/RED AL3 79 P8
Farriday Cl STALW/RED AL3 120 D4
Farrier Ct ROY SG8 20 B3
Farriers WARE SG12 108 F6
Farriers Cl BLDK SG7 26 A8
HHS/BOV HP3 132 E7
HTCHE/RSTV SG4 84 C4
Farriers End BROX EN10 142 E5
Farriers Wy BORE WD6 165 K5
CSHM HP5 130 F7
DUN/HR/TOD LU5 60 D2
Farringford Cl
LCOL/BKTW AL2 135 P5
Farrow Cl LTNN/LIM LU3 46 C6
Farr Rd ENC/FH EN2 155 L9
Farr's La LTNE LU2 82 A4
Farthingale La WAB EN9 157 M4
Farthing Cl WAT WD17 13 H7
Farthing Dr LWTH SG6 36 F5
The Farthings HHW HP1 117 L8
Fauna Cl STAN HA7 164 D9
Faverolle Gn CHES/WCR EN8 142 C7
Faversham Cl TRING HP23 95 P8
Fawcett Rd STVGE SG2 51 L7
Fawn Ct BRKMPK AL9 122 F4
Fay Gn ABLGY WD5 148 E3
Feacey Down HHW HP1 117 K6
Fearney Md
RKW/CH/CXG WD3 160 E7
Fearnley Rd WGCW AL8 104 F7
Fearnley St WATW WD18 12 E5
Featherbed La ABLGY WD5 135 J5
HHS/BOV HP3 133 M3
Feather Dell HAT AL10 122 C6
Feathers Hl RBSF CM22 93 M3
Featherstone Gdns
BORE WD6 165 K3
Featherston Rd STVGE SG2 67 M3
Federal Wy WATN WD24 149 K9
Felbridge Av STAN HA7 172 G5
Felbrigg Cl LTNE LU2 63 N4
Felden Cl GSTN WD25 149 L4
PIN HA5 171 N4
Felden Dr HHS/BOV HP3 133 K3
Felden La HHS/BOV HP3 133 K3
Felden Lawns HHS/BOV HP3 133 K3
Felix Av LTNE LU2 63 H4
Fellowes La STALE/WH AL4 138 A2
Fellowes Wy STVGE SG2 67 J4
Fell Pth BORE WD6 * 165 K4
Fells Cl HTCH/STOT SG5 35 L8
Felmersham Ct LTN LU1 62 C7
Felmersham Rd LTN LU1 62 B7
Felmongers HLW CM20 129 L1
Felstead Cl LTNE LU2 * 62 G3
Felstead Rd CHES/WCR EN8 156 D2
Felstead Wy LTNE LU2 62 G4
Felton Cl BORE WD6 * 151 K8
BROX EN10 142 E4
LTNE LU2 63 L5
Fen End HTCH/STOT SG5 25 K1
Fennells HLWW/ROY CM19 128 E8
The Fennings AMS HP6 145 J6
Fennycroft Rd HHW HP1 117 J5
Fensome Dr
DUN/HR/TOD LU5 61 H1
Fensomes Aly HHNE HP2 117 N7
Fenton Gra HLWE CM17 129 M4
Fenwick Cl LTNN/LIM LU3 62 C1
Fenwick Rd
DUN/HR/TOD LU5 61 H1
Ferguson Gv
CHES/WCR EN8 * 142 C8
Fermor Crs LTNE LU2 63 K5
Fern Cl BROX EN10 142 E2
Ferndale MHAD SG10 90 C3
Ferndale Rd LTN LU1 62 C7
PEND EN3 156 D7
Ferndale Ter HRW HA1 172 F8
Fern Dells HAT AL10 122 C7

Ferndene LCOL/BKTW AL2 149 N1
Ferndown NTHWD HA6 171 J6
Ferndown Cl PIN HA5 171 N4
Ferndown Rd OXHEY WD19 162 E9
Fern Dr HHNE HP2 5 G4
Fernecroft STAL AL1 136 B2
Ferney Rd CHESW EN7 141 L5
EBAR EN4 167 L6
Fern Gv WGCW AL8 104 G2
Fernheath LTNN/LIM LU3 46 B6
Fernhill HLWS CM18 129 H7
Fern Hill La HLWS CM18 129 J7
Fernhills KGLGY WD4 148 E4
Fernhurst Gdns EDGW HA8 173 N3
Fernleigh Ct
RYLN/HDSTN HA2 172 B6
Fernley Cl PIN HA5 171 J8
Fernleys STALE/WH AL4 121 H5
Ferns Cl PEND EN3 156 D6
Fernside Av MLHL NW7 165 K9
Fernsleigh Cl CFSP/GDCR SL9 168 C3
The Ferns STALW/RED AL3 120 C4
Fernville La HHNE HP2 4 E1
Fern Wy GSTN WD25 149 J5
Fernwood Crs
TRDG/WHET N20 167 K9
Ferny Hl EBAR EN4 154 A8
Ferrars Cl LTNW/LEA LU4 61 L5
Ferrers La HARP AL5 102 E7
Ferrier Rd STVGE SG2 51 M9
Ferryhills Cl OXHEY WD19 162 E9
Fesants Cft HLW CM20 111 L9
Fetherstone Cl
POTB/CUF EN6 153 N2
Fiddle Bridge La HAT AL10 122 C5
Fidler Pl BUSH WD23 163 K5
Field Cl CSHM HP5 131 K7
HARP AL5 102 C5
STALE/WH AL4 120 F4
Field Crs ROY SG8 20 E3
Field End BAR EN5 165 P3
Field End Cl LTNE LU2 63 K2
OXHEY WD19 162 G6
TRING HP23 114 C2
Field End Rd PIN HA5 171 K9
Fielders Wy RAD WD7 151 K3
Fieldfare LWTH SG6 25 J8
STVGE SG2 67 N3
Field Fare Gn LTNW/LEA LU4 61 K1
Fieldfares LCOL/BKTW AL2 137 J6
Fieldfare Wy ROY SG8 20 D2
Fieldgate Rd LTNW/LEA LU4 61 N3
Fieldings Rd CHES/WCR EN8 142 E8
Field La LWTH SG6 36 C4
Field Rd HHNE HP2 118 B9
OXHEY WD19 162 G5
Fields End TRING HP23 95 P6
Fields End La HHW HP1 116 G6
Fieldside Cots
TRDG/WHET N20 * 166 D6
Fieldview Cots
STHGT/OAK N14 * 167 P8
Field View Ri LCOL/BKTW AL2 135 M8
Field View Rd POTB/CUF EN6 153 K3
Field Wy CFSP/GDCR SL9 168 B4
HHS/BOV HP3 132 D6
HOD EN11 126 G1
AMSS HP7 158 B2
RKW/CH/CXG WD3 160 F7
Fieldway BERK HP4 116 B9
TRING HP23 114 C2
WARE SG12 108 G8
Fifth Av GSTN WD25 149 L5
LWTH SG6 36 F2
Fifth Avenue Allende Av
HLW CM20 2 E3
Figtree Hl HHNE HP2 117 N7
Filey Cl STVG SG1 50 D8
Fillingham Wy HAT AL10 122 B4
Filmer Rd LTNW/LEA LU4 61 P2
Finch Cl BAR EN5 166 E4
HAT AL10 122 D8
LTNW/LEA LU4 61 K2
Finchdale HHW HP1 117 K8
Finches End STVGE SG2 52 C7
The Finches HERT/BAY SG13 108 A6
HTCHE/RSTV SG4 35 M9
Finch Gn RKW/CH/CXG WD3 160 D3
Finch La AMSS HP7 158 G1
BUSH WD23 163 J4
Finchmoor HLWS CM18 128 G6
Finch Rd BERK HP4 115 M7
Finley Rd HARP AL5 102 C1
Finsbury Rd LTNW/LEA LU4 61 N1
Finucane Ri BUSH WD23 163 L8
Finway LTN LU1 62 B6
Finway Ct WATW WD18 * 12 B7
Finway Rd HHNE HP2 118 C4
Firbank WGCW AL8 * 104 F6
Firbank Cl LTNN/LIM LU3 45 M7
Firbank Dr OXHEY WD19 162 G6
Firbank Rd STALW/RED AL3 120 E4
Fir Cl STVGE SG2 67 J5
Firecrest LWTH SG6 25 J8
Firlands BSF CM23 73 P8
Fir Pk HLWW/ROY CM19 128 E6
Firs WAB EN9 157 P5
Firs Cl HAT AL10 122 E7
HTCH/STOT SG5 35 J8
Firs Dr STALE/WH AL4 83 H8
Firs La POTB/CUF EN6 153 L3
The Firs Pk BRKMPK AL9 * 139 K2
First Av AMSS HP7 158 C1
DUN/WHIP LU6 60 E7
GSTN WD25 149 K5
HLW CM20 3 G3
STSD CM24 59 J9
First Avenue Mandela Av
HLW CM20 2 E3
The Firs CHESW EN7 141 M5
HARP AL5 * 102 C2
STAL AL1 136 G3
TRDG/WHET N20 167 H7
TRING HP23 114 C2
WGCW AL8 104 F2
Firs Wk NTHWD HA6 170 F3
WLYN AL6 85 N8
Fir Tree Cl HHS/BOV HP3 118 B9
Fir Tree Ct BORE WD6 164 F3
Fir Tree Hl RKW/CH/CXG WD3 148 B7
Firway WLYN AL6 85 J6
Firway Cl WLYN AL6 85 J6
Firwood Av STALE/WH AL4 121 K8
Fisher Cl
AMP/FLIT/BLC MK45 32 C5
KGLGY WD4 134 B8
PEND EN3 156 F7
Fishermans Wy HOD EN11 127 J3
Fisher Rd
KTN/HRWW/WS HA3 172 F6
Fishers Cl BUSH WD23 162 G3
CHES/WCR EN8 156 F4
STDN SG11 71 J5
Fishers Gn STVG SG1 50 D6
Fisher's Green Rd STVG SG1 50 E7
Fishers Hatch HLW CM20 3 H4
Fishers Md STDN SG11 71 J3
Fishery Pas HHW HP1 4 A5
Fishery Rd HHW HP1 133 K1
Fish Hl ROY SG8 20 C4
Fishponds Rd
HTCH/STOT SG5 35 K8
Fishpool St STALW/RED AL3 8 B3
Fish St STALW/RED AL3 101 J7
Fish Street Farm
STALW/RED AL3 101 J7
Fitzjohn Av BAR EN5 166 C4
Fitzroy Av LTNN/LIM LU3 62 C3
Fitzwarin Cl LTNN/LIM LU3 45 P8
Fitzwilliam Cl
TRDG/WHET N20 167 K7
Fitzwilliams Ct HLWE CM17 111 P8
Five Acres CSHM HP5 145 J3
HLWS CM18 129 H6
KGLGY WD4 134 A8
LCOL/BKTW AL2 137 J4
STSD CM24 58 F3
Five Acres Av
LCOL/BKTW AL2 135 N8
Five Fields Cl OXHEY WD19 163 H8
Five Oaks HAT AL10 * 122 E9
LTN LU1 80 A1
Five Springs LTNN/LIM LU3 45 P9
Flagstaff Cl WAB EN9 156 G3
Flagstaff Rd WAB EN9 156 G3
The Flags HHNE HP2 118 C8
Flamsteadbury La
STALW/RED AL3 101 H8
Flamstead End Rd
CHES/WCR EN8 142 A7
Flandrian Cl PEND EN3 156 F9
Flash La ENC/FH EN2 155 K7
Flatfield Rd HHS/BOV HP3 134 B1
Flaunden Bottom CSHM HP5 146 B7
Flaunden Hl HHS/BOV HP3 146 C3
Flaunden La HHS/BOV HP3 132 F8
HHS/BOV HP3 146 E2
Flavian Cl STALW/RED AL3 135 N1
Flaxen Fld
RAYLNE/WEN HP22 112 A1
Flax Ms STALW/RED AL3 * 79 P8
Flecker Cl STAN HA7 172 F2
Flecks La ROY SG8 15 P4
The Fleet ROY SG8 20 B4
Fleetwood Crs STVG SG1 50 E8
Fleetwood Wy OXHEY WD19 171 L1
Fleming Cl CHESW EN7 141 P5
Fleming Crs HERT/WAT SG14 107 H6
Fleming Dr HTCH/STOT SG5 24 G7
Fleming Rd WAB EN9 156 G5
Fletcher Wy HHNE HP2 117 M6
Flexley Wd WGCE AL7 105 J3
Flex Meadow
HLWW/ROY CM19 128 B4
Flinders Cl STAL AL1 136 F1
STVGE SG2 67 M1
Flint Cl LTNN/LIM LU3 45 P8
Flint Copse STALW/RED AL3 101 K6
The Flintings HHNE HP2 99 J4
Flint Rd LWTH SG6 25 N9
Flint Wy STALW/RED AL3 120 B4
Flitch Wy RBSF CM22 75 L3
Flora Cl STAN HA7 164 D9
Flora Gv STAL AL1 9 J5
Floral Dr LCOL/BKTW AL2 137 J5
Florence Av LTNN/LIM LU3 45 N9
Florence Cl
DUN/HR/TOD LU5 61 H5
GSTN WD25 149 H5
HLWE CM17 129 M5
Florence St HTCH/STOT SG5 35 L8
Florida Cl BUSH WD23 163 M8
Floriston Cl STAN HA7 173 H5
Floriston Gdns STAN HA7 173 H5
Flowers Wy LTN LU1 6 E5
Flowmere Rd ROY SG8 22 C2
Flowton Gv HARP AL5 101 P5
Fogerty Cl PEND EN3 156 G7
Fold Cft HLW CM20 2 A4
Foldingshott KNEB SG3 85 N2
Follett Dr ABLGY WD5 148 G1
Folly Av STALW/RED AL3 8 D1
Folly Cl HTCHE/RSTV SG4 49 M2
RAD WD7 150 E6
Folly Flds STALE/WH AL4 102 G2
Folly La LTN LU1 79 N1
STALW/RED AL3 8 C2
Folly Pathway RAD WD7 150 E5
The Folly BUNT SG9 40 C9
HERT/WAT SG14 107 L6
Folly Vw WARE SG12 108 G7
Fontmell Cl STALW/RED AL3 120 D5
Fontwell Cl
KTN/HRWW/WS HA3 172 E4
Football Cl BLDK SG7 26 A8
Forbes Av POTB/CUF EN6 153 N3
Force End HTCHE/RSTV SG4 37 M7
Ford Cl BUSH WD23 163 L3
Ford Fld STDN SG11 72 D6
Fordham Cl BLDK SG7 17 N5
Fordham Rd EBAR EN4 167 H2
ROY SG8 20 D5
Fordham Ter ROY SG8 * 28 F2
Ford Hl STDN SG11 72 E6
Ford La STVGE SG2 68 A3
Ford St STDN SG11 55 K9
Fordwich Cl
HERT/WAT SG14 107 H6
Fordwich Hl
HERT/WAT SG14 107 H6
Fordwich Ri
HERT/WAT SG14 107 H6
Fordwich Rd WGCW AL8 104 F7
Forebury Av SBW CM21 92 A7
The Forebury SBW CM21 92 A7
Forefield LCOL/BKTW AL2 135 P6
Forelands Wy CSHM HP5 145 H2
Forest Av HHS/BOV HP3 5 F6
Forest Cl RAYLNE/WEN HP22 112 C7
WAB EN9 157 N7
Foresters Cl CHESW EN7 141 M6
Foresthall Rd STSD CM24 58 E7
Forest La RAD WD7 150 G1
Fore St BRKMPK AL9 122 F5
HERT/WAT SG14 107 L6
HLWE CM17 111 M8
HTCHE/RSTV SG4 37 L7
PIN HA5 171 H8
Forest Rd CHES/WCR EN8 142 C8
GSTN WD25 149 J3
PEND EN3 156 D6
Forest Rw STVGE SG2 67 J5
Forest Wk BUSH WD23 149 N9
Forest Wy HLWS CM18 129 L7
LOU IG10 157 P8
RBSF CM22 75 K4
RBSF CM22 93 K9
Forge Cl HTCH/STOT SG5 35 L8
KGLGY WD4 147 K1
LTNW/LEA LU4 45 H5
Forge End LCOL/BKTW AL2 135 P5
Forge La NTHWD HA6 170 G4
WLYN AL6 84 E8
Formby Av
KTN/HRWW/WS HA3 173 J7
Form Cl RAD WD7 151 K1
Forres Cl HOD EN11 126 F3
Forrest Crs LTNE LU2 63 H3
Forresters Dr WGCE AL7 105 M7
Fortnums Acre STAN HA7 172 F3
Fortuna Cl STVG SG1 51 M7
Fortune La BORE WD6 164 D5
The Fortunes HLWS CM18 129 J5
Forty Hl ENC/FH EN2 155 N7
Forum Pl HAT AL10 * 122 D5
Forumside EDGW HA8 173 N3
The Forum STVG SG1 10 C4
Forum Wy EDGW HA8 173 N3
Forward Dr
KTN/HRWW/WS HA3 172 F8
Foster Av DUN/HR/TOD LU5 60 E3
Foster Cl CHES/WCR EN8 142 C9
STVG SG1 50 F6
Foster Dr HTCHE/RSTV SG4 49 M2
Foster Rd HHW HP1 4 A5
Foston Cl LTNN/LIM LU3 62 A1
Fotherley Rd
RKW/CH/CXG WD3 160 D8
Founceley Av WARE SG12 69 N6
Foundary Ga CHES/WCR EN8 156 D3
Founders Rd HOD EN11 126 G2
Fountain Dr HERT/BAY SG13 107 N5
Fountain Farm HLWS CM18 129 J5
Fountain Pl WAB EN9 157 H4
Fountains Rd LTNN/LIM LU3 62 D3
Fouracres LWTH SG6 36 D6
PEND EN3 156 D9
Four Acres STVG SG1 10 D1
WGCE AL7 105 H8
Fouracres Dr HHS/BOV HP3 5 K6
The Four Acres SBW CM21 92 B7
Fouracres Wk HHS/BOV HP3 5 K6
Fourdrinier Wy
HHS/BOV HP3 133 N2
Four Limes STALE/WH AL4 103 J4
Four Oaks CSHM HP5 130 F6
Fourth Av GSTN WD25 149 L5
HLWW/ROY CM19 2 B5
LTNN/LIM LU3 45 N8
LWTH SG6 36 F1
Four Trees LCOL/BKTW AL2 136 A3
The Four Tubs BUSH WD23 163 M6
Fourways RBSF CM22 59 K2
Fovant Cl HARP AL5 102 B6
Fowley Cl CHES/WCR EN8 156 E4
Fowley Mead Pk
CHES/WCR EN8 * 156 E4
Foxbury Cl LTNE LU2 46 E9
Fox Cl BGSW SG18 14 C6
BORE WD6 164 D5
BUSH WD23 163 K4
TRING HP23 114 B2
Fox Cnr ROY SG8 15 L6
Foxcroft STAL AL1 136 F1
Foxdell NTHWD HA6 170 F3
Fox Dells DUN/WHIP LU6 60 F9
Foxdells HERT/WAT SG14 106 D9
Foxdells La BSF CM23 58 A9
Foxdell Wy CFSP/GDCR SL9 168 C2
Foxes Cl HERT/BAY SG13 108 A6
Foxes Dr CHESW EN7 141 N8
Foxes La POTB/CUF EN6 140 F7
Foxes Pde WAB EN9 * 157 H3
Foxfield STVGE SG2 67 M3
Foxfield Cl NTHWD HA6 171 H3
Foxglove Bank ROY SG8 20 E5
Foxglove Cl BSF CM23 73 M8
HAT AL10 122 E7
HOD EN11 127 H2
The Foxgloves HHW HP1 117 H9
Foxglove Wy LTNN/LIM LU3 62 E4
WLYN AL6 85 H5
Foxgrove Pth OXHEY WD19 171 M2
Foxhill LTNE LU2 62 F1
Fox Hl ROY SG8 15 L6
Foxhill WATN WD24 149 H6
Fox Hill Rd ROY SG8 15 L6
Foxholes Av HERT/BAY SG13 107 N6
Foxhollows HAT AL10 122 E4
LCOL/BKTW AL2 137 H5
Foxlands Cl GSTN WD25 149 H4
Foxley Dr BSF CM23 74 B2
Foxley Gv WLYN AL6 85 H9
Foxleys OXHEY WD19 162 G9
Fox Rd STVG SG1 10 E5
TRING HP23 114 B1
Fox's La BRKMPK AL9 139 H3
Foxton Rd HOD EN11 126 E5
Foxwood Cha WAB EN9 157 H6
Foyle Cl STVG SG1 51 M4
Frampton Rd POTB/CUF EN6 139 M9
Frampton St
HERT/WAT SG14 107 L6
Frances St CSHM HP5 131 H9
Franchise St CSHM HP5 131 H9
Francis Av STALW/RED AL3 120 C5
Francis Cl HTCH/STOT SG5 25 J3
HTCHE/RSTV SG4 49 M2
Francis Rd BLDK SG7 16 F5
PIN HA5 171 L9
WARE SG12 108 C2
WATW WD18 12 E4
Francis St LTN LU1 6 B3
Francis Yd CSHM HP5 * 144 G1
Francklyn Gdns EDGW HA8 164 G9
Frankland Cl
RKW/CH/CXG WD3 161 L6
Frankland Rd
RKW/CH/CXG WD3 161 M5
Frank Lester Wy LTNE LU2 63 L6
Franklin Av
AMP/FLIT/BLC MK45 32 C5
CHESW EN7 141 P9
Franklin Cl HHS/BOV HP3 * 133 P2
HTCH/STOT SG5 34 C4
STALE/WH AL4 138 B1
TRDG/WHET N20 166 G6
Franklin Gdns
HTCHE/RSTV SG4 35 N7
Franklin Rd DUN/WHIP LU6 60 C6
WAT WD17 13 F1
Franklin's Rd STVG SG1 50 F7
Frank Martin Ct CHESW EN7 141 P9
Franshams BUSH WD23 * 163 N8
Fraser Cnr STVGE SG2 * 51 L8
Fraser Rd CHES/WCR EN8 142 D7
Frederick St LTNE LU2 6 E2
Frederick Street Pas
LTNE LU2 6 E1
Fred Millard Ct STVG SG1 * 11 F5
Freeman Av LTNN/LIM LU3 46 C7
Freeman Ct CSHM HP5 131 H9
Freemans Cl
DUN/HR/TOD LU5 60 D2
HTCH/STOT SG5 35 H7
Freewaters Cl
HTCH/STOT SG5 35 K4
Freewood La SAFWS CB11 23 K7
Freman Dr BUNT SG9 40 C8
French Horn Ct
WARE SG12 * 108 C3
French Horn La HAT AL10 122 E5
Frenchmans Cl
DUN/HR/TOD LU5 44 B2
French's Av DUN/WHIP LU6 60 B4
French's Cl WARE SG12 108 G7
French's Ga DUN/WHIP LU6 60 C4
Frensham CHESW EN7 141 N6
Frensham Dr
HTCHE/RSTV SG4 35 P6
Freshfield Dr
STHGT/OAK N14 167 M6
Freshwater Cl LTNN/LIM LU3 46 A8
Freshwaters HLW CM20 3 H3
Fresson Rd STVG SG1 50 G7
Freston Gdns EBAR EN4 167 L4
Fretherne Chambers
WGCW AL8 * 104 G6
Fretherne Rd WGCW AL8 104 G6
Friars Av TRDG/WHET N20 167 J9
Friars Cl LTN LU1 62 C9
Friarscroft BROX EN10 126 F8
Friars Fld BERK HP4 115 K4
Friars La RBSF CM22 93 J8
Friars Rd HTCHE/RSTV SG4 37 L7
STDN SG11 55 M8
The Friars HLWW/ROY CM19 128 E5
Friars Wk DUN/WHIP LU6 60 E7
STHGT/OAK N14 167 M7
TRING HP23 95 P8
Friars Wash
STALW/RED AL3 * 100 G2
Friars Wy BUSH WD23 149 N9
KGLGY WD4 134 B9
LTN LU1 62 C9
Friars Wd BSF CM23 74 D2
Friary Fld DUN/WHIP LU6 60 E6
The Friary CHES/WCR EN8 * 156 E3
Friday Furlong
HTCH/STOT SG5 35 H8
Friedberg Av BSF CM23 91 N2
Friendless La STALW/RED AL3 99 P1
Friends Av CHES/WCR EN8 156 C2
Friern Barnet La
TRDG/WHET N20 167 H9
Friern Cl CHESW EN7 141 M5
Friern Mount Dr
TRDG/WHET N20 166 G6
Friesian Cl LTNW/LEA LU4 61 K3
Frimley Rd HHW HP1 117 H7
Fringewood Cl NTHWD HA6 170 D5
Frinton Cl OXHEY WD19 162 D8
Friston Gn LTNE LU2 63 L5
Frithsden Copse BERK HP4 116 C3
Frithwood Av NTHWD HA6 171 H3
Frobisher Cl BUSH WD23 163 J5
Frobisher Dr STVGE SG2 51 L8
Frobisher Rd STAL AL1 137 H1
Frobisher Wy HAT AL10 122 A3
Froghall La STVGE SG2 52 C6
Frogmoor La
RKW/CH/CXG WD3 161 H8
Frogmore LCOL/BKTW AL2 136 D6
Frogmore Hl HERT/WAT SG14 68 B8
Frogmore Rd HHS/BOV HP3 * 133 N2
Frogmore St TRING HP23 95 P8
Frognal Av HRW HA1 172 F8
Frogs Hall La STDN SG11 69 N3
Frome Cl LTNW/LEA LU4 61 P2
Frome Sq HHNE HP2 118 B3
Front St LTN LU1 80 D4
The Front BERK HP4 116 E4
Frowick Cl BRKMPK AL9 138 E2
Frowycke Crs POTB/CUF EN6 152 D2
Fryent Wy CDALE/KGS NW9 173 N9
Fryer Cl CSHM HP5 145 J3
Fry Rd STVGE SG2 67 M1
Fryth Md STALW/RED AL3 8 A2
Fulbeck Wy
RYLN/HDSTN HA2 172 C6
Fulbourne Cl LTNW/LEA LU4 61 P4
Fulford Gv OXHEY WD19 162 D8
Fuller Cl BUSH WD23 163 M6
Fuller Ct BSF CM23 74 B3
Fuller Gdns WATN WD24 149 J7
Fuller Rd WATN WD24 149 J7
Fuller's Cl CSHM HP5 144 G2
Fullers Cl WAB EN9 157 L3
Fullers Ct LWTH SG6 36 B1
Fuller's Hl AMS HP6 144 E4
Fullers Md HLWE CM17 129 M4
Fullerton Cl STALW/RED AL3 79 P7
Fuller Wy RKW/CH/CXG WD3 161 L4
Fulling Mill La WLYN AL6 84 E8
Fulmar Crs HHW HP1 117 K9
Fulmore Cl HARP AL5 82 C9
Fulton Cl STVG SG1 10 A5
Fulton Crs BSF CM23 74 D1
Furham Fld PIN HA5 172 A4
Furlay Cl LWTH SG6 36 A1
Furlongs HHW HP1 117 K7
The Furlong TRING HP23 * 95 P9
Furlong Wy WARE SG12 108 E5
Furmston Ct LWTH SG6 36 D1
Furness Av DUN/WHIP LU6 60 F7
Furriers Cl BSF CM23 73 M9
The Furrows LTNN/LIM LU3 46 C8
Furse Av STALE/WH AL4 120 F5
Furtherfield ABLGY WD5 148 F2
Furtherground HHNE HP2 5 G3
Furzebushes La
LCOL/BKTW AL2 135 M4
Furze Cl LTNE LU2 46 E8
OXHEY WD19 171 L2
Furzedown STVGE SG2 67 L2
Furzedown Ct HARP AL5 102 A4
Furzefield CHES/WCR EN8 142 A7
Furzefield Ct
POTB/CUF EN6 * 153 H1
Furzefield Rd WGCE AL7 105 H7
Furze Gv ROY SG8 20 D5
Furzehill Pde BORE WD6 * 164 G3
Furzehill Rd BORE WD6 165 H3
Furzen Cl DUN/WHIP LU6 60 F9
Furzen Crs HAT AL10 122 C9
Furze Rd HHW HP1 117 H9
Furze Vw RKW/CH/CXG WD3 160 A5

G

Gable Cl ABLGY WD5 148 F2
PIN HA5 172 A4
Gables Av BORE WD6 164 F2
Gables Cl CFSP/GDCR SL9 168 C1
RAYLNE/WEN HP22 112 B7
Gaddesden Crs GSTN WD25 149 L4
Gaddesden Gv WGCE AL7 105 L7
Gaddesden La
STALW/RED AL3 100 B8
Gaddesden Rw HHNE HP2 99 K4
Gade Av WATW WD18 162 A3
Gade Bank
RKW/CH/CXG WD3 161 P3
Gadebridge La HHW HP1 117 L6
Gadebridge Rd HHW HP1 117 L7
Gade Cl HHW HP1 117 L5
WATW WD18 162 A3
Gade Valley Cl KGLGY WD4 134 B7
Gade View Gdns KGLGY WD4 148 D2
Gade View Rd HHS/BOV HP3 133 M3
Gadmore La TRING HP23 113 M4
Gadswell Cl GSTN WD25 149 M6
Gage Cl ROY SG8 20 C2
Gainsborough Av STAL AL1 9 J2
Gainsborough Dr
DUN/HR/TOD LU5 60 G1
Gainsborough Gdns
EDGW HA8 173 M6
Gainsford Crs
HTCHE/RSTV SG4 35 P6
Gainswood WGCE AL7 105 H7
Galdana Av BAR EN5 166 G2
Gale Ct AMP/FLIT/BLC MK45 32 D6
Gallants Farm Rd EBAR EN4 167 J6
Gall End La STSD CM24 58 G4
The Galleons AMSS HP7 * 145 H8
Galley Gn HERT/BAY SG13 126 F1
Galley Hl HHW HP1 117 K6
Galleyhill Rd WAB EN9 157 K3
Galley La BAR EN5 165 P2
Galliard Cl LTNN/LIM LU3 62 C2
Galloway Cl BROX EN10 142 E5
BSF CM23 74 A2
Galloway Rd BSF CM23 74 A2
Gallows Hl KGLGY WD4 148 D1
Gallows Hill La ABLGY WD5 148 D2
Galston Rd LTNN/LIM LU3 45 N7
Galva Cl EBAR EN4 167 L3
Games Rd EBAR EN4 167 J2
Gammon Cl HHNE HP2 5 K4
Gammons Farm Cl
WATN WD24 148 G6
Gammons La WATN WD24 149 H7
Gamnel Ms TRING HP23 96 A6
Ganders Ash GSTN WD25 149 H3
Gandhi Ct WATN WD24 162 F1
Gangies Hl SBW CM21 111 K1
Gant Ct WAB EN9 157 L4
Ganton Wk OXHEY WD19 * 171 N1
Ganymede Pl HHNE HP2 118 A5
Gaping La HTCH/STOT SG5 35 J9
Garden Av HAT AL10 122 D9
Garden City EDGW HA8 173 N3
Garden Cl BAR EN5 166 A3
HARP AL5 101 P7
RAYLNE/WEN HP22 112 D3
ROY SG8 20 D3
STAL AL1 120 G7
WAT WD17 12 A1
Garden Ct LTNN/LIM LU3 62 B2
STALE/WH AL4 103 J3
WGCE AL7 105 H5
Garden End AMS HP6 145 K7
Garden Fld STVGE SG2 67 P4
Garden Field La BERK HP4 116 C9
Gardenia Av LTNN/LIM LU3 62 B2
Garden La ROY SG8 20 C5

Garden Reach CSTG HP8........159 K2
Garden Rd ABGLY WD5........148 F1
  BUNT SG9........40 D8
  DUN/WHIP LU6........60 F7
  KNEB SG3........35 L8
Garden Wy HTCH/STOT SG5........35 L8
Gardens End
  DUN/HR/TOD LU5 *........26 A9
The Gardens BLDK SG7........26 A9
  BRKMPK AL9........139 H6
  HTCH/STOT SG5........25 J3
  WAT WD17........162 B1
Garden Ter WARE SG12 *........87 M9
Garden Terrace Rd
  HLWE CM17........111 M8
Garden Wk ROY SG8........20 D3
  STVC SG1........10 E5
Gardiners La BLDK SG7........17 N6
The Gardiners HLWE CM17........129 C4
Gardner's Ct DUN/WHIP LU6........60 B7
Gardners Cl FBAR/BDGN N11........167 L8
Garfield St WATN WD24........149 J8
Garland Cl CHES/WCR EN8........156 D1
Garland Rd STAN HA7........173 K5
  WARE SG12........108 C9
Garland Wy
  RAYLNE/WEN HP22........94 F7
Garnault Rd EN EN1........155 N8
Garner Dr BROX EN10........142 D5
Garners End CFSP/GDCR SL9........168 C3
Garners Rd CFSP/GDCR SL9........168 C3
Garnett Cl WATN WD24........149 L6
Garnett Dr LCOL/BKTW AL2........135 M8
Garrard Wy STALW/RED AL4........103 J4
Garrard Rd EDGW HA8........173 N4
Garratts Rd BUSH WD23........165 L6
Garrett Cl CSHM HP5........145 H3
  DUN/WHIP LU6........60 C9
Garretts Cl HERT/WAT SG14........107 K6
Garretts Md LTNE LU2........63 J5
Garsmouth Wy GSTN WD25........149 L6
Garson Gv CSHM HP5........130 F8
Garston Crs GSTN WD25........149 K4
Garston Dr GSTN WD25........149 K4
Garston La GSTN WD25........149 L4
Garthland Dr BAR EN5........165 P4
Garth Rd LWTH SG6........36 E5
The Garth ABGLY WD5........148 E3
Gartlet Rd WAT WD17........13 F2
Gascoyne Cl POTB/CUF EN6........152 D2
Gascoyne Wy
  HERT/BAY SG13........107 L7
Gas La ROY SG8........30 A6
Gatcombe Wy EBAR EN4........167 K2
Gate Cl BORE WD6........151 P9
Gate Cots CFSP/GDCR SL9 *........164 C8
Gatecroft HHS/BOV HP3 *........5 K6
Gate End NTHWD HA6........171 J4
Gatehall Gdns LTNN/LIM LU3........46 C6
Gatehall Rd NTHWD HA6........171 H4
Gater Dr ENC/FH EN2........155 J3
Gatesbury Wy STDN SG11........71 J3
Gatesdene Cl BERK HP4........97 P4
Gateshead Rd BORE WD6........164 F1
Gates Orch
  RAYLNE/WEN HP22........94 E7
Gates Wy STVG SG1........10 E3
Gateway Cl NTHWD HA6........171 H4
The Gateways WATW WD18........141 L7
The Gateway WATW WD18........162 A4
Gatwick Ct BSF CM23........74 C1
Gauldie Wy STDN SG11........71 J4
Gaumont Ap WAT WD17 *........13 F2
Gaunts Wy LWTH SG6........25 K7
Gaveston Dr BERK HP4........115 N5
Gawdrey Cl CSHM HP5........145 H3
Gayland Av LTNE LU2........63 J6
Gayton Ct AMS HP6........145 K5
  LTNN/LIM LU3........62 B2
Gaywood Av CHES/WCR EN8........156 C4
Geddes Rd BUSH WD23 *........149 L9
Geddings Rd HOD EN11........126 C5
Geescroft Wk HARP AL5........101 P6
Geisthorp Ct WAB EN9........157 M3
Gelding Cl LTNN/LEA LU4........46 C3
The Generals Wk PEND EN3........156 D7
Gentlemens Fld WARE SG12........108 E1
George Gange Wy
  KTN/HRWW/WS HA3........172 E2
George La ROY SG8........20 C4
George Leighton Ct
  STVG SG2 *........67 L1
George Lighton Ct
  STVG SG2 *........67 L2
George Lovell Dr PEND EN3........156 E7
George Md BORE WD6........164 E5
George St BERK HP4........191 H9
  CSHM HP5........144 C2
  DUN/WHIP LU6........60 D5
  HERT/WAT SG14........107 K5
  HHNE HP2........117 N7
  LTN LU1........6 B3
  STALW/RED AL3........8 E4
  STALW/RED AL3........79 P8
  WATW WD18........13 G5
George St West LTN LU1........6 E5
George's Wood Rd
  BRKMPK AL9........139 K5
George V Av PIN HA5........171 P6
George V Wy
  RKW/CH/CXG WD3........147 K6
George Wk WARE SG12........108 C3
Georgewood Rd
  HHS/BOV HP3........134 A4
Georgian Cl STAN HA7........172 C4
Germains Cl CSHM HP5........144 C2
Germain St CSHM HP5........144 C2
Gernon Rd LWTH SG6........36 C3
Gernon Wk LWTH SG6........36 C3
Gerrard Gdns PIN HA5........171 J9
Gertrude Peake Pl
  STALW/RED AL3 *........101 J7
Gew's Cnr CHES/WCR EN8........142 C8
Ghyll Gdns BERK HP4 *........115 J4
Giant Tree HI BUSH WD23........163 M8
Gibb Cft HLWS CM18........129 H7

Gibbons Cl BORE WD6........151 K9
  STALE/WH AL4........121 H2
Gibbons Wy KNEB SG3........85 J1
Gibbs Cl CHES/WCR EN8........142 C8
Gibbs Couch OXHEY WD19........162 F9
Gibbs Fld BSF CM23........73 N9
Gibson Cl HTCHE/RSTV SG4........35 N9
Gidian Ct LCOL/BKTW AL2........136 B6
Gifford's La STDN SG11........69 P4
Gilbert Cl HARP AL5........82 A9
Gilbert Rd DEN/HRF UB9........169 P6
  PIN HA5........171 M8
Gilbert's HI TRING HP23........113 M8
Gilbert St PEND EN3........156 B7
Gilbey Av BSF CM23........74 C4
Gilbey Crs STSD CM24........58 F5
Gildea Cl PIN HA5........172 A4
Gilded Acre DUN/WHIP LU6........60 F9
Gilden Cl HLWE CM17........111 P8
Gilden Wy HLWE CM17........111 N9
Gilder Cl LTNN/LIM LU3........46 B7
Gilderdale LTNE LU2 *........45 L9
Gilders SBW CM21........111 N2
Giles Cl STALE/WH AL4........121 H2
Gillam St LTNE LU2........7 J1
Gillan Gn BUSH WD23........163 L8
Gillan Rd WD18........161 N5
Gillian Av STAL AL1........136 B3
Gilliat's Gn
  RKW/CH/CXG WD3........160 B3
Gillison Cl LWTH SG6........36 E3
Gills Hill La RAD WD7........150 E5
Gills Hollow RAD WD7........150 E6
Gillum Cl EBAR EN4........167 K7
Gilmour Cl CHESW EN7........155 P5
Gilpin Cl DUN/HR/TOD LU5........60 C1
Gilpin Gn HARP AL5........102 B3
Gilpin's Gallop WARE SG12........108 G8
Gilpin's Ride BERK HP4........116 N6
Gilpin St DUN/WHIP LU6........60 D4
Gilroy Rd HHNE HP2........117 N7
Gilsland Wk HHW HP2........157 K5
Gilsted Ct STALW/RED AL3........120 C4
Gilston Pk HLW CM20........110 F5
Gingers Cl
  RAYLNE/WEN HP22........94 F7
Ginns Rd BUNT SG9........56 C3
Gippeswyck Cl PIN HA5........171 M5
Gipsy La BSF CM23........58 D7
  KNEB SG3........85 H2
  LTN LU1........6 D2
Girdle Rd HTCHE/RSTV SG4........35 M4
Girons Ct HTCHE/RSTV SG4........35 N9
Girtin Rd BUSH WD23........163 K4
Girton Av CDALE/KGS NW9........173 N7
Girton Ct CHES/WCR EN8........142 A7
Girton Wy RKW/CH/CXG WD3........161 N4
Gisburne Wy WATN WD24........149 H7
Gladden Ct HLWS CM18........129 H7
Gladding Rd CHESW EN7........141 J8
Gladeside STALE/WH AL4........121 J5
The Glades HHW HP1........117 H7
The Glade LWTH SG6........36 C5
  WCCW ALB........104 F4
The Gladeway WAB EN9........157 J3
Gladsdale Dr PIN HA5........171 J8
Gladsmuir Rd BAR EN5........166 C1
Gladstone Av LTN LU1........6 B5
Gladstone Pl BAR EN5........166 B5
Gladstone Rd CSHM HP5........145 H1
  HOD EN11........126 C4
  WARE SG12........69 N6
  WAT WD17........108 B2
  WAT WD17 *........13 H3
Gladstone Wy
  KTN/HRWW/WS HA3........172 E2
Glaisdale LTNN/LEA LU4........61 M1
Glamis Cl CHESW EN7........141 P8
  HHNE HP2........118 C2
Glamis Pl HHNE HP2........118 C2
Glanfield HHW HP2........117 P5
Glanleam Rd STAN HA7........173 K1
Glanville Ms STAN HA7........172 G2
Gleave Cl STAL AL1........120 C7
Glebe Av ARL/CHE SG15........24 C3
  KTN/HRWW/WS HA3........173 L7
Glebe Cl BRKMPK AL9........124 A5
  CFSP/GDCR SL9........168 B5
  HERT/WAT SG14........86 E2
  HTCH/STOT SG5........25 L5
Glebe Cots BRKMPK AL9........124 A5
Glebe Ct BSF CM23........74 C2
  STAN HA7........173 J2
Glebe Crs
  KTN/HRWW/WS HA3........173 L7
Glebe End RBSF CM22........59 K2
Glebelands HLW CM20........111 J9
Glebe La BAR EN5........165 N4
  KTN/HRWW/WS HA3........173 L7
Glebe Rd CFSP/GDCR SL9........168 A5
  HERT/WAT SG14........107 L4
  LWTH SG6........36 D1
  STAN HA7........173 J2
  WARE SG12........84 E8
The Glebe CSTN WD25........173 L7
  HLW CM20........3 H5
  HTCHE/RSTV SG4 *........49 P5
  KGLY WD4........134 B8
  RAYLNE/WEN HP22........112 A1
  STVG SG2........51 J7
Glebe Wy AMS HP6........145 J6
Gleed Av BUSH WD23........163 M8
Glemsford Cl LTNN/LEA LU4........45 L9
Glemsford Dr HARP AL5........102 C2
Glenalmond Rd
  KTN/HRWW/WS HA3........173 L8
Glencoe Rd BUSH WD23........163 J5
Glencorse Gv OXHEY WD19 *........171 M1
Glendale HHW HP1........117 H2
Glendale Av EDGW HA8........173 M1
Glendevon Cl EDGW HA8........165 H9
Gleneagles STAN HA7........173 H5
Gleneagles Dr LTNE LU2........46 F9
Glenester Cl HOD EN11........126 F2

Glen Faba Rd
  HLWW/ROY CM19........127 L5
Glenferrie Rd STAL AL1........120 F8
Glenfield Ct HERT/WAT SG14........106 C5
Glenfield Rd LTNN/LIM LU3........46 D9
Glengall Pl STAL AL1 *........136 D2
Glengad Rd EDGW HA8........165 H9
Glenhaven Av BORE WD6........164 G2
Glenister Rd CSHM HP5........131 H7
Glen Luce CHES/WCR EN8........142 C9
Glenlyn Av STAL AL1........120 G9
Glenmore Gdns ABGLY WD5........149 H1
The Glen LTN LU1........79 P2
  NTHWD HA6........170 F4
Glenview Rd HHW HP1........4 A2
Glenville Av ENC/FH EN2........155 K8
Glen Wy WAT WD17........148 F8
Glenwood BROX EN10........126 E7
  WGCE AL7........105 M7
Glenwood Cl HRW HA1........172 F9
  STVGE SG2........67 M4
Glenwood Rd MLHL NW7........165 L9
Glevum Cl STALW/RED AL3........135 N1
Globe Cl HARP AL5........102 B5
Globe Crs BSF CM23........57 N9
Glossop Wy ARL/CHE SG15........24 F2
Gloucester Av
  CHES/WCR EN8........156 D3
Gloucester Cl STVG SG1........51 H5
Gloucester Ct HAT AL10........122 D3
Gloucester Gdns EBAR EN4........167 L5
Gloucester Rd BAR EN5........166 F4
  ENC/FH EN2........155 K8
  HRW HA1........172 B9
  LTN LU1........7 G5
Gloucester Ter LTN LU1 *........7 J1
  STHGT/OAK N14 *........167 P7
Glover Rd CHESW EN7........141 N6
Glovers Cl HERT/BAY SG13........107 K8
Glovers La HLWE CM17........129 P8
Glyn Av EBAR EN4........167 K3
Glyn Ct STAN HA7........173 H3
Glynswood CFSP/GDCR SL9........168 D4
Glynswood Pl NTHWD HA6........170 D4
Goat La EN EN1........155 N8
Goblins Wy POTB/CUF EN6........139 L7
Goblins Gn WGCE AL7........104 C7
Goddard End STVGE SG2........67 M5
Goddards Cl HERT/BAY SG13........124 D7
Godfrey Cl STVGE SG2........67 L3
Godfreys Cl LTN LU1........62 D8
Godfries Cl WLYN AL6........105 P1
Godwin Cl CHING E4........157 H8
Goffs Crs CHESW EN7........141 K8
Goff's La CHESW EN7........141 L6
Goff's Oak Av CHESW EN7........141 J6
Golda Cl BAR EN5........166 B5
Gold Cl BROX EN10........126 D8
Gold Crest Cl LTNN/LEA LU4........61 K1
Goldcrest Wy BUSH WD23........163 J8
Goldcroft HHS/BOV HP3........134 B1
Golden Bell WGCE AL7........102 E3
Golders Cl EDGW HA8........173 P2
Goldfield Cl HARP AL5........102 D2
Goldfinch Wy BORE WD6........164 C3
Gold HI North
  CFSP/GDCR SL9........168 A5
Gold HI West CFSP/GDCR SL9........168 A5
Goldings BSF CM23........74 C2
Goldings Crs HAT AL10........122 C5
Goldings La HERT/WAT SG14........107 H5
Goldington Cl HOD EN11........126 E2
Goldon LWTH SG6........36 E4
Goldrill Dr FBAR/BDGN N11........167 L8
Goldring Wy LCOL/BKTW AL2........136 F6
Goldsmith Wy
  STALW/RED AL3........120 B6
Goldstone Cl WARE SG12........108 C2
Goldstone Crs
  DUN/HR/TOD LU5........60 G4
  STAN HA7 *........173 J4
Golf Club Rd BRKMPK AL9........139 K5
Golf Ride ENC/FH EN2........155 J1
Golfside Ct TRDG/WHET N20........167 J9
Gombards STALW/RED AL3........8 A3
Gomer Cl HTCHE/RSTV SG4........84 B4
Gonville Av
  RKW/CH/CXG WD3........161 N5
Gonville Crs STVGE SG2........67 M4
Goodey Meade STVGE SG2........51 L5
Goodhall Cl STAN HA7........172 G3
Goodison Cl BUSH WD23........149 L9
Goodliffe Pk BSF CM23........58 C9
Goodrich Cl GSTN WD25........150 C9
Goodrich Cl CHES/WCR EN8........142 D7
Goodwins Md LBUZ LU7........79 P6
Goodwin Stile BSF CM23........72 B3
Goodwood Av PEND EN3........156 B7
  WATN WD24........148 F5
Goodwood Rd CHES/WCR EN8........126 E4
Goodwood Rd ROY SG8........20 E4
Goodyers Av RAD WD7........150 E3
Goose Acre CSHM HP5........131 M9
  LBUZ LU7........79 P5
Goosacre La
  KTN/HRWW/WS HA3........173 K9
Gooseberry HI LTNN/LIM LU3........46 C3
Goosecroft HHW HP1........117 J7
Gooserfields
  RKW/CH/CXG WD3........160 C5
Goose La RBSF CM22........92 E2
Goral Md RKW/CH/CXG WD3........161 H7
Gordian Wy STVGE SG2........51 P4
Gordon Av STAN HA7........172 F3
Gordon Cl STAL AL1........136 E1
Gordon Gdns EDGW HA8........173 M6
Gordon HI ENC/FH EN2........155 K9
Gordon Rd CSHM HP5........145 J2
  ENC/FH EN2........155 L9
  HARP AL5........102 C6
  LTNE LU2........7 J2
Gordon St LTN LU1........6 C4
Gordons Wk HARP AL5........102 D6
Gordon Wy BAR EN5........166 D5

CSTG HP8........159 H9
Gore HI DEN/HRF UB9........169 M8
Gore HI AMSS HP7........158 B3
Gorelands La CSTG HP8........159 K7
Gore La STDN SG11........89 H2
Gorham Dr STAL AL1........136 D2
Gorham Wy
  DUN/HR/TOD LU5........60 G2
Gorle Cl GSTN WD25........149 H4
Gorleston Cl STVG SG1........50 D6
Gorse Cl HAT AL10........122 C9
Gorse Cnr STVGE SG2 *........102 B4
  STALW/RED AL3........51 M6
Gorse Rd HTCHE/RSTV SG4........49 L4
Gorselands HARP AL5........102 A5
Gorseway HAT AL10........122 C2
Gorst Cl LWTH SG6........36 B5
Gosforth La OXHEY WD19........162 C9
Gosforth Pth OXHEY WD19........162 C9
Goshawk Cl LTNN/LEA LU4........61 K2
Gosling Av HTCH/STOT SG5........49 M2
Gosmore Ley Cl
  HTCHE/RSTV SG4........49 L4
Gosmore Rd
  HTCHE/RSTV SG4........49 L2
The Gossamers GSTN WD25........149 M6
Gosse Cl HOD EN11........126 E2
Gosselin Rd HERT/WAT SG14........107 H4
Gossoms Ryde BERK HP4........115 M6
Gossom's End BERK HP4........115 M6
Gothic Wy ARL/CHE SG15........24 E4
Gould Cl BRKMPK AL9........138 E3
Government Rw PEND EN3........157 H8
Governors Av DEN/HRF UB9........169 K9
Governors Cl AMS HP6........145 L7
Gowar Fld POTB/CUF EN6........152 D1
Gower Rd ROY SG8........20 B5
The Gowers AMS HP6........145 K7
  HLW CM20........3 K1
Grace Av RAD WD7........151 J5
Grace Cl BORE WD6........152 A9
Grace Gdns BSF CM23........74 A4
Grace Wy STVG SG1........51 H1
Graemes Dyke Rd
  BERK HP4........115 M8
Grafton Cl STALE/WH AL4........121 J9
Grafton Gdns LTNN/LIM LU3........71 L5
Grafton Rd HRW HA1........172 B9
Graham Av BROX EN10........126 D8
Graham Ct STAL AL1........136 C2
Graham Gdns LTNN/LIM LU3........61 N7
  KTN/HRWW/WS HA3........172 E7
Grahams BSF CM23........73 N6
Grammar School Wk
  HTCH/STOT SG5........25 J3
Grampian Pl STVG SG1........51 L3
Grampian Wy LTNN/LIM LU3........46 B8
The Granaries WAB EN9........157 K4
Granary Cl STALE/WH AL4........103 J4
Granary La HARP AL5........102 D2
The Granary ARL/CHE SG15........24 E4
  HLWW/ROY CM19........127 P3
  WARE SG12........109 H9
Granby Av HARP AL5........102 D2
Granby Park Rd CHESW EN7........141 L6
Granby Rd LTNN/LEA LU4........61 N3
  STVG SG1........50 F7
Grandfield Av WAT WD17........149 H9
Grand Union Canal Wk
  TRDG/WHET N20........166 F7
Great Cambridge Rd EN EN1........155 M5
Great Conduit WCCE AL7........105 M5
Great Dell WCCW AL8........104 C4
Great Eastern Cl BSF CM23........74 B4
Great Elms Rd HHS/BOV HP3........134 A3
Great Gables STVG SG1........51 J9
Great Ganett WGCE AL7........105 L8
Great Gn HTCH/STOT SG5........34 C4
Great Gv BUSH WD23........163 K5
Great Groves CHESW EN7........141 M7
Great Hadham Rd BSF CM23........73 K3
Great Heart HHNE HP2........117 P6
Great Heath HAT AL10........122 E3
Great Innings North
  HERT/WAT SG14........86 E2
Great Innings South
  HERT/WAT SG14........86 E2
Great Lawne KNEB SG3........85 N5
Great Leylands HLWS CM18........129 K4
Great Meadow BROX EN10........142 F1
Great Molewood
  HERT/WAT SG14........107 J3
Great Northern Rd
  DUN/HR/TOD LU5........60 F7
Great North Rd BAR EN5........166 D1
  BLDK SG7........26 A7
  BRKMPK AL9........122 E2
  HAT AL10........122 E2
  STVG SG1........35 N5
  WLYN AL6........68 G7
Great Palmers HHNE HP2........118 A3
Great Pk KGLY WD4........134 B9
Great Plumtree HLW CM20........3 K1
Great Rd HHNE HP2........118 A7
Great Slades POTB/CUF EN6........152 A2
Great Stockwood Rd
  CHESW EN7........141 L5
Great Sturgess Rd HHW HP1........117 J8
Great Westwood
  KGLY WD4 *........147 P5
Great Whites Rd
  HHS/BOV HP3........5 K6
Greenacre Cl BAR EN5........153 J8
Greenacres BUSH WD23........163 K6
  HHNE HP2........134 C1
  HTCHE/RSTV SG4........49 L3
  STVGE SG2........67 M5
  WGCE AL7........105 J9
Greenacres Dr STAN HA7........173 H4
Greenacres Pk
  DUN/WHIP LU6........79 J3
Greenacre Wk
  STHGT/OAK N14........167 P9
Greenall Cl CHES/WCR EN8........142 C8
Greenbank Rd WAT WD17........148 C6
Greenbanks STAL AL1........9 K7

Greenbrook Av EBAR EN4 ...... 153 M9
Greenbury Cl
  RKW/CH/CXG WD3......... 160 A2
  ROY SG8 .... 21 L9
Green Cl BRKMPK AL9......... 139 H5
  CHES/WCR EN8 .... 156 D2
  LTNW/LEA LU4 .... 61 L1
  STVGE SG2 .... 67 J5
Greencoates HERT/BAY SG13... 107 M7
Greencourt La EDGW HA8...... 173 N5
Green Cft HAT HA7 .... 122 D3
Green Dell Wy HHS/BOV HP3 .. 118 C8
Green Drift ROY SG8 .... 20 A5
Greene Field Rd BERK HP4...... 115 P7
Green End WLYN AL6 .... 84 C5
Green End La HHW HP1 .... 117 J9
Green End Gdns HHW HP1 ...... 117 K9
Green End Rd HHW HP1......... 117 K8
Green End St
  RAYLNE/WEN HP22 .... 94 E7
Greenes Ct BERK HP4 .... 115 P6
Green Wk BERK HA4.............. 116 A8
Greenfield BRKMPK AL9 .... 122 C3
  ROY SG8 .... 20 A3
  WGCW AL8 .... 104 C9
Greenfield Av
  HTCH/STOT SG5 .... 35 J4
  OXHEY WD19 .... 162 G8
Greenfield End DUN/WHIP LU6.. 60 B5
Greenfield End
  CFSP/GDCR SL9 .... 168 D4
Greenfield La HTCH/STOT SG5.. 35 K4
Greenfield Rd STVG SG1 .... 10 E1
Greenfields POTB/CUF EN6 *... 140 F9
  STSD CM24 .... 58 F4
Greenfield St WAB EN9 .... 157 H4
Greenfield Wy BGSW SG18 ..... 14 C6
  RYLN/HDSTN HA2 .... 172 B7
Greengate LTNN/LIM LU3....... 45 M7
Greenheys Cl NTHWD HA6 ..... 170 C5
Green Hill Cl STDN SC11 .... 55 L9
Greenhill Av LTNE LU2 .... 62 E3
Greenhill Cl BAR EN5 .... 166 E4
Greenhill Crs WATW WD18 .... 162 A5
Greenhill Pde BAR EN5 * 166 F4
Greenhills HLW CM20 .... 3 C5
  WARE SG12 .... 108 B1
Greenhills Cl
  RKW/CH/CXG WD3 .... 160 E4
Greenland Rd BAR EN5.......... 166 A5
Green La AMS HP6 .... 145 N3
  BLDK SG7 .... 17 P5
  BROX EN10 .... 142 G2
  CSHM HP5 .... 145 N3
  DUN/WHIP HA8 .... 79 H5
  EBAR EN4 .... 173 M1
  HHNE HP2 .... 8 A7
  HHS/BOV HP3 .... 132 C7
  HTCHE/RSTV SG4 .... 35 N7
  LTNE LU2 .... 63 J2
  LWTH SG6 .... 25 M8
  NTHWD HA6 .... 170 H4
  OXHEY WD19 .... 162 E7
  RKW/CH/CXG WD3 .... 161 K4
  STAL AL1 .... 136 F5
  STALW/RED AL3 .... 80 A9
  STAN HA7 .... 171 M1
  STDN SG11 .... 55 L8
  WGCE AL7 .... 105 M8
Green Lane Cl HARP AL5 .... 102 D4
Green Lane Cots STAN HA7 *.. 173 H1
Green Lanes HAT AL10 .... 122 C3
Greenleaf Wy
  KTN/HRWW/WS HA3 .... 172 F7
Green Meadow
  POTB/CUF EN6 .... 139 K9
Green Milverton
  LTNN/LIM LU3 .... 46 B8
Greenoak Pl EBAR EN4......... 167 K1
Green Oaks LTNE LU2 .... 62 C3
Green Pth
  RAYLNE/WEN HP22 .... 95 K8
Greenriggs LTNE LU2 .... 63 N4
Green Rd STHGT/OAK N14 .... 167 M5
Greenside BORE WD6 .... 151 M8
Greenside Cl
  TRDG/WHET N20 .... 167 H8
Greenside Dr HTCH/STOT SG5.. 35 J8
Greenside Pk LTNE LU2 .... 62 F3
Greensleeves Cl
  STALE/WH AL4 .... 121 H9
Greenstead GSTN CM21 .... 111 P3
Green St BORE WD6 .... 151 M7
  BRKMPK AL9 .... 123 L8
  HLW CM17 .... 129 N2
  RKW/CH/CXG WD3 .... 160 A1
  STVG SG1 .... 10 A1
Greensward BUSH WD23....... 163 K5
The Green BERK HP4 .... 116 E5
  BSF CM23 .... 74 A6
  CHES/WCR EN8 .... 142 B7
  DUN/WHIP HA8 .... 60 F2
  HTCH/STOT SG5 .... 25 K2
  HTCHE/RSTV SG4 .... 84 B4
  KNEB SG3 .... 66 E9
  LCOL/BKTW AL2 * 137 J6
  LTNE LU2 .... 82 B2
  LTNW/LEA LU4 .... 61 M1
  ROY SG8 .... 161 K4
  ROY SG8 .... 20 C5
  STHGT/OAK N14 .... 167 P8
  WAB EN9 .... 157 H4
  WARE SG12 .... 108 C1
  WLYN AL6 .... 84 C6
Green Verges STAN HA7 .... 175 K4
Green View Cl HHS/BOV HP3 .. 132 D8
Greenway BERK HP4............ 115 M7
  BSF CM23 .... 59 K4
  CSHM HP5 .... 130 G7
  HARP AL5 .... 102 C4
  HHNE HP2 .... 118 C3
  HLWW/ROY CM19 .... 128 B3

  KTN/HRWW/WS HA3 .... 173 L9
  LWTH SG6 .... 36 D6
  PIN HA5 .... 171 K6
  STVGE SG2 .... 52 C7
  TRDG/WHET N20 .... 166 E8
Greenway Cl
  TRDG/WHET N20 .... 166 E8
Green Way Gdns
  KTN/HRWW/WS HA3 .... 172 G6
Greenways ABLGY WD5 .... 148 E1
  BUNT SG9 .... 40 C8
  CHESW EN7 .... 141 J8
  HERT/WAT SG14 .... 107 J6
  LTNE LU2 .... 63 J1
  STVG SG1 .... 10 C2
  WLYN AL6 .... 105 H1
The Green Wy
  KTN/HRWW/WS HA3 .... 172 E5
The Greenway
  CFSP/GDCR SL9 .... 168 B7
  PEND EN3 .... 156 C5
  POTB/CUF EN6 .... 133 K5
  RKW/CH/CXG WD3 .... 160 E6
  TRING HP23 .... 95 N7
Greenwich Wy WAB EN9 .... 157 H6
Greenwood Av CHESW EN7 ... 156 A1
Greenwood Cl AMS HP6 .... 145 K8
  CHESW EN7 .... 156 A1
Greenwood Dr GSTN WD25 ... 149 J4
Greenwood Rd RAD WD7 ...... 151 K2
The Greenwood
  RAYLNE/WEN HP22 .... 94 E7
Greenyard WAB EN9 .... 157 H3
Greer Rd
  KTN/HRWW/WS HA3 .... 172 C5
Gregories Ct LTNN/LIM LU3 ...... 6 C1
Gregory Av POTB/CUF EN6 ... 153 M1
Gregory Ms WAB EN9 .... 156 G6
Gregson Cl BORE WD6 .... 165 J1
Grenadier Cl STALE/WH AL4 .. 121 H9
Grenadine Cl CHESW EN7 ..... 141 N6
Grenadine Wy TRING HP23 ..... 95 P7
Grenfell Cl BORE WD6 .... 151 P6
Grenville Av BROX EN10....... 126 E9
  RAYLNE/WEN HP22 .... 94 E7
Grenville Cl CHES/WCR EN8... 156 C2
Grenville Wy STVGE SG2 .... 67 K5
Gresford Cl STALE/WH AL4.... 121 J8
Gresham Cl LTNE LU2 .... 63 L5
Gresham Ct BERK HP4 .... 115 M8
Gresham Rd EDGW HA8 .... 173 H3
Gresley Cl WCCW AL8 .... 105 H4
Gresley Ldg ROY SG8 * 20 B3
Gresley Wy STVGE SG2 .... 51 N9
Greville Cl BRKMPK AL9 .... 138 E3
Greycaine Rd WATN WD24 .... 149 L7
Greydells Rd STVG SG1 .... 10 E1
Greyfell Cl STAN HA7 .... 173 H2
Greyfriars STALE/WH AL4 ..... 108 A1
Greyfriars La HARP AL5 .... 101 P5
Greygoose Pk
  HLWW/ROY CM19 .... 128 D5
Greyhound La
  POTB/CUF EN6 .... 152 D3
Greystoke Av PIN HA5 .... 172 A7
Greystoke Cl BERK HP4 .... 115 M8
Greystoke Gdns ENC/FH EN2.. 167 J3
Griffiths Wy STAL AL1 .... 8 D7
Griffon Wy GSTN WD25 .... 148 C4
Grimsdells Cnr AMS HP6 *..... 145 J7
Grimsdell's La AMS HP6 .... 145 J7
Grimsdyke Crs BAR EN5 .... 166 A2
Grimsdyke Rd PIN HA5 .... 171 N4
  TRING HP23 .... 96 C2
Grimstone Rd
  HTCHE/RSTV SG4 .... 50 B3
Grimston Rd STAL AL1 .... 9 H4
Grimthorpe Cl
  STALW/RED AL3 .... 8 B1
Grindcobbe Cl STAL AL1 ...... 136 C2
Grinders End
  HTCHE/RSTV SG4 .... 50 E4
Grindleford Av
  FBAR/BDGN N11 .... 167 L8
Grinstead La RBSF CM22 .... 92 D5
Groom Rd BROX EN10 .... 142 E5
Grooms Cots CSHM HP5 .... 131 N9
Grooms Dr PIN HA5 .... 171 J9
Grosvenor Av KGLGY WD4 .... 134 D7
Grosvenor Cl BSF CM23 .... 91 N2
Grosvenor Ct
  RKW/CH/CXG WD3 * 161 L8
Grosvenor Crs
  CDALE/KGS NW9 .... 173 N8
Grosvenor Gdns
  STHGT/OAK N14 .... 167 P4
Grosvenor Rd BLDK SG7 .... 26 B8
  BORE WD6 .... 164 C2
  BROX EN10 .... 126 E8
  LTNW/LIM LU3 .... 62 C1
  NTHWD HA6 ....171 H2
  STAL AL1 .... 9 H5
  WAT WD17 .... 13 H5
Grosvenor Rd West
  BLDK SG7 .... 26 B8
Grosvenor Sq KGLGY WD4 .... 134 D7
Grosvenor Ter HHW HP1 ...... 117 K9
The Grotto WARE SG12 .... 108 C4
Ground La HAT AL10 .... 122 C5
Grove Av HARP AL5 .... 102 C5
  PIN HA5 .... 171 N8
Grove Bank OXHEY WD19 *... 162 F7
Grovebury Cl DUN/WHIP LU6.. 60 D3
Grovebury Ct
  STHGT/OAK N14 .... 167 N6
Grovebury Gdns
  LCOL/BKTW AL2 .... 136 B6
Grove Cl CFSP/GDCR SL9 ..... 168 A5
  STHGT/OAK N14 * 167 N6
Grove Ct WAB EN9 .... 155 D5
Grove Crs RKW/CH/CXG WD3.. 161 L3
Grovedale Cl CHESW EN7 ..... 141 N9
Grove End CFSP/GDCR SL9 ... 168 A5
  LTN LU1 .... 62 C9
Grove Farm Pk NTHWD HA6 .. 156 C9
Grove Gdns PEND EN3 .... 156 A5
Grove Hall Rd BUSH WD23 .... 162 G3
Grove Hl CFSP/GDCR SL9 ..... 168 A5
  STSD CM24 .... 58 F4

Grovelands HHNE HP2 .... 118 D6
  LCOL/BKTW AL2 .... 136 A6
Grovelands Cl
  HTCHE/RSTV SG4 .... 35 P6
Grovelands Ct
  STHGT/OAK N14 .... 167 P6
Groveland Wy
  HTCH/STOT SG5 .... 25 L4
Grove La CSHM HP5 .... 131 N6
Grove Lea HAT AL10 .... 122 D9
Grove Leys TRING HP23 .... 96 B7
The Grovells BERK HP4 * 98 C5
Grove Md HAT AL10 .... 122 C6
Grove Meadow WCCE AL7 .... 105 M6
Grove Mill La
  RKW/CH/CXG WD3 .... 148 D8
Grove Pk TRING HP23 .... 96 B7
Grove Park Rd LTN LU1 .... 80 B2
Grove Pl BRKMPK AL9 .... 138 F3
  GSTN WD25 * 150 A9
Grover Cl HHNE HP2 .... 117 N7
Grove Rd AMS HP6 .... 145 L7
  BORE WD6 .... 151 M9
  DUN/WHIP HA8 .... 44 F8
  DUN/HR/TOD LU5 .... 60 C2
  EBAR EN4 .... 167 J2
  EDGW HA8 .... 173 N3
  HARP AL5 .... 102 C5
  HHW HP1 .... 133 K1
  HTCH/STOT SG5 .... 35 L7
  NTHWD HA6 .... 170 F2
  PIN HA5 .... 171 P9
  RKW/CH/CXG WD3 .... 160 E8
  STAL AL1 .... 8 E6
  STVG SG1 .... 10 E1
  TRING HP23 .... 96 B7
  WARE SG12 .... 108 C2
Grove Rd West PEND EN3 ..... 156 B7
Grover Rd OXHEY WD19 ...... 162 F5
Groves Rd
  RAYLNE/WEN HP22 .... 112 B5
Groves Wy CSHM HP5 .... 130 E8
The Grove AMS HP6 .... 145 J5
  BRKMPK AL9 .... 139 K6
  CSHM HP5 .... 145 J5
  HARP AL5 .... 102 D5
  KGLGY WD4 * 133 M9
  LTN LU1 .... 62 C9
  POTB/CUF EN6 .... 153 M2
  RAD WD7 .... 150 F4
  RBSF CM22 .... 93 J4
  RKW/CH/CXG WD3 .... 161 L3
  STDN SG11 .... 73 H7
  TRING HP23 .... 96 B7
Grove Wk HERT/WAT SG14 ... 107 K4
Grove Wy RKW/CH/CXG WD3.. 159 P3
Grovewood Cl
  RKW/CH/CXG WD3 .... 159 P4
Grubbs La BRKMPK AL9 .... 139 K1
Guernsey Cl LTNW/LEA LU4 .... 46 C5
Guessens Gv WGCW AL8 .... 104 F6
Guessens Rd WGCW AL8 .... 104 F6
Guessens Wk WGCW AL8 .... 104 F5
Guildford Cl STVG SG1 .... 51 H5
Guildford Rd STAL AL1 .... 120 C9
Guildhall St LTN LU1 * 6 F3
Guilfords HLWE CM17 .... 111 N7
Guinery Gv HHS/BOV HP3 ..... 134 A3
Guinevere Gdns
  CHES/WCR EN8 .... 142 C9
Guildhall Cl BUSH WD23 .... 163 L4
Gullbrook HHW HP1 * 117 K9
Gullet Wood Rd GSTN WD25 .. 149 H5
The Gulphs HERT/BAY SG13 .. 107 L7
Gun La KNEB SG3 .... 67 J9
Gun Meadow Av KNEB SG3 .... 85 K1
Gunnels Wood Pk STVG SG1 *.. 66 C3
Gunnels Wood Rd STVG SG1 .. 50 B8
Gunner Dr PEND EN3 .... 156 F7
Gun Road Gdns KNEB SG3 ..... 85 K1
Gunters Md STAN HA7 .... 173 L1
Gurney's La HTCH/STOT SG5 .. 34 C1
Gustard Wd STALE/WH AL4 ... 83 H8
Gwent Cl GSTN WD25 .... 149 L4
Gwynne Cl CI WLYN AL6 .... 84 C6
Gwynn Cl TRING HP23 .... 96 A7
Gwynns Wk HERT/BAY SG13 . 107 M6
Gyles Pk STAN HA7 .... 173 J5
Gypsy Cl WARE SG12 .... 108 E8
Gypsy La KGLGY WD4 .... 148 E5
  WARE SG12 .... 108 E8
  WGCE AL7 .... 123 J2
Gypsy Moth Av HAT AL10 .... 122 B4

Hadley Gv BAR EN5 .... 166 C1
Hadley Highstone
  BAR EN5 .... 153 J8
Hadley Pde BAR EN5 * 166 C2
Hadley Rdg BAR EN5 .... 166 D2
Hadley Rd BAR EN5 .... 166 F2
  EBAR EN4......................... 154 B9
Hadley Wood Rd BAR EN5 .... 166 E1
Hadlow Down Cl
  LTNN/LIM LU3 .... 62 D1
Hadrian Av DUN/HR/TOD LU5.. 61 H4
Hadrian Cl STALW/RED AL3 .. 135 N1
Hadrians Wk STVG SG1 .... 51 M7
Hadrian Wy GSTN WD25 .... 36 G1
Hadwell Cl STVGE SG2 .... 52 C9
Haggeld Rd LTN LU1 .... 62 D9
Hagden La WATW WD18 .... 12 A5
Haggerston Rd BORE WD6 ... 151 K8
Haglis Dr
  RAYLNE/WEN HP22 .... 112 B5
Hagsdell Rd HERT/BAY SG13.. 107 L7
Haig Cl STAL AL1 .... 122 C9
Haig Rd STAN HA7 .... 173 J2
Hailes Wd RBSF CM22 .... 59 L1
Hailey Av HOD EN11 .... 126 D1
Hailey La HERT/BAY SG13 .... 125 P5
Hailey Pl SBW CM21 .... 111 P2
Hailsham Dr HRW HA1 .... 149 H4
Haines Wy GSTN WD25 .... 136 G8
Haldane Ct PEND EN3 .... 156 D5
Haldens WGCE AL7 .... 105 J3
Hale La RAYLNE/WEN HP22 .. 112 F8
  RAYLNE/WEN HP22 .... 112 D9
Hales Meadow HARP AL5 ..... 102 D4
Hales Pk HHNE HP2 .... 118 D7
Hales Park Cl HHNE HP2 ...... 118 D7
Haleswood Rd HHNE HP2 .... 118 D7
Half Acre HTCH/STOT SG5 ...... 49 J1
Halfacre HI CFSP/GDCR SL9 . 168 C5
Halfacre La BUNT SG9 .... 41 M7
Half Acres BSF CM23 .... 74 A2
Halfhide La CHES/WCR EN8 .. 142 C5
Halfhides WAB EN9 .... 157 J5
Half Moon La
  HHNE HP2 .... 118 D3
Half Moon Ms STAL AL1 .... 9 F4
Half Moon Pl
  DUN/WHIP LU5 .... 60 C7
Halford Cl EDGW HA8 .... 173 P6
Halford Ct STAL AL10 .... 122 B5
Halfway Av LTNW/LEA LU4 .... 61 N5
Halifax Cl LCOL/BKTW AL2 ... 149 N1
Halifax Rd RKW/CH/CXG WD3.. 160 A6
Halifax Wy WCCE AL7 .... 105 P6
Halings La DEN/HRF UB9 ..... 169 H8
Hallam Cl WATN WD24 .... 149 H1
Hallam Gdns PIN HA5 .... 171 N4
Halland Wy NTHWD HA6 ...... 170 D3
Hall Cl RKW/CH/CXG WD3 ... 160 E7
Hall Dr DEN/HRF UB9 .... 169 N5
Halley Rd HERT/WAT SG14 .. 107 J4
Halley's Wy
  DUN/HR/TOD LU5 .... 60 C2
Hall Farm Cl STAN HA7 .... 173 H1
Hall Gdns STALE/WH AL4 .... 105 L8
Hall Heath Cl STAL AL1 .... 120 C9
Halliday Cl RAD WD7 .... 151 K2
Hallingbury Cl RBSF CM22 ..... 74 C6
Hallingbury Rd RBSF CM22 ... 74 C6
  SBW CM21 .... 92 B5
Halling Hl HLW CM20 .... 4 F1
  HTCHE/RSTV SG4 .... 85 K3
  KNEB SG3 .... 85 K3
  ROY SG8 .... 35 P2
Hall marl LWTH SG6 .... 35 P2
Hallmores BROX EN10 .... 126 F7
Hallowell Rd NTHWD HA6 .... 170 C4
Hallowes Crs OXHEY WD19 .. 162 C9
Hall Pk BERK HP4 .... 116 B9
Hall Park Ga BERK HP4 .... 116 B9
Hall Pl STAL AL1 * 9 G2
Hall Place Cl STAL AL1 .... 9 G2
Hall Place Gdns STAL AL1 ...... 9 G2
Hall Rd HHNE HP2 .... 118 C6
  RBSF CM22 .... 59 L2
Halls Cl WLYN AL6 .... 84 F9
Hallside Rd EN EN1 .... 156 A5
Hallside Rd EN EN1 .... 156 A5
The Hall Wk BERK HP4 .... 63 J3
Hallwicks Rd LTNE LU2 .... 63 J3
Halsbury Cl STAN HA7 .... 173 H2
Halsey Dr HHW HP1 .... 117 J6
  HTCHE/RSTV SG4 .... 34 C4
Halsey Pl LCOL/BKTW AL2 ... 137 L6
Halsey Pl WATN WD24 .... 149 J8
Halsey Rd WATW WD18 .... 12 E3
Halstead Hl CHESW EN7 ...... 141 M9
Halter Ct BORE WD6 .... 164 C1
Halton Cl LCOL/BKTW AL2 ... 136 B7
Halton La RAYLNE/WEN HP22.. 112 B4
Haltside HAT AL10 .... 122 E6
Haitside HAT AL10 .... 122 A7
Halwick Cl HHW HP1 .... 118 B9
Halyard Cl LTNE LU2 .... 63 H1
Hamberlins La TRING HP23 .. 114 C4
Hambling's Pl HHW HP1 .... 118 B9
Hamblings Cl RAD WD7 .... 151 J3
Hambridge Wy
  HTCH/STOT SG5 .... 35 L9
Hambro Cl LTNE LU2 .... 81 N6
Hambrook Crs CHES/WCR EN8.. 142 C7
Hamel Cl
  KTN/HRWW/WS HA3 .... 173 K8
Hamels Dr HERT/BAY SG13 .. 108 A5
Hamels La BUNT SG9 .... 54 E8
Hamer Cl HHS/BOV HP3 ...... 134 F6
Hamilton Av HOD EN11 .... 126 F5
Hamilton Cl EBAR EN4 .... 167 K1
  LCOL/BKTW AL2 .... 135 P5

  POTB/CUF EN6 .... 152 D3
Hamilton Ct AL10 * 122 E8
Hamilton Md BERK HP4 .... 132 D6
Hamilton Rd BERK HP4 .... 115 N7
  EBAR EN4 .... 167 J3
  HRW HA1 .... 172 E9
  KGLGY WD4 .... 148 C3
  OXHEY WD19 .... 161 P7
  STAL AL1 .... 120 F7
Hamilton St WATW WD18 ..... 13 H7
Hamlet Cl LCOL/BKTW AL2 .. 135 M3
Hamlet HI HLWW/ROY CM19. 127 M7
The Hamlet BERK HP4 .... 116 D4
Hamlins LTNE LU2 .... 63 N4
Hamlyn Cl EDGW HA8 .... 164 E9
Hammarskjold Rd HLW CM20.. 2 D3
Hammer Pde GSTN WD25 .... 149 H3
Hammersfield Cl STDN SG11.. 71 J2
Hammers Ga LCOL/BKTW AL2.. 135 P5
Hammersmith Cl
  DUN/HR/TOD LU5 .... 60 F1
Hammersmith Gdns
  DUN/HR/TOD LU5 .... 60 F1
Hammond Cl LTN LU1 * 80 D4
Hammond End La HARP AL5 .. 101 M7
Hammond Rd STAL AL1 .... 101 N7
Hammonds La STALE/WH AL4 103 M9
Hammonds Rd RBSF CM22 ... 93 J8
Hammondstreet Rd
  CHESW EN7 .... 141 J4
Hammondswick HARP AL5 ... 101 N8
Hampden Cl LTNE LU2 .... 165 H8
Hampden HTCHE/RSTV SG4 .. 83 H4
Hampden Av CSHM HP5 .... 130 F9
Hampden Cl LWTH SG6 .... 25 M9
Hampden Crs CHESW EN7 .... 156 A1
Hampden HI LA WARE SG12 .. 108 E2
Hampden PI LCOL/BKTW AL2. 136 D8
Hampden Ri CFSP/GDCR SL9.. 168 C6
Hampden Rd ROY SG8 .... 20 C6
  KTN/HRWW/WS HA3 .... 172 C5
  RAYLNE/WEN HP22 .... 112 D7
Hampden Wy
  STHGT/OAK N14 .... 167 M9
Hampendell LTNE LU2 .... 148 F6
Hampshire Wy LTNE LU2 * 45 N6
Hampstead Cl
  LCOL/BKTW AL2 .... 149 N1
Hampton Ct BORE WD6 .... 165 J4
  STVGE SG2 .... 52 C7
Hampton Gdns SBW CM21 ... 111 L5
Hampton Rd LTNW/LEA LU4 .. 60 C5
Hamstel Rd HLW CM20 .... 2 B5
Hanaper Dr ROY SG8 .... 21 L9
Hanbury Cl CHES/WCR EN8 .. 142 C9
Hanbury Dr WARE SG12 .... 83 J5
Hanbury Ms WARE SG12 * ... 108 A6
Hancock Dr LTNE LU2 .... 5 K6
Hancroft Rd HHS/BOV HP3 ... 134 C2
Handa Cl HHS/BOV HP3 .... 134 C2
Handcross Rd LTNE LU2 .... 46 F8
Handel Cl EDGW HA8 .... 173 M3
Handel Pde EDGW HA8 * 173 M3
Handel La SBW CM21 .... 173 N4
Handley Page Wy
  LCOL/BKTW AL2 .... 136 E9
Handpost Lodge Gdns
  HHNE HP2 .... 118 E3
Handside Cl WGCW AL8 .... 104 F6
Handside La WGCW AL8 .... 104 E6
Handside La WCCW AL8 .... 104 F5
Handsworth Cl OXHEY WD19.. 162 C9
Hangar Rd DEN/HRF UB9 .... 169 H9
Hangar Ruding OXHEY WD19. 162 F5
Hanger Cl HHW HP1 * 3 J5
Hangmans La WLYN AL6 .... 85 J5
Hankins La MLHL NW7 .... 165 J8
Hanover Cl STVGE SG2 .... 67 J5
Hanover Gdns ABLGY WD5 * . 134 C9
Hanover Gra HARP AL5 .... 51 K5
Hanover Gn HHW HP1 .... 133 K1
Hanover Pl
  AMP/FLIT/BLC MK45 .... 32 D4
Hanover Wk HAT AL10 .... 122 C9
Hansart Wy ENC/FH EN2 ..... 155 H9
Hanselin Cl STAN HA7 .... 172 F2
Hanover Pl
  HLWW/ROY CM19 .... 127 M3
Hanswick Cl LTNE LU2 .... 63 J4
Hanworth Cl LTNE LU2 .... 63 N4
Hanyards La POTB/CUF EN6 . 140 F7
Harbert Gdns
  LCOL/BKTW AL2 .... 136 A8
Harberts Rd
  HLWW/ROY CM19 .... 2 B7
Harborne Cl OXHEY WD19 ... 171 L2
Harbury Dell LTNN/LIM LU3 ... 46 C8
Harcamlow Wy BSF CM23 ..... 57 M8
  HLWW/ROY CM19 .... 127 N1
  RBSF CM22 .... 92 F5
  ROY SG8 .... 21 J6
  SAFWS CB11 .... 31 P6
Harcourt Rd EDGW HA8 ...... 122 E8
Harcourt Rd BUSH WD23 ..... 163 L4
  TRING HP23 .... 96 B8
Harcourt St LTN LU1 .... 80 B7
Harding Cl STDN WD25 .... 149 K3
Harding Cl LTNE LU2 .... 149 K3
  STALW/RED AL3 .... 101 J7
Harding Pde HARP AL5 * 102 A3
Harding Rd CSHM HP5 .... 131 J9
Hardings WGCE AL7 .... 105 L2
Hardy Cl HHS/BOV HP3 .... 173 L2
Hardwick Cl STAN HA7 .... 173 L2
  STVGE SG2 .... 67 J5
Hardwicke Gdns AMS HP6 ... 145 K8
Hardwicke Pl
  LCOL/BKTW AL2 .... 137 J6
Hardwick Gn BLDK SG7 .... 8 B7
Hardy Cl BAR EN5 .... 166 C4

H

Hackforth Cl BAR EN5 .... 165 N4
Hackney Cl BORE WD6 .... 165 K4
Hadar Cl TRDG/WHET N20 ... 166 E7
Haddenham Ct
  OXHEY WD19 * 162 F9
Haddestoke Ga
  CHES/WCR EN8 .... 142 E5
Haddington Cl
  RAYLNE/WEN HP22 .... 112 E6
Haddon Cl BORE WD6 .... 164 C1
  HHS/BOV HP3 .... 118 B9
Haddon Rd LTNE LU2 .... 7 H3
  RKW/CH/CXG WD3 .... 160 A4
Hadham Cl BSF CM23 .... 73 N6
Hadham Gv BSF CM23 .... 73 M6
Hadham Rd STDN SG11 .... 71 H1
Hadland Cl HHS/BOV HP3 .... 118 D5
Hadleigh Ct BROX EN10 ...... 142 E1
Hadleigh Cl BROX EN10 ...... 142 E1
  HARP AL5 .... 86 A9
Hadley Cl BORE WD6 .... 164 B1
Hadley Common BAR EN5 .... 166 C1
Hadley Gra HLWE CM17 ...... 129 M3
Hadley Gn BAR EN5 .... 166 B1
Hadley Green Rd BAR EN5 ... 166 C1
Hadley Green West BAR EN5 . 166 B1

HTCHE/RSTV SG4 .... 35 P9
Hardy Dr ROY SG8 .... 20 C2
Hardy Rd HHNE HP2 .... 118 A7
Hardy Wy ENC/FH EN2 .... 155 H9
Harebell WCCE AL7 .... 123 H1
Harebell Cl HERT/BAY SG13 .. 108 A6
Hareridge La
 RAYLNE/WEN HP22 .... 112 F1
Hare Crs STVGE SG2 .... 149 H2
Harefield Cl ENC/FH EN2 .... 155 H9
Harefield HLW CM20 .... 129 K2
 STVGE SG2 .... 67 M3
Harefield PI STALE/WH AL4 .. 121 J5
Harefield Rd LTN LU1 .... 62 A6
 RKW/CH/CXG WD3 .... 169 P2
Hare La HAT AL10 .... 122 E8
Harepark Ct HHW HP1 .... 117 J7
Hare St HLWW/ROY CM19 .... 128 C4
Hare Street Bunt BUNT SG9 .... 40 E9

Harewood
 RKW/CH/CXG WD3 .... 160 C4
Harewood Rd CSTG SG6 .... 159 J2
 OXHEY WD19 .... 162 D8
Harford Dr WAT WD17 .... 13 H4
Harforde Ct HERT/BAY SG13 *.. 107 P6
Hargrave Ct STSD CM24 .... 58 F3
Hargreaves Av CHESW EN7 .. 156 A1
Hargreaves Cl CHESW EN7 ... 156 A1
Hargreaves Rd STVGE SG8 .. 20 C5
Harkett Cl
Harkness CHESW EN7 .... 142 A8
Harkness Rd HHNE HP2 .... 117 N7
Harkness Wy
 HTCHE/RSTV SG4 .... 35 P6
Harlech Rd ABLGY WD5 .... 149 H1
The Harlequin WAT WD17 .... 13 H4
Harlesden Rd STAL AL1 .... 120 F8
Harlestone Cl LTNN/LIM LU3 .. 46 B6
Harley Ct STALE/WH AL4 * .. 121 J4
Harley Crs HRW HA1 .... 172 D8
Harley Rd HHW HA1 .... 172 D8
The Harlings HERT/BAY SG13 .. 126 E1

Harlow Common
 HLWE CM17 .... 129 N6
Harlow Ct HHNE HP2 .... 118 A4
Harlow Rd HLWW/ROY CM19 .. 127 P2
 SBW CM21 .... 111 N4
Harlyn Dr PIN HA5 .... 171 K7
Harmer Dell WLYN AL6 .... 85 K9
Harmer Green La WLYN AL6 .. 85 J7
Harmony Cl HAT AL10 .... 122 D4
Harmsworth Wy
 TRDG/WHET N20 .... 166 D7
Harness Wy STALE/WH AL4 .. 121 J5
Harold Cl HLWW/ROY CM19 .. 128 C4
Harold Crs WAB EN9 .... 157 H2
Harold Rd
 AMP/FLIT/BLC MK45 .... 32 D5
Harolds Rd HLWW/ROY CM19 .. 128 C4
Harpenden La
 STALW/RED AL3 .... 101 J6
Harpenden Ri HARP AL5 .... 101 M1
Harpenden Rd
 STALE/WH AL4 .... 102 C4
 STALW/RED AL3 .... 101 K8
Harper Cl STHGT/OAK N14 .. 167 N4
Harper Ct STVG SG1 * 11 C5
Harper La RAD WD7 .... 137 H9
Harpsfield Broadway
 HAT AL10 .... 122 C5
Harptree Wy STAL AL1 .... 120 E6
Harrier Wy WAB EN9 .... 157 M4
Harries Cl CHAMP HA6 .... 130 C8
Harriescourt WAB EN9 .... 157 M2
Harriet Walker Wy
 RKW/CH/CXG WD3 .... 160 D6
Harrington Hts
 DUN/HR/TOD LU5 .... 60 D1
Harris Cl ENC/FH EN2 .... 155 J9
Harris La HTCH/STOT SG5 .... 48 C5
 RAD WD7 .... 151 M4
Harrison Cl HTCHE/RSTV SG4 .. 34 E3
 NTHWD HA6 .... 170 E3
 TRDG/WHET N20 .... 167 J7
Harrison Rd WAB EN9 .... 157 L5
Harrisons BSF CM23 .... 58 B4
Harrison Wk CHES/WCR EN8 .. 142 C9
Harris Rd GSTN WD25 .... 149 H5
Harrods Gn EDGW HA8 .... 173 N2
Harrogate Rd OXHEY WD19 .. 162 D9
Harrowband Rd LTNE LU2 .. 70 E4
Harrow Ct STVG SG1 .... 10 E4
Harrowdene STVGE SG2 .... 67 M2
Harrowden Rd LTNE LU2 .... 63 J6
Harrowes Meade EDGW HA8 .. 164 G9
Harrow Vw HHW HA1 .... 172 D8
Harrow Wy OXHEY WD19 .... 162 G9
Harrow Weald Pk
 KTN/HRWW/WS HA3 .... 172 G3
Harry Scott Ct LTNW/LEA LU4 .. 45 M9
Harston Dr PEND EN3 .... 156 F8
Hartcroft Cl HHS/BOV HP3 .. 118 C9
Hartfield Av BORE WD6 .... 164 G3
Hartfield Rd BORE 164 G4
Hartford Av
 KTN/HRWW/WS HA3 .... 172 G7
Hartforde Rd BORE WD6 .... 164 G1
Harthall La KGLGY WD4 .... 134 C7
Hartham Common
 HERT/WAT SG14 .... 107 L5
Hartham La HERT/WAT SG14 .. 107 K6
Hart Hill Dr LTNE LU2 .... 7 H3
Hart Hill La LTNE LU2 .... 7 H3
Hartland Cl EDGW HA8 .... 164 G8
Hartland Rd EDGW HA8 .... 164 G8
 CHES/WCR EN8 .... 142 C9
Hart La LTNE LU2 .... 7 J1
Hartley Rd LTNE LU2 .... 7 J1
Hartmoor Ms PEND EN3 .... 156 C7
Hartmore Rd HAT AL10 .... 111 M7
 STAL AL1 .... 5 H5
Hartsbourne Av BUSH WD23 .. 163 L8
Hartsbourne Cl BUSH WD23 .. 163 M8

Hartsbourne Rd BUSH WD23 .. 163 M8
Hartsbourne Wy HHNE HP2 .. 118 D9
Harts Cl BUSH WD23 .... 163 J1
Hartsfield Rd LTNE LU2 .... 63 H4
Hartspring La BUSH WD23 .... 163 J1
 GSTN WD25 .... 150 A9
Hartswood Cl BUSH WD23 .. 163 J1
Hartswood Gn BUSH WD23 .. 163 M8
Hart Wk LTNE LU2 * 7 J1
Hartwell Gdns HARP AL5 .... 101 M3
Harvest Bank AMS HP6 .... 144 B4
Harvest Cl LTNW/LEA LU4 .... 61 K3
Harvest Ct LHTH SG6 * 36 F2
 STALE/WH AL4 .... 121 H4
 WLYN AL6 .... 85 H6
Harvest End GSTN WD25 ...... 149 L6
Harvesters Ms
 STALE/WH AL4 * 121 J4
Harvest La STVGE SG2 .... 51 M8
Harvest Md HAT AL10 .... 122 E5
Harvest Rd BUSH WD23 ...... 163 K3
Harveyfields WAB EN9 .... 157 H4
Harvey Rd DUN/WHIP LU6 .... 60 A7
 LCOL/BKTW AL2 .... 137 K7
 RKW/CH/CXG WD3 .... 161 L5
 STVGE SG2 .... 51 L9
Harvey's HI LTNE LU2 .... 62 G1
Harvil Rd DEN/HRF UB9 ...... 169 N8
Harwood Av WCCW AL8 ...... 105 H2
Harwood Rd WATW WD18 .... 12 C4
Hasedines Rd HHW HP1 ...... 117 K7
Haseldine Mdw HAT AL10 .... 122 C7
Haseldine Rd LCOL/BKTW AL2 .. 137 J5
Haselfoot LHTH SG6 .... 36 B2
Hasketon Dr LTNW/LEA LU4 .. 45 L9
Haslemere BSF CM23 .... 74 B6
Haslemere Av EBAR EN4 ...... 167 K7
Haslewood Av HOD EN11 .... 126 F4
Hasluck Gdns BAR EN5 ...... 101 L1
Hastings Cl BAR EN5 .... 166 C5
Hastings Rd
 AMP/FLIT/BLC MK45 .... 32 D5
Hastings St LTN LU1 .... 6 D6
Hastings Wy
 RKW/CH/CXG WD3 .... 161 M3
Hastingwood Rd HLWE CM17 .. 129 P8
Hastoe HI TRING HP23 .... 113 P2
Hastoe La TRING HP23 .... 113 P1
Hatch Gn RBSF CM22 .... 92 C1
Hatching Green Cl HARP AL5 .. 101 P6
Hatch La BLDK SG7 .... 27 J5
The Hatch PEND EN3 .... 156 C9
Hatfield Av BSF CM23 .... 122 B3
Hatfield Crs HHNE HP2 .... 118 A4
Hatfield Rd BRKMPK AL9 .... 123 P2
 POTB/CUF EN6 .... 153 M1
 STAL AL1 .... 9 G3
 STALE/WH AL4 .... 121 H8
 WATN WD24 .... 149 J9
Hatfield Tnl HAT AL10 .... 122 C5
Hathaway Cl LTNW/LEA LU4 .. 61 L4
 STAN HA7 .... 172 C2
Hathaway Ct STALE/WH AL4 .. 121 K4
Hatherleigh Gdns
 POTB/CUF EN6 .... 153 N2
Hatherley Cha LTNE LU2 .... 62 F4
Hatters La WATW WD18 .... 161 H5
Hatters Wy LTN LU1 .... 61 L5
Hatton Rd CHES/WCR EN8 .. 142 C8
Havelock Cl KGLGY WD4 ...... 134 A7
 KTN/HRWW/WS HA3 .... 172 E9
 LTNE LU2 .... 62 F5
Haven Cl HAT AL10 .... 122 C5
Havenfield KGLGY WD4 ...... 147 L1
Havercroft Cl
 STALW/RED AL3 .... 136 A1
Haverdale LTNW/LEA LU4 .... 61 M2
Haverford Wy EDGW HA8 .... 173 M5
Havers La BSF CM23 .... 74 A5
Haward Rd HOD EN11 .... 127 H3
Hawbush Cl WLYN AL6 .... 84 E9
Hawbush Ri WLYN AL6 .... 84 E9
Hawes Cl NTHWD HA6 .... 171 H4
Hawes La CHING E4 .... 157 H8
Haweswater Dr GSTN WD25 .. 149 K3
Hawfield Gdns
 LCOL/BKTW AL2 .... 136 C5
Hawk Cl WAB EN9 .... 157 M4
Hawkenbury
 HLWW/ROY CM19 .... 128 D5
Hawkes Dr STALW/RED AL3 .. 101 J7
Hawkesley Ct RAD WD7 ...... 151 J8
Hawkfields LTNE LU2 .... 46 F9
Hawkings Wy HHS/BOV HP3 .. 135 J1
Hawkins Cl BORE WD6 .... 165 J1
Hawkins Hall La KNEB SG3 .. 85 J8
Hawkshead La BRKMPK AL9 .. 139 H7
Hawkshead Rd
 POTB/CUF EN6 .... 139 K8
Hawkshill STAL AL1 .... 120 F9
Hawkshill Dr HHS/BOV HP3 .. 133 H2
Hawksmead Cl PEND EN3 .... 156 C6
Hawksmoor RAD WD7 .... 151 M3
Hawkwell Dr TRING HP23 .... 96 B8
Hawridge La CSHM HP5 ...... 130 D2
Hawsley Av CSHM HP5 .... 130 E1
Hawsley Rd HARP AL5 .... 101 P3
Hawthorn Av STVG SG1 ...... 63 J2
Hawthorn Centre HRW HA1 .. 172 F8
Hawthorn Cl STALE/WH AL4 .. 148 G2
 DUN/WHIP LU6 .... 60 D7
 HARP AL5 .... 101 L4
 HERT/WAT SG14 .... 107 H5
 HTCH/STOT SG5 .... 49 J1
 ROY SG8 .... 20 E3
 WAT WD17 .... 148 E2
Hawthorn Crs LTN LU1 .... 79 P2
Hawthorne Av CHESW EN7 .. 142 A9
Hawthorne Cl CHESW EN7 .. 142 A9
Hawthorne Rd RAD WD7 ...... 150 F4
Hawthorn Gv ENC/FH EN2 .. 155 L8
Hawthorn HI LWTH SG6 .... 36 A6
Hawthorn La HHW HP1 .... 117 J7

Hawthorn Ri BSF CM23 ...... 74 A7
Hawthorn Rd HOD EN11 ...... 126 G3
Hawthorns HHNE HP2 .... 118 C7
Hawthorns WAB EN9 .... 104 G4
The Hawthorns BERK HP4 .. 115 M6
 CSTG SG6 .... 159 J1
 HHS/BOV HP3 .... 133 J3
 RKW/CH/CXG WD3 .... 169 N2
 STVG SG1 .... 11 H6
 WARE SG12 .... 108 C1
Hawthorn Wy CSHM HP5 .... 131 J8
 LCOL/BKTW AL2 .... 135 P3
Hawtrees Rad WD7 .... 150 D5
Haybluff Dr STVG SG1 .... 51 K3
Haybourn Md HHW HP1 .... 4 B4
Hay Cl BORE WD6 .... 165 J1
Haycroft BSF CM23 .... 74 D4
 LTNE LU2 .... 46 F9
Haycroft Rd STVG SG1 .... 10 C1
Hayden Dell BUSH WD23 .... 163 H5
Hayden Rd WAB EN9 .... 157 H5
Haydens Rd HLWW/ROY CM19 .. 128 A5
Haydon Dell Farm
 BUSH WD23 * 163 H6
Haydon Rd OXHEY WD19 .... 162 C5
Hayes Cl LTNE LU2 .... 63 J1
Hayfield Cl BUSH WD23 ...... 163 K3
Haygarth KNEB SG3 .... 85 K1
Hay Gn ROY SG8 .... 28 F3
Hayhurst Rd LTNN/LEA LU4 .. 61 L4
Hay La HARP AL5 .... 101 P3
Hayley Bell Gdns BSF CM23 .. 74 A7
Hayley Common STVGE SG2 .. 67 M2
Hayley Ct DUN/HR/TOD LU5 .. 60 F1
Hayling Dr LTNE LU2 .... 63 K3
Hayling Rd OXHEY WD19 .... 162 B9
Haymarket Rd LTNW/LEA LU4 .. 61 H7
Haymeads WGCW AL8 .... 105 H3
Haymeads La BSF CM23 .... 74 C6
Haymoor LWTH SG6 .... 36 B1
Haynes Cl FBAR/BDGN N11 .. 167 L2
 WGCE AL7 .... 105 K7
Haynes Md BERK HP4 .... 115 M5
Haysman Cl LWTH SG6 .... 36 B1
Hay St ROY SG8 .... 15 N9
Hayton Cl LTNN/LIM LU3 ...... 46 C5
Hay Wains KNEB SG3 .... 68 D9
Hayward Rd
 TRDG/WHET N20 .... 166 G8
Haywood Cl PIN HA5 .... 171 M6
Haywood Copse
 RKW/CH/CXG WD3 .... 161 H3
Haywood Ct WAB EN9 ...... 157 L4
Haywood Dr
 RKW/CH/CXG WD3 .... 160 D5
Haywood La ROY SG8 .... 28 C3
Haywood Pk
 RKW/CH/CXG WD3 .... 161 H3
Hazely TRING HP23 .... 96 B8
Heacham Cl LTNW/LEA LU4 .. 61 L3
Headingley Cl CHESW EN7 .. 141 M5
 RAD WD7 .... 151 K2
 STVG SG1 .... 50 F6
Headlands Dr BERK HP4 .... 116 B6
Headstone Dr HRW HA1 .... 172 G7
 KTN/HRWW/WS HA3 .... 172 E7
Headstone Gdns
 RYLN/HDSTN HA2 .... 172 C9
Headstone La
 RYLN/HDSTN HA2 .... 172 B6
Headstone Rd HRW HA1 .... 172 E9
Healey Rd WATW WD18 ...... 162 B5
Hearlewary HAT AL10 .... 122 B4
Heath Av ROY SG8 .... 20 C6
 STALW/RED AL3 .... 120 C6
Heathbourne Rd BUSH WD23 .. 163 M6
Heath Brow HHW HP1 * 4 A1
Heathbrow Rd WLYN AL6 .... 85 H5
Heathcliff Av HTCH/STOT SG5 .. 47 P2
Heathcote Av HAT AL10 ...... 122 D6
Heathcote Gdns HLWE CM17 .. 129 P5
Heathcroft WGCE AL7 .... 105 M5
Heathdene Mnr WAT WD17 * .. 148 C3

Heath Dr POTB/CUF EN6 .... 139 K9
 WARE SG12 .... 108 C1
Heather Cl ABLGY WD5 ...... 149 H2
 BSF CM23 .... 73 N8
Heatherfold Wy PIN HA5 .... 171 H7
Heather Hollow
 HTCHE/RSTV SG4 .... 34 E7
Heathermere LWTH SG6 ...... 25 K8
Heather Rd WGCW AL8 ...... 104 F8
Heathers AMS HP6 .... 144 A7
Heather Wk EDGW HA8 ...... 164 C4
Heather Wy HHNE HP2 ...... 117 N7
 POTB/CUF EN6 .... 153 J2
 STAN HA7 .... 172 F3
Heath Farm La
 STALW/RED AL3 .... 120 D6
Heathfield Cl BUSH WD23 .. 20 A4
 OXHEY WD19 .... 162 E6
Heathfield Rd BUSH WD23 .. 138 J3
 HTCH/STOT SG5 .... 35 L6
 LTNN/LIM LU3 .... 62 D2
Heathgate HERT/BAY SG13 .. 108 A9
 POTB/CUF EN6 .... 139 L9
Heathland Rd BUSH WD23 .. 164 A2
Heathlands WLYN AL6 ...... 85 J4
Heathlands Dr
 STALW/RED AL3 .... 120 D6
Heath La HERT/BAY SG13... 126 B1
 HHW HP1 .... 4 C5
 HTCHE/RSTV SG4 .... 64 C5
Heath Ldg BUSH WD23 * 163 M7
Heath Rd AMS HP6 .... 144 B8
 HTCHE/RSTV SG4 .... 64 C5
 OXHEY WD19 .... 162 F6
 POTB/CUF EN6 .... 139 L9
 STAL AL1 .... 120 C5
 WLYN AL6 .... 85 H5
Heath Rw BSF CM23 .... 74 C1
Heathside STALE/WH AL4 .... 137 N2
 STALW/RED AL3 .... 120 D6
Heathside Cl NTHWD HA6 .. 170 F2
Heathside Rd NTHWD HA6 .. 170 F2
The Heath HTCHE/RSTV SG4 .. 64 C4
 RAD WD7 .... 150 F3
Heath Wy HHW HP1 .... 137 H9
Heaton Dell LTNE LU2 .... 63 K5
Heavens Cl LTNW/LEA LU4 .. 61 L1
Heay Flds WCCE AL7 .... 105 M5
Hebden Cl LTNW/LEA LU4 .. 61 L2
Heckford Cl WATW WD18 .... 161 P5
Heddon Court Av EBAR EN4 .. 167 K4
Heddon Ct Pde
 EBAR EN4 * 167 L4
Heddon Rd EBAR EN4 .... 167 K4
Hedgebrooms WGCE AL7 .... 105 M3
Hedge HI ENC/FH EN2 .... 155 J9
Hedge Rw HHW HP1 .... 117 K5
Hedgerow STVGE SG2 .... 51 N8
Hedgerow La ROY SG8 ...... 28 C3
Hedgerow Wk
 RKW/CH/CXG WD3 .... 161 H5
Hedgerows SBW CM21 ...... 92 A7
The Hedgerows BSF CM23 .. 74 C4
 STVGE SG2 .... 51 N7
The Hedgerow
 LTNW/LEA LU4 .... 61 M1
Hedges Cl HAT AL10 .... 122 C5
Hedgeside BERK HP4 .... 116 D4
Hedley Cl RAYLNE/WEN HP22 .. 172 D5
Hedley Ri LTNE LU2 .... 63 K5
Hedley Rd STAL AL1 .... 122 C8
Hedworth Av CHES/WCR EN8 .. 142 E5
Heighams HLWW/ROY CM19 .. 128 C5
The Heights HHW HA3 ...... 143 N4
Helena Cl EBAR EN4 .... 153 N7
Helena Ga CHES/WCR EN8 .. 142 E5
Hellions Rd HLWW/ROY CM19 .. 2 H6
Hellards Rd STVG SG1 ...... 50 G8
Helston Cl PIN HA5 .... 171 N4
Helston Gv HHNE HP2 * 117 N5
Helston La STALW/RED AL3 .. 148 G2
Hemel Hempstead Rd
 BERK HP4 .... 98 C3
 HHS/BOV HP3 .... 134 F1
 STALW/RED AL3 .... 8 A3
 STALW/RED AL3 .... 118 E2
Hemingford Dr LTNE LU2 .... 62 G1
Hemingford Rd WAT WD17 .. 148 F6
Heming Rd EDGW HA8 ...... 173 P3
The Hemmings BERK HP4 .. 115 K8
Hemming Wy GSTN WD25 .. 149 H5
Hemp La TRING HP23 .... 96 F6
Hempstall WCCE AL7 .... 105 L8
Hempstead Rd HHS/BOV HP3 .. 134 A6
 KGLGY WD4 .... 134 F4
 WAT WD17 .... 12 C1
Henbury Wy OXHEY WD19 .. 162 F9
Henderson Cl
 STALW/RED AL3 .... 120 B4
Henderson PI ABLGY WD5 .. 134 G6
Hendon Wood La BARE HA4 .. 165 N6
Henge Wy LTNN/LIM LU3 .... 45 N9
Henham Rd RBSF CM22 ...... 59 M2
Henley Cl DUN/HR/TOD LU5 .. 61 H1
Henley Gdns PIN HA5 .... 171 K7
Henry Cl ENC/FH EN2 .... 155 M8
Henry Rd EBAR EN4 .... 167 H4
Henrys Grant STAL AL1 ...... 10 F7
Henry St HHS/BOV HP3 ...... 133 N3
 TRING HP23 .... 95 P9
Henry Wells Sq HHNE HP2 * .. 118 A4
Hensley Cl HTCHE/RSTV SG4 .. 49 H1
 WLYN AL6 .... 85 K4
Henstead PI LTNE LU2 .... 63 L5
Heracles Cl LCOL/BKTW AL2 .. 136 D7
Herald Cl BSF CM23 .... 73 N8
Herberts Hole CSHM HP5 .. 143 J1
Herbert St HHNE HP2 .... 117 N7
Hereford Av EBAR EN4 ...... 167 K7
Hereford Gdns PIN HA5 .... 171 M9
Hereford Rd LTNW/LEA LU4 .. 61 J7
Hereward Cl WAB EN9 .... 157 H2
Herga Ct WAT AL17 .... 162 C1
Herga Rd
 KTN/HRWW/WS HA3 .... 172 F8
Heriots Cl STAN HA7 .... 172 G1
Heritage Cl STALW/RED AL3 .. 8 E4

Heritage Wk
 RKW/CH/CXG WD3 * 160 C2
Herkomer Cl BUSH WD23 .... 163 K5
Herkomer Rd BUSH WD23 .. 163 J4
Hermitage Cots STAN HA7 * .. 172 G2
Hermitage Ct POTB/CUF EN6 .. 153 M5
Hermitage Rd
 HTCH/STOT SG5 .... 35 L9
The Hermitage
 ARL/CHE SG15 .... 24 C1
Hermitage Wy STAN HA7 .... 172 G5
Herne Cl BUSH WD23 * 163 L7
Herne Rd BUSH WD23 .... 163 K5
 STVG SG1 .... 50 E6
Henneshaw HAT AL10 .... 122 C8
Herns La WGCE AL7 .... 105 L6
Herns Wy WGCE AL7 .... 105 K6
Heron Cl HHS/BOV HP3 ...... 134 A4
 RKW/CH/CXG WD3 .... 161 H6
Heron Ct EBAR CM23 .... 74 B3
Heron Dr LTNE LU2 .... 63 K5
 STVG SG1 .... 109 H9
Heronfield POTB/CUF EN6 .. 139 M9
Herongate Rd
 CHES/WCR EN8 .... 142 C6
Heron Md PEND EN3 .... 156 F8
Heron PI DEN/HRF UB9 ...... 169 L3
Herons Elm BERK HP4 .... 115 K4
Heronsgate EDGW HA8 ...... 173 N2
Heronsgate Rd
 RKW/CH/CXG WD3 .... 159 P5
Heronslea GSTN WD25 .... 149 K6
Heronslea Dr STAN HA7 .... 173 L2
Herons Ri EBAR EN4 .... 167 J3
Herons Wy STAL AL1 .... 136 F5
Herons Wd HLW CM20 ...... 2 B4
Heronswood PI WCCE AL7 * .. 105 K7
Heronswood Rd WCCE AL7 .. 105 J6
Heron Wk NTHWD HA6 ...... 170 G1
Heron Wy HAT AL10 .... 122 D8
 HTCH/STOT SG5 .... 25 J3
Hertford Cl EBAR EN4 .... 167 H2
Hertford Ct STAN HA7 * 173 K4
Hertford End Ct
 NTHWD HA6 * 170 G2
Hertford La ROY SG8 .... 22 C5
Hertford Rd BRKMPK AL9 .. 122 C4
 EBAR EN4 .... 166 C2
 HOD EN11 .... 126 D3
 PEND EN3 .... 156 B9
 STVGE SG2 .... 51 M7
 WARE SG12 .... 108 E8
 WLYN AL6 .... 84 F9
 WLYN AL6 .... 106 A2
Hertfordshire Wy BUNT SG9 .. 41 M8
 HERT/WAT SG14 .... 87 H7
 LWTH SG6 .... 36 D9
 STVG SG1 .... 91 J3
Hertingfordbury Rd
 HERT/WAT SG14 .... 106 F8
Hertswood Ct BAR EN5 * 166 A5
Hervines Ct AMS HP6 .... 143 H7
Hervines Rd AMS HP6 .... 144 C7
Heswall Ct LTN LU1 .... 7 G7
Heswell Gn OXHEY WD19 * .. 162 C9
Hetchleys HHW HP1 .... 117 K5
Hever Ct LBUZ LU7 .... 4 J2
Hewett Cl STAN HA7 .... 173 H1
Hewins Ct WAB EN9 .... 157 K2
Hewitt Cl LTNW/LEA LU4 .... 103 J5
Hewlett Rd LTNN/LIM LU3 .. 61 P2
Hexham Rd BAR EN5 .... 166 F3
Hexton Rd
 AMP/FLIT/BLC MK45 .... 32 C4
 HTCH/STOT SG5 .... 34 D8
 LTNE LU2 .... 47 J3
Heybridge Ct
 HERT/WAT SG14 * 106 C3
Heybridge Ct STALW/RED AL3 .. 101 H7
Heydon La ROY SG8 .... 22 E5
Heydon Rd ROY SG8 .... 22 B8
Heydons Cl STALW/RED AL3 .. 120 D6
Heyford End LCOL/BKTW AL2 .. 136 D2
Heyford Rd RAD WD7 .... 150 E7
Heyford Wy HAT AL10 ...... 122 F4
Heysham Dr OXHEY WD19 .. 171 L2
Heywood Dr LTNE LU2 ...... 62 G3
Hibbert Av WATN WD24 .... 149 L8
Hibbert Rd
 KTN/HRWW/WS HA3 .... 172 F6
Hibbert St LTN LU1 .... 6 E7
Hibberts Wy CFSP/GDCR SL9 .. 168 F7
Hickling Cl LTNE LU2 .... 63 L5
Hickling Wy HARP AL5 .... 102 B1
Hickman Cl BROX EN10 .... 126 C8
Hicks Rd STALE/WH AL4 .... 79 P8
High Acres ABLGY WD5 ...... 142 D8
Higham Dr LTNE LU2 .... 63 L5
Higham Rd
 AMP/FLIT/BLC MK45 .... 32 D4
 CSHM HP5 .... 131 H9
High Ash Rd STALE/WH AL4 .. 103 H5
High Av LWTH SG6 .... 36 A3
Highbanks Rd PIN HA5 ...... 172 B3
Highbarns HHS/BOV HP3 .... 134 B4
High Beech Rd
 LTNN/LIM LU3 .... 45 N8
High Bois La AMS HP6 ...... 145 J5
Highbridge St WAB EN9 .... 156 F3
Highbury Rd HOD EN11 ...... 126 F3
Highbury Rd
 HTCHE/RSTV SG4 .... 35 M9
 LTNN/LIM LU3 .... 6 B1
Highbush Rd HTCH/STOT SG5 .. 25 J4
High Canons BORE WD6 .... 151 P7
Highclere Dr HHS/BOV HP3 .. 134 D5
High Cl RKW/CH/CXG WD3 .. 160 C4
High Coppice AMSS HP7 .... 145 H9
Highcroft Rd HHS/BOV HP3 .. 133 K4

Highcroft Trailer Gdns
  HHS/BOV HP3 * 132 E5
High Cross GSTN WD25 .... 145 J8
High Dane HTCHE/RSTV SC4 ...... 35 M6
High Dells HAT AL10 .... 122 C7
High Elms HARP AL5 .... 101 P6
High Elms La NTHWD HA6 .... 170 C5
High Elms La GSTN WD25 .... 149 J1
  STVGE SG2 .... 68 F6
Highfield CSTG HP8 .... 159 K8
  HLWS CM18 .... 129 K4
  KGLGY WD4 .... 135 P7
  LWTH SG6 .... 42 D4
  OXHEY WD19 .... 163 H9
Highfield Av BSF CM23 .... 74 D4
  HARP AL5 .... 102 B4
  PIN HA5 .... 171 P9
Highfield Cl AMSS HP6 .... 145 J7
  NTHWD HA6 .... 170 C5
Highfield Crs NTHWD HA6 .... 170 C5
Highfield Dr BROX EN10 .... 126 D9
Highfield La HHNE HP2 .... 118 A6
  STALE/WH AL4 .... 137 H1
Highfield Ov HARP AL5 .... 101 P1
Highfield Park Dr
  STALE/WH AL4 .... 137 H2
Highfield Rd BERK HP4 .... 116 A8
  BUSH WD23 .... 162 C4
  CHESW EN7 .... 141 M5
  CSHM HP5 .... 130 C8
  HERT/BAY SG13 .... 107 L8
  LTNW/LEA LU4 .... 62 C5
  NTHWD HA6 .... 170 C5
  STALE/WH AL4 .... 120 G2
  TRING HP23 .... 95 M9
Highfields KGLGY WD4 * 135 P7
  POTB/CUF EN6 .... 140 F7
  RAD WD7 .... 150 E5
Highfields Cl
  DUN/HR/TOD LU5 .... 61 K4
Highfield Wy POTB/CUF EN6 ..... 153 L1
High Firs RAD WD7 .... 150 F5
High Firs Crs HARP AL5 .... 102 C4
Highgate Gv SBW CM21 .... 111 N2
High Gv STALW/RED AL3 .... 120 C6
  WGCW AL8 .... 104 E5
Highland Dr BUSH WD23 .... 163 K6
  HHS/BOV HP3 .... 118 C8
Highland Rd AMSS HP7 .... 145 J9
  BSF CM23 .... 74 A7
  NTHWD HA6 .... 171 J6
  WAB EN9 .... 143 K1
Highlands BRKMPK AL9 .... 122 F3
  OXHEY WD19 .... 46 B2
  ROY SG8 .... 20 D4
Highlands Cl CFSP/GDCR SL9 .... 168 D4
Highlands End
  CFSP/GDCR SL9 .... 168 D4
Highlands La CFSP/GDCR SL9 .... 168 C4
Highlands Rd BAR EN5 .... 166 E4
The Highlands BAR EN5 .... 166 E4
  EDGW HA8 .... 175 P6
  POTB/CUF EN6 .... 153 M1
  RKW/CH/CXG WD3 .... 160 F6
High La STSD CM24 .... 58 F3
High Md HRW HA1 .... 172 E9
  LTNW/LEA LU4 .... 62 B3
Highmead STSD CM24 .... 58 F3
High Meadow Cl PIN HA5 .... 171 K9
High Meads STALE/WH AL4 .... 103 H4
Highmoor AMSS HP7 .... 145 J9
  ROY SG8 .... 81 P9
High Moors
  RAYLNE/WEN HP22 .... 112 C3
High Oak Rd WARE SG12 .... 108 C2
High Oaks ENC/FH EN2 .... 154 C8
  STALW/RED AL3 .... 120 B5
High Oaks Rd WGCW AL8 .... 104 E5
Highover Cl LTNE LU2 .... 63 J5
Highover Pk AMSS HP7 .... 158 C1
Highover Rd LWTH SG6 .... 36 A6
Highover Wy
  HTCHE/RSTV SC4 .... 35 N7
High Pastures RBSF CM22 .... 92 E9
High Plash STVG SG1 * 10 E5
High Rdg HARP AL5 .... 101 M1
  LTNE LU2 .... 63 K5
  POTB/CUF EN6 .... 140 F6
High Ridge Cl HHS/BOV HP3 ..... 133 L8
Highridge Pl ENC/FH EN2 * 154 D8
High Ridge Rd HHS/BOV HP3 ..... 133 N4
High Rd BRKMPK AL9 .... 122 C1
  BROX EN10 .... 126 E9
  BUSH WD23 .... 163 M7
  GSTN WD25 .... 148 G4
  HERT/WAT SG14 .... 86 C7
  HTCH/STOT SG5 .... 33 M1
  KTN/HRWW/WS HA3 .... 172 E5
  TRDG/WHET N20 .... 166 F6
High Road Broxbourne
  BROX EN10 .... 126 E9
High Road Eastcote PIN HA5 .... 171 K9
High Road Turnford
  CHES/WCR EN8 .... 142 D5
High Road Wormley
  BROX EN10 .... 142 E3
High St ABLGY WD5 .... 134 C9
  AMSS HP7 .... 144 F9
  ARL/CHE SG15 .... 24 F5
  BAR EN5 .... 166 C2
  BERK HP4 .... 115 K4
  BCSW SG18 .... 16 F4
  BLDK SG7 .... 14 F4
  BLDK SG7 .... 17 N6
  BLDK SG7 .... 24 A3
  BSF CM23 .... 74 A3
  BUNT SG9 .... 40 D9
  CFSP/GDCR SL9 .... 168 C5
  CHES/WCR EN8 .... 142 C7
  CHES/WCR EN8 .... 156 C5
  CSHM HP5 .... 144 C1
  DEN/HRF UB9 .... 169 N6
  DUN/HR/TOD LU5 .... 44 C1
  DUN/HR/TOD LU5 .... 60 E2

HARP AL5 .... 101 P2
HERT/WAT SG14 .... 86 E1
HHNE HP2 .... 117 N7
HHS/BOV HP3 .... 132 D6
HLWE CM17 .... 111 M8
HLWW/ROY CM19 .... 127 N2
HOD EN11 .... 126 F7
HTCH/STOT SG5 .... 25 K3
HTCH/STOT SG5 .... 34 C4
HTCH/STOT SG5 .... 35 K9
HTCHE/RSTV SC4 .... 48 B4
HTCHE/RSTV SC4 .... 50 F5
HTCHE/RSTV SC4 .... 83 H4
HTCHE/RSTV SC4 .... 84 C4
KGLGY WD4 .... 134 B8
KTN/HRWW/WS HA3 .... 172 E7
LBUZ LU7 .... 77 P6
LCOL/BKTW AL2 .... 137 H4
LTNW/LEA LU4 .... 61 M2
MHAD SG10 .... 90 C2
NTHWD HA6 .... 171 H5
PIN HA5 .... 171 N7
POTB/CUF EN6 .... 153 N2
RAYLNE/WEN HP22 .... 112 C7
RBSF CM22 .... 59 L2
RBSF CM22 .... 93 N3
RKW/CH/CXG WD3 .... 160 B6
ROY SG8 .... 15 L7
ROY SG8 .... 21 L8
ROY SG8 .... 22 C7
ROY SG8 .... 29 L4
SAFWS CB11 .... 43 M4
SDY/GAM/POT SG19 .... 14 E3
STALE/WH AL4 .... 103 J3
STALE/WH AL4 .... 120 G2
STALE/WH AL4 .... 137 N1
STALW/RED AL3 .... 8 E4
STALW/RED AL3 .... 79 N7
STDN SG11 .... 71 J3
STHGT/OAK N14 .... 167 P7
STVG SG1 .... 50 F8
STVG SG2 .... 52 C7
TRING HP23 .... 95 P9
WARE SG12 .... 90 B9
WARE SG12 .... 109 H8
WARE SG12 .... 110 A3
WAT WD17 .... 13 F3
WGCE AL7 .... 148 B3
High Street Gn HHNE HP2 .... 118 B5
High St South
  DUN/WHIP LU6 .... 60 F6
High Town Rd LTNE LU2 .... 7 F5
High Trees EBAR EN4 .... 167 J4
High Vw BSF CM23 .... 58 D8
  CSTG HP8 .... 159 K8
  HAT AL10 .... 122 C8
  HTCH/STOT SG5 .... 49 J1
  PIN HA5 .... 171 L8
  RKW/CH/CXG WD3 .... 160 E3
  STALW/RED AL3 .... 79 P9
  WATW WD18 .... 162 B5
Highview Gdns
  POTB/CUF EN6 .... 153 M3
  STALE/WH AL4 .... 121 H5
Highview Rd
  HHS/BOV HP3 .... 134 B4
Highwood Hl MLHL NW7 .... 165 M8
High Wood Rd HOD EN11 .... 126 E2
High Wd La SBW CM21 .... 111 H6
High Wych Rd SBW CM21 .... 111 H6
Hilberry Cl BUSH WD23 * 163 K6
Hilbury HAT AL10 .... 145 H5
Hilbury Cl AMS HP6 .... 145 H5
Hiliary Gdns STAN HA7 .... 173 J6
Hiljon Crs CFSP/GDCR SL9 ...... 168 C5
Hillary Crs LTN LU1 .... 6 A6
Hillary Rd ARL/CHE SG15 .... 24 F1
  BAR EN5 .... 166 C3
Hillary Rd HHNE HP2 .... 118 B7
Hill Av AMS HP6 .... 145 H8
Hillborough Crs
  DUN/HR/TOD LU5 .... 44 F8
Hillborough Rd LTN LU1 .... 6 C7
Hillbrow LWTH SG6 .... 36 A3
Hillbury Av
  KTN/HRWW/WS HA3 .... 173 H9
Hill Cl BAR EN5 .... 166 A4
  HARP AL5 .... 82 B9
  LBUZ LU7 .... 44 A6
  LTNN/LIM LU3 .... 45 N8
  STAN HA7 .... 173 H1
Hill Common HHS/BOV HP3 .... 134 B3
Hill Crs HRW HA1 .... 172 G9
  TRDG/WHET N20 .... 166 F1
Hill Crest HTCHE/RSTV SC4 ..... 65 K8
  POTB/CUF EN6 .... 153 N1
Hillcrest BLDK SG7 .... 37 J1
  HAT AL10 .... 122 D7
  STALW/RED AL3 * 9 F1
  STVG SG1 .... 11 F4
Hillcrest Av EDGW HA8 .... 173 P1
  LTNE LU2 .... 63 P2
  PIN HA5 .... 171 M8
Hillcrest Pk LWTH SG6 * 35 P2
Hillcrest Rd RAD WD7 .... 151 M3
Hillcroft DUN/WHIP LU6 .... 60 D5
Hill Croft Cl LTNW/LEA LU4 .... 61 N3
Hillcroft Crs OXHEY WD19 ...... 162 D7
Hillcroft Rd CSHM HP5 .... 131 J8
Hill Dyke Rd STALE/WH AL4 ..... 103 H5
Hill End Farm La
  HTCHE/RSTV SC4 .... 65 N2
Hill End La STAL AL1 .... 137 H2
Hill End Rd DEN/HRF UB9 .... 169 M3
Hillersdon Av EDGW HA8 .... 173 M2
Hill Farm Av CSHM HP5 .... 143 H3
Hill Farm La LTN LU1 .... 62 A9
  STALW/RED AL3 .... 83 M7

Hill Farm Rd CFSP/GDCR SL9 .... 168 C4
  CSHM HP5 .... 145 J4
Hillfield HAT AL10 .... 122 C3
Hillfield Av HTCHE/RSTV SC4 ... 35 M6
Hillfield Cl RYLN/HDSTN HA2 ... 172 C8
Hillfield Rd CFSP/GDCR SL9 .... 5 C2
Hillfield La South
  BUSH WD23 .... 163 N5
Hillfield Rd CFSP/GDCR SL9 .... 5 N5
  HHNE HP2 .... 5 F2
Hillfield Sq CFSP/GDCR SL9 .... 5 N5
Hillfield HTCHE/RSTV SC4 ...... 35 M5
Hill House Av STAN HA7 .... 172 F4
Hill House Cl CFSP/GDCR SL9 ... 168 A4
Hilliard Rd NTHWD HA6 .... 171 H5
Hillier Cl BAR EN5 .... 166 D5
Hillingdon Rd GSTN WD25 .... 149 H4
Hillingdon Trail
  DEN/HRF UB9 .... 169 L6
Hill Ley HAT AL10 .... 122 C6
Hill Leys POTB/CUF EN6 .... 140 F7
Hill Md BERK HP4 .... 115 M8
Hillmead STVG SG1 .... 11 J3
Hillpoint RKW/CH/CXG WD3 ...... 160 C4
Hill Ri CFSP/GDCR SL9 .... 168 B6
  LTNN/LIM LU3 .... 46 E9
  LTNE LU2 .... 6 C3
  POTB/CUF EN6 .... 140 E6
  POTB/CUF EN6 .... 153 M4
  RKW/CH/CXG WD3 .... 160 B6
Hillrise Av WATN WD24 .... 149 L8
Hill Rise Crs CFSP/GDCR SL9 ... 168 B6
Hill Rd HRW HA1 .... 172 C9
  HTCHE/RSTV SC4 .... 84 B4
  HTCHE/RSTV SC4 .... 170 F5
Hillsborough Gn
  OXHEY WD19 * 162 C9
Hillshott LWTH SG6 .... 36 D2
Hill Side BAR EN5 .... 166 C4
  LBUZ LU7 .... 77 N7
Hillside BAR EN5 .... 165 N4
  CSHM HP5 .... 130 F7
  DEN/HRF UB9 .... 169 N9
  DUN/HR/TOD LU5 .... 44 C6
  HAT AL10 .... 122 D6
  HLWE CM17 .... 129 M5
  HOD EN11 .... 126 E4
  HTCHE/RSTV SC4 .... 98 C9
  ROY SG8 .... 20 C5
  STVG SG1 .... 11 H4
  WARE SG12 .... 108 C4
  WGCE AL7 .... 105 L9
Hillside Av BORE WD6 .... 164 A3
  BSF CM23 .... 74 B3
  CFSP/GDCR SL9 .... 168 C3
  CSTG HP8 .... 159 H3
Hillside Crs CHES/WCR EN8 ..... 155 L8
  ENC/FH EN2 .... 155 M8
  NTHWD HA6 .... 171 J5
  OXHEY WD19 .... 162 F5
  WARE SG12 .... 108 C4
Hillside Dr EDGW HA8 .... 173 P1
Hillside Gdns AMSS HP7 .... 158 C1
  BAR EN5 .... 166 A4
  BRKMPK AL9 .... 116 A8
  EDGW HA8 .... 173 M1
  NTHWD HA6 .... 171 K7
Hillside Gv STHGT/OAK N14 ..... 167 P6
Hillside La WARE SG12 .... 108 F7
Hillside Ri NTHWD HA6 .... 171 J4
Hillside Rd BUSH WD23 .... 60 G7
  DUN/HR/TOD LU5 .... 60 D7
  HARP AL5 .... 101 N1
  LTNN/LIM LU3 .... 6 C1
  NTHWD HA6 .... 171 J4
  OXHEY WD19 .... 162 F5
  WARE SG12 .... 108 C4
Hillside Ter HERT/BAY SG13 .... 107 K8
Hillside Wy WLYN AL6 .... 85 K5
Hills La NTHWD HA6 .... 170 C5
Hill St STALW/RED AL3 .... 4 C3
Hills Vw LTNN/LIM LU3 .... 45 L3
The Hill HLWE CM17 .... 111 M8
  STALE/WH AL4 .... 103 J5
Hill Top BLDK SG7 .... 37 H1
  STALW/RED AL3 .... 98 B8
  STVG SG1 .... 11 N1
Hilltop Cl CHESW EN7 .... 141 N5
Hilltop Rd BERK HP4 .... 115 P8
  KGLGY WD4 .... 134 E6
Hilltop Wy STAN HA7 .... 164 A9
Hill Vw CSBW CM21 .... 111 N3
Hill Vw BERK HP4 .... 115 M5
  BUNT SG9 .... 29 K9
  HTCHE/RSTV SC4 .... 65 K8
Hillview La
  RKW/CH/CXG WD3 .... 146 D8
Hillview Cl PIN HA5 .... 171 P5
Hillview Crs LTNN/LIM LU3 ..... 46 C8
Hillview Gdns CHES/WCR EN8 .... 142 C6
  RYLN/HDSTN HA2 .... 172 A7
Hillway LTNN/LIM LU3 .... 45 M7
Hilly Fld HLWS CM18 .... 129 J7
Hillyfields DUN/WHIP LU6 ...... 60 F8
Hill Yd WARE SG12 * 108 C3
Hinchley Cl DUN/WHIP LU6 ...... 60 E8
Hinkley Cl DEN/HRF UB9 .... 169 N8
Hinton Wk DUN/HR/TOD LU5 ...... 45 H9
Hinxworth Rd BLDK SG7 .... 16 E8
Hipkins BSF CM23 .... 91 P1
Hipkins Pl BROX EN10 .... 126 D8
Hispano Ms PEND EN3 .... 156 G9
Hitchen Hl HTCHE/RSTV SC4 ..... 98 C3
Hitchens Yd WARE SG12 * 108 C3
Hitchin Hl HTCHE/RSTV SC4 ..... 98 C3
Hitchin Rd ARL/CHE SG15 .... 24 E9

Hitchin Rd HTCH/STOT SG5 ...... 33 L7
  HTCHE/RSTV SC4 .... 83 J3
  LTNE LU2 .... 7 G2
  LWTH SG6 .... 36 B5
  STVG SG1 .... 51 H1
Hitchin St BLDK SG7 .... 26 A9
Hitchwood La
  HTCHE/RSTV SC4 .... 65 L1
Hitherbaulk WCCE AL7 .... 104 C8
Hither Fld WARE SG12 .... 108 G4
Hitherfield La HARP AL5 .... 101 P2
Hither Meadow
  CFSP/GDCR SL9 * 168 C5
Hitherway WGCW AL8 .... 104 C2
Hitherwell Dr
  KTN/HRWW/WS HA3 .... 172 D5
Hive Cl BUSH WD23 .... 163 M8
Hive Rd BUSH WD23 .... 163 M8
Hiving's Hl CSHM HP5 .... 130 F7
Hivings Pk CSHM HP5 .... 130 F6
Hobart Cl TRDG/WHET N20 .... 165 P1
Hobart Ct HHNE HP2 .... 120 C4
Hobbs Cl CHES/WCR EN8 .... 142 C8
  STALE/WH AL4 .... 121 K9
Hobbs Hill Rd HHS/BOV HP3 ..... 133 P5
Hobby Horse Cl CHESW EN7 ...... 141 L5
Hobletts Rd HHNE HP2 .... 118 A7
Hobsons Cl HOD EN11 .... 126 E4
Hobsons Wk TRING HP23 .... 95 N7
Hobtoe Rd HLWW/ROY CM19 .... 128 C4
Hockeridge Vw BERK HP4 .... 115 L8
Hockerill St BSF CM23 .... 74 A2
Hocklands WGCE AL7 .... 105 M5
Hockwell Ring LTNW/LEA LU4 .... 61 L1
Hoddesdon Rd WARE SG12 .... 109 H8
Hodds Wood Rd CSHM HP5 .... 145 H5
Hodgemoor Vw CSTG HP8 .... 158 F9
Hodges Wy WATW WD18 .... 162 C5
Hodgkins Ms STAN HA7 .... 172 F2
Hodson Pl PEND EN3 .... 156 F8
Hodwell BLDK SG7 .... 37 H1
Hoecroft WAB EN9 .... 143 L1
Hoe La EN EN1 .... 156 A8
  WAB EN9 .... 143 L1
  WARE SG12 .... 108 C4
Hoestock Rd SBW CM21 .... 111 N2
The Hoe OXHEY WD19 .... 162 F8
Hogarth Rd EDGW HA8 .... 173 N6
Hogg End La STALW/RED AL3 ..... 119 H6
Hogg La BORE WD6 .... 150 G1
Hogpits Bottom
  HHS/BOV HP3 .... 146 D2
Hogsdell La HERT/BAY SG13 ..... 108 A3
Hog's La POTB/CUF EN6 .... 152 G7
Hogtrough La
  RAYLNE/WEN HP22 .... 112 C9
Holbeck La CHESW EN7 .... 141 N5
Holbein Ga NTHWD HA6 .... 170 D5
Holbrache Cl EN EN1 .... 155 N9
Holbrook Gdns GSTN WD25 .... 155 N9
Holcombe Hl MLHL NW7 .... 165 N9
Holcroft Rd HARP AL5 .... 102 B4
Holdbrook HTCHE/RSTV SC4 ...... 35 N9
Holden Cl HERT/BAY SG13 .... 107 M5
  HTCHE/RSTV SC4 .... 35 P9
Holders La STVG SG1 .... 67 P1
The Holdings BRKMPK AL9 .... 122 C4
Holecroft WAB EN9 .... 143 K4
Holford Wy LTNW/LEA LU4 .... 46 C6
Holgate Dr LTNW/LEA LU4 .... 61 K2
Holkham Cl LTNW/LEA LU4 .... 61 K2
Holland Cl BAR EN5 .... 167 H6
  RAYLNE/WEN HP22 .... 112 A1
  STAN HA7 .... 173 J2
Holland Gdns GSTN WD25 .... 149 K5
Holland Rd LTNW/LEA LU4 .... 62 C4
Holland's Cft WARE SG12 .... 110 A3
Holland Wy STAN HA7 .... 172 G3
Hollick's La DUN/WHIP LU6 ..... 78 C3
Holliday St BERK HP4 .... 116 A8
Holliers Wy HAT AL10 .... 122 D6
Hollies Wk BUNT SG9 .... 29 N9
The Hollies BAR EN5 .... 165 N4
  HHS/BOV HP3 .... 132 D9
  KTN/HRWW/WS HA3 .... 172 G8
  STAL AL1 * 11 J5
Hollies Wy POTB/CUF EN6 .... 153 M1
Holliwick Rd
  DUN/HR/TOD LU5 .... 61 H4
Holloway La
  RKW/CH/CXG WD3 .... 146 D8
Holloways La BRKMPK AL9 .... 138 G2
The Holloway
  RAYLNE/WEN HP22 .... 95 K3
Hollow La HTCHE/RSTV SC4 ...... 35 L9
Hollow Wy STVG SG1 .... 130 D9
Hollow Way La AMS HP6 .... 145 J9
Holly Av STAN HA7 .... 173 L6
Hollybush Av STALE/WH AL4 ..... 135 P3
Hollybush Cl BERK HP4 .... 115 K8
  KTN/HRWW/WS HA3 .... 172 G5
  OXHEY WD19 .... 162 E6
  WLYN AL6 .... 85 H5
Hollybush Hl LTNE LU2 .... 63 K5
Hollybush La AMS HP6 .... 145 J7
  HARP AL5 .... 102 A1
  HHW HP1 .... 117 J7
  HTCHE/RSTV SC4 .... 64 G6
  KNEB SG3 .... 83 N3
  STALW/RED AL3 .... 100 B1
  WGCE AL7 .... 105 J8
Hollybush Rd CSHM HP5 .... 130 F6
  LTNE LU2 .... 63 K5
Hollybush Rw TRING HP23 * 114 C3
Hollybush Wy CHESW EN7 .... 141 N7
Holly Cl CHESW EN7 .... 141 N7
Holly Copse STVG SG1 .... 11 L6
Holly Ct HERT/WAT SG14 .... 86 B4
Hollycross Rd WARE SG12 .... 109 H6
Holly Dell HERT/BAY SG13 ...... 107 K8

Holly Dr BERK HP4 .... 116 A8
  POTB/CUF EN6 .... 153 L3
Holly Farm Cl LTN LU1 .... 79 P1
Holly Fld HLWW/ROY CM19 .... 128 F6
Hollyfield HAT AL10 .... 122 D9
  TRING HP23 .... 96 B7
Hollyfield Ct TRING HP23 ...... 96 B7
Hollygrove BUSH WD23 .... 163 M6
Holly Gv PIN HA5 .... 171 N5
Holly Grove Rd
  HERT/WAT SG14 .... 106 D1
Holly Hall Ct WLYN AL6 .... 84 F8
Holly Hedges La
  HHS/BOV HP3 .... 132 F9
Holly La HARP AL5 .... 102 B4
Holly Leys STVGE SG2 .... 67 L6
  PEND EN3 .... 156 C6
Holly Shaws STVGE SG2 .... 67 L4
Holly St LTN LU1 .... 7 F2
Hollytree Cl CFSP/GDCR SL9 .... 168 C2
  CSHM HP5 .... 145 N1
Holly Tree Ct HHNE HP2 .... 118 C8
Holly Wk HARP AL5 .... 102 C3
  WGCW AL8 .... 104 D5
Holmbrook Av LTNN/LIM LU3 ..... 62 F7
Holmbury Ct BUSH WD23 .... 163 N8
Holmdale LWTH SG6 .... 36 D3
Holmdale Rd BORE WD6 .... 164 F1
Holmdene Av
  RYLN/HDSTN HA2 .... 172 B7
Holmebury Cl BUSH WD23 * 163 N8
Holme Cl CHES/WCR EN8 .... 156 D1
  HAT AL10 .... 122 C5
Holme Lea GSTN WD25 .... 149 N5
Holme Pk BORE WD6 .... 164 F1
Holme Pl HHNE HP2 .... 118 D7
Holme Rd HAT AL10 .... 122 C3
Holmesdale CHES/WCR EN8 .... 156 B5
Holmes Meadow
  HLWW/ROY CM19 .... 128 C9
Holme Wy STAN HA7 .... 172 F3
Holmfield Cl
  DUN/HR/TOD LU5 .... 44 B2
  LTN LU1 .... 62 E9
Holm Oak Pk WATW WD18 * 12 C7
Holmscroft Rd LTNN/LIM LU3 .... 45 M4
Holmshill La BORE WD6 .... 152 C7
Holmside Ri OXHEY WD19 .... 162 D9
Holmwood Cl
  RYLN/HDSTN HA2 .... 172 C7
Holmwood Rd PEND EN5 * 156 C6
  CR BLDK SG7 .... 37 H1
Holsworth Cl
  RYLN/HDSTN HA2 .... 172 C9
Holt Cl BORE WD6 .... 164 F3
Holts Meadow
  STALW/RED AL3 .... 101 J6
Holtsmere Cl GSTN WD25 .... 149 K5
  LTNE LU2 .... 63 L5
Holtwhites End La
  STALW/RED AL3 .... 100 C3
The Holt HHNE HP2 .... 5 H3
  WGCE AL7 .... 105 N7
Holtwhite's Hl ENC/FH EN2 ..... 155 J9
Holwell Hyde WGCE AL7 .... 105 M8
Holwell Hyde La WGCE AL7 ...... 105 N9
Holwell Rd WGCE AL7 .... 171 N6
Holwell Rd HTCH/STOT SG5 ...... 34 C4
  WGCE AL7 .... 105 H7
Holy Cross Hl BROX EN10 .... 141 P2
Holyfield Rd WAB EN9 .... 143 L4
Holyrood Crs STAL AL1 .... 136 C3
Holyrood Gdns EDGW HA8 .... 173 P6
Holyrood Rd BAR EN5 .... 166 C5
Holywell Cl DUN/WHIP LU6 ...... 78 E7
  STAL AL1 .... 11 F6
Holywell Rd DUN/WHIP LU6 ...... 78 E6
  WATW WD18 .... 12 D7
Home Cl BROX EN10 .... 142 E3
  HLW CM20 .... 3 J5
  HTCH/STOT SG5 .... 35 J8
  LTNW/LEA LU4 .... 61 M2
  RAYLNE/WEN HP22 .... 112 A1
  STAL AL1 * 88 D3
Home Ct LTNW/LEA LU4 * 61 M2
Homedale Dr LTNW/LEA LU4 ...... 61 N4
Home Farm TRING HP23 * 113 P8
Home Farm Ct CSTG HP8 .... 158 C9
  STVG SG1 .... 71 J3
Home Farm Rd BERK HP4 .... 115 J4
  RKW/CH/CXG WD3 .... 170 C1
Homefield BERK HP4 .... 116 C4
  BLDK SG7 .... 16 C4
  HHS/BOV HP3 .... 132 E7
  WAB EN9 .... 157 M2
Homefield Cl
  HTCHE/RSTV SC4 .... 66 C4
Homefield Rd BUSH WD23 .... 163 J4
  HHNE HP2 .... 116 B8
  RAD WD7 .... 150 E7
  RKW/CH/CXG WD3 .... 160 B3
  WGCE AL7 .... 108 C2
Homeleigh Ct
  CHES/WCR EN8 .... 142 A9
Home Ley WGCE AL7 .... 105 H6
Home Mead STAN HA7 .... 173 J5
Home Meadow WGCE AL7 .... 105 H6
Home Park Mill Link Rd
  KGLGY WD4 .... 148 C1
Home Pastures RBSF CM22 .... 92 C1
Homefield WGCW AL8 .... 104 C6
Homerswood La WLYN AL6 .... 104 D2
Home Rd LTNN/LIM LU3 .... 45 M2
Homestead Cl
  LCOL/BKTW AL2 .... 136 B6
Homestead Ct WGCE AL7 .... 105 J3
Homestead Moat STVG SG1 .... 11 J5
Homestead Paddock
  STHGT/OAK N14 .... 167 M4
Homestead Rd HAT AL10 .... 122 D3
  RKW/CH/CXG WD3 .... 161 N6
  LTNN/LIM LU3 .... 62 A9
Home Wy
  RKW/CH/CXG WD3 .... 160 D2
Homewood Av
  POTB/CUF EN6 .... 140 F6

Homewood La
  POTB/CUF EN6...........140 D6
Homewood Rd STAL AL1....120 C5
Honey Banks
  RAYLNE/WEN HP22........112 D7
Honeybourne BF CM23......91 P1
Honeycroft WCCW AL8.....157 K3
Honeycroft Dr
  STALE/WH AL4...........137 H2
Honeycross Rd HLWW HP1...117 H9
Honeygate LTNE LU2.......62 F2
Honey La BUSH SC9........40 D8
  SAFWS CB11.............43 J5
  WAB EN9................157 K4
Honeymeade SBW CM21.....111 M5
Honeypot CI CDALE/KGS NW9...173 M8
Honeypot La STAN HA7....173 K5
Honeysuckle CI BSF CM23...73 M8
  HERT/BAY SC13..........107 P6
Honeysuckle Fld CSHM HP5...131 H9
Honeysuckle Gdns HAT AL10...122 E7
Honeywood CI
  POTB/CUF EN6...........155 N3
Honister CI STAN HA7....173 H5
Honister Gdns STAN HA7...173 H5
Honister PI STAN HA7....173 H5
Honor St HLWE CM17......129 N2
Honours Md HHS/BOV HP3 *...132 D6
Hood Av STHGT/OAK N14...161 M5
Hook Fld HLWS CM18......129 H5
Hook Ga EN1.............156 A7
Hooking Gn
  RYLN/HDSTN HA2.........172 B9
Hook La POTB/CUF EN6.....154 A2
The Hook BAR EN5........167 H5
Hoopers Ms BUSH WD23....163 R5
Hoops La ROY SG8........28 F3
Hoo St LTN LU1 *........62 F9
The Hoo HLWE CM17.......111 M7
Hope Gn GSTN WD25.......149 H5
Hopbine Rd BUSH SC9 *...25 P9
Hop Garden Wy GSTN WD25...149 K1
Hopground CI STAL AL1....130 C5
Hopkins Crs STALE/WH AL4...120 C2
Hopkins Yd STAL AL1.....9 G5
Hopton Bd STVG SC1......56 D8
Hopton Rd WAT WD17......148 E6
Hopwood CI WAT WD17.....148 E6
Horace Gay Gdns LWTH SG6...36 B3
Hordle Gdns STAL AL1....9 K6
Hornbeam CI BORE WD6....151 H9
  MLHL NW7...............165 M9
Hornbeam La BRKMPK HP3...129 P9
Hornbeams LCOL/BKTW AL2...135 L9
  WCCE AL7 *.............105 L7
Hornbeams Av EN EN1.....156 B5
Hornbeam Spring KNEB SG3...85 J1
The Hornbeams HLW CM20...2 B1
  STVGE SC2..............67 L2
Hornbeam Wy CHESW EN7...141 M4
Hornbeam Wd WAT WD18....12 E5
Horn HI HTCHE/RSTV SG4...65 K8
Hornhill Rd
  RKW/CH/CXG WD3........168 G2
Hornsby CI LTNE LU2.....63 K3
Horns CI HERT/BAY SG13...107 K8
Horns End PI PIN HA5....171 L8
Hornsfield WCCE AL7.....105 M5
Horrocks CI WARE SG12...108 C1
Horsa Gdns HAT AL10.....122 A5
Horseblock La CSHM HP5...133 K1
Horsecroft Rd HHW HP1...133 K1
  HLWW/ROY CM19.........128 B4
Horse Cross STDN SG11...71 N2
Horse HI CSHM HP5.......146 A2
Horselers HHS/BOV HP3...134 B2
Horsemans Dr
  LCOL/BKTW AL2..........135 P5
Horseshoe La BCGSW SG18...14 C6
Horseshoe La
  STVG SC1...............77 N6
  ROY SG8................23 L6
  SAFWS CB11.............23 J6
  WAB EN9................157 M4
Horseshoe HI BUNT SG9...41 M8
  WAB EN9................157 P3
Horseshoe La
  GSTN WD25..............41 L9
  TRDG/WHET N20.........166 B7
The Horseshoe HHS/BOV HP3...134 C1
Horsham CI LTNE LU2.....63 L3
Horsler CI
  AMP/FLIT/BLC MK45......32 D6
Horsleys RKW/CH/CXG WD3...169 K2
Horton Gdns HHNE HP2....118 B2
Horton Rd LBUZ LU7......77 P3
Hospital Circular Rd
  RAYLNE/WEN HP2 *......112 C5
Hospital HI CSHM HP5....145 H2
Hospital Rd ARL/CHE SG15...24 D6
Houghton Pde
  DUN/HR/TOD LU5........60 D4
Houghton Park Rd
  DUN/HR/TOD LU5........45 H9
Houghton Rd
  DUN/HR/TOD LU5........60 D3
Housden CI STALE/WH AL4...103 K5
Housefield Wy
  STALE/WH AL4...........137 H2
House La ARL/CHE SG15...24 E2
  STALE/WH AL4...........121 H2
Housewood End HHW HP1...117 L5
Housman Av ROY SG8......20 B1
Howard Agne CI
  HHS/BOV HP3............132 D6
Howard CI BUSH WD23.....163 N6
  FBAR/BDGN N11.........167 L8
  HTCH/STOT SG5 *.......25 J4
  LTNN/LIM LU3...........46 A2
  STAL AL1...............137 H2
  WAB EN9................157 J4
  WATN WD24..............149 H7
Howard Dr BORE WD6......165 K3
Howarde Ct STVG SG1.....10 B2

Howard Ga LWTH SG6......36 E4
Howard PI DUN/HR/TOD LU5...60 G7
Howard Rd CHSM HP5......130 C7
Howards CI PIN HA5 *....171 K6
Howards Dr HHW HP1......117 J5
Howardsgate WGCW AL8....104 C5
Howards Wd LWTH SG6.....36 E5
Howard Wy BAR EN5.......166 B4
  HLWS CM18..............129 K3
Howberry CI EDGW HA8....175 K3
Howberry Gn ARL/CHE SG15...24 D6
Howberry Rd EDGW HA8....175 K3
Howe Cl RAD WD7.........151 K2
Howe Dell HAT AL10......135 L3
Howe Hi HHS/BOV HP3.....134 D1
How Fld HARP SG5........101 M1
Howfield Gn HOD EN11....126 E2
Howicks Gn WCCE AL7.....105 K9
Howland Ct PIN HA5 *....172 A5
Howland Garth STAL AL1...136 B2
Howlands WCCE AL7.......123 J1
Howse Rd WAB EN9........156 C5
Howton PI BUSH WD23.....163 M1
How Wd LCOL/BKTW AL2....137 H7
Hoylake Gdns OXHEY WD19...171 M1
Hubbards Rd
  RKW/CH/CXG WD3........160 B4
Huckleberry CI LTTN/LIM LU3...46 B7
Huckleby Wy LTNN/LIM LU3...6 C2
Hudnall La BERK HP4.....116 B6
Hudson CI STAL AL1......136 B2
  WATN WD24..............148 G6
Hudson Rd STVGE SG2.....51 L8
Huggins La BRKMPK AL9...138 E2
Hughenden Av
  KTN/HRWW/WS HA3........173 H9
Hughenden Rd
  STALE/WH AL4...........120 C5
Hugo Ct WATW WD18.......162 A3
Hull CI CHESW EN7.......141 L5
Hull Gv HLWW/ROY CM19...128 D8
Hull La STDN SG11.......55 K8
Humber Ct STVG SG1......51 J3
Humberstone CI
  LTNN/LEA LU4...........61 P4
Humberstone Rd
  LTNN/LEA LU4...........61 P4
Humphery Talbot Av
  DUN/WHIP LU6...........78 C6
Humphrys Rd
  DUN/HR/TOD LU5........60 G3
Hundred Acres
  CHES/WCR EN8 *.........156 F4
Hundred Acres La AMSS HP7...158 F2
Hunsdon Rd STVGE SG2....51 L8
Hunston Rd WARE SG12....90 A9
Hunston CI LTNN/LEA LU4...61 L9
Hunt CI STALE/WH AL4....121 J5
Hunter D BORE WD6.......165 L4
  POTB/CUF EN6...........153 L3
Huntercombe Gdns
  OXHEY WD19.............171 L2
Hunters CI CSHM HP5.....130 F9
  HHS/BOV HP3............132 D8
  HTCH/STOT SG5..........25 J3
  STVGE SC2..............51 N8
  TRING HP23.............96 A7
Hunters Gv
  KTN/HRWW/WS HA3........173 J8
Hunter's La GSTN WD25...148 C4
Hunters Oak HHNE HP2....118 C5
Hunters Pk BERK HP4.....116 B6
Hunters Reach CHESW EN7...141 N8
Hunters Ride LCOL/BKTW AL2...149 P1
Hunters Wy ENC/FH EN2...155 H9
  ROY SG8................80 E4
  WCCE AL7...............105 J9
Huntingdon Rd BROX EN10...142 D3
Huntingdon Rd STVGE SG2...50 E7
Hunting Ga HHNE HP2.....117 P4
  HTCHE/RSTV SG4........35 M5
Hunton Bridge HI
  KGLGY WD4..............148 D3
Hunts CI LTN LU1........6 B7
Huntsman CI STDN SG11...71 J3
Huntsmill Rd HHW HP1....117 H9
Hurlock CI DUN/WHIP LU6...60 A6
Hurlock Wy LTNN/LEA LU4...61 M1
Hurn Gv BSF CM23........74 D1
  STSD CM24..............58 F5
Huron Rd BROX EN10......142 D5
Hurricane Wy ABLGY WD5...149 H5
Hurst CI BLDK SG7.......26 C8
  BSF CM23...............73 P7
  WCCE AL7...............105 M7
Hurst Dr CHES/WCR EN8...156 C4
Hurstings WGCE AL7......105 L8
Hurst PI HHNE HP2.......170 D5
Hurst Ri BAR EN5........166 E2
Hurst Wy LTNN/LIM LU3...61 P1
Hutton CI HERT/WAT SG14...107 H6
  LTNN/LEA LU4...........61 N3
Hutton La
  KTN/HRWW/WS HA3........172 C4
Hutton Wk
  LTNN/LEA LU4...........61 P4
Hyatts Yd CSHM HP5 *....144 C2
Hyburn CI HHS/BOV HP3...118 C9
Hydean Wy STVGE SG2.....67 K3
Hyde Av HTCH/STOT SG5...25 J4
  POTB/CUF EN6...........153 L4
Hyde CI BAR EN5.........166 D2
  HARP AL5...............82 A9
Hyde Gn STVGE SG2.......67 L3
Hyde Gn East STVGE SG2...67 L3
Hyde Gn South STVGE SG2...67 L3
Hyde La HHS/BOV HP3......132 D6
  HHS/BOV HP3............136 D7
  LCOL/BKTW AL2..........136 D7
Hyde Md WAB EN9.........143 K2
Hyde Mdw HHS/BOV HP5....132 D7
Hyde Rd LTN LU1.........80 A1
  WAT WD17...............12 D2
The Hyde RAYLNE/WEN HP22...112 A1
Hyde St STVGE SG2.......67 M3

WARE SG12..............108 A2
Hyde Va WCCE AL7........105 J8
Hyde View Rd HARP AL5...82 A9
Hyde Wy WCCE AL7........105 H6
Hyperion Ct HHNE HP2....118 A5
Hyrons CI AMS HP6.......145 K8
Hyrons La AMS HP6.......145 K8
Hyver HI BAR EN5........165 K5

I

Ibberson Wy
  HTCHE/RSTV SG4........35 M9
Ibsley Wy EBAR EN4......167 J4
Iceni Ct LWTH SG6.......36 E1
Ickleford Rd HTCH/STOT SG5...35 L8
Ickleton Rd SAFWS CB11...23 K6
Ickley CI LTNN/LEA LU4...61 L1
Icknield CI HTCH/STOT SG5...35 L9
  RAYLNE/WEN HP22.......112 D6
  STALW/RED AL3.........135 N1
Icknield Gn LTNE/LIM LU3...36 B2
  TRING HP23.............95 P6
Icknield Rd LTNN/LIM LU3...62 A2
Icknield Wk ROY SG8.....20 D3
Icknield Wy BERK HP4....97 J4
Icknield Wy East BLDK SG7...26 G8
Icknield Way Pth BLDK SG7...17 M7
  BLDK SG7...............27 J9
  HTCH/STOT SG5..........33 N8
  LTNN/LEA LU4...........61 M3
  LTNN/LEA LU4...........61 M3
  ROY SG8................18 C4
  ROY SG8................50 E6
The Icon STVG SG1 *.....10 D5
Ilford CI LTNE LU2......63 K3
Ilkley Rd OXHEY WD19....171 M2
Imber CI STHGT/OAK N14...167 N6
Imberfield LTNN/LEA LU4...61 N1
Imperial PI BORE WD6....165 H2
Imperial Wy WATN WD24...149 K9
Indells HAT AL10........122 C7
Index Dr DUN/WHIP LU6...60 A7
Ingelheim Ct STVG SG1...10 D1
Ingersoll Rd PEND EN3...156 B8
Ingle CI PIN HA5........171 P7
Inglefield POTB/CUF EN6...139 K9
Ingles WGCW AL8.........105 H3
Ingleside Dr STVG SG1...50 E6
Inglewood Gdns
  LCOL/BKTW AL2..........136 E4
Ingram CI STAN HA7......173 J2
Ingram Gdns LTNE LU2....46 E9
Inkerman Rd STAL AL1....9 G5
Inkerman St LTN LU1.....9 D3
Inkerman Ter CSHM HP5...145 H3
Inkwell CI
  NFNCH/WDSPK N12.......166 G9
Innes CI HHS/BOV HP3....5 F7
Innova Wy PEND EN3......155 M9
Inn's CI STVG SG1.......10 C2
Inskip Crs STVG SG1.....11 F4
Inverness Av EN EN1.....155 M9
Iona Ct STVG SG1........51 J5
Ionian Wy HHW HP2.......118 A5
Iredale Vw BLDK SG7......26 C8
Ireton CI STVG SG1......10 B2
Irkdale Av EN EN1.......155 N9
Iron Dr HERT/BAY SG13...108 A5
Irvine Av
  KTN/HRWW/WS HA3........172 G7
Irvine Dr TRDG/WHET N20...167 J3
Irving CI BSF CM23.......91 N1
Irving Crs LBUZ LU7......77 P5
Isabel CI HOD EN11......126 G3
Isabel Ga CHES/WCR EN8...142 E5
Isabella CI LTNN/LEA LU4...61 L9
Isabelle CI CHESW EN7...141 K8
Isenburg Wy HHNE HP2....117 N9
Isherwood Cl ROY SG8....51 J3
Island Centre Wy PEND EN3...156 F8
Isle of Wight La
  DUN/WHIP LU6...........78 L2
Islington Wy STVG SG1...51 J5
Ivanhoe Dr
  KTN/HRWW/WS HA3........173 H6
Ivatt Ct HTCHE/RSTV SG4...35 P9
Iveagh Ct HHNE HP2......10 D5
Ivel Ct AMP/FLIT/BLC MK45...32 E5
Ivel Rd STVG SG1........51 H4
Ivel Wy BLDK SG7........37 K2
  HTCH/STOT SG5..........25 K1
Ivere Dr BAR EN5........166 E2
Ives Rd HERT/WAT SG14...107 J5
Ivinghoe CI GSTN WD25...149 L5
  STALE/WH AL4...........121 H3
Ivinghoe Rd BUSH WD23...163 M5
  RKW/CH/CXG WD3........160 D6
Ivory CI STALE/WH AL4...137 H1
Ivory Ct HHNE HP2.......118 B5
Ivybridge BROX EN10.....126 F7
Ivy CI DUN/WHIP LU6.....60 D5
Ivy House La BERK HP4...116 D7
Ivy Lea RKW/CH/CXG WD3 *...160 E7
Ivy Rd LTNE LU2.........62 F1
Ivy Ter HOD EN11........127 H5
Ivy Wk NTHWD HA6 *......170 G5

J

Jackdaw St STVGE SG2....67 N2
Jackdaws WCCE AL7.......105 M6
Jackets La NTHWD HA6....170 C4
Jacketts Rd ABLGY WD5...148 G1
Jackman's PI LWTH SG6...36 F4
Jacks Hill Pk
  HTCHE/RSTV SG4 *......50 F1

Jacks La DEN/HRF UB9....169 L5
Jackson Rd EBAR EN4.....167 J5
Jacksons Dr CHESW EN7...141 P7
Jackson's La ROY SG8....29 L4
Jackson St BLDK SG7.....26 A8
Jakes Vw LCOL/BKTW AL2...135 M9
James Bedford CI PIN HA5...171 L6
James CI BUSH WD23......162 G4
James Ct LTN LU1........6 E7
James Lee Sq PEND EN3...156 F8
Jameson Rd HARP AL5.....102 A1
James Wy OXHEY WD19.....171 M1
  STVG SG1...............50 F8
Jane CI HHW HP2.........118 A5
Jarden LWTH SG6.........36 F4
Jardine Wy DUN/HR/TOD LU5...61 H7
Jarman HHNE HP2.........5 H6
Jarman Wy HHNE HP2......5 J4
  ROY SG8................20 D3
Jarvis Cleys CHESW EN7...141 N5
Jarvis CI BAR EN5.......166 B4
Jasmin CI BSF CM23......75 M8
  NTHWD HA6..............171 H5
Jasmine Dr HERT/BAY SG13...107 P6
Jasmine Gdns HAT AL10...122 C4
Jasmine Wk CSHM HP5.....130 F9
Jasmin Wy HHW HP1.......117 H7
Jasons HI CSHM HP5......131 N8
Jasper CI PEND EN3......156 B5
Jay CI LWTH SG6.........25 J9
Jaycroft ENC/FH EN2.....141 H8
Jays CI LCOL/BKTW AL2...149 P1
Jaywood LTNE LU2........63 K1
Jeans La BSF CM23.......73 P7
Jeans Wy DUN/HR/TOD LU5...61 H6
Jeffries Rd WARE SG12...108 D3
Jellicoe Gdns STAN HA7...173 G5
Jellicoe Rd WAT WD18....162 D5
Jenkins Av LCOL/BKTW AL2...135 M9
Jenkins Dr
  RAYLNE/WEN HP22.......76 D2
Jenkins La RBSF CM22....113 M8
  TRING HP23.............96 A7
Jennings CI STVG SG1....67 H3
Jennings Rd STAL AL1....9 K1
Jennings Wy BAR EN5.....166 A2
  HHNE HP2 *.............5 K6
Jenning Wd WLYN AL6.....5 F7
Jepps CI CHESW EN7......141 M6
Jepps La ROY SG8........29 J2
Jeremiah Ct
  AMP/FLIT/BLC MK45......32 D5
Jerome Dr STALW/RED AL3...135 N1
Jerounds HLWW/ROY CM19...128 E5
Jersey Av
  KTN/HRWW/WS HA3........173 H6
Jersey CI HOD EN11......142 A1
Jersey La STAL AL1......121 H8
Jervis Av PEND EN3......156 D5
Jervis Rd BSF CM23......74 A4
Jessamine Wy STAN HA7...173 L2
Jessop Rd STVG SG1......51 H8
Jeve CI BLDK SG7........26 C8
Jill Grey PI HTCHE/RSTV SG4...35 L8
Jillifer Rd LTNN/LEA LU4...61 L1
The Jennings WCCE AL7...105 M7
Jocelyns HLWE CM17......111 M8
Jocketts Hi HHW HP1.....117 J8
Jocketts Rd HHW HP1.....117 J8
Joel St NTHWD HA6.......171 J6
  PIN HA5................171 J6
John Barker PI
  HTCH/STOT SG5..........35 H7
John Bradshaw Rd
  STHGT/OAK N14.........167 P7
John Bunyan Trail
  HTCH/STOT SG5..........33 H5
  LTNN/LIM LU3...........46 B4
Johnby CI PEND EN3......156 D7
John Dyde CI BSF CM23...74 B4
John Eliot CI WAB EN9...143 K1
John Gooch Dr ENC/FH EN2...155 J9
John Howland CI HNLW SG16...24 B1
John Lamb Ct
  KTN/HRWW/WS HA3........172 E5
John Sale CI BLDK SG7...17 M6
Johnson Ct HHNE HP2 *...5 J5
Johns Rd BSF CM23.......74 B1
John St LTN LU1.........6 C4
  STVG SG1...............20 C4
John Tate Rd HERT/BAY SG13...107 N7
Joiner's CI CFSP/GDCR SL9...168 D4
Joiners La CFSP/GDCR SL9...168 C5
Joiners Wy CFSP/GDCR SL9...168 C4
The Joint ROY SG8.......29 N3
Jones Rd CHESW EN7......141 M6
Jonquil CI WGCE AL7.....105 L8
Jordan CI GSTN WD25.....148 G5
Jordans WGCE AL7........105 M5
Jordan Rd RKW/CH/CXG WD3...160 C2
Jordan's Wy LCOL/BKTW AL2...135 M9
Joshua Wk CHES/WCR EN8...156 F4
Joslyn CI PEND EN3......156 F8
Joyce Ct WAB EN9........157 J4
Jubilee CI ARL/CHE SG15...24 D5
Jubilee Cr RKW/CH/CXG WD3...160 C2
Jubilee Rd LWTH SG6.....36 E7
  STVG SG1...............50 E7
  WATW WD18..............149 H8
Jubilee St LTNE LU2.....7 G1
Judge's HI POTB/CUF EN6...140 A8
Judge St WATN WD24......149 J8
Julia Ga STVGE SG2......51 M7
Julian CI BAR EN5.......166 F2
Julian's Rd STVG SG1....50 D7
Julius Caesar Wy STAN HA7...164 C9
Julius Gdns LTNN/LIM LU3...46 A8
Juniper Av LCOL/BKTW AL2...149 P1

Juniper CI BAR EN5......166 B4
  BROX EN10..............142 E4
  LTNW/LEA LU4...........61 P4
  RKW/CH/CXG WD3........161 H9
Juniper Ct
  KTN/HRWW/WS HA3 *......172 F5
  NTHWD HA6..............171 J1
Juniper Gdns RAD WD7....151 K3
  WLYN AL6...............85 H6
Juniper Ga
  RKW/CH/CXG WD3........161 H8
Juniper Gn HHW HP1......117 H8
Juniper Gv WAT WD17.....149 H8
Jupiter Dr HHNE HP2.....5 H5
Jupiter Ga STVGE SG2....51 N7
Juson's Glebe
  RAYLNE/WEN HP22.......112 D6
Juxon CI KTN/HRWW/WS HA3...172 B5

K

Kaduna PI PIN HA5.......171 K9
Kardwell CI HTCHE/RSTV SG4...49 M1
Kates CI BAR EN5........165 N4
Katescroft WGCE AL7.....123 H1
Katherine CI HHS/BOV HP3 *...5 H8
Katherine Dr
  DUN/HR/TOD LU5........61 H4
Katherine PI ABLGY WD5...149 H2
Katherine Wy
  HLWW/ROY CM19.........128 C6
Kay CI HHW HP2..........117 N4
Kay CI STDN SG11........71 N4
Kay Wk STALE/WH AL4.....121 J7
Keaton CI DUN/WHIP LU6...60 C1
Keats CI HHNE HP2.......118 C2
  ROY SG8................51 L7
  STVGE SG2..............51 L7
Keats Wy HTCHE/RSTV SG4...35 P9
Keble Ter ABLGY WD5.....148 G2
Kecksy's SBW CM21.......92 A5
Keeble CI LTNE LU2......63 M5
Keele CI WATN WD24......149 H6
Keepers CI LBUZ LU7.....77 P6
  LTNE LU2...............63 K4
Keiths Rd HHNE HP2......118 B9
Keiths Wd KNEB SG3......85 M5
Kelbys WGCE AL7.........105 M5
Keller Ct STVGE SG2.....67 L2
Kelling CI LTNE LU2.....46 D7
Kelly O BORE WD6........165 J4
Kelman CI CHES/WCR EN8...156 C1
Kelmscott Crs WATW WD18...12 C5
Kelmscott Gdns
  RKW/CH/CXG WD3........160 E5
Kelshall STVGE SG2......67 L2
Kelshall St ROY SG8.....28 C5
Kelvin CI LTN LU1.......6 E7
Kelvin Crs
  KTN/HRWW/WS HA3........172 E4
Kemble CI POTB/CUF EN6...153 N3
Kemble Pde POTB/CUF EN6 *...153 M2
Kemp CI STAL AL1........136 B3
Kempe Rd EN EN1.........156 A6
Kemprow GSTN WD25......150 C5
Kempsey Dr SG NTHWD HA6...171 H4
Kempsey CI LTNE LU2.....63 L3
Kendal CI LTNN/LIM LU3...45 N8
  TRDG/WHET N20.........167 J3
Kendale HHS/BOV HP3.....118 C9
Kendal Rd HTCHE/RSTV SG4...49 L1
  LTNN/LEA LU4...........61 L1
Kendall CI WGCE AL7.....123 J1
Kendal Rd WAB EN9.......157 H5
Kendals CI RAD WD7......150 D6
Kenerne Dr BAR EN5......166 C4
Kenetic Av PEND EN3.....156 B6
Kenetic Crs PEND EN3....156 E6
Kenford CI GSTN WD25....149 J2
Kenilworth CI WAT WD17 *...67 M7
Kenilworth Ct WAT WD17...155 M9
Kenilworth Dr BORE WD6...165 J2
  RKW/CH/CXG WD3........161 M3
Kenilworth Gdns
  LTN LU1................6 A3
Kenilworth Rd EDGW HA8...165 J8
  LTN LU1................167 J3
Kenley CI BAR EN5.......167 J3
Kenmare Ct STVG SG1.....50 C8
  STVG SG1...............51 J4
Kenmore Av
  KTN/HRWW/WS HA3........173 C9
Kenmore Gdns EDGW HA8...173 P6
Kenmore Rd
  KTN/HRWW/WS HA3........173 K7
Kennedy Av HOD EN11.....126 E5
Kennedy CI CHES/WCR EN8...142 D7
  LCOL/BKTW AL2..........137 J5
  PIN HA5................171 P3
Kennedy Rd WARE SG12....69 M7
Kennelwood La HAT AL10...123 H6
Kenneth Rd LTNE LU2.....63 H5
Kennett Wy STVG SG1.....51 K4
Kenning Rd HOD EN11.....126 E5
Kennington Rd
  LTNN/LIM LU3...........62 C4
Kensington Av WATW WD18...12 B5
Kensington CI
  STAL AL1...............136 F1
Kensworth Rd
  DUN/WHIP LU6...........78 F9
Kent CI BORE WD6........152 A8
Kent Crs BSF CM23.......91 P1
Kent Dr EBAR EN4........167 L3
Kentish La BRKMPK AL9...139 M3
Kenton Gdns
  KTN/HRWW/WS HA3........173 J9
  STAL AL1...............9 J6
Kenton La
  KTN/HRWW/WS HA3........172 F4

Kenton Park Av
  KTN/HRWW/WS HA3 ....173 K8
Kenton Park Cl
  KTN/HRWW/WS HA3 ....173 J8
Kenton Park Crs
  KTN/HRWW/WS HA3 ....173 K8
Kenton Park Pde
  KTN/HRWW/WS HA3 * 173 J9
Kenton Park Rd
  KTN/HRWW/WS HA3 ....173 J9
Kenton Rd
  KTN/HRWW/WS HA3 ....173 L9
Kent Pl HTCH/STOT SC5 * 44 C9
Kent Rd DUN/HR/TOD LU5 ......44 C9
  LTN LU1 ....62 A6
Kents Av HHS/BOV HP3 ....133 N3
Kent's La STDN SG11 ....71 H4
Kenway Dr AMSS HP7 ....145 N9
Kenwood Dr
  RKW/CH/CXG WD3 ....160 D8
Kenworth Cl CHES/WCR EN8 ..156 C5
Kenyngton Pl
  KTN/HRWW/WS HA3 ....173 J9
Kenyon Pl WCCE AL7 ....105 H9
Kerdistone Cl POTB/CUF EN6 ..139 L9
Kerri Cl KNEB SG3 ....67 J9
Kerri Ct BAR EN5 ....166 A3
Kerril Cft HLW CM20 ....128 C2
Kerris Av RKW/CH/CXG WD3 ..231 J1
Kerry Ct STAN HA7 ....173 K1
Kershaw Cl LTNN/LIM LU3 ......46 B7
Kershaw's
  HTCHE/RSTV SC4 ....49 L1
Kessingland Av STVG SG1 ......50 D6
Kesters Rd CSHM HP5 ....145 J2
Keston Ms WAT WD17 ....162 D1
Kestral Wy ROY SG8 ....20 B2
Kestrel Cl BERK HP4 ....115 P8
  GSTN WD25 ....150 D7
Kestrel Gdns BSF CM23 ....73 M8
Kestrel Gn HAT AL10 ....122 D7
Kestrel Rd WAB EN9 ....157 N4
The Kestrels LCOL/BKTW AL2 ..188 E1
Kestrel Vw STVG SG2 ....36 C5
Kestrel Wy LTNW/LEA LU4 ......61 K1
Keswick Cl DUN/WHIP LU6 ......60 E7
  STAL AL1 ....168 E6
Keswick Dr PEND EN3 ....156 B6
Keswick Gdns RSLP HA4 ....170 F9
Kettering Rd PEND EN3 ....156 C7
Kettle Green Rd MHAD SG10 ....90 B3
Ketton Cl LTNE LU2 * 5 J5
Kewferry Dr NTHWD HA6 ....170 D2
Kewferry Rd NTHWD HA6 ....170 D3
Keyfield Ct STAL AL1 * 9 F5
Keyfield Ter STAL AL1 ....9 F5
Keymer Cl LTNE LU2 ....63 K5
Keynton Ct HERT/WAT SG14 ..106 C5
Keysers Rd BROX EN10 ....153 K4
Kibes La WARE SG12 ....108 C3
Kidner Cl LTNE LU2 ....62 F1
Kilbride Ct HHNE HP2 ....118 A4
Kilby Rd GSTN WD25 ....149 L5
Kilfillan Gdns BERK HP4 ....115 M8
Kilmarnock Dr OXHEY WD19 ....171 M1
Kiln Av AMS HP6 ....145 P8
Kiln Cl BERK HP4 ....115 N5
Kilncroft HHS/BOV HP3 ....134 C1
Kilnfield WCCE AL7 ....105 J3
Kiln Gnd HHS/BOV HP3 ....134 B1
Kiln La CSHM HP5 ....145 N1
  HLWE CM17 ....129 M4
Kiln House Ct WARE SG12 ......145 N1
Kiln Wy DUN/HR/TOD LU5 ......61 K5
  NTHWD HA6 ....170 C3
Kilmore La CHES/WCR EN8 ....162 C7
Kilvinton Dr ENC/FH EN2 ......155 L8
Kilworth Ct WCCE AL7 ....105 L8
Kimberley LWTH SG6 ....25 K7
Kimberley Cl BSF CM23 ....74 B5
Kimberley Rd STALW/RED AL3 ..8 D1
Kimberwell Cl
  HTCHE/RSTV SC4 ....44 C3
Kimble Cl WATW WD18 * 162 A5
Kimble Crs BUSH WD23 ....163 L6
Kimbolton Crs STVGE SG2 ......67 K6
Kimbolton Gn BORE WD6 ......165 J3
Kimps Wy HHS/BOV HP3 ....134 B2
Kimpton Cl HHNE HP2 ....118 C3
Kimpton Pl GSTN WD25 ....149 L4
Kimpton Bottom HARP AL5 ......82 D6
Kimpton Rd HTCHE/RSTV SC4 ..82 D3
  LTNE LU2 ....7 K7
  STALW/WH AL4 ....83 H7
  WLYN AL6 ....84 B7
Kimptons Cl POTB/CUF EN6 ....152 C5
Kimptons Md POTB/CUF EN6 ....152 C5
Kinderscout HHNE HP2 ....134 B1
Kindersley Cl WLYN AL6 ....84 F7
Kindersley Wy ABLGY WD5 ....148 D1
Kinderton Cl STHGT/OAK N14 ..167 H4
Kinfauns Ct
  CHES/WCR EN8 ....156 C1
King Arthur Ct
  CHES/WCR EN8 ....156 D1
King Charles Rd RAD WD7 ....151 K2
King Croft Rd HARP AL5 ....102 C5
King Edgar Yd ROY SG8 * 21 M8
King Edward Rd
  STALW/WH AL4 ....103 J3
King Edward Rd BAR EN5 ......166 E3
  CHES/WCR EN8 ....156 D5
  OXHEY WD19 ....162 C5
  RAD WD7 ....151 L4
King Edward's Rd
  WARE SG12 ....108 D2
King Edward St
  HHS/BOV HP3 ....133 N1
Kingfisher
  KTN/HRWW/WS HA3 ......172 F4
  NTHWD HA6 ....170 D4
  STALW/WH AL4 ....103 J3
  WARE SG12 ....109 H9
Kingfisher Ct
  HTCHE/RSTV SC4 ....49 M1

Kingfisher Dr HHS/BOV HP3 ..134 A4
Kingfisher Lure KGLGY WD4 * ..134 C8
Kingfisher Meadow
  RBSF CM22 ....75 N3
Kingfisher Ri STVGE SG2 ......67 H4
Kingfisher Wy BSF CM23 ......73 M8
King George Av WAB EN9 ....157 H4
King George Sq STVG SG1 ......10 C3
King George Rd WAB EN9 ....157 H4
  WARE SG12 ....108 D2
Kingsbury Av
  WATW WD18 ....12 A5
King Georges Cl
  HTCH/STOT SC5 ....35 J6
King George's Wy
  HTCH/STOT SC4 ....65 K8
Kingham Rd WARE SG12 ....89 K8
Kinghamway LTNE LU2 ....6 E1
King Harry La
  STALW/RED AL3 ....119 P9
King Harry St HHNE HP2 ....4 E2
The Kingit LTNN/LIM LU3 ......46 C9
King Henry's Ms PEND EN3 ..156 E7
King James Av
  POTB/CUF EN6 ....140 F8
King James Wy ROY SG8 ......20 C4
Kingley Pk KGLGY WD4 ....134 C8
Kings Av HHS/BOV HP3 ....134 A3
  WATW WD18 ....12 B5
Kingsbridge Rd BSF CM23 ......74 B2
Kingsbury Av
  DUN/HR/TOD LU5 ....61 H5
  STALW/RED AL3 ....8 C2
Kingsbury Ct
  DUN/HR/TOD LU5 ....60 F6
Kingsbury Gdns
  DUN/HR/TOD LU5 ....61 J5
Kingsbury Rd
  CDALE/KGS NW9 ....173 N9
Kings Cl CSTG SG8 ....159 K8
King's Cl KGLGY WD4 ....147 L1
Kings Cl NTHWD HA6 ....171 H3
  WARE SG12 ....13 C5
Kings Ct BSF CM23 * 74 B2
Kingscroft WCCE AL7 ....105 L5
Kingscroft Av
  DUN/HR/TOD LU5 ....60 E5
Kingsdale Rd BERK HP4 ....115 M8
Kingsdon La HLWE CM17 ......129 M4
Kingsdown HTCHE/RSTV SC4 ....35 N9
Kings Dr EDGW HA8 ....173 M1
Kings Farm Rd
  RKW/CH/CXG WD3 ....160 B5
Kingsfield HOD EN11 ....126 F3
Kingsfield Rd
  RYLN/HDSTN HA2 ....172 B9
Kingsfield Ct OXHEY WD19 ....162 F5
Kingsfield Rd OXHEY WD19 ....162 F6
  WARE SG12 ....109 M7
Kingsgate STALW/RED AL3 ......8 B7
Kings Head Pde
  RAYLNE/WEN HP22 * 112 C7
Kings Heath Pk HARP AL5 ......82 B7
Kings Hedges
  HTCH/STOT SC5 ....35 H8
Kingshill Av
  KTN/HRWW/WS HA3 ......173 H8
  STALW/WH AL4 ....120 C5
Kingshill Ct BAR EN5 ....166 C3
Kingshill Dr
  KTN/HRWW/WS HA3 ......173 H7
Kingshill Wy BERK HP4 ....115 M9
Kingsland HLWS CM18 ....128 F5
Kingsland Cl
  DUN/HR/TOD LU5 ....61 H2
Kingsland Ct LTN LU1 ....7 G7
Kingsland Rd HHW HP1 * 133 K1
  LTN LU1 ....7 G7
Kingsland Wy BLDK SG7 ....17 P7
Kings La KGLGY WD4 ....147 K1
Kingsley Av BORE WD6 ....164 F1
Kingsley Ct EDGW HA8 * 165 H8
  WCCE AL7 ....123 J1
Kingsley Rd LTNN/LIM LU3 ....46 B7
  PIN HA5 ....171 P8
Kingsley Wy TRING HP23 ......95 P8
Kingsmead BAR EN5 ....166 C3
  CHES/WCR EN8 ....142 C7
  POTB/CUF EN6 ....140 A8
  SBW CM21 ....111 P5
  STVG SG1 ....3 J1
  WAB EN9 * 143 H1
Kingsmead Cl
  HLWW/ROY CM19 ....127 N4
Kings Meadow KGLGY WD4 ....134 B7
Kingsmill Cl HAT AL10 ....122 E8
Kingsmoor Rd
  HLWW/ROY CM19 ....128 B6
Kings Pond Cl BGSW SG18 ....14 C6
Kings Rd BAR EN5 ....166 A2
  BERK HP4 ....115 M5
King's Rd CHES/WCR EN8 ......156 D4
  CSTG SG8 ....159 K8
King's Rd HERT/BAY SG13 ....107 P5
  HTCH/STOT SC5 ....35 L8
  LCOL/BKTW AL2 ....137 H5
  STALW/RED AL3 ....8 B5
Kings Rd STVG SG1 ....10 C7
Kings Sq HAT AL10 ....122 A3
Kingston Pl
  KTN/HRWW/WS HA3 ......172 F4
Kingston Rd EBAR EN4 ....167 H4
  LTNE LU2 ....62 D5
Kingston V ROY SG8 ....20 C5
King St BSF CM23 ....74 A3
  CHES/WCR EN8 ....144 C2
  DUN/HR/TOD LU5 ....6 E5
  LTN LU1 ....20 C4
  ROY SG8 ....79 P8
  STALW/RED AL3 ....95 P9
  TRING HP23 ....13 C5
  WATW WD18 ....51 M8
Kings Walden Ri STVGE SG2 ....48 B5
King's Walden Rd
  HTCH/STOT SC5 ....

Kings Wk ROY SG8 * 20 D5
Kings Wy HRW HA1 ....172 E8
  STVG SG1 ....10 A6
Kingsway CFSP/GDCR SL9 ....168 C7
  DUN/HR/TOD LU5 ....60 E5
  LTNW/LEA LU4 ....61 L5
  POTB/CUF EN6 ....140 F9
  ROY SG8 ....20 B2
  WARE SG12 ....108 C2
Kingsway Crs
  RYLN/HDSTN HA2 ....172 C8
Kingsway Gdns
  HTCHE/RSTV SC4 ....25 J2
Kingsway North Orbital Rd
  WARE 149 H4
Kingswell Ride
  POTB/CUF EN6 ....140 F9
Kingswood Av
  HTCHE/RSTV SC4 ....36 A3
Kingswood Cl CHES/WCR EN8 ..156 C5
Kingswood Rd GSTN WD25 ....149 J4
  KTN/HRWW/WS HA3 * 161 J7
Kingswell Rd EBAR EN4 ......153 N8
King William Cl
  AMP/FLIT/BLC MK45 ......32 E4
King William Cl WAB EN9 * 157 H5
King William Rd
  LTNN/LIM LU3 ....45 N7
Kinross Cl
  KTN/HRWW/WS HA3 ......173 M9
Kinross Crs LTNN/LIM LU3 ....45 N7
Kinsbourne Cl HARP AL5 ......81 K9
Kinsbourne Crs HARP AL5 ....81 L9
Kinsbourne Green La
  HARP AL5 ....101 J1
Kipling Cl HTCHE/RSTV SC4 ....35 P9
Kipling Gv HHNE HP2 ....118 C2
The Kipling LTNN/LIM LU3 ......46 C9
Kipling Wy HARP AL5 ....102 A3
Kirby Cl NTHWD HA6 ....171 H3
Kirby Dr LTNN/LIM LU3 ....46 A6
Kirby Rd DUN/WHIP LU6 ......80 E9
Kirkdale Rd HARP AL5 ....162 E9
Kirkdale Rd HARP AL5 ....101 P2
Kirkland Dr ENC/FH EN2 ......155 K9
Kirklands WCCW AL8 ....105 H2
Kirkstone Dr DUN/WHIP LU6 ....60 A5
Kirkwick Av HARP AL5 ....101 N5
Kirkwood Rd LTNW/LEA LU4 ....61 J3
Kirtle Rd CSHM HP5 ....145 H1
Kitcheners Ct STAL AL1 * 120 F9
Kitcheners La STVGE SG2 ......52 C6
Kitchen Garden Ct
  HTCH/STOT SC5 ....49 K1
Kite Fld BERK HP4 ....115 K4
Kitsbury Rd BERK HP4 ....115 N7
Kitsbury Ter BERK HP4 ....115 N7
Kitson Wy HLW CM20 ....27 L9
Kitt's End Rd BAR EN5 ....153 H7
Kitts End Rd BAR EN5 ....153 H7
Knebworth Cl BAR EN5 ....166 F3
Knebworth Ga STVGE SG2 ......67 J5
Knebworth Pth BORE WD6 ....165 K3
Kneesworth St ROY SG8 ......20 B3
Knella Gn WCCE AL7 ....123 J1
Knella Rd WCCE AL7 ....123 J1
Knifton Ct POTB/CUF EN6 * ..152 C1
Knightsbridge Wy
  HHNE HP2 ....117 P7
Knights Cl BSF CM23 ....73 L6
  BUNT SG9 ....39 J1
Knightscote Cl DEN/HRF UB9 ..169 P6
Knoll Crs NTHWD HA6 ....170 C6
Knolles Crs BRKMPK AL9 ......138 E3
Knights Fld LTNE LU2 ....62 E5
Knightsfield WGCW AL8 ......104 C2
Knights Orch HHW HP1 ....117 J6
Knights Rd STAN HA7 ....173 J1
Knights Wy BSF CM23 ....73 P8
Knight St SBW CM21 ....111 P2
Knightswood Ct EDGW HA8 ..173 M1
Knoll Crs NTHWD HA6 ....170 C6
Knoll Gn STHGT/OAK N14 ....167 H6
Knoll Ri LTNE LU2 ....62 E5
Knolls Cl RAYLNE/WEN HP22 ....60 C7
Knolls Vw DUN/WHIP LU6 ......60 C7
The Knoll HERT/BAY SG13 ....108 A5
The Knowle HOD EN11 ....126 F6
Knowl Piece
  HTCHE/RSTV SC4 ....35 M5
Knowl Wy BORE WD6 ....164 E4
Knutsford Av WATN WD24 ....149 L8
Koh-i-Noor Av BUSH WD23 ....163 M3
Kristiansand Wy LWTH SG6 ....25 N9
Krymsweld Rd STVGE SG2 ......67 M2
Kynance Cl LTNE LU2 ....63 J3
Kynance Gdns STAN HA7 ....173 J5
Kynaston Cl
  KTN/HRWW/WS HA3 ......173 J1
Kynaston Rd ENC/FH EN2 ....155 K7
Kynaston Wd
  KTN/HRWW/WS HA3 ......173 J1
Kyrkeby LWTH SG6 ....25 J5
Kytes Dr GSTN WD25 ....149 L3

L

Laburnum Cl CHES/WCR EN8 ..156 C1
  LTNN/LIM LU3 ....46 B3
  RBSF CM22 ....92 D9
Laburnum Ct STAN HA7 ....173 J1
Laburnum Gv
  LCOL/BKTW AL2 ....135 P4
  LTNN/LIM LU3 ....46 B3
Laburnum Rd HOD EN11 ......126 G3
Laburnum Wy CHESW EN7 ....141 H7

Lacemaker Ct AMSS HP7 * 158 C1
Lacey Dr EDGW HA8 ....173 L1
Laceys Yd LTNW/LEA LU4 * ..144 C1
Lachbury Cl LTN LU1 ....62 B8
Lackmore Rd EN EN1 ....156 B5
Lacre Wy LWTH SG6 ....36 F1
Ladbrook Cl PIN HA5 ....171 P9
Ladbrooke Dr POTB/CUF EN6 ..153 K2
Ladbrooke Dr POTB/CUF EN6 ..153 K2
  WARE SG12 * 8 B1
Ladies Gv STALW/RED AL3 ......8 B1
Lady Aylesford Av STAN HA7 ..173 H2
Ladycroft Wk STAN HA7 ......173 K5
Lady Gv WGCE AL7 ....123 H1
Ladyhill LTNW/LEA LU4 ....45 L9
Lady Margaret Gdns
  WARE SG12 ....108 D1
Lady Meadow KGLGY WD4 ....133 N6
Lady St John Sq
  HERT/WAT SG14 ....107 H6
Lady's Cl WATW WD18 ....13 D5
Ladysmith Rd
  KTN/HRWW/WS HA3 ......172 E6
  STALW/RED AL3 ....8 E1
Ladywalk RKW/CH/CXG WD3 ..169 J2
Ladywell Prospect
  SBW CM21 ....92 A8
Ladywood Cl
  RKW/CH/CXG WD3 ....160 F2
Ladywood Rd
  HERT/WAT SG14 ....106 G6
Lagger Cl HHW HP1 ....159 H9
Lagger Cl HHW HP1 ....159 H9
The Lagger CSTG HP8 ....158 D6
Lagley Meadow BERK HP4 ....115 M6
Laidon Sq HHW HP1 ....117 N4
Lake Dr BUSH WD23 ....163 L8
Lakefield Av
  DUN/HR/TOD LU5 ....44 C2
Lakeland Cl
  KTN/HRWW/WS HA3 ......172 D3
Lakenheath STHGT/OAK N14 ..167 P4
Lake Rd WAB EN9 ....143 K1
Lakeside ENC/FH EN2 ....167 P5
  TRING HP23 ....95 P7
Lakeside Crs EBAR EN4 ......167 K5
Lakeside Ri LCOL/BKTW AL2 ..137 J7
Lakeside Rd CHES/WCR EN8 ..142 B7
The Lake BUSH WD23 ....163 H7
Lake Vw STALW/RED AL3 ......173 L4
  POTB/CUF EN6 ....139 K7
  KGLGY WD4 * 153 M3
Laleham Av MLNL NW7 ....165 K9
Lalleford Rd LTNE LU2 ....63 K5
Lamb Cl GSTN WD25 ....149 K4
  HAT AL10 ....122 E7
Lamb Ct STALW/WH AL4 * 103 J1
Lambe Rd
  RAYLNE/WEN HP22 ....112 F5
Lamb La STALW/RED AL3 ......101 J7
Lamb Meadow
  ARC/CHES L6 ....24 D6
Lambourn Cha RAD WD7 ......150 D6
Lambourn Dr LTNE LU2 ....62 E5
Lambourn Gdns HARP AL5 ....101 N1
Lambourne Av
  DUN/HR/TOD LU5 ....60 F6
  LTNE LU2 ....62 E5
Lambourn Gv STVGE SG2 ......67 J5
Lambscroft Wy
  CFSP/GDCR SL9 ....168 C6
Lambs Gdns WARE SG12 ......90 A3
Lambton Av CHES/WCR EN8 ..156 C5
Lamer La STALW/WH AL4 ......83 J9
Lamers Rd LTNE LU2 ....63 J4
Lammas Md HTCH/STOT SC5 ..35 K6
Lammas Rd STVGE SG2 ....67 J2
Lammas Rd HERT/WAT SG14 ..7 P6
  LBUZ LU7 ....88 C4
  WATW WD18 ....13 G7
Lammas Wy LWTH SG6 ....25 K9
Lamorna Cl LTNN/LIM LU3 ....45 L9
Lampits Rd HOD EN11 ....126 G5
Lampitts Cross
  LTNN/LIM LU3 * 62 B1
Lamplighters Cl WAB EN9 ....157 M4
Lamsey Rd HHNE HP2 ....118 C3
Lancaster Av EBAR EN4 ......153 N8
  HTCH/STOT SC5 ....35 J8
  LTNE LU2 ....46 E7
Lancaster Cl
  AMP/FLIT/BLC MK45 ......32 E4
  STVG SG1 ....51 H5
Lancaster Dr HHS/BOV HP3 ..132 C6
Lancaster Rd EBAR EN4 ......167 H3
  ENC/FH EN2 ....155 L9
  RYLN/HDSTN HA2 ....172 A9
  STAL AL1 ....120 B6
Lancaster Wy ABLGY WD5 ....148 C1
  BSF CM23 ....73 L6
Lancelot Ct DUN/WHIP LU6 ....60 B7
Lancet Av DUN/WHIP LU6 ......60 B7
Lancing Dr ENC/FH EN2 ......155 M7
Lancing Wy
  RKW/CH/CXG WD3 ....161 M4
Landau Wy BROX EN10 ....142 E4
Landford Cl
  RKW/CH/CXG WD3 ....161 J8
Landmead Rd
  CHES/WCR EN8 ....142 D6
Landridge Dr EN EN1 ....156 A8
Landseer Cl EDGW HA8 ......173 N6
Lands' End BORE WD6 ....164 D5
Lane End BERK HP4 ....115 J7
  HAT AL10 ....129 H7
  HLWE CM17 ....129 H7
Lane Gdns BUSH WD23 ......163 N1
The Lane LTNW/LEA LU4 ......85 L6
Lane Wood Cl AMSS HP7 ....145 L9
Langbridge Ct
  HTCHE/RSTV SC4 ....49 M2
Langdale Av DUN/WHIP LU6 ....60 F7
Langdale Dr
  RKW/CH/CXG WD3 ....148 C5

Langdale Ct HHNE HP2 ....117 P5
Langdale Gdns PEND EN3 ......156 C5
Langdale Rd DUN/WHIP LU6 ....60 E7
Langdale Ter BORE WD6 * 165 P3
Langdon St TRING HP23 ....95 P9
Langfield Cl WAB EN9 ....143 K1
Langford Cl STALE/WH AL4 ..121 H6
Langford Crs EBAR EN4 ......167 K3
Langford Rd EBAR EN4 ......167 K3
Langham Cl LTNE LU2 * 46 E8
  STALE/WH AL4 ....121 H5
Langholme BUSH WD23 ....163 L7
Langland Ct NTHWD HA6 ......170 E4
Langland Dr PIN HA5 ....171 K6
Langland Dr PIN HA5 ....171 N4
Langleigh LWTH SG6 ....25 K8
Langley Av HHS/BOV HP3 ....5 H7
Langleybury La
  RKW/CH/CXG WD3 ....148 C5
Langley Cr CHESW EN7 ....141 K7
Langley Crs EDGW HA8 ....165 J9
  KGLGY WD4 ....134 B9
  STALW/RED AL3 ....120 B6
Langley Gv STVG SG1 ....3 H1
Langley Gv STALW/RED AL3 ..134 A9
Langley Hl KGLGY WD4 ....134 A8
Langley Hill Cl KGLGY WD4 ..134 B8
Langley La ABLGY WD5 ....148 C5
Langley Lodge La
  KGLGY WD4 ....147 P2
Langley Rd ABLGY WD5 ......148 F1
  KGLGY WD4 ....133 L9
Langley Rw BAR EN5 ....165 N1
Langley Sidings STVG SG1 * 67 H4
Langley St LTN LU1 ....7 F6
Langley Wy WAT WD17 ....162 A2
Langley Whf KGLGY WD4 * ..134 B6
Langmead Dr BUSH WD23 ....163 N7
Langney Crs STHGT/OAK N14 ..167 P2
Langstone Ley WGCE AL7 ....105 L7
Langthorne Av ROY SG8 ......10 E2
Langton Av STALW/WH AL4 ..83 N8
Langton Gn NTHWD HA6 * 170 D4
  KTN/HRWW/WS HA3 ......172 C4
Langwood Gdns WAT WD17 ..149 H9
Lankester Rd ROY SG8 ....20 B5
Lannock LWTH SG6 ....36 C6
Lannock Hl HTCHE/RSTV SC4 ..36 C6
Lanrick Copse BERK HP4 ....116 D6
Lansbury Rd PEND EN3 ....156 E5
Lansdowne Rd BROX EN10 ..126 F8
Lansdowne Rd CSHM HP5 ....131 H8
  LTN LU1 ....62 D5
  STAN HA7 ....173 J5
Lansdown Rd
  CFSP/GDCR SL9 ....168 B8
Lanterns La CFSP/GDCR SL9 ..51 N9
The Lanterns ROY SG8 ....20 C4
Lanthorn Cl BRKMPK AL9 ....124 A7
Laporte Wy LTNW/LEA LU4 ....61 K4
Lapwing Cl HHNE HP2 ....117 P4
Lapwing Dell LWTH SG6 ......36 E6
Lapwing Ri STVGE SG2 ......149 K2
Lapwing Rd STVGE SG2 ......67 H4
Lapwing Wy LTNW/LEA LU4 ..149 K5
Larch Av HTCHE/RSTV SC4 ..135 M3
  LCOL/BKTW AL2 ....135 M3
Larches Av EN EN1 ....156 B5
The Larches BERK HP4 ....115 J4
  BUSH WD23 ....162 G4
  LTNE LU2 ....6 D1
  STALW/WH AL4 ....121 J4
Larch Ri BERK HP4 ....115 M6
Larchwood BSF CM23 ....73 N9
Larchwood Rd HHNE HP2 ....118 A6
Larken Cl BUSH WD23 ....163 L8
Larken Dr BUSH WD23 ......163 L8
Larkens Cl STDN SG11 ....71 J3
Larkfield
  KTN/HRWW/WS HA3 ......173 H7
Larkin Pl BUSH WD23 ....163 J8
Larkins Cl BLDK SG7 ....26 E8
Larkins La BKMAP SG10 ......90 C4
Lark Hl HAT AL10 ....122 A4
Larksfield WARE SG12 ....108 D1
Larksfield Gn EN EN1 ....156 A4
Larkspur Cl BSF CM23 ....73 J8
  CDALE/KGS NW9 ....173 N9
Larkspur Gdns LTNW/LEA LU4 ..62 A4
Larks Rdg LCOL/BKTW AL2 ..135 P5
Larks Rdg LCOL/BKTW AL2 ..135 P5
Larkswy BSF CM23 ....73 J8
Larkswood HLWE CM17 ......129 M5
Larkswood Ri PIN HA5 ....171 L8
Larmans Rd PEND EN3 ....156 E8
Larsen Dr WAB EN9 ....157 J4
Larwood Gv STVG SG1 ....51 K7
Latchford Ms STALW/WH AL4 ..103 J1
Latchmoor Av
  CFSP/GDCR SL9 ....168 B8
Latchmoor Gv
  CFSP/GDCR SL9 ....168 B8
Latchmoor Wy
  CFSP/GDCR SL9 ....168 B8
Latchmore Ct
  HTCHE/RSTV SC4 * 49 L2
Latimer Cl AMS HP6 ....145 P9
  HHNE HP2 ....118 C3
  PIN HA5 ....171 H6
  WATW WD18 ....162 A6
Latimer Gdns PIN HA5 ....171 H6
  WCCE AL7 ....105 L6
Latimer Rd BAR EN5 ....166 F2
  CSHM HP5 ....131 H9
  LTN LU1 ....62 A1
  RKW/CH/CXG WD3 ....146 C8
Latium Cl STAL AL1 ....8 E6
Lattimore Rd STAL AL1 ....9 F5
  STALW/WH AL4 ....103 H4
Latton Gn HLWS CM18 ....129 J2
Latton Hall Cl HLW CM20 ....129 K2

Latton House *HLWS* CM18.... 129 L6
Latton St *HLWE* CM17.... 129 L4
Lauderdale Rd *KGLGY* WD4.... 148 D3
Launceston
 RKW/CH/CXG WD3.... 159 P5
Laundry La *WAB* EN9.... 143 L4
Launton St *LTNN/LIM* LU3.... 46 C6
Laureate Wy *HHW* HP1.... 117 L6
Laurel Av *STAL/WH* HP3.... 153 J2
Laurel Bank *HHS/BOV* HP3.... 153 J2
Laurel Bank Rd *ENC/FH* EN2.... 155 J1
Laurel Cl *HHNE* HP2.... 118 A7
 OXHEY WD19.... 162 F6
Laurel Ct *AMS* HP6.... 145 H6
Laureldene *MHAD* SC10.... 90 C4
Laurel Flds *POTB/CUF* EN6.... 153 J1
Laurel Gdns *MLHL* NW7.... 165 K9
Laurel Pk
 KTN/HRWW/WS HA3.... 172 F4
Laurel Rd *CFSP/GDCR* SL9.... 168 B5
 STAL AL1.... 9 K3
The Laurels *BERK* HP4.... 116 E5
 BORE WD6.... 151 M9
 BUSH WD23 *....
 CHESW EN7.... 141 M6
Laurel Vw *TRDG/WHET* N20.... 166 F9
Laurel Wy *HTCH/STOT* SC5.... 35 K5
 TRDG/WHET N20.... 166 E9
Lauret Cl *HHW* HP1.... 132 E1
Laurimel Cl *STAN* HA7.... 173 H5
Laurino Pl *BUSH* WD23.... 163 L8
Lavender Av *BSF* CM23.... 78 N8
 CHESW EN7.... 141 N6
 HAT AL10.... 122 C3
 HLW CM20.... 3 H5
 LTNE LU2.... 48 F8
Lavender Cl *BLDK* SG7.... 26 A8
Lavender Crs *STALW/RED* AL3.... 120 B6
Lavender Gdns *ENC/FH* EN2.... 155 J8
 KTN/HRWW/WS HA3.... 172 E5
Lavender Hl *ENC/FH* EN2.... 155 H9
Lavender Rd *ENC/FH* EN2.... 155 H9
Lavender Wk *HHNE* HP2.... 117 N6
Lavender Wy *HTCH/STOT* SC5.... 35 J9
Lavinia Av *GSTN* WD25.... 149 K4
Lavrock La
 RKW/CH/CXG WD3.... 161 K6
Lawford Av
 RKW/CH/CXG WD3.... 160 A5
Lawford Cl *LTN* LU1.... 6 B5
 RKW/CH/CXG WD3.... 160 A5
Law Hall La *HTCHE/RSTV* SC4.... 51 N5
Lawley Rd *STHGT/OAK* N14.... 167 M6
Lawn Av *NTHWD* HA6.... 83 H4
Lawn Cl *HTCH/STOT* SC5.... 48 B5
Lawns Cl *HTCH/STOT* SC5.... 48 B5
The Lawns Dr *BROX* EN10.... 142 E1
The Lawns *HHW* HP1.... 117 H7
 PIN HA5.... 172 B4
 RAD WD7.... 151 K3
 STVGE SG2.... 67 N2
 WCCW AL8.... 104 C3
Lawnswood *BAR* EN5 *.... 166 C4
Lawn V *PIN* HA5.... 171 M6
Lawrence Gdns
 CHES/WCR EN8.... 142 B8
Lawrence Rd *STALW/RED* AL3.... 120 B4
 SBW CM21.... 91 P9
 STVG SG1.... 51 H8
Lawrence Campe Cl
 TRDG/WHET N20.... 167 H9
Lawrence Cl *HERT/WAT* SG14.... 106 F5
Lawrence Ct *OXHEY* WD19 *.... 162 F9
Lawrence Crs *EDGW* HA8.... 173 N6
Lawrence Ernd Rd *LTNE* LU2.... 82 B2
Lawrence Gdns *MLHL* NW7.... 165 H8
Lawrence Md
 HTCHE/RSTV SC4 *.... 50 C3
Lawrence Moorings
 SBW CM21.... 92 A7
Lawrence Rd *PIN* HA5.... 171 M9
 DUN/WHIP LU6.... 60 C4
Lawrence Rd *PEND* EN3.... 156 B9
Lawton Rd *EBAR* EN4.... 167 H2
Laxton Cl *LTNE* LU2.... 63 H5
Laxton Gdns *BLDK* SG7.... 37 K1
Layard Rd EN1.... 155 N9
Lay Brook *STALW/RED* AL4.... 120 F4
Layham Dr *LTNE* LU2.... 63 L5
Layhill *HHNE* HP2....
Layston Meadow *BUNT* SG9.... 64 E1
Layston Pk *ROY* SG8.... 20 C5
Layter's Av South
 CFSP/GDCR SL9.... 168 A6
Layter's Cl *CFSP/GDCR* SL9.... 168 A6
Layter's End *CFSP/GDCR* SL9.... 168 A6
Layters Wy *CFSP/GDCR* SL9.... 168 B9
Lea Bushes *GSTN* WD25.... 149 M5
Leachcroft *CFSP/GDCR* SL9.... 168 A5
Lea Cl *BSF* CM23....
 BUSH WD23.... 163 K4
Leaders Cl
 RAYNLE/WEN HP22.... 76 C2
Lea Ct CH *NTHWD* HA6.... 170 F4
Leafield *LTNN/LIM* LU3.... 61 J3
Leafields *DUN/HR/TOD* LU5.... 44 F9
Leaford Crs *WATN* WD24.... 148 C2
Leaforis Rd *CHESW* EN7.... 141 M7
Lea Ford Rd *DUN/HR/TOD* LU5.... 44 F9
Leaf Wy *STAL* AL1.... 136 C2
Leafy La *TRING* HP23.... 113 M2
Leagrave High St
 LTNW/LEA LU4.... 61 J3
Lea Gn *BRKMPK* AL9.... 123 H3
Lea Gv *BSF* CM23.... 74 C1
Leahoe Gdns *HERT/BAY* SG13.... 107 K7
Leamington Rd
Lea Mt *CHESW* EN7.... 48 B8
Leander Av *GSTN* WD25 *.... 149 M7
Lea Rd *ENC/FH* EN2.... 155 L9
 HARP AL5.... 102 A1
 HOD EN11.... 127 H3
 LTN LU1.... 7 G5

WAB EN9.... 156 F4
WATN WD24 *.... 149 J8
Leasey Bridge La *HARP* AL5.... 102 E3
Leasey Dell Dr *STALE/WH* HA9.... 102 E3
Leaside *HHNE* HP2.... 118 D9
The Leas *BLDK* SG7.... 37 H1
 BUSH WD23.... 163 H1
 HHS/BOV HP3.... 153 B3
Leat Cl *SBW* CM21.... 92 A6
Leathersellers Cl *BAR* EN5 *.... 166 C2
Leathwaite Cl *LTNN/LIM* LU3.... 62 A1
Lea Valley Wk *BRKMPK* AL9.... 122 F1
 BRKMPK AL9.... 124 A2
 BROX EN10.... 142 F5
 HARP AL5.... 102 B1
 HERT/WAT SG14.... 106 B9
 HOD EN11.... 127 J6
 LTN LU1.... 63 K9
 STVG SG1.... 81 N6
 PEND EN3.... 156 F7
 WARE SG12.... 108 B3
Leavesden Rd *STAN* HA7.... 172 C5
 WATN WD24.... 149 J8
Leaves Spring *STVGE* SG2.... 67 J4
Leaview *WAB* EN9.... 156 C5
Lebanon Cl *WAT* WD17.... 162 F1
Le Corte Cl *LTNN/LIM* LU3.... 134 A8
Lectern La *STAL* AL1.... 136 D3
Lea Av *PEND* EN3.... 156 C9
Ledgemore La *HHNE* HP2.... 99 J6
Ledwell Rd *LTN* LU1 *.... 80 A2
Leeches Wy *LBUZ* LU7.... 77 P6
Lee Cl *HERT/BAY* SG13.... 107 K8
 WARE SG12.... 109 H8
Leecroft Rd *BAR* EN5.... 166 C3
Lee Farm Cl *CSHM* HP5.... 131 M9
Leefe Rd *LTN/LIM* LU3.... 140 E7
Leeming Rd *BORE* WD6.... 151 L9
Lees Av *NTHWD* HA6.... 171 H5
Lees Cl *EDGW* HA8.... 173 P5
Leeside *BAR* EN5.... 166 C4
 POTB/CUF EN6.... 153 N2
Lee Pk *ROY* SG8.... 20 B5
The Lee *NTHWD* HA6.... 171 H2
Lee Vw *ENC/FH* EN2.... 155 J9
Left Side *STHGT/OAK* N14 *.... 167 N7
Leggatts Cl *WATN* WD24.... 148 C6
Leggatts Ri *WATN* WD24.... 149 H5
Leggatts Wood Av
 WATN WD24.... 149 J6
Leggatt Gv *STVG* SG1.... 51 H7
Leggfield Ter *HHW* HP1.... 117 J8
Leghorn Crs *LTNW/LEA* LU4.... 61 K3
Legions Wy *BSF* CM23.... 74 B2
Legra Av *HOD* EN11.... 126 F5
Leicester Rd *BAR* EN5.... 166 D4
 LTNW/LEA LU4.... 61 P5
Leigh Cl *DUN/HR/TOD* LU5.... 44 C1
Leigh Common *WCCE* AL7.... 105 H8
Leigh Dr *RAD* WD7.... 151 M3
Leigh Rd *RBSF* CM22.... 59 K2
Leigh Hunt Dr
 STHGT/OAK N14.... 167 P7
Leigh Rodd *OXHEY* WD19.... 162 G9
Leighton Av *PIN* HA5.... 171 N7
Leighton Buzzard Rd
 HHNE HP2.... 4 D2
Leighton Cl *EDGW* HA8.... 173 N6
Leighton Ct *DUN/WHIP* LU6.... 60 D6
Leighton Rd
 DUN/HR/TOD LU5.... 44 B2
 KTN/HRWW/WS HA3.... 172 D6
 RAYNLE/WEN HP22.... 76 D2
Lemark Cl *STAN* HA7.... 173 J3
Lemonfield Dr *GSTN* WD25.... 149 M2
Lemon Field Dr *CSTN* WD25.... 149 M2
Lemsford Cl *BORE* WD6.... 165 J3
Lemsford La *WCCW* AL8.... 104 F7
Lemsford Rd *HAT* AL10.... 122 C5
 STAL AL1.... 9 J2
Lemsford Village *WCCW* AL8.... 104 C5
Lennox Cl *LTNE* LU2.... 63 N4
Lensbury Cl *CHES/WCR* EN8.... 142 D7
Leonard's Cl *WLYN* AL6.... 85 H5
Lesbury Cl *LTNE* LU2.... 63 M5
Leslie Cl *STVGE* SG2.... 67 M4
Lester Ms *LTNE* LU2.... 63 M4
Leston Cl *DUN/WHIP* LU6.... 60 C9
Letchfield Ter
 KTN/HRWW/WS HA3 *.... 172 B5
Letchmore Cl *STVG* SG1.... 10 C2
Letchmore Rd *RAD* WD7.... 150 F6
 STVG SG1.... 51 J6
Letchworth Cl *OXHEY* WD19.... 171 M2
Letchworth Ga *LWTH* SG6.... 36 C5
Leven Cl *CHES/WCR* EN8.... 36 C5
Leven Cl *CHES/WCR* EN8.... 156 C3
Levendale *LTNW/LEA* LU4.... 61 M1
Leven Dr *CHES/WCR* EN8.... 156 C3
Leven Wy *HHNE* HP2.... 117 N4
Leveret Cl *STVG* SG1.... 51 L5
Leverstock Green Rd
 HHNE HP2.... 118 B7
Leverton Wy *WAB* EN9.... 157 H3
Leveson Wy *RKW/CH/CXG* WD3.... 161 M3
Lewins Rd *CFSP/GDCR* SL9.... 168 B7
Lewis La *ARL/CHE* SC15.... 24 A1
Lewis Cl *IDEN/HRF* UB9.... 169 N6
 STHGT/OAK N14.... 167 N6
Lewsey Park Ct
 LTNW/LEA LU4.... 61 K2
Lewsey Rd *LTNW/LEA* LU4.... 61 L3
Lexden Ter *WAB* EN9 *.... 157 H4
Lexham Gdns *AMS* HP6.... 145 H7
Lexington Cl *BORE* WD6.... 163 N5
Lexington Ct *POTB/CUF* EN6.... 152 C1
Lexington Wy *BAR* EN5.... 166 B3
Leybourne Rd
 CDALE/KGS NW9.... 173 N9

Leyburne Rd *LTNN/LIM* LU3.... 46 C9
Leycroft Cl *HARP* AL5.... 102 D5
Leyden Rd *STVG* SG1.... 66 G3
Leygreen Cl *LTNE* LU2.... 7 K2
Leyhill Dr *LTN* LU1.... 80 C1
Leyland Av *STAL* AL1.... 136 C1
Leyland Cl *CHES/WCR* EN8.... 142 B8
Leys Av *LWTH* SG6.... 36 C2
Leys Cl *DEN/HRF* UB9.... 169 P5
 HRW HA1.... 172 D8
Leysdown *WCCE* AL7.... 105 N6
Leys Gdns *BAR* EN5.... 167 J4
Leys Rd *HHS/BOV* HP3.... 5 J6
Leys Rd East *PEND* EN3.... 156 D9
The Leys *AMS* HP6.... 144 G5
 RAD WD7.... 150 F7
 STALE/WH AL4.... 121 J5
 TRING HP23.... 96 A8
Leyton Gn *HARP* AL5.... 101 P3
Leyton Rd *HARP* AL5.... 101 P3
Ley Wk *WGCE* AL7.... 105 M6
Liberty Cl *HARP* AL5.... 102 A4
Liberty Hl *HERT/BAY* SG13.... 107 K8
Liberty Wk *STAL* AL1.... 121 H9
Library Rd *LTN* LU1.... 6 E4
Lichfield Cl *EBAR* EN4.... 167 K2
Lichfield Ms *LTNE* LU2.... 9 J1
Lichfield Rd *NTHWD* HA6.... 171 H8
Lichfield Wy *BROX* EN10.... 142 E1
Liddel Cl *LTNN/LIM* LU3.... 62 B3
Liddell Cl
 KTN/HRWW/WS HA3.... 173 K9
Lidding Rd
 KTN/HRWW/WS HA3.... 173 K9
Lidgate Cl *LTNN/LIM* LU4.... 45 J9
Lieutenant Ellis Wy
 CHESW EN7.... 155 N1
Life Cl *LTNW/LEA* LU4.... 61 J2
Liffre Dr *RAYLNE/WEN* HP22.... 112 C5
Lighthorne Ri *LTNN/LIM* LU3.... 46 B8
Lightswood Cl *CHESW* EN7.... 141 L6
Lilac Av *EN* EN1.... 156 B6
Lilac Cl *CHESW* EN7.... 141 J9
Lilac Gv *LTNN/LIM* LU3.... 45 M6
Lilbourne Dr *HERT/BAY* SG13.... 107 P5
Lilley Bottom Rd
 HTCHE/RSTV SC4.... 64 D3
Lilleyhoo La *HTCH/STOT* SC5.... 47 N5
Lilliard Cl *HOD* EN11.... 126 C1
Lilly La *HHNE* HP2.... 118 E4
The Limberlost *WLYN* AL6.... 85 N1
Limbrick Rd *HARP* AL5.... 102 A6
Limbury Rd *LTNN/LEA* LU4.... 62 A2
Lime Av *LWTH* SG6.... 36 A4
 STALE/WH AL4.... 82 G7
Lime Cl *LAMP/FLIT/BLC* MK45.... 32 D5
 KTN/HRWW/WS HA3.... 172 C6
 OXHEY WD19.... 162 F6
 STVGE SG2.... 67 N2
 WARE SG12.... 108 D2
Lime Gv *ROY* SG8.... 20 D2
 TRDG/WHET N20.... 166 C7
Limekiln Cl *ROY* SG8.... 20 D2
Limekiln La *BLDK* SG7.... 37 J1
Lime Rd *CHES/WCR* EN8.... 156 C3
The Limes *AMS* HP6.... 144 C5
 HTCH/STOT SC5.... 24 E1
 RKW/CH/CXG WD3 *.... 160 D6
 STAL AL1.... 120 D6
Limetree Av *LTN/LIM* LU3.... 45 M6
Lime Tree Cl *LTNN/LIM* LU3.... 45 M6
Lime Tree Ct *HHS/BOV* HP3.... 172 A4
Lime Tree Dr *BCSW* SC18.... 14 C4
Limetree Pl *STAL* AL1.... 9 H6
Lime Tree Wk *AMSS* HP7.... 145 L9
 BUSH WD23.... 163 N7
 ENC/FH EN2.... 155 K8
Limewalk *DUN/HR/TOD* LU5.... 60 C6
Lime Wk *HHS/BOV* HP3.... 5 K5
Lime Wy *RAD* WD7.... 137 H9
Linacres *LTNW/LEA* LU4.... 61 M1
Linbridge Wy *LTNE* LU2.... 63 M4
Linces Wy *WGCE* AL7.... 105 L8
Lincoln Av *STHGT/OAK* N14.... 167 L8
 LTNW/LEA LU4.... 62 C5
 NTHWD HA6.... 171 H7
 RYLN/HDSTN HA2.... 171 P9
 WCCE AL7.... 105 L5
Lincoln's Cl *STAL* AL1.... 121 H3
Lincoln Dr *OXHEY* WD19.... 162 C9
 RKW/CH/CXG WD3.... 161 M3
Lincoln Rd *CFSP/GDCR* SL9.... 168 C5
 LTNW/LEA LU4.... 62 C5
 NTHWD HA6.... 171 H9
 RYLN/HDSTN HA2.... 171 P9
Lincoln Wy
 RKW/CH/CXG WD3.... 161 M3
Lincut La *HTCHE/RSTV* SC4.... 65 P7
Lindbergh *WGCE* AL7.... 105 N6
Linden Av *EN* EN1.... 155 P9
 WATW WD18.... 161 P4
Linden Cl *CHESW* EN7.... 141 M6
 RYLN/HDSTN HA2.... 171 P6
 STAN HA7.... 173 H2
 STHGT/OAK N14.... 167 M5
Linden Ct *DUN/HR/TOD* LU5.... 61 J4
 HARP AL5.... 102 A4

Linden Lea *GSTN* WD25.... 149 H3
 PIN HA5 *.... 171 P4
 RAYLNE/WEN HP22.... 112 C6
Linden Rd *DUN/HR/TOD* LU5.... 61 J4
 FBAR/BDGN N11.... 167 K8
 LTNW/LEA LU4.... 61 J7
 STALW/RED AL3.... 101 H6
Lindens WD23.... 163 L8
Linden Sq *DEN/HRF* UB9.... 169 L5
The Lindens *BSF* CM23.... 74 A4
 DUN/HR/TOD LU5.... 60 D2
 HAT AL10 *.... 122 C5
 HHS/BOV HP3.... 133 J2
 STVG SG1.... 11 F6
 WAB EN9.... 157 H3
Linden Wy *STHGT/OAK* N14.... 167 N5
Lindiswara Ct
 RKW/CH/CXG WD3 *.... 161 L5
Lindley Cl *HARP* AL5.... 81 P9
Lindlings *HHW* HP1.... 171 P4
Lindo Cl *CSHM* HP5.... 130 C9
Lindsay Av *HTCHE/RSTV* SC4.... 49 N2
Lindsay Cl *STVG* SG1.... 20 B1
Lindsay Dr *CSTN* WD25.... 149 K3
Lindsey Cl *BSF* CM23.... 74 A1
 LTNE LU2.... 9 H3
Lindsey Rd *BSF* CM23.... 74 A1
Lindum Pl *STALW/RED* AL5.... 135 N1
Linfield Ct *HERT/WAT* SG14.... 106 G5
Linford Cl *HLWW/ROY* CM19.... 128 F5
Linford End
 HLWW/ROY CM19.... 128 F5
Lingfield Cl *NTHWD* HA6.... 170 G4
Lingfield Rd *ROY* SG8.... 20 D4
 STVG SG1.... 51 M6
Lingholm Wy *BAR* EN5.... 166 B4
Lingmoor Dr *CSTN* WD25.... 149 K3
Lington Av *CSHM* HP5.... 131 M9
Link Cl *HAT* AL10.... 122 E6
Link Dr *HAT* AL10.... 122 E6
Linkfield *WGCE* AL7.... 123 H1
Links Av *HERT/BAY* SG13.... 108 B5
Links Dr *BORE* WD6.... 151 J8
 RAD WD7.... 150 F2
 TRDG/WHET N20.... 166 F7
Linkside Rd *BSF* CM23.... 74 D4
The Links *CHES/WCR* EN8.... 142 C5
Links Vw *WAT/RED* AL5.... 120 A6
Links View Cl *STAN* HA7.... 173 J2
Links Wy *LTNE* LU2.... 46 D7
 NTHWD HA6.... 170 D5
Linksway *NTHWD* HA6.... 170 F5
Linkswood Av *CSTN* WD25.... 149 H4
The Link *BSF* CM23.... 73 P8
Link Wy *BSF* CM23.... 73 P8
Linkway *PIN* HA5.... 171 M5
Linkways East *STVG* SG1.... 11 C4
Linkways West *STVG* SG1.... 11 C4
The Linkway *BAR* EN5.... 166 F5
Linley Dell *LTNE* LU2.... 63 N5
Linnet Cl *BUSH* WD23.... 163 L7
 LWTH SG6.... 23 H9
Linnet Cl *PIN* HA5.... 171 M6
Linney Head *DUN/WHIP* LU6 *.... 78 E1
Linnins Pond *STAL* AL4.... 136 B2
Linsey Cl *HHS/BOV* HP3.... 100 C5
Linslade Cl *PIN* HA5.... 171 K7
Linster Gv *BORE* WD6.... 165 J4
Linton Cl *HTCHE/RSTV* SG4.... 49 J1
Linthorpe Rd *EBAR* EN4.... 167 J2
Linton Av *BORE* WD6.... 164 F1
Lintons Cl *HOD* EN11.... 126 C4
Lintott Cl *STVG* SG1.... 10 C2
Linwood *SBW* CM21.... 91 N9
Linwood Crs *EN* EN1.... 155 P9
Linwood Rd *HARP* AL5.... 102 A3
Lion Ct *BORE* WD6.... 151 P9
Lionel Rd *RAYLNE/WEN* HP22.... 112 B6
Lionel Cl *RAYLNE/WEN* HP22.... 112 B6
Liphook Rd *OXHEY* WD19.... 171 M1
Lippitts Hl *LTNE* LU2.... 62 F1
Liscombe Rd
 BRKMPK AL9.... 124 A8
Lismore *HHS/BOV* HP3.... 134 D1
 STVGE SG2.... 67 M5
Lister Cl *STVG* SG1.... 49 L2
Lister Rd *LTNW/LEA* LU4.... 62 C5
Litlington Cl *STVG* SG1.... 11 L1
Little Acre *STALW/RED* AL3.... 120 C5
Little Acre *WARE* SG12.... 108 C4
Little Almshoe Rd
 HTCHE/RSTV SC4.... 49 M7
Little Berkhamsted La
 BRKMPK AL9.... 124 A8
Little Berries *LTNN/LIM* LU3.... 45 P8
Little Brays *HLWS* CM18.... 129 K4
Little Bridge Rd *BERK* HP4 *.... 116 C3
Littlebrook Gdns
 CHES/WCR EN8.... 142 C9
Little Brook Rd
 HLWW/ROY CM19.... 127 P3
Little Burrow *WCCE* AL7.... 104 G8
Littlebury Ct *HTCH/STOT* SC5.... 25 L4
Little Bushey La *BUSH* WD23.... 163 J2
Little Catherells *HHW* HP1.... 117 H6
Little Cattins
 HLWW/ROY CM19.... 128 C7
Little Cl *STAL* AL1.... 121 H7
Littlecroft *WGCE* AL7.... 105 L8
Littlecote PI *PIN* HA5.... 171 N5
Little Dell *WCCW* AL8.... 104 G4
Littlefield Rd *EDGW* HA8.... 173 P7
Little Foxes *HOD* EN11.... 127 M8
Little Ganett *WGCE* AL7.... 105 L8
Little Graylings *ABLGY* WD5.... 148 E5
Little Greencroft *CSHM* HP5.... 130 F6
Littlegreen La *BSF* CM23.... 79 P5
Little Green La
 RKW/CH/CXG WD3.... 161 K2
 BUSH WD23.... 163 K3

Littlegrove *EBAR* EN4.... 167 J5
Little Grove Av *CHESW* EN7.... 141 M6
Little Grove Fld
 HLWW/ROY CM19.... 2 C5
Little Hampden Cl
 RAYLNE/WEN HP22.... 112 C7
Little Hardings *WCCE* AL7.... 105 M5
Little Hayes *KGLGY* WD4.... 134 B8
Little Heath *RBSF* CM22.... 92 C6
Little Heath La *HHW* HP1.... 116 E9
Little Hill *RKW/CH/CXG* WD3.... 160 A5
Little Hivings *CSHM* HP5.... 130 F6
Little Hoo *TRING* HP23.... 95 N8
Little How Cft Av *ABLGY* WD5.... 148 D1
Little Hyde *STVGE* SG2....
Little Lake *WGCE* AL7.... 105 L9
Little La *HARP* AL5.... 102 B6
 HTCH/STOT SC5.... 34 C3
Little Ley *WGCE* AL7.... 105 H9
Little Martins *BUSH* WD23.... 163 K4
Little Meadow *LTN* LU1 *.... 80 C2
Little Mimms *HHNE* HP2....
Little Moss La *PIN* HA5.... 171 N6
Little Mundells *WCCE* AL7.... 105 J5
Little Orch *HHNE* HP2.... 118 B6
Little Oxhey La *OXHEY* WD19.... 171 N2
Little Pk *HHS/BOV* HP3.... 132 D7
Little Piper's Cl *CHESW* EN7.... 141 J8
Little Potters *BUSH* WD23.... 163 M6
Little Pynchons *HLWS* CM18.... 129 K4
Little Reeves Av *AMSS* HP7.... 145 L9
Little Rdg *WGCE* AL7.... 105 K6
Little Rivers *WGCE* AL7.... 105 K5
Little Ridge *HHNE* HP2.... 117 P7
Little Shardeloes *AMSS* HP7.... 145 H9
Little Spring *CSHM* HP5.... 130 G7
Little Stock Rd *CHESW* EN7.... 141 L5
Little Stream Cl *NTHWD* HA6.... 170 C2
Little St *WAB* EN9.... 157 H6
Little Thistle *WGCE* AL7.... 105 M8
Little Tring Rd *TRING* HP23.... 113 N8
Little Twye Rd *TRING* HP23.... 113 N8
Littss Av *HERT/BAY* SG13.... 105 J9
Little Wk *HLW* CM20.... 2 E4
Little Widbury La *WARE* SG12.... 108 E3
Little Widbury *WARE* SG12.... 108 E3
Little Windmill Hl *KGLGY* WD4.... 147 N2
Little Wood Cft
 LTNN/LIM LU3.... 45 P8
Little Youngs *WCCW* AL8.... 104 F6
Liverpool Rd *LTN* LU1.... 6 C4
 STAL AL1.... 13 G6
 WATW WD18.... 13 G4
Livingstone Link *STVGE* SG2.... 51 L7
Livingstone Wk *HHNE* HP2.... 118 A4
Lloyd Ct *PIN* HA5.... 171 M9
Lloyd Ms *PEND* EN3.... 156 F8
Lloyd-Taylor Cl *STVG* SG11.... 72 E4
Lloyd Wy *HTCHE/RSTV* SG4.... 83 H4
Loates La *WAT* WD17.... 13 C3
Loates Pasture *STSD* CM24.... 59 H2
Local Board Rd *WAT* WD17.... 13 E6
Locarno Av *RAYLNE/WEN* HP22.... 45 M9
Lochnell Rd *BERK* HP4.... 115 L5
Lockers Park La *HHW* HP1.... 4 B2
Locket Rd
 KTN/HRWW/WS HA3.... 172 F6
Locket Road Ms
 KTN/HRWW/WS HA3.... 172 E6
Lockhart Cl *DUN/WHIP* LU6.... 60 G8
Lockington Crs
 DUN/HR/TOD LU5.... 61 H4
Lockley Crs *HAT* AL10.... 122 E4
Locksleys Dr *WLYN* AL6.... 84 F8
Lockyer Cl *PEND* EN3.... 156 G8
Lockyer Av *BORE* WD6.... 164 F4
 KTN/HRWW/WS HA3.... 173 L8
Lodge Cl *EDGW* HA8.... 173 M3
 HERT/WAT SG14.... 107 K4
 LBUZ LU7.... 77 P6
Lodge Ct *HTCH/STOT* SC5.... 35 K5
Lodge Crs *CHES/WCR* EN8.... 156 C1
 RKW/CH/CXG WD3.... 160 C3
Lodge End *RAD* WD7.... 150 G4
 RKW/CH/CXG WD3.... 161 P3
Lodge Gdns *DUN/HR/TOD* LU5.... 60 D2
Lodge Dr *BRKMPK* AL9.... 122 C3
Lodge Gdns *DUN/HR/TOD* LU5.... 60 D2
Lodge Fld *WGCE* AL7.... 105 J7
Lodge Gn *RKW/CH/CXG* WD3.... 160 C3
Lodge Hall *HLWS* CM18.... 129 H7
Lodge La *CSTG* HP8.... 159 M1
 WAB EN9.... 157 J5
Loftus Cl *LTNN/LEA* LU4.... 61 L2
Logan Cl *PEND* EN3.... 156 C9
The Logans *BAR* EN5.... 166 B2
Loire Ms *HAT* AL10.... 122 E4
Lollard Cl *LTNW/LEA* LU4.... 61 H3
Lollards Cft *AMS* HP6.... 145 H7
Lombard Av *PEND* EN3.... 156 B9
Lombardy Dr *BERK* HP4.... 118 E9
Lombardy Dr *BERK* HP4.... 92 C6
Lombardy Wk *BORE* WD6.... 151 K9
Lomond Dr *HHNE* HP2.... 117 N4
Lomond Wy *STVG* SG1.... 51 N5
London Loop *BORE* WD6.... 165 H5
 EN EN1.... 156 A9
London Rd *BERK* HP4.... 116 E6
 BGSW SG18.... 16 A1
 BLDK SG7.... 37 J2
 BSF CM23.... 74 A7
 BUSH....
 BUSH WD23.... 164 E5
 CSTG HP8.... 159 J8
 DUN/HR/TOD LU5.... 44 B2
 ENC/FH EN2.... 155 M8
 HARP AL5.... 102 E5
 HERT/BAY SG13.... 107 M6
 HHW HP1.... 2 A2
 HLWE CM17.... 129 L2
 HTCHE/RSTV SC4.... 49 L2
 KNEB SG3.... 67 K9
 RAD WD7.... 151 L3
 RAYLNE/WEN HP22.... 76 C3
 ROY SG8.... 20 C8
 SBW CM21.... 111 P2

STAL AL1 9 F5
STALW/RED AL3 79 P8
STAN HA7 173 J2
STVG SG1 10 D7
STVGE SG2 67 H5
TRING HP23 96 A9
WARE SG12 108 D5
WLYN AL6 84 F9
London Rd East AMSS HP7 158 E2
London Rd West AMSS HP7 158 C1
London Rw ARL/CHE SG15 24 E6
Londrina Ter BERK HP4 116 A7
Long Acre HLWE CM17 111 L8
Longacres STALE/WH AL4 121 J8
Long Arrotts HHW HP1 117 L6
Long Banks HLWS CM18 128 G6
Long Barn Cl GSTN WD25 149 H2
Long Border Rd STSD CM24 75 M1
Longbridge Cl TRING HP23 95 P6
Longbrooke
DUN/HR/TOD LU5 60 G2
Long Buftlers HARP AL5 102 E4
Long Chaulden HHW HP1 117 H9
Longcliffe Pth OXHEY WD19 162 C9
Long Cl LTNE LU2 63 K3
Long Cft OXHEY WD19 162 D6
Longcroft
RAYLNE/WEN HP22 94 G7
Long Cft STSD CM24 58 E3
Longcroft Av HARP AL5 101 N3
RAYLNE/WEN HP22 112 E5
Longcroft Dr
AMP/FLIT/BLC MK45 32 C6
Long Croft Dr
CHES/WCR EN8 156 E4
Longcrofte Rd EDGW HA8 173 K4
Longcroft Gdns WGCW AL8 104 G7
Longcroft Gn WGCW AL8 104 G8
Longcroft La HHS/BOV HP3 132 F7
WGCW AL8 104 G7
Long Croft Rd LTN LU1 62 B7
RKW/CH/CXG WD3 169 H2
Longcroft Rd STVG SG1 51 H8
Long Cutt STALW/RED AL3 101 H6
Longdean Pk HHS/BOV HP3 134 B3
Long Elmes
KTN/HRWW/WS HA3 172 B5
Long Elms ABLGY WD5 148 E3
Long Elms Cl ABLGY WD5 148 E3
Long Fallow LCOL/BKTW AL2 135 P6
Longfield HHS/BOV HP3 134 C1
HLWS CM18 129 K5
Longfield Av PEND EN3 156 B7
Longfield Dr AMS HP6 144 G8
LTNW/LEA LU4 61 N5
Longfield Gdns TRING HP23 95 M9
Longfield La CHESW EN7 141 N6
Longfield Rd CSHM HP5 130 E8
HARP AL5 102 B5
TRING HP23 95 M9
Longfields STVGE SG2 67 M5
Long Grove Cl BROX EN10 126 D7
Long Hale LBUZ LU7 96 B1
Long Hedge
DUN/HR/TOD LU5 60 G6
Long Hyde STVGE SG2 67 L2
Long John HHNE HP2 5 K5
Longland Dr
TRDG/WHET N20 166 F9
Longlands HHNE HP2 5 K1
Longlands Cl CHES/WCR EN8 156 C2
Longlands Rd WGCE AL7 105 J8
Long La HHS/BOV HP3 132 D9
HHS/BOV HP3 146 C1
HTCHE/RSTV SG4 64 F7
RKW/CH/CXG WD3 160 A5
STVGE SG2 67 P1
Long Leaves STVGE SG2 67 K4
Long Ley HLW CM20 3 K5
LBUZ LU7 77 P6
WGCE AL7 105 M6
Longley Rd HRW HA1 172 D9
Longmans Cl WATW WD18 161 N5
Long Marston La LBUZ LU7 77 N6
Long Marston Rd
TRING HP23 95 M2
Long Md DUN/HR/TOD LU5 44 E9
Longmead BUNT SG9 40 C9
HAT AL10 122 D3
KNEB SG3 85 K3
LWTH SG6 36 B1
Long Meadow BSF CM23 73 N8
CSHM HP5 131 H7
DUN/WHIP LU6 60 D6
HERT/WAT SG14 * 86 E1
STALW/RED AL3 79 P8
Longmeadow Dr
HTCH/STOT SG5 35 K3
Long Mimms HHNE HP2 117 P7
Long Moor CHES/WCR EN8 142 D8
Longmore Av BAR EN5 166 G5
Longmore Cl
RKW/CH/CXG WD3 169 K1
Longmore Gdns WGCE AL7 105 J6
Long Pk AMS HP6 145 H6
Long Park Cl AMS HP6 145 H6
Long Park Wy AMS HP6 145 H5
Long Plough
RAYLNE/WEN HP22 94 E7
Longridge RAD WD7 150 G4
Long Rdg STVGE SG2 67 N5
Long Spring STALW/RED AL3 120 D3
Longspring WATN WD24 149 J7
Long Vw BERK HP4 115 M5
Long Wk CSTG HP8 159 L2
Long Wd HLWS CM18 128 G8
Longwood La AMSS HP7 145 J9
Longwood Rd
HERT/WAT SG14 106 G5
The Loning PEND EN3 156 B8
Lonsdale HHNE HP2 117 P5
Lonsdale Cl LTNN/LIM LU3 62 B1
Lonsdale Ct STVG SG1 51 J8
Lonsdale Dr ENC/FH EN2 167 P3
Lonsdale Rd STVG SG1 11 G1
Loom La RAD WD7 150 E7
Loop Rd WAB EN9 156 G2
Lord Mead La WLYN AL6 83 P6
Lords Av BSF CM23 73 L7
Lords Cl RAD WD7 151 K2
Lord's Hl DUN/HR/TOD LU5 44 C6
Lordship La LWTH SG6 36 E4
Lordship Rd CHESW EN7 142 A9
Lords Meadow
STALW/RED AL3 101 H7
Lords Mill Ct CSHM HP5 145 H2
Lord St HOD EN11 126 D5
WAT WD17 13 G3
Lords Wd WGCE AL7 105 M6
Loretto Gdns
KTN/HRWW/WS HA3 173 L8
Loring Rd BERK HP4 115 P8
DUN/WHIP LU6 60 C6
TRDG/WHET N20 167 J8
Lorne Rd
KTN/HRWW/WS HA3 172 F6
Lorraine Pk
KTN/HRWW/WS HA3 172 E4
Lorrimer Cl LTNE LU2 46 F9
Lothair Rd LTNE LU2 63 H2
Loudhams Rd AMSS HP7 145 P9
Loudhams Wood La
CSTG HP8 159 K1
Loudwater Dr
RKW/CH/CXG WD3 160 G3
Loudwater Hts
RKW/CH/CXG WD3 160 F2
Loudwater La
RKW/CH/CXG WD3 160 G4
Loudwater Rdg
RKW/CH/CXG WD3 160 G3
Louise Wk HHS/BOV HP3 132 D7
Louisville Cl WARE SG12 109 H8
Louvain Wy GSTN WD25 149 J2
Lovatt Cl EDGW HA8 173 P3
Lovatts RKW/CH/CXG WD3 161 L3
Loveday Cl ROY SG8 22 G7
Lovelace Rd EBAR EN4 167 J6
Love La BLDK SG7 17 K5
KGLGY WD4 133 P8
PIN HA5 171 N7
Lovel Cl HHW HP1 117 K8
Lovel End CFSP/GDCR SL9 168 A4
Lovell Cl HTCHE/RSTV SG4 49 M1
Lovell Rd EN EN1 156 A5
Lovel Md CFSP/GDCR SL9 168 A4
Lovel Rd CFSP/GDCR SL9 168 A4
Lovering Rd CHESW EN7 141 K4
Lovers' Wk DUN/HR/TOD LU5 60 F6
Lovet Rd HLWW/ROY CM19 128 D4
Lovett Rd DEN/HRF UB9 169 N7
LCOL/BKTW AL2 136 F5
Lovett Wy DUN/HR/TOD LU5 60 G3
Lowbell La LCOL/BKTW AL2 137 K6
Lower Adeyfield Rd
HHNE HP2 117 N7
Lower Barn HHS/BOV HP3 134 A2
Lower Bourne Gdns
WARE SG12 108 B1
Lower Clabdens WARE SG12 108 E3
Lower Dagnall St
STALW/RED AL3 8 D3
Lower Derby Rd WAT WD17 13 H5
Lower Emms HHNE HP2 118 D3
Lower End
RAYLNE/WEN HP22 76 C3
Lowerfield WGCE AL7 105 K7
Lower Gower Rd ROY SG8 20 C2
Lower Harpenden Rd LTN LU1 63 J9
Lower Hatfield Rd
HERT/BAY SG13 124 G2
Lower High St WAT WD17 13 H5
Lower Icknield Wy
RAYLNE/WEN HP22 95 H7
Lower Innings
HTCH/STOT SG5 35 J8
Lower Island Wy WAB EN9 156 G5
Lower Kenwood Av
ENC/FH EN2 * 167 P4
Lower Kings Rd BERK HP4 115 N7
Lower King St ROY SG8 20 C4
Lower Luton Rd HARP AL5 82 B9
STALE/WH AL4 102 F2
Lower Mardley Hl WLYN AL6 85 J5
Lower Meadow
CHES/WCR EN8 142 C6
HLWS CM18 129 H7
Lower Paddock Rd
OXHEY WD19 162 G5
Lower Park Crs BSF CM23 74 A5
Lower Paxton Rd STAL AL1 9 G5
Lower Plantation
RKW/CH/CXG WD3 160 G2
Lower Rd CFSP/GDCR SL9 168 C7
HHS/BOV HP3 134 B5
HTCHE/RSTV SG4 64 E5
RBSF CM22 92 D2
RKW/CH/CXG WD3 160 B3
STDN SG11 73 H7
WARE SG12 108 E6
Lower Sales HHW HP1 117 J9
Lower Sean STVGE SG2 67 K3
Lower Shott CHESW EN7 141 N5
Lower St STSD CM24 58 F5
Lower Tail OXHEY WD19 162 G9
Lower Titmore Gn
HTCHE/RSTV SG4 50 B6
Lower Tub BUSH WD23 163 M6
Lower Yott HHNE HP2 5 H3
Lowes Cl STVG SG1 51 M5
Lowestoft Rd WATN WD24 149 J9
Loweswater Cl GSTN WD25 149 K3
Lowfield SBW CM21 111 P3
Lowfield La HOD EN11 126 F5
Lowgate La WARE SG12 87 P1
Low Hill Rd HLWW/ROY CM19 127 L5
Lowick Rd HRW HA1 172 E8
Lowlands BRKMPK AL9 122 F3
Lowndes Av CSHM HP5 130 G9
Low Rd BRKMPK AL9 124 A3
Lowry Dr DUN/HR/TOD LU5 60 G1
Lowson Gv OXHEY WD19 162 G6
Lowswood Cl NTHWD HA6 170 E5
Lowther Cl BORE WD6 164 F4
Lowther Rd DUN/WHIP LU6 60 F8
STAN HA7 173 M7
Loxley Ct WARE SG12 * 108 D3
Loxley Rd BERK HP4 115 K5
Lucan Rd BAR EN5 166 C2
Lucas Ct WAB EN9 157 L3
Lucas Gdns LTNN/LIM LU3 46 C7
Lucas La BLDK SG7 17 P6
HTCH/STOT SG5 35 J9
Lucern Cl CHESW EN7 141 M6
Lucerne Wy LTNN/LIM LU3 62 D2
Lucks Hl HHW HP1 117 H8
Ludgate TRING HP23 95 N8
Ludlow Av LTN LU1 80 F1
Ludlow Md OXHEY WD19 162 D9
Ludlow Wy
RKW/CH/CXG WD3 161 N3
Ludun Cl DUN/HR/TOD LU5 61 H6
Ludwick Cl WGCE AL7 * 105 J8
Ludwick Gn WGCE AL7 * 105 J7
Ludwick Wy WGCE AL7 105 J6
Lukes La TRING HP23 95 L1
Lukes Lea TRING HP23 95 P3
Lullington Cl LTNE LU2 63 K3
Lullington Garth BORE WD6 * 165 J4
Lulworth Av CHESW EN7 141 J8
Lumbards WGCE AL7 105 K3
Lumen Rd ROY SG8 20 C3
Lunardi Ct STDN SG11 71 H3
Lundin Wk OXHEY WD19 * 171 M1
Luther Cl EDGW HA8 165 J8
Luther King Rd
HLWW/ROY CM19 2 D6
The Luton Dr LTN LU1 63 H9
Luton La STALW/RED AL3 101 H4
Luton Rd
AMP/FLIT/BLC MK45 32 C7
DUN/HR/TOD LU5 44 D2
DUN/HR/TOD LU5 60 G6
HARP AL5 81 M9
HTCH/STOT SG5 47 P5
HTCHE/RSTV SG4 82 F3
LTN LU1 80 A1
LTNE LU2 63 M3
LTNN/LIM LU3 46 C2
LTNW/LEA LU4 44 G5
STALW/RED AL3 79 P6
Luton White Hl LTNE LU2 47 P7
Luxembourg Cl LTNN/LIM LU3 45 N7
Luxford Pl SBW CM21 92 A8
Luynes Ri BUNT SG9 54 D1
Lybury La STALW/RED AL3 100 F5
Lycaste Cl STAL AL1 9 K5
Lych Ga GSTN WD25 149 L3
Lycrome La CSHM HP5 131 J7
Lycrome Rd CSHM HP5 131 K7
Lydia Ms BRKMPK AL9 138 F3
Lye Green Rd CSHM HP5 131 K9
Lye Hl HTCHE/RSTV SG4 64 C7
Lye La LCOL/BKTW AL2 135 P9
The Lye BERK HP4 98 A6
Lygean Av WARE SG12 108 D3
Lygetun Dr LTNN/LIM LU3 45 P9
Lygrave STVGE SG2 67 M6
Lyles La WGCW AL8 105 H4
Lyle's Rw HTCHE/RSTV SG4 49 L1
Lymans Rd ARL/CHE SG15 24 E3
Lyme Av BERK HP4 115 J4
Lymington Ct GSTN WD25 * 149 H4
Lymington Rd STVG SG1 50 E7
Lynch Hl DUN/WHIP LU6 79 K5
The Lynch HOD EN11 126 G5
Lyncroft Av PIN HA5 171 M9
Lyndale STVG SG1 10 E6
Lyndhurst Av PIN HA5 171 K5
Lyndhurst Cl HARP AL5 102 B2
Lyndhurst Dr HARP AL5 102 B2
Lyndhurst Gdns PIN HA5 171 K5
Lyndhurst Rd CSHM HP5 130 G7
LTN LU1 6 B4
Lyndon Av PIN HA5 171 N3
Lyndon Md STALE/WH AL4 121 H1
Lyndsey Pl CHESW EN7 * 142 A9
Lyne Wy HHW HP1 117 J6
Lynford Cl BAR EN5 165 M4
Lynford Gdns EDGW HA8 165 H9
Lynmouth Rd WGCE AL7 105 J6
Lynn Cl KTN/HRWW/WS HA3 172 D6
Lynn St ENC/FH EN2 155 L9
Lynsey Cl STALW/RED AL3 101 H5
Lynton Av ARL/CHE SG15 24 E4
STAL AL1 121 H9
Lynton Md TRDG/WHET N20 166 E9
Lynton Pde CHES/WCR EN8 142 C9
Lynton Rd CSHM HP5 130 G7
Lynwood Av LTNE LU2 63 H3
Lynwood Dr NTHWD HA6 170 G5
Lynwood Hts
RKW/CH/CXG WD3 160 F4
Lyon Meade STAN HA7 173 J5
Lyonsdown Av BAR EN5 166 G5
Lyonsdown Rd BAR EN5 166 G4
Lyon Wy STALE/WH AL4 121 M8
Lyrical Wy HHW HP1 117 L6
Lysander Cl HHS/BOV HP3 132 C6
Lysander Wy ABLGY WD5 149 H2
WGCE AL7 105 N5
Lys Hill Gdns HERT/WAT SG14 107 J4
Lysley Pl BRKMPK AL9 139 M6
Lytchet Wy PEND EN3 156 B9
Lytham Av OXHEY WD19 171 M2
Lytton Av LWTH SG6 36 C3
PEND EN3 156 D8
Lytton Flds KNEB SG3 67 J9
Lytton Gdns WGCW AL8 104 G6
Lytton Rd BAR EN5 166 G3
PIN HA5 171 N4
Lyttons Wy HOD EN11 126 F2
Lytton Wy STVG SG1 10 A1

M

Mabbutt Cl LCOL/BKTW AL2 135 M9
Mabey's Wk SBW CM21 111 L3
Macaret Cl TRDG/WHET N20 166 F6
Macaulay Rd LTNW/LEA LU4 61 K4
Macdonald Cl AMS HP6 145 H5
Macdonnell Gdns GSTN WD25 148 G5
Macer's La BROX EN10 142 E3
Macintosh Cl CHESW EN7 141 L5
Mackenzie Sq STVGE SG2 67 L3
Mackerel Hall ROY SG8 20 A4
Maddesfield Ct RAD WD7 151 K3
Maddles LWTH SG6 36 G4
Maddox Rd HHNE HP2 118 C8
HLW CM20 3 G3
Made Feld STVG SG1 11 G4
Madeley Cl AMS HP6 145 J6
Madgeways Cl WARE SG12 * 108 E7
Madgeways La WARE SG12 108 E7
Magdalene Cl BGSW SG18 14 C6
Magellan Cl STVGE SG2 67 N1
Magna Cl HARP AL5 102 C6
Magnaville Rd BSF CM23 91 P1
BUSH WD23 163 N6
Magnolia Av ABLGY WD5 148 G2
Magnolia Cl HERT/BAY SG13 107 P6
LCOL/BKTW AL2 136 C5
Magpie Cl EN EN1 155 P9
Magpie Crs STVGE SG2 67 N2
Magpie Hall Rd STAN HA7 163 N8
Magpie La AMSS HP7 158 A7
Magpie Pl GSTN WD25 * 149 K2
The Magpies LTNE LU2 46 E9
Mahon Cl EN EN1 155 N9
Maidenbower Av
DUN/WHIP LU6 60 C5
Maidenhall Rd
LTNW/LEA LU4 62 B4
Maidenhead St
HERT/WAT SG14 107 L6
Maidenhead Yd
HERT/WAT SG14 107 L6
Maidens Br ENC/FH EN2 * 155 P7
Maidensfield WGCW AL8 104 G3
Maiden St HTCHE/RSTV SG4 37 M7
Mailers La BSF CM23 58 A1
Main Av NTHWD HA6 161 N9
Main Dr CFSP/GDCR SL9 168 A9
Main Rd HERT/WAT SG14 106 D1
Main Rd South BERK HP4 98 A1
Maitland Rd
RAYLNE/WEN HP22 112 E4
STSD CM24 58 F5
Major Haddock Cl ROY SG8 20 B3
Malcolm Ct STAN HA7 173 J2
Malcolms Wy
STHGT/OAK N14 * 167 N4
Malden Flds BUSH WD23 13 K5
Malden Rd BORE WD6 164 G2
WAT WD17 12 D1
Maldon Ct HARP AL5 102 A2
Malham Cl LTNW/LEA LU4 62 A3
Malins Cl BAR EN5 * 165 P4
Malkin Dr HLWE CM17 129 P4
Malkin Wy WATW WD18 162 A3
Mallard Cl BAR EN5 * 167 H5
Mallard Gdns LTNN/LIM LU3 62 B1
Mallard Ms HARP AL5 102 B1
Mallard Rd ABLGY WD5 149 H1
ROY SG8 20 B4
STVGE SG2 67 N4
Mallards Ct OXHEY WD19 163 H9
Mallards Ri HLWE CM17 129 M3
The Mallards HHS/BOV HP3 134 A4
Mallard Wy GSTN WD25 149 M6
NTHWD HA6 170 E4
Mallion Ct WAB EN9 157 L3
Mallory Gdns EBAR EN4 167 L6
Mallows Gn
HLWW/ROY CM19 128 D7
Mallows Green Rd BSF CM23 57 M5
The Mallow LTNN/LIM LU3 * 62 A3
Mallow Wk CHESW EN7 141 L7
ROY SG8 20 D5
The Mall DUN/HR/TOD LU5 60 F5
LCOL/BKTW AL2 136 B6
Malm Cl RKW/CH/CXG WD3 161 H8
Malmesbury Cl PIN HA5 171 H8
Malmes Cft HHS/BOV HP3 134 D1
Malms Cl DUN/WHIP LU6 78 G4
Malmsdale WGCW AL8 104 G2
Malpas Dr PIN HA5 171 M9
Maltby Dr EN EN1 156 A8
Malthouse Gn LTNE LU2 63 N5
Malthouse La
HTCH/STOT SG5 25 L2
Malthouse Ms
DEN/HRF UB9 * 169 N5
The Malthouse
HERT/WAT SG14 * 107 L6
Malting La MHAD SG10 90 C3
STDN SG11 55 K8
TRING HP23 97 J7
Malting Md HAT AL10 * 122 F5
Malting Ms HERT/BAY SG13 * 107 K7
Maltings Cl BLDK SG7 26 C8
ROY SG8 20 B3
Maltings Dr STALE/WH AL4 103 H5
Maltings La ROY SG8 22 B8
The Maltings
Norton Hall Farm
LWTH SG6 * 25 N8
Maltings Orch
HTCH/STOT SG5 34 C5
The Maltings AMSS HP7 * 144 G9
HERT/BAY SG13 * 107 M6
KGLGY WD4 148 D3
ROY SG8 * 20 B3
STVGE SG2 52 C7
Maltmans La CFSP/GDCR SL9 168 A7
Malus Cl HHNE HP2 118 B8
Malvern Cl BUSH WD23 163 L5
HAT AL10 122 C5
STALE/WH AL4 120 G4
Malvern Gdns
KTN/HRWW/WS HA3 173 L8
Malvern Rd LTN LU1 62 C7
PEND EN3 156 D7
Malvern Wy HHNE HP2 117 P6
RKW/CH/CXG WD3 161 M4
Malzeard Rd LTNN/LIM LU3 6 B1
Manan Cl HHS/BOV HP3 134 D1
Manchester Cl STVG SG1 51 J4
Manchester Pl
DUN/WHIP LU6 60 E5
Manchester St LTN LU1 6 D4
Mancroft Rd LTN LU1 80 A4
Mandela Av HLW CM20 3 H2
Mandela Pl WATN WD24 13 J1
Mandelyns BERK HP4 115 K4
Mander Cl DUN/HR/TOD LU5 44 C1
Mandeville STVGE SG2 67 M5
Mandeville Cl BROX EN10 126 E8
HERT/BAY SG13 107 K9
WAT WD17 148 G8
Mandeville Dr STAL AL1 136 C2
Mandeville Ri WGCW AL8 104 G4
Mandeville Rd
HERT/BAY SG13 107 K9
PEND EN3 156 D6
POTB/CUF EN6 153 M2
STHGT/OAK N14 167 M8
Mangrove Dr
HERT/BAY SG13 107 M8
Mangrove La
HERT/BAY SG13 125 N4
Mangrove Rd
HERT/BAY SG13 107 M7
LTNE LU2 63 K3
Manhattan Av WATW WD18 12 A4
Manland Av HARP AL5 102 B2
Manland Wy HARP AL5 102 B2
Manley Hwy HTCH/STOT SG5 34 G9
Manly Dixon Dr PEND EN3 156 D7
Mannicotts WGCW AL8 104 E6
Manning Pl LTNE LU2 63 M4
Manns Rd EDGW HA8 173 N3
Manor Av HHS/BOV HP3 133 N2
Manor Cl BAR EN5 166 C3
BERK HP4 * 115 P7
CDALE/KGS NW9 173 P8
HARP AL5 101 P6
HAT AL10 122 C3
HERT/WAT SG14 107 L4
HTCH/STOT SG5 35 K5
LWTH SG6 36 C5
Manor Cots NTHWD HA6 171 H5
Manor Ct CHES/WCR EN8 * 156 C1
DEN/HRF UB9 169 N6
EN EN1 156 A6
POTB/CUF EN6 * 153 J2
RAD WD7 150 E7
Manor Crs HTCHE/RSTV SG4 49 N1
RAYLNE/WEN HP22 112 D6
Manor Cft EDGW HA8 * 173 N3
Manor Croft Pde
CHES/WCR EN8 * 142 C9
Manor Dr AMS HP6 144 G6
LCOL/BKTW AL2 135 P6
STHGT/OAK N14 167 M6
TRDG/WHET N20 167 J9
Manor Farm Cl
AMP/FLIT/BLC MK45 32 D5
LTNW/LEA LU4 61 M3
Manor Farm Rd EN EN1 156 A5
Manor Farm Stables
KNEB SG3 66 F9
Manor Hatch HLWS CM18 129 K4
Manor Hatch Cl HLWS CM18 129 L4
Manor House Dr
NTHWD HA6 170 D4
STVGE SG2 51 N8
Manor House Gdns
ABLGY WD5 148 E1
Manor Links BSF CM23 74 D3
Manor Pde HAT AL10 122 C3
Manor Pk DUN/HR/TOD LU5 60 E2
Manor Park Crs EDGW HA8 173 N3
Manor Park Dr
RYLN/HDSTN HA2 172 B7
Manor Park Gdns EDGW HA8 173 N2
Manor Pl BORE WD6 * 165 J2
Manor Pound Rd LBUZ LU7 77 P6
Manor Rd
AMP/FLIT/BLC MK45 32 E6
BAR EN5 166 C3
BSF CM23 74 B3
CSHM HP5 130 G8
HAT AL10 122 C3
HLWE CM17 111 M7
HOD EN11 126 F3
LBUZ LU7 77 N6
LCOL/BKTW AL2 137 H5
LOU IG10 157 N8
LTN LU1 7 G6
LTN LU1 79 P2
LTNN/LIM LU3 45 L4
POTB/CUF EN6 153 J1
RAYLNE/WEN HP22 112 D6
STAL AL1 9 H2
STALE/WH AL4 102 E2
STSD CM24 58 F6
TRING HP23 95 P7
WAB EN9 157 J3
WAT WD17 149 J9
Manorside BAR EN5 166 C3
Manor St BERK HP4 116 A7
Manor Vw STVGE SG2 67 L5
Manorville Rd HHS/BOV HP3 133 M3
Manor Wy BORE WD6 165 J3
CSHM HP5 131 J9
LWTH SG6 36 C5
POTB/CUF EN6 139 K9
RKW/CH/CXG WD3 161 L3
RYLN/HDSTN HA2 172 B8
Mansard Cl PIN HA5 171 M7
TRING HP23 95 P9
Manscroft Rd HHW HP1 117 L6
Mansdale Rd
STALW/RED AL3 100 G8
Mansefield Cl CSHM HP5 130 G7
Mansells La HTCHE/RSTV SG4 84 B2
Mansfield SBW CM21 111 K3
Mansfield Av EBAR EN4 167 K5
Mansfield Gdns
HERT/WAT SG14 107 K4
Mansfield Rd BLDK SG7 37 H1
LTNW/LEA LU4 62 C5
Mansion Dr TRING HP23 96 A9
Mansion Hl
RAYLNE/WEN HP22 112 F3
Manston Cl CHES/WCR EN8 142 B9
Manston Dr BSF CM23 74 C1
Manston Rd HLW CM20 3 H6
Manston Wy STALE/WH AL4 121 J9
Manton Dr LTNE LU2 62 E2
Manton Rd DUN/WHIP LU6 60 A9
HTCHE/RSTV SG4 49 N1
PEND EN3 156 F7
Manus Wy TRDG/WHET N20 166 G8
Manx Cl LTNW/LEA LU4 62 B4
Maple Av BSF CM23 73 N6

STALW/RED AL3 120 B4
Maple Cl BSF CM23 73 N6
BUSH WD23 162 G1
HAT AL10 122 D7
Maplecroft La WAB EN9 127 K9
Maplefield LCOL/BKTW AL2 136 A8
Maplefield La CSTG HP8 159 H2
Maple Gn HHW HP1 117 H6
Maple Gv BSF CM23 73 N6
WAT WD17 149 H9
WGCE AL7 105 J3
Maple Leaf Cl ABLGY WD5 149 H2
Maple Lodge Cl
RKW/CH/CXG WD3 169 J1
Maple Rd HARP AL5 101 N3
Maple Rd East
LTNW/LEA LU4 62 C6
Maple Rd West
LTNW/LEA LU4 62 C6
Maples WAB EN9 157 P5
Maple Spring BSF CM23 73 M6
Maple Springs WAB EN9 157 M3
The Maples CHESW EN7 141 M7
HLWW/ROY CM19 128 E8
HTCHE/RSTV SG4 49 L2
RAYLNE/WEN HP22 112 D6
STVGE SG2 * 67 L6
Mapleton Crs PEND EN3 156 B8
Maple Wy DUN/HR/TOD LU5 45 H9
DUN/WHIP LU6 79 H5
ROY SG8 20 D2
Maplewood WARE SG12 108 B1
Maran Av WLYN AL6 84 F9
Marbury Pl LTNN/LIM LU3 * 62 A2
Marchmont Gn HHNE HP2 117 N6
Marconi Wy STALE/WH AL4 121 J8
Mardale Av DUN/WHIP LU6 60 F8
Mardle Cl LTN LU1 79 P3
Mardley Av WLYN AL6 85 J5
Mardleybury KNEB SG3 85 K4
Mardleybury Ct KNEB SG3 * 85 K3
Mardleybury Rd KNEB SG3 85 K4
Mardley Dell WLYN AL6 85 J4
Mardley Hts WLYN AL6 85 K5
Mardley Hl WLYN AL6 85 J5
Mardley Wd WLYN AL6 85 J4
Mardyke Rd HLW CM20 129 K1
Marford Rd STALE/WH AL4 103 L4
WGCW AL8 104 A6
Margaret Av STALW/RED AL3 120 C6
Margaret Cl ABLGY WD5 148 G2
POTB/CUF EN6 153 M3
WAB EN9 157 J3
Margaret Rd EBAR EN4 167 H3
Margeholes OXHEY WD19 162 G8
Margery Wd WGCE AL7 105 K2
Margherita Pl WAB EN9 157 L4
Margrave Gdns BSF CM23 73 P9
Margrett La
AMP/FLIT/BLC MK45 32 C3
Marguerite Wy BSF CM23 73 M8
Marian Gdns GSTN WD25 149 J3
Maricas Av
KTN/HRWW/WS HA3 172 D5
Marigold Pl HLWE CM17 * 111 L8
Marina Dr DUN/WHIP LU6 60 B7
Marina Gdns CHES/WCR EN8 142 B9
Mariner Wy HHNE HP2 118 B9
Marion Cl BUSH WD23 149 N9
Marion Wk HHNE HP2 * 118 A3
Marish La DEN/HRF UB9 168 G8
Mark Dr CFSP/GDCR SL9 168 B1
Markeston Gn OXHEY WD19 171 M1
Market Hl BUNT SG9 40 D9
ROY SG8 20 C4
Market Oak La HHS/BOV HP3 134 B3
Market Pl CFSP/GDCR SL9 168 B5
HAT AL10 122 E5
HERT/WAT SG14 107 L6
HTCH/STOT SG5 35 K9
STALW/RED AL3 8 E4
STVG SG1 10 D5
WAT WD17 13 G4
Market Sq BSF CM23 74 A3
DUN/HR/TOD LU5 44 D1
HLW CM20 2 E4
LTN LU1 62 C8
STVG SG1 10 D5
Market St HERT/WAT SG14 107 L6
HLWE CM17 111 M8
WATW WD18 13 F5
Market Wk AMSS HP7 * 158 B1
Markfield Cl LTNN/LIM LU3 46 D9
Mark Hall Moors HLW CM20 111 L9
Markham Cl BORE WD6 164 F2
Markham Crs
DUN/HR/TOD LU5 61 H4
Markham Rd CHESW EN7 141 K5
LTNN/LIM LU3 46 D7
Mark Rd HHNE HP2 118 B6
Markwells RBSF CM22 59 L1
Markwell Wd
HLWW/ROY CM19 128 E9
Markyate Rd STALW/RED AL3 80 B5
Marlands SBW CM21 92 A5
Marlborough Av EDGW HA8 165 H9
STHGT/OAK N14 167 N9
Marlborough Cl BSF CM23 74 A5
HTCHE/RSTV SG4 37 L8
TRDG/WHET N20 167 K9
WLYN AL6 85 J5
Marlborough Gdns
TRDG/WHET N20 167 K9
Marlborough Ga STAL AL1 9 G4
Marlborough Hl HRW HA1 172 E8
Marlborough Pk HARP AL5 102 B5
Marlborough Pl
DUN/HR/TOD LU5 44 C1
Marlborough Ri HHNE HP2 117 P5
Marlborough Rd
LTNN/LIM LU3 62 D5
STAL AL1 9 G4
STVGE SG2 67 M1
WATW WD18 12 E4
Marle Gdns WAB EN9 157 H2
Marley Rd WGCE AL7 105 K8
Marlin Cl BERK HP4 115 L6
Marlin Copse BERK HP4 115 M8
Marlin Ct LTNW/LEA LU4 61 H2
Marlin Hl TRING HP23 113 P2
Marlin Rd LTNW/LEA LU4 61 H3
Marlins Cl RKW/CH/CXG WD3 160 C1
Marlins End BERK HP4 115 L8
Marlins Meadow
WATW WD18 161 P5
Marlin Sq ABLGY WD5 148 G1
The Marlins NTHWD HA6 171 H3
Marlins Turn HHW HP1 117 L5
Marlow Av LTN LU1 62 B6
Marlowe Cl STVGE SG2 51 M7
Marlowes HHNE HP2 4 E2
Marmet Av LWTH SG6 36 B2
Marnham Ri HHW HP1 117 K6
Marquis Cl BSF CM23 73 L7
HARP AL5 102 C2
Marquis La HARP AL5 102 C2
Married Quarters
EDGW HA8 * 173 P4
Marrilyne Av PEND EN3 156 E8
Marriott Rd BAR EN5 166 B2
LTNN/LIM LU3 46 C9
Marriotts Wy HHNE HP2 5 F5
Marriotts Yd BAR EN5 * 166 B2
Marriott Ter
RKW/CH/CXG WD3 160 D3
Marryat Rd EN EN1 156 A5
Marschefield HTCH/STOT SG5 25 J3
Marsden Cl WGCW AL8 104 E8
Marsden Gn WGCW AL8 104 E7
Marsden Rd WGCW AL8 104 E7
Marshall Av STALW/RED AL3 120 D5
Marshall Rd LTNE LU2 63 K4
Marshalls Heath La HARP AL5 82 F8
Marshall's La STDN SG11 88 C3
WARE SG12 87 P1
Marshalls Wy STALE/WH AL4 102 E2
Marshal's Dr STAL AL1 120 F5
Marshalswick La STAL AL1 120 F5
Marsham La CFSP/GDCR SL9 168 D9
Marsham Wy
CFSP/GDCR SL9 168 C9
Marshbarns BSF CM23 73 M6
Marsh Cl CHES/WCR EN8 156 E3
MLHL NW7 165 M9
Marshcroft Dr
CHES/WCR EN8 142 D9
Marshcroft La TRING HP23 96 C6
Marshe Cl POTB/CUF EN6 153 N2
Marshgate STVG SG1 10 D4
Marshgate Dr
HERT/BAY SG13 107 M5
Marsh Hl WAB EN9 143 K6
Marsh La HLWE CM17 111 P7
MLHL NW7 165 L9
STAN HA7 173 J2
WARE SG12 109 J9
Marshmoor Crs BRKMPK AL9 138 G1
Marshmoor La BRKMPK AL9 138 F1
Marsh Rd LTNN/LIM LU3 61 P1
PIN HA5 171 N8
The Marsh ROY SG8 * 29 L4
Marsom Gv LTNN/LIM LU3 46 C7
Marston Cl CSHM HP5 130 F6
HHS/BOV HP3 118 B9
Marston Ct TRING HP23 * 77 J9
Marston Gdns LTNE LU2 62 E2
Marston Rd HOD EN11 126 G4
Marsworth Av PIN HA5 171 M5
Marsworth Cl WATW WD18 * 162 A5
Marten Ga STALE/WH AL4 120 F4
Marthorne Crs
KTN/HRWW/WS HA3 172 D6
Martian Av HHNE HP2 118 A5
Martin Cl HAT AL10 122 D8
Martindale Rd HHW HP1 117 J7
The Martindales LTNE LU2 * 7 H4
Martinfield WGCE AL7 105 J5
Martingale Rd ROY SG8 20 D4
Martini Dr PEND EN3 156 F7
Martins Cl RAD WD7 150 D6
Martins Dr CHES/WCR EN8 142 D7
HERT/BAY SG13 108 A6
Martins Mt BAR EN5 166 E3
Martins Wy STVG SG1 50 F7
Martin Wy LWTH SG6 36 A3
Martlesham WGCE AL7 105 P6
Martock Cl
KTN/HRWW/WS HA3 172 G8
Martyr Cl STAL AL1 136 C3
Marwood Cl KGLGY WD4 134 A8
Mary Cl KTN/HRWW/WS HA3 173 M8
Mary Cross Cl TRING HP23 114 C2
Marygold Wk AMS HP6 145 P9
Maryland HAT AL10 122 C6
Mary McArthur Pl STSD CM24 58 F3
Marymead Ct STVGE SG2 67 K6
Marymead Dr STVGE SG2 67 K6
Mary Park Gdns BSF CM23 74 A6
Maryport Rd LTNW/LEA LU4 62 B4
Mary Proud Ct WLYN AL6 * 85 H6
Maryrose Wy
TRDG/WHET N20 167 H7
Mary Wy OXHEY WD19 171 L1
Masefield HTCHE/RSTV SG4 35 P9
Masefield Av BORE WD6 165 H4
STAN HA7 172 F2
Masefield Ct HARP AL5 82 A9
Masefield Crs
STHGT/OAK N14 167 N4
Masefield Rd HARP AL5 102 A1
Masefield Wy ROY SG8 20 C1
Mason Cl BORE WD6 165 K1
WAB EN9 157 L4
Masons Av
KTN/HRWW/WS HA3 172 E7
Masons Ct BSF CM23 73 P7
Masons Pde CHESW EN7 * 141 K7
Masons Rd EN EN1 156 A6
HHNE HP2 118 C7
Mason Wy WAB EN9 157 K3
Masters Cl LTN LU1 62 C9
Matching La BSF CM23 73 N6
Matching Rd RBSF CM22 93 J9
Mathams Dr BSF CM23 73 N9
Mathews Cl STVG SG1 50 G6
Matlock Cl BAR EN5 166 B4
Matlock Crs LTNW/LEA LU4 61 M5
OXHEY WD19 162 E9
Matthew Ga
HTCHE/RSTV SG4 49 M2
Matthew St DUN/WHIP LU6 60 E6
Mattocke Rd HTCH/STOT SG5 35 H7
Maude Crs WATN WD24 149 J7
Maulden Cl LTNE LU2 63 K5
Maundsey Cl DUN/WHIP LU6 60 F9
Maunds Hatch HLWS CM18 128 G7
Maxfield Cl TRDG/WHET N20 166 G6
Maxted Cl HHNE HP2 118 D6
Maxted Cnr HHNE HP2 * 118 C5
Maxted Rd HHNE HP2 118 C5
Maxwell Cl
RKW/CH/CXG WD3 160 E8
Maxwell Ri OXHEY WD19 162 G6
Maxwell Rd BORE WD6 165 H2
NTHWD HA6 170 F4
STAL AL1 120 G9
STVG SG1 66 E1
Mayall Cl PEND EN3 156 F8
Maybank Gdns PIN HA5 171 J9
Maybury Av CHES/WCR EN8 142 A7
Maybury Cl EN EN1 156 A8
Maychurch Cl STAN HA7 173 K5
May Cl STALW/RED AL3 120 C6
Maycock Gv NTHWD HA6 171 H3
Maycroft LWTH SG6 25 L8
PIN HA5 171 K6
Maycroft Rd CHESW EN7 141 M5
Maydencroft La
HTCH/STOT SG5 49 J3
Maydwell Ldg BORE WD6 164 F1
Mayer Wy DUN/HR/TOD LU5 60 D3
Mayes Cl BSF CM23 74 E2
Mayfair Cl STALE/WH AL4 121 H3
Mayfair Ct EDGW HA8 173 M2
Mayfair Ter STHGT/OAK N14 167 P6
Mayfare RKW/CH/CXG WD3 161 P4
Mayfield WGCW AL8 104 F2
Mayfield Av
KTN/HRWW/WS HA3 173 H9
STHGT/OAK N14 167 N8
Mayfield Cl HARP AL5 101 M1
Mayfield Dr PIN HA5 171 P8
Mayfield Pk BSF CM23 91 N2
Mayfield Rd DUN/WHIP LU6 60 G8
LTNE LU2 63 J2
Mayflower Av HHNE HP2 5 F1
Mayflower Cl
HERT/WAT SG14 106 F8
HTCHE/RSTV SG4 84 C4
WAB EN9 143 K2
Mayflower Gdns BSF CM23 73 L8
Mayflower Rd
LCOL/BKTW AL2 136 A6
May Gdns BORE WD6 164 D5
Mayhall La AMS HP6 144 G5
Mayhill Rd BAR EN5 166 C4
Maylands Av HHNE HP2 118 C6
Maylands Rd OXHEY WD19 171 L1
Mayles Cl STVG SG1 50 E8
Maylin Cl HTCHE/RSTV SG4 35 P8
Maylins Dr SBW CM21 111 N2
Maynard Dr STAL AL1 136 C2
Maynard Pl POTB/CUF EN6 140 F8
Maynard Rd HHNE HP2 4 E3
Mayne Av LTNW/LEA LU4 61 M2
STALW/RED AL3 135 N1
Mayo Cl CHES/WCR EN8 142 B7
Mayo Gdns HHW HP1 4 B4
Maypole St HLWE CM17 129 M2
Maypole Yd DUN/WHIP LU6 * 60 E6
Mayshades Cl KNEB SG3 85 K3
May's La BAR EN5 165 P6
May St LTN LU1 7 F7
ROY SG8 22 B8
Maythorne Cl WATW WD18 162 A3
Maytree Cl EDGW HA8 165 J9
Maytree Crs WATN WD24 148 G6
Maytree La STAN HA7 172 F3
Maytrees HTCHE/RSTV SG4 49 M1
RAD WD7 150 F7
May Wk STSD CM24 59 H2
Maze Green Hts BSF CM23 73 M7
Maze Green Rd BSF CM23 73 N7
Mazoe Cl BSF CM23 74 A5
Mazoe Rd BSF CM23 74 A5
McAdam Cl HOD EN11 126 F3
McDonald Ct HAT AL10 122 D8
McDougall Rd BERK HP4 116 A7
McEwen Ride
RAYLNE/WEN HP22 112 E2
McGredy CHESW EN7 142 A8
Mc Kellar Cl BUSH WD23 163 L8
Mc Kenzie Rd BROX EN10 126 F8
Mead Cl KTN/HRWW/WS HA3 172 D5
STVG SG1 11 H3
Mead Ct WAB EN9 156 G4
Meades La CSHM HP5 144 G2
Meadfield EDGW HA8 165 H8
Meadgate Rd WAB EN9 127 J8
Meadhook Dr
AMP/FLIT/BLC MK45 32 C5
Mead La HERT/BAY SG13 107 M5
Meadow Av RAD WD7 151 H1
Meadowbank
HTCHE/RSTV SG4 35 N7
KGLGY WD4 134 B9
OXHEY WD19 162 E6
Meadow Bank Cl AMSS HP7 145 K8
Meadowbank Cl
HHS/BOV HP3 132 E7
Meadowbanks BAR EN5 165 M4
Meadowbrook TRING HP23 96 A6
Meadow Cl BAR EN5 166 D5
BRKMPK AL9 138 G3
CSHM HP5 * 130 F6
HERT/BAY SG13 107 N5
KNEB SG3 85 N3
LCOL/BKTW AL2 135 P8
PEND EN3 156 D9
RAD WD7 137 H9
STALE/WH AL4 121 H5
TRING HP23 95 P8
Meadow Cft HAT AL10 122 C6
Meadowcroft BERK HP4 115 J4
BUSH WD23 * 163 K5
CFSP/GDCR SL9 168 B6
STAL AL1 136 F2
STSD CM24 58 F3
Meadowcross WAB EN9 157 K4
Meadow Dell HAT AL10 122 C6
Meadow Dr AMS HP6 145 K7
Meadow Gdns EDGW HA8 173 P3
Meadow Gn WGCW AL8 104 F6
Meadowlands BAR EN5 165 M4
BSF CM23 74 B1
Meadow La
DUN/HR/TOD LU5 60 E1
LBUZ LU7 96 D1
Meadow Rd BERK HP4 115 N5
BORE WD6 165 H1
BUSH WD23 163 K4
DUN/HR/TOD LU5 44 B2
GSTN WD25 149 H4
HHS/BOV HP3 134 B4
LTNN/LIM LU3 62 C2
PIN HA5 171 M8
Meadow Road Cl BERK HP4 115 M5
Meadowside GSTN WD25 149 J1
The Meadows AMSS HP7 145 K9
BSF CM23 73 P9
HHW HP1 117 H7
HTCHE/RSTV SG4 64 D5
LBUZ LU7 44 B6
SBW CM21 92 B7
Meadowsweet Cl BSF CM23 73 M8
The Meadow HERT/BAY SG13 126 D1
STALW/RED AL3 * 101 J7
WGCE AL7 105 M6
Meadow Vw BUNT SG9 54 C1
CSTG HP8 158 G9
HTCHE/RSTV SG4 65 L8
STALW/RED AL3 101 H4
Meadow Wk HARP AL5 102 B4
STDN SG11 71 K4
Meadow Wy AMS HP6 144 B5
HHS/BOV HP3 133 J2
HTCH/STOT SG5 25 J3
HTCH/STOT SG5 35 K8
HTCHE/RSTV SG4 84 B4
LTN LU1 79 P1
LWTH SG6 36 C3
POTB/CUF EN6 153 K4
RKW/CH/CXG WD3 160 G6
ROY SG8 28 G3
SBW CM21 92 B8
STVG SG1 11 H4
The Meadow Wy
KTN/HRWW/WS HA3 172 E5
Mead Pl RKW/CH/CXG WD3 160 F7
Mead Rd EDGW HA8 173 N3
RAD WD7 151 M3
Meads Cl DUN/HR/TOD LU5 60 E1
Meads Ctyd STVGE SG2 * 51 M8
Meads La STALE/WH AL4 103 J3
Meads Rd PEND EN3 156 D9
The Meads BERK HP4 115 L5
LCOL/BKTW AL2 135 N8
LTNN/LIM LU3 62 B3
LWTH SG6 36 B2
The Mead BROX EN10 * 126 G9
CHES/WCR EN8 142 B8
HTCH/STOT SG5 35 K6
OXHEY WD19 162 G9
Mead Vw BUNT SG9 57 H1
Meadview Rd WARE SG12 108 B4
Meadway BAR EN5 166 E3
BERK HP4 116 B6
Mead Wy BUSH WD23 162 G1
Meadway DUN/WHIP LU6 60 D7
HARP AL5 102 D5
HOD EN11 126 F7
KNEB SG3 85 J1
PEND EN3 156 C6
STALE/WH AL4 138 A2
STHGT/OAK N14 167 P8
STVG SG1 50 D9
WGCE AL7 105 J8
Meadway Cl BAR EN5 166 E2
PIN HA5 172 B3
The Meadway
POTB/CUF EN6 140 G7
Meautys STALW/RED AL3 135 N1
Medalls Link STVGE SG2 67 K3
Medalls Pth STVGE SG2 67 K3
Medcalf Rd PEND EN3 156 E7
Medina Rd LTNW/LEA LU4 62 B5
Medlars Md RBSF CM22 93 N4
Medlows HARP AL5 101 M2
Medow Md RAD WD7 150 E3
Medway Cl GSTN WD25 149 K4
Medway Rd HHNE HP2 118 A3
Medwick Ms HHNE HP2 118 C3
Mees Cl LTNN/LIM LU3 46 A6
Meeting Aly WAT WD17 * 13 G4
Meeting House La BLDK SG7 26 A8
BUNT SG9 40 D9
Megg La KGLGY WD4 133 L8
Melbourne Av PIN HA5 172 B7
Melbourne Cl HTCH/STOT SG5 25 K4
STALW/RED AL3 120 E4
Melbourne Ct WGCW AL8 104 E7
Melbourne Rd BUSH WD23 163 K4
Melbourn Rd ROY SG8 20 D3
Melbourn St ROY SG8 20 C4
Melbury Rd
KTN/HRWW/WS HA3 173 M9
Melford Cl LTNE LU2 63 L5
Melia Cl GSTN WD25 149 K5
The Melings HHNE HP2 118 C3
Melling Dr EN EN1 155 P9
Melne Rd STVGE SG2 67 L6
Melrose Av BORE WD6 165 H4
POTB/CUF EN6 153 L3
Melrose Gdns EDGW HA8 173 P7
Melrose Pl WAT WD17 148 G8
Melrose Rd PIN HA5 171 P8
Melson St LTN LU1 7 F4
Melsted Rd HHW HP1 4 A1
Melton Wk DUN/HR/TOD LU5 45 H9
Melvern Cl STVGE SG2 67 L7
Melvyn Cl CHESW EN7 141 J7
Memorial Rd LTNN/LIM LU3 62 A2
Mendip Cl STALE/WH AL4 121 H3
Mendip Rd BUSH WD23 163 L5
Mendip Wy HHNE HP2 117 P5
LTNN/LIM LU3 45 M7
STVG SG1 51 K4
Mendlesham WGCE AL7 105 P6
Mentley La STDN SG11 70 D2
Mentley La East STDN SG11 71 J2
Mentley La West STDN SG11 70 G2
Mentmore Crs
DUN/WHIP LU6 60 F9
Mentmore Rd LBUZ LU7 77 N5
STAL AL1 136 C1
Mentmore Vw TRING HP23 95 N7
Mepham Crs
KTN/HRWW/WS HA3 172 C4
Mepham Gdns
KTN/HRWW/WS HA3 172 C4
Mercer Pl PIN HA5 171 L6
Mercers HHNE HP2 117 P6
HLWW/ROY CM19 128 D6
Mercers Av BSF CM23 91 L1
Mercers Meadow
RAYLNE/WEN HP22 112 C5
Mercers Rw STAL AL1 136 B1
Merchant Dr HERT/BAY SG13 107 N5
Merchants Wk BLDK SG7 26 D8
Mercia Rd BLDK SG7 26 C9
Mercury Wk HHNE HP2 118 A5
Meredews LWTH SG6 36 E1
Meredith Cl PIN HA5 171 M4
Meredith Rd STVG SG1 51 K8
Merefield SBW CM21 111 P3
Meriden Wy GSTN WD25 149 M7
Meridian Wy WAB EN9 156 G4
WARE SG12 108 G7
Merle Av DEN/HRF UB9 169 N6
Merlin Cl WAB EN9 157 M4
Merlin Crs EDGW HA8 173 M5
Merling Cft BERK HP4 115 K5
Merlin Wy GSTN WD25 148 G4
Mermaid Cl HTCHE/RSTV SG4 35 N9
Merrick Cl STVG SG1 51 L3
Merrifield Ct WGCE AL7 104 G9
Merrill Pl BSF CM23 73 P9
Merring Wy WAB EN9 128 C9
Merrion Av STAN HA7 173 K2
Merritt Wk BRKMPK AL9 138 E2
Merrivale STHGT/OAK N14 167 P4
Merrow Dr HHW HP1 117 H7
Merrows Cl NTHWD HA6 170 E3
Merryfield Gdns STAN HA7 173 J2
Merryfields STALE/WH AL4 121 K8
Merry Hill Mt BUSH WD23 163 K7
Merry Hill Rd BUSH WD23 163 J6
Mersey Pl HHNE HP2 118 A3
LTN LU1 6 C4
Mersham Dr CDALE/KGS NW9 173 N9
Merton Rd ENC/FH EN2 155 L8
WATW WD18 12 E5
Meryfield Cl BORE WD6 164 F1
Metford Crs PEND EN3 156 F8
Methuen Cl EDGW HA8 173 N4
Methuen Rd EDGW HA8 173 N4
Metropolitan Ms
WATW WD18 162 A3
Metropolitan Station Ap
WATW WD18 12 A4
Meux Cl CHESW EN7 155 P1
The Mews Norton Hall Farm
LWTH SG6 * 25 N8
The Mews HARP AL5 * 102 A3
RBSF CM22 74 B7
SBW CM21 111 P1
WATW WD18 * 13 G5
Meyer Gn EN EN1 155 P8
Meyrick Av LTN LU1 6 A6
Mezen Cl NTHWD HA6 170 F2
Michaels Rd BSF CM23 58 B9
Michigan Cl BROX EN10 142 D5
Micholls Av CFSP/GDCR SL9 168 C2
Micklefield Rd HHNE HP2 118 D8
Micklefield Wy BORE WD6 151 K8
Micklem Dr HHW HP1 117 J7
Midcot Wy BERK HP4 115 L5
Mid Cross La CFSP/GDCR SL9 168 D2
Middle Dene MLHL NW7 165 K9
Middle Down GSTN WD25 150 A6
Middle Drift ROY SG8 20 B4
Middle Fld
RAYLNE/WEN HP22 94 A9
Middlefield HAT AL10 122 D5
WGCE AL7 123 H1
Middlefield Av HOD EN11 126 F3
Middlefield Cl HOD EN11 126 F3
STALE/WH AL4 121 H5
Middlefield Rd HOD EN11 126 F3
Middlefields LWTH SG6 25 K9
Middlefields Ct LWTH SG6 * 25 K8
Middle Furlong BUSH WD23 163 K3
Middlehill HHW HP1 117 H8
Middleknights Hl HHW HP1 117 K6
Middle La HHS/BOV HP3 146 D1
Middle Meadow CSTG HP8 159 H9
Middle Ope WATN WD24 149 J7
Middle Rd BERK HP4 115 N7
EBAR EN4 167 J5
WAB EN9 156 G2
Middle Rw BSF CM23 74 A4
STVG SG1 10 B1
Middlesborough Cl STVG SG1 51 J5
Middle St SAFWS CB11 43 M4
WAB EN9 143 K1
Middleton Dr PIN HA5 171 J7
Middleton Rd LTNE LU2 63 L2
RKW/CH/CXG WD3 160 E7
Middle Wy WATN WD24 149 J7
The Middle Wy
KTN/HRWW/WS HA3 172 F6
Midhurst LWTH SG6 25 J9
Midhurst Gdns LTNN/LIM LU3 62 D1
Midland Rd HHNE HP2 4 E1
LTNE LU2 6 E3
Midway STALW/RED AL3 136 A2
Milburn Cl LTNN/LIM LU3 46 C6
Mildmay Rd STVG SG1 51 L7
Mildred Av BORE WD6 164 G3
WATW WD18 12 B5
Mile Cl WAB EN9 157 H3
Mile House Cl STAL AL1 136 F2
Mile House La STAL AL1 136 E2
Miles Cl HLWW/ROY CM19 128 E4
Milestone Cl STVGE SG2 67 N2
Milestone Rd HLWE CM17 129 M1
HTCH/STOT SG5 35 J7
KNEB SG3 67 K9
Miles Wy TRDG/WHET N20 167 J8
Miletree Crs DUN/WHIP LU6 60 G8

Milford Cl STALE/WH AL4 * 121 J4
Milford Gdns EDGW HA8 ...... 173 N4
Milford Hl HARP AL5 .... 82 C9
Milksey La HTCHE/RSTV SC4 ... 50 E2
Millacres WARE SG12 * 108 D3
Millais Gdns EDGW HA8 .... 173 N6
Millard Ct BORE WD6 .... 152 A9
Millard Wy HTCHE/RSTV SC4 ... 36 B5
Millbank HHS/BOV HP3 .... 133 N3
Mill Br BAR EN5 * 166 D4
HERT/WAT SG14 .... 107 K6
Millbrook Rd BUSH WD23 ...... 149 N9
Mill Cswy ROY SG8 .... 22 F5
Mill Ct BUNT SG9 .... 40 D9
CSHM HP5 .... 145 K4
HHS/BOV HP3 .... 134 B4
HHW HP1 .... 117 L4
HTCH/STOT SG5 .... 25 J5
HTCHE/RSTV SC4 .... 36 A8
RAYLNE/WEN HP22 * 59 K2
RBSF CM22 .... 59 K2
Mill Cnr BAR EN5 .... 153 J9
HLWW/ROY CM19 .... 127 M2
ROY SG8 .... 29 L4
Millcrest Rd CHESW EN7 ...... 147 J7
Millcroft BSF CM23 .... 74 B1
Mill End STDN SG11 .... 71 L4
Millennium Whf
RKW/CH/CXG WD3 * 161 J7
Miller Av PEND EN3 .... 156 F8
Miller Cl STALW/RED AL3 ...... 101 J7
Miller Pl CFSP/GDCR SL9 ...... 168 B9
Millers Cl BSF CM23 .... 73 M9
Millersdale HLWW/ROY CM19 .. 128 E7
Millers La WARE SG12 .... 109 H8
Millers Lay DUN/HR/TOD LU5 .. 65 J4
Millers Ri STAL AL1 * 9 G6
Millers Vw MHAD SG10 .... 90 B4
Millers Wy DUN/HR/TOD LU5 .. 66 D2
Miller Wy STVG SG1 .... 10 E2
Mill Farm CI PIN HA5 .... 171 L6
Mill Fld HLWE CM17 .... 111 M8
Millfield BERK HP4 .... 116 A6
WARE SG12 .... 108 B7
WCCE AL7 .... 104 D7
Millfield La HTCHE/RSTV SC4 ... 49 L5
LTN LU1 .... 79 M2
STDN SG11 .... 72 C6
Millfield Ms HLWE CM17 ...... 79 N3
Millfield Rd LTNN/LIM LU3 .... 45 J5
SBW CM21 .... 92 A6
STSD CM24 .... 58 F5
Millfields HHS/BOV HP3 ...... 134 B2
Millfield Wk HLWE CM17 ...... 79 N3
Mill Green La HERT/BAY SG13 .. 98 A8
Mill Green La ABLGY WD5 ..... 123 H2
Mill Green Rd WCCE AL7 ...... 105 H7
Mill HI BSF CM23 .... 73 P1
ROY SG8 .... 20 C6
Millhouse La ABLGY WD5 ...... 135 H6
Millhurst Ms HLWE CM17 ..... 111 P8
Milligan Cl LTNW/LEA LU4 .... 61 N2
Milliners Wy BSF CM23 .... 59 K1
LTNN/LIM LU3 .... 62 D5
Mill La AMP/FLIT/BLC MK45 ... 32 C5
AMSS 144 F9
ARL/CHE SG15 .... 24 D5
BROX EN10 .... 157 K4
BUNT SG9 .... 42 D3
CFSP/GDCR SL9 .... 168 D9
CHES/WCR EN8 .... 142 D7
CSTG HP8 .... 158 C8
HERT/WAT SG14 .... 68 G9
HLWE CM17 .... 111 P8
HTCH/STOT SG5 .... 25 L3
HTCH/STOT SG5 .... 33 J5
HTCHE/RSTV SC4 .... 37 M7
HTCHE/RSTV SC4 .... 49 H4
KGLCY WD4 .... 134 B8
RAYLNE/WEN HP22 .... 76 D3
RAYLNE/WEN HP22 .... 94 B9
RBSF CM22 .... 92 C5
ROY SG8 .... 28 F1
SBW CM21 .... 92 A6
STALW/RED AL3 .... 100 B3
STDN SG11 .... 56 C9
WARE SG12 .... 69 H7
WLYN AL6 .... 84 F8
Mill Lane Cl BROX EN10 ...... 126 E9
Mill Md RAYLNE/WEN HP22 ... 112 C6
Millmead Wy HERT/WAT SG14 . 107 J3
Mill Race WARE SG12 .... 109 J3
Mill Rdg EDGW HA8 .... 173 M2
Mill Rd DUN/HR/TOD LU5 ..... 66 C5
HERT/WAT SG14 .... 107 L6
HTCHE/RSTV SC4 .... 49 L4
ROY SG8 .... 20 C5
Mill Side STSD CM24 .... 58 E5
Millson Ct TRDG/WHET N20 .. 167 H8
Millstream
RAYLNE/WEN HP22 .... 112 A1
Millstream CI HERT/WAT SG14 . 107 J6
HTCHE/RSTV SC4 .... 35 M6
Mill St BERK HP4 .... 115 P7
BSF CM23 .... 74 B5
HHS/BOV HP3 .... 133 N3
HLWE CM17 .... 129 P6
LTN LU1 .... 6 D3
Milltome Ct
RKW/CH/CXG WD3 * 161 K4
Mill View Rd TRING HP23 ..... 95 N8
Mill Wy RKW/CH/CXG WD3 ... 160 D7
BUSH WD23 .... 162 G1
Mill Yd LTN LU1 * 7 F4
Milman Cl PIN HA5 .... 171 M7
Milne Cl LWTH SG6 .... 23 L5
Milne Fld PIN HA5 .... 172 A4
Milner Cl GSTN WD25 .... 149 L4
Milner Ct BUSH WD23 .... 163 K5
Milneway DEN/HRF UB9 ...... 169 M5

Milton Av BAR EN5 .... 166 D4
CDALE/KGS NW9 .... 175 P7
CFSP/GDCR SL9 .... 168 B8
Milton Cl ROY SG8 .... 20 B1
Milton Ct WAB EN9 .... 157 H4
Milton Dr BORE WD6 .... 165 H3
Milton Dr BORE WD6 .... 165 H3
Milton Flds CSTG HP8 .... 159 H9
Milton Lawns AMS HP6 ...... 145 J6
Milton Rd CSHM HP5 .... 130 C8
HARP AL5 .... 119 L4
HHW HP1 .... 172 E8
LTN LU1 .... 6 A6
RAYLNE/WEN HP22 .... 94 G7
WARE SG12 .... 108 C2
Milton St WATN WD24 .... 149 J9
Milton Vw HTCHE/RSTV SC4 .. 35 P9
Milton Wy DUN/HR/TOD LU5 . 65 J3
Milverton Cl LTNN/LIM LU3 ... 46 B8
Milwards HLWW/ROY CM19 ... 128 C7
Mimas Rd HHW HP2 .... 118 A5
Mimms Hall Rd
POTB/CUF EN6 .... 152 C1
Mimms La RAD WD7 .... 151 M3
Mimram CI HTCHE/RSTV SC4 . 65 K7
Mimram Pl WLYN AL6 .... 84 F8
Mimram Rd HERT/WAT SG14 . 107 J7
WLYN AL6 .... 84 F8
Minall Cl TRING HP23 .... 95 N8
Minchenden Crs
STHGT/OAK N14 .... 167 P9
Minchen Rd HLWE CM17 ...... 3 K2
Minehead Wy STVG SG1 .... 50 D8
Mineral Cl BAR EN5 .... 166 A5
Mineral La CSHM HP5 .... 145 H2
Minerva Cl STVGE SG2 .... 51 M6
Minerva Dr WATT WD17 ...... 148 F6
Minister Ct HARP AL5 .... 122 D4
Minister Ct LCOL/BKTW AL2 . 136 D7
Minoan Dr HHS/BOV HP3 ..... 133 P5
Minorca Wy LTNW/LEA LU4 .. 61 K3
Minsden Rd STVGE SG2 .... 52 B2
Minster Cl HAT AL10 .... 122 D8
Minster Rd ROY SG8 .... 20 B2
Minstrel Cl HHW HP1 .... 117 L7
Minterne Rd
KTN/HRWW/WS HA3 .... 173 M9
Minton La HLWE CM17 .... 129 M3
Mirrie La DEN/HRF UB9 ...... 168 C9
Misbourne Av
CFSP/GDCR SL9 .... 168 C2
Misbourne Cl CFSP/GDCR SL9 . 168 C2
Misbourne Ct AMSS HP7 * 158 B1
Missden Dr HHS/BOV HP3 ..... 134 D1
Missenden Rd CSHM HP5 ..... 130 C5
Miss Joans Ride BERK HP4 .... 78 B6
Mistletoe Hl LTNE LU2 .... 63 K6
Mistley Rd HLWE CM17 .... 129 M3
Miswell La TRING HP23 .... 95 N9
Mitchell Cl ABLGY WD5 ...... 149 H2
HHS/BOV HP3 .... 132 C6
STAL AL1 .... 136 C3
Mitchell Wk AMS HP6 .... 145 K8
Mitre Cl HERT/WAT SG14 * ... 107 K8
Mitre Gdns BSF CM23 .... 74 B6
Mixes Hill Rd LTNE LU2 ...... 62 G2
The Mixies HTCH/STOT SG5 .. 25 J3
The Moakes LTNN/LIM LU3 ... 45 P8
Moat CI BUSH WD23 .... 163 K4
Moat Dr HRW HA1 .... 172 C8
Moatfield Rd BUSH WD23 ..... 163 K4
Moat La LTNN/LIM LU3 .... 62 C5
RAYLNE/WEN HP22 .... 76 C3
Moatside BUNT SG9 .... 41 M1
The Moat STDN SG11 .... 71 J3
Moatwood Gn WGCE AL7 ..... 105 H7
Mobbsbury Wy STVGE SG2 .... 51 L8
Mobley Gn LTNE LU2 .... 63 G9
Moelyn Ms HHW HP1 .... 172 C9
Moffats CI BRKMPK AL9 ...... 139 K5
Moffats La BRKMPK AL9 ...... 139 H6
Moira Cl LTNN/LIM LU3 ...... 62 A4
Molescroft HARP AL5 .... 81 L9
Moles La BUNT SG9 .... 40 L5
Molesworth HOD EN11 .... 126 F1
Molewood Rd
HERT/WAT SG14 .... 107 J5
Mollison Av PEND EN3 .... 156 F8
Mollison Wy EDGW HA8 ...... 173 N6
Motteno Rd WATT WD17 ...... 149 H9
Molyneaux Av HHS/BOV HP3 . 132 C6
Momples Rd HLW CM20 ...... 129 K2
Monach's Wy
RKW/CH/CXG WD3 * 156 D3
Monarch Wk RAD WD7 * 151 L3
Monastery Cl STALW/RED AL3 . 8 D4
Moneyhill Rd
RKW/CH/CXG WD3 * 160 F7
Money Hill Rd
RKW/CH/CXG WD3 .... 160 G7
Money Hole La WLYN AL6 ..... 85 H1
Monica Cl WATN WD24 .... 15 J1
Monkfrith Av
STHGT/OAK N14 .... 167 M6
Monkfrith Wy
STHGT/OAK N14 .... 167 M6
Monklands LWTH SG6 .... 36 A2
Monks Av BAR EN5 .... 165 N2
Monksbury HLWS CM18 .... 129 K6
Monks Cl BROX EN10 .... 126 F8
DUN/HR/TOD LU5 .... 65 H5
LWTH SG6 .... 35 P2
STAL AL1 .... 136 F4
STALW/RED AL3 .... 8 C2
Monks Horton Wy STAL AL1 . 120 F6
Monkshead BORE WD6 .... 165 J3
Monks Ri WGCW AL8 .... 104 C2
Monks Rw BARE EN5 .... 166 D4
Monks Vw BUNT SG9 .... 40 C9
Monkswick Rd HLW CM20 .... 3 H2
Monkswood WGCW AL8 ...... 104 F2
Monkswood Av WAB EN9 ..... 157 J5
Monkswood Dr BSF CM23 .... 73 N8
Monkswood Gdns BORE WD6 . 165 K4
Monkswood Wy STVG SG1 .... 10 E7
Monmouth Cl
DUN/HR/TOD LU5 .... 44 B1
Monmouth Rd WAT WD17 .... 13 F2

Monroe Crs EN EN1 .... 156 A9
Monro Gdns
KTN/HRWW/WS HA3 .... 172 E4
Mons Av BLDK SG7 .... 13 J7
Mons Cl HARP AL5 .... 102 C6
Monson Rd BROX EN10 .... 126 E8
Montacute Rd BUSH WD23 .... 163 N6
Montagu Cl BAR EN5 .... 166 D3
Montague Hall Pl
BUSH WD23 .... 163 J5
Montague Rd BERK HP4 ...... 115 N7
Montague Rd CHES/WCR EN8 . 156 C2
Montesole Ct PIN HA5 .... 171 L6
Montgomery Av STVGE SG2 .. 51 N8
Montgomerie Ct BERK HP4 ... 115 M5
Montgomery Av HHNE HP2 ... 118 B7
Montgomery Dr 142 D7
Montgomery Rd EDGW HA8 .. 173 M3
Monton CI LTNN/LIM LU3 .... 46 A9
Montrose Av LTNN/LIM LU3 .. 62 C3
Montrose Rd
KTN/HRWW/WS HA3 .... 172 E6
Monument La
CFSP/GDCR SL9 .... 168 C3
Moolinnock Rd PEND EN5 .... 156 C7
Moon La BAR EN5 .... 166 D2
Moorcroft EDGW HA8 .... 173 P5
Moorcroft Wy PIN HA5 ...... 171 N9
Moore Crs DUN/HR/TOD LU5 . 105 K9
Moorend WGCE AL7 .... 105 K9
Moore End Rd HHNE HP2 ..... 4 D4
Moore Rd BERK HP4 .... 115 L5
Moorfield Rd PEND EN3 ...... 156 B9
Moorfields HLWS CM18 .... 128 D8
Moor Hall La BSF CM23 ...... 91 L2
Moorhall Rd DEN/HRF UB9 ... 169 M3
Moorhen Wy
HLWW/ROY CM19 .... 127 M2
Moorhouse Rd
KTN/HRWW/WS HA3 .... 173 K7
Moorhurst Av CHESW EN7 .... 141 J8
The Moorings BSF CM23 ...... 74 B4
Moorland Gdns LTNE LU2 .... 6 D2
Moorland Rd HARP AL5 .... 82 A9
Moorlands HHW HP1 * 133 J1
Moorlands
LCOL/BKTW AL2 * 136 D7
WGCE AL7 .... 105 K9
Moorlands Reach SBW CM21 . 92 A8
Moor La RKW/CH/CXG WD3 .. 147 H6
Moor Lane Crossing
WATW WD18 .... 161 N6
Moormead Rd
HTCH/STOT SG5 .... 49 H1
Moormead HI
HTCH/STOT SG5 .... 49 H1
Moor Mill La LCOL/BKTW AL2 . 136 D3
Moor Pk RAYLNE/WEN HP22 . 112 C4
Moor Park Gdns
KTN/HRWW/WS HA3 .... 172 E5
Moor Park Rd NTHWD HA6 ... 170 F3
Moor Rd CSHM HP5 .... 145 H3
Moorside WGCE AL7 .... 105 K9
Moors Ley STVGE SG2 .... 52 B6
The Moors WGCE AL7 .... 105 K5
Moor St LTN LU1 .... 6 C5
Moors Wk WGCE AL7 .... 105 L5
Moortown Rd OXHEY WD19 .. 171 L1
Moor Vw WATW WD18 .... 162 C6
Moorymead Cl
WATW WD14 .... 86 C2
Moran Cl LCOL/BKTW AL2 .... 149 N1
Moray Cl EDGW HA8 * 173 P1
Morcambe Cl LTNW/LEA LU4 . 61 L3
Morcom Rd
DUN/HR/TOD LU5 .... 61 N8
Morecambe Cl STVG SG1 ...... 50 E8
Morecambe Gdns STAN HA7 . 173 K1
Morefields TRING HP23 ...... 95 P6
Moreland Av WAB EN9 .... 157 J5
Moreton Av HARP AL5 .... 82 A9
Moreton Cl CHESW EN7 ...... 142 A1
Moreton End Cl HARP AL5 .... 101 N2
Moreton End La HARP AL5 ... 101 N2
Moreton Pl HARP AL5 .... 101 N1
Moreton Rd North LTNE LU2 . 63 H4
Moreton Rd South LTNE LU2 . 63 H4
Morgan Cl LTNW/LEA LU4 .... 61 P3
NTHWD HA6 .... 171 H2
STVG SG1 .... 50 C6
Morgan Gdns GSTN WD25 .... 150 D8
Morgan's Rd HERT/BAY SG13 . 107 L8
Morgan's Rd HERT/BAY SG13 . 107 L8
Morgan's Wk HERT/BAY SG13 . 107 L9
Morice Rd HOD EN11 .... 115 J5
Morland Cl DUN/WHIP LU6 ... 60 D7
Morland Rd
KTN/HRWW/WS HA3 .... 173 K7
Morland Wy CHES/WCR EN8 . 142 D7
Morley Av EDGW HA8 .... 165 J8
Morley Crs East STAN HA7 ... 173 J7
Morley Crs West STAN HA7 .. 173 J7
Morley Gv HLW CM20 .... 2 C5
Morley HI ENC/FH EN2 .... 155 L1
Mornington WLYN AL6 .... 85 K8
Mornington Rd RAD WD7 .... 150 F4
Morningtons
HLWW/ROY CM19 .... 128 F7
Morpeth Av BORE WD6 .... 151 L8
Morpeth Cl HHNE HP2 .... 8 C5
Morrel Cl BAR EN5 .... 166 C2
Morrell Cl LTNN/LIM LU3 .... 46 B8
Morrell Ct WGCE AL7 .... 105 J5
Morrello Gdns
HTCHE/RSTV SC4 .... 49 M2
Morris Cl CFSP/GDCR SL9 .... 168 C5
HNLW SG16 .... 24 A4
Morris Ct WAB EN9 .... 157 L4
Morriston Cl OXHEY WD19 ... 171 H4
Morris Wy LCOL/BKTW AL2 ... 136 E3
Morse Cl DEN/HRF UB9 ...... 169 H4
Mortain Dr BERK HP4 .... 115 K4
Mortens Wd AMSS HP7 ...... 158 D4
Mortimer Cl BUSH WD23 ..... 149 L9
Mortimer Gdns CHES/WCR EN8 142 E6
Mortimer Ga CHES/WCR EN8 . 142 E6
Mortimer HI TRING HP23 ..... 96 A8

Mortimer Ri TRING HP23 ..... 96 A8
Mortimer Rd ROY SG8 .... 20 D4
Morton St BORE WD6 .... 151 L8
Morven Cl POTB/CUF EN6 .... 153 M1
Mosquito Wy HAT AL10 ...... 122 E5
Mossbank CI LTNE LU2 .... 63 K6
Moss Cl PIN HA5 .... 171 P8
Mossdale Ct LTNW/LEA LU4 * . 61 M1
Mossendew Cl DEN/HRF UB9 . 169 P5
Moss Gn WGCE AL7 .... 105 H8
Moss Rd GSTN WD25 .... 149 J4
Moss Side LCOL/BKTW AL2 ... 135 N9
Moss Wy HTCH/STOT SG5 ..... 35 H7
Mostyn Rd BUSH WD23 .... 163 N6
LTNN/LIM LU3 .... 61 P2
Motts Cl HERT/WAT SG14 .... 86 D1
Mott St CHING E4 .... 157 K9
Moules Yd BLDK SG7 .... 13 N6
Moulton Rt LTNE LU2 * 7 G3
Mountbatten Cl STAL AL1 .... 136 C2
Mountbatten Ct WAB EN9 * . 172 G6
Mount Cl EBAR EN4 .... 167 L3
HHW HP1 .... 117 J8
RAYLNE/WEN HP22 .... 94 G8
Mount Dr LCOL/BKTW AL2 ... 136 F6
HRW HA1 .... 171 P9
STSD CM24 .... 58 D5
Mounteagle ROY SG8 .... 20 C5
Mountfield Rd HHNE HP2 .... 5 G4
LTNE LU2 .... 62 F4
Mountfitchet Rd STSD CM24 . 58 C4
Mount Carrison
HTCHE/RSTV SC4 .... 35 L9
Mount Grace Rd LTNE LU2 ... 47 K9
POTB/CUF EN6 .... 153 K1
Mount Gv EDGW HA8 .... 165 P9
Mountjoy HTCHE/RSTV SC4 .. 35 P7
Mount Nugent CSHM HP5 .... 130 F6
Mount Pde EBAR EN4 * 167 J3
Mount Park Rd PIN HA5 ..... 171 J9
Mount Pleasant
DEN/HRF UB9 .... 169 L5
EBAR EN4 .... 167 K3
HERT/BAY SG13 .... 108 B8
HTCH/STOT SG5 .... 49 J1
STAL AL1 .... 10 A6
Mount Pleasant Av
DUN/HR/TOD LU5 .... 44 C3
Mount Pleasant Cl
BRKMPK AL9 .... 122 F3
Mount Pleasant La
BRKMPK AL9 .... 122 F3
LTNE LU2 .... 63 M9
Mount Pleasant Rd
LTNN/LIM LU3 .... 61 P1
STALE/WH AL4 .... 87 H9
Mountsfield
KTN/HRWW/WS HA3 .... 172 F5
Mountsorrel HERT/BAY SG13 . 107 N6
The Mount CHESW EN7 ...... 142 A1
LTNN/LIM LU3 .... 6 D2
POTB/CUF EN6 .... 139 L9
RKW/CH/CXG WD3 .... 160 C5
ROY SG8 .... 21 K9
TRDG/WHET N20 .... 154 C8
Mount Vw ENC/FH EN2 ...... 154 C8
LCOL/BKTW AL2 .... 137 K6
NTHWD HA6 .... 171 J3
Mountview Rd CHESW EN7 ... 141 M5
Mountway POTB/CUF EN6 .... 139 K9
Mowbray Cl STVGE SG2 ...... 105 J9
Mowbray Ct HTCH/STOT SG5 . 25 K9
Mowbray Gdns
HTCHE/RSTV SC4 .... 49 M2
Mowbray Rd BAR EN5 .... 166 C3
EDGW HA8 .... 173 N1
STAN HA7 .... 173 J1
Moxes Wd LTNN/LIM LU3 .... 45 P8
Moxom Av CHES/WCR EN8 ... 142 D9
Moxon St BAR EN5 .... 166 D2
Mozart Ct STVG SG1 .... 10 A4
Muddy La LWTH SG6 .... 36 C5
Mudd La HARP AL5 .... 102 C7
Muirfield LTNE LU2 .... 46 F9
Muirfield Cl OXHEY WD19 .... 171 J3
Muirfield Gn OXHEY WD19 ... 171 J3
Muirfield Rd OXHEY WD19 ... 171 K1
Muirhead Wy KNEB SG3 ...... 67 J9
Mulberry Cl BROX EN10 ...... 142 E5
EBAR EN4 .... 167 H3
LCOL/BKTW AL2 .... 136 A7
TRING HP23 .... 95 P7
Mulberry Cl BSF CM23 .... 74 B5
Mulberry Gdns RAD WD7 .... 151 L3
Mulberry La HAT AL10 .... 111 N8
Mulberry PI HAT AL10 .... 122 B2
Mulberry Pl STALW/RED AL3 . 101 M5
Mulberry Wy HTCH/STOT SG5 . 35 H5
Mullion Cl
KTN/HRWW/WS HA3 .... 172 E5
LTNE LU2 .... 63 J2
Mullion Wk OXHEY WD19 .... 171 M1
Mullway LWTH SG6 .... 35 P2
Mulready Wy HHS/BOV HP3 . 133 P3
Mundells CHESW EN7 .... 141 P6
Munden CI WATN WD24 ...... 149 L8
Munden Rd WARE SG12 ...... 69 M1
Mundesley CI OXHEY WD19 .. 171 J3
Munro Av WATN WD24 ...... 149 K8
Munro Rd BUSH WD23 .... 163 H4
The Muntings STVGE SG2 .... 67 K5
Munts Meadow
HTCHE/RSTV SC4 .... 37 M7
Murchison Rd HOD EN11 ..... 126 C3
Muriel Av WATW WD18 ...... 13 H7

Murray Crs PIN HA5 .... 171 M5
Murray Rd BERK HP4 .... 115 P6
NTHWD HA6 .... 170 C5
Murrell La HTCH/STOT SG5 ... 25 J3
Murton Ct STAL AL1 * 9 H2
Musca Ct LTNW/LEA LU4 * ... 62 A5
Musgrave Cl EBAR EN4 ...... 153 M9
Muskalls Cl CHESW EN7 ...... 141 J6
Muskham Rd HLW CM20 ..... 111 K9
Musk Hl HHW HP1 .... 117 H9
Musleigh Mnr WARE SG12 ... 108 C3
Musley Hl WARE SG12 .... 108 C3
Musley La WARE SG12 .... 108 C3
Mussons CI WATN WD24 * ... 149 J9
Mussons Pth LTNE LU2 ...... 6 E2
Muswell Cl LTNN/LIM LU3 ... 46 C9
Mutchetts Cl GSTN WD25 .... 149 M3
Mutford Cft LTNE LU2 .... 63 L5
Mutton La POTB/CUF EN6 .... 152 C1
Myddelton Av EN EN1 .... 155 M8
Myddelton Pk
TRDG/WHET N20 .... 167 H9
Myddleton Cl STAN HA7 ..... 164 A8
Myddleton Rd WARE SG12 ... 108 C2
Myers CI RAD WD7 .... 151 K2
Myles Ct CHESW EN7 .... 141 K8
Mylne Cl CHES/WCR EN8 ..... 142 B6
Mymms Dr BRKMPK AL9 ..... 139 K6
Myrtle Cl EBAR EN4 .... 167 K7
Myrtle Gv ENC/FH EN2 ...... 155 L8
Myrtleside Cl NTHWD HA6 ... 170 F4
Myson Wy BSF CM23 .... 74 C3

N

Nails La BSF CM23 .... 74 A3
Nairn Cl HARP AL5 .... 102 C6
Nairn Gn OXHEY WD19 ...... 162 C9
Nalders Rd CSHM HP5 .... 131 J8
Nan Aires RAYLNE/WEN HP22 . 76 B2
Nan Clark's La MLHL NW7 ... 165 M8
Nancy Downs OXHEY WD19 .. 171 H1
Napier Cl LCOL/BKTW AL2 ... 137 J4
Napier Dr BUSH WD23 .... 162 G3
Napier Rd LTN LU1 .... 6 A5
Nappsbury Av LTNW/LEA LU4 . 61 N1
Nappsbury Rd LCOL/BKTW AL2 . 137 K9
Nappsbury La STAL AL1 ...... 136 D4
The Nap KGLCY WD4 .... 134 B8
Narcot Rd CSTG HP8 .... 158 B9
Nascot Pl WATT WD17 .... 162 D1
Nascot Rd WATT WD17 .... 162 D1
Nascot Wood Rd WAT WD17 . 148 F7
Naseby Rd LTN LU1 .... 62 C7
Nash Cl BORE WD6 .... 164 F3
BRKMPK AL9 .... 138 C2
DUN/HR/TOD LU5 .... 60 C1
KNEB SG3 .... 51 L9
Nash Gn HHS/BOV HP3 ...... 134 A5
Nashleigh HI CSHM HP5 ..... 131 J5
Nash Mills La HHS/BOV HP3 . 134 A5
Nash Rd ROY SG8 .... 20 B6
Nathaniel Wk TRING HP23 ... 84 F6
Nathans Cl WLYN AL6 .... 84 F6
Nayland Cl LTNE LU2 .... 62 F3
Naylor Rd TRDG/WHET N20 .. 167 J8
Nazeingbury Cl WAB EN9 .... 143 J1
Nazeingbury Pde WAB EN9 * . 143 J1
Nazeing Common WAB EN9 .. 143 P3
Nazeing New Rd BROX EN10 . 126 F7
Neagh Cl STVG SG1 .... 51 M4
Neagle Cl BORE WD6 .... 152 B5
Neal Cl NTHWD HA6 .... 171 J5
Neal St HERT/WAT SG14 ..... 86 C5
Neal St WATW WD18 .... 13 C6
Necton Rd STALE/WH AL4 .... 103 K4
Needham Rd LTNW/LEA LU4 . 61 P2
Neild Wy RKW/CH/CXG WD3 . 160 D6
Nell Gwynn Cl RAD WD7 .... 136 G2
Nelson Av STAL AL1 .... 136 C2
Nelson Rd BSF CM23 .... 74 B5
STAN HA7 .... 173 J2
Nelson St HERT/WAT SG14 ... 107 J5
Neptune Ct BORE WD6 * 164 G2
Neptune Dr HHNE HP2 .... 117 P6
Neptune Ga STVGE SG2 ...... 51 N6
Nesbitts Aly BAR EN5 .... 166 D2
Neston Rd WATN WD24 ...... 149 K7
Netherby Cl TRING HP23 ..... 96 A1
Nethercott Cl LTNE LU2 ..... 63 K5
Nethercott Av LTNW/LEA LU4 . 109 J9
Nethercott HHW HP1 .... 102 A3
Netherfield La WARE SG12 ... 108 A9
Netherhall Rd
HLWW/ROY CM19 .... 127 L5
Netherlands Rd BAR EN5 .... 167 H5
Netherstones
HTCH/STOT SG5 .... 25 K2
Nether St WARE SG12 .... 90 B8
Netherway STALW/RED AL3 .. 8 B6
Netley Dell LWTH SG6 .... 36 E5
Nettleden Rd
HLWS CM18 .... 3 J7
Nettleswell Orch HLW CM20 . 3 J7
Nettleswell Rd HLW CM20 ... 3 G1
Nettle Cl LTNW/LEA LU4 ..... 61 N1
Nettlecroft HHW HP1 .... 117 J7
WGCE AL7 .... 105 L5
Nettleden Rd BERK HP4 ..... 97 P5
Nevells Gn LWTH SG6 .... 36 C2
Nevells Rd LWTH SG6 .... 36 C2
Nevill Cl NTHWD HA6 .... 146 C9
Neville Cl POTB/CUF EN6 .... 153 J1
Neville Rd LTNN/LIM LU3 ... 62 B1
Neville St BSF CM23 .... 74 D3
Nevill Gv WATN WD24 ...... 149 J2
Nevis Rd STVG SG1 .... 51 M4
The New Ar
HERT/WAT SG14 .... 107 L6
Newark Cl ROY SG8 .... 20 A1
Newark Gn BORE WD6 .... 165 K2
Newark Rd LTNW/LEA LU4 ... 61 N2
New Barnes Av STAL AL1 .... 136 F2
New Barn Farm La
DUN/HR/TOD LU5 .... 44 D9

New Barn La RBSF CM22 74 D9
New Barns La MHAD SG10 90 B1
New Bedford Rd LTN LU1 6 D3
Newberries Av RAD WD7 150 G5
Newbiggin Pth OXHEY WD19 171 L1
Newbold Rd LTNN/LIM LU3 46 C8
Newbolt Rd STAN HA7 172 F3
Newbury Av PEND EN3 156 E7
Newbury Cl BSF CM23 73 P6
LTNW/LEA LU4 61 P4
STVG SG1 50 G6
New Bury Meadow
RBSF CM22 93 N4
Newbury Rd
DUN/HR/TOD LU5 45 H9
Newcastle Cl STVG SG1 51 J5
New Chilterns AMSS HP7 * 145 K9
New Cl KNEB SG3 67 J8
Newcombe Rd LTN LU1 6 A4
Newcome Rd RAD WD7 151 M4
New Cots BRKMPK AL9 138 F7
New Ct KNEB SG3 * 85 K3
Newdigate Gn DEN/HRF UB9 169 P5
Newdigate Rd DEN/HRF UB9 169 N5
Newdigate Rd East
DEN/HRF UB9 169 P5
Newell La STVGE SG2 38 D9
Newell Ri HHS/BOV HP3 133 P2
Newell Rd HHS/BOV HP3 133 P2
Newells LWTH SG6 36 G4
New England Cl
HTCHE/RSTV SG4 49 L3
New England St
STALW/RED AL3 8 D3
New Farm La NTHWD HA6 170 G5
New Fiddlers Hl HARP AL5 * 81 K8
Newfield La HHNE HP2 5 J2
Newfields WGCW AL8 104 E7
Newfield Wy STALE/WH AL4 137 H1
Newford Cl HHNE HP2 118 C7
New Ford Rd CHES/WCR EN8 156 E4
Newgale Gdns EDGW HA8 173 M5
Newgate STVGE SG2 67 K3
Newgate Cl STALE/WH AL4 121 J5
Newgatestreet Rd
CHESW EN7 141 J5
Newgate Street Village
HERT/BAY SG13 140 E2
New Greens Av
STALW/RED AL3 120 C3
Newground Rd TRING HP23 96 G9
New Hall Cl HHS/BOV HP3 132 D6
Newhall Cl HHS/BOV HP3 * 132 D6
Newhall Ct WAB EN9 157 L3
Newhouse Crs GSTN WD25 149 J3
New House Pk STAL AL1 136 F2
Newhouse Rd HHS/BOV HP3 132 D5
New Inn Rd BLDK SG7 16 G6
New Kent Rd STAL AL1 9 F4
Newland Cl PIN HA5 171 N3
STAL AL1 136 F2
Newland Dr EN EN1 156 A9
Newland Gdns
HERT/BAY SG13 107 M6
Newlands LWTH SG6 36 D5
Newlands Av RAD WD7 150 E4
Newlands Cl EDGW HA8 164 E9
Newlands Cl East
HTCHE/RSTV SG4 49 L3
Newlands Cl West
HTCHE/RSTV SG4 49 L3
Newlands La
HTCHE/RSTV SG4 49 L3
Newlands Pk ABLGY WD5 * 134 G5
Newlands Pl BAR EN5 166 B4
Newlands Rd HHW HP1 117 H7
LTN LU1 80 E3
Newlands Wk GSTN WD25 149 L3
Newlands Wy POTB/CUF EN6 139 L9
Newlyn Cl LCOL/BKTW AL2 135 M9
STVG SG1 50 D9
Newlyn Rd BAR EN5 166 D3
Newman Av ROY SG8 20 E4
Newmans Dr HARP AL5 101 N2
Newman's Wy EBAR EN4 166 G1
Newmarket Ct
STALW/RED AL3 8 D1
Newmarket Rd ROY SG8 20 D4
Newnham Cl LTNE LU2 63 L5
Newnham Pde
CHES/WCR EN8 * 142 C9
Newnham Rd BLDK SG7 25 P4
Newnham Wy BLDK SG7 17 K9
KTN/HRWW/WS HA3 173 L9
New Pde RKW/CH/CXG WD3 * 161 K5
New Park Dr HHNE HP2 118 C7
New Park La STVGE SG2 67 P4
New Park Rd DEN/HRF UB9 169 N5
HERT/BAY SG13 140 D3
New Pl WLYN AL6 84 E9
Newport Cl PEND EN3 156 D7
Newport Md OXHEY WD19 * 171 M1
Newports SBW CM21 111 M3
Newquay Gdns OXHEY WD19 162 D8
New River Av WARE SG12 108 G8
New River Cl HOD EN11 126 G4
New Rd AMS HP6 145 K7
BERK HP4 115 K5
BORE WD6 164 D5
BROX EN10 126 E7
CSTG HP8 159 L2
GSTN WD25 150 D9
HERT/WAT SG14 107 L4
HLWE CM17 111 N8
KGLGY WD4 133 J9
KNEB SG3 85 L2
POTB/CUF EN6 152 D3
RAD WD7 150 D6
RAD WD7 151 M4
RAYLNE/WEN HP22 94 A9
RBSF CM22 59 J1
RKW/CH/CXG WD3 147 J9
RKW/CH/CXG WD3 161 K4
ROY SG8 15 M6
ROY SG8 21 N1
STDN SG11 72 D7
TRING HP23 95 K3
WARE SG12 108 D3
WAT WD17 13 H5
WGCW AL8 104 D9
WLYN AL6 105 J1
Newstead HAT AL10 122 C9
New St BERK HP4 116 A7
LBUZ LU7 77 N6
LTN LU1 6 D6
SBW CM21 111 P1
WAT WD17 13 G4
Newteswell Dr WAB EN9 157 J2
Newton Cl HARP AL5 102 C6
HOD EN11 126 G1
Newton Crs BORE WD6 165 J3
Newtondale LTNW/LEA LU4 61 M1
Newton Dr SBW CM21 111 N3
Newton Rd
KTN/HRWW/WS HA3 172 E5
STVGE SG2 51 L9
Newtons Wy
HTCHE/RSTV SG4 49 L1
New Town HTCHE/RSTV SG4 84 C4
Newtown Rd BSF CM23 74 A4
New Town Rd LTN LU1 7 F7
New Town St LTN LU1 7 F7
New Wd WGCE AL7 105 M5
New Woodfield Gn
DUN/HR/TOD LU5 61 H8
Niagara Cl CHES/WCR EN8 142 C8
Nibthwaite Rd HRW HA1 172 E9
Nicholas Cl STALW/RED AL3 120 C5
WATN WD24 149 J7
Nicholas La HERT/WAT SG14 107 L6
Nicholas Pl STVG SG1 50 G6
Nicholas Rd BORE WD6 164 F5
Nicholas Wy
DUN/WHIP LU6 * 60 E6
HHNE HP2 118 A6
NTHWD HA6 170 E5
Nichol Cl STHGT/OAK N14 167 P7
Nicholls Cl
AMP/FLIT/BLC MK45 32 C5
STALW/RED AL3 100 G7
Nicholls Fld HLWS CM18 129 L4
Nichols Cl LTNE LU2 63 J4
Nicholson Dr BUSH WD23 163 L7
Nickleby Wy HTCH/STOT SG5 24 G7
Nicky Line HHNE HP2 118 A5
Nicola Cl KTN/HRWW/WS HA3 172 D6
Nicol Cl CFSP/GDCR SL9 168 A5
Nicol End CFSP/GDCR SL9 168 A5
Nicoll Wy BORE WD6 165 K4
Nicol Rd CFSP/GDCR SL9 168 A5
Nidderdale HHNE HP2 118 A5
Nightingale Cl ABLGY WD5 149 H1
LTNE LU2 47 K9
PIN HA5 171 L9
RAD WD7 150 E6
Nightingale Ct
LTNN/LIM LU3 * 6 C2
Nightingale La STAL AL1 137 H2
Nightingale Pl
RKW/CH/CXG WD3 161 H6
Nightingale Rd BUSH WD23 163 J4
CHESW EN7 141 K4
CSHM HP5 * 130 G8
HTCH/STOT SG5 35 L8
RAYLNE/WEN HP22 112 C6
RKW/CH/CXG WD3 160 G6
Nightingales La CSTG HP8 159 K7
Nightingale Ter
ARL/CHE SG15 24 E6
Nightingale Wk STVGE SG2 67 M1
Nightingale Wy BLDK SG7 37 H2
ROY SG8 20 D2
Nightingles BSF CM23 74 C4
Nimbus Wy HTCHE/RSTV SG4 35 P9
Nimmo Dr BUSH WD23 163 M6
Nimrod Cl STALE/WH AL4 121 H6
Nimrod Dr HAT AL10 122 A5
Nine Acre La HAT AL10 122 C7
Nine Ashes WARE SG12 110 A5
Ninefields WAB EN9 157 L3
Ninesprings Wy
HTCHE/RSTV SG4 49 P1
Ninian Rd HHNE HP2 117 P3
Ninnings Cots HARP AL5 * 101 P4
Ninning's La WLYN AL6 84 G3
Ninnings Rd CFSP/GDCR SL9 168 D4
Ninnings Wy CFSP/GDCR SL9 168 D4
Ninth Av LTNN/LIM LU3 45 N8
STSD CM24 59 J8
Niton Cl BAR EN5 166 B5
Niven Cl BORE WD6 151 P9
Noahs Court Gdns
HERT/BAY SG13 107 L7
Noake Mill La HHW HP1 117 K3
The Nobles BSF CM23 73 N8
Nodes Dr STVGE SG2 67 K5
Node Way Gdns WLYN AL6 104 F1
Noke La LCOL/BKTW AL2 135 M5
Noke Shot HARP AL5 82 B9
Noke Side LCOL/BKTW AL2 135 P6
Nokeside STVGE SG2 67 L6
The Nokes HHW HP1 117 K6
The Noke STVGE SG2 67 L6
Nolton Pl EDGW HA8 173 M5
The Nook WARE SG12 108 G8
Norbury Av WATN WD24 149 K9
Norbury Gv MLHL NW7 165 L9
Norcott Cl DUN/HR/TOD LU5 60 G7
Norfolk Av WATN WD24 149 K8
Norfolk Cl EBAR EN4 167 L3
Norfolk Ct BAR EN5 * 166 C3
Norfolk Gdns BORE WD6 165 K3
Norfolk House
RKW/CH/CXG WD3 * 161 J7
Norfolk Rd BAR EN5 166 E2
BUNT SG9 40 C8
DUN/HR/TOD LU5 61 H8
HRW HA1 172 B9
LTNE LU2 7 K4
RKW/CH/CXG WD3 161 J7
Norfolk Wy BSF CM23 74 A5
Norgrove Pk CFSP/GDCR SL9 168 C8
Norman Av BSF CM23 73 N8
Norman Cl STAL AL1 136 D2
WAB EN9 157 J3
Norman Ct POTB/CUF EN6 139 M9
Norman Crs PIN HA5 171 L5
Normandy Av BAR EN5 166 D4
Normandy Ct HHNE HP2 5 F1
Normandy Dr BERK HP4 115 M6
Normandy Rd
STALW/RED AL3 8 E1
Normandy Wy HOD EN11 127 J3
Norman Rd
AMP/FLIT/BLC MK45 32 D5
LTNN/LIM LU3 62 C4
WLYN AL6 104 E1
Normans Cl LWTH SG6 25 K8
Normansfield Cl BUSH WD23 163 K6
Norman's La ROY SG8 20 C5
Normans La WLYN AL6 85 H3
Norman's Wy STSD CM24 58 F4
Norman Wy DUN/WHIP LU6 60 B6
Norrington End
STALW/RED AL3 100 F3
Norris Cl BSF CM23 74 D3
LCOL/BKTW AL2 136 G5
Norris Gv BROX EN10 126 D8
Norris La HOD EN11 126 F4
Norris Ri HOD EN11 126 E4
Norris Rd HOD EN11 126 F5
Norrys Cl EBAR EN4 167 K4
Norrys Rd EBAR EN4 167 K3
North Ap GSTN WD25 149 H4
NTHWD HA6 161 N8
North Av LWTH SG6 25 M9
RAD WD7 151 K2
Northaw Cl HHNE HP2 118 C3
Northaw Pl POTB/CUF EN6 * 139 P9
Northaw Rd West
POTB/CUF EN6 140 B9
North Barn BROX EN10 142 G1
North Bridge Rd BERK HP4 115 L5
Northbrook Dr NTHWD HA6 170 G5
North Brook End ROY SG8 15 N5
Northbrook Rd BAR EN5 166 C5
Northbrooks
HLWW/ROY CM19 2 B7
Northchurch La CSHM HP5 115 H9
Northcliffe Dr
TRDG/WHET N20 166 D7
North Cl BAR EN5 166 A4
LCOL/BKTW AL2 136 A4
ROY SG8 20 B3
North Common Rd
STALW/RED AL3 101 H8
Northcourt
RKW/CH/CXG WD3 * 160 E7
North Dene MLHL NW7 165 K9
Northdown Rd
CFSP/GDCR SL9 168 C3
HAT AL10 122 D9
North Drift Wy LTN LU1 62 C8
North Dr HAT AL10 122 F4
HTCH/STOT SG5 24 G6
STALE/WH AL4 121 K6
STDN SG11 88 E4
Northend HHS/BOV HP3 134 C1
Northfield STDN SG11 55 L8
Northfield Av PIN HA5 171 M8
Northfield Gdns WATN WD24 149 K7
Northfield Rd BLDK SG7 17 M2
BORE WD6 151 N9
CHES/WCR EN8 156 D2
EBAR EN4 167 J2
HARP AL5 82 B9
SBW CM21 91 P9
TRING HP23 96 D4
Northfields
DUN/HR/TOD LU5 60 C3
LWTH SG6 25 K8
North Ga HLW CM20 2 D4
Northgate NTHWD HA6 170 E4
Northgate End BSF CM23 74 A2
Northgate Pth BORE WD6 151 L8
North Gv HLWS CM18 129 K4
North Hl RKW/CH/CXG WD3 160 C1
Northlands POTB/CUF EN6 153 N1
North Mt TRDG/WHET N20 * 166 G8
Northolme Gdns EDGW HA8 173 N5
Northolt Av BSF CM23 74 C1
North Orbital Rd
DEN/HRF UB9 169 K8
LCOL/BKTW AL2 135 M9
North Orbital Road
St Albans Rd GSTN WD25 149 L3
North Pde EDGW HA8 * 173 N6
North Pk CFSP/GDCR SL9 168 C7
North Pl HLW CM20 111 K7
WAB EN9 156 G3
North Ride WLYN AL6 84 F7
Northridge Wy HHW HP1 117 J9
North Riding LCOL/BKTW AL2 135 P9
North Rd AMS HP6 145 H6
BERK HP4 115 N7
CHES/WCR EN8 156 D3
EDGW HA8 173 P5
HERT/WAT SG14 107 H5
HOD EN11 126 F4
RKW/CH/CXG WD3 160 B4
STVG SG1 50 F5
North Road Av
HERT/WAT SG14 107 H5
North Road Gdns
HERT/WAT SG14 107 J6
North St BSF CM23 74 A2
LTNE LU2 6 E2
WAB EN9 143 K1
North Ter BSF CM23 74 A2
Northumberland Av EN EN1 156 A8
Northumberland Rd
BAR EN5 166 G5
RYLN/HDSTN HA2 171 P9
Northview Rd
DUN/HR/TOD LU5 60 D4
LTNE LU2 62 G4
North Wy CDALE/KGS NW9 173 P7
PIN HA5 171 L7
Northway RKW/CH/CXG WD3 161 H6
WGCE AL7 105 J3
Northwell Dr LTNN/LIM LU3 46 A7
North Western Av
WATN WD24 148 G5
North Western Avenue Coln
WATN WD24 149 K6
North Western Avenue
Gade Side WAT WD17 148 E5
Northwick Rd OXHEY WD19 171 L1
Northwold Dr PIN HA5 171 L7
Northwood WGCE AL7 105 N6
Northwood Cl CHESW EN7 141 N6
Northwood Rd DEN/HRF UB9 170 A5
Northwood Wy
DEN/HRF UB9 169 P5
NTHWD HA6 171 J4
Nortoft Rd CFSP/GDCR SL9 168 D3
Norton Bury La LWTH SG6 25 N7
Norton Cl BORE WD6 151 M9
Norton Crs BLDK SG7 26 A9
Norton Gn STVG SG1 * 66 E3
Norton Green Rd STVG SG1 10 B7
Norton Rd LTNN/LIM LU3 62 A2
LWTH SG6 25 L9
STVG SG1 10 B7
Norton Street La
HTCHE/RSTV SG4 65 M8
Norton Wy North LWTH SG6 25 L9
Norton Wy South LWTH SG6 36 D3
Norvic Rd TRING HP23 95 P3
Norwich Cl STVG SG1 51 L6
Norwich Rd NTHWD HA6 171 H7
Norwich Wy
RKW/CH/CXG WD3 161 M2
Norwood Cl HERT/WAT SG14 106 G5
Norwood Ct AMSS HP7 * 158 B1
Norwood Rd CHES/WCR EN8 142 D9
Nottingham Cl GSTN WD25 149 H4
Nottingham Rd
RKW/CH/CXG WD3 160 A7
Novello Wy BORE WD6 152 A9
Nower Hl PIN HA5 171 P8
Nugents Ct PIN HA5 * 171 N5
Nugent's Pk PIN HA5 171 N5
Numbers Farm KGLGY WD4 * 134 D8
Nunnery Cl STAL AL1 9 G7
Nunnery La LTNN/LIM LU3 62 C1
Nunnery Stables STAL AL1 9 F7
Nunsbury Dr BROX EN10 142 D4
Nun's Cl HTCH/STOT SG5 35 K9
Nuns La STAL AL1 136 D3
Nup End Cl
RAYLNE/WEN HP22 76 C2
Nup End La
RAYLNE/WEN HP22 76 B2
Nupton Dr BAR EN5 166 A5
Nurseries Rd STALE/WH AL4 103 K5
Nursery Cl AMSS HP7 145 K9
DUN/WHIP LU6 60 D6
OXHEY WD19 162 D7
PEND EN3 156 C9
STVGE SG2 67 K6
Nursery Crs LWTH SG6 36 C2
Nursery Flds SBW CM21 111 N2
Nursery Gdns CHESW EN7 141 L7
PEND EN3 156 C9
TRING HP23 96 A8
WARE SG12 108 D3
WGCE AL7 105 H3
Nursery Hl WGCE AL7 105 H3
Nurserymans Rd
FBAR/BDGN N11 167 L8
Nursery Pde LTNN/LIM LU3 * 61 P1
Nursery Rd BROX EN10 * 142 D4
BSF CM23 74 A4
HOD EN11 126 G2
LTNN/LIM LU3 62 A1
PIN HA5 171 L7
STHGT/OAK N14 167 N6
WAB EN9 143 J1
Nursery Rw BAR EN5 * 166 C2
Nutcroft KNEB SG3 85 N3
Nutfield WGCE AL7 105 K3
Nut Gv WGCW AL8 104 G3
Nuthampstead Rd ROY SG8 30 B7
Nutkins Wy CSHM HP5 131 H8
Nutleigh Gv HTCH/STOT SG5 35 J7
Nut Slip BUNT SG9 54 D1
Nuttfield Cl
RKW/CH/CXG WD3 * 161 M5
Nutt Gv EDGW HA8 164 D8
Nutwood Gdns CHESW EN7 141 M5
Nye Wy HHS/BOV HP3 132 D7
Nymans Cl LTNE LU2 63 L3

O

Oak Av ENC/FH EN2 154 G9
LCOL/BKTW AL2 135 P9
Oak Cl DUN/HR/TOD LU5 60 G6
HHS/BOV HP3 134 A3
STHGT/OAK N14 167 M6
WAB EN9 157 J4
Oakcroft Cl PIN HA5 171 K6
Oakdale STHGT/OAK N14 167 M7
WGCW AL8 104 G2
Oakdale Av
KTN/HRWW/WS HA3 173 L9
NTHWD HA6 171 J6
Oakdale Cl OXHEY WD19 171 L1
Oakdale Rd OXHEY WD19 162 E9
Oakdene CHES/WCR EN8 142 D9
Oakdene Cl PIN HA5 171 P4
Oakdene Rd HHS/BOV HP3 134 A3
WATN WD24 149 J6
Oakdene Wy STAL AL1 121 H8
Oak Dr BERK HP4 116 A8
SBW CM21 111 M4
Oak End BUNT SG9 54 C1
HLWS CM18 * 129 J5
Oak End Wy CFSP/GDCR SL9 168 D9
Oaken Gv WGCE AL7 105 H9
Oak Farm BORE WD6 165 J4
Oak Fld CSHM HP5 130 G9
Oakfield RKW/CH/CXG WD3 160 E6
Oakfield Av HTCHE/RSTV SG4 49 N2
KTN/HRWW/WS HA3 173 H7
Oakfield Cl POTB/CUF EN6 153 J1
Oakfield Ct BORE WD6 * 165 H3
Oakfield Rd HARP AL5 101 N7
Oakfields STVGE SG2 67 L5
Oakfields Av KNEB SG3 67 K8
Oakfields Cl STVGE SG2 67 M5
Oakfields Rd KNEB SG3 67 K8
Oak Gld NTHWD HA6 170 D5
Oak Gn ABLGY WD5 148 F2
Oak Gv HAT AL10 122 C6
HERT/BAY SG13 107 M8
Oakhill LWTH SG6 36 G4
Oakhill Av PIN HA5 171 N6
Oakhill Cl RKW/CH/CXG WD3 169 J1
Oakhill Dr WLYN AL6 84 D7
Oakhill Rd RKW/CH/CXG WD3 169 H1
Oakhurst Av EBAR EN4 167 J6
HARP AL5 101 N6
Oakhurst Pl WATW WD18 * 12 A5
Oakhurst Rd PEND EN3 156 C6
Oakington WGCE AL7 105 N6
Oakington Av AMS HP6 146 B9
Oaklands BERK HP4 115 M7
Oaklands Av BRKMPK AL9 139 H6
OXHEY WD19 162 D7
Oaklands Cl BSF CM23 58 C9
Oaklands Ct WAT WD17 149 H9
Oaklands Dr BSF CM23 74 C1
HLWE CM17 129 M4
Oaklands Ga NTHWD HA6 170 G3
Oaklands Gv BROX EN10 142 D3
Oaklands La BAR EN5 165 P3
STALE/WH AL4 121 L6
Oaklands Pk BSF CM23 58 C9
Oaklands Ri WLYN AL6 85 J6
Oaklands Rd CHESW EN7 141 M5
TRDG/WHET N20 166 D6
Oaklands Wd HAT AL10 122 D6
Oakland Vw WLYN AL6 85 J5
Oak La HTCHE/RSTV SG4 50 E3
POTB/CUF EN6 140 G7
TRING HP23 113 N9
Oaklea WLYN AL6 85 H6
Oaklea Cl WLYN AL6 85 H5
Oaklea Wd WLYN AL6 85 H6
Oakleigh Av EDGW HA8 173 P6
TRDG/WHET N20 167 H7
Oakleigh Cl TRDG/WHET N20 167 K9
Oakleigh Crs
TRDG/WHET N20 167 J9
Oakleigh Dr
RKW/CH/CXG WD3 161 N5
Oakleigh Gdns EDGW HA8 173 M2
TRDG/WHET N20 166 G7
Oakleigh Ms
TRDG/WHET N20 166 G8
Oakleigh Pk North
TRDG/WHET N20 167 H7
Oakleigh Pk South
TRDG/WHET N20 167 J7
Oakleigh Rd PIN HA5 171 P3
Oakleigh Rd North
TRDG/WHET N20 167 H8
Oakley Cl LTNW/LEA LU4 61 N2
Oakley Rd HARP AL5 102 C5
LTNW/LEA LU4 61 N2
Oak Lodge Cl STAN HA7 173 J2
Oakmeade PIN HA5 172 A3
Oakmere Av POTB/CUF EN6 153 M3
Oakmere Cl POTB/CUF EN6 153 N1
Oakmere La POTB/CUF EN6 153 M2
Oak Piece WLYN AL6 84 G6
Oakridge LCOL/BKTW AL2 135 N8
Oakridge Av RAD WD7 150 E3
Oak Rd KNEB SG3 85 L4
LTNW/LEA LU4 6 A2
Oakroyd Av POTB/CUF EN6 153 J3
Oakroyd Cl POTB/CUF EN6 153 J4
Oaks Cl HTCHE/RSTV SG4 49 L2
RAD WD7 150 E5
Oaks Cross STVGE SG2 67 L6
The Oaks BERK HP4 115 M7
BORE WD6 * 151 M9
LTN LU1 80 D4
OXHEY WD19 162 E7
Oak St BSF CM23 74 A4
HHS/BOV HP3 134 A3
Oak Tree Cl ABLGY WD5 148 E2
Oaktree Cl BSF CM23 74 A3
CHESW EN7 141 K7
Oak Tree Cl HAT AL10 122 D5
HERT/BAY SG13 108 B9
LWTH SG6 36 B4
STAN HA7 173 J4
STVGE SG2 68 G3
Oak Tree Ct BORE WD6 * 164 D5
WLYN AL6 * 85 H5
Oak Tree Dr TRDG/WHET N20 166 F7
Oaktree Gdns HLWE CM17 129 N4
Oaktree Garth WGCE AL7 105 H7
Oakview WATW WD18 162 A2
Oakview Cl CHESW EN7 142 A7
HARP AL5 101 N7
OXHEY WD19 162 E5
Oakway AMS HP6 144 G5
DUN/WHIP LU6 78 E6
Oak Wy HARP AL5 101 P7
STHGT/OAK N14 167 L6
Oakway Pl RAD WD7 150 F4
Oakwell Cl DUN/WHIP LU6 60 C7
STVGE SG2 67 N7
Oakwell Dr POTB/CUF EN6 154 C3
Oak Wd BERK HP4 115 L8
Oakwood Av BORE WD6 165 H3
DUN/HR/TOD LU5 61 H7
STHGT/OAK N14 167 P6
Oakwood Cl STHGT/OAK N14 167 N5
STVGE SG2 67 M4
Oakwood Dr HARP AL5 101 N7
LTNN/LIM LU3 45 M7
STALE/WH AL4 121 H7
Oakwood Ms HLWE CM17 111 M8
Oakwood Pde
STHGT/OAK N14 * 167 N4
Oakwood Rd LCOL/BKTW AL2 135 N8
PIN HA5 171 K6
Oak Yd WAT WD17 * 13 G4
Oatfield Cl LTNW/LEA LU4 61 J2
Oatlands Rd PEND EN3 156 B9
Oban Ter LTN LU1 62 C6
Oberon Cl BORE WD6 151 P9
Obrey Wy BSF CM23 91 P2
Observer Dr WATW WD18 162 A3
Occupation Rd WATW WD18 12 E6
Octavia Ct WATN WD24 13 H1
Oddy Hl TRING HP23 96 B9
Odeon Pde
RKW/CH/CXG WD3 * 161 J7
Odsey Mdw BLDK SG7 * 18 D9
Odyssey Rd BORE WD6 151 N9
Offa Rd STALW/RED AL3 8 C3

Offas Wy STALE/WH AL4 103 J4
Offley Hl HTCH/STOT SG5 48 B4
Offley Rd HTCH/STOT SG5 49 J1
Ogard Rd HOD EN11 127 H3
Okeford Cl TRING HP23 95 N8
Okeford Dr TRING HP23 95 N9
Okeley La TRING HP23 95 M9
The Old Bakery LTN LU1 * 62 F9
Old Barn La
RKW/CH/CXG WD3 161 K4
Old Bedford Rd LTNE LU2 6 D1
Old Bell Cl STSD CM24 58 E5
Old Bells Ct CSHM HP5 144 G2
Old Bourne Wy STVG SG1 51 K4
Old Brewery Cl
HTCH/STOT SG5 25 K2
Old Burylodge La STSD CM24 59 H7
Old Chantry La STVG SG1 50 D5
Old Charlton Rd
HTCH/STOT SG5 49 K1
Old Chorleywood Rd
RKW/CH/CXG WD3 161 H5
Old Church La STAN HA7 173 H3
WARE SG12 88 D6
The Old Coach Rd
HERT/WAT SG14 106 A9
Old Common Rd
RKW/CH/CXG WD3 160 B3
Old Crabtree La HHNE HP2 5 H4
Old Cross HERT/WAT SG14 107 K6
Old Dairy Ct
DUN/HR/TOD LU5 61 J4
Old Dean HHS/BOV HP3 132 D6
The Old Dr WGCW AL8 104 E7
Old Earls La POTB/CUF EN6 152 D3
Olden Md LWTH SG6 36 E5
Olde Swann Ct STVG SG1 50 F7
Old Farm Av STHGT/OAK N14 167 N6
Old Farm Cl LBUZ LU7 77 P2
Old Farm La AMSS HP7 158 E2
Old Farm Yd RBSF CM22 92 D9
Old Field Cl AMS HP6 146 B9
Oldfield Cl STAN HA7 172 G2
Oldfield Ri HTCHE/RSTV SG4 65 K7
Oldfield Rd HHW HP1 117 H9
LCOL/BKTW AL2 137 J4
Old Fishery La HHW HP1 133 J1
Old Fold Cl BAR EN5 * 153 J9
Old Fold La BAR EN5 153 J9
Old Fold Vw BAR EN5 166 A2
Old Forge Cl GSTN WD25 149 H3
STAN HA7 172 G1
WLYN AL6 105 J2
Old Forge Rd EN EN1 155 N8
Old Forge Rw
HERT/BAY SG13 * 108 A9
Old French Horn La HAT AL10 122 E5
Old Gannon Cl NTHWD HA6 170 E1
Old Garden Ct
STALW/RED AL3 8 D3
Old Grove Cl CHESW EN7 141 L5
Old Hale Wy HTCH/STOT SG5 35 K7
Old Hall Cl PIN HA5 171 N5
Old Hall Dr PIN HA5 171 N5
Old Hall Ri HLWE CM17 129 P3
Oldhall St HERT/WAT SG14 107 L6
Old Harpenden Rd
STALW/RED AL3 120 D4
Old Herns La WGCE AL7 105 M4
Old Hertford Rd BRKMPK AL9 122 F4
Old Hwy HOD EN11 126 G3
Oldhill DUN/WHIP LU6 60 F8
Oldhouse Ct HHNE HP2 5 J1
Oldhouse Cft HLW CM20 3 H2
Old House La
HLWW/ROY CM19 128 A6
KGLGY WD4 148 B5
Old House Rd HHNE HP2 5 J1
Oldings Cnr BRKMPK AL9 122 E2
Old Kenton La
CDALE/KGS NW9 173 P9
Old Knebworth La KNEB SG3 66 F8
Old La KNEB SG3 67 L9
Old Leys HAT AL10 138 D1
Old Library La
HERT/WAT SG14 * 107 K6
Old Lodge Wy STAN HA7 172 G2
Old London Rd
HERT/BAY SG13 107 M6
STAL AL1 9 F5
The Old Maltings BSF CM23 74 B3
HERT/BAY SG13 * 107 K7
Old Maple HHNE HP2 118 A2
Old Md CFSP/GDCR SL9 168 C3
Old Meadow Cl BERK HP4 115 M9
Old Mill Gdns BERK HP4 116 A7
Old Mill La RBSF CM22 92 C3
Old Mill Rd KGLGY WD4 148 D4
Old Nazeing Rd BROX EN10 126 F9
Old North Rd ROY SG8 20 B2
Old Nursery Wy WLYN AL6 86 D4
Old Oak STAL AL1 136 D2
Old Oak Cl ARL/CHE SG15 24 E1
Old Oak Gdns BERK HP4 * 115 K4
Old Oaks WAB EN9 157 K2
Old Orch HLWS CM18 128 G5
LCOL/BKTW AL2 136 C5
LTN LU1 62 E9
Old Orchard Cl EBAR EN4 153 N8
Old Orchard Ms BERK HP4 115 P8
Old Parkbury La
LCOL/BKTW AL2 136 E6
Oldpark Ride CHESW EN7 155 L2
Old Park Rd HTCH/STOT SG5 35 K9
Old Rectory Cl HARP AL5 101 P2
Old Rectory Dr HAT AL10 122 E6
Old Rectory Gdns
EDGW HA8 173 N3
STALE/WH AL4 103 J3
Old Redding
KTN/HRWW/WS HA3 172 B2
Old River La BSF CM23 74 A3
Old Rd AMP/FLIT/BLC MK45 32 D7
HLWE CM17 111 M6
PEND EN3 156 B9
Old's Ap WATW WD18 161 N7
Old Sax La CSHM HP5 130 C6
Old School Cl
HTCHE/RSTV SG4 84 C4
RAYLNE/WEN HP22 112 D2
Old School Gdns
AMP/FLIT/BLC MK45 32 D5
Old School Gn STVGE SG2 68 F1
Old School Wk ARL/CHE SG15 24 E5
Old's Cl WATW WD18 161 M7
Old Shire La
RKW/CH/CXG WD3 159 N6
WAB EN9 157 M4
Old Shire Lane Circular Wk
CSTG HP8 159 N8
DEN/HRF UB9 169 H6
Old Solesbridge La
RKW/CH/CXG WD3 160 E2
Old Sopwell Gdns STAL AL1 9 F7
Old South Cl PIN HA5 171 M5
Old Street Hl RBSF CM22 93 K4
Old Uxbridge Rd
RKW/CH/CXG WD3 169 J4
Old Vicarage Gdns
STALW/RED AL3 79 N7
The Old Walled Gdn
STVG SG1 50 F6
Old Watford Rd
LCOL/BKTW AL2 135 M9
Old Watling St
STALW/RED AL3 80 C9
Oldwood WLYN AL6 85 H6
Olive Cl STAL AL1 120 G9
Oliver Cl HHS/BOV HP3 133 P3
HOD EN11 126 G3
LCOL/BKTW AL2 136 C6
Oliver Ct WARE SG12 * 87 M9
Oliver Ri HHS/BOV HP3 133 P3
Oliver Rd HHS/BOV HP3 134 A3
Olivers Cl BERK HP4 116 F4
Oliver's La HTCH/STOT SG5 25 K2
Olivia Gdns DEN/HRF UB9 169 N5
Olleberrie La
RKW/CH/CXG WD3 147 H2
Olma Rd DUN/HR/TOD LU5 60 D4
Olwen Ms PIN HA5 171 M6
Olyard Ct LTN LU1 62 C9
Olympic Cl LTNN/LIM LU3 45 P6
Omega Ct WARE SG12 * 108 C2
Omega Maltings
WARE SG12 * 108 D3
One Tree Pl AMS HP6 * 145 H8
Onslow Cl HAT AL10 122 E6
Onslow Pde
STHGT/OAK N14 * 167 M7
Onslow Rd LTNW/LEA LU4 61 N1
Ontario Cl BROX EN10 142 D4
On The Hl OXHEY WD19 162 G8
The Opening
HTCHE/RSTV SG4 84 C5
Openshaw Wy LWTH SG6 36 D2
Oram Pl HHS/BOV HP3 5 F7
Orbital Crs GSTN WD25 148 G5
Orchard Av BERK HP4 115 M7
GSTN WD25 149 J1
HARP AL5 101 N3
TRDG/WHET N20 167 H8
Orchard Cl
AMP/FLIT/BLC MK45 32 D7
BORE WD6 164 F3
BUSH WD23 163 M7
DUN/HR/TOD LU5 44 C1
DUN/HR/TOD LU5 60 E3
EDGW HA8 173 L3
HERT/BAY SG13 124 D7
HHNE HP2 118 A6
HTCHE/RSTV SG4 49 L4
LTN LU1 79 P1
LWTH SG6 25 K9
POTB/CUF EN6 140 F7
RAD WD7 150 D7
RAYLNE/WEN HP22 76 C3
RAYLNE/WEN HP22 112 B5
RBSF CM22 92 D9
RKW/CH/CXG WD3 160 B2
STAL AL1 9 K6
WARE SG12 108 C2
WARE SG12 109 H8
WAT WD17 162 B1
Orchard Crs EN EN1 155 N9
STVG SG1 50 F8
Orchard Cft HLW CM20 129 K1
Orchard Dr EDGW HA8 173 M2
LCOL/BKTW AL2 136 A5
RAYLNE/WEN HP22 94 F8
RKW/CH/CXG WD3 160 A2
STDN SG11 71 K4
WAT WD17 148 G9
Orchard End Av AMSS HP7 145 L9
Orchard Gdns WAB EN9 156 G4
Orchard Gv CFSP/GDCR SL9 168 A5
EDGW HA8 173 N5
KTN/HRWW/WS HA3 173 M9
Orchard House La STAL AL1 8 E5
Orchard La AMS HP6 145 J8
Orchard Md HAT AL10 122 C6
The Orchard on The Green
RKW/CH/CXG WD3 161 K4
Orchard Pde
POTB/CUF EN6 * 152 G1
Orchard Pl CHES/WCR EN8 142 C9
Orchard Ri PIN HA5 171 H7
Orchard Rd BAR EN5 166 C3
BLDK SG7 26 A9
BSF CM23 74 C1
CSTG HP8 159 J8
HTCHE/RSTV SG4 35 N7
ROY SG8 20 A3
STVG SG1 50 E7
WLYN AL6 68 B9
WLYN AL6 85 M8
Orchard Sq BROX EN10 142 E3
The Orchards LTN LU1 80 D3
SBW CM21 111 P1
TRING HP23 95 N9
Orchard St HHS/BOV HP3 133 N3
STALW/RED AL3 8 D5
The Orchard BLDK SG7 26 B9
BROX EN10 * 126 F8
HERT/WAT SG14 107 J3
HTCHE/RSTV SG4 84 B4
KGLGY WD4 134 B8
RAYLNE/WEN HP22 112 D3
TRDG/WHET N20 166 F7
TRING HP23 * 95 N9
WARE SG12 87 M6
WGCW AL8 104 G4
Orchard Vw BLDK SG7 18 B7
Orchard Wy CHESW EN7 141 J6
HHS/BOV HP3 132 D7
HTCHE/RSTV SG4 64 D5
KNEB SG3 67 H9
LTNW/LEA LU4 61 M2
LWTH SG6 25 K9
POTB/CUF EN6 139 L7
RKW/CH/CXG WD3 160 E6
ROY SG8 20 B2
Orchehill Av CFSP/GDCR SL9 168 B8
Orchehill Ri CFSP/GDCR SL9 168 C9
Orchid Cl CHESW EN7 141 K9
DUN/WHIP LU6 60 B5
HAT AL10 122 C2
LTNN/LIM LU3 45 M9
Orchid Rd STHGT/OAK N14 167 N6
Ordelmere LWTH SG6 25 K8
Ordnance Rd PEND EN3 156 C7
Oregon Wy LTNN/LIM LU3 46 B7
Organ Hall Rd BORE WD6 151 K9
Orient Cl STAL AL1 9 H7
Oriole Cl ABLGY WD5 149 H1
Oriole Wy BSF CM23 73 M8
Orion Wy NTHWD HA6 171 H1
Orlando Cl HTCHE/RSTV SG4 49 M1
Ormesby Dr POTB/CUF EN6 152 G2
Ormonde Rd NTHWD HA6 170 F1
Ormsby Cl LTN LU1 62 F9
Ormskirk Rd OXHEY WD19 171 M1
Oronsay HHS/BOV HP3 134 C1
Orphanage Rd WAT WD17 13 G1
Orpington Cl LTNW/LEA LU4 61 K3
Orton Cl STALE/WH AL4 120 F4
Orton Gv EN EN1 155 N9
Orwell Av STVG SG1 51 J4
Orwell Ct WATN WD24 13 J2
Orwell Vw BLDK SG7 26 D8
Osborne Cl EBAR EN4 167 K2
Osborne Gdns
POTB/CUF EN6 139 L9
Osborne Rd BROX EN10 126 F7
CHES/WCR EN8 142 D6
DUN/WHIP LU6 60 E7
LTN LU1 7 H7
POTB/CUF EN6 139 L9
WATN WD24 149 K8
Osborne Wy TRING HP23 114 C2
Osborn Rd
AMP/FLIT/BLC MK45 32 E5
Osborn Wy WGCW AL8 104 G7
Osbourne Av KGLGY WD4 134 A7
Osbourne Ct
RYLN/HDSTN HA2 * 172 B8
Osidge La STHGT/OAK N14 167 L7
The Osiers RKW/CH/CXG WD3 161 N4
Osmington Pl TRING HP23 95 N8
Osprey Cl GSTN WD25 149 M4
Osprey Gdns STVGE SG2 67 N4
Osprey Rd WAB EN9 157 M4
Ostell Crs PEND EN3 156 F8
Osterley Cl STVGE SG2 67 M7
Oster St STALW/RED AL3 8 D2
Ostler Cl BSF CM23 91 M1
Oswald Rd STAL AL1 9 H5
Otley Wy OXHEY WD19 162 E9
Ottawa Ct BROX EN10 142 D4
Otter Gdns HAT AL10 122 E7
Otterspool La GSTN WD25 149 M8
Otterspool Wy GSTN WD25 149 N9
Otterton Cl HARP AL5 101 N1
Ottoman Ter WAT WD17 13 H3
Ottway Wk WLYN AL6 84 E9
Otway Gdns BUSH WD23 163 N6
Otways Cl POTB/CUF EN6 153 L3
Oudle La MHAD SG10 90 C2
Oughton Cl HTCH/STOT SG5 35 J8
Oughtonhead La
HTCH/STOT SG5 34 G8
Oughton Head La
HTCH/STOT SG5 35 J8
Oughton Head Wy
HTCH/STOT SG5 35 J8
Oulton Crs POTB/CUF EN6 152 G2
Oulton Ri HARP AL5 102 B1
Oulton Wy OXHEY WD19 171 P1
Oundle Av BUSH WD23 163 L5
Oundle Ct STVGE SG2 67 M6
Oundle Pth STVGE SG2 67 M6
The Oundle STVGE SG2 67 M5
Ousden Cl CHES/WCR EN8 142 D9
Ousden Dr CHES/WCR EN8 142 D9
Ouseley Cl LTNW/LEA LU4 61 N3
Outfield Rd CFSP/GDCR SL9 168 B4
Outlook Dr CSTG HP8 159 K9
The Oval BROX EN10 142 D4
HNLW SG16 24 A6
Ovaltine Dr KGLGY WD4 134 C8
Oval Wy CFSP/GDCR SL9 168 C8
Overbrook Wk EDGW HA8 173 N4
Overdale Rd CSHM HP5 130 G7
Overfield Rd LTNE LU2 63 K5
Overlord Cl BROX EN10 126 D8
Overstone Rd HARP AL5 102 B3
LTNW/LEA LU4 61 N5
Overstrand
RAYLNE/WEN HP22 94 F7
Overstream
RKW/CH/CXG WD3 160 F3
Oving Cl LTNE LU2 63 L4
Owen Dr ROY SG8 20 C1
Owen Jones Cl HNLW SG16 24 A4
Owens Wy
RKW/CH/CXG WD3 161 L4
Owles La BUNT SG9 54 E1
Oxcroft BSF CM23 74 A7
Oxendon Dr HOD EN11 126 F6
Oxen Rd LTNE LU2 7 H1
Oxfield Cl BERK HP4 115 M8
Oxford Av STAL AL1 121 H9
STHGT/OAK N14 167 N7
Oxford Cl CHES/WCR EN8 142 B8
NTHWD HA6 170 E1
Oxford Gdns
TRDG/WHET N20 167 H7
Oxford Pl HAT AL10 122 B4
Oxford Rd HTCHE/RSTV SG4 64 D5
KTN/HRWW/WS HA3 172 F7
LTN LU1 7 F6
Oxford St WATW WD18 12 E6
Oxhey Av OXHEY WD19 162 F6
Oxhey Dr NTHWD HA6 171 K2
OXHEY WD19 162 E9
Oxhey La OXHEY WD19 162 F6
PIN HA5 171 P1
Oxhey Ridge Cl NTHWD HA6 171 J2
Oxhey Rd OXHEY WD19 162 E6
Ox La HARP AL5 102 A1
Oxlease Dr HAT AL10 122 E7
Oxleys Cl SAFWS CB11 43 M5
Oxleys Rd STVGE SG2 67 L3
WAB EN9 157 M3
The Oxleys HLWE CM17 111 N8
Oysterfields STALW/RED AL3 8 C1
Oziers RBSF CM22 59 K1

P

Pacatian Wy STVG SG1 51 M7
Packhorse Cl STALE/WH AL4 121 H5
Packhorse La POTB/CUF EN6 152 A1
Packhorse Pl
DUN/WHIP LU6 * 79 M5
Paddick Cl HOD EN11 126 E4
Paddock Cl LTNW/LEA LU4 61 J1
LWTH SG6 36 C3
OXHEY WD19 162 G5
WARE SG12 110 A3
Paddock La BAR EN5 165 L3
Paddock Md HLWS CM18 128 F8
Paddock Rd BUNT SG9 40 D8
Paddocks Cl STVGE SG2 67 L3
The Paddocks EBAR EN4 167 K2
HERT/BAY SG13 108 A9
HTCHE/RSTV SG4 84 C4
RAYLNE/WEN HP22 112 C6
RKW/CH/CXG WD3 160 D3
STALE/WH AL4 82 G7
STALE/WH AL4 * 137 N1
STVGE SG2 67 L3
WGCE AL7 105 L5
The Paddock BROX EN10 126 F8
BSF CM23 91 N2
CFSP/GDCR SL9 168 C2
HAT AL10 122 D5
HTCHE/RSTV SG4 49 M2
Paddock Vw LTNE LU2 * 63 L2
Paddock Wd HARP AL5 102 D5
Pageant Rd STAL AL1 9 F5
Page Cl BLDK SG7 37 J2
Page Hl WARE SG12 108 A2
Page Rd HERT/BAY SG13 107 P6
Pages Cl BSF CM23 73 N9
Pages Cft BERK HP4 115 M5
Paget Ct RBSF CM22 59 K2
Pagitts Gv EBAR EN4 153 L9
Paignton Cl LTNW/LEA LU4 61 N2
Paines Cl PIN HA5 171 N7
Paine's La PIN HA5 171 N6
Paines Orch LBUZ LU7 77 P5
Painters La PEND EN3 156 D5
Paisley Cl LTNW/LEA LU4 61 N3
Palace Cl KGLGY WD4 134 A9
Palace Gdns BSF CM23 73 P9
ROY SG8 20 B4
Palfrey Cl STALW/RED AL3 120 C6
Pallas Rd HHNE HP2 118 A6
Pallett Ct HOD EN11 126 G7
Palliser Rd CSTG HP8 158 G9
Palma Cl DUN/WHIP LU6 60 C3
Palmer Av BUSH WD23 163 K5
Palmer Cl HERT/WAT SG14 107 K4
Palmer Gdns BAR EN5 166 B4
Palmer Rd HERT/WAT SG14 107 L4
Palmers Gv WAB EN9 143 L1
Palmers La PEND EN3 156 B9
ROY SG8 22 F6
Palmers Rd BORE WD6 151 P9
Palmerston Cl WGCW AL8 104 F6
Palmerston Dr
STALE/WH AL4 103 J3
Palmerston Rd
KTN/HRWW/WS HA3 172 F7
Palmerston Wy
HTCH/STOT SG5 25 H7
Palmers Wy CHES/WCR EN8 142 D8
Pamela Av HHS/BOV HP3 5 J7
Pamela Gdns BSF CM23 74 A7
PIN HA5 171 K9
Pams La HTCHE/RSTV SG4 83 J4
Pancake La HHNE HP2 118 E9
Pangbourne Dr STAN HA7 173 K2
Pank Av BAR EN5 167 H4
Pankhurst Crs STVGE SG2 67 M1
Pankhurst Pl WATN WD24 13 H2
Pankridge OXHEY WD19 * 162 F8
Panshanger Dr WGCE AL7 105 L6
The Pantiles BUSH WD23 163 M7
Panxworth Rd HHNE HP2 5 F5
Paper Mill La STDN SG11 71 K5
The Parade DUN/WHIP LU6 * 60 D5
HAT AL10 * 122 F4
LTNN/LIM LU3 45 M8
LWTH SG6 * 25 K8
OXHEY WD19 162 F9
WAT WD17 12 E2
Paradise HHNE HP2 4 E4
Paradise Cl CHESW EN7 142 A7
Paradise Rd WAB EN9 157 H4
Parchment Cl AMS HP6 145 K7
Par Cl HERT/BAY SG13 108 A5
Paringdon Rd
HLWW/ROY CM19 128 E7
Parish Cl GSTN WD25 149 K4
Parishes Md STVGE SG2 67 N2
Park Av BSF CM23 74 A7
BUSH WD23 13 K2
DUN/HR/TOD LU5 60 F1
HLWE CM17 129 M6
LTNN/LIM LU3 45 M8
POTB/CUF EN6 153 M3
RAD WD7 150 G3
RKW/CH/CXG WD3 160 E4
STAL AL1 120 F7
WATW WD18 12 D4
Park Av North HARP AL5 101 N3
Park Av South HARP AL5 101 M3
Park Cl BLDK SG7 37 H1
BRKMPK AL9 122 F5
BRKMPK AL9 139 J5
BUSH WD23 13 K2
KTN/HRWW/WS HA3 172 E5
RKW/CH/CXG WD3 170 D1
STALW/RED AL3 79 N8
STVGE SG2 67 L5
Park Ct HLW CM20 3 F3
Park Crs BLDK SG7 37 H1
BORE WD6 164 F2
KTN/HRWW/WS HA3 172 E5
Park Dr BLDK SG7 37 H1
KTN/HRWW/WS HA3 172 D3
POTB/CUF EN6 153 L1
RBSF CM22 93 J7
STDN SG11 71 J3
Parkend HLWW/ROY CM19 128 A3
Parker Av HERT/WAT SG14 107 L4
Parker Cl LWTH SG6 36 B4
Parker's Fld STVGE SG2 67 M2
Parker St WATN WD24 149 J9
Park Farm Cl HNLW SG16 24 B1
PIN HA5 171 K9
Park Farm La ROY SG8 30 G7
Parkfield LWTH SG6 36 G4
RKW/CH/CXG WD3 160 D3
STALW/RED AL3 79 N8
Parkfield Av AMS HP6 145 J7
RYLN/HDSTN HA2 172 C6
Parkfield Cl EDGW HA8 173 P3
Parkfield Crs
HTCHE/RSTV SG4 83 J4
RYLN/HDSTN HA2 172 C6
Parkfield Gdns
RYLN/HDSTN HA2 172 B7
Park Flds HLWW/ROY CM19 127 M3
Parkfields WGCW AL8 104 G6
Parkfield Vw POTB/CUF EN6 153 L2
Park Gdns BLDK SG7 37 H1
CDALE/KGS NW9 173 P7
Park Ga HTCHE/RSTV SG4 49 L1
Parkgate Av EBAR EN4 153 M9
Parkgate Crs EBAR EN4 153 M9
Parkgate Rd WATN WD24 149 K7
Park Gv CSTG HP8 159 K2
EDGW HA8 173 M2
Park Hl HARP AL5 101 N2
HLWE CM17 111 L8
Park Hill Rd HHW HP1 4 B2
Park Homes LCOL/BKTW AL2 137 H5
Parkhurst Rd
HERT/WAT SG14 107 J5
Parkins Cl STDN SG11 70 F8
Parkinson Cl STALE/WH AL4 103 J4
Parkland Cl HOD EN11 126 G2
Parkland Dr LTN LU1 62 E9
Parklands BUSH WD23 * 163 L5
HHW HP1 117 J6
ROY SG8 20 D4
WAB EN9 157 K2
Parklands Cl EBAR EN4 153 N8
Parklands Dr STALW/RED AL3 119 P9
Park La BROX EN10 126 D8
BSF CM23 74 A6
CHES/WCR EN8 156 B3
CHESW EN7 141 P6
DEN/HRF UB9 169 L5
HHNE HP2 4 E4
HLW CM20 3 F2
HTCHE/RSTV SG4 83 H3
KNEB SG3 66 E9
SAFWS CB11 31 L7
STALE/WH AL4 137 P2
STAN HA7 164 A9
STDN SG11 71 J3
Park Lane Paradise
CHESW EN7 141 P3
Park Md HLW CM20 2 B3
Park Meadow BRKMPK AL9 122 F5
Park Meadow Cl
AMP/FLIT/BLC MK45 32 C5
Park Ms BRKMPK AL9 * 122 F5
Park Mt HARP AL5 101 M2
Park Nook Gdns ENC/FH EN2 155 L7
Park Pl AMS HP6 145 K8
DEN/HRF UB9 * 169 N5
LCOL/BKTW AL2 136 C6
STVG SG1 10 D5
Park Ri BERK HP4 115 K5
HARP AL5 101 M1
KTN/HRWW/WS HA3 172 E5
Park Rise Cl HARP AL5 101 M1
Park Rd AMS HP6 145 L7
BAR EN5 166 D3
BUNT SG9 41 M8
BUSH WD23 163 J5
CHES/WCR EN8 156 C3
CSHM HP5 144 G1
DUN/HR/TOD LU5 60 F7
EBAR EN4 167 H3
HERT/BAY SG13 107 M6
HHW HP1 4 D5
HOD EN11 126 F5
PEND EN3 156 D6
POTB/CUF EN6 140 B9
RAD WD7 150 F5
RBSF CM22 59 L1
RKW/CH/CXG WD3 161 J6
STHGT/OAK N14 167 P6
STSD CM24 58 F5
TRING HP23 113 N1
WARE SG12 108 A3
WAT WD17 149 H9
Park Rd North
DUN/HR/TOD LU5 60 F1
Parkside BUNT SG9 40 B5
CFSP/GDCR SL9 168 D9
CHES/WCR EN8 156 D4
HHS/BOV HP3 * 134 B6
OXHEY WD19 * 162 E5
WLYN AL6 84 F8
Parkside Cl
DUN/HR/TOD LU5 60 G1
Parkside Dr
DUN/HR/TOD LU5 60 G1
EDGW HA8 164 G9
WAT WD17 12 B1

Parkside Gdns *EBAR* EN4........... 167 K7
Parkside Rd *NTHWD* HA6........... 171 H2
Parkside Wy
  RYLN/HDSTN HA2........... 172 B8
Park St *BERK* HP4........... 115 N6
  BLDK SG7........... 26 A9
  BRKMPK AL9........... 122 F5
  DUN/WHIP LU6........... 60 D5
  HTCHE/RSTV SC4........... 49 K1
  LCOL/BKTW AL2........... 136 C6
  LTN LU1........... 7 F5
  TRING HP23........... 95 P9
Park Street La
  LCOL/BKTW AL2........... 136 A8
Park St West *LTN* LU1........... 7 F5
Park Ter *GSTN* WD25 *........... 149 L3
  LTN LU1........... 7 C6
  PEND EN3 *........... 156 D8
The Park *HERT/WAT* SG14 *........... 68 A3
  STAL AL1........... 120 F6
  STALW/RED AL3........... 101 L5
Park Vlad *LTN* LU1........... 7 J8
Park Vw *BRKMPK* AL9........... 122 F4
  HOD EN11........... 126 F6
  PIN HA5........... 171 P5
  POTB/CUF EN6........... 153 M5
  STVGE SG2........... 67 L5
Park View *EDGW* HA8........... 173 P5
  HTCH/STOT SG5........... 49 K1
  RKW/CH/CXG WD3........... 160 C7
Park View Dr *STALW/RED* AL3........... 79 N7
Park Vw Rd *BERK* HP4........... 115 K7
  PIN HA5........... 171 K3
Parkway *LTN/WGCW* AL8........... 123 B8
  STVGE SG2........... 67 L5
Parkway Cl *STAL* AL1........... 136 C2
Parkway Gdns *WGCW* AL8........... 106 F7
Parkway Rd *LTN* LU1........... 8 B3
Parkwood Cl *BROX* EN10........... 126 C7
Parkwood Dr *HHW* HP1........... 117 J8
Parliament Sq
  HERT/WAT SG14........... 107 L6
Parnall Rd *HLWS* CM18........... 128 C7
Parndon Mill La *HLW* CM20........... 110 E9
Parndon Wood Rd
  HLWW/ROY CM19........... 128 F8
Parnell Cl *ABLGY* WD5........... 134 G9
  EDGW HA8........... 173 P4
Parnel Rd *WARE* SG12........... 108 E2
Parpins *KGLCY* WD4 *........... 133 P7
Parr Crs *HHNE* HP2........... 118 C3
Parr Cl *DUN/HR/TOD* LU5........... 61 H5
Parrotts Cl
  RKW/CH/CXG WD3........... 161 L3
Parrotts Fld *HOD* EN11........... 126 C4
Parrott's La *TRING* HP23........... 113 P8
Parr Rd *STAN* HA7........... 173 K5
Parsley Cl *RAYLNE/WEN* HP22........... 94 D7
Parsloe Rd *EPP* CM16........... 128 D9
Parsonage Cl *ABLGY* WD5........... 134 F9
  TRING HP23........... 95 P8
Parsonage Farm
  RAYLNE/WEN HP22........... 76 C2
Parsonage La *BRKMPK* AL9........... 138 E2
  BSF CM23........... 74 C2
  HTCHE/RSTV SC4........... 64 F1
  SAFWS CB11........... 43 L5
  STDN SG11........... 56 F2
  STSD CM24........... 58 C7
Parsonage Leys *HLW* CM20........... 3 J4
  TRING HP23........... 95 P9
Parsonage Rd *BRKMPK* AL9........... 138 E2
  CSTG HP8........... 159 H9
  RKW/CH/CXG WD3........... 161 H6
Parson's Cl *STALW/RED* AL3........... 100 C3
Parsons Crs *EDGW* HA8........... 164 G9
Parsons Green Est
  STVG SG1 *........... 51 M5
Parthia Cl *ROY* SG8........... 20 D4
Parton Cl *RAYLNE/WEN* HP22........... 94 B5
Partridge Cl *BAR* EN5........... 166 A5
  BUSH WD23 *........... 161 L8
  CSHM HP5........... 131 K7
  LTNW/LEA LU4........... 61 K1
  STAN HA7........... 173 L1
Partridge Ct *HHNE* HP2........... 118 C6
Partridge Hl *BLDK* SG7........... 17 M7
Partridge Rd *HLWS* CM18........... 128 G5
  STALW/RED AL3........... 120 C4
The Partridges *HHS/BOV* HP3........... 146 B7
Parvills *WAB* EN9........... 102 C6
Pascoe La *DUN/WHIP* LU3........... 46 F9
Pascal Wy *LWTH* SG6........... 36 E1
Pascomb Rd *DUN/WHIP* LU6........... 60 C6
Pasfield *WAB* EN9........... 157 J3
Passingham Av
  HTCHE/RSTV SC4........... 49 M1
Paston Rd *HHNE* HP2........... 117 N6
Pasture Cl *BUSH* WD23........... 163 L6
Pasture La *HTCHE/RSTV* SC4........... 64 D6
Pasture Rd *LWTH* SG6........... 23 J9
The Pastures *HAT* AL10........... 122 E7
  HHW HP1........... 117 H7
  LCOL/BKTW AL2........... 135 P3
  OXHEY WD19........... 162 D6
  STVGE SG2........... 51 N7
  TRDC/WHET N20........... 102 B1
  WARE SG12........... 108 B1
  WGCE AL7........... 105 K8
Pastures Wy *LTNW/LEA* LU4........... 61 J1
Paternoster Cl *WAB* EN9........... 157 L3
Paternoster Hl *WAB* EN9........... 157 L2
Path Stort Valley Wy
  HERT/BAY SG15........... 141 J1
The Pathway *OXHEY* WD19........... 162 F7
Patmer Rd *WD7........... 150 E6
Patmore Cl *BSF* CM23........... 73 M6
Patmore Link Rd *HHNE* HP2........... 118 D5
Patmore Rd *HHNE* HP2........... 157 K4
Patricia Gdns *BSF* CM23........... 73 P9
Patrick Gv *WAB* EN9........... 156 C3
Patterdale Cl *DUN/WHIP* LU6........... 60 E7

Patterson Rd *CSHM* HP5........... 130 G7
Paul Cl *CHESW* EN7........... 141 K4
Paulhan Rd
  KTN/HRWW/WS HA3........... 173 K8
Pauls Ct *HOD* EN11 *........... 126 F5
Pauls La *HOD* EN11 *........... 126 F5
The Pavilion
  CHES/WCR EN8........... 156 D4
Pavilion Wy *AMS* HP6........... 145 P9
Paxton Dr *HTCH/STOT* SG5........... 24 G7
Paxton Rd *BERK* HP4 *........... 116 B7
Paycock Rd
  HLWW/ROY CM19........... 128 D5
Payne End *BUNT* SG9........... 28 B8
Paynes Cl *LWTH* SG6........... 25 L8
Paynes Field Cl *BERK* HP4........... 115 J5
Paynesfield Rd *BUSH* WD23........... 165 P6
Paynes La *WAB* EN9........... 143 H5
Payne's Pk *HTCH/STOT* SG5........... 35 K9
Peace Cl *CHESW* EN7........... 142 A8
  STHGT/OAK N14........... 167 M4
Peace Gv *WLYN* AL6........... 85 K6
Peach Cl *LTN* LU1........... 7 G6
Peacocks *HLWW/ROY* CM19........... 128 C5
Peacocks Cl *BERK* HP4........... 115 L4
Peakes La *CHESW* EN7........... 141 N6
Peakes Pl *STAL* AL1 *........... 9 J4
Peakes Wy *CHESW* EN7........... 141 N6
Pea La *BERK* HP4........... 115 J5
Pearce Rd *CSHM* HP5........... 131 M1
Pearces Wk *STAL* AL1 *........... 9 F5
Peareswood Gdns *STAN* HA7........... 173 K5
Pearl Ct *BLDK* SG7 *........... 26 B8
Pearman Dr *WARE* SG12........... 69 M7
Pearsall Cl *LWTH* SG6........... 36 G5
Pearson Av *HERT/BAY* SG15........... 107 K9
Pearson Cl *BAR* EN5........... 166 F2
Pearsons Cl *HERT/BAY* SG15........... 107 K8
Pear Tree La *AMSS* HP7........... 145 L9
Peartree Cl *DUN/HR/TOD* LU5........... 44 B2
  HHW HP1........... 117 K7
  WGCE AL7........... 105 H6
Peartree Ct *WGCE* AL7........... 105 H7
Peartree La *WGCE* AL7........... 105 H7
Pear Tree Md *HLWS* CM18........... 129 K6
Peartree Rd *HHW* HP1........... 117 K7
  LTNE LU2........... 63 K2
Peartree Wy *STVGE* SG2........... 67 K3
Pearwood Cots *STAN* HA7 *........... 164 C8
Peascroft Rd *HHNE* HP2........... 119 P5
Peasmead *BUNT* SG9........... 54 C1
Peck Ct *AMP/FLIT/BLC* MK45........... 32 C4
Peck's Hl *WAB* EN9........... 127 K9
Pedlars La *ROY* SG8........... 28 E2
Pedley Hl *BERK* HP4........... 137 P9
Pednor Dr *CSHM* HP5........... 130 A7
Pednormead End *CSHM* HP5........... 144 G2
Pednor Rd *CSHM* HP5........... 144 F1
Peel Cl *HERT/WAT* SG14........... 107 J3
Peel Pl *LTN* LU1 *........... 6 B5
Peel Rd *KTN/HRWW/WS* HA3........... 173 H7
Peel St *KTN/HR/TOD* LU5........... 60 E1
  LTN LU1 *........... 6 D4
Peerless Dr *DEN/HRF* UB9........... 169 M8
Pegasus Pl *STALW/RED* AL3........... 120 C6
Peggs La *RAYLNE/WEN* HP22........... 94 C7
Pegmire La *GSTN* WD25........... 150 B9
Pegrams Rd *HLWS* CM18........... 128 F6
Pegsdon Cl *LTNN/LIM* LU3........... 46 C8
Pegsdon Wy *HTCH/STOT* SG5........... 33 L7
Peg's La *HERT/BAY* SG15........... 107 L7
Pegs La *WARE* SG12........... 90 A8
Peldon Rd *HLWW/ROY* CM19........... 128 D5
Pelham Ct *HHW* HP1........... 118 D8
  WGCE AL7 *........... 105 M7
Pelham Rd *SAFWS* CB11........... 43 L4
  STDN SG11........... 55 L8
The Pelhams *GSTN* WD25........... 149 L5
Pelican Wy *LWTH* SG6........... 25 K8
Pemberton Cl *STAL* AL1 *........... 136 C2
Pembridge Cha
  HHS/BOV HP3........... 132 C7
Pembridge Cl *HHS/BOV* HP3........... 132 C7
Pembridge La *BROX* EN10........... 125 N9
Pembridge Rd *HHS/BOV* HP3........... 132 C7
Pembroke Av *EN* EN1........... 156 A9
  KTN/HRWW/WS HA3........... 172 G7
  LTNW/LEA LU4........... 61 P3
Pembroke Cl *BROX* EN10........... 142 D5
Pembroke Dr *CHESW* EN7........... 141 J8
Pembroke Ldg *STAN* HA7 *........... 173 J5
Pembroke Pl *EDGW* HA8........... 173 N4
Pembroke Rd *BLDK* SG7........... 26 B9
  NTHWD HA6........... 161 N9
Pemsel Ct *HHNE* HP2 *........... 5 G6
  HHS/BOV HP3........... 5 G6
Penda Cl *LTNN/LIM* LU3........... 46 A9
Pendall Cl *EBAR* EN4........... 167 J3
Pendennis Ct *HARP* AL5........... 102 C5
Penfold Rd *HHW* HP1........... 117 K4
Penfold *LTNN/LIM* LU3........... 45 P8
Penfold Cl *BLDK* SG7........... 37 K1
Pengelly Cl *CHESW* EN7........... 141 J6
Penhill *LTNN/LIM* LU3........... 45 P8
Penlow Rd *HLWS* CM18........... 128 F6
Penman Cl *LCOL/BKTW* AL2........... 135 P6
Penn Cl *HTCH/STOT* SG5........... 130 F9
Penn Cl *KTN/HRWW/WS* HA3........... 173 J4
Penn Gaskell La
  CFSP/GDCR SL9........... 168 D2
Pennine Av *LTNN/LIM* LU3........... 45 M7
Pennine La *HHNE* HP2........... 118 A3
The Pennings
  RAYLNE/WEN HP22........... 112 C6
Pennington *LA* STSD* CM24........... 58 E5
Pennington Dr
  CFSP/GDCR SL9........... 168 B4
Penningtons *BSF* CM23........... 73 M9
The Pennings *AMS* HP6........... 145 K7
Penn Rd *LCOL/BKTW* AL2........... 136 B6
  RKW/CH/CXG WD3........... 160 B5
Penn Wy *LWTH* SG6........... 36 E5
  RKW/CH/CXG WD3........... 160 B5
Penny Cft *HARP* AL5........... 101 P8

Pennyfather Av *KNEB* SG3........... 85 P3
Pennyfathers La *WLYN* AL6........... 85 K9
Pennymead *HLW* CM20........... 129 K2
Penrith Av *DUN/WHIP* LU6........... 60 E7
Penrose Av *DUN/WHIP* WD19........... 162 G8
Penrose Ct *HHNE* HP2........... 117 P4
Penscroft Gdns *BORE* WD6........... 165 K3
Penshurst *HLWE* CM17........... 111 L9
Penshurst Rd *CFSP/GDCR* SL9........... 168 B6
  HARP AL5........... 81 L9
Penshurst Gdns *EDGW* HA8........... 173 P2
Penshurst Rd *POTB/CUF* EN6........... 153 L7
Pensilver Cl *EBAR* EN4........... 167 J3
Penta Ct *BORE* WD6 *........... 164 C3
Pentland *HHNE* HP2........... 118 A5
Pentland Av *EDGW* HA8........... 165 H8
Pentland Rd *STVG* SG1........... 51 M4
Pentland Rd *BUSH* WD23........... 163 L5
Pentley Pk *WGCW* AL8........... 104 F5
Penton Dr *CHES/WCR* EN8........... 142 C8
Pentrich Av *EN* EN1........... 155 P8
Penylan Pl *EDGW* HA8 *........... 173 N5
Penzance Cl *DEN/HRF* UB9 *........... 169 J3
Peplins Cl *BRKMPK* AL9........... 139 H5
Peplins Wy *BRKMPK* AL9........... 139 H4
Peppard Cl *STALW/RED* AL3........... 101 N6
Peppercorn Wk
  HTCHE/RSTV SC4........... 35 N9
Peppercorn Wy
  DUN/WHIP LU6........... 60 C4
Pepper Hl *WARE* SG12........... 108 G4
Peppett's Gn *CSHM* HP5........... 130 C2
Pepsal End *STVGE* SG2........... 67 L5
Pepsal End Rd *LTN* LU1........... 7 L9
Pepys Crs *BAR* EN5........... 166 A4
Pepys Wy *BLDK* SG7........... 25 P9
Percheron Dr *LTNW/LEA* LU4........... 61 K3
Percheron Rd *BORE* WD6........... 165 K5
Perch Mdw
  RAYLNE HP22........... 112 C3
Percival Av *LTNE* LU2........... 63 K7
Percy Rd *WATW* WD18........... 13 F4
Percy Ter *CSTC* HP8........... 158 C9
Peregrine Cl *BSF* CM23........... 73 N8
  STVGE SG2........... 67 N1
Peregrine Rd *LTNW/LEA* LU4........... 61 K2
Peregrin Rd *WAB* EN9........... 143 M3
Perham Wy *LCOL/BKTW* AL2........... 137 J5
Perivale Gdns *GSTN* WD25........... 149 J4
Periwinkle Cl *ROY* SG8........... 30 A4
Periwinkle La *DUN/WHIP* LU6........... 60 F7
  HTCH/STOT SG5........... 35 L7
Periwinkle Ter
  CFSP/GDCR SL9........... 168 A4
Perowne Wy *STDN* SG11........... 71 K3
Perram Cl *RAD* WD7........... 151 K3
Perram Ct *LTNW/LEA* LU4........... 61 M3
Perrett Gdns *HERT/WAT* SG14........... 106 F5
Perriors Cl *CHESW* EN7........... 141 P6
Perry Dr *ROY* SG8........... 20 D5
Perry Gn *HHNE* HP2........... 118 B2
Perry Hl *WAB* EN9........... 143 L2
Perry Md *BUSH* WD23........... 163 L5
Perrymead *LTNE* LU2........... 63 N4
Perry Rd *HLWS* CM18........... 128 F6
Perrysfield Rd
  CHES/WCR EN8........... 142 D5
Perry Spring *HLWE* CM17........... 129 M5
Perry St *RAYLNE/WEN* HP22........... 112 B6
Perrywood La *WCCW* AL8........... 104 G4
Perrywood La
  HERT/WAT SG14........... 86 B6
Pescot Hl *HHW* HP1........... 117 L6
Petard Cl *LTNW/LEA* LU4........... 61 L2
Peterhill Ct *CFSP/GDCR* SL9........... 168 C2
Peterlee Ct *HHNE* HP2........... 118 A4
Peters Av *LCOL/BKTW* AL2........... 137 H5
Peters Cl *STAN* HA7........... 173 K3
Petersfield *STALW/RED* AL3........... 120 D4
Petersfield Gdns
  LTNN/LIM LU3........... 45 P6
Peter's Pl *HARP* AL5........... 115 K5
Peters Wy *KNEB* SG3........... 67 J8
Peterswood *HLWS* CM18........... 128 G7
Peters Wood Hl *WARE* SG12........... 108 C5
Pettys Ct *CHES/WCR* EN8........... 142 C7
Petunia Ct *LTNN/LIM* LU3........... 62 D5
Petworth Ct *STVGE* SG2........... 63 L2
Pevensey Cl *LTNE* LU2........... 63 L2
Pewterers Av *BSF* CM23........... 91 M1
Pheasant Cl *BERK* HP4........... 115 P8
  TRING HP23........... 96 A6
Pheasant Hl *CSTG* HP8........... 159 J8
Pheasant Ri *AMS* HP7........... 145 J3
Pheasants Wy
  RKW/CH/CXG WD3........... 160 F6
Pheasant Wk *CFSP/GDCR* SL9........... 168 D6
Phelips Rd *HLWW/ROY* CM19........... 128 D1
Phillimore Ct *RAD* WD7........... 150 D6
Phillimore Pl *RAD* WD7........... 150 D6
Philips Av *ROY* SG8........... 20 B2
Phipps Hatch La *ENC/FH* EN2........... 155 K8
Phoebe Rd *HHNE* HP2........... 118 C5
Phoenix Ct *NTHWD* HA6........... 171 H1
The Phygtle *CFSP/GDCR* SL9........... 168 C5
Piccotts End La *HHW* HP1........... 117 M5
Piccotts End Rd *HHW* HP1........... 117 L4
Pickard Cl *STHGT/OAK* N14........... 167 P7
Pickets Cl *BUSH* WD23........... 163 M7
Pickets St *BUSH* WD23........... 173 K5
Pickets *WGCW* AL8........... 104 C6
Pickford Hl *HARP* AL5........... 102 B1
Pick Hl *WAB* EN9........... 157 M2
Picknage Rd *ROY* SG8........... 21 M8
Pie Cnr *LTNW/RED* AL3........... 100 D3
Pie Gdn *STALW/RED* AL3........... 100 D3
Pierian Spring *HHW* HP1........... 117 L6
Pietley Hl *STALW/RED* AL3........... 100 B3
Pigeonwick *HARP* AL5........... 101 P1
Piggottshill La *HARP* AL5........... 102 B2
Piggotts La *LTNW/LEA* LU4........... 61 N2
Piggotts Orch *HARP* AL5........... 158 B1
Piggotts Wy *BSF* CM23........... 73 P8
Piggy La *RKW/CH/CXG* WD3........... 159 M1
The Pightle *LBUZ* LU7........... 96 C1
Pig La *RBSF* CM22........... 74 B7
Pigotts Wy *BSF* CM23........... 73 P8

Pike End *STVG* SG1........... 10 D1
Pike's End *PIN* HA5........... 171 K8
Pikes Leap *STALE/WH* AL4........... 103 J3
Pilgrim Cl *GSTN* WD25........... 149 L3
  LCOL/BKTW AL2........... 136 B6
Pilgrim's Ri *EBAR* EN4........... 167 J4
Pilgrims Wy *STVG* SG1........... 51 L5
Pikingtons *HLWE* CM17........... 129 N3
Piltdown Rd *OXHEY* WD19........... 171 M1
Pinceybrook Rd *HLWS* CM18........... 128 F7
Pincey Rd *STSD* CM24........... 59 N8
Pinchfield *RKW/CH/CXG* WD3........... 169 H1
Pindar Rd *HOD* EN11........... 127 H4
Pineapple Rd *AMSS* HP7........... 145 L9
Pine Cl *HARP* AL5........... 81 J8
  CHES/WCR EN8........... 142 B7
  STAN HA7........... 173 H1
  STHCT/OAK N14........... 167 N6
Pine Crest *WLYN* AL6........... 85 H5
Pinecroft *HHS/BOV* HP3........... 134 A3
  KTN/HRWW/WS HA3........... 173 M9
Pinecroft Crs *BAR* EN5........... 166 C3
Pine Gv *BRKMPK* AL9........... 139 L4
  BSF CM23........... 73 N4
  BUSH WD23........... 149 N9
  LCOL/BKTW AL2........... 135 N3
  TRDG/WHET N20........... 166 D7
Pinehurst La *ABLGY* WD5........... 148 F2
Pinelands *BSF* CM23........... 74 A1
Pine Rdg *STAL* AL1 *........... 136 F2
Pine Rd *FBAR/BDGN* N11........... 167 L8
Pines Av *EN* EN1........... 156 B6
Pines Cl *AMS* HP6........... 144 G7
  NTHWD HA6........... 170 G3
Pines Hl *STSD* CM24........... 58 E6
The Pines *BORE* WD6........... 164 F1
  HHS/BOV HP3........... 133 H3
  STHGT/OAK N14........... 167 N4
Pinetree Cl *CFSP/GDCR* SL9........... 168 A4
Pine Wk *BERK* HP4........... 115 M8
Pinewood Av *PIN* HA5........... 172 B5
Pinewood Cl *BORE* WD6........... 152 A9
  HLWE CM17........... 129 N3
  LTNN/LIM LU3........... 45 M6
  NTHWD HA6........... 171 J2
  PIN HA5........... 171 H4
  STALE/WH AL4........... 121 H8
  WAT WD17........... 150 A6
Pinewood Dr *POTB/CUF* EN6........... 153 J1
Pinewood Gdns *HHNE* HP2 *........... 5 H5
  HHW HP1........... 5 H5
Pinewood Ldg *BUSH* WD23 *........... 163 M7
Pinewoods *STVGE* SG2 *........... 51 J7
Pinfold Rd *BUSH* WD23........... 149 J9
Pinford Dell *LTNE* LU2........... 63 L5
Pinkeneys *ROY* SG8........... 20 E6
Pinnacles *WAB* EN9........... 157 K4
Pinnate Pl *WGCE* AL7........... 123 H1
Pinn Cl *PIN* HA5........... 171 J4
Pinner Cl *PIN* HA5........... 172 A8
Pinner Gn *PIN* HA5........... 171 K1
Pinner Hl *PIN* HA5........... 171 K4
Pinner Hill Rd *PIN* HA5........... 171 K3
Pinner Pk *PIN* HA5........... 171 P1
Pinner Park Av
  RYLN/HDSTN HA2........... 172 C6
Pinner Park Gdns
  RYLN/HDSTN HA2........... 172 A6
Pinner Rd *HRW* HA1........... 172 B5
  OXHEY WD19........... 161 N9
  PIN HA5........... 171 P9
Pinner Vw *HRW* HA1........... 172 C5
  RYLN/HDSTN HA2........... 172 B5
Pinnocks La *BLDK* SG7........... 37 J1
Pintail Cl *LTNW/LEA* LU4........... 61 J2
Pin Ct *BORE* WD6 *........... 165 K5
Pioneer Wy *WATW* WD18........... 162 B3
Pipers Av *HARP* AL5........... 102 C5
Pipers Cft *DUN/WHIP* LU6........... 60 C7
Pipers Green La *STAN* HA7........... 164 E9
Pipers Hl *HHW* HP1........... 117 H5
Pipers La *HARP* AL5........... 102 D5
Pippens *WGCW* AL8........... 105 H3
Pippin Cl *RAD* WD7........... 151 K3
Pippin Gv *ROY* SG8........... 21 K5
The Pippins *WD25........... 149 K4
Pirton Cl *HTCH/STOT* SG5........... 35 J9
Pirton Rd *HTCH/STOT* SG5........... 34 F2
  LTNW/LEA LU4........... 61 J2
Pishiobury Dr *SBW* CM21........... 111 N4
Pitfield Wy *PEND* EN3........... 156 B9
Pitsfield *WGCW* AL8........... 104 G3
Pitstone Cl *STALE/WH* AL4........... 121 H3
Pitt Dr *STALE/WH* AL4........... 137 H2
Pittman's Fld *HLW* CM20........... 3 J3
Pix Ct *ARL/CHE* SG15........... 24 E1
Pix Farm La *HHW* HP1........... 116 E9
Pixies Hill Crs *HHW* HP1........... 133 J1
Pixies Hill Rd *HHW* HP1........... 117 J9
Pixmore Av *LWTH* SG6........... 36 E2
Pixmore Est *LWTH* SG6 *........... 36 E2
Pixmore Wy *LWTH* SG6........... 25 J4
  LWTH SG6........... 36 E2
Place Farm *STALE/WH* AL4........... 103 J3
Plaistow Wy *ROY* SG8........... 22 B8
Plaiters Ct *TRING* HP23........... 95 P8
Plaiters Wy
  DUN/HR/TOD LU5........... 60 D1
Plaitford Cl
  RKW/CH/CXG WD3........... 161 J6
Plantaganet Pl *WAB* EN9........... 156 C3
Plantagenet Rd *BAR* EN5........... 166 G3
Plantation Rd *AMS* HP6........... 145 H8
  LTNN/LIM LU3........... 45 N8
Plantation Wk *HHW* HP1........... 117 K5
Plash Dr *STVG* SG1........... 10 E4
Plashes Dr *BUNT* SG9........... 54 D3
Plashets *RBSF* CM22........... 92 D8
The Plashets *RBSF* CM22........... 92 D9
Platt Cl *LTNW/LEA* LU4........... 61 N2
Platts Rd *PEND* EN3........... 156 B9
The Platt *AMSS* HP7........... 158 B1
Plaw Hatch Cl *BSF* CM23........... 74 C2

Playford Sq *LTNW/LEA* LU4 *........... 61 N1
Playhouse Sq *HLW* CM20........... 2 D5
The Pleasance *HARP* AL5........... 81 L9
Pleasant Pl
  RKW/CH/CXG WD3........... 169 J4
Pleasant Ri *BRKMPK* AL9........... 122 F3
Pleasant Rd *BSF* CM23........... 73 P6
The Pleasaunce
  RAYLNE/WEN HP22........... 94 F7
Plewes Cl *DUN/WHIP* LU6........... 79 H5
Plomer Av *HOD* EN11........... 126 C2
Plough Cl *LTNW/LEA* LU4........... 61 H2
Plough Ct *LTNW/LEA* LU4 *........... 61 H2
Plough Dr *HOD* EN11........... 126 C2
Plough La *BERK* HP4........... 138 B9
  DEN/HRF UB9........... 169 N3
  HTCHE/RSTV SC4........... 64 F1
  RKW/CH/CXG WD3........... 147 J3
Ploughmans Cl *BSF* CM23........... 73 M9
Ploughmans End *WGCE* AL7........... 105 M7
Plough Rbt *HHNE* HP2........... 5 F2
Plover Cl *BERK* HP4........... 115 P8
Ployters Rd
  HLWW/ROY CM19........... 128 F7
Plummers La *LTNE* LU2........... 82 C4
Plumpton Cl *LTNE* LU2........... 63 P3
Plumpton Rd *HOD* EN11........... 127 H3
Pluto Rd *HHNE* HP2........... 117 P7
Plymouth Cl *LTNE* LU2........... 63 A5
Plymouth Dr *HHW* HP1........... 117 L6
Poets Cl *HARP* AL5........... 102 A3
Poets Ga *CHESW* EN7........... 141 L7
Poets Wk *WAB* EN9........... 61 K4
  LTNW/LEA LU4........... 172 E8
Polayn Garth *WGCW* AL8........... 104 F5
Polegate *LTNE* LU2........... 63 L4
Polehanger La *HHW* HP1........... 117 H6
Poles Hl *CSHM* HP5........... 130 E8
  RKW/CH/CXG WD3........... 147 H3
Poles La *WGCE* AL7........... 108 B1
Police Rw *ROY* SG8........... 88 B7
  *........... 28 F2
Polish Av
  RAYLNE/WEN HP22........... 112 F3
Pollard Gdns *STVG* SG1........... 51 J7
Pollard Hatch
  HLWW/ROY CM19........... 128 E6
Pollards Cl *TRDG/WHET* N20........... 167 H2
Pollards Cl *CHESW* EN7........... 169 H2
Pollards Cl *CHESW* EN7........... 141 K8
Pollards Wy *HTCH/STOT* SG5........... 34 B4
Pollywick Rd *TRING* HP23........... 114 C2
Polsten Ms *PEND* EN3........... 156 F7
Polzeath Cl *LTNE* LU2........... 63 K6
Pomeroy Cl *AMSS* HP7........... 158 D1
Pomeroy Crs *WATN* WD24........... 149 J6
Pomeroy Gv *LTNE* LU2........... 63 N3
Pomfret Av *LTNE* LU2........... 7 H2
Pond Cl *DEN/HRF* UB9........... 169 N6
  LTNW/LEA LU4........... 61 L1
Pond Cft *STVGE* SG2........... 50 F8
Pond Ct *HTCHE/RSTV* SC4 *........... 84 C4
  WGCE AL7........... 122 C5
Pondcroft Rd *KNEB* SG3........... 85 K1
Pondfield Crs *STALE/WH* AL4........... 120 G5
Pond La *BERK* HP4........... 138 G1
  BLDK SG7........... 26 A9
  RBSF CM22........... 93 H6
Pond Park Rd *CSHM* HP5........... 130 C8
Pondside *HTCHE/RSTV* SC4........... 134 B4
  *........... 50 F5
Pondsmeade
  STALW/RED AL3........... 101 J7
Pondwick Rd *HARP* AL5........... 101 M1
Pondwicks *AMSS* HP7........... 144 G9
Pondwicks Cl *LTN* LU1........... 8 D5
Pondwicks Rd *LTN* LU1........... 7 J4
Pooleys La *BRKMPK* AL9........... 138 E2
Popes La *WATN* WD24........... 149 J7
Pope's Rd *ABLGY* WD5........... 148 F1
Popes Rw *WARE* SG12........... 108 D2
Popis Gdns *WARE* SG12........... 108 D1
Poplar Av *AMSS* HP7........... 145 L9
  HAT AL10........... 122 A6
  LTNN/LIM LU3........... 62 C2
Poplar Cl *CSHM* HP5........... 131 H7
  HTCHE/RSTV SC4........... 64 M2
  PIN HA5........... 171 M5
  ROY SG8........... 20 D3
  STAN HA7........... 88 E4
Poplar Dr *ROY* SG8........... 20 D3
Poplar Rd *DUN/WHIP* LU6........... 60 B5
Poplars Cl *HAT* AL10........... 122 C5
The Poplars *ARL/CHE* SG15........... 24 E1
  BORE WD6 *........... 151 M9
  CHESW EN7........... 141 M5
  DEN/HRF UB9 *........... 169 N5
  *........... 4 A4
  HTCH/STOT SG5........... 35 L3
  RAYLNE/WEN HP22........... 112 D6
  STAL AL1........... 34 D4
  STHGT/OAK N14........... 167 M4
Poppy Cl *HHW* HP1........... 117 H7
  LTNN/LIM LU3........... 62 E4
Poppyfields *WGCE* AL7........... 105 M6
Poppy Md *STVG* SG1........... 11 H6
Poppy Wk *CHESW* EN7........... 141 L7
Porch Wy *TRDG/WHET* N20........... 166 E3
Porlock Dr *LTNE* LU2........... 63 K5
Portal Rd *RAYLNE/WEN* HP22........... 112 C3
Porters Cl *BUNT* SG9........... 40 D8
Porters Hl *HARP* AL5........... 102 B2
Porters Ms *HTCHE/RSTV* SC4........... 84 C4
Porters Park Dr *RAD* WD7........... 151 K2
Porters Wd *STALW/RED* AL3........... 120 E4
Port Hl *HERT/WAT* SG14........... 107 K6
Portland Cl *DUN/HR/TOD* LU5........... 60 E3
Portland Cl *LTNW/LEA* LU4........... 61 B5
Portland Crs *STAN* HA7........... 173 K6
Portland Crs West *STAN* HA7........... 173 K7
Portland Dr *CHESW* EN7........... 155 P1
  ENC/FH EN2........... 155 M8
Portland Pl *BSF* CM23........... 74 A3
  HERT/BAY SG15........... 108 B8

Portland Ride
DUN/HR/TOD LU5....... 60 E4
Portland Rd BSF CM23....... 74 A3
    LTNW/LEA LU4....... 62 B5
Portland St STALW/RED AL3....... 8 C3
Portman Dr HTCH/STOT SG5....... 35 J6
    STALE/WH HA4....... 121 H3
Portmill La HTCH/STOT SG5....... 35 L9
Portobello Cl
AMP/FLIT/BLC MK45....... 32 D6
    CSHM HP5....... 130 F8
Port V HERT/WAT SG14....... 107 K6
Porz Av DUN/HR/TOD LU5....... 60 G3
Postfield WGCE AL7....... 105 K3
Post Office Rd HLW CM20....... 2 E4
Post Office Rw
HTCHE/RSTV SG4....... 37 L7
Postwood Gn
HERT/BAY SG13....... 108 B9
Post Wood Rd WARE SG12....... 108 D5
Potash La TRING HP23....... 76 D9
Potten End Hl HHW HP1....... 117 H3
Potterells BRKMPK AL9 *....... 138 C4
The Potteries BAR EN5....... 33 L9
Potters Bar Station Yd
POTB/CUF EN6 *....... 153 K1
Potterscrouch La
LCOL/BKTW AL2....... 135 L3
Potters Fld HLWE CM17 *....... 123 J8
Potters Gn ROY SG8....... 15 K5
Pottersheath Rd WLYN AL6....... 84 C4
Potters Heights Cl PIN HA5....... 171 K4
Potters La BAR EN5....... 166 E3
Potters Rd BORE WD6....... 151 P9
Potter St BSF CM23....... 74 A3
    HLWE CM17....... 124 M4
    NTHWD HA6....... 161 J6
Potter Street Hl PIN HA5....... 171 K3
Potters Wood Cl WARE SG12....... 70 B8
Pottery Cl LTNW/LIM LU3....... 46 A8
Potton Dr ROY SG8....... 15 K5
Pouchen End La HHW HP1....... 116 C9
Poulteney Rd STSD CM24....... 58 F6
Poultney Cl RAD WD7....... 151 K2
Pound Av STVG SG1....... 10 C2
Pound Cl STALE/WH AL4....... 121 H1
    WAB EN9....... 143 K2
Pound Ct STVG SG1....... 10 C1
Pound Fld CSTN WD25....... 148 C5
Pound Gn ROY SG8....... 15 L6
Pound La CSHM HP5....... 130 E1
    RAD WD7....... 151 L3
Pound Wy RAYLNE/WEN HP22....... 112 C9
Poundwell WGCE AL7....... 105 K7
Powdermill La WAB EN9....... 156 C3
Powdermill Ms WAB EN9....... 156 C3
Powdermill Wy WAB EN9....... 156 C3
Powell Cl EDGW HA8....... 173 M5
Power Ct LTN LU1 *....... 4 C4
Power Dr PEND EN3....... 156 E6
Powis Ct BUSH WD23 *....... 163 M7
    POTB/CUF EN6....... 153 M4
Powys Ct BORE WD6....... 165 K2
Poynders Hl HHW HP1....... 118 D9
Poynders Meadow
HTCHE/RSTV SG4....... 84 C4
Poynings Cl HARP AL5....... 102 E4
Poynters Gn PIN HA5....... 61 H5
Prae Cl STALW/RED AL3....... 8 A2
Praetorian Ct STAL AL1....... 136 B2
Prebendal Dr LTN LU1....... 80 C3
The Precinct BROX EN10 *....... 126 E8
Premier Pl WATW UB18....... 12 E6
Prentice Wy LTNE LU2....... 5 L8
Prescelly Hl EDGW HA8....... 173 M5
Prescott Rd CHES/WCR EN8....... 142 D6
Presdales Dr WARE SG12....... 108 C4
President Wy LTNE LU2....... 63 L6
Prestatyn Cl STVG SG1....... 50 E8
Preston Ct BAR EN5....... 153 L7
Preston Gdns LTNE LU2....... 63 C4
    PEND EN3....... 156 D7
Preston Hl CSHM HP5....... 131 J8
Preston Pth LTNE LU2....... 62 C4
Preston Rd DUN/HR/TOD LU5....... 44 D2
Prestwick Cl LTNE LU2....... 62 C4
Prestwick Dr BSF CM23....... 74 C1
Prestwood OXHEY WD19 *....... 162 G8
Prestwood Av
KTN/HRWW/WS HA3....... 173 H1
Prestwood Cl
KTN/HRWW/WS HA3....... 173 H1
Pretoria Rd WATW WD18....... 12 D5
Prevost Rd
FBAR/BDGN N11....... 167 L8
Pricklers Hl BAR EN5....... 166 F4
Priestland Gdns BERK HP4....... 116 B5
Priestleys LTN LU1....... 67 L1
Priestly Rd STVGE SG2....... 69 J6
Primary Wy ARL/CHE SG15....... 24 E5
Primett Rd STVG SG1....... 10 D2
Primley La RBSF CM22....... 92 D8
Primrose Av ENC/FH EN2....... 155 L9
Primrose Cl ARL/CHE SG15....... 24 E5
    BSF CM23....... 73 M8
    HAT AL10....... 122 E7
    HHW HP1....... 117 H9
    LTNW/LIM LU3....... 45 L7
Primrose Ct STVG SG1....... 10 D1
Primrose Gdns BUSH WD23....... 163 K6
Primrose Hl KGLCY WD4....... 134 C7
Primrose La ARL/CHE SG15....... 24 D8
Primrose Pth CHESW SG12 *....... 155 F1
Primrose Vw ROY SG8....... 20 C5
Prince Andrew's Cl ROY SG8....... 20 C5
Prince Charles Av
HTCH/STOT SG5....... 34 B1
Prince Edwards St BERK HP4....... 115 P7
Prince Edward Wy
HTCH/STOT SG5....... 25 L4

Prince George Av
STHGT/OAK N14....... 167 N4
Prince of Wales Cl
ARL/CHE SG15....... 24 D6
Prince Pk HHW HP1....... 117 K9
Princes Av CDALE/KGS NW9....... 173 N8
    PEND EN3....... 156 D6
    WATW WD18....... 12 B6
Princes Cl BERK HP4....... 115 M5
    CDALE/KGS NW9....... 173 N8
    EDGW HA8....... 173 M2
Princes Ct BSF CM23....... 73 M7
Princes Dr HRW HA1....... 172 E7
Princesfield Rd WAB EN9....... 157 N3
Princes Ga BSF CM23....... 73 M7
Princes Ms ROY SG8....... 20 D5
Princes Pde POTB/CUF EN6 *....... 153 L5
Princess Diana Dr
STALE/WH AL4....... 121 H9
Princess St LTN LU1....... 6 C6
Princes St DUN/HR/TOD LU5....... 44 C2
    DUN/WHIP LU6....... 60 D6
Prince's St HTCH/STOT SG5....... 26 E7
Prince St WARE SG12....... 108 C2
Prince St WD17....... 13 G2
Prince Wy LTNE LU2....... 63 L6
Priors Cl HERT/BAY SG13....... 108 A9
Priors Gv CSHM HP5....... 131 H9
Priors Hl HTCH/STOT SG5....... 34 B4
Priors Pk EN1....... 155 M9
Priors Wood Rd
HERT/BAY SG13....... 108 B9
Priory Cl DEN/HRF UB9....... 169 N8
    HLWE CM17....... 111 M7
Priory Ct BROX CM23....... 142 D3
    DEN/HRF UB9....... 169 N8
    HOD EN11....... 126 F6
    ROY SG8....... 20 D4
    STAN HA7....... 157 M4
    STHGT/OAK N14....... 167 M4
    TRDG/WHET N20....... 166 D6
Priory Cr BSF CM23....... 73 P7
    HLWS CM18....... 129 L6
Priory Dell STVG SG1....... 11 F5
Priory Dr HRW HA1....... 172 F9
    STSD CM24....... 58 F6
Priory End HTCHE/RSTV SG4....... 49 L2
Priory Field Dr EDGW HA8....... 173 P1
Priory Flds WD17....... 148 A3
Priory Gdns BERK HP4....... 115 P7
    DEN/HRF UB9....... 169 N8
    LTNE LU2....... 62 E5
Priory Ga CFSP/GDCR SL9....... 168 A7
Priory La HTCHE/RSTV SG4....... 50 C3
    ROY SG8....... 20 C5
Priory Orch STALW/RED AL3....... 100 C2
Priory Rd CFSP/GDCR SL9....... 168 A7
    DUN/HR/TOD LU5....... 44 B3
Priory St HERT/WAT SG14....... 107 L6
    WARE SG12....... 108 B3
The Priory STALW/RED AL3 *....... 101 J7
Priory Vw BUSH WD23....... 163 N6
Priory Wk HTCHE/RSTV SG4....... 50 C3
Priory Wy CFSP/GDCR SL9....... 168 B7
    RYLN/HDSTN HA2....... 172 B8
Priory Wood Rbt RBSF CM22....... 75 H2
Pritchett Cl PEND EN3....... 156 C7
Proctors Wy BSF CM23....... 74 B6
Proctor Wy LTN LU2....... 63 K7
Progress Pk LTNW/LEA LU4 *....... 45 L8
Progress Wy LTNW/LEA LU4....... 45 L8
The Promenade EDGW HA8 *....... 173 N2
Prospect La HARP AL5....... 101 N8
Prospect Rd BAR EN5....... 84 F8
    CHES/WCR EN8....... 142 B8
    STAL AL1....... 8 E7
Prospect Wy LTNE LU2....... 63 K7
Protea Wy LTN SG6....... 16 J5
Providence Gv STVG SG1....... 51 H7
Providence Wy BLDK SG7....... 37 J1
Provost Wy LTNE LU2....... 63 K6
Prowse Av BUSH WD23....... 163 L8
Pruden Cl STHGT/OAK N14....... 167 N8
Pryor Cl ABLGY WD5....... 135 M6
Pryor Ct STVG SG1....... 50 C7
Pryor Gn HTCH/STOT SG5....... 25 K1
Pryor Rd BLDK SG7....... 37 J1
Pryors Cl BSF CM23....... 74 B4
Pryor Wy LTN SG6....... 16 J5
Puddephat's La
STALE/WH AL4....... 99 N5
Pudding La HHW HP1....... 117 K6
    ROY SG8....... 21 M9
Puddingstone Dr
STALE/WH AL4....... 137 H1
Pulham Av BROX EN10....... 126 D8
Puller Rd BAR EN5....... 166 B1
    HHW HP1....... 117 J7
Pulleys La HHW HP1....... 117 J7
Pulleyfields CSHM HP5....... 130 F9
Pullman Cl STAL AL1....... 9 H7
Pullman Dr HTCHE/RSTV SG4....... 35 M5
Pulpit Cl CSHM HP5....... 130 F8
Pulter's Wy HTCHE/RSTV SG4....... 49 M1
Pump Hl HERT/BAY SG13....... 108 A9
Pump La CSHM HP5....... 145 K3
Punchard Crs PEND EN3....... 156 E6
Punch Bowl La CSHM HP5....... 145 H2
    HHW HP1....... 118 E5
Punchowl Pk HHW HP1....... 118 E5
Purbrook Av GSTN WD25....... 149 K6
Purcell Cl BORE WD6....... 151 J9
    WLYN AL6....... 85 K7
Purcell Rd LTNW/LEA LU4....... 45 L9
Purdom Rd WGCE AL7....... 105 H9
Purford Gn HLWS CM18....... 129 K4
Purkiss Rd HERT/BAY SG13....... 107 K3
Purlings Rd BUSH WD23....... 149 M8
Purryus LTN LU1....... 4 B5
Purwell La HTCHE/RSTV SG4....... 35 P8
Putnams Dr
RAYLNE/WEN HP22....... 94 E7

Putney Rd PEND EN3....... 156 C6
Puttenham Cl OXHEY WD19....... 162 E9
Putteridge Pde LTNE LU2 *....... 63 J2
Putteridge Rd LTNE LU2....... 63 J3
Putters Cft HHW HP1....... 118 A5
Puttocks Cl BRKMPK AL9....... 138 F2
Puttocks Dr BRKMPK AL9....... 138 F2
Pye Gdns BSF CM23....... 73 N6
Pyenest Rd
RKW/ROY CM19....... 128 E6
The Pyghtle BUNT SG9....... 40 C8
    LTN LU1....... 62 B7
Pym Cl EBAR EN4....... 167 H4
Pymmes Brook Trail....... 167 J4
Pymmes Brook Dr EBAR EN4....... 167 J3
Pyms Cl LWTH SG6....... 25 M9
Pynchbek BSF CM23....... 91 P2
Pynchon Paddocks
RBSF CM22....... 92 E2
Pynders La DUN/HR/TOD LU5....... 61 H4
Pynest Green La LOU IG10....... 157 M7
Pynnacles Cl STAN HA7....... 173 H2
Pyot Pth BORE WD6....... 151 M7
Pytchley Cl LTNE LU2....... 62 F1
Pytt Fld HLWE CM17....... 129 L4

Q

The Quadrangle WGCW AL8....... 104 F5
The Quadrant
DUN/HR/TOD LU5....... 60 F1
    HLWW/ROY CM19....... 173 N3
    LWTH SG6....... 36 C2
    ROY SG8....... 20 B2
    RYLN/HDSTN HA2 *....... 172 D7
    STALE/WH AL4....... 120 C5
    STVG SG1....... 10 D5
Quail Wk ROY SG8....... 15 K4
Quaker La WAB EN9....... 157 H4
Quaker Rd WARE SG12....... 108 D3
Quakers La POTB/CUF EN6....... 139 L9
Quakers Md
RAYLNE/WEN HP22....... 94 A9
Quantock Cl LTNN/LIM LU3....... 46 C7
    STALE/WH AL4....... 121 H4
    STVG SG1....... 51 N4
Quantock Ct LTNN/LIM LU3 *....... 46 C7
Quantock Rd LTNN/LIM LU3....... 46 C7
Quantocks HHW HP1....... 118 A5
Quarrendon Rd AMSS HP7....... 158 D1
Quarry Rd LBUZ LU7....... 96 C2
Quarry Springs HLW CM20....... 129 K3
Quarry Wk LTNN/LIM LU3....... 46 C7
Quartermass Cl HHW HP1....... 117 K7
Quartermass Rd HHW HP1....... 117 K7
Queen Anne's Cl
HTCH/STOT SG5....... 25 K4
Queen Bee Ct HAT AL10....... 122 A4
Queen Elizabeth Ct
WAB EN9 *....... 157 J5
Queen Hoo La KNEB SG3....... 86 A7
Queen Mary's Av
WATW WD18....... 162 A3
Queen Marys Ct WAB EN9 *....... 157 H5
Queens Av
KTN/HRWW/WS HA3....... 173 H7
    TRDG/WHET N20....... 166 E5
    WATW WD18....... 12 B5
Queens Cl LTN SG6 *....... 173 M2
    SBW CM21....... 92 A5
Queens Ct STSD CM24....... 58 F8
Queens Cr BSF CM23....... 73 P9
    STALE/WH AL4....... 120 E5
Queen's Dr ABLGY WD5....... 148 C2
Queen's Dr HTCH/STOT SG5....... 34 B1
The Queen's Dr
RKW/CH/CXG WD3....... 160 D5
Queens Md EDGW HA8....... 173 M3
Queens Pl WAT WD17....... 13 G1
Queens Rd BAR EN5....... 166 B2
    BERK HP4....... 115 M6
Queen's Rd CHES/WCR EN8....... 142 B8
    HARP AL5....... 119 P5
    ROY SG8....... 21 H2
    WARE SG12....... 108 E2
Queen's Rd WAT WD17....... 13 J2
The Queen's Sq HHNE HP2 *....... 5 K1
The Queen's Dr DUN/HR/TOD LU5....... 25 L4
Queens Sq HHNE HP2 *....... 5 K1
Queensway CHES/WCR EN8....... 142 B8
    HAT AL10....... 147 H1
    STALW/RED AL3....... 8 D3
    STVGE SG2....... 51 N9
    TRING HP23....... 95 P9
Queens Wk HRW HA1....... 172 E8
Queens Wy RAD WD7....... 151 K1
    CHES/WCR EN8....... 156 E4
Queensway DUN/WHIP LU6....... 60 E5
    HAT AL10....... 122 D6
    HHNE HP2....... 5 J3
    ROY SG8....... 15 K5
    STVG SG1....... 50 E7
Queensway Pde....... 60 E5
The Queensway
CFSP/GDCR SL9....... 168 B8
Queensway Crs
GSTN WD25....... 149 H3
Queensway Dr
HTCHE/RSTV SG4....... 35 P7
Quendell Wk HHNE HP2....... 5 H1
Quendon Dr WAB EN9....... 157 H4
Quickbeams WGCE AL7....... 105 K3
Quickberry Pl AMSS HP7....... 158 E1
Quickley Brow
RKW/CH/CXG WD3 *....... 159 P5
Quickley La
RKW/CH/CXG WD3....... 160 A5
Quickley Ri
RKW/CH/CXG WD3....... 159 P5
Quickly Brow
RKW/CH/CXG WD3 *....... 159 P5
Quickmoor La KGLGY WD4....... 147 L3
Quickset Rd SAFWS CB11....... 23 L5
Quickswood LTNN/LIM LU3....... 46 B8

Quickwood Cl
RKW/CH/CXG WD3....... 160 D5
Quills LWTH SG6....... 36 C4
Quilter Cl LTNN/LIM LU3....... 62 A2
Quinces Cft HHW HP1....... 117 P3
Quincey Rd WARE SG12....... 108 B1
Quin Ct STDN SG11....... 55 L8
Quinn Wy LWTH SG6....... 36 B5
Quinta Dr BAR EN5....... 165 P4
Quinton Wy WAB EN9....... 157 H5

R

Raans Rd AMS HP6....... 145 L8
Raban Cl STVGE SG2....... 67 M5
Rabley Heath Rd WLYN AL6....... 84 D4
Rackman Dr LTNN/LIM LU3....... 63 J2
Radburn Cl HLWS CM18....... 129 K7
Radburn Ct DUN/WHIP LU6....... 60 D5
Radburn Wy LWTH SG6....... 36 A5
Radcliffe Av ENC/FH EN2....... 155 K9
Radcliffe Rd HTCH/STOT SG5....... 35 M8
    KTN/HRWW/WS HA3....... 172 C6
Radlett La RAD WD7....... 151 J4
Radlett Park Rd RAD WD7....... 150 D8
Radlett Rd GSTN WD25....... 150 B8
    LCOL/BKTW AL2....... 136 D2
    WAT WD17....... 13 H2
    WAT WD24....... 149 L9
Radley Gdns
KTN/HRWW/WS HA3....... 173 L8
Radnor Av HRW HA1....... 172 E9
Radnor Gdns EN1....... 155 M9
Radnor Hall BORE WD6 *....... 164 F4
Radnor Rd HRW HA1....... 172 D9
    WAT WD17....... 12 C1
Radnor St LTN LU1....... 61 J2
Radstock Av
KTN/HRWW/WS HA3....... 173 G7
Radstone Pl LTNE LU2....... 63 H5
Radwell La BLDK SG7....... 26 B4
Raebarn Gdns BAR EN5....... 165 P4
Raeburn Rd EDGW HA8....... 173 N6
Raffin Cl KNEB SG3....... 85 N2
Raffin Green La
HERT/BAY SG13....... 68 A9
    KNEB SG3....... 85 P2
Ragged Hall La
LCOL/BKTW AL2....... 135 L3
Raglan Av CHES/WCR EN8....... 156 C4
Raglan Cl LTNW/LEA LU4 *....... 61 J3
Raglan Gdns OXHEY WD19....... 162 D7
Rags La CHESW SG12....... 141 M6
Railway Ap HRW HA1....... 172 F8
Railway Cl HERT/BAY SG13....... 107 M6
Railway Rd CHES/WCR EN8....... 55 J3
Railway St HERT/WAT SG14....... 107 L3
Railway Ter KGLCY WD4....... 134 B6
Rainbow Cl OXHEY WD19....... 162 E5
Rainbow Ct STALW/RED AL3....... 100 C3
Rainer Cl CHES/WCR EN8....... 142 C8
Rainsford Rd STSD CM24....... 58 F6
Raisins Hl PIN HA5....... 171 J1
Raith Av OXHEY WD19....... 162 E9
Raleigh Crs STVGE SG2....... 51 K8
Raleigh Dr TRDG/WHET N20....... 167 J9
Raleigh Wy STHGT/OAK N14....... 167 N9
The Rally ARL/CHE SG15....... 24 E2
Ralston Wy OXHEY WD19....... 162 F8
Rambler Cl HLWE CM17....... 129 L5
Ramblers Wy WGCE AL7....... 105 L2
Rambling Wy BERK HP4....... 116 E5
Ramerick Gdns
ARL/CHE SG15....... 24 D7
Ram Gorse HLW CM20....... 2 A2
Ramillies Rd MLHL NW7....... 165 L8
Ramney Dr PEND EN3....... 156 D6
The Ramparts
STALW/RED AL3....... 8 A7
Ramridge Rd LTNE LU2....... 63 H4
Ramsay Cl BROX EN10....... 126 D9
Ramsbury Rd STAL AL1....... 8 A4
Ramscote La HLWE CM17....... 130 E4
Ramsdell STVG SG1....... 11 H6
Ramsey Cl BRKMPK AL9....... 139 N6
    LTNW/LEA LU4....... 61 J3
    STAL AL1....... 9 H2
Ramsey Lodge Ct STAL AL1 *....... 9 H2
Ramsey Rd
AMP/FLIT/BLC MK45....... 32 D5
    STHGT/OAK N14....... 167 N6
Ramson Ri HHW HP1....... 117 N6
Randall Dr DUN/HR/TOD LU5....... 44 C4
Randalls Ride HHNE HP2....... 117 P6
Randalls Hl LCOL/BKTW AL2....... 149 N1
Randalls Hl STVGE SG2....... 67 L3
Rands Meadow
HTCH/STOT SG5....... 34 G1
Ranelagh Dr EDGW HA8....... 173 N1
Ranelagh Rd HHNE HP2....... 117 N8
Raneleigh Wk HARP AL5....... 143 H4
Ranmoor Cl HRW HA1....... 172 D8
Rannoch Gdns HRW HA1....... 172 D8
Rannoch Wk HHNE HP2....... 117 N4
Rannoch Cl LTNN/LIM LU3....... 45 M7
Ranskill Rd BORE WD6....... 151 M9
Ransom Cl HTCHE/RSTV SG4....... 49 L3
    OXHEY WD19....... 162 E6
Rant Meadow HHS/BOV HP3....... 118 F8
Ranulf Wy HLWE CM17....... 126 E5
Ranworth Av HOD EN11....... 126 C4
    STVGE SG2....... 67 N7
Ranworth Cl HHNE HP2....... 5 F5
Ranworth Rd
POTB/CUF EN6....... 152 C1
Raphael Dr WATN WD24....... 12 B2
Raphael St WATN WD24....... 12 C5
Rasehill Cl RKW/CH/CXG WD3....... 160 G4
Rasper Rd TRDG/WHET N20....... 166 F9
Rathlin HHS/BOV HP3....... 134 C1
Ranworth Cl HHNE HP2....... 5 F5
Ratty's La HOD EN11....... 127 J5

Ravenbank Rd LTNE LU2....... 63 K1
Raven Cl RKW/CH/CXG WD3....... 160 C6
Raven Ct HAT AL10....... 122 D8
Ravenhill Wy LTNW/LEA LU4....... 61 K2
Ravensburgh Cl
AMP/FLIT/BLC MK45....... 60 C5
Ravenscourt DUN/WHIP LU6....... 57 J9
Ravenscroft BROX EN10 *....... 126 E8
    GSTN WD25....... 149 M5
    HARP AL5....... 102 C6
Ravenscroft Cots BAR EN5 *....... 166 E5
Ravenscroft Pk BAR EN5....... 166 E2
Ravensdell HHW HP1....... 117 J7
Ravens La BERK HP4....... 116 A7
Ravensmead CFSP/GDCR SL9....... 168 C7
Ravensthorpe LTNE LU2....... 63 J2
Ravenswood Gdns
HHW HP1....... 117 J3
Rawdon Dr HOD EN11....... 126 E8
Rawlings La BEAC HP9....... 158 D9
Rayburn Rd HHW HP1....... 117 K6
Raydean Rd BAR EN5....... 166 E4
Rayfield WGCW AL8....... 104 C5
Ray Gdns STAN HA7....... 173 H2
Raylands Rd CFSP/GDCR SL9....... 168 A3
Raymer Cl STAL AL1....... 9 H1
Raymond Cl ABLGY WD5....... 148 E2
Raymonds Cl WGCE AL7....... 105 H8
Raymonds Pln WGCE AL7....... 105 H8
Rayners La PIN HA5....... 171 P9
Raynham Rd BSF CM23....... 74 C2
Raynham St HERT/BAY SG13....... 108 A9
Raynham Wy LTNE LU2....... 63 L5
Raynsford Rd WARE SG12....... 108 E3
Raynton Rd PEND EN3....... 156 C7
Ray's Hl CSHM HP5....... 114 B9
Read Ct WAB EN9....... 157 M3
Readers Cl DUN/WHIP LU6....... 60 E5
The Readings HLWS CM18....... 129 J6
    RKW/CH/CXG WD3....... 160 D2
Reaper Cl LTNW/LEA LU4....... 61 J3
Recreation Gnd STSD CM24....... 58 E5
Recreation Rd
DUN/HR/TOD LU5....... 44 F9
Rectory Cl BRKMPK AL9....... 123 P9
    BSF CM23....... 91 N2
    STAN HA7....... 173 H5
    WARE SG12....... 108 D2
Rectory Fld
HLWW/ROY CM19....... 128 E5
Rectory Gdns HAT AL10....... 145 H9
Rectory La AMSS HP7....... 144 G9
    BERK HP4....... 115 P7
    BSF CM23....... 57 H9
    BUSH WD23....... 163 J5
    EDGW HA8....... 173 N3
    HLWW/ROY CM19....... 128 E5
    KGLCY WD4....... 134 C7
    KNEB SG3....... 85 P5
    LTNE LU2....... 47 L5
    RAD WD7....... 151 L3
    RKW/CH/CXG WD3....... 161 K7
    STVG SG1....... 50 F6
Rectory Mnr
HTCH/STOT SG5 *....... 34 B4
Rectory Rd
RKW/CH/CXG WD3....... 161 K6
    WGCW AL8....... 104 F2
Rectory Wd HLW CM20....... 108 D5
Redan Rd WARE SG12....... 108 D5
Redbournbury La
STALW/RED AL3....... 119 L1
Redbourn La HARP AL5....... 101 M6
Redbourn Rd HHNE HP2....... 118 B4
    STALW/RED AL3....... 119 M4
Redcar Dr STVG SG1....... 50 D9
Redcote La HARP AL5....... 101 P5
Redding Av BARE HA6....... 144 C7
Redding La STALW/RED AL3....... 100 F4
Reddings HHS/BOV HP3....... 133 H7
    WGCW AL8....... 104 F5
Reddings Av BUSH WD23....... 163 K4
Reddings Cl
RAYLNE/WEN HP22....... 112 C9
The Reddings BORE WD6....... 164 F2
    MLHL NW7....... 165 M9
Redditch Ct HHNE HP2....... 5 G4
Redferns Ct LTN LU1....... 63 B8
Redfield Cl DUN/WHIP LU6....... 60 E5
    STALW/RED AL3....... 100 C3
Redgrave Gdns
LTNN/LIM LU3....... 46 A7
Redhall Cl HAT AL10....... 122 C9
Redhall Dr HAT AL10....... 122 C9
Redhall La RKW/CH/CXG WD3....... 148 A5
    GSTN WD25....... 148 C5
Redhill Dr EDGW HA8....... 173 P6
Redhill Rd HTCH/STOT SG5....... 35 H8
Redhoods Wy East LWTH SG6....... 36 B2
Redhoods Wy West
LWTH SG6....... 36 B2
Red House Cl WARE SG12....... 108 D5
Redlands BLDK SG7 *....... 26 D5
Redlands Rd PEND EN3....... 156 D9
Red Lion Cl GSTN WD25....... 150 F1
Red Lion Crs HLWE CM17....... 129 M5
Red Lion La HHS/BOV HP3....... 134 A5
    HLWE CM17....... 129 M5
    HHW HP1....... 147 N5
Red Lion Pde PIN HA5 *....... 171 N7
Red Lion St CSHM HP5....... 144 C2
Red Lodge Gdns BERK HP4....... 115 M8
Redmire Cl LTNW/LEA LU4....... 45 J9
Red Rails LTN LU1....... 62 C4
Redricks La SBW CM21....... 111 J6
Red Rd BORE WD6....... 164 F2
Redvers Ct BSF CM23....... 58 B9
Red White & Blue Rd
BSF CM23....... 58 C9
Redwing Cl STVGE SG2....... 67 M2
Redwing Gv ABLGY WD5....... 149 H1
Redwing Rd STVGE SG2....... 67 M2
Redwood Cl OXHEY WD19....... 171 L1
    STHGT/OAK N14....... 167 P6
Redwood Dr HHNE HP2....... 5 G5

Redwood Ri BORE WD6...45 M7
Redwoods HERT/WAT SC14...107 K5
WGCW AL8...104 C1
Redwood Wy BAR EN5...166 B4
Reed Cl LCOL/BKTW AL2...151 M7
Reedham Ct LCOL/BKTW AL2...135 P8
Reedings Wy SBW CM21...92 A5
Reed Pl HARP AL5 *...101 N1
Reeds Crs WAT WD17...13 C1
Reedsdale LTNE LU2...63 N4
The Reeds WCCE AL7...104 G7
Reenglass Rd STAN HA7 *...173 K1
Rees Dr STAN HA7...173 L1
Reeves Av LTNN/LIM LU3...62 C2
Reeves La HERT/WAT SC14...107 L4
Reeves Pightle ROY SG8...22 C7
Regal Cl STDN SG11...71 K4
Regal Wy WATN WD24...149 K8
Regency Cl BSF CM23...73 P7
Regency Ct DUN/WHIP LU6...60 F7
HLWS...128 K6
Regent Cl KGLCY WD4...134 B8
STALE/WH AL4...105 H7
WCCE AL7...105 H7
Regent Ct HTCH/STOT SG5...25 K2
Regent Rd RAD WD7...150 F4
Regent St DUN/WHIP LU6...25 K5
HTCH/STOT SG5...25 K5
LTN LU1...6 D5
WATN WD24...149 J8
Reginald Ms HLWE CM17...129 M2
Reginald Rd NTHWD HA6...171 H5
Reginald St LTNE LU2...6 E1
Regis Rd LTNW/LEA LU4...61 H2
Reid Cl PIN HA5 *...171 J4
Rembrandt Rd EDGW HA8 *...173 N6
Remus Cl STAL HA1...4 A4
Rendlesham Av RAD WD7...150 E7
Rendlesham Cl WARE SG12...108 A2
Rendlesham Rd ENC/FH EN2...155 J9
Rendlesham Wy
RKW/CH/CXG WD3...160 A5
Rennison Cl CHESW EN7...141 N6
Renshaw Cl LTNE LU2...63 M4
Repton Cl LTNN/LIM LU3...46 A9
Repton Gn STALW/RED AL3...120 C5
Repton Pl AMSS HP7 *...145 M9
Repton Rd
KTN/HRWW/WS HA3...173 M8
Repton Wy
RKW/CH/CXG WD3...161 L4
Reservoir Rd RSLP HA4...170 E9
STHGT/OAK N14 *...9 H1
Reson Wy HHW HP1 *...4 A4
Reston Cl BORE WD6...151 M8
Retford Cl BORE WD6...151 M8
Retreat Cl
KTN/HRWW/WS HA3...173 J9
The Retreat AMSS HP6...146 B9
DUN/HR/TOD LU5...61 J5
Revels Av HERT/WAT SC14...107 L4
Revels Rd HERT/WAT SC14...107 L4
Reynard Copse BSF CM23...74 A1
Reynard Rd WLYN AL6...84 E6
Reynard's Wy
LCOL/BKTW AL2...135 N8
Reynard Wy HERT/BAY SG13...107 P6
Reynolds Cl HHW HP1...117 K7
Reynolds Ct LTNW/LEA LU4...120 C3
Reynolds Dr EDGW HA8...173 J8
Reynolds Yd CSHM HP5...144 C2
Rhee Spring BLDK SG7...26 D8
Rhodes Av BSF CM23...74 A5
Rhodes Wy WATN WD24...149 M7
Rhymes HHW HP1 *...117 H7
Ribbledale LCOL/BKTW AL2...137 L6
Ribblesdale HHW HP1...117 P5
Rib Cl STDN SG11...71 K4
Ribocon Wy LTNW/LEA LU4...45 L8
Ribston Cl RAD WD7...137 J1
Rib V HERT/WAT SC14...107 L5
Rib Wy BUNT SG9...40 D9
Riccat La STVC SG9...51 J4
Richards Cl BUSH WD23...163 M6
HRW HA1...172 C9
LTN LU1...62 C8
Richardson Cl
LCOL/BKTW AL2...137 K6
Richardson Crs CHESW EN7...141 J4
Richardson Pl
STALE/WH AL4...137 N1
Richards St HAT AL10...122 A4
Richard Stagg Cl STAL HA1...136 C1
Richard St DUN/HR/TOD LU5...60 F7
Richfield Rd BUSH WD23...163 L6
Richmond Cl BORE WD6...150 D3
BSF CM23...73 M7
WARE SG12...108 A1
Richmond Ct BROX EN10...126 E8
LTNE LU2...62 G5
POTB/CUF EN6 *...153 M1
Richmond Dr WAT WD17...162 A1
Richmond Gdns
KTN/HRWW/WS HA3...172 F4
Richmond Hi LTNE LU2...62 G4
Richmond Rd BAR EN5...166 F4
POTB/CUF EN6...153 M1
Richmond Wy
RKW/CH/CXG WD3...161 N3
Rickmansworth La
CFSP/GDCR SL9...168 C3
Rickmansworth Rd
RKW/CH/CXG WD3...160 C2
WAT WD17...12 E2
Rickyard Cl LTNE LU2...63 J3
Rickyard Meadow
STALW/RED AL3...101 H7
The Rickyard
Norton Hall Farm
LWTH SG6 *...25 N8
The Rickyard BLDK SG7...17 N6
Riddel Gdns BLDK SG7...26 B9
Riddings La HLWS CM18...129 J7
Riddy Hill Cl...
Riddy La LTNN/LIM LU3 *...49 M1
The Riddy HTCHE/RSTV SG4...84 C5
Ridge Av HARP AL5...81 M9

LWTH SG6...36 D2
Ridge Crest ENC/FH EN2...154 G9
Ridgedown LCOL/BKTW AL2...101 H7
Ridgefield WAT WD17...13 C3
Ridgehurst Av GSTN WD25...148 G3
Ridge La WAT WD17...148 F6
Ridge Lea HHW HP1...117 J9
Ridgemont End
CFSP/GDCR SL9...168 C2
Ridge Rd LWTH SG6...36 D2
Ridge St WATN WD24...149 J8
The Ridge BAR EN5...166 D4
Ridgeway LCOL/BKTW AL2...137 L7
Ridge Vw TRING HP23...96 B7
Ridgeview Cl BAR EN5...166 B5
Ridgeview Rd
TRDG/WHET N20...166 F9
Ridgeway BERK HP4...115 L7
DUN/WHIP LU6...79 H5
HARP AL5 *...81 J7
LBUZ LU7...96 F2
RAD WD7...151 H1
RAYLNE/WEN HP22...112 A8
Ridge Wy RKW/CH/CXG WD3...160 F6
Ridgeway STDN SG11...71 J5
STVC SG1...51 H4
TRING HP23...113 J7
WAT WD17...13 C3
Ridgeway Av
DUN/HR/TOD LU5...60 G4
EBAR EN4...167 K5
Ridgeway Cl CSHM HP5...130 C7
HHS/BOV HP3...134 A4
Ridgeway Dr
DUN/HR/TOD LU5...61 H5
Ridgeway Rd CSHM HP5...130 C7
ROY SG8 *...20 E3
The Ridgeway AMSS HP7...158 C1
ENC/FH EN2...154 D6
HERT/WAT SC14...106 C5
HTCH/STOT SG5...49 J1
HTCHE/RSTV SG4...84 C4
POTB/CUF EN6...140 B6
POTB/CUF EN6...154 A5
RAD WD7...150 E7
RYLN/HDSTN HA2...171 P9
STALE/WH AL4...120 F4
STAN HA7...173 J3
WARE SG12...108 B1
WAT WD17...148 F7
Ridgewood Dr HARP AL5...101 M1
Ridgewood Gdns HARP AL5...81 M9
Ridgmont Rd STAL AL1...9 H6
Ridgway Rd LTNE LU2...7 C1
The Ridings AMS HP6...145 J5
BSF CM23...91 N1
CSHM HP5...146 A6
HERT/WAT SC14...106 C5
LTNN/LIM LU3...79 P7
STALW/RED AL3...79 P7
STVGE SG2...67 L3
Ridler Rd EN EN1...155 M8
Ridley Gdns BUSH WD23...59 K1
Ridlins End STVGE SG2...67 N5
Rigby Pl PEND EN3...156 F7
Rigery La STDN SG11...70 E8
Right Side STHGT/OAK N14 *...167 P7
Riley Rd PEND EN3...156 B8
Ringshall Gn BERK HP4...97 N4
Ringshall Rd BERK HP4...97 N4
Ringtale Pl BLDK SG7...26 D8
Ringway Rd
LCOL/BKTW AL2...136 A6
Ringwood Cl PIN HA5 *...171 J7
Ringwood Rd LBUZ LU7...46 E9
Ripley Rd ENC/FH EN2...155 K9
LTNW/LEA LU4...61 M5
Ripley Wy CHESW EN7...142 A9
HHW HP1...117 H7
Ripon Rd STVG SG1...51 J5
Ripon Wy BORE WD6...165 J4
Risdens HLWS CM18...128 F7
Risedale Av HHW HP1...117 H9
Risedale Hl HHNE HP2...5 H7
Risedale Rd HHNE HP2...5 H7
The Rise AMSS HP7...145 H9
BORE WD6...37 H1
BORE WD6...164 F4
EDGW HA8...173 P2
LCOL/BKTW AL2...136 C4
Rising Hill Cl NTHWD HA6 *...170 E3
Risinghoime Cl
BUSH WD23...163 K6
Risinghome Rd
KTN/HRWW/WS HA3...172 E6
Ritcroft Cl HHS/BOV HP3...118 C9
Ritcroft Dr HHS/BOV HP3...118 C9
Ritcroft St HHS/BOV HP3...118 C9
Ritz Ct POTB/CUF EN6...153 K1
Rivenhall End WCCE AL7...105 M6
River Av HOD EN11...126 G6
Riverbank HHW HP1...117 M4
Riverbanks Cl HARP AL5...82 B9
River Cl CHES/WCR EN8...156 D5
River Ct HTCH/STOT SG5...35 L4
WARE SG12 *...108 B1
Riverford Cl HARP AL5...82 A9
River Hi STALW/RED AL3...100 C2
River Md HTCH/STOT SG5...35 H6
River Meads WARE SG12...109 H7
Rivermill HLW CM20...2 C1
River Pk HHW HP1...133 K1
Riversend Rd
HHS/BOV HP3...133 M2
Rivershill HERT/WAT SC14...85 A3
Riverside Av BROX EN10...142 F1
Riverside Cl KGLCY WD4...134 C4
Riverside Ct CSHM HP5 *...146 A6
CSHM HP5 *...111 M6
Riverside Dr
RKW/CH/CXG WD3...161 H7

Riverside Gdns BERK HP4...115 M6
Riverside Ms BROX EN10 *...142 D2
WARE SG12 *...108 B1
Riverside Pl
FBAR/BDGN N11 *...167 N9
Riverside Rd LTNN/LIM LU3...62 B1
OXHEY WD19...12 D5
River St HTCH/STOT SG5 *...9 G6
Riversmead HOD EN11...126 F6
Riversmeet HERT/WAT SC14...85 A3
River St WARE SG12...108 D3
River Vw WGCE AL7...105 H2
River Wy HLW CM20...111 K7
LTNN/LIM LU3...61 P1
Rivett Cl BLDK SG7...26 C8
Robarts Cl PIN HA5...171 K9
Robbery Bottom La
WLYN AL6...85 J5
Robb Rd STAN HA7...172 C3
Robbs Cl HHW HP1...117 K6
Robe End HHW HP1...117 J6
Robert Av STAL AL1...136 B3
Robert Cl CHES/WCR EN8...65 L8
Roberts Cl CHES/WCR EN8...142 D9
Roberts La CFSP/GDCR SL9...168 E2
Roberts Rd BERK HP4...116 A7
Robertson Cl BROX EN10...142 D5
Robertson Rd WATW WD18...13 C6
Robeson St LTNW/LEA LU4...62 C7
Robeson Wy BORE WD6...151 P9
Robina Cl NTHWD HA6...171 H6
Robin Cl MLWL NW7...165 L9
WARE SG12...109 H9
Robin Ct HARP AL5 *...82 A9
Robin Hi BERK HP4...115 P8
Robin Hood Dr BUSH WD23...149 N9
KTN/HRWW/WS HA3...172 F4
Robin Hood La HAT AL10...122 C5
Robin Hood Meadow
HHNE HP2...118 A3
Robin Hood Rd RBSF CM22...59 K2
Robin Md WCCE AL7...105 K8
Robin Pl IN GSTN WD25 *...149 J2
Robins Cl LCOL/BKTW AL2...137 K6
Robinsfield HHNE HP2...117 K8
Robins Nest Hl
HERT/BAY SG13...124 D6
Robinson Av CHESW EN7...141 J7
Robinson Crs BUSH WD23...163 L7
Robins Orch CFSP/GDCR SL9...168 C3
Robins Wy HAT AL10...122 B5
Robinswood Cl HARP AL5...82 A9
Robin Wy POTB/CUF EN6...140 F7
Robson Cl CFSP/GDCR SL9...168 B4
Robsons Cl CHES/WCR EN8...142 B8
Roch Av EDGW HA8...173 M6
Rochester Av LTNE LU2...63 H4
Rochester Cl EN EN1...155 M9
Rochester Dr GSTN WD25 *...149 K5
PIN HA5...171 M9
Rochester Wy
RKW/CH/CXG WD3...161 M3
Rochford Av WAB EN9...143 J7
Rochford Ct BROX EN10...142 D5
Rochford Dr LTNE LU2...63 M4
Rochford Rd BSF CM23...74 C1
Rockcliffe Av KGLCY WD4...134 C9
Rockfield Av WARE SG12...108 C1
Rockingham Ga
BUSH WD23...163 L5
Rockingham Wy STVC SG1...67 H3
Rocklands Dr
KTN/HRWW/WS HA3...173 H6
Rockleigh HERT/WAT SC14...107 K6
Rockley Rd LTN LU1...62 B8
Rock Rd ROY SG8...20 E3
Rockways BAR EN5...165 M5
Rodeheath LTNW/LEA LU4...45 H8
Rodgers Ct BORE WD6...166 D5
Rodings Rw BAR EN5 *...166 C5
Rodney Av STAL AL1...135 N4
Rodney Cl LTNW/LEA LU4...61 J3
Rodney Crs HOD EN11...126 F5
Rodney Gdns PIN HA5...171 K9
Rodwell Yd TRING HP23...95 P9
Roebuck Cl HARP AL5...82 A9
Roebuck Ga STVGE SG2...67 H6
Roe End HTCH/STOT SG5...25 J4
Roe End La
STALW/RED AL3...79 A9
Roefields Cl HHS/BOV HP3...133 L6
Roe Green La HAT AL10...122 D3
Roe Green La HAT AL10...122 C7
Roe Hill Cl HAT AL10...122 C7
Roehyde Wy HAT AL10...122 B9
Roe La CDALE/KGS NW9...173 P8
Roestock Gdns
STALE/WH AL4...138 B1
Rostock La STALE/WH AL4...138 A2
Rossiter Flds BAR EN5...166 B5
Rogate Rd LTNE LU2...63 J7
Rogers Cl CHESW EN7...141 L6
Rogers Ruff NTHWD HA6...170 E5
Rogers Wk
NFNCH/WDSPK N12 *...165 P4
Roland St STAL AL1...168 A7
Rolfe Cl EBAR EN4...167 J3
Rollason Wy BORE WD6...164 A4
Rollswood WCCE AL7...105 H6
Rollswood Rd WLYN AL6...84 D6
Rollys La BLDK SG7...26 B9
Roman Cl DEN/HRF UB9...169 L5
Roman Gdns
DUN/HR/TOD LU5...60 E2

KGLCY WD4...134 C9
Roman Rd BORE WD6...164 D5
Roman Ri SBW CM21...111 N2
Roman Rd
AMP/FLIT/BLC MK45...32 E5
HHW HP1...116 E2
LTNW/LEA LU4...61 P3
RAD WD7...150 F5
Romans End STALW/RED AL3...186 B1
Roman St HOD EN11...126 G6
Roman V CM17...111 M7
Roman Wk RAD WD7...150 E6
LTNN/LIM LU3...79 P7
STDN SG11...71 J3
WAB EN9...156 G5
WLYN AL6...156 G5
Romeland HI STALW/RED AL3...8 D4
Romeland BORE WD6...164 D5
STALW/RED AL3...8 D4
WAB EN9...157 H3
Romilly Dr OXHEY WD19...171 N1
Romany Cl LWTH SG6...26 B9
Romany Ct HHNE HP2...118 D7
Romeland BORE WD6...164 D5
Ronart St...
Rondini Av LTNN/LIM LU3...62 C4
Ronsons Wy STALE/WH AL4...120 F4
Rookery Dr WARE SG12...46 F9
The Rookery STSD SM24...58 F3
Rookery Wy STVC SG1...10 B1
Rookes Cl LWTH SG6...36 E5
Rooks Cl WGCE AL7...104 E1
Rooks Hi RKW/CH/CXG WD3...160 C3
WGCW AL8...104 E1
Rooks Nest La ROY SG8...28 F2
Rook Tree Cl
HTCH/STOT SG5...25 L3
Rook Tree La HTCH/STOT SG5...25 L3
Rookwood Dr STVGE SG2...67 L5
Rosary Ct POTB/CUF EN6...139 L9
Rosary Gdns BUSH WD23...163 N6
Roscoff Cl EDGW HA8...173 P5
Rose Acre STALW/RED AL3...100 C6
Roseacres SBW CM21...111 N1
Rosebank WAB EN9...157 K4
Rosebarn La TRING HP23...95 J3
Roseberry Ct WAT WD17...149 H9
Rosebery BSF CM23...73 P8
Rosebery Av HARP AL5...101 N2
Rosebery Ms LBUZ LU7...77 L2
Rosebery Rd BUSH WD23...163 J5
RAYLNE/WEN HP22...94 C7
Rosebery Wy TRING HP23...96 A1
Rose Cots ARL/CHE SG15...24 E5
Rose Ct AMS HP6...145 L6
CHESW EN7...141 P6
Rosecroft Ct NTHWD HA6 *...170 C5
Rosecroft Dr WAT WD17...148 F7
Rosecroft Wk PIN HA5...171 J3
Rosedale DUN/HR/TOD LU5...61 H1
WGCE AL7...105 J2
Rosedale Av CHESW EN7...141 N8
Rosedale Cl
LCOL/BKTW AL2...135 M9
LTNN/LIM LU3...45 M8
STAN HA7...173 H3
Rosedale Wy CHESW EN7...141 N8
Rose Dr CSHM HP5...145 J2
Rose Garden Cl EDGW HA8...173 J5
Rose Gdns WATW WD18...12 D7
Rosehath HHW HP1...117 H7
Rosehill BERK HP4...115 M6
Rosehill Cl HOD EN11...126 E5
Rosehill Gdns ABLGY WD5...148 D2
Roselands Av HOD EN11...126 E5
Rose La STALE/WH AL4...103 H2
Rose Lawn BUSH WD23...163 L7
Rosemary Av ENC/FH EN2...155 L9
Rosemount Dr
LCOL/BKTW AL2...136 F5
Rose Md POTB/CUF EN6...139 M9
Rosemead
RAYLNE/WEN HP22...112 F2
Rose Meadow STDN SG11...55 K3
Rosemont Cl LWTH SG6...36 B2
Rosemoor Ct WCCE AL7...105 J7
Rose Mt...
HLWW/ROY CM19...128 G3
Rosens Wk EDGW HA8...165 H9
Rose Wk HARP AL5...101 N2
Rose Wk DUN/HR/TOD LU5...60 F7
ROY SG8...20 B3
STALE/WH AL4...120 G4
The Rose Wk RAD WD7...150 G6
Rose Wood Cl LTNE LU2...63 L3
Rosewood Ct HHW HP1 *...117 H7
Rosewood Dr ENC/FH EN2...155 H5
Roslyn Cl BROX EN10...126 C9
Roslyn Wy
HLWW/ROY CM19...128 B2
Ross Cl KTN/HRWW/WS HA3...172 C4
LTN LU1...62 C8
Ross Ct STVGE SG2...51 L8
Ross Crs GSTN WD25...149 H5
Rossendale Ct LTNE LU2...155 J7
Rossetti Ldg ROY SG8 *...21 L7
Rossfold Rd LTNN/LIM LU3...45 N7
Rossington Av BORE WD6...151 K8
Rossington Cl EN EN1...156 A8
Rossiter Flds BAR EN5...166 C5
Rosslyn Crs HRW HA1...172 F8
LTNN/LIM LU3...79 P8
Rosslyn Rd WATW WD18...12 E5
Rossway LTN LU1...80 C4
Rossway Dr BUSH WD23...163 L4
Rossway La TRING HP23...114 F3
Rossway Rd BUSH WD23...163 L4
Roswell Cl CHES/WCR EN8...142 D9
Rothamsted Av HARP AL5...101 L4
Rotheram Av LTN LU1...62 D9
Rother Cl GSTN WD25...149 J2
Rother Fld LTNE LU2...63 L3
Rotherfield Rd PEND EN3...156 C7
Rotherwood Cl
DUN/WHIP LU6...60 B5

Rothesay Rd LTN LU1...6 C5
Rothschild Av
RAYLNE/WEN HP22...94 F7
Roughdown Av
HHS/BOV HP3...133 K2
Roughdown Rd HHW HP1...4 A7
Roughdown Villas Rd
HHS/BOV HP3...133 K2
The Roughs NTHWD HA6...162 A9
Roughwood Cl WAT WD17...148 F8
Roughway La CSTG HP8...159 L5
Roundabout La WLYN AL6...85 J5
Roundbush La GSTN WD25...150 B8
Round Coppice Rd
STSD CM24...75 H2
Roundfield Av HARP AL5...82 C9
Roundhaye STDN SG11...71 J5
Roundhedge Wy
ENC/FH EN2...154 C8
Roundhills WAB EN9...157 K4
The Roundings
HERT/BAY SG13...126 A2
Roundmoor Dr
CHES/WCR EN8...142 D8
The Roundway WATW WD18...162 B5
Roundway RAD WD7...133 P6
Roundwood Cl
HTCHE/RSTV SG4...35 P6
WLYN AL6...84 G5
Roundwood Dr WGCW AL8...104 F5
Roundwood Gdns HARP AL5...101 M1
Roundwood La HARP AL5...101 J1
Roundwood Pk HARP AL5...101 M1
Round Wood Rd AMS HP6...145 L7
Rounton Rd WAB EN9...157 K3
Rousebarn La
RKW/CH/CXG WD3...161 M1
Rouse Ct CFSP/GDCR SL9...168 D3
Rowan Cl HTCHE/RSTV SG4...37 L8
LCOL/BKTW AL2...149 P1
LTN LU1...62 C7
STALE/WH AL4...120 F4
STAN HA7...172 F3
Rowan Crs LWTH SG6...36 B2
STVG SG1...50 G8
Rowan Dr BROX EN10...142 E3
Rowan Gv HTCHE/RSTV SG4...49 M5
Rowans WGCE AL7...105 H5
The Rowans BLDK SG7...37 H1
BROX EN10...126 D7
CFSP/GDCR SL9...168 A7
HHW HP1...117 H5
Rowan Wk SBW CM21...111 P2
Rowan Wy HARP AL5...102 B4
Rowben Cl TRDG/WHET N20...166 F7
Rowborough Rd...
RAYLNE/WEN HP22...112 A4
Rowcroft HHW HP1...117 H9
Rowelfield LTNE LU2...63 K5
Rowen Wk LTNE LU2...130 C9
Rowington Cl LTNE LU2...63 N4
Rowland Av
KTN/HRWW/WS HA3...173 J7
Rowland Pl NTHWD HA6...170 C4
Rowland Rd STVG SG1...11 F7
Rowlands Av PIN HA5...172 A3
Rowlands Cl
CHES/WCR EN8...142 C9
Rowlandsfields
CHES/WCR EN8 *...142 C9
Rowlatt Dr WATW WD18...12 C5
Rowley Cl WATN WD24...150 A6
Rowley Ct CHENT WD3...162 C5
Rowley Green Rd BAR EN5...165 N4
Rowley La BAR EN5...165 K1
Rowley's Rd HERT/BAY SG13...107 N5
Rowney Gdns SBW CM21...111 N4
Rowney Gdns SBW CM21...111 N4
Rowney La WARE SG12...70 A9
The Rows HLW CM20...2 D4
Roxborough Rd HRW HA1...172 D9
Royal Av CHES/WCR EN8...156 B5
Royal Ct HHS/BOV HP3...5 G7
Royal Oak Gv BSF CM23...40 C3
Royal Oak La
HTCH/STOT SG5...34 C4
Royal Rd STAL AL1...120 C8
Royal Wk DUN/WHIP LU6...60 F7
DUN/WHIP LU6...60 F7
Royce Cv GSTN WD25...148 G4
Roydon Cl LTNW/LEA LU4...61 K2
Roydon Ct HHNE HP2...118 B2
Roydon Rd
HLWW/ROY CM19...128 B2
Roy Rd NTHWD HA6...171 H4
Royse Gv ROY SG8...20 C6
Royston Cl HERT/WAT SC14...107 J6
Royston Ct LTNE LU2...155 J3
Royston La SAFWN CB10...23 K2
Royston Park Rd PIN HA5...171 P3
Royston Rd BLDK SG7...26 C8
ROY SG8...21 J7
STAL AL1...9 H1
Rubin Pl PEND EN3...156 F7
Rucklers La KGLCY WD4...133 K7
Ruckles Cl STVG SG1...11 F4
Ruckles Wy AMSS HP7...158 C1
Rudd Cl STVGE SG2...67 J2
Rudham Gv LWTH SG6...36 A5
Rudolph Rd BUSH WD23...163 J5
Rudyard Cl LTNW/LEA LU4...61 K6
Rue De St Lawrence...
WAB EN9...157 H4
Rueley Dell Rd LTNE LU2...47 L5
Rufford Cl WAT WD17...148 G7
Rugby Cl HRW HA1...172 D7
Rugby La CDALE/KGS NW9...173 N8
Ruhemann St LTNE LU2...63 L3
The Ruins STALW/RED AL3...101 J7
Rumballs Ct BSF CM23...91 H1
Rumballs Rd HHS/BOV HP3...134 B2
Rumbold Rd HOD EN11...127 H3

Rumsley *CHESW* EN7 .... 141 P6
Runcie Cl *STALE/WH* AL4 ...... 120 F4
Runcorn Cl *HHNE* HP2 .... 118 A4
Rundells *HLWS* CM18 .... 129 K7
  LWTH SG6 .... 36 G4
Runfold Av *LTNW/LIM* LU5 ...... 62 B1
Runham Cl *LTNW/LEA* LU4 ...... 61 L2
Runham Rd *HHNE* HP2 .... 5 L5
Runley Rd *LTN* LU1 .... 62 A7
Runnalow *LWTH* SG6 .... 36 A1
Runnymede Ct
  LTNN/LIM LU3 * 46 A9
Runrig Hl *AMS* HP6 .... 145 K5
Runsley *WGCE* AL7 .... 105 K3
The Runway *HAT* AL10 .... 122 A4
Ruscombe Dr
  LCOL/BKTW AL2 .... 136 A5
Rushall Gn *LTN* LU1 .... 63 L4
Rushby Md *LWTH* SG6 .... 36 D2
Rushby Pl *LWTH* SG6 .... 36 D2
Rushby Wk *LWTH* SG6 .... 36 D2
Rushden Av *EBAR* EN4 .... 167 J6
Rushden Rd *BUNT* SG9 .... 28 B9
Rushen Dr *WAB* EN9 .... 79 P5
Rushes Md *HLWS* CM18 .... 129 H5
Rushfall *POTB/CUF* EN6 .... 152 C3
  SBW CM21 .... 111 P2
Rushfield Rd *WARE* SG12 ...... 108 E1
Rush Gn *WARE* SG12 .... 89 H6
Rush La *RBSF* CM22 .... 59 K3
Rushleigh Av
  CHES/WCR EN8 .... 142 C9
Rushleigh Gn *BSF* CM23 .... 91 N2
Rushmere La *CSHM* HP5 .... 171 K8
  RKW/CH/CXG WD3 .... 168 H5
Rushmore Ct *WATW* WD18 * ... 161 P5
Rushton Av *GSTN* WD25 .... 124 E5
Rushton Gv *HLWE* CM17 .... 129 N3
Ruskin Av *WAB* EN9 .... 157 K4
Ruskin Cl *CHESW* EN7 .... 141 M5
Ruskin Gdns
  KTN/HRWW/WS HA3 .... 173 M9
Ruskin La *HTCHE/RSTV* SG4 ... 35 P9
Rusland Park Rd *HRW* HA1 .... 172 E8
Rusper Cl *STAN* HA7 .... 173 J1
Rusper Gn *LTNE* LU2 .... 63 L3
Russell Av *STALW/RED* AL3 ...... 8 E3
Russell Cl *AMS* HP6 .... 146 A9
  DUN/WHIP LU6 .... 78 N3
  NTHWD HA6 .... 170 E2
  ROY SG8 .... 15 N9
  STVGE SG2 .... 69 L4
Russell Ct *BAR* EN5 * 166 C3
  CSHM HP5 .... 131 H8
Russell Crs *GSTN* WD25 ...... 148 C5
Russelcroft Rd *WGCW* AL8 ... 104 C5
Russell Gdns
  TRDG/WHET N20 .... 167 J8
Russell La *TRDG/WHET* N20 .. 167 K8
Russell Ms *LTN* LU1 .... 62 C7
Russell Pl *HHS/BOV* HP3 ...... 133 L2
  HHW HP1 .... 1 J6
Russell Ri *LTN* LU1 .... 6 C7
Russell Rd *DUN/HR/TOD* LU5 ... 44 C2
  EN1 N1 .... 155 N4
  HHW HP1 .... 161 N9
  TRDG/WHET N20 .... 167 J8
Russell's Dr *CHES/WCR* EN8 . 142 D9
Russell's Ride
  CHES EN8 .... 156 C1
Russell St *LTN* LU1 * 5 L5
Russell Wy *OXHEY* WD19 .... 162 D6
Russet Cl *CHESW* EN7 * 141 M5
Russet Dr *RAD* WD7 .... 151 J1
  STALE/WH AL4 .... 121 H9
The Russets *CFSP/GDCR* SL9 . 168 C7
Russett Hl *CFSP/GDCR* SL9 ... 168 C7
Russett Wd
  DUN/HR/TOD LU5 .... 60 G5
Ruston Gdns *STHGT/OAK* N14 . 141 L5
Ruth Cl *STAN* HA7 .... 173 M8
Rutherford Cl *BORE* WD6 .... 165 J1
  STVG SG1 .... 50 D9
Rutherford Wy *BUSH* WD23 .... 9 K9
Ruthin Cl *LTN* LU1 .... 62 E9
Ruthven Av *CHES/WCR* EN8 ... 156 D3
Rutland Crs *LTNE* LU2 .... 7 K4
Rutland Pl *BUSH* WD23 * 163 M7
The Rutts *BUSH* WD23 .... 163 M7
Ryall Cl *LCOL/BKTW* AL2 ...... 135 H8
Ryan Ct *OXHEY* WD19 * 162 G6
Ryan Wy *WATN* WD24 .... 149 K9
Rydal Mt *POTB/CUF* EN6 * ... 153 H3
Rydal Wy *LTNN/LIM* LU3 .... 62 A1
Ryder Av *HTCH/STOT* SG5 ..... 25 J5
Ryder Cl *BUSH* WD23 .... 163 K5
  HERT/BAY SG13 .... 51 P9
  HHS/BOV HP3 .... 132 D7
Ryders Av *STALE/WH* AL4 .... 122 B8
Ryder Seed Ms *STAL* AL1 .... 8 E5
Ryders Hl *STVG* SG1 .... 51 M4
The Ryde *BRKMPK* AL9 .... 137 J1
Rye Cl *HARP* AL5 .... 82 A9
  STVG SG1 .... 51 J4
Ryecroft *HAT* AL10 .... 122 C8
  HLWW/ROY CM19 .... 2 A6
Ryecroft Cl *HLWW/ROY* CM19 . 2 A6
Ryecroft Crs *BAR* EN5 .... 165 P4
Ryecroft Rd *CSHM* HP5 .... 144 F1
Ryecroft Wy *LTNE* LU2 .... 63 H3
Ryefeld Cl *HOD* EN11 .... 115 J7
Ryefield *LTNN/LIM* LU3 .... 46 B6
Ryefield Crs *PIN* HA5 * 171 J6
Ryefield Pde *NTHWD* HA6 * . 171 J6
Rye Gdns *BLDK* SG7 .... 26 D8
Rye Hl *HARP* AL5 .... 82 A9
  HOD EN11 .... 126 C7
Rye Hill Rd *HLWS* CM18 ...... 128 G8
Ryelands *WGCE* AL7 .... 105 K8
Rye Rd *HOD* EN11 .... 126 C4
Ryes La *RBSF* CM22 .... 93 J2
The Rye *STHGT/OAK* N14 .... 167 N6
Rye Wy *EDGW* HA8 .... 173 M3
Rylands Heath *LTU* LU2 .... 63 N4

Rymill Cl *HHS/BOV* HP3 ...... 132 D7
Ryton Cl *LTN* LU1 .... 62 C7

S

Saberton Cl *STALW/RED* AL3 . 100 G8
Sacombe Gn *LTNN/LIM* LU3 ... 46 C6
Sacombe Green Rd
  WARE SG12 .... 87 M1
Sacombe Pound *WARE* SG12 .. 87 L3
Sacombe Rd *HERT/WAT* SG14 . 87 J9
  HHW HP1 .... 117 J6
Sacombs Ash La *SBW* CM21 ... 91 H6
Saddlers Cl *BAR* EN5 .... 165 P4
  BLDK SG7 .... 26 A9
  BORE WD6 * 165 K4
  BSF CM23 .... 91 M1
  PIN HA5 .... 172 A2
Saddlers Pl *ROY* SG8 .... 20 D3
Saddlers Wk *KGLGY* WD4 * .. 134 B8
Sadleir Rd *STAL* AL1 .... 136 D1
Sadler Cl *CHESW* EN7 .... 141 K4
Sadlers Md *HLWS* CM18 ...... 129 K4
Sadlers Wy *HERT/WAT* SG14 . 107 H6
Sadlier Rd *STDN* SG11 .... 56 D3
Saffron Cl *ARL/CHE* SG15 ...... 24 E2
  HOD EN11 .... 126 E4
  LTNE LU2 .... 46 E9
Saffron Hl *LWTH* SG6 .... 36 B2
Saffron La *HHW* HP1 .... 117 K7
Saffron Mdw *STDN* SG11 ...... 71 K4
Saffron St *ROY* SG8 .... 20 E5
Sainfoin End *HHNE* HP2 ...... 118 B6
St Agnells Ct *HHNE* HP2 ..... 118 B4
St Agnells La *HHNE* HP2 ...... 118 A3
St Agnes Ga
  RAYLNE NW6 * 112 B6
St Albans Dr *STVG* SG1 .... 51 H6
St Albans Hwy
  HTCHE/RSTV SG4 .... 49 L9
St Albans Hl *HHS/BOV* HP3 * .. 5 L9
St Albans La *ABLGY* WD5 .... 134 G5
St Albans Link *STVG* SG1 ...... 51 H6
St Albans Rd *BAR* EN5 .... 153 H9
  GSTN WD25 .... 149 K5
  HHNE HP2 .... 9 H1
  HHS/BOV HP3 .... 118 B9
  HTCHE/RSTV SG4 .... 84 B5
  POTB/CUF EN6 .... 152 B1
  STALE/WH AL4 .... 120 F4
  STALW/RED AL3 .... 9 L1
  WAT WD17 .... 12 E1
  WATN WD24 .... 149 J6
St Albans Rd East *HAT* AL10 . 122 A4
St Albans Rd West *HAT* AL10 . 122 A4
St Andrew Ms
  HERT/WAT SG14 .... 107 K6
St Andrew's Av *HARP* AL5 ... 101 N3
St Andrews Cl *LTN* LU1 .... 80 C4
St Andrews Dr *STAN* HA7 .... 173 J4
St Andrews Dr *STAN* HA7 .... 149 J9
  STVG SG1 .... 51 H5
St Andrews La
St Andrew's Meadow
  HLWS CM18 .... 3 J7
St Andrew's Pl
  HTCHE/RSTV SG4 .... 49 L1
St Andrews Rd
  HHS/BOV HP3 * 133 M3
St Andrews Ter
  OXHEY WD19 * 171 L2
St Andrew St
  HERT/WAT SG14 .... 107 K6
St Anna Rd *BAR* EN5 * 166 B4
St Anne's Cl *CHESW* EN7 .... 141 M7
St Annes Cl *OXHEY* WD19 * . 171 L1
St Anne's Ct
  RAYLNE NW6 * 112 B6
St Anne's Pk *BROX* EN10 .... 126 F8
St Annes Rd *DEN/HRF* UB9 ... 169 N7
St Anne's Rd
  HTCH/STOT SG5 .... 25 J5
St Annes Rd *STALE/WH* AL4 .. 137 J6
St Ann's Rd *LTN* LU1 .... 7 F5
St Anthonys Av
  HHS/BOV HP3 .... 134 C1
St Audreys Cl *HAT* AL10 ..... 123 H5
St Audreys Gn *WGCE* AL7 ... 105 J7
St Augusta Ct
  STALW/RED AL3 .... 120 C6
St Augustine Av
  LTNN/LIM LU3 .... 62 C2
St Augustine Cl
  HTCH/STOT SG5 .... 35 L8
St Augustines Cl *BROX* EN10 . 126 E8
St Augustines Dr *BROX* EN10 . 126 E8
St Austell Cl *EDGW* HA8 .... 173 H5
St Bernard's Cl *LTNN/LIM* LU3 . 62 D3
St Bernard's Rd
  STALW/RED AL3 .... 9 F1
St Brelades Br *STALE/WH* AL4 . 121 J4
St Bride's Av *EDGW* HA8 .... 173 M5
St Catharine's Rd
  BROX EN10 .... 126 F7
St Catherines Av
  LTNN/LIM LU3 .... 62 C2
St Catherines Rd *RSLP* HA4 . 170 E9
St Christopher's Cl
  DUN/HR/TOD LU5 .... 61 J5
St Christophers Ct
  RKW/CH/CXG WD3 * 160 B3
St Cross Ct *HOD* EN11 .... 126 C7
St Cuthberts Gdns *PIN* HA5 * 171 P4
St Cuthberts Rd *HOD* EN11 .. 127 J2
St David's Cl *HHS/BOV* HP3 .. 134 C1
  STALE/WH AL4 .... 121 J4
St David's Dr *BROX* EN10 ..... 51 J4
  EDGW HA8 .... 173 M5
St Dunstan's Rd *WARE* SG12 . 110 A4
St Edmunds *BERK* HP4 .... 115 P4
St Edmunds Dr *STAN* HA7 ... 173 J2
St Edmunds Wk
  STALE/WH AL4 * 121 J4
St Edmund's Wy *HLWE* CM17 . 111 M4
St Elmo Ct *HTCHE/RSTV* SG4 * 49 L2
St Ethelbert Av
  LTNN/LIM LU3 .... 62 C2
St Etheldreda's Dr *HAT* AL10 . 122 F6
St Evroul Ct *WARE* SG12 ..... 108 C2
St Faith's Cl *ENC/FH* EN2 .... 155 K9
St Faiths Ct *HTCHE/RSTV* SG4 . 35 L8
St Francis Cl *BUNT* SG9 .... 54 E1
  STVG SG1 .... 109 D7
  POTB/CUF EN6 .... 155 M3
St George's Cl
  DUN/HR/TOD LU5 .... 44 C1
St George's Dr *OXHEY* WD19 . 162 C9
St George's Rd *EN* N1 .... 155 N6
  HHS/BOV HP3 .... 133 M3
  WATN WD24 .... 149 J8
St George's Wy *STVG* SG1 .... 10 D4
St Giles' Av *POTB/CUF* EN6 .. 152 D3
St Giles Rd *HTCHE/RSTV* SG4 . 84 C3
St Helen's Cl *STALE/WH* AL4 . 103 J4
St Heliers Rd *STALE/WH* AL4 . 120 C3
St Ives Cl *LTNN/LIM* LU3 ..... 62 C3
  LTNE LU2 .... 105 J1
St James Av *TRDG/WHET* N20 . 167 J9
St James Cl
  DUN/HR/TOD LU5 .... 61 H2
  EBAR EN4 .... 167 H2
St James Ct *HARP* AL5 .... 102 A1
St James Rd *HARP* AL5 ...... 102 A1
St James Rd *LTNN/LIM* LU3 .. 62 B2
St James's Dr *WD18* 13 F6
St James's Rd *CHESW* EN7 .. 141 K7
St James's Rd *WGCE* AL7 .... 105 J1
St John Cl *LTN* LU1 .... 62 C9
St Johns *STDN* SG11 .... 71 K3
St John's Av *HLWE* CM17 ... 111 M8
St John's Cl *POTB/CUF* EN6 . 153 M3
St John's Ct *HARP* AL5 * 102 B5
St Johns Ct *STSD* CM24 .... 58 F4
St Johns La *STSD* CM24 ...... 58 E4
St John's Rd *ARL/CHE* SG15 .. 24 E5
St John's Rd *HARP* AL5 .... 102 B5
St John's Rd *HHW* HP1 .... 1 J5
  HTCHE/RSTV SG4 .... 49 L2
  STSD CM24 .... 58 F4
  WAT WD17 .... 13 F1
St John's St *HLWE* CM17 ..... 111 M8
St Johns Ter *ENC/FH* EN2 .... 155 L7
St Johns Wk *HLWE* CM17 ... 111 M8
St John's Well Ct *BERK* HP4 . 115 N6
St John's Well La *BERK* HP4 . 115 N6
St Joseph's Cl *LTNN/LIM* LU3 . 62 B2
St Joseph's Gn *WGCE* AL7 .. 104 D9
St Joseph's Rd
  CHES/WCR EN8 .... 156 D3
St Julian's Rd *STAL* AL1 .... 8 E7
St Katharines Cl
  HTCH/STOT SG5 .... 35 J5
St Katherine's Wy *BERK* HP4 . 115 L4
St Kilda Rd *LTNW/LEA* LU4 ... 61 J2
St Laurence Dr *BROX* EN10 .. 142 D2
St Lawrence Av *ABLGY* WD5 . 134 F9
  EDGW HA8 .... 173 M4
St Lawrence Dr *PIN* HA5 ..... 171 K9
St Lawrences Av
  LTNN/LIM LU3 .... 62 D2
St Lawrence Wy
  STALW AL2 .... 135 N9
St Leonards Av
  KTN/HRWW/WS HA3 .... 173 J9
St Leonards Cl *WARE* SG12 .. 108 D1
  HERT/WAT SG14 .... 107 M4
St Leonard's Ct
  STALE/WH AL4 .... 121 H2
St Leonards Crs
  STALE/WH AL4 .... 121 H2
St Leonard's Rd *WAB* EN9 ... 143 J3
St Louis Cl *POTB/CUF* EN6 .. 153 M3
St Luke's Av *ENC/FH* EN2 .... 155 L8
St Luke's Cl *LTNW/LEA* LU4 .. 61 J4
St Magnus Cl *HHS/BOV* HP3 . 134 C1
St Margarets *STVGE* SG2 ...... 67 J4
St Margarets Av
  LTNN/LIM LU3 .... 62 C2
  TRDG/WHET N20 .... 166 G7
St Margaret's Cl
  LTNN/LIM LU3 .... 46 A1
St Margarets Rd *EDGW* HA8 . 173 P2
St Marie's Cl *BAR* EN5 .... 166 F2
St Marks Cl *STALE/WH* AL4 .. 137 N1
St Martins *NTHWD* HA6 ...... 170 F2
St Martins Cl *EN* N1 .... 156 A9
St Martins Cl *HARP* AL5 ...... 82 B9
  OXHEY WD19 .... 171 L1
St Martins Rd *HOD* EN11 .... 127 H6
St Martins Rd *KNEB* SG3 ...... 67 K9
St Mary's Av *WLYN* AL6 .... 67 J2
St Mary's Ga *DUN/WHIP* LU6 . 60 E6
St Mary's La *HTCHE/RSTV* SG4 . 64 C5
St Mary's Pk *ROY* SG8 .... 20 C4
St Mary's Rd *CHES/WCR* EN8 . 142 B8
  DEN/HRF UB9 .... 169 M7
St Mary's Sq
  HERT/WAT SG14 * 107 L6
St Mary's Vw
  KTN/HRWW/WS HA3 .... 173 J9
  WATW WD18 * 13 G5
St Mary's Wk *STALE/WH* AL4 . 103 L1
St Marys Wy *BLDK* SG7 .... 37 H2
  CFSP/GDCR SL9 .... 168 B6
  CSHM HP5 .... 144 C2
St Matthews Cl *LTNE* LU2 ...... 7 F2
St Michaels Av
  HHS/BOV HP3 * 118 C9
St Michaels Av *HHS/BOV* HP3 . 118 C9
St Michaels Cl *HLW* CM20 ..... 3 H4
St Michaels Ct
  RAYLNE NW6 * 112 D2
St Michael's Crs
  LTNN/LIM LU3 .... 62 C3
St Michaels Dr *GSTN* WD25 . 149 J3
St Michaels Mt
  HTCHE/RSTV SG4 .... 35 M8
St Michael's Rd *BROX* EN10 . 126 E8
St Michaels Rd
  STALW/RED AL3 .... 8 A3
St Michaels Wy
  POTB/CUF EN6 .... 139 L9
St Mildreds Av *LTNN/LIM* LU3 . 62 C2
St Monicas Av *LTNN/LIM* LU3 . 62 D2
St Neots Cl *BORE* WD6 .... 151 M8
St Nicholas Cl *AMSS* HP7 .... 145 N9
  BORE WD6 .... 151 M8
St Nicholas Cl *HLWE* CM17 . 129 K7
St Nicholas Mt *HHW* HP1 ... 117 J8
St Ninian's Ct
  TRDG/WHET N20 .... 167 K9
St Olam's Cl *LTNN/LIM* LU3 .. 46 C9
St Olives *HTCH/STOT* SG5 ..... 25 J1
St Pauls Av
  KTN/HRWW/WS HA3 .... 173 M9
St Paul's Cl *BORE* WD6 ...... 165 J4
St Pauls Gdns *LTN* LU1 .... 62 F9
St Pauls Pl *STAL* AL1 .... 121 H2
St Pauls Rd *HHNE* HP2 ...... 117 P7
  LTN LU1 .... 62 F9
St Pauls Wy *WAB* EN9 .... 157 J3
  WATN WD24 .... 13 H1
St Peter's Av *ARL/CHE* SG15 . 24 E2
St Peter's Ct *BAR* EN5 .... 165 P4
  BUSH WD23 .... 163 H7
St Peters Cl *HAT* AL10 .... 122 D5
St Peters Cl
  RKW/CH/CXG WD3 .... 160 F8
  STAL AL1 .... 9 F2
St Peters Crs
  CFSP/GDCR SL9 .... 168 C5
St Peters Hl *TRING* SG4 .... 95 P8
St Peter's Rd
  DUN/HR/TOD LU5 .... 60 F6
St Peter's Rd *STVG* SG1 .... 51 L8
St Peter's St *STAL* AL1 .... 9 F3
St Peters Wy
  RKW/CH/CXG WD3 .... 159 P3
St Ronans Ct *EBAR* EN4 ..... 153 M8
St Saviour's Crs *LTN* LU1 ..... 4 C6
St Stephen's Av
  STALW/RED AL3 .... 136 A1
St Stephen's Cl
  STALW/RED AL3 .... 136 A2
St Stephen's Hl
  STALW/RED AL3 .... 136 B1
St Stephens Rd *BAR* EN5 .... 156 C4
St Stephens Rd *PEND* EN3 .. 156 C7
St Thomas' Dr *PIN* HA5 ...... 172 A1
St Thomas Pl *STALW/RED* AL3 * 103 J4
St Thomas Rd
  STHGT/OAK N14 .... 167 H6
St Thomas's Cl *LTNN/LIM* LU2 . 63 H2
  WAB EN9 .... 63 J2
St Thomas's Rd *LTNE* LU2 .... 63 H2
St Ursula Gv *PIN* HA5 .... 171 M9
St Vincent Dr *STAL* AL1 ...... 136 F1
St Vincent Gdns
  LTNE LU2 * 61 N3
St Vincents Cots
  WATW WD18 * 13 F4
St Vincent's Wy
  POTB/CUF EN6 .... 153 M4
St Wilfrid's Cl *EBAR* EN4 * .. 167 H4
St Wilfrid's Rd *EBAR* EN4 .... 167 H4
St Winifreds Av
  LTNN/LIM LU3 .... 62 D2
Sakins Cft *HLWS* CM18 ...... 129 J6
Salehurst Cl
  KTN/HRWW/WS HA3 .... 173 L9
Salisbury Av *HARP* AL5 ...... 101 N3
  STAL AL1 .... 145 J3
Salisbury Cl *AMSS* HP7 ...... 145 N9
  BSF CM23 .... 74 A5
  HTCH/STOT SG5 .... 25 K3
  POTB/CUF EN6 .... 153 M2
Salisbury Crs
  CHES EN8 .... 156 C2
Salisbury Gdns *WGCE* AL7 ... 105 J7
Salisbury Hall Dr *HAT* AL10 . 122 D8
Salisbury Rd *BAR* EN5 .... 166 C2
  BLDK SG7 .... 26 A8
  HARP AL5 .... 102 C1
  HRW HA1 .... 172 C6
  LTN LU1 .... 62 C6
  PEND EN3 .... 156 F1
  PIN HA5 .... 171 K5
  WATN WD24 .... 149 J8
  WGCE AL7 .... 105 J7

Sallowsprings
  DUN/WHIP LU6 .... 78 C4
Sally Deards La *WLYN* AL6 ... 84 E1
Salmon Cl *WGCE* AL7 .... 105 K3
Salmond Cl *STAN* HA7 .... 172 C3
Salmon Cl *STAN* HA7 .... 172 C3
Saltdean Cl *LTNE* LU2 .... 63 L2
Salters *BSF* CM23 .... 91 M1
Salter's Cl *BERK* HP4 .... 115 L4
Salters Cl *RKW/CH/CXG* WD3 . 161 J7
Salters Wy *DUN/WHIP* LU6 .. 149 K9
Saltfield Crs *LTNW/LEA* LU4 . 61 J4
Salusbury Ct *HTCH/STOT* SG5 . 48 A5
Salwey Crs *BROX* EN10 ...... 126 E8
Sampson Av *BAR* EN5 .... 166 B4
Samuel Ct *STAL* AL1 .... 164 A8
Samuel Sq *STAL* AL1 .... 8 E5
Sancroft Rd
  KTN/HRWW/WS HA3 .... 173 L9
Sanctuary Cl *DEN/HRF* UB9 . 169 N4
Sandals Spring *HHW* HP1 ...... 1 J6
Sandalwood Cl *LTNN/LIM* LU3 . 46 C6
Sandbrook La *TRING* HP23 .... 95 K5
Sandell Cl *LTNE* LU2 .... 63 J1
Sandeman Gdns *WARE* SG12 . 108 D2
Sanderling Cl *LWTH* SG6 ...... 25 J9
Sanders Cl *LCOL/BKTW* AL2 . 137 J6
Sanders Cnr *ENC/FH* EN2 * . 155 J5
Sandfield Rd *STAL* AL1 .... 145 H3
Sandgate Rd *LTNW/LEA* LU4 . 61 N4
Sandhurst Rd
  CDALE/KGS NW9 .... 173 N7
Sandifield *HAT* AL10 .... 122 E9
Sandiland Cl *DUN/WHIP* LU6 . 60 D5
Sand La *AMP/FLIT/BLC* MK45 . 32 C1
Sandle Rd *BSF* CM23 .... 74 B5
Sandmere Cl *HHNE* HP2 * ... 118 D5
Sandown Cl *TRING* HP23 ...... 95 N8
Sandon Rd *CHES/WCR* EN8 .. 142 B9
Sandover Cl *HTCHE/RSTV* SG4 . 49 N1
Sandown Rd *STVG* SG1 .... 51 M6
  WATN WD24 .... 149 K8
Sandpit La *STAL* AL1 .... 121 J6
  STALE/WH AL4 .... 121 K6
Sandpit Rd *WGCE* AL7 .... 105 H8
Sandridgebury La
  STALW/RED AL3 .... 120 D4
Sandridge Cl *EBAR* EN4 ..... 153 P7
  HHNE HP2 .... 118 B2
  HRW HA1 .... 172 E8
Sandridge Pk
  STALW/RED AL3 .... 120 E3
Sandridge Rd *STAL* AL1 ...... 120 D6
Sandringham Av
  HLWW/ROY CM19 .... 128 B3
Sandringham Crs
  STALE/WH AL4 .... 120 F4
Sandringham Dr
  DUN/HR/TOD LU5 .... 61 H2
Sandringham Gdns
  BSF CM23 .... 73 P9
Sandringham Rd
  POTB/CUF EN6 .... 139 L2
  WATN WD24 .... 149 J7
Sandringham Wy
  CHES/WCR EN8 .... 156 F4
Sandwood Ms *CSHM* HP5 .... 130 C9
Sandy Gr *HERT/WAT* SG14 ... 107 J6
Sandycroft Rd *AMS* HP6 ..... 145 N9
Sandy Gv *HTCH/STOT* SG5 .... 25 J6
Sandy La *BUSH* WD23 .... 163 L2
  NTHWD HA6 .... 171 J2
Sandy Ldg *PIN* HA5 * 172 A3
Sandy Lodge Ct
  NTHWD HA6 * 170 C2
Sandy Lodge Rd
  NTHWD HA6 .... 161 P8
Sandy Lodge Wy
  NTHWD HA6 .... 170 C2
Sandymount Av *STAN* HA7 .. 173 J2
Sandy Ri *CFSP/GDCR* SL9 ... 168 C5
Sanfoine Cl *HTCHE/RSTV* SG4 . 35 P8
Sanfton Rd *LTNW/LEA* LU4 ... 61 J4
Santers La *POTB/CUF* EN6 .. 153 H5
Santingfield North *LTN* LU1 .. 62 A7
Santingfield South *LTN* LU1 .. 62 A7
Sappers Cl *SBW* CM21 .... 92 A7
Saracens Head *HHNE* HP2 ... 118 B7
Sargents *STDN* SG11 .... 71 L5
Sarita Cl
  KTN/HRWW/WS HA3 .... 172 D6
Sarratt Av *RKW/CH/CXG* WD3 . 118 B3
Sarratt La *RKW/CH/CXG* WD3 . 160 F1
Sarum Pl *HHNE* HP2 .... 117 P4
Satinwood Ct *HHNE* HP2 .... 5 H1
Saturn Wy *HHNE* HP2 .... 118 A5
Sauncey Av *HARP* AL5 .... 102 A1
Saunders Cl *WARE* SG12 ..... 92 D2
Sauncey Wood La *HARP* AL5 . 102 D8
Saunders Cl *CHES/WCR* EN8 . 142 B1
  LWTH SG6 .... 36 E1
Saunders End *AMS* HP6 ...... 144 B4
Savernake Ct *STAN* HA7 * .. 173 J3
Savile Cl *CHESW* EN7 .... 141 M5
Saville Cl *SAFWS* CM11 .... 4 A8
Savoy Cl *DEN/HRF* UB9 ...... 169 P6
Savoy Wd *HLWW/ROY* CM19 . 2 B7
Savoy Ms *STAL* AL1 .... 136 A2
Savoy Wd *HLWW/ROY* CM19 . 2 B7
Sawbridgeworth Rd
  RBSF CM22 .... 92 C4
Sawells *BROX* EN10 .... 126 E9
Sawpit La *BSF* CM23 .... 43 K9
Sawtry Cl *LTNN/LIM* LU3 ...... 46 C6
Sawtry Wy *BORE* WD6 .... 151 M8
Sawyers La *POTB/CUF* EN6 . 152 C4
Sawyers Wy *HHNE* HP2 .... 5 K1
Saxon Av *HTCH/STOT* SG5 .... 25 K1
Saxon Cl *LWTH* SG6 .... 145 J8
  DUN/WHIP LU6 .... 60 E6
  HARP AL5 .... 82 B9
  LWTH SG6 .... 36 E1
Saxon Ct *BORE* WD6 .... 151 K9

Saxon Crs
AMP/FLIT/BLC MK45....... 32 D4
Saxon Rd LTNN/LIM LU3... 62 C4
STALE/WH AL4............ 103 J5
WLYN AL6............... 104 E1
Saxon Wy BLDK SC7....... 26 D8
STHGT/OAK N14.......... 167 P5
Saxtead Cl LTNE LU2..... 51 L5
Saxton Ms WAT WD17 *... 149 H9
Sayers Gdns BERK HP4.... 115 M4
Sayer Wy KNEB SG3....... 85 J1
Saysbury Av SBW CM21.... 111 P2
Saysbury Rd SBW CM21.... 111 P2
Sayes Gdns SBW CM21..... 92 A7
Sayward Cl CSHM HP5..... 131 J8
Saywell Rd LTNE LU2..... 63 J5
Scammell Wy WAT WD18.... 162 B5
Scarborough Av STVG SG2. 50 D8
Scarlett Av
RAYLNE/WEN HP22........ 112 F5
Scatterdells La KGLGY WD4. 133 J4
Scatterdells Pk KGLGY WD4 *.. 133 K9
Scawsby Cl DUN/WHIP LU6. 60 B5
Scholars Cl BAR EN5...... 166 C3
Scholar's Wk HARE SG12... 89 L9
Scholars Ms WGCW AL8.... 104 C4
Scholars Wk CFSP/GDCR SL9. 168 C3
Scholars Wy AMS HP6..... 143 L1
School Cl BRKMPK AL9.... 124 A5
CSHM HP5............... 130 C7
STVGE SG2.............. 67 L3
Schoolfields LWTH SG6... 36 F5
School Gdns BERK HP4.... 116 E5
School La AMSS HP7...... 134 C5
BRKMPK AL9............. 124 A5
BUSH WD23.............. 163 K7
CFSP/GDCR SL9.......... 168 B6
DUN/WHIP LU6........... 78 E9
HAT AL10............... 122 E5
HERT/WAT SG14.......... 86 F2
HLW CM20............... 3 G1
HTCH/STOT SC5.......... 48 B4
HTCHE/RSTV SG4......... 37 M7
HTCHE/RSTV SG4......... 49 K9
LCOL/BKTW AL2.......... 149 N4
LTNW/LEA LU4........... 61 N2
PIN HA5 *.............. 171 N8
ROY SG8................ 21 M9
STVGE SG2.............. 52 C4
STVGE SG2.............. 67 L3
WLYN AL6............... 84 E9
School Md ABLGY WD5..... 148 C4
School Pde DEN/HRF UB9 *.. 169 N6
School Rd POTB/CUF EN6.. 139 N9
School Rw HHW HP1....... 117 J9
School Wk WATN SG6...... 36 E2
Schubert Rd BORE WD6.... 164 D5
Scot Co PIN HA5......... 171 M4
Scotscraig RAD WD7...... 150 E5
Scots Hl RKW/CH/CXG WD3. 161 K5
Scots Hill Cl
RKW/CH/CXG WD3......... 161 K5
Scots Mill La
RKW/CH/CXG WD3......... 161 K5
Scott Av WARE SG12...... 108 C4
Scott Cl HOD EN11....... 127 H5
ROY SG8................ 21 M9
Scott Rd BSF CM23....... 73 P8
EDGW HA8............... 173 P6
LTNN/LIM LU3........... 45 M8
STVGE SG2.............. 51 L9
Scotts Cl WARE SG12..... 108 C4
Scotts Rd WARE SG12..... 108 C4
Scotts Vw WGCW AL8...... 104 F7
Scottswood Ct BUSH WD23. 162 C1
Scottswood Rd BUSH WD23. 162 C1
Scriveners Cl HHNE HP2.. 5 G2
Scrubbits Sq RAD WD7.... 150 F5
Scrubbits Park Rd RAD WD7. 150 F5
Seabrook LTNW/LEA LU4... 61 L5
Seabrook Rd KGLGY WD4... 134 E7
Seacroft Gdns OXHEY WD19. 162 F9
Seaford Cl LTNW/LEA LU4.. 63 K3
Seaforth Dr CHES/WCR EN8. 156 C4
Sea Cl LTNN/LIM LU3..... 61 N3
Seaman Cl LCOL/BKTW AL2. 136 C4
Seamons Cl DUN/WHIP LU6. 60 C8
Searches La ABLGY WD5... 135 K6
Seaton Rd HHS/BOV HP3... 5 F7
LCOL/BKTW AL2.......... 137 J6
LTNW/LEA LU4........... 61 L5
Sebright Rd BAR EN5..... 166 B1
HHW HP1................ 117 K9
STALW/RED AL3.......... 79 P8
Secker Crs
KTN/HRWW/WS HA3........ 172 C5
Second Av GSTN WD25..... 149 L5
HLW CM20............... 3 G6
HLWE CM17.............. 129 L4
HLWS CM18.............. 3 J6
LWTH SG6............... 36 F2
STSD CM24.............. 59 J9
Sedbury Cl LTNN/LIM LU3.. 46 B9
Sedgecombe Av
KTN/HRWW/WS HA3........ 173 J9
Sedge Gn HLWW/ROY CM19. 127 L7
WAB EN9................ 127 K8
Sedgewick Rd LTNW/LEA LU4. 45 L8
Sedley Cl EN EN1........ 156 A8
Sedley Gv DEN/HRF UB9... 169 N6
Sedum Cl CDALE/KGS NW9.. 173 P9
Seebohm Cl HTCH/STOT SC5. 35 H7
The Seedbed Centre
HLWW/ROY CM19.......... 128 D4
Seeleys HLWE CM17....... 111 M8
Sefton Av
KTN/HRWW/WS HA3........ 172 C5
Sefton Cl STAL AL1...... 9 K1
Sefton Rd STVG SG1...... 51 L6
Selby Av STALW/RED AL3.. 8 E5
Selden Hl HHW HP1....... 4 E4
Sele Mi HERT/WAT SG14... 107 J3
Sele Rd HERT/WAT SG14... 107 J3
Selina Cl LTNN/LIM LU3.. 45 M8
Selin Cl CHESW EN7...... 141 J4
Sells Rd WARE SG12...... 108 C2
Sellwood Dr BAR EN5..... 166 B4

Selsey Dr LTNE LU2...... 63 L1
Selway Cl PIN HA5....... 171 K8
Selwyn Av HAT AL10...... 122 B6
Selwyn Ct EDGW HA8...... 173 P4
Selwyn Crs HAT AL10..... 122 B6
Selwyn Dr HAT AL10...... 122 B6
Sempil Rd HHW HP1....... 117 K7
Senate Pl STVG SG1...... 51 L5
September Wy STAN HA7... 173 H5
Sequoia Cl BUSH WD23.... 163 M7
Sequoia Pk PIN HA5...... 172 B3
Serby Av ROY SG8........ 20 B2
Sergeants Green La WAB EN9. 157 P5
Sergehill La ABLGY WD5.. 135 H5
Serpentine Cl STVG SG1.. 51 M5
The Service Rd
POTB/CUF EN6........... 153 K2
Seven Acres NTHWD HA6... 171 J3
Severalls Av CSHM HP5... 131 H9
The Severalls LTNE LU2.. 63 J3
Severn Dr EN EN1........ 142 B9
Severnmead HHNE HP2..... 5 F4
Severnvale LCOL/BKTW AL2 *. 137 L6
Severn Wy GSTN WD25..... 149 K4
STVG SG1............... 51 J4
Sewardstone Rd WAB EN9.. 157 H4
Sewardstone St WAB EN9.. 157 H6
Sewardstone Wy WAB EN9.. 157 H6
Sewell Cl STALE/WH AL4.. 121 K8
Sewell Harris Cl HLW CM20. 3 K2
Sewell La DUN/WHIP LU6.. 60 A4
Sewells WGCW AL8........ 105 H3
Sexton Cl CHESW EN7..... 141 J4
Seymour Av LTN LU1...... 7 C7
Seymour Cl PIN HA5...... 171 P5
Seymour Crs HHNE HP2.... 5 G1
Seymour Rd BERK HP4..... 115 K5
CSTG HP8............... 168 A1
LTN LU1................ 62 C3
STALW/RED AL3.......... 120 D5
Seymours HLWW/ROY CM19.. 128 C6
Shackledell STVGE SG2... 67 J4
Shacklegate La
HTCHE/RSTV SG4......... 65 L8
Shackleton Gdns BSF CM23. 73 N8
Shackleton Spring
STVGE SG2.............. 67 K3
Shackleton Wy ABLGY WD5 *. 149 H2
WGCE AL7............... 105 N6
Shady Bush Cl BUSH WD23. 163 L6
Shady La WAT WD17....... 13 M3
Shaftenhoe End Rd ROY SG8. 21 M9
Shaftesbury Av BAR EN5.. 166 C3
Shaftesbury Ct
RKW/CH/CXG WD3......... 161 N4
Shaftesbury Dr
HTCH/STOT SG5.......... 24 C6
Shaftesbury Rd LTNW/LEA LU4. 62 C6
WAT WD17............... 13 H9
Shaftesbury Wy ROY SG8.. 20 D5
Shaftsbury La KGLGY WD4. 134 D6
Shakespeare Av STVG SG8. 20 C2
Shakespeare Rd HARP AL5. 102 A3
Shakespeare St WATN WD24. 149 J8
Shalcross Dr CHES/WCR EN8. 142 E9
Shaldon Rd EDGW HA8..... 173 M6
Shallcross Crs HAT AL10. 122 C9
Shambrook Rd CHESW EN7.. 141 J4

Shanwick Wy
STHGT/OAK N14.......... 167 M7
Shangani Rd BSF CM23.... 74 A5
Shanklin Cl CHESW EN7... 141 N8
LTNN/LIM LU3........... 46 B8
Shanklin Gdns OXHEY WD19. 171 L1
Shantock Hall La
HHS/BOV HP3............ 132 B8
Shantock La HHS/BOV HP3. 132 B9
Shantung Pl CSHM HP5.... 145 H5
Sharmans Cl WLYN AL6.... 85 J9
Sharose Ct STALW/RED AL3. 79 P8
Sharpcroft HHNE HP2..... 117 N6
Sharpecroft
HLWW/ROY CM19.......... 2 D5
Sharpenhoe Rd
LTNN/LIM LU3........... 46 B2
Sharples La HHW HP1..... 116 E9
Sharples Gn LTNN/LIM LU3. 46 C7
Sharps Wy HTCHE/RSTV SG4. 35 M8
Shawbridge
HLWW/ROY CM19.......... 128 F6
Shaw Cl BUSH WD23....... 163 N8
CHES/WCR EN8........... 142 B8
Shaw Rd PEND EN3........ 156 C9
The Shaws WGCE AL7...... 105 M4
The Shaw RBSF CM23...... 93 H6
The Shearers BSF CM23... 91 L1
Sheares Hoppit WARE SG12. 110 A2
Shearwater Cl WARE SG12. 67 N2
Sheepcot Dr GSTN WD25... 149 K4
Sheepcote WGCE AL7...... 105 K9
Sheepcote La BSF CM23... 57 P4
STALE/WH AL4........... 108 K4
Sheepcote Rd HHNE HP2... 5 J3
Sheepcot La HARP AL5.... 149 H5
Sheepcroft Hl STVGE SG2. 67 N5
Sheepfold La AMSS HP7... 145 J9
Sheephouse Rd HHNE HP2. 5 J5
Sheering Dr HLWE CM17... 111 P9
Sheering Mill La SBW CM21. 92 A7
Sheering Rd HLWE CM17... 111 P8
Sheethanger La
HHS/BOV HP3............ 133 K3
Shefton Ri NTHWD HA6.... 171 J4
Shelbourne Cl PIN HA5... 171 P7
Sheldon Cl CHESW EN7.... 141 L5
Shelford Rd BAR EN5..... 166 A5
Shelley La DEN/HRF UB9.. 169 L4
Shelley Ms HHS/BOV HP3 *. 133 N2
Shelley Rd CSHM HP5..... 130 C8
LTN LU1................ 61 K4
Shelly Cl BORE WD6...... 164 G3
Shelton Av DUN/HR/TOD LU5. 44 C3
Shelton Wy LTNE LU2..... 63 H5
Shenfield Cl HLWS CM18.. 128 F6

Shenleybury RAD WD7..... 137 K9
Shenleybury Cots RAD WD7. 151 K1
Shenley Cl LTNE LU2..... 63 H4
Shenley La LCOL/BKTW AL2. 136 G4
Shenley Rd BORE WD6..... 164 C2
HHNE HP2............... 118 C2
RAD WD7................ 151 J5
Shenstone Hl BERK HP4... 116 B6
Shephall Gn STVGE SG2... 67 L4
Shephall La STVGE SG2... 67 J5
Shephall Vw STVG SG1.... 11 J4
Shephall Wy STVGE SG2... 67 L2
Shepherd Cl ABLGY WD5... 135 G9
ROY SG8................ 20 D5
Shepherds Cl BSF CM23... 91 M1
STAN HA7............... 172 G2
Shepherds Ct HERT/WAT SG14. 107 K3
Shepherds Farm
RKW/CH/CXG WD3......... 160 E7
Shepherds Gn HHW HP1.... 117 H9
Shepherd's La
RKW/CH/CXG WD3......... 160 B5
Shepherds Md
HTCH/STOT SC5.......... 35 K6
Shepherds Rd WAT WD18... 12 B3
Shepherds Wk BUSH WD23. 163 M8
Shepherds Wy BRKMPK AL9. 124 E7
CSHM HP5............... 145 J5
HARP AL5............... 81 L9
Shepherds Wd STVGE SG2. 67 L4
Shepley Ms PEND EN3..... 156 F8
Sheppard Cl EN EN1...... 156 A8
Sheppards HLWW/ROY CM19. 128 C6
Sheppards Cl STALW/RED AL3. 120 D5
Shepperton Cl BORE WD6. 152 A9
Sheppey's La KGLGY WD4. 134 F7
Sherards Orch
HLWW/ROY CM19.......... 128 E5
Sheraton Cl BAR EN5..... 164 F4
Sheraton Ms WAT WD18 *.. 162 A3
Sherborne Av LTNE LU2... 46 E9
Sherborne Gdns
CDALE/KGS NW9.......... 173 N7
Sherborne Pl NTHWD HA6. 170 F3
Sherborne Wy
RKW/CH/CXG WD3......... 161 M3
Sherbourne Cl HHNE HP2. 5 H4
Sherd Cl LTNN/LIM LU3... 46 A8
Sheredes Dr HOD EN11.... 126 E6
Sherfield Av
RKW/CH/CXG WD3......... 161 H9
Sheridan Cl HHW HP1..... 4 A3
Sheridan Rd LTNN/LIM LU3. 46 B7
OXHEY WD19............. 162 F6
Sheridan Wk BROX EN10.. 126 B8
Sheriff Wy GSTN WD25.... 149 H3
Sheringham Av
STHGT/OAK N14.......... 167 P4
STVG SG1............... 50 E6
Sheringham Dr LTNE LU2. 46 D8
Sherington Av PIN HA5... 172 A4
Sherland Ct RAD WD7..... 150 F5
Shernbroke Rd WAB EN9.. 157 L4
Sherrardspark Rd WGCW AL8. 104 F4
Sherrards Wy BAR EN5.... 166 C4
Shervington Cv
LTNN/LIM LU3........... 62 C3
Sherwood Av HLWW/ROY CM19. 128 C6
Sherwood Av POTB/CUF EN6. 153 H2
STALE/WH AL4........... 120 C5
Sherwood Pl HHNE HP2.... 118 A4
Sherwood Rd LTNW/LEA LU4. 62 B4
Sherwoods Rd OXHEY WD19. 162 G6
Sherwood St
TRDG/WHET N20.......... 167 H9
Sherwood Ter
TRDG/WHET N20.......... 167 H9
Shetland Cl BORE WD6.... 165 K5
Shillington Rd
HTCH/STOT SG5.......... 33 M2
Shillitoe Av POTB/CUF EN6. 152 C2
Shingle Cl WAB EN9...... 157 M3
Ship La LBUZ LU7........ 96 C1
Shire Cl BROX EN10 *.... 142 E5
Shire Ct STVG SG1....... 50 F8
Shire La CFSP/GDCR SL9.. 168 F4
CSTG HP8............... 159 P9
TRING HP23............. 113 M4
Shiremade BORE WD6...... 164 F4
Shires Pk WGCE AL7 *.... 105 H4
The Shires GSTN WD25.... 149 J1
LTNE LU2............... 63 H9
ROY SG8................ 20 D4
Shirley Cl BROX EN10.... 142 E3
CHES/WCR EN8........... 142 B8
Shirley Rd ABLGY WD5.... 148 C2
LTN LU1................ 6 A3
Shortacre HHNE HP2...... 5 J5
Shortcroft BSF CM23..... 74 E2
Shortcroft Ct
AMP/FLIT/BLC MK45...... 32 C6
Short Hale LBUZ LU7..... 96 C1
Shortlands On WGCE AL7. 105 J7
Shortlands Pl BSF CM23. 74 A2
Short La LCOL/BKTW AL2.. 135 M8
STVGE SG2.............. 67 P2
Shortmead Dr
CHES/WCR EN8........... 156 D1
Shorts Cft CDALE/KGS NW9. 173 N8
Shortway CSHM HP5....... 130 D8
Shothanger Wy
HHS/BOV HP3............ 132 G4
Shott Cl LWTH SG6....... 36 D2

Shrewsbury Av
KTN/HRWW/WS HA3........ 173 L8
The Shrubberies STAL AL1 *. 8 E7
Shrubbery Cv ROY SG8.... 20 C6
The Shrubbery HHW HP1... 117 H7
Shrub Hill Rd HHW HP1.. 117 J9
Shrubland Cl
TRDG/WHET N20 *........ 167 H8
Shrublands BRKMPK AL9.. 139 L5
Shrublands Av BERK HP4. 115 M7
Shrublands Cl
TRDG/WHET N20.......... 167 H8
Shrublands Rd BERK HP4. 115 M6
The Shrublands
POTB/CUF EN6........... 153 J1
Shrubs Rd RKW/CH/CXG WD3. 170 B3
Shugars Gn TRING HP23... 96 A7
Shurland Av EBAR EN4.... 167 H5
Sibley Av HARP AL5...... 102 C5
Sibley Ct LTNE LU2...... 63 J5
Sibneys Gn HLWS CM18.... 129 H7
Sibthorpe Rd BRKMPK AL9. 138 F3
Siccut Rd HTCHE/RSTV SG4. 50 B5
Sicklefield Cl CHESW EN7. 141 H5
Siddons Rd STVG SG2..... 67 H4
Sidford Cl HHW HP1...... 117 J8
The Sidings BROX EN10... 142 E1
HAT AL10............... 122 B7
HHNE HP2............... 5 H3
Siding Wy LCOL/BKTW AL2. 136 F5
Sidmouth Cl OXHEY WD19. 162 D8
Sidney Rd RYLN/HDSTN HA2. 172 C7
Sidney Ter BSF CM23..... 74 A4
Sidney Wy TRING HP23.... 95 P3
Silam Rd STVG SG1....... 10 E5
Silecroft Rd LTNE LU2... 7 K3
Silk Mill Rd OXHEY WD19. 162 B3
STALW/RED AL3.......... 101 J8
Silk Mill Wy TRING HP23. 95 P5
Silverbirch Av
HTCH/STOT SG5.......... 25 K1
Silvercliffe Gdns EBAR EN4. 167 J2
Silver Cl KTN/HRWW/WS HA3. 172 D4
Silver Ct WGCE AL7 *.... 105 K5
Silverdale Rd BUSH WD23. 163 N5
Silver Dell WATN WD24... 148 G4
Silverfield BROX EN10... 142 E1
Silver Hl BORE WD6...... 151 P6
CSTG HP8............... 159 H8
Silverston Wy STAN HA7. 173 J3
Silver St BLDK SC7...... 17 N6
CHESW EN7.............. 141 L9
LTN LU1................ 6 E4
ROY SG8................ 21 J4
STSD CM24.............. 58 E5
WAB EN9................ 157 H4
Silverthorn Dr HHS/BOV HP3. 134 C3
Silver Trees LCOL/BKTW AL2. 135 N9
Silverwood Cl NTHWD HA6. 170 E5
Silvesters HLWW/ROY CM19. 128 C5
Simmonds Ri HHW HP1.... 117 H6
Simmons Ct TRDG/WHET N20. 167 J7
Simmons' Wy
TRDG/WHET N20.......... 167 J8
Simon Dean HHS/BOV HP3. 132 D6
Simpkins Dr
AMP/FLIT/BLC MK45...... 32 D4
Simplicity La HLWE CM17. 129 N2
Simpson Cl LTNW/LEA LU4. 61 N4
Simpson Dr BLDK SC7..... 26 B9
Sinclare Cl EN EN1...... 155 N9
Sinderby Cl BORE WD6.... 151 K9
Sinfield Cl STVG SG1.... 11 J4
Singlets La STALW/RED AL3. 100 D2
Sir John Newsom Wy
WGCE AL7............... 105 H9
Sir Joseph's Wk HARP AL5. 101 P4
Sir Peter's Wy BAR EN5. 78 A6
Sirus Rd NTHWD HA6..... 171 J2
Sish Cl STVG SG1........ 10 C2
Sish La STVG SG1........ 10 C2
Siskin Cl BORE WD6...... 164 G3
BUSH WD23.............. 162 G3
ROY SG8................ 20 D4
Sisson Cl STVGE SG2..... 67 M4
Six Acres HLWS CM18 *... 128 B2
Six Hills Wy STVG SG1... 10 C7
Six Hills Wy STVG SG1... 11 K7
STVGE SG2.............. 11 K7
Sixth Av GSTN WD25...... 149 L5
LWTH SG6............... 36 F2
STSD CM24.............. 59 K8
Skannings Ct WAB EN9.... 157 M3
Skegness Rd STVG SG1.... 50 D7
Skegsbury La
HTCHE/RSTV SG4......... 82 K4
Skeins Wy SAFWS CB11... 43 M4
Skelton Cl LTNN/LIM LU3. 46 C6
Skidmore Wy
RKW/CH/CXG WD3......... 161 J7
Skimpans Cl BRKMPK AL9. 138 G3
Skimpot Rd LTNW/LEA LU4. 61 J7
Skinners St BSF CM23.... 91 M1
Skipton Cl STVGE SG2.... 67 M4
Skua Cl LTNW/LEA LU4.... 61 K1
Skylark Cnr STVGE SG2... 67 N3
Skylark Pl ROY SG8...... 20 E5
Skys Wood Rd STALE/WH AL4. 120 C4
Slacksbury Hatch
HLWW/ROY CM19.......... 2 B6
Slade Ct RAD WD7........ 150 F5
Slade End STVGE SG2 *... 67 N3
Sladegreen La STALE/WH AL4. 45 K3
Sleaford Cl OXHEY WD19. 162 F9
Sleapcross Gdns
STALE/WH AL4........... 121 N9
Sleaps Hyde STVGE SG2... 67 M5
Sleapshyde La STALE/WH AL4. 121 P9
Sleddale HHNE HP2....... 5 H5
Sleets End HHW HP1...... 117 J6
Slimmons Dr STALE/WH AL4. 120 E6
Slipe La BROX EN10...... 142 E3
The Slipe LBUZ LU7...... 77 P6
Slip La KNEB SG3........ 69 M7
Slippers Hl HHNE HP2... 117 N6
Sloan Ct STVG SG1....... 11 H6
Sloansway WGCE AL7...... 105 J3
Slowmans Cl LCOL/BKTW AL2. 136 B4
The Slype STALW/RED AL3. 82 F8
Small Acre HHW HP1...... 117 J8

Smallcroft WGCE AL7..... 105 L5
Smallford La STALE/WH AL4. 121 L9
Smallwood Cl STALE/WH AL4. 103 K5
Smarts Gn CHESW EN7..... 141 N5
Smeaton Cl WAB EN9...... 157 K5
Smeaton Rd PEND EN3.... 156 F7
Smithcombe Cl
AMP/FLIT/BLC MK45...... 32 D5
Smithfield HHW HP2...... 117 N6
Smith's End La ROY SG8. 21 K9
Smiths Sq WATW WD18.... 13 C5
Smith St WATW WD18..... 13 C5
The Smithy STDN SG11.... 72 E4
Smug Oak La LCOL/BKTW AL2. 136 B4
Snailswell La HTCH/STOT SG5. 35 K5
Snakes La EBAR EN4...... 167 M2
RBSF CM23.............. 59 H1
Snaresbrook Dr STAN HA7. 173 K1
Snatchup STALW/RED AL3. 101 H7
Snells La AMSS HP7...... 159 H1
Snells Md BUNT SG9...... 40 D9
Snells Wood Ct AMSS HP7. 159 J1
The Snipe HTCHE/RSTV SG4. 37 K7
Snowdonia Wy STVG SG1.. 51 K3
Snowdrop Cl BSF CM23.... 73 L6
Snowford Cl LTNN/LIM LU3. 46 B8
Snowhill Cots CSHM HP5. 131 L3
Soham Rd BORE WD6....... 156 E7
Solar Ct WATW WD18 *.... 12 A6
Solar Wy PEND EN3...... 156 E5
Solesbridge Cl
RKW/CH/CXG WD3......... 160 D2
Solesbridge La
RKW/CH/CXG WD3......... 160 D2
Sollershott East LWTH SG6. 36 C4
Sollershott Hall LWTH SG6 *. 36 C4
Sollershott West LWTH SG6. 36 B4
Solomon's Hl
RKW/CH/CXG WD3......... 161 H6
Solway HHNE HP2......... 118 A6
Solway Rd North
LTNN/LIM LU3........... 62 B2
Solway Rd South
LTNN/LIM LU3........... 62 B2
Somaford Gv EBAR EN4.... 167 H5
Somerby Cl BROX EN10... 126 E7
Somercoates Cl EBAR EN4. 167 J2
Somerford Cl PIN HA5.... 171 J8
Someries Rd HARP AL5.... 82 B9
HHW HP1................ 117 J6
Somersby Cl LTN LU1.... 62 F9
Somerset Av LTNE LU2.... 63 H4
Somerset Rd BAR EN5..... 166 F4
PEND EN3............... 156 F8
Somersham WGCE AL7..... 105 N6
Somers Rd BRKMPK AL9... 138 E6
Somers St BRKMPK AL9... 138 F2
Somers Wy BUSH WD23.... 163 L6
Sommers Ct WARE SG12 *. 108 D4
Sonia Cl OXHEY WD19.... 162 E6
The Sonnets HHW HP1.... 117 L7
Soothouse Spring
STALW/RED AL3.......... 120 E4
Soper Ms PEND EN3....... 156 F8
Soper Sq HLWE CM17..... 129 M2
Sopers Rd POTB/CUF EN6. 140 C8
Sopwell La STAL AL1.... 8 B5
Sorrel Cl LTNN/LIM LU3. 46 B7
ROY SG8................ 20 E5
Sorrel Garth
HTCHE/RSTV SG4......... 49 H7
Sotheron Rd WAT WD17... 13 G1
Souberie Av LWTH SG6... 36 C3
Souldern St WATW WD18.. 13 D2
Southall Cl WARE SG12.. 108 C2
Southampton Gdns
.... 45 N6
South Ap NTHWD HA6..... 161 P9
South Bank Rd BERK HP4. 115 L5
Southbrook SBW CM21.... 111 P3
Southbury Dr
CHES/WCR EN8........... 142 C7
South Bucks Wy AMSS HP7. 144 B8
CFSP/GDCR SL9.......... 168 B4
CSTG HP8............... 158 G5
South Charlton Mead La
.... 127 H6
Southcliffe Dr
CFSP/GDCR SL9.......... 168 C2
South Cl BAR EN5........ 166 D2
BLDK SC7............... 37 J1
LCOL/BKTW AL2.......... 136 A4
ROY SG8................ 20 A3
South Cottage Dr
RKW/CH/CXG WD3......... 160 D4
South Cottage Gdns
RKW/CH/CXG WD3......... 160 D4
South Dene AMSL NW7.... 165 K9
Southdown Ct HAT AL10.. 122 D9
Southdown Rd HARP AL5.. 102 A3
HAT AL10............... 122 D9
South Drift Wy LTN LU1. 62 C8
South Dr POTB/CUF EN6.. 140 F7
STALE/WH AL4........... 121 J8
Southend Cl STVG SG1... 10 B1
Southend La WAB EN9.... 157 N4
Southern Ri LTNE LU2... 81 N6
Southern Ter HOD EN11.. 126 F6
Southern Wy DUN/WHIP LU6. 78 F7
HLWW/ROY CM19.......... 128 D6
LWTH SG6............... 25 J9
Southernwood Cl
HHNE HP2............... 118 B7
Southerton Wy RAD WD7.. 151 K3
Southfield BAR EN5..... 166 B5
STDN SG11.............. 55 L8
WGCE AL7............... 104 C8
Southfield Av WATN WD24. 149 K8
Southfield Pk
RYLN/HDSTN HA2......... 172 B8
Southfield Rd
CHES/WCR EN8........... 142 D5
HOD EN11............... 126 F3
Southfields LWTH SG6... 25 K8
STDN SG11.............. 71 K4
Southfields Rd
DUN/WHIP LU6........... 60 G8
South Ga HLW CM20...... 2 E5
Southgate STVG SG1..... 10 D6

Southgate Rd *POTB/CUF EN6*... 153 M3
South Hl *NTHWD HA6 *... 170 G5
South Hill Ct
  *HTCHE/RSTV SC4 *... 49 M1
South Hill Rd *HLW HP1 *... 4 C2
South Hill La *PIN HA5 *... 171 J8
South Ley *WGCE AL7 *... 105 H9
South Lodge *ENC/FH EN2 *... 167 P3
South Lodge Dr
  *STHGT/OAK N14 *... 167 P3
Southmead Crs
  *CHES/WCR EN8 *... 142 D9
Southmill Rd *BSF CM23 *... 74 B4
South Mt *TRDG/WHET N20 *... 166 G8
South Ordnance Rd
  *PEND EN3 *... 156 F7
Southover
  *HTCHN/WDSPK N12 *... 166 F1
South Pde *EDGW HA8 *... 173 N6
South Pk *CFSP/GDCR SL9 *... 168 D9
South Park Av
  *RKW/CH/CXG WD3 *... 160 D4
South Park Crs
  *CFSP/GDCR SL9 *... 168 D9
South Park Dr
  *CFSP/GDCR SL9 *... 168 C8
South Park Gdns *BERK HP4 *... 115 N6
South Pl *HLW CM20 *... 6 E3
  *HTCH/STOT SG5 *... 35 J8
South Riding *LCOL/BKTW AL2 *... 135 D9
Southron Rd *HLWE HP6 *... 145 H6
  *BLDK SG7 *... 37 J1
  *BSF CM23 *... 74 B5
  *EDGW HA8 *... 173 P5
  *HLW CM20 *... 111 K9
  *LTN LU1 *... 6 E7
  *RKW/CH/CXG WD3 *... 160 A4
  *STDN SG11 *... 71 J4
Southsea Av *WATW WD18 *... 12 C4
Southsea Rd *STVG SG1 *... 50 E7
South Side *CFSP/GDCR SL9 *... 74 A4
South St *BSF CM23 *... 74 B3
  *HERT/WAT SG14 *... 107 L6
  *RAYLNE/WEN HP22 *... 112 C7
  *WARE SG12 *... 109 H8
South Vw *LWTH SG6 *... 36 C5
Southview Cl *CHING E4 *... 35 L8
South View Rd *PIN HA5 *... 171 K3
  *CFSP/GDCR SL9 *... 168 B8
Southview Rd *HARP AL5 *... 102 B1
South Wy *CHING E4 *... 51 L6
South Wy *CHING E4 *... 138 D1
  *HAT AL10 *... 148 E3
  *RYLN/HDSTN HA2 *... 172 A4
Southway *TRDG/WHET N20 *... 166 E8
South Weald Dr *WAB EN9 *... 157 J3
Southwold Rd *WATN WD24 *... 149 K7
Southwood Rd
  *DUN/HR/TOD LU5 *... 61 H8
Sovereign Ct
  *HLWW/ROY CM19 *... 128 E6
Sovereign Ms *EBAR EN4 *... 167 K2
Sovereign Pk *HHNE HP2 *... 118 C6
  *LTNW/LEA LU4 *... 62 A5
  *STALE/WH AL4 *... 121 J9
Sovereign Pl *HRW HA1 *... 172 F9
Sowerby Av *LTNE LU2 *... 63 L8
Sparhawke *LWTH SG6 *... 25 L8
Sparkbridge Rd *HRW HA1 *... 172 F6
Sparrow Cl *LTNW/LEA LU4 *... 61 K2
Sparrow Dr *STVGE SG2 *... 67 M2
Sparrows Herne *BUSH WD23 *... 163 L6
Sparrows Wk *BUSH WD23 *... 163 L7
Sparrowswick Ride
  *STALW/RED AL3 *... 120 B3
Sparrow Wk *WATN WD25 *... 149 H6
Spear Cl *LTNN/LIM LU3 *... 45 P9
Speedwell Cl *HHW HP1 *... 117 N9
  *LTNN/LIM LU3 *... 46 B7
Speke Cl *STVGE SG2 *... 67 N1
Spellbrooke *HTCH/STOT SG5 *... 35 J8
Spellbrook La East
  *RBSF CM22 *... 92 A1

STSD CM24... 58 F5
STVGE SG2... 51 N8
WAT WD17... 149 H9
WGCE AL7... 105 M7
Spinning Wheel Md
  *HLWS CM18 *... 129 K6
The Spire Green Centre
  *HLWW/ROY CM19 *... 128 B4
The Spires *HHNE HP2 *... 4 E5
Spittlesea Rd *LTNE LU2 *... 63 K8
Spoondell *DUN/WHIP LU6 *... 60 C7
Spooners Dr *LCOL/BKTW AL2 *... 136 B6
Spratts La *DUN/WHIP LU6 *... 79 J4
Spring Cl *BAR EN5 *... 166 B4
  *BORE WD6 *... 164 C1
  *CSHM HP5 *... 145 P5
  *DEN/HRF UB9 *... 169 P5
Spring Court Rd *ENC/FH EN2 *... 155 H8
Spring Crofts *BUSH WD23 *... 163 J4
Spring Dr *STVGE SG2 *... 67 K6
Springett Pl *AMS HP6 *... 145 L7
Spring Field *BDCW SG18 *... 74 D7
  *BUSH WD23 *... 163 M7
Springfield Crs *HARP AL5 *... 81 P9
Spring Field Rd *BERK HP4 *... 115 L4
Springfield Rd
  *CHES/WCR EN8 *... 156 D2
  *CSHM HP5 *... 145 H2
  *DUN/WHIP LU6 *... 60 C7
  *GSTN WD25 *... 149 J3
  *HHNE HP2 *... 118 A7
  *LTNN/LIM LU3 *... 46 D9
  *LTNW/LEA LU4 *... 120 F9
  *STAL AL1 *... 145 H7
Springfields *AMS HP6 *... 126 E7
  *BROX EN10 *... 157 K4
  *WAB EN9 *... 104 E8
Spring Garden La *BERK HP4 *... 115 J6
Spring Gdns *WATN WD25 *... 149 P5
Spring Glen *HAT AL10 *... 122 C2
Springhall La *BSF CM23 *... 111 P3
Springhall Rd *SBW CM21 *... 111 P2
Springhead *BLDK SG7 *... 42 A2
Spring Hills *HLW CM20 *... 7 H2
Spring Lake *STAN HA7 *... 173 H1
Spring La *BUNT SG9 *... 53 K2
Spring Rd *HARP AL5 *... 117 K7
Springle La *HERT/BAY SG13 *... 6 D6
Spring Pl *LTN LU1 *... 81 H9
Spring Rd *HARP AL5 *... 36 B3
  *LWTH SG6 *... 36 B3
Springshott *LWTH SG6 *... 36 B3
The Springs *BROX EN10 *... 142 D4
  *HERT/BAY SG13 *... 107 N5
Spring Valley
  Enterprise Centre
  *STALW/RED AL3 *... 120 D4
Spring View Rd *WARE SG12 *... 108 B4
Spring Villa Rd *EDGW HA8 *... 173 N4
Spring Wk *DEN/HRF UB9 *... 126 D9
Spring Wy *HHNE HP2 *... 118 C6
Springwell Av
  *RKW/CH/CXG WD3 *... 160 E8
Springwell Ct
  *RKW/CH/CXG WD3 *... 160 E8
  *WARE SG12 *... 108 B4
Springwell La *DEN/HRF UB9 *... 169 M2
  *RKW/CH/CXG WD3 *... 160 E9
Springwood *CHESW EN7 *... 141 N5
Springwood Cl *DEN/HRF UB9 *... 169 P5
Springwood Crs *EDGW HA8 *... 165 J3
Springwood Wk
  *STALE/WH AL4 *... 121 H5
Spruce Hl *HLWS CM18 *... 129 H7
Spruce Wy *LCOL/BKTW AL2 *... 135 H5
Spur Cl *ABLGY WD5 *... 148 E3
Spurcroft *LTNN/LIM LU3 *... 46 D6
Spur Rd *EDGW HA8 *... 173 L1
Spurrs Rd *HTCHE/RSTV SC4 *... 35 N9
The Spur *CHES/WCR EN8 *... 142 C9
  *STVG SG1 *... 11 F6
Square St *HLWE CM17 *... 129 M2
The Square *BROX EN10 *... 142 D4
  *BUNT SG9 *... 40 B3
  *DUN/WHIP LU6 *... 60 E6
  *HHNE HP2 *... 4 C5
  *MHAD SG10 *... 90 C2
  *SBW CM21 *... 111 P3
  *STALW/RED AL3 *... 100 G6
  *WATW WD24 *... 4 D3
Squires Cl *BSF CM23 *... 73 M6
Squires Pl *DUN/HR/TOD LU5 *... 44 C1
Squires Ride *HHNE HP2 *... 118 A2
Squirrel Cha *HHW HP1 *... 117 H7
Squirrels Cl *DUN/WHIP LU6 *... 60 C7
The Squirrels *BUSH WD23 *... 163 M5
  *HERT/BAY SG13 *... 107 P6
  *PIN HA5 *... 171 P7
Stablebridge Rd
  *RAYLNE/WEN HP22 *... 94 D9
Stable Rd
  *RAYLNE/WEN HP22 *... 112 E4
Stables Ms *BRKMPK AL9 *... 139 N7
The Stables *GSTN WD25 *... 150 A6
Stable Yd *LTN LU1 *... 81 H4
Stackfield *HLW CM20 *... 6 A3
Stacklands *WGCW AL8 *... 104 E8
Staddles *RBSF CM22 *... 74 C9
Stadium Wy
  *HLWW/ROY CM19 *... 128 C2
Stafford Rd *CHES/WCR EN8 *... 142 A8
  *HRW HA1 *... 167 N4
Stafford Dr *BROX EN10 *... 126 F8
Stafford Rd
  *KTN/HRWW/WS HA3 *... 172 C4
  *LTNN/LIM LU3 *... 111 P8
  *RKW/CH/CXG WD3 *... 173 P6
Stagg Green Av *BRKMPK AL9 *... 122 F4
Stag La *BERK HP4 *... 115 M6
  *EDGW HA8 *... 172 G2
  *RKW/CH/CXG WD3 *... 160 A5
Stainer Rd *BORE WD6 *... 151 J9
Staines Sq *DUN/WHIP LU6 *... 60 F7
Stains Cl *CHES/WCR EN8 *... 142 D7

Stainton Rd *PEND EN3 *... 156 B3
Stake Piece Rd *ROY SG8 *... 20 B5
Stakers Ct *HARP AL5 *... 102 A3
Stamford Av *ROY SG8 *... 20 C3
Stamford Cl
  *KTN/HRWW/WS HA3 *... 172 C4
  *POTB/CUF EN6 *... 153 N2
Stamford Ct *ROY SG8 *... 162 O1
Stanborough Rd *WAT WD17 *... 162 O1
Stanborough Av *BORE WD6 *... 151 M8
Stanborough Cl *WGCW AL8 *... 104 F7
Stanborough Gn *WGCW AL8 *... 104 F8
Stanborough La *WGCW AL8 *... 104 G8
Stanborough Ms *WGCW AL8 *... 104 G8
Stanborough Rd *WGCW AL8 *... 104 F7
Stanbury Av *WAT WD17 *... 148 F7
Standale Gv *RSLP HA4 *... 170 E9
Standard Rd *PEND EN3 *... 156 D8
Standfield *ABLGY WD5 *... 148 F1
Standfield Cl *HTCHE/RSTV SC4 *... 49 L1
Standhill Cl *HTCHE/RSTV SC4 *... 49 L1
Standingford
  *HLWW/ROY CM19 *... 128 B8
Standon Ct *STDN SG11 *... 71 L5
Standon Hl *STDN SG11 *... 71 H4
Standon Rd *STDN SG11 *... 71 J3
Standing Rd *HHS/BOV HP3 *... 133 L2
Stane Cl *BSF CM23 *... 74 A2
Stane Fld *LWTH SG6 *... 26 B8
Stanelow Crs *STDN SG11 *... 71 J4
Stane St *BLDK SG7 *... 26 C3
Stanfields Ct *HLW CM20 *... 3 C4
Stanford Ct *WAB EN9 *... 157 M3
Stanford Rd *LTNW/LEA LU4 *... 63 H5
Stangate Dr *BORE WD6 *... 165 L4
Stangate Gdns *STAN HA7 *... 173 H1
Stanhope Av
  *RAYLNE/WEN HP22 *... 112 B4
Stanhope Rd *BAR EN5 *... 166 B5
  *CHES/WCR EN8 *... 156 D3
  *STAL AL1 *... 9 J4
Stanier Ri *BERK HP4 *... 115 L4
Stanley Av *LCOL/BKTW AL2 *... 135 P4
Stanley Ct *HLW CM20 *... 122 E8
Stanley Dr *HAT AL10 *... 122 A7
Stanley Gdns *BORE WD6 *... 151 K9
Stanley Hl *AMSS HP7 *... 158 E1
Stanley Hl Av *AMSS HP7 *... 158 F1
Stanley Rd *HERT/BAY SG13 *... 107 M7
  *LTNN/LIM LU3 *... 46 B7
  *NTHWD HA6 *... 171 J5
  *STVGE SG2 *... 51 L8
Stanley St *LTN LU1 *... 4 E4
Stanmore Cha *STALE/WH AL4 *... 121 J9
Stanmore Hl *STAN HA7 *... 62 A2
Stanmore Hl *STAN HA7 *... 173 H1
Stanmore Rd *STVG SG1 *... 51 J5
Stanmount Rd
  *LCOL/BKTW AL2 *... 135 P4
Stansted Dr *HOD EN11 *... 126 E3
Stansted Pl *AMSS HP7 *... 145 H9
Stansted Rd
  *HERT/BAY SG13 *... 107 P5
  *HOD EN11 *... 126 E3
  *WARE SG12 *... 108 C2
Stansted Hl *MHAD SG10 *... 90 B2
Stansted Rd *BSF CM23 *... 59 J3
Stanton Cl *STALE/WH AL4 *... 121 J4
Stanton Rd *LTNW/LEA LU4 *... 61 M4
Stanway Rd *WAB EN9 *... 157 N4
Staplefield Cl *PIN HA5 *... 171 J1
Stapleford *WGCE AL7 *... 105 M4
Stapleford Rd *LTNE LU2 *... 63 J2
Stapleton Cl
  *POTB/CUF EN6 *... 153 N1
Stapleton Rd *BORE WD6 *... 151 M8
Stapley Rd *STAL AL1 *... 8 E2
Staplyton Rd *BAR EN5 *... 166 C4
Star Holme Ct *WARE SG12 *... 108 D3
Starkey Cl *CHESW EN7 *... 141 K4
Starlight Wy *STALE/WH AL4 *... 137 H1
Star Pl *LTN LU1 *... 171 J7
Star La *POTB/CUF EN6 *... 153 J5
Starling La *POTB/CUF EN6 *... 142 G8
Starling Pl *GSTN WD25 *... 149 K2
Star St *WARE SG12 *... 108 D3
Statham Ct *STVGE SG2 *... 66 G8
Station Ap *BAR EN5 *... 166 C5
  *CFSP/GDCR SL9 *... 168 C5
  *CHES/WCR EN8 *... 156 D3
  *HARP AL5 *... 102 A3
  *KNEB SG3 *... 85 M8
  *NTHWD HA6 *... 171 H8
  *OXHEY WD19 *... 162 F9
  *RAD WD7 *... 162 C7
  *RAYLNE/WEN HP22 *... 112 C7
  *RKW/CH/CXG WD3 *... 160 A3
  *WATW WD18 *... 12 A4
Station Cl *BRKMPK AL9 *... 139 H5
  *POTB/CUF EN6 *... 153 P1
  *RKW/CH/CXG WD3 *... 145 H8
Stationers Pl *HHS/BOV HP3 *... 133 N4
Station Footpath
  *KGLGY WD4 *... 134 C7
Station Ms *POTB/CUF EN6 *... 153 K1
Station Pde *EBAR EN4 *... 167 L3
  *EDGW HA8 *... 173 J4
  *KTN/HRWW/WS HA3 *... 171 H6
  *STHGT/OAK N14 *... 167 P7
Station Pl *LWTH SG6 *... 36 C7
Station Rd *AMSS HP7 *... 145 J6
  *ARL/CHE SG15 *... 24 E1
  *BAR EN5 *... 166 C4
  *BERK HP4 *... 116 A6
  *BLDK SG7 *... 42 A2
  *BRKMPK AL9 *... 138 G5
  *BSF CM23 *... 74 A5
  *BUNT SG9 *... 40 C3
  *CFSP/GDCR SL9 *... 168 D9

CHES/WCR EN8... 156 F4
CSHM HP5 *... 144 C5
DUN/HR/TOD LU5 *... 25 K8
EDGW HA8 *... 173 N3
HARP AL5 *... 86 E2
HERT/WAT SG14 *... 87 P5
HHS/BOV HP3 *... 133 L1
HHW HP1 *... 4 B6
HLWE CM17 *... 121 M8
HRW HA1 *... 172 B9
KGLGY WD4 *... 67 J9
KNEB SG3 *... 85 P8
LBUZ LU7 *... 77 P4
LCOL/BKTW AL2 *... 135 J1
LTN LU1 *... 6 E3
LTNN/LEA LU4 *... 36 C2
LWTH SG6 *... 36 C7
MHAD SG10 *... 90 B4
POTB/CUF EN6 *... 128 B4
RAD WD7 *... 150 F5
RBSF CM22 *... 92 A6
RKW/CH/CXG WD3 *... 161 H6
ROY SG8 *... 172 B9
RYLN/HDSTN HA2 *... 172 B9
SBW CM21 *... 92 A6
STALE/WH AL4 *... 121 H9
STDN SG11 *... 71 J3
STSD CM24 *... 58 F5
TRING HP23 *... 77 H9
TRING HP23 *... 96 A3
WARE SG12 *... 108 D3
WAT WD17 *... 162 D1
WLYN AL6 *... 105 H1
The Stone Wy *LWTH SG6 *... 36 B3
Stonea Rd *HHS/BOV HP3 *... 133 K9
Stonea Wk
  *KTN/HRWW/WS HA3 *... 172 D5
Stratford Cl *HHW HP1 *... 153 K2
Stratford Ct *KNEB SG3 *... 67 K9
Stratford Ga *POTB/CUF EN6 *... 153 L2
Stratford Rd *BAR EN5 *... 166 C2
The Straits *WAB EN9 *... 156 G9
Strandburgh Pl
  *HHS/BOV HP3 *... 134 C1
Strangers Wy *LTNW/LEA LU4 *... 61 M2
Stratways Wy *WAT WD17 *... 148 E3
Stratfield Dr *BROX EN10 *... 126 D3
Stratfield Rd *BORE WD6 *... 164 F2
Stratford Cl
  *DUN/HR/TOD LU5 *... 62 C5
  *WAT WD17 *... 62 B1
Stratford Wy *HHS/BOV HP3 *... 133 L2
  *HHW HP1 *... 4 B1
  *LCOL/BKTW AL2 *... 135 N8
  *WAT WD17 *... 12 B1
Strathearn Cots
  *TRDG/WHET N20 *... 166 E9
Strathmore Av
  *HTCH/STOT SG5 *... 35 K7
  *LTNE LU2 *... 62 F9
Strathmore Gdns *EDGW HA8 *... 173 P6
Strathmore Rd
  *HTCHE/RSTV SC4 *... 49 L1
Strathmore Wk *LTN LU1 *... 5 K8
Stratton Av *ENC/FH EN2 *... 155 L7
Stratton Chase Dr *CSTG HP8 *... 158 C8
Stratton Cl *EDGW HA8 *... 173 M3
Stratton Gdns *LTNE LU2 *... 63 H4
Stratton Pl *AMSS HP7 *... 145 L9
Strawberry Crs
  *LCOL/BKTW AL2 *... 136 G5
Strawberry Fld *HAT AL10 *... 122 D9
  *LTNN/LIM LU3 *... 45 P8
Strawberry Flds *WARE SG12 *... 108 A3
Strawfields *WGCE AL7 *... 105 L4
Strawmead *HAT AL10 *... 122 E4
Straw Plait Wy
  *ARL/CHE SG15 *... 24 D5
Straws Hadley Ct
  *RAYLNE/WEN HP22 *... 76 C3
Strayfield Rd *ENC/FH EN2 *... 155 H6
Stream La *EDGW HA8 *... 173 P3
Streatfield Rd
  *KTN/HRWW/WS HA3 *... 173 J7
Streatley Rd *LTNN/LIM LU3 *... 45 P6
The Street *BLDK SG7 *... 27 L9
Streatfield Rd *BLDK SG7 *... 43 L9
  *BUNT SG9 *... 52 C8
  *KGLGY WD4 *... 147 K1
  *RBSF CM22 *... 92 E8
  *STDN SG11 *... 55 L8
  *STDN SG11 *... 71 N3
Stretton Wy *BORE WD6 *... 151 M6
Stringers La *STVGE SG2 *... 67 P5
Stripling Wy *WATW WD18 *... 12 A4
Strombolo Cl *HHS/BOV HP3 *... 134 C1
Stromberg Cl *LTNE LU2 *... 63 H5
Stromnell Cl *LTNE LU2 *... 63 H5
Stronsay Cl *HHS/BOV HP3 *... 134 D1
Stuart Ct *AMS HP6 *... 145 J8
  *BORE WD6 *... 35 N9
Stuart Pl *HTCHE/RSTV SC4 *... 35 N9
Stuart Pl *LTN LU1 *... 6 D5
Stuart Rd
  *AMP/FLIT/BLC MK45 *... 32 D5
  *BERK HP4 *... 167 J6
  *KTN/HRWW/WS HA3 *... 172 F7
  *WLYN AL6 *... 84 E9
Stuarts Cl *HHS/BOV HP3 *... 134 C1
Stuart St *DUN/WHIP LU6 *... 60 E6
Stuart Wy *CHES/WCR EN8 *... 156 A1
Stubbs Cl *DUN/HR/TOD LU5 *... 60 C1
Stubbs End Cl *AMS HP6 *... 145 K6

Stubbs Wd AMS HP6 145 K6
Stud Gn GSTN WD25 149 H2
Studham La BERK HP4 78 B9
DUN/WHIP LU6 78 D5
The Studios BUSH WD23 163 J5
Studio Wy BORE WD6 151 P9
Studlands Ri ROY SG8 20 D4
Studley Rd LTNN/LIM LU3 6 C1
Sturgeon's Wy
HTCHE/RSTV SG4 35 N6
Sturla Cl HERT/WAT SG14 107 J5
Sturlas Wy CHES/WCR EN8 156 C3
Sturmer Cl STALE/WH AL4 121 H9
Sturrock Wy
HTCHE/RSTV SG4 49 P1
Stylecroft Rd CSTG HP8 159 K8
Styles Cl LTNE LU2 63 K4
Such Cl LWTH SG6 36 E1
Sudbury Rd LTNW/LEA LU4 45 L9
Sudicamps Ct WAB EN9 157 M3
Suffolk Cl BORE WD6 165 K4
LCOL/BKTW AL2 137 H4
LTNW/LEA LU4 61 K3
Suffolk Rd DUN/HR/TOD LU5 61 J8
POTB/CUF EN6 153 H2
ROY SG8 20 D4
Sugar La HHW HP1 132 E1
Sugden Ct DUN/WHIP LU6 60 D6
Sulgrave Crs TRING HP23 96 B7
Sullivan Crs DEN/HRF UB9 169 P6
Sullivan Wy BORE WD6 164 C5
Summer Ct HHNE HP2 117 N6
Summer Dl WGCW AL8 104 G2
Summerfield HAT AL10 122 D9
Summerfield Cl
LCOL/BKTW AL2 137 H5
Summerfield Rd GSTN WD25 149 H5
LTN LU1 62 A6
Summer Gv BORE WD6 164 D5
Summer Hl BORE WD6 164 G4
Summerhill Ct STAL AL1 * 9 J1
Summerhouse La
DEN/HRF UB9 169 L4
GSTN WD25 150 B9
Summerhouse Wy
ABLGY WD5 134 G9
Summerleas Cl HHNE HP2 5 H1
Summer Pl WATW WD18 * 162 B5
Summersland Rd
STALE/WH AL4 121 H4
Summers Rd LTNE LU2 63 K5
Summer St LTN LU1 80 D3
Summers Wy
LCOL/BKTW AL2 * 137 K6
Summers Wd BORE WD6 * 165 H3
Summerswood La
BORE WD6 152 B5
Summer Wk STALW/RED AL3 79 P8
Summit Cl EDGW HA8 173 N4
STHGT/OAK N14 167 N8
Summit Rd POTB/CUF EN6 139 H9
Summit Wy STHGT/OAK N14 167 M8
Sumners Farm Cl
HLWW/ROY CM19 128 D8
Sumpter Yd STAL AL1 8 E4
Sunbower Av
DUN/WHIP LU6 60 B3
Sunbury Ct BAR EN5 * 166 C3
Suncote Av DUN/WHIP LU6 60 B3
Suncote Cl DUN/WHIP LU6 60 B4
Sunderland Av STAL AL1 120 F7
Sunderland Gv GSTN WD25 148 G4
Sundew Rd HHW HP1 133 H1
Sundon Park Rd
LTNN/LIM LU3 45 M7
Sundon Rd
DUN/HR/TOD LU5 60 F1
LTNN/LIM LU3 46 A2
Sundown Av
DUN/HR/TOD LU5 60 G7
Sun Hl ROY SG8 20 B5
Sun La HARP AL5 101 P2
Sunmead Rd HHNE HP2 117 N6
Sunningdale BSF CM23 73 P8
LTNE LU2 62 G3
Sunningdale Cl STAN HA7 172 G4
Sunningdale Ldg
EDGW HA8 * 173 M2
Sunningdale Ms
WGCE AL7 * 105 J2
Sunny Bank LBUZ LU7 77 N6
Sunnybank Rd
POTB/CUF EN6 153 K3
Sunny Brook Cl
RAYLNE/WEN HP22 94 E6
Sunny Cft HLWS CM18 129 J6
Sunnydell LCOL/BKTW AL2 136 A5
Sunnyfield BRKMPK AL9 122 G3
Sunny Hl BUNT SG9 40 D9
Sunnyhill Rd HHW HP1 4 A1
RKW/CH/CXG WD3 169 H3
Sunnymead Orch BLDK SG7 18 B7
Sunnymede Av CSHM HP5 131 K7
The Sunny Rd PEND EN3 156 C9
Sunnyside STSD CM24 58 F5
WAB EN9 143 L1
Sunnyside Rd CSHM HP5 130 G9
HTCHE/RSTV SG4 49 M1
Sunridge Av LTNE LU2 62 F4
Sunrise Crs HHS/BOV HP3 5 H7
Sunset Dr LTNE LU2 62 G3
Sunset Vw BAR EN5 166 C1
Sun St BLDK SG7 26 A9
HTCH/STOT SG5 49 K1
SBW CM21 92 A8
WAB EN9 157 H3
Surrey Pl TRING HP23 95 P9
Surrey St LTN LU1 7 F7
Sursham Ct
STALW/RED AL3 79 P8
Sussex Cl CSTG HP8 159 H8
HOD EN11 126 F4
LTNW/LEA LU4 61 J2
Sussex Pl CFSP/GDCR SL9 * 168 C3
LTNE LU2 63 L4
Sussex Rd HRW HA1 172 C9
WATN WD24 149 H8
Sussex Wy EBAR EN4 167 M4
Sutcliffe Cl BUSH WD23 163 L3
STVG SG1 51 K7
Sutherland Av
POTB/CUF EN6 140 E7
Sutherland Cl BAR EN5 166 C3
Sutherland Ct
CDALE/KGS NW9 173 P8
WGCE AL7 105 J5
Sutherland Pl LTN LU1 62 E9
Sutherland Wy
POTB/CUF EN6 140 E7
Sutton Acres RBSF CM22 92 E2
Sutton Cl BROX EN10 126 D8
PIN HA5 171 J9
TRING HP23 96 A6
Sutton Ct WARE SG12 * 108 D4
Sutton Crs BAR EN5 166 B4
Sutton Gdns LTN LU1 79 N2
LTNN/LIM LU3 45 N9
Sutton La BGSW SG18 14 A5
Sutton Rd
SDY/GAM/POT SG19 14 A2
STAL AL1 120 G9
WAT WD17 13 G3
Swale Cl STVG SG1 51 K4
Swallow Cl BUSH WD23 163 K7
LTNW/LEA LU4 61 K2
RKW/CH/CXG WD3 160 G6
Swallow Ct WGCE AL7 * 105 J6
Swallowdale La HHNE HP2 118 B5
Swallow End WGCE AL7 105 J6
Swallowfields WGCE AL7 105 J6
Swallow Gdns HAT AL10 122 D8
Swallow La STAL AL1 136 G2
Swallow Oaks ABLGY WD5 148 G1
Swallow Pk HHNE HP2 118 C4
Swallows HLWE CM17 111 M8
The Swallows WGCE AL7 105 J2
Swallowtail Wk BERK HP4 115 L4
Swan Cl CSHM HP5 130 G6
RKW/CH/CXG WD3 161 H6
Swan Ct BSF CM23 74 A4
HHNE HP2 4 D2
Swanells Wd DUN/WHIP LU6 78 E9
Swanfield Rd
CHES/WCR EN8 156 D3
Swangley's La KNEB SG3 67 K9
Swanhill WGCE AL7 105 K3
Swanland Rd BRKMPK AL9 138 E6
POTB/CUF EN6 152 E3
Swan La ROY SG8 15 L7
TRDG/WHET N20 166 G9
Swanley Bar La
POTB/CUF EN6 139 L7
Swanley Crs POTB/CUF EN6 139 L8
Swan Md HHS/BOV HP3 134 A4
LTNW/LEA LU4 61 K2
Swan Ms
RAYLNE/WEN HP22 112 C6
Swann Rd
RAYLNE/WEN HP22 112 D3
Swan & Pike Rd PEND EN3 156 F8
Swan Rd CHES/WCR EN8 156 C4
Swans Cl STALE/WH AL4 121 K9
Swanstand LWTH SG6 36 G4
Swanston Gra
LTNW/LEA LU4 * 61 L4
Swanston Pth
OXHEY WD19 162 E9
Swan St BLDK SG7 17 N6
Swasedale Rd LTNN/LIM LU3 46 A9
Sweet Briar BSF CM23 73 L8
WGCE AL7 105 K8
Sweetbriar Cl HHW HP1 117 K5
Sweetmans Av PIN HA5 171 M7
Sweets Wy TRDG/WHET N20 167 H8
Sweyne HLWE CM17 129 M6
Sweyns Md STVGE SG2 51 M7
Swift Cl LWTH SG6 25 J9
ROY SG8 20 C1
WARE SG12 109 H9
Swiftfields WGCE AL7 105 J5
Swifts Green Cl LTNE LU2 63 J1
Swifts Green Rd LTNE LU2 63 J1
Swinburne Av
HTCH/STOT SG5 35 H7
Swinburne Cl ROY SG8 20 C1
Swingate STVG SG1 10 C5
Swing Gate La BERK HP4 132 A1
Swiss Av WATW WD18 162 A3
Swiss Cl WATW WD18 162 A2
Sword Cl BROX EN10 126 C8
Sworder Cl LTNN/LIM LU3 46 A6
Sworders Yd BSF CM23 74 A3
Sycamore Ap
RKW/CH/CXG WD3 161 N4
Sycamore Av HAT AL10 122 D7
Sycamore Cl AMS HP6 145 J7
BUSH WD23 162 G1
CHESW EN7 141 N6
EBAR EN4 167 H5
GSTN WD25 149 J5
HTCHE/RSTV SG4 49 M3
LTNN/LIM LU3 45 M6
Sycamore Dene CSHM HP5 131 J7
Sycamore Dr
LCOL/BKTW AL2 136 C6
TRING HP23 96 A8
Sycamore Fld
HLWW/ROY CM19 128 D7
Sycamore Pl AMS HP6 * 145 H8
Sycamore Ri BERK HP4 116 A8
CSTG HP8 158 G9
Sycamore Rd AMS HP6 145 H7
CSTG HP8 158 G9
DUN/HR/TOD LU5 44 F9
RKW/CH/CXG WD3 161 N4
The Sycamores BLDK SG7 26 A8
BSF CM23 74 C4
HHS/BOV HP3 133 J2
RAD WD7 150 G4
Sydney Chapman Wy
BAR EN5 166 D1
Sydney Rd WATW WD18 162 A4
Sylam Cl LTNN/LIM LU3 45 P8
Sylvan Cl HHS/BOV HP3 118 B9
Sylvandale WGCE AL7 105 M7
Sylvan Wy WGCE AL7 105 M7
Sylvesters HLWW/ROY CM19 128 C5
Sylvia Av PIN HA5 171 P3
Symonds Ct CHES/WCR EN8 142 C7
Symonds Green La STVG SG1 50 D8
Symonds Rd HTCH/STOT SG5 35 J8
Symphony Cl EDGW HA8 173 P4

T

Tabbs Cl LWTH SG6 25 M9
Tacitus Cl STVG SG1 51 M7
Tailors BSF CM23 73 L9
Takeley Cl WAB EN9 157 J3
Talbot Av OXHEY WD19 162 G6
Talbot Ct HHS/BOV HP3 * 5 F6
Talbot Rd HAT AL10 122 D3
KTN/HRWW/WS HA3 172 F6
LTNE LU2 62 G5
RAYLNE/WEN HP22 94 F7
RKW/CH/CXG WD3 161 J7
Talbot St HERT/BAY SG13 107 M6
HTCH/STOT SG5 35 J8
Talbot Wy LWTH SG6 25 M9
Talisman St HTCHE/RSTV SG4 35 P9
Tallack Cl
KTN/HRWW/WS HA3 172 E4
Tallents Crs HARP AL5 102 C1
Tallis Wy BORE WD6 151 J9
Tall Oaks AMS HP6 145 J7
Tall Trees HTCHE/RSTV SG4 49 M3
ROY SG8 20 D4
Talman Gv STAN HA7 173 K3
Tamar Cl STVG SG1 51 K4
Tamar Gn HHNE HP2 118 A3
Tamarisk Cl STALW/RED AL3 120 C4
Tamarix Crs LCOL/BKTW AL2 136 F5
Tameton Cl LTNE LU2 63 M4
Tamworth Rd
HERT/BAY SG13 107 N5
Tancred Rd LTNE LU2 63 H2
Tanfield Cl CHESW EN7 141 P6
Tanfield Gn LTNE LU2 63 M5
Tanglewood WLYN AL6 85 K6
Tanglewood Cl STAN HA7 163 N8
Tankerfield Pl
STALW/RED AL3 8 D4
Tanners Cl STALW/RED AL3 8 C1
Tanners Crs HERT/BAY SG13 107 K8
Tanners Hl ABLGY WD5 148 G1
Tanners Wy WARE SG12 109 P3
Tanners Wood La ABLGY WD5 148 F2
Tannery Cl ROY SG8 20 B4
Tannery Drift ROY SG8 20 B3
The Tannery BUNT SG9 40 D9
Tannery Yd
HTCHE/RSTV SG4 * 65 L8
Tannsfield Dr HHNE HP2 118 A6
Tannsmore Cl HHNE HP2 118 A6
Tansycroft WGCE AL7 105 L5
Tanworth Cl NTHWD HA6 170 E3
Tanworth Gdns PIN HA5 171 K6
Tanyard La HTCHE/RSTV SG4 83 P5
The Tanyard
RAYLNE/WEN HP22 * 112 D7
Tanys Ct HLW CM20 111 J9
Tanys Dell HLW CM20 111 K9
Tany's Dell HLW CM20 111 K9
Tapster St BAR EN5 166 D2
Taransey HHS/BOV HP3 134 C1
Tarnside Cl DUN/WHIP LU6 60 E8
Tarpan Wy BROX EN10 142 E5
Tarrant Dr HARP AL5 102 B5
Tassell Hall STALW/RED AL3 100 G6
Tate Gdns BUSH WD23 163 N6
Tate Rd CFSP/GDCR SL9 168 D2
Tates Wy STVG SG1 50 E5
Tatlers La STVGE SG2 67 N1
Tatsfield Av WAB EN9 143 J2
Tattershall Dr HHNE HP2 118 B2
Tattle Hl HERT/WAT SG14 106 F2
Tattlers Hl
RAYLNE/WEN HP22 76 C2
Tatton St HLWE CM17 129 M2
Tauber Cl BORE WD6 164 F3
Taunton Av LTNE LU2 63 J5
Taunton Wy STAN HA7 173 L6
Taverners HHNE HP2 117 P6
Taverners Wy HOD EN11 126 F5
Tavistock Av STAL AL1 136 B2
Tavistock Cl POTB/CUF EN6 153 N1
STAL AL1 136 C2
Tavistock Crs LTN LU1 62 F9
Tavistock Pl
STHGT/OAK N14 * 167 M5
Tavistock Rd EDGW HA8 173 M5
WATN WD24 149 L9
Tavistock St DUN/WHIP LU6 60 D4
LTN LU1 6 E7
Tawneys Rd HLWS CM18 129 J5
Taylifers HLWW/ROY CM19 128 D8
Taylor Cl STALE/WH AL4 120 F4
Taylors Av HOD EN11 126 F6
Taylors End Rd STSD CM24 75 M1
Taylor's La BAR EN5 153 J9
Taylors La TRING HP23 113 K8
Taylors Rd CSHM HP5 131 J8
Taylor's Rd HTCH/STOT SG5 25 K1
Taylor St LTNE LU2 7 G2
Tayside Dr EDGW HA8 165 H9
Taywood Cl STVGE SG2 67 L4
Teal Cl PEND EN3 156 B7
Teal Dr NTHWD HA6 170 E4
Teal Wy HHS/BOV HP3 134 A4
Teasdale Cl ROY SG8 20 C1
Teasel Cl ROY SG8 20 D5
Tedder Rd HHNE HP2 118 B7
RAYLNE/WEN HP22 112 E6
Tees Cl STVG SG1 51 J4
Teesdale HHNE HP2 117 P5
LTNW/LEA LU4 61 M1
Tee Side HERT/BAY SG13 108 A5
Teignmouth Cl EDGW HA8 173 M6
Telford Av STVGE SG2 11 K2
Telford Cl GSTN WD25 149 L5
Telford Rd LCOL/BKTW AL2 137 H5
Telford Wy LTN LU1 6 C3
Telscombe Wy LTNE LU2 63 K3
Temperance St
STALW/RED AL3 8 D3
Tempest Av POTB/CUF EN6 153 M2
Templar Av BLDK SG7 37 J2
Templars Dr
KTN/HRWW/WS HA3 * 172 D3
Templars La HTCHE/RSTV SG4 49 J9
Temple Av TRDG/WHET N20 167 H6
Temple Bank HLW CM20 111 L7
Temple Cl CHESW EN7 155 P1
HTCHE/RSTV SG4 48 G3
LTNE LU2 * 62 F1
WAT WD17 162 B1
Temple Ct BLDK SG7 * 37 J2
POTB/CUF EN6 152 G1
Temple Flds HERT/WAT SG14 107 K3
Temple Gdns LWTH SG6 * 25 N9
RKW/CH/CXG WD3 161 M9
Temple La WARE SG12 87 M6
Temple Md HHNE HP2 117 N6
HLWW/ROY CM19 127 N3
Temple Mead Cl STAN HA7 173 H3
Templepan La
RKW/CH/CXG WD3 147 P7
Temple Pde BAR EN5 * 167 H6
Temple Vw STALW/RED AL3 120 B6
Templewood WGCW AL8 104 G3
Tempsford WGCE AL7 105 N6
Tempsford Av BORE WD6 165 K3
Temsford Cl
RYLN/HDSTN HA2 172 C6
Tenby Av
KTN/HRWW/WS HA3 173 H6
Tenby Dr LTNW/LEA LU4 62 A3
Tenby Ms LTNW/LEA LU4 61 P3
Tenby Rd EDGW HA8 173 M5
Tendring Rd HLWS CM18 128 F5
The Tene BLDK SG7 26 B9
Tennand Cl CHESW EN7 141 N5
Tennison Av BORE WD6 165 H4
Tenniswood Rd EN EN1 155 M9
Tennyson Av
DUN/HR/TOD LU5 60 G2
HTCHE/RSTV SG4 49 P1
WAB EN9 157 K4
Tennyson Cl ROY SG8 20 C1
Tennyson Rd HARP AL5 101 P1
LCOL/BKTW AL2 135 P5
LTN LU1 62 F9
Tenth Av LTNN/LIM LU3 45 M8
STSD CM24 59 K9
Tenzing Gv LTN LU1 6 B7
Tenzing Rd HHNE HP2 118 B8
Teresa Gdns CHES/WCR EN8 156 B4
Terminus St HLW CM20 2 E4
Terrace Gdns WAT WD17 162 D1
The Terrace TRING HP23 * 95 P9
Terrilands PIN HA5 171 P7
Tethys Rd HHNE HP2 118 A5
Tewin Cl STALE/WH AL4 121 H4
WLYN AL6 85 M8
Tewin Ct WGCE AL7 105 J5
Tewin Hl WLYN AL6 105 P1
Tewin Rd HHNE HP2 118 D8
WGCE AL7 105 J5
Tewkesbury Av PIN HA5 171 N9
Tewkesbury Gdns
CDALE/KGS NW9 173 P7
Thackeray Cl ROY SG8 20 C1
Thames Av HHNE HP2 118 A3
Thames Ct LTNN/LIM LU3 62 C3
Thamesdale LCOL/BKTW AL2 137 L6
Thatcham Gdns
TRDG/WHET N20 166 G6
Thatch Cl LTNW/LEA LU4 61 J2
Thatchers Cft HHNE HP2 117 P4
Thatchers End
HTCHE/RSTV SG4 36 A8
The Thatchers BSF CM23 91 M1
Thaxted Cl LTNE LU2 63 N4
Thaxted Wy WAB EN9 157 J3
Thaynesfield
POTB/CUF EN6 153 N1
The Laurels LCOL/BKTW AL2 135 P7
Thelby Cl LTNN/LIM LU3 46 A9
Thele Av WARE SG12 109 J8
Theleway Cl HOD EN11 126 G2
Thellusson Wy
RKW/CH/CXG WD3 160 D6
Thelusson Ct RAD WD7 * 150 F5
Theobald Crs
KTN/HRWW/WS HA3 172 B5
Theobald's Cl POTB/CUF EN6 140 G9
Theobald's Gv
CHES/WCR EN8 * 156 C2
Theobald's La
CHES/WCR EN8 156 A2
Theobalds Park Rd
ENC/FH EN2 155 J5
Theobald's Rd
POTB/CUF EN6 140 F9
Theobald St BORE WD6 164 F2
RAD WD7 151 H6
Theodora Wy PIN HA5 171 H7
Therfield Rd
STALW/RED AL3 120 C5
Therfield Wk
DUN/HR/TOD LU5 45 H9
Thetford Gdns LTNE LU2 46 E9
Theydon Ct WAB EN9 157 N3
Thieves La HERT/WAT SG14 106 G6
Third Av GSTN WD25 149 L5
HLW CM20 2 E6
LTNN/LIM LU3 45 N8
LWTH SG6 36 F1
STSD CM24 59 J9
Thirlestone Rd
LTNW/LEA LU4 61 N5
Thirlmere STVG SG1 51 M5
Thirlmere Dr STAL AL1 136 G1
Thirlmere Gdns NTHWD HA6 170 D2
Thirsk Rd BORE WD6 151 M8
Thirtieth St STSD CM24 59 N8
Thistle Cl HHW HP1 117 H9
Thistlecroft HHW HP1 4 A4
Thistlecroft Gdns STAN HA7 173 K5
Thistle Dr HAT AL10 122 C3
Thistle Gv WGCE AL7 105 M9
Thistle Rd LTN LU1 7 H5
The Thistles HHW HP1 117 L7
Thistley La HTCHE/RSTV SG4 49 L5
Thomas Rochford Wy
CHES/WCR EN8 142 E6
Thomas Wy ROY SG8 20 C1
Thompsons Cl CHESW EN7 141 N8
HARP AL5 101 P3
Thompsons Meadow
ROY SG8 15 L7
Thompson Wy
RKW/CH/CXG WD3 160 E6
Thomson Rd
KTN/HRWW/WS HA3 172 E7
Thorley Hl BSF CM23 74 A5
Thorley La BSF CM23 91 L1
Thorley Park Rd BSF CM23 74 A6
Thornage Cl LTNE LU2 46 E8
Thorn Av BUSH WD23 163 L7
Thornbera Cl BSF CM23 74 A6
Thornbera Gdns BSF CM23 74 A6
Thornbera Rd BSF CM23 74 A6
Thornbury DUN/HR/TOD LU5 61 J4
HARP AL5 102 C3
Thornbury Cl HOD EN11 126 G1
STVGE SG2 67 K6
Thornbury Ct
DUN/HR/TOD LU5 44 F8
Thornbury Gdns BORE WD6 165 J3
Thorncroft HHS/BOV HP3 134 C1
Thorndene Av
TRDG/WHET N20 167 L7
Thorndyke Ct PIN HA5 171 P4
Thorne Cl HHW HP1 4 A5
Thorne Wy
RAYLNE/WEN HP22 95 H8
Thorneycroft Cl LTNN/LIM LU3 62 A2
Thorneycroft Dr PEND EN3 156 F8
Thornfield Rd BSF CM23 73 P6
Thorn Gv BSF CM23 74 C4
Thornhill Cl AMSS HP7 158 A1
DUN/HR/TOD LU5 44 G8
Thornhill Rd LTNW/LEA LU4 62 A5
NTHWD HA6 170 E1
Thorn Rd DUN/HR/TOD LU5 44 B9
Thornton Crs
RAYLNE/WEN HP22 112 B6
Thorntondale LTNW/LEA LU4 61 M1
Thornton Gv PIN HA5 172 A3
Thornton Rd BAR EN5 166 C2
POTB/CUF EN6 139 M9
Thornton St HERT/WAT SG14 107 L6
STALW/RED AL3 8 D2
Thorn Tree Dr TRING HP23 95 N8
Thorn View Rd
DUN/HR/TOD LU5 * 60 E1
Thorpe Crs OXHEY WD19 162 D6
Thorpefield Cl STALE/WH AL4 121 J5
Thorpe Rd STAL AL1 9 F6
Thrales Cl LTNN/LIM LU3 45 P8
Thrales End La HARP AL5 81 M8
Thrales End Rd HARP AL5 81 M8
Three Cherry Trees La
HHNE HP2 118 C4
Three Close La BERK HP4 115 P8
Three Closes HTCH/STOT SG5 34 B4
Three Corners
HHS/BOV HP3 * 134 B1
Three Forests Wy
HLWW/ROY CM19 127 L3
WAB EN9 157 P6
Three Forest Wy RBSF CM22 75 J5
Three Horseshoes Rd
HLWW/ROY CM19 128 E5
Three Houses La
HTCHE/RSTV SG4 83 P2
Three Meadows Ms
KTN/HRWW/WS HA3 172 F5
Three Stiles STVGE SG2 68 F2
Three Valleys Wy
BUSH WD23 13 K6
Thremhall Av RBSF CM22 74 G2
STSD CM24 75 N1
Thresher Cl BSF CM23 73 M9
LTNW/LEA LU4 61 J1
Thricknells Cl LTNN/LIM LU3 45 P8
Thrift Farm La BORE WD6 165 J1
Thriftfield HHNE HP2 117 N6
Thristers Cl LWTH SG6 * 36 E5
Throcking La BUNT SG9 40 B7
Throcking Rd BUNT SG9 39 L8
Throstle Pl GSTN WD25 * 149 K2
Thrums WATN WD24 149 J7
Thrush Av HAT AL10 122 D8
Thrush Gn
RKW/CH/CXG WD3 160 G6
RYLN/HDSTN HA2 172 A8
Thrush La POTB/CUF EN6 140 F7
Thumbswood WGCE AL7 105 K9
Thumpers HHNE HP2 117 P6
Thundercourt WARE SG12 108 C2
Thundridge Cl WGCE AL7 105 L7
Thurgood Rd HOD EN11 126 F3
Thurlow Cl LTNW/LEA LU4 61 J3
STVG SG1 50 G6
Thurnall Av ROY SG8 20 C5
Thurnall Cl BLDK SG7 26 B9
Thurstans HLWW/ROY CM19 128 E8
Thyme Cl LTNE LU2 46 F8
Tibbett Cl DUN/WHIP LU6 60 F8
Tibbles Cl GSTN WD25 149 M5
Tibbs Hill Rd ABLGY WD5 134 G9
Tiberius Rd LTNN/LIM LU3 46 A9
Tichborne
RKW/CH/CXG WD3 169 H2
Tickenhall Dr HLWE CM17 129 N3
Tiger Moth Wy HAT AL10 122 A5
Tilbury Cl PIN HA5 * 171 P4
Tilbury Md HLWS CM18 129 K4
Tilecroft WGCW AL8 104 G3
Tilegate Rd HLWS CM18 129 J5
Tilehouse Cl BORE WD6 164 F2
Tilehouse La DEN/HRF UB9 169 J9
Tilehouse St HTCH/STOT SG5 35 K9
Tilekiln Cl CHESW EN7 141 N8
Tile Kiln Cl HHS/BOV HP3 118 C9
Tile Kiln Crs HHS/BOV HP3 118 C9
Tile Kiln La HHS/BOV HP3 118 B9
Tilgate LTNE LU2 63 L3
Tillers Link STVGE SG2 67 K4
Tillingham Ct WAB EN9 157 M3
Tillotson Rd
KTN/HRWW/WS HA3 172 B4
Tillwicks Rd HLWS CM18 129 J4
Tilsworth Wk STALE/WH AL4 121 H3
Timbercroft WGCE AL7 105 J3

Timber Orch HERT/WAT SG14 ... 107 H2
Timberridge
  RKW/HRWW/WS WD3 ... 160 G3
Timbers Ct HARP AL5 ... 101 N2
Times Cl HTCH/STOT SG5 ... 35 J6
Timplings Rw HHW HP1 ... 117 L6
Tinworth Cl LTNE LU4 ... 63 L5
Tingeys Cl STALW/RED AL3 ... 101 H7
Tinkers La TRING ... 114 F5
Tinsley Cl LTN LU1 ... 62 C9
Tintagel Cl HHNE HP2 ... 117 N3
  LTNN/LIM LU3 ... 62 C2
Tintagel Dr STAN HA7 ... 173 K2
Tintern Av CDALE/KGS NW9 ... 173 P7
Tintern Cl HARP AL5 ... 81 K9
  STVGE SG2 ... 67 K7
Tinwell Ms BORE WD6 ... 165 K4
Tippendell La
  LCOL/BKTW AL2 ... 135 P4
Tippet Ct STVG SG1 ... 66 C3
Tippetts Cl ENC/FH EN2 ... 155 K9
Tiree Cl HHS/BOV HP3 ... 134 C1
Titan Ct LTNW/LEA LU4 ... 62 A5
Titan Rd HHNE HP2 ... 118 A5
Titchfield Cl ROY SG8 ... 7 P8
Titchmarsh Cl ROY SG8 ... 21 M5
Tithe Barn Cl STAL AL1 ... 136 E2
Tithe Barn Ct ABGLY WD5 ... 134 G8
Tithe Cl HTCH/RSTV SG4 ... 84 C4
Tithe Farm Rd
  DUN/HR/TOD LU5 ... 44 E9
Tithelands HLWW/ROY CM19 ... 128 C6
Titian Av BUSH WD23 ... 163 N6
Titmus Cl STVG SG1 ... 11 F2
Titmus Rd
  RAYLNE/WEN HP22 ... 112 F4
Tiverton Ct HARP AL5 ... 102 D6
Tiverton Rd EDGW HA8 ... 173 M6
  POTB/CUF EN6 ... 153 N1
Toddbrook HLWW/ROY CM19 ... 2 B7
Toddington Rd
  LTNW/LEA LU4 ... 61 N1
Toland Ct LTNW/LEA LU4 ... 61 M5
Tolcarne Dr PIN HA5 ... 171 J6
Tollgate Cl RKW/CH/CXG WD3 ... 160 D3
Tollgate Rd CHES/WCR EN8 ... 145 J3
  STALE/WH AL4 ... 138 B3
Tolpit End HHW HP1 ... 117 K5
Tollsworth Wy STDN SG11 ... 71 H5
Tolmers Rd POTB/CUF EN6 ... 140 F7
Tolmers Gdns POTB/CUF EN6 ... 140 F6
Tolpits Cl WATW WD18 ... 12 C1
Tolpits La WATW WD18 ... 161 P6
Tomkins Cl LTNW/LEA LU4 ... 61 J2
Tomlins Cl ROY SG8 ... 21 L9
Tomlinson Av LTNW/LEA LU4 ... 61 J2
Tompkins Cl
  RAYLNE/WEN HP22 ... 94 C8
Toms Cft HHNE HP2 ... 5 E3
Toms Fld HAT AL10 ... 122 B7
Toms Hill Cl TRING HP23 ... 97 J7
Toms Hill Rd TRING HP23 ... 97 J7
Tom's La KGLGY WD4 ... 134 D7
Tonbridge Crs
  KTN/HRWW/WS HA3 ... 173 L8
Tooke Cl PIN HA5 ... 171 N5
Toorack Rd
  KTN/HRWW/WS HA3 ... 173 L7
Tooveys Mill Cl KGLGY WD4 ... 134 B8
Topland Rd CFSP/GDCR SL9 ... 158 B7
Toplars Hl BGSW SG18 * ... 16 C5
Topstreet Wy HARP AL5 ... 102 B4
Topridge Cl EDGW HA8 ... 173 L4
Torquay Crs STVG SG1 ... 50 E8
Torquay Dr LTNW/LEA LU4 ... 62 B2
Torrington Dr
  POTB/CUF EN6 ... 153 N2
Torrington Rd BERK HP4 ... 115 N7
Tortoiseshell Wy BERK HP4 ... 115 L5
Torver Rd HHW HA1 ... 172 E8
Torwood Ct BERK HP4 ... 115 L7
Torworth Rd BORE WD6 ... 151 M3
Tot La BSF CM23 ... 58 E8
Totteridge Common
  TRDG/WHET N20 ... 165 N8
Totteridge La
  TRDG/WHET N20 ... 166 A6
Totteridge Rd PEND SG5 ... 156 C7
Totteridge Village
  TRDG/WHET N20 ... 165 P7
Totternhoe Cl
  KTN/HRWW/WS HA3 ... 173 J9
Totternhoe Rd
  DUN/WHIP LU6 ... 60 B7
Totton Rd STALW/RED AL3 ... 101 J7
Totts La STVGE SG2 ... 32 B4
Toulmin Dr STALW/RED AL3 ... 120 C3
Tovey Av HOD EN11 ... 126 E5
Tovey Cl LCOL/BKTW AL2 ... 137 J5
Towan Cl LTNE LU4 ... 143 K2
Tower Cl BERK HP4 ... 115 M8
  HTCHE/RSTV SG4 ... 50 B4
Tower Hl KGLGY WD4 ... 133 H8
  MHAD SG10 ... 90 C3
Tower Hill La
  STALE/WH AL4 ... 103 L7
Tower Rd AMSS HP7 ... 158 A4
  HTCHE/RSTV SG4 ... 84 B3
  LTNE LU2 ... 7 J2
  WARE SG12 ... 127 P2
Towers Rd HHNE HP2 ... 117 P7
  PIN HA5 ... 171 N5
  STVG SG1 ... 10 D6
The Towers STVG SG1 ... 10 D6
Tower St HERT/WAT SG14 ... 107 K4
Tower Vw BUSH WD23 ... 163 N6
  HTCHE/RSTV SG4 ... 67 J8
Tower Wy LTNE LU2 ... 63 J3
Town Bridge Ct CSHM HP5 ... 144 G2
Towne Rd ROY SG8 ... 20 C5
Town Farm LBUZ LU7 ... 77 P6
Town Farm Cl ROY SG8 ... 21 K5
Town Farm Crs STDN SG11 ... 71 L4
Townfield CSHM HP5 ... 144 C2
  RKW/CH/CXG WD3 ... 160 G6
Town Field La CSTG HP8 ... 159 J9
Town Flds HAT AL10 ... 122 D5
Town Hall Ar BERK HP4 * ... 115 P7

Town La STVGE SG2 ... 68 E3
Townley LWTH SG6 ... 36 F4
Town Mead Rd WAB EN9 ... 157 H4
Townsend HHNE HP2 ... 117 N6
Townsend Cl STVG SG1 ... 9 G1
Townsend Cl HARP AL5 ... 101 N3
  HTCHE/RSTV SG4 ... 49 M5
  ROY SG8 ... 30 A6
Townsend Dr
  STALW/RED AL3 ... 120 C5
Townsend Farm Rd
  DUN/HR/TOD LU5 ... 60 E3
Townsend La HARP AL5 ... 101 L3
Townsend Rd CSHM HP5 ... 130 G9
  HARP AL5 ... 101 P2
Townsend Wy NTHWD HA6 ... 171 J4
Townshend St
  HERT/BAY SG13 ... 107 M6
Townsley Cl LTN LU1 ... 6 E7
Town Sq STVG SG1 ... 10 D5
Tracyes Rd HLWS CM18 ... 129 L5
Trafalgar Av BROX EN10 ... 126 E9
Trafford Cl RAD WD7 ... 151 J4
  STVG SG1 ... 49 L2
Traherne Cl HTCHE/RSTV SG4 ... 49 L2
Trajan Ga STVGE SG2 ... 67 N8
Trapp's Cl CSHM HP5 ... 145 H3
Trapp's La CSHM HP5 ... 145 H3
Trap Rd ROY SG8 ... 15 M7
Trapstyle Rd WARE SG12 ... 107 P2
Trastrum Rd BRKMPK AL9 ... 138 F1
Travellers La HAT AL10 ... 122 D8
Treacher's Cl CSHM HP5 ... 144 G1
Treacle La BUNT SG9 ... 38 C5
Treacy Cl BUSH WD23 ... 163 L8
Trebellan Dr HHNE HP2 ... 118 A7
Treehanger Cl TRING HP23 ... 96 A8
Treetops Cl NTHWD HA6 ... 170 F9
Trefoil Cl LTNE LU2 ... 61 J2
Trefusis Wk WAT WD17 ... 148 F9
Tregelles Rd HOD EN11 ... 126 F5
Tregenna Cl STHGT/OAK N14 ... 167 N4
Tremaine Gv HHNE HP2 ... 117 P4
Trenchard Av
  RAYLNE/WEN HP22 ... 112 E5
Trenchard Cl STAN HA7 ... 173 H5
Trent Cl RAD WD7 ... 151 K2
  STVG SG1 ... 51 H6
Trent Gdns STHGT/OAK N14 ... 167 M5
Trent Pk EBAR EN4 * ... 167 H4
Trent Rd LTNN/LIM LU3 ... 62 C3
Tresco Rd BERK HP4 ... 115 L6
Trescott Cl LTNE LU2 ... 63 M4
Trevalga Wy HHNE HP2 ... 117 N3
Treveliance Wy GSTN WD25 ... 149 K3
Trevelyan Wy BERK HP4 ... 115 N5
Trevera Ct CHES/WCR EN8 ... 156 D3
  HOD EN11 * ... 126 F4
Trevor Cl EBAR EN4 ... 167 H5
  KTN/HRWW/WS HA3 ... 172 F4
Trevor Rd HTCHE/RSTV SG4 ... 85 M8
Trevose Wy OXHEY WD19 ... 162 E9
Trewenna Dr POTB/CUF EN6 ... 153 N2
Triangle Pas EBAR EN4 * ... 166 C3
Trident Av HAT AL10 * ... 122 B5
Trident Ct LTNW/LEA LU4 ... 44 C9
Trident Rd GSTN WD25 ... 148 C4
Triggs Wy LTNE LU2 ... 63 M3
Trigg Ter STVG SG1 ... 11 F2
Trimley Cl LTNW/LEA LU4 ... 61 L1
Trinder Rd BAR EN5 ... 166 A4
Tring Ford Rd TRING HP23 ... 95 K9
Tring Hl TRING HP23 ... 95 K9
Tring Rd BERK HP4 ... 115 H4
  DUN/WHIP LU6 ... 78 A1
  RAYLNE/WEN HP22 ... 76 D4
  RAYLNE/WEN HP22 ... 112 D6
  TRING HP23 ... 74 A4
Trinity Cl BSF CM23 ... 74 A4
  RKW/CH/CXG WD3 * ... 170 C3
Trinity Ct
  RKW/CH/CXG WD3 * ... 161 J8
Trinity Gv HERT/WAT SG14 ... 107 K5
Trinity Hall Cl WATN WD24 ... 13 H2
Trinity La CHES/WCR EN8 ... 156 D2
Trinity Ms WARE SG12 ... 118 E9
Trinity Pl BAR EN5 * ... 108 B9
Trinity Rd HERT/BAY SG13 ... 108 B9
  HTCH/STOT SG5 ... 25 J2
  LTNN/LIM LU3 ... 62 B2
  STVG SG1 ... 10 B2
  WARE SG12 ... 108 C2
Trinity St BSF CM23 ... 74 A4
Trinity Wk HERT/BAY SG13 ... 108 A8
  STSD CM24 ... 74 A4
Tripton Rd HLWS CM18 ... 3 H7
Tristan Ldg BUSH WD23 * ... 162 G3
Triton Rd
  HTCHE/RSTV SG4 ... 35 M6
Triton Wy HHNE HP2 ... 118 A6
Trojan Ct LTNW/LEA LU4 ... 62 A5
Troon Gdns LTNE LU2 ... 46 F9
Trotters Rd TRING HP23 ... 97 H7
Trotters Bottom BAR EN5 ... 152 D7
Trotters Gap WARE SG12 ... 109 K8
Trotters Rd HLWS CM18 ... 129 K5
Trout Ri RKW/CH/CXG WD3 ... 160 F2
Troutstream Wy
  RKW/CH/CXG WD3 ... 160 F3
Trouvere Av HHW HP1 * ... 117 L5
Trowbridge Gdns LTNE LU2 ... 62 F5
Trowley Bottom
  STALW/RED AL3 ... 100 C4
Trowley Hill Rd
  STALW/RED AL3 ... 100 C4
Trowley Ri ABGLY WD5 ... 148 F1
Trueman Cl EDGW HA8 * ... 173 P4
Truemans Rd
  HTCH/STOT SG5 ... 35 J3
Truesdale Dr
  DEN/HRF UB9 ... 169 N8
Trumper Rd STVG SG1 ... 51 J7
Trumpington Dr STAL AL1 ... 135 G2
Trundlers Wy BUSH WD23 ... 163 N7
Truro Ct STVG SG1 * ... 51 H6
Truro Gdns LTNN/LIM LU3 ... 62 C1
Trustees Wy DEN/HRF UB9 ... 169 K4
Trust Rd CHES/WCR EN8 ... 156 D2
Tubbs Cft WGCE AL7 ... 123 K7
Tucker's Rw BSF CM23 ... 74 A4

Tucker St WATW WD18 ... 13 C6
Tudor Av CHESW EN7 ... 156 A1
  WATN WD24 ... 149 L7
Tudor Cl HARP/FLIT/BLC MK45 ... 32 A7
  CHESW EN7 ... 156 A1
  HAT AL10 ... 122 B9
  PIN HA5 ... 171 J9
  STAL AL1 ... 136 D1
Tudor Ct AMS HP6 ... 145 J8
  BORE WD6 ... 164 E1
  DUN/WHIP LU6 ... 49 J1
Tudor Crs ENC/FH EN2 ... 155 K9
Tudor Dr DUN/HR/TOD LU5 ... 61 H2
  WATN WD24 ... 149 L8
Tudor Manor Gdns
  GSTN WD25 ... 149 L2
Tudor Orch BERK HP4 ... 115 K5
Tudor Pk AMS HP6 ... 145 H7
Tudor Rd BROX EN10 ... 126 D9
  HAT AL10 ... 122 B9
  KTN/HRWW/WS HA3 ... 172 E4
  LTNN/LIM LU3 ... 62 C4
  PIN HA5 ... 171 L6
  STALW/RED AL4 ... 120 C4
Tudor Sq WARE SG12 * ... 108 C3
Tudor Vls CHESW EN7 ... 141 M8
Tudor Wk WARE SG12 ... 108 C3
Tudor Wy HERT/WAT SG14 ... 107 H6
  RKW/CH/CXG WD3 ... 160 E7
  STHGT/OAK N14 ... 167 P7
  WAB EN9 ... 157 J3
Tudor Well Cl STAN HA7 ... 173 H2
Tuffnells Wy HARP AL5 ... 81 K9
Tumber Cl HLWS CM18 ... 129 K4
Tumbling Bay Weir
  WARE SG12 * ... 108 C2
Tunfield Rd HOD EN11 ... 126 C2
Tunmers End CFSP/GDCR SL9 ... 168 A5
Tunnel Wy LBUZ LU7 * ... 96 B2
Tunnel Wood Cl WAT WD17 ... 148 C7
Tunnel Wood Rd WAT WD17 ... 148 C7
Tunmeade HLW CM20 ... 129 K2
Turf La HTCHE/RSTV SG4 ... 50 E3
Turkey St EN EN1 ... 155 P6
Turmer Dr WCCW AL8 ... 104 F7
Turnberry Cl OXHEY WD19 * ... 162 E9
Turnberry Dr LCOL/BKTW AL2 ... 135 M9
Turner Cl DUN/HR/TOD LU5 ... 60 D4
  STVG SG1 ... 50 F5
Turner Rd BUSH WD23 ... 163 L3
  EDGW HA8 ... 173 H5
Turners Cl HARP AL5 ... 82 B9
  HERT/WAT SG14 ... 106 D7
  TRDG/WHET N20 ... 167 K9
Turners Crs BSF CM23 ... 91 M1
Turner's Hl CHES/WCR EN8 ... 142 C9
Turners Hl HHNE HP2 ... 5 G3
Turners Meadow
  RAYLNE/WEN HP22 ... 94 C6
Turners Rd North LTNE LU2 ... 63 H4
Turners Rd South LTNE LU2 ... 63 H4
Turners Wk CSHM HP5 ... 131 H9
Turners Wood Dr CSTG HP8 ... 159 J9
Turneys Orch
  RKW/CH/CXG WD3 ... 160 B4
Turnford Pl BROX EN10 * ... 142 D5
Turnford Vls BROX EN10 * ... 142 E5
Turnors HLW CM20 ... 129 K2
Turnpike Dr DUN/WHIP LU6 ... 60 F6
Turnpike Dr LTNN/LIM LU3 ... 46 B3
Turnpike Gn HHNE HP2 * ... 118 A4
Turnpike La HTCH/STOT SG5 ... 35 J5
Turnpike Rd PEND EN3 ... 156 F7
The Turnstones GSTN WD25 ... 149 M6
Turpin Cl PEND EN3 ... 156 F7
Turpins Cha WLYN AL6 ... 85 L4
Turpin's Cl HERT/WAT SG14 ... 106 C4
Turpin's Ride WLYN AL6 ... 85 H6
Turpin's Ri STVGE SG2 ... 67 H5
Turpin's Wy BLDK SG7 ... 37 J1
Turvey Cl RAYLNE/WEN HP22 ... 94 F7
Tussauds Cl
  RKW/CH/CXG WD3 ... 161 L4
Tuxford Cl BORE WD6 ... 151 K8
Tweed Cl BERK HP4 ... 115 N6
Tweenways CSHM HP5 ... 131 J9
Twelve Acres WGCE AL7 ... 105 H9
Twelve Leys
  RAYLNE/WEN HP22 ... 76 B2
Twentyfirst St STSD CM24 ... 59 N9
Twickenham Gdns
  KTN/HRWW/WS HA3 ... 172 E4
Twin Foxes KNEB SG3 ... 85 K3
Twinwoods HLWS CM18 ... 11 H6
The Twist TRING HP23 ... 114 C1
Twitchell La
  RAYLNE/WEN HP22 ... 94 F7
The Twitchell BLDK SG7 ... 26 B3
Two Acres WGCE AL7 ... 105 J9
Two Beeches HHNE HP2 ... 118 A4
Two Dells La CSHM HP5 ... 130 C5
Two Gates La CSHM HP5 ... 130 C5
Two Oaks Dr WLYN AL6 ... 85 M7
Two Ponds La BERK HP4 ... 115 H5
Two Waters Rd
  HHS/BOV HP3 ... 4 D7
Twyford Bury La BSF CM23 ... 74 B5
Twyford Cl BSF CM23 ... 74 B5
Twyford Dr LTNE LU2 ... 63 L5
Twyford Gdns BSF CM23 ... 74 B5
Twyford Rd BSF CM23 ... 74 B4
  STAL AL1 ... 121 H4
Tye End STVGE SG2 ... 67 K7
Tye Green Rd RBSF CM22 ... 59 K4
Tye Green Village
  HLWS CM18 ... 129 J6
Tyfield Ct CHESW EN7 ... 142 B9
Tylers HARP AL5 ... 102 C3
Tylers Cswy HERT/BAY SG13 ... 140 D1
Tylers Ct STVG SG1 * ... 50 D5
Tylers La BUNT SG9 ... 40 A8
Tylersfield ABGLY WD5 ... 148 G1
Tylers Hl Rd CSHM HP5 ... 131 J9
Tylers Md LTNE LU2 ... 62 F1
Tylers Rd HLWW/ROY CM19 ... 128 A8

Tylers Wd WLYN AL6 ... 85 M7
Tylney Cft
  HLWW/ROY CM19 ... 128 E5
Tynedale LCOL/BKTW AL2 ... 137 L6
Tynemouth Dr EN EN1 ... 117 N6
Tyrells Rd HLWS CM18 ... 129 J6
Tysea Cl HLWS CM18 ... 129 J6
Tysea Rd HLWS CM18 ... 129 J6
Tysoe Av PEND EN3 ... 156 E6
Tythe Rd LTNW/LEA LU4 ... 44 M9
Tyttenhanger Gn
  STALE/WH AL4 ... 137 J2

U

Uckfield Rd PEND EN3 ... 156 C7
Ufford Cl
  KTN/HRWW/WS HA3 ... 172 B4
Ufford Rd
  KTN/HRWW/WS HA3 ... 172 B4
Ullswater Cl STVG SG1 ... 51 M5
Ullswater Rd DUN/WHIP LU6 ... 60 E8
  HHS/BOV HP3 ... 134 C1
Ulverston Cl STAL AL1 ... 9 K4
Ulverston Rd DUN/WHIP LU6 ... 60 D8
Undercares Cl HHNE HP2 ... 118 B7
Underhill BAR EN5 ... 166 E4
Underhill Ct BAR EN5 * ... 166 E4
Underhill La STHGT/OAK N14 ... 167 M8
Underwood Cl
  LTNN/LIM LU3 ... 45 P6
Underwood Rd STVG SG1 ... 50 F5
Union St BAR EN5 ... 166 C3
  DUN/WHIP LU6 ... 60 D6
  EN EN1 ... 156 B5
Union Ter BUNT SG9 ... 40 D9
Unity Rd PEND EN3 ... 156 B7
University Cl BUSH WD23 ... 163 H5
Unwin Cl LWTH SG6 ... 36 B4
Unwin Pl STVGE SG2 ... 67 M3
Unwin Rd STVGE SG2 ... 67 M3
Up Cnr CSTG HP8 ... 159 H8
Updale Cl POTB/CUF EN6 ... 153 H3
Upland Av CSHM HP5 ... 130 G3
Upland Dr BRKMPK AL9 ... 139 L4
Uplands LTNN/LIM LU3 ... 45 N1
  RKW/CH/CXG WD3 ... 161 K5
  STDN SG11 ... 55 L9
  STVGE SG2 ... 51 N7
  WARE SG12 ... 108 E2
  WGCW AL8 ... 104 F2
Uplands Av HTCHE/RSTV SG4 ... 49 N1
Uplands Rd EBAR EN4 ... 167 L1
The Uplands HARP AL5 ... 101 P8
Upper Ashlyns Rd BERK HP4 ... 115 N8
Upper Barn HHS/BOV HP3 ... 134 A2
Upper Belmont Rd
  CSHM HP5 ... 130 G7
Upper Bourne End La
  HHW HP1 * ... 116 C4
Upper Claddens WARE SG12 ... 108 E3
Upper Culver St STAL AL1 ... 120 D6
Upper Dagnall St
  STALW/RED AL3 ... 8 C3
Upperfield Rd WGCE AL7 ... 123 K6
Upper George St CSHM HP5 ... 131 H9
  LTN LU1 ... 6 B4
Upper Gladstone Rd
  CSHM HP5 ... 131 H9
Upper Gn WLYN AL6 ... 105 P1
Upper Green Rd WLYN AL6 ... 105 P1
Upper Hall Pk BERK HP4 ... 115 P8
Upper Heath Rd STAL AL1 ... 120 E6
Upper Hwy KGLGY WD4 ... 148 D2
Upper Hill Rd
  RKW/CH/CXG WD3 ... 160 F5
Upper Hitch OXHEY WD19 ... 162 F7
Upper Hook HLWS CM18 ... 129 J5
Upper Icknield Wy
  RAYLNE/WEN HP22 ... 112 E4
  TRING HP23 ... 96 C4
Upper King St ROY SG8 ... 20 C4
Upper Lattimore Rd STAL AL1 ... 8 E4
Upper Lea Valley Wk LTN LU1 ... 63 K9
Upper Marlborough Rd
  STAL AL1 ... 9 G4
Upper Marsh La HOD EN11 ... 126 E5
Upper Maylins LWTH SG6 ... 36 F4
Upper Meadow HLWS CM18 ... 129 K6
Upper Paddock Rd
  OXHEY WD19 * ... 162 G5
Upper Pk HLW CM20 ... 129 G4
Upper Sales HHW HP1 ... 117 J9
Upper Sean STVGE SG2 ... 67 K3
Upper Shot WGCE AL7 ... 105 K5
Upper Shott CHESW EN7 ... 141 M9
Upper Station Rd RAD WD7 ... 150 F5
Upperstone Cl
  HTCH/STOT SG5 ... 25 K3
Upper Stonyfield
  HLWW/ROY CM19 * ... 2 B5
Upper Tail OXHEY WD19 ... 162 G9
Upper Tilehouse St
  HTCH/STOT SG5 ... 49 J1
Uppingham Av STAN HA7 ... 173 H4
Upshire Rd WAB EN9 ... 157 L2
Upton Av STALW/RED AL3 ... 8 E2
Upton Cl LCOL/BKTW AL2 ... 46 C9
  LTNE LU2 ... 46 E9
Upton Lodge Cl BUSH WD23 ... 163 L2
Upway CFSP/GDCR SL9 ... 158 D5
Upwell Rd LTNE LU2 ... 46 E8
Uranus Rd HHNE HP2 ... 117 P6
Urban Rd BSF CM23 ... 74 C3
Uxbridge Rd
  KTN/HRWW/WS HA3 ... 160 D8
Uxbridge Road
  (Harrow Weald)
  KTN/HRWW/WS HA3 ... 172 G4
Uxbridge Road
  (Pinner End) PIN HA5 ... 171 N5
Uxbridge Road
  (Pinner) PIN HA5 ... 171 M6

Uxbridge Road
  (Stanmore) STAN HA7 ... 172 F3

V

Vache La CSTG HP8 ... 159 J8
Vache Ms CSTG HP8 ... 159 K6
Vadis Cl LTNN/LIM LU5 ... 45 P8
Valance Rd SAFWS CB11 ... 43 K1
Vale Av BORE WD6 ... 165 H4
Vale Cl CFSP/GDCR SL9 ... 168 B5
  HARP AL5 ... 81 L9
Vale Ct STALE/WH AL4 ... 103 J5
Vale Cft PIN HA5 ... 171 N9
Vale Dr BAR EN5 ... 166 D5
Valence Dr CHESW EN7 ... 141 N1
Valence End DUN/WHIP LU6 ... 60 C8
Valencia Rd STAN HA7 ... 173 J1
Valency Cl NTHWD HA6 ... 170 G4
Valentine Wy CSTG HP8 ... 159 K9
Valerian Wy STVG SG1 ... 51 N7
Valerie Cl STAL AL1 ... 120 C8
Vale Ri CSHM HP5 ... 131 H7
Vale Rd BUSH WD23 ... 130 C3
  CSHM HP5 ... 130 C3
Valeside HERT/WAT SG14 ... 106 C6
The Vale CFSP/GDCR SL9 ... 168 B5
  HARP AL5 ... 102 B5
Vallans Cl WARE SG12 ... 108 C1
Vallansgate STVGE SG2 ... 67 L5
Valley Cl BERK HP4 ... 78 B6
  DUN/WHIP LU6 ... 107 L7
  HTCH/RSTV SG13 ... 19 K1
  WAB EN9 ... 157 H2
  WARE SG12 ... 108 A2
Valley Dr CDALE/KGS NW9 ... 118 C2
The Valley Gn WGCW AL8 ... 104 F5
Valley La STALW/RED AL3 ... 99 P3
Valley Pk WATW WD17 ... 161 N6
Valley Ri GSTN WD25 ... 149 H8
  STVG SG1 ... 20 D4
  STALE/WH AL4 ... 102 E2
Valley Rd BERK HP4 ... 115 L5
  LTNE LU2 ... 78 E9
  HTCHE/RSTV SG4 ... 86 C1
  RKW/CH/CXG WD3 ... 160 E4
  STALW/RED AL3 ... 120 D4
  WGCW AL8 ... 104 E6
Valley Rd South
  HTCHE/RSTV SG4 ... 84 C5
Valleyside HHW HP1 ... 117 J8
The Valley HTCHE/RSTV SG4 ... 65 K7
Valley Vw BAR EN5 ... 166 C5
  CHESW EN7 ... 141 K7
Valley Wk RKW/CH/CXG WD3 ... 161 N4
Valley Wy STVGE SG2 ... 67 J4
Vanbrugh Dr
  DUN/HR/TOD LU5 ... 60 C1
Vancouver Man CSHM HP5 * ... 131 H9
Vancouver Rd BROX EN10 ... 142 C4
  EDGW HA8 ... 173 P5
Vanda Crs STAL AL1 ... 9 K5
Vantorts Cl SBW CM21 ... 111 P2
Vantorts Rd SBW CM21 ... 111 P2
Vardon Rd STVG SG1 ... 51 J7
Varna Cl LTNN/LIM LU3 ... 62 B3
Varney Cl CHESW EN7 ... 141 P6
  HHW HP1 ... 116 F3
Varney Rd HHW HP1 ... 117 J8
Vaughan Md STALW/RED AL3 ... 101 H8
Vaughan Rd HARP AL5 ... 102 A3
  HTCH/STOT SG5 ... 25 J3
Vauxhall Rd HHNE HP2 ... 118 B8
  LTNE LU2 ... 63 J9
Vega Crs NTHWD HA6 ... 163 L6
Vega Rd BUSH WD23 ... 2 E3
Velizy Av HLW CM20 ... 129 G4
Venables Ter STVGE SG1 * ... 50 F8
Venetia Rd LTNE LU2 ... 63 H2
Venice Av WATW WD18 ... 173 H5
Ventnor Dr TRDG/WHET N20 ... 173 P5
Ventnor Gdns LTNN/LIM LU3 ... 46 A8
Ventura Pk LCOL/BKTW AL2 ... 136 E8
Venus Hl HHS/BOV HP3 ... 146 D1
Vera Ct OXHEY WD19 ... 162 F6
Ver-colne Valley Wk
  HHS/BOV HP3 ... 132 A2
Ver-colne Valley Wk
  STALW/RED AL3 ... 8 A3
Ver-Colne Valley Wk
  STALW/RED AL3 ... 101 J8
  STALW/RED AL3 ... 119 M2
  WAT WD17 ... 13 J5
  WATN WD24 ... 149 M8
Verdure Cl GSTN WD25 ... 149 M9
Vere Rd HTCH/STOT SG5 ... 60 F4
Verity's HAT AL10 ... 122 D4
Verity Wy STVG SG1 ... 51 K6
Verney Cl BERK HP4 ... 115 L6
  TRING HP23 ... 96 D6
Vernon Av PEND EN3 ... 156 D6
Vernon Crs EBAR EN4 ... 167 L4
Vernon Dr DEN/HRF UB9 ... 169 N5
  STAN HA7 ... 172 C5
Vernon Pl DUN/HR/TOD LU5 ... 60 C1
Vernon Rd BUSH WD23 ... 163 J1
  LTN LU1 ... 6 C4
Vernon's Cl STAL AL1 ... 9 G5
Ver Rd STALW/RED AL3 ... 101 K6
  STALW/RED AL3 ... 8 A2
Verulam Cl WGCE AL7 ... 123 K6
Verulam Gdns LTNN/LIM LU3 ... 46 A9
Verulam Rd HTCH/STOT SG5 ... 35 L8
  STALW/RED AL3 ... 8 B3
Verwood Dr EBAR EN4 ... 167 K2
Verwood Rd
  RYLN/HDSTN HA2 ... 172 C6
Vespers Cl LTNW/LEA LU4 ... 61 K4
Vesta Av STAL AL1 ... 136 B2
Vestry Cl LTN LU1 ... 4 A5
Veysey Cl HHW HP1 ... 116 E3
Viaduct Rd WARE SG12 ... 108 C4

Viaduct Wy WGCE AL7 — 105 J3
Vian Av PEND EN3 — 156 D5
Vicarage Cswy
  HERT/BAY SG13 — 108 A8
Vicarage Ct ARL/CHE SG15 — 24 E1
  HHW HP1 * — 128 C5
  POTB/CUF EN6 — 140 A9
  RAYLNE/WEN HP22 — 112 B6
  STAL AL1 — 136 B2
  STDN SG11 — 71 K4
Vicarage Gdns BERK HP4 — 116 E4
  STALW/RED AL3 — 100 C3
  TRING HP23 — 95 P2
Vicarage La BSF CM23 — 43 L8
  HERT/WAT SG14 — 107 L4
  HHS/BOV HP3 — 132 E5
  KGLGY WD4 — 134 A8
Vicarage Rd BERK HP4 — 116 D4
  BUNT SG9 — 40 D8
  DUN/HR/TOD LU5 — 60 E1
  TRING HP23 — 95 N2
  WARE SG12 — 114 C2
  WATW WD18 — 12 D7
Vicarage St DUN/WHIP LU6 — 60 D5
Viceroy Cl LTN LU1 — 7 C5
Vicerons Br BSF CM23 — 91 N1
Victoria Cl EBAR EN4 — 167 H5
  RKW/CH/CXG WD3 — 161 H6
  STVG SG1 — 10 C1
Victoria Crs ROY SG8 — 20 C3
Victoria Ga HLWE CM17 — 129 L3
Victoria La BAR EN5 — 166 D3
Victoria Rd BERK HP4 — 115 P8
  BUSH WD23 — 163 K7
  CSHM HP5 — 145 H1
  EBAR EN4 — 167 H3
  HARP AL5 — 118 B2
  HTCH/STOT SG5 — 35 J8
  WAB EN9 — 157 H4
  WATW WD18 — 149 J8
Victoria St DUN/WHIP LU6 — 60 D5
  LTN LU1 — 5 G4
Victor Rd RYLN/HDSTN HA2 — 172 C7
Victor Smith Ct
  LCOL/BKTW AL2 * — 149 P1
Victors Wy BAR EN5 — 166 D2
Victory Rd BERK HP4 — 115 M6
  RAYLNE/WEN HP22 — 112 C6
View Cl HRW HA1 — 172 D8
View Rd POTB/CUF EN6 — 153 M2
Vigors Cft HAT AL10 — 122 J3
Village Cl HOD EN11 — 127 J3
Village St HTCHE/RSTV SG4 — 66 C5
Village Wy HHS HP7 — 159 K1
  BLDK SG7 — 18 B7
Villa Rd LTNW/LIM LU4 — 6 C2
Villiers Av ENC/FH EN2 — 156 L8
Villiers Crs STALE/WH AL4 — 121 J5
Villiers Rd OXHEY WD19 — 162 C5
Villiers St HERT/BAY SG13 — 107 M6
Villiers-sur-Marne Av
  BSF CM23 — 91 N1
Vincent Cl LWTH SG6 — 36 F4
Vincent Ct BAR EN5 — 166 E2
  CHES/WCR EN8 — 142 D7
Vincent Rd LTNW/LEA LU4 — 172 C7
Vincenzo Cl BRKMPK AL9 — 138 F2
Vine Cl WCCW AL8 — 105 H4
Vine Gv HLW CM20 — 110 C2
The Vineries STHGT/OAK N14 — 167 N5
Vinetrees RAYLNE/WEN HP22 — 112 C7
Vineyards Rd POTB/CUF EN6 — 140 C8
The Vineyard WARE SG12 — 108 E2
  WCCW AL8 — 105 H4
Vinters Av STVG SG1 — 11 G5
Violet Av ENC/FH EN2 — 155 L8
Violets La BUNT SG9 — 53 J4
Violet Wy RKW/CH/CXG WD3 — 160 C3
Virgil Dr BROX EN10 — 142 E2
Virginia Cl LTNW/LIM LU3 — 62 C5
Viscount Cl LTNW/LIM LU3 — 62 C5
Vivian Cl OXHEY WD19 — 162 C8
Vivian Gdns OXHEY WD19 — 162 C7
Vixen Cl HAT AL10 — 122 E4
Vixen Dr HERT/BAY SG13 — 107 P6
Vyse Rd BAR EN5 — 166 A3

W

Wacketts CHESW EN7 — 141 P6
Waddesdon Cl LTNE LU2 — 63 L4
Waddington Rd
  STALW/RED AL3 — 8 E5
Waddling La STALE/WH AL4 — 103 J3
Wadesmill Rd
  HERT/WAT SG14 — 107 L3
  WARE SG12 — 87 M8
The Wades HAT AL10 — 122 D9
The Wade WGCE AL7 — 105 J8
Wadham Rd ABLGY WD5 — 168 D7
Wadhurst Av LTNW/LIM LU3 — 62 D2
Wadley Cl HHNE HP2 * — 5 K3
Wadnall Wy KNEB SG3 — 85 J1
Waggoners Yd WARE SG12 — 108 C2
Waggon Rd BAR EN5 — 153 K5
Waghorn Rd
  KTN/HRWW/WS HA3 — 173 J7
Wagon Md RBSF CM22 — 93 H6
Wagon Wy
  RKW/CH/CXG WD3 — 160 C2
Wagtail Cl HAT AL10 — 156 A9
Waight Cl HAT AL10 — 122 B4
Wain Cl POTB/CUF EN6 — 153 N3
Wainwright St BSF CM23 — 73 M9
Wakefields Wk
  CHES/WCR EN8 — 156 D1
Wakehams Hi PIN HA5 — 171 P7
Walcot Av LTN LU2 — 63 H4
Waldeck Rd LTN LU1 — 6 B2
Waldegrave Pk HARP AL5 — 52 E7
Walden End STVG SG1 — 10 E6
Walden Pl WGCW AL8 — 104 C4
Walden Rd WGCW AL8 — 104 C4
Waleran Cl STAN HA7 — 172 F3
Waleys Cl LTNN/LIM LU3 — 45 P7

Walfield Av TRDG/WHET N20 — 166 F6
Walgrave Rd
  DUN/HR/TOD LU5 — 61 J4
Walkden's BLDK SG7 — 17 P6
Walken Rd STVG SG1 — 50 C7
  STVGE SG2 — 68 B2
Walkers Cl HARP AL5 — 102 B5
Walkers Ct HARP AL5 — 102 B5
Walkers Rd HARP AL5 — 102 A5
Walkley Rd DUN/HR/TOD LU5 — 60 E2
The Walk POTB/CUF EN6 — 153 K2
Wallace Wy HTCHE/RSTV SG4 — 35 M5
The Walled Gdn WLYN AL6 * — 105 K2
Waller Av LTNW/LEA LU4 — 62 A3
Waller Dr NTHWD HA6 — 171 J5
Waller's Cl ROY SG8 — 22 C8
Wallers Wy HOD EN11 — 126 C2
Wallingford Wk STAL AL1 — 136 C2
Wallington Rd BLDK SG7 — 26 C9
  CSHM HP5 — 130 C9
Walmar Cl EBAR EN4 — 153 N9
Walnut Acre
  DUN/HR/TOD LU5 * — 44 C1
Walnut Av BLDK SG7 — 37 K1
Walnut Cl HTCH/STOT SG5 — 25 K3
  LCOL/BKTW AL2 — 49 M1
  LTNE LU2 — 63 J3
  MHAD SG10 — 90 C3
  ROY SG8 — 20 C4
Walnut Gr WGCE AL7 — 105 H9
Walnut Dr BSF CM23 — 91 N2
  RAYLNE/WEN HP22 — 112 C5
Walnut Gn BUSH WD23 — 163 H1
Walnut La HHNE HP2 — 5 F2
  WGCE AL7 — 105 H9
Walnut Tree Av SBW CM21 — 91 P9
Walnut Tree Cl
  CHES/WCR EN8 — 156 C1
  HOD EN11 — 126 A2
  STVGE SG2 — 67 N2
Walnut Tree Crs SBW CM21 * — 111 J7
Walnut Tree Rd
  HTCH/STOT SG5 — 34 C5
Walnut Tree Wk WARE SG12 — 108 C6
Walnut Wy HERT/WAT SG14 — 107 M6
Walnut Wy AMS HP6 — 144 B5
  HTCH/STOT SG5 — 35 K4
Walpole Cl PIN HA5 — 172 A3
Walsham Cl STVGE SG2 — 67 M7
Walsh Cl HTCH/STOT SG5 — 35 J9
Walshford Wy BORE WD6 — 151 M8
Walsingham Cl HAT AL10 — 122 C5
  LTNE LU2 — 46 E8
Walsingham Wy
  LCOL/BKTW AL2 — 137 H6
Walsworth Rd
  HTCHE/RSTV SG4 — 35 M9
Walters Cl CHESW EN7 — 141 J4
Waltham Dr EDGW HA8 — 173 H6
Waltham Gdns PEND EN3 — 156 B6
Waltham Ga CHES/WCR EN8 — 142 D5
Waltham Rd
  HTCHE/RSTV SG4 — 49 L1
  WAB EN9 — 143 K5
Walton Cl HRW HA1 — 172 D1
Walton Dr HRW HA1 — 172 C1
Walton Gdns WAB EN9 — 156 C3
Walton Pl RAYLNE/WEN HP22 — 94 A9
Walton Rd BUSH WD23 — 13 K4
  HOD EN11 — 126 C3
  HRW HA1 — 172 C2
  STVGE SG2 — 108 C4
Walton St ENC/FH EN2 — 155 L9
  STAL AL1 — 11 J1
Walverns Cl OXHEY WD19 — 162 E5
Wander Whf KGLGY WD4 — 134 C8
Wandon Cl LTNE LU2 — 63 K2
Wannions Cl CSHM HP5 — 131 M9
Wansbeck Cl STVG SG1 — 51 K4
Wansford Pk BORE WD6 — 165 K3
Warburton Cl
  KTN/HRWW/WS HA3 — 172 F6
Warden Cl CHESW EN7 — 141 P6
  WARE SG12 — 108 B2
Warden Hill Cl LTNE LU2 — 46 D7
Warden Hill Gdns LTNE LU2 — 46 D7
Warden Hill Rd LTNE LU2 — 46 D7
Ward Hatch HLW CM20 — 111 L9
Wardown Crs LTNE LU2 — 62 F4
Ward Pl AMSS HP7 — 158 B1
Wards La BORE WD6 — 163 P1
Wareham's La
  HERT/WAT SG14 — 107 K7
Warenford Wy BORE WD6 — 151 M9
Ware Park Rd
  HERT/WAT SG14 — 107 L4
Ware Rd HERT/BAY SG13 — 107 M6
  HERT/WAT SG14 — 86 F3
  HOD EN11 — 126 F4
  WARE SG12 — 89 P9
Wareside HHNE HP2 — 118 B2
Wareside Cl WGCE AL7 — 105 L7
Warham Rd
  KTN/HRWW/WS HA3 — 172 F6
Warlow Cl PEND EN3 — 156 F7
Warmark Rd HHW HP1 — 117 H6
Warminster Cl LTNE LU2 — 63 N5
Warneford Av
  RAYLNE/WEN HP22 — 112 C6
Warneford Pl OXHEY WD19 — 162 G5
Warneford Rd
  KTN/HRWW/WS HA3 — 173 K7
Warner Cl EBAR EN4 — 153 P8
Warner Rd WARE SG12 — 108 C4
Warners Av HOD EN11 — 126 F7
Warners Cl STVGE SG2 — 67 L3
Warners End Rd HHW HP1 — 117 K8
Warners La HAT AL10 — 122 E3
Warren Cl WGCW AL8 — 104 C3
Warrender Rd CSHM HP5 — 131 K8
The Warren Dr LTN LU1 — 81 J4
Warrenfield Cl CHESW EN7 — 155 P1
Warren Flds STAN HA7 — 173 J1
Warrengate La
  POTB/CUF EN6 — 152 A3
Warrengate Rd BRKMPK AL9 — 138 F7
Warren Gn HAT AL10 — 122 E3

Warren Gv BORE WD6 — 165 K3
Warren La BLDK SG7 — 37 N1
  BUNT SG9 — 53 J2
  STAN HA7 — 164 A8
Warren Park Rd
  HERT/WAT SG14 — 107 K5
Warren Pl HERT/WAT SG14 * — 107 L6
Warren Rd BUSH WD23 — 163 L7
  LTN LU1 — 62 A6
  STAL AL1 — 136 B3
Warrensgreen La
  HTCHE/RSTV SG4 — 51 N2
Warren Shawe La
  EDGW HA8 — 165 H8
Warren Ter HERT/WAT SG14 — 107 L4
The Warren CFSP/GDCR SL9 — 168 D4
  CSHM HP5 — 130 D7
  HARP AL5 — 101 P7
  KGLGY WD4 — 134 C8
  RAD WD7 — 150 A9
  ROY SG8 — 20 C5
Warren Wy WLYN AL6 — 105 H1
Warrington Rd HRW HA1 — 172 E9
Warwick Av EDGW HA8 — 165 H9
  POTB/CUF EN6 — 140 E6
Warwick Cl BUSH WD23 — 163 N6
  EBAR EN4 — 167 H4
  HARP AL5 — 107 K8
  POTB/CUF EN6 — 140 E6
  RAYLNE/WEN HP22 — 112 C4
Warwick Ct LTNW/LEA LU4 — 62 C6
Warwick Dr CHES/WCR EN8 — 142 C7
Warwick Ms
  RKW/CH/CXG WD3 — 161 L5
Warwick Pde
  KTN/HRWW/WS HA3 * — 173 H6
Warwick Pl BORE WD6 — 165 K2
Warwick Rd BORE WD6 — 165 K2
  BSF CM23 — 74 C4
  LBUZ LU7 — 96 C1
  PEND EN3 — 156 E1
  STAL AL1 — 120 E6
  STVGE SG2 — 51 M9
Warwick Rd East
  LTNW/LEA LU4 — 62 C6
Warwick Rd West
  LTNW/LEA LU4 — 62 C5
Warwick Wy
  RKW/CH/CXG WD3 — 161 N3
Washbrook Cl
  AMP/FLIT/BLC MK45 — 32 D7
Washington Av HHNE HP2 — 117 P3
Wash La POTB/CUF EN6 — 152 E3
The Wash BUNT SG9 — 56 B8
  HERT/WAT SG14 — 107 L6
Watchlytes WGCE AL7 — 105 M6
Watchmead WGCE AL7 — 105 K6
Waterbeach WGCE AL7 — 105 N6
Watercress Cl STVGE SG2 — 67 P3
Watercress Wy HERT/WAT SG14 — 107 L5
Waterdale HERT/BAY SG13 — 107 K8
Waterdell La
  HTCHE/RSTV SG4 — 49 L5
Water End Cl BORE WD6 — 164 F1
Water End La LTNW/LEA LU4 — 61 N4
Waterend La STALW/RED AL3 — 103 P4
  STALW/RED AL3 — 101 J7
Water End Rd BERK HP4 — 116 E5
Waterfall Cl HOD EN11 — 126 E4
Waterfall Rd STHGT/OAK N14 — 167 M1
Waterfield
  RKW/CH/CXG WD3 — 160 A6
  WGCE AL7 — 105 K3
Waterfields Wy BUSH WD23 — 13 K4
Waterford Common
  HERT/WAT SG14 — 107 J2
Waterford Gn WGCE AL7 — 105 L6
The Waterfront BORE WD6 * — 164 B5
The Watergate WGCE AL7 — 162 F8
Waterhouse Moor
  HLWS CM18 — 3 H7
Waterhouse St HHNE HP2 — 4 D2
Water La BERK HP4 — 115 P7
  BSF CM23 — 74 E5
  HHS/BOV HP3 — 132 E8
  HLWW/ROY CM19 — 128 B7
  HTCH/STOT SG5 — 35 L7
  KGLGY WD4 — 134 C8
  STSD CM24 — 58 F5
  WAT WD17 — 13 F3
Waterloo La HTCH/STOT SG5 — 34 F2
Waterlow Rd DUN/WHIP LU6 — 60 D5
Waterman Cl OXHEY WD19 — 162 D5
Watermark Ms
  HERT/BAY SG13 — 107 N6
Water Meadow CSHM HP5 — 144 G2
Watermeadow
  LCOL/BKTW AL2 — 136 C7
Water Meadow Wy
  RAYLNE/WEN HP22 — 112 C5
Watermead Rd
  LTNN/LIM LU3 — 46 A9
Watermill La HERT/WAT SG14 — 107 L3
Waters End HTCH/STOT SG5 — 25 J3
Watersfield Wy EDGW HA8 — 173 H9
Waterside CSHM HP5 — 145 H2
  HARP AL5 — 102 B1
  KGLGY WD4 — 134 B8
  LCOL/BKTW AL2 — 137 K6
  RAD WD7 — 150 C4
  STSD CM24 — 58 F5
  WGCE AL7 — 105 H7
Waterside Ct KGLGY WD4 — 134 C8
Waterside Ms DEN/HRF UB9 — 169 L3
Watersmeet
  HLWW/ROY CM19 — 128 E2
Watersplash Ct
  LCOL/BKTW AL2 * — 137 L6
Waterwick Hl SAFWS CB11 — 31 M8
Watery La BSF CM23 — 57 M6
  STALW/RED AL3 — 100 F1

Watery Stones SAFWS CB11 * — 43 L4
Watford Field Rd
  WATW WD18 — 13 H6
Watford Heath OXHEY WD19 — 162 F6
Watford Heath Farm
  OXHEY WD19 * — 162 F6
Watford Int WATN WD24 — 149 K9
Watford Rd BORE WD6 — 164 C5
  KGLGY WD4 — 148 C3
  LCOL/BKTW AL2 — 148 C5
  NTHWD HA6 — 171 H4
  RAD WD7 — 150 D6
  STAL AL1 — 135 N3
Watkin Ms PEND EN3 — 156 F7
Watkins Ri POTB/CUF EN6 — 153 L2
Watling Cl HHW HP1 — 117 P5
Watling Farm Cl BORE WD6 — 164 C1
Watling Gdns DUN/WHIP LU6 — 60 C8
Watling Knoll RAD WD7 — 150 C3
Watling Pl DUN/HR/TOD LU5 — 60 E2
Watling St BORE WD6 — 163 M6
  DUN/HR/TOD LU5 — 60 E2
  LCOL/BKTW AL2 — 136 C4
  RAD WD7 — 150 B2
  STAL AL1 — 136 B2
Watlington Rd HLWE CM17 — 111 N8
Watling Vw STAL AL1 — 136 B2
Watson Cl STALW/RED AL3 — 120 C5
Watson Rd STVG SG1 — 10 A3
Watson's Wk STAL AL1 — 11 J3
Watton Rd HERT/WAT SG14 — 86 D5
  KNEB SG3 — 67 K9
Watts Cl STVG SG11 — 72 E4
Waulds Bank Dr
  LTNN/LIM LU3 — 45 N7
Wavell Cl CHES/WCR EN8 — 142 D6
Waveney HHNE HP2 — 118 A3
Waveney Rd HARP AL5 — 102 B1
Waverley Cl STVGE SG2 — 67 N6
Waverley Gdns NTHWD HA6 — 171 J5
Waverley Rd STALW/RED AL3 — 120 B6
Waxwell La PIN HA5 — 171 M1
Wayfarers Pk BERK HP4 — 115 L2
Wayletts Dr BSF CM23 — 74 C5
Wayre St HLWE CM17 — 111 M8
Waysbrook LWTH SG6 — 36 E4
Wayside DUN/WHIP LU6 — 60 C9
  KGLGY WD4 — 133 L9
  POTB/CUF EN6 — 139 N8
  RAD WD7 — 151 J3
Wayside Av BUSH WD23 — 163 M5
Wayside Cl STHGT/OAK N14 — 167 N5
The Wayside HHS/BOV HP3 — 118 D9
Waytemore Rd BSF CM23 — 73 P8
Weald La
  KTN/HRWW/WS HA3 — 172 D6
Weald Ri
  KTN/HRWW/WS HA3 — 172 F4
Wealdwood Gdns PIN HA5 — 172 B3
Weall Gn GSTN WD25 — 149 J2
Weardale Gdns ENC/FH EN2 — 155 L9
Weatherby DUN/WHIP LU6 — 60 B6
Weatherby LTNW/LEA LU4 — 61 N4
Weavers Orch ARL/CHE SG15 — 24 E5
Weavers Rd TRING HP23 — 95 M8
Weaver St BSF CM23 — 91 M1
Weavers Wy BLDK SG7 — 26 C9
Webb Cl CSHM HP5 — 130 D9
  LWTH SG6 —
Webber Cl BORE WD6 — 164 D5
Webb Ri STVG SG1 — 11 J5
Webster Cl WAB EN9 — 157 M3
Wedgewood Cl
  HTCHE/RSTV SG4 — 35 P9
  NTHWD HA6 — 170 E4
Wedgewood Ct STVG SG1 — 51 M4
Wedgewood Dr HLW CM20 — 51 M4
Wedgewood Ga STVG SG1 — 51 M4
Wedgewood Rd
  HTCHE/RSTV SG4 — 35 N9
  LTNW/LEA LU4 — 61 J2
Wedgwood Ct STVG SG1 — 51 L5
Wedgwood Ga STVG SG1 — 51 L5
Wedgwood Wy STVG SG1 — 51 L5
Wedhey HLW CM20 — 120 D8
Wedmore Rd
  HTCHE/RSTV SG4 — 49 M1
Wedon Wy BLDK SG7 — 26 A5
Weedon Hi AMS HP6 — 144 F6
Weedon La AMS HP6 — 144 F6
Weighton Rd
  KTN/HRWW/WS HA3 — 172 D5
Weirdale Rd TRDG/WHET N20 — 166 F7
Welbeck Cl BORE WD6 — 164 C2
Welbeck Ri HARP AL5 — 102 C6
Welbeck Rd EBAR EN4 — 167 H5
Welburn Av LTNN/LIM LU3 — 46 D8
Welch Pl PIN HA5 — 171 L5
Welclose St STALW/RED AL3 — 8 C5
Weldon Cl LTNE LU2 — 63 M5
Welham Ct BRKMPK AL9 — 138 F3
  BRKMPK AL9 — 138 F3
Welkin Gn HHNE HP2 — 118 D7
Wellands HAT AL10 — 122 D4
Well Ap BAR EN5 — 165 P5
Wellbrook Ms TRING HP23 — 96 A8
Welbury Ter HHNE HP2 — 118 C6
Well Cft HHW HP1 — 117 M5
Wellcroft Cl WGCE AL7 — 105 K8
Wellcroft Rd WGCE AL7 — 105 K8
Well End Rd BORE WD6 — 151 P7
Weller Rd AMS HP6 — 145 K7
Weller St HHS/BOV HP3 — 132 C8
Wellers Gv CHESW EN7 — 141 P4
Wellesley HLWW/ROY CM19 — 128 D8
Wellesley Av NTHWD HA6 — 170 E6
Wellesley Crs POTB/CUF EN6 — 153 H5
Wellesley Rd HLW CM20 — 110 D4
Wellfield Av LTNN/LIM LU3 — 45 N7
Wellfield Cl HAT AL10 — 122 D5
Wellfield Rd HAT AL10 — 122 D5

Wellgate Rd LTNW/LEA LU4 — 61 N4
Well Gn HERT/WAT SG14 — 86 D9
Well Gv TRDG/WHET N20 — 166 C2
Wellhouse Cl LTN LU1 — 62 E7
Wellhouse La BAR EN5 — 166 A3
Wellingham Av
  HTCH/STOT SG5 — 35 J7
Wellington Av PIN HA5 — 171 P5
Wellington Cl OXHEY WD19 — 162 C9
Wellington Dr WGCE AL7 — 105 M6
Wellington Hl LOU IG10 — 157 N8
Wellington Pl BROX EN10 * — 142 B2
Wellington Rd
  KTN/HRWW/WS HA3 — 172 E7
  LCOL/BKTW AL2 — 137 J5
  PIN HA5 — 171 P5
  STVGE SG2 — 67 M1
  WAT WD17 — 13 F1
Wellington St
  HERT/WAT SG14 — 107 J5
  LTN LU1 — 6 D5
Wellington Ter
  DUN/HR/TOD LU5 — 60 F6
Well La HLW CM20 — 128 D3
Wellonhead Br
  RAYLNE/WEN HP22 — 94 C9
Well Rd BAR EN5 — 166 A4
  POTB/CUF EN6 — 139 P8
Well-Row RAYLNE/WEN SG13 — 124 C5
Wells Cl CHESW EN7 — 141 K4
  HARP AL5 — 81 H9
  STALW/RED AL3 — 8 C1
Wellsfield BUSH WD23 — 162 G4
The Wells STHGT/OAK N14 — 167 P7
Wellstones WAT WD17 — 13 F3
Wellswood Cl HHNE HP2 — 118 C7
Wells Yd WARE SG12 * — 108 C3
Welsummer Wy
  CHES/WCR EN8 — 142 C6
Weltmore Rd LTNN/LIM LU3 — 45 K6
Welwyn By-Pass Rd
  WLYN AL6 — 104 F1
Welwyn Ct HHNE HP2 — 118 A4
Welwyn Hall Gdns WLYN AL6 — 84 F8
Welwyn Rd HERT/WAT SG14 — 106 F5
Wemborough Rd STAN HA7 — 173 H5
Wendover Cl HARP AL5 — 121 H3
Wendover Ct WLYN AL6 — 84 F8
Wendover Dr WLYN AL6 — 84 F8
Wendover Hts
  RAYLNE/WEN HP22 — 112 E6
Wendover Ldg WLYN AL6 * — 84 F8
Wendover Rd
  RAYLNE/WEN HP22 — 112 A4
  BUSH WD23 — 163 L5
  LTNE LU2 — 46 F5
Wengeo La WARE SG12 — 108 A2
Wenham Pl HAT AL10 — 122 D5
Wenlock Rd EDGW HA8 — 173 P3
Wenlock St LTNE LU2 — 63 K5
Wensley Cl HARP AL5 — 102 C6
Wensleydale HHNE HP2 — 117 P5
  LTNE LU2 — 62 C5
Wensum Rd STVG SG1 — 51 J4
Wensum Wy
  RKW/CH/CXG WD3 — 161 N7
Wentbridge Pth BORE WD6 — 151 M8
Wentworth Av BORE WD6 — 164 F4
  LTNW/LEA LU4 — 62 B7
Wentworth Cl
  POTB/CUF EN6 — 153 K1
  WAT WD17 — 148 G8
Wentworth Cots STDN SG11 — 69 N4
Wentworth Dr BSF CM23 — 73 J8
  PIN HA5 — 171 J9
Wentworth Gdns
  DUN/HR/TOD LU5 — 44 D1
Wentworth Pl CSHM HP5 * — 145 K2
  STAN HA7 — 173 J3
Wentworth Rd BAR EN5 — 166 B1
  HERT/BAY SG13 — 107 K9
Wentworth Wy PIN HA5 — 171 M8
Wenwell Cl
  RAYLNE/WEN HP22 — 95 H9
Wesley Cl ARL/CHE SG15 — 24 E5
  CHESW EN7 — 141 K7
Wesley Hi CSHM HP5 — 144 C9
Wesley Rd STALW/RED AL3 — 79 P8
Wessex Dr PIN HA5 — 171 N4
West Acres AMSS HP7 — 158 D1
Westall Cl HERT/BAY SG13 — 107 K7
West Av LCOL/BKTW AL2 — 136 A4
  LTNW/LIM LU3 — 45 J9
Westbere Dr STAN HA7 — 173 K2
Westbourne Ms STAL AL1 — 11 J5
Westbourne Rd
  LTNW/LEA LU4 — 62 C5
Westbrook Cl EBAR EN4 — 167 H4
  ROY SG8 — 18 B2
Westbrook Crs EBAR EN4 — 167 H4
West Burrowfield WGCE AL7 — 104 D8
Westbury CHES/WCR EN8 — 142 C9
Westbury Cl
  DUN/HR/TOD LU5 — 60 E3
  STVG SG1 — 35 H8
Westbury Farm Cl
  HTCH/STOT SG5 — 48 B4
Westbury Gdns LTNE LU2 — 62 E3
Westbury Lodge Cl PIN HA5 — 171 M7
Westbury Pl LWTH SG6 — 36 B3
Westbury Rd LTNE LU2 — 120 C9
Westbury Rd NTHWD HA6 — 170 C1
  WATW WD18 — 13 H7
Westbush Cl HOD EN11 — 126 E2
West Chantry
  KTN/HRWW/WS HA3 — 172 B5
West Cl BAR EN5 — 165 P4
  EBAR EN4 — 167 L3
  HOD EN11 — 126 F3
  HTCHE/RSTV SG4 — 35 N6
  STVG SG1 — 11 G4
Westcombe Dr BAR EN5 — 166 E4
West Common
  CFSP/GDCR SL9 — 168 B3
  HARP AL5 — 101 P5

West Common Cl HARP AL5 ... 102 A6
West Common Rd HARP AL5 ... 102 A6
West Common Wy HARP AL5 ... 101 P7
Westcott WCCE AL7 ... 105 N5
West Ct ROY SG8 * ... 20 B4
Westcott Cl PEND EN3 ... 156 B8
Westcroft Cl BROX EN10 ... 126 F7
Westdean La CSHM HP5 ... 130 B7
West Dene HHNE HP2 ... 99 J4
Westdown Gdns
  DUN/WHIP LU6 ... 60 C7
West Dr ARL/CHE SG15 ... 24 C5
  GSTN WD25 ... 149 J6
  GSTN WD25 ... 24 C6
  KTN/HRWW/WS HA3 ... 172 D3
West Drive Gdns
  KTN/HRWW/WS HA3 ... 172 D3
Westell Cl BLDK SG7 ... 26 C9
West End BLDK SG7 ... 26 C9
West End Av PIN HA5 ... 171 M4
West End La BAR EN5 ... 166 B3
  BRKMPK AL9 ... 123 H6
  PIN HA5 ... 171 N5
West End Rd BROX EN10 ... 141 N2
  LBUZ LU7 ... 77 N6
Westerdale HHNE HP2 ... 117 P5
  LTNW/LEA LU4 ... 61 J1
Western Cl LWTH SG6 ... 25 J8
Western Man BAR EN5 * ... 166 F4
Western Pde BAR EN5 ... 166 E4
Western Rd LTN LU1 ... 6 C6
  TRING HP23 ... 95 N9
  WAB EN9 ... 143 K1
Western Ter HHNE HP11 * ... 126 C2
Western Wy BAR EN5 ... 166 E5
  DUN/HR/TOD LU5 ... 61 H5
  LWTH SG6 ... 25 J8
Westfield AMS HP6 ... 144 B5
  BRKMPK AL9 ... 123 G6
  HLWS CM18 ... 12 A7
  WGCE AL7 ... 105 K5
Westfield Av HARP AL5 ... 101 P1
  WATN WD24 ... 149 L8
Westfield Cl BSF CM23 ... 75 P6
  CHES/WCR EN8 ... 156 E1
  HTCH/STOT SG5 ... 35 J4
Westfield Dr HARP AL5 ... 82 A9
  KTN/HRWW/WS HA3 ... 173 K9
Westfield Gdns
  KTN/HRWW/WS HA3 ... 173 K8
Westfield Pk PIN HA5 ... 171 P4
Westfield Pl HARP AL5 ... 82 A9
Westfield Rd BERK HP4 ... 73 P5
  BSF CM23 ... 75 J6
  DUN/WHIP LU6 ... 60 C5
  HARP AL5 ... 82 A9
  HERT/WAT SG14 ... 151 J1
  HOD EN11 ... 126 D4
  LBUZ LU7 ... 96 B1
  MLHL NW7 ... 165 K9
Westfields STALW/RED AL3 ... 135 P1
West Ga HLW CM20 ... 7 D1
  LWTH SG6 ... 25 L5
Westgate Ct DUN/WHIP LU6 * ... 60 D6
Westgate Ct
  KTN/HRWW/WS HA3 ... 173 K9
West Hayes RBSF CM22 ... 93 H6
West La HTCH/STOT SG5 ... 34 C3
  HTCH/STOT SG5 ... 48 B5
Westlea Av BROX EN10 ... 141 N7
Westlea Cl BROX EN10 ... 142 E3
Westlea Rd BROX EN10 ... 142 E3
Westlecote Gdns LTNE LU2 ... 62 E2
Westleigh Gdns EDGW HA8 ... 173 N5
West Leith TRING HP23 ... 113 M2
Westly Wd WGCE AL7 ... 105 K5
West Md WGCE AL7 ... 105 L9
Westmede Cl CHESW EN7 ... 142 A4
Westmere Dr MLHL NW7 ... 165 H1
Westmill La HTCH/STOT SG5 ... 35 H6
Westmill Lawns
  HTCH/STOT SG5 ... 35 J7
Westmill Rd HTCH/STOT SG5 ... 35 J8
  WARE SG12 ... 127 K8
Westminster Ct HARP AL5 * ... 102 B5
  ... 8 C1
Westminster Gdns
  DUN/HR/TOD LU5 ... 44 F9
Westminster Ldg STAL AL1 * ... 8 C7
Westmoreland Rd HRW HA1 ... 172 B9
Westmorland Av
  LTNN/LIM LU3 ... 62 A1
Weston Av ROY SG8 ... 20 B3
Weston Ct POTB/CUF EN6 ... 142 D6
Weston Dr STAN HA7 ... 173 H5
Weston Rd
  RAYLNE/WEN HP22 ... 94 C8
  STVG SG1 ... 51 H7
West Wy BLDK SG7 ... 37 H2
West Pde DUN/WHIP LU6 ... 60 D6
Westpole Av EBAR EN4 ... 167 N4
Westray HHS/BOV HP3 ... 134 D1
West Reach STVGE SG2 ... 67 J4
Westridge Ct CSHM HP5 ... 119 J8
West Riding LCOL/BKTW AL2 ... 135 N9
  WLYN AL6 ... 86 B6
West Rd BERK HP4 ... 115 M6
  BSF CM23 ... 73 P6
  EBAR EN4 ... 167 L7
  HLW CM20 ... 111 K8

STSD CM24 ... 58 F6
Westron Gdns TRING HP23 ... 96 A8
West Side BROX EN10 ... 142 D4
West Sq HLW CM20 ... 2 D4
West St HERT/BAY SG13 ... 107 K7
  LTNE LU2 ... 47 L6
  WAT WD17 ... 108 C3
  WAT WD17 ... 162 D1
West Valley Rd HHS/BOV HP3 ... 133 M3
West Vw CSHM HP5 ... 131 J8
  HAT AL10 ... 122 D4
West Vw Gdns BORE WD6 ... 36 A4
Westview Ct BORE WD6 ... 164 D5
West View Gdns BORE WD6 ... 164 D5
Westview Ri HHNE HP2 ... 117 M7
West View Rd
  STALW/RED AL3 ... 8 E2
West Wk BERK EN4 ... 167 L7
Westway LTNE LU2 ... 63 K2
West Wy EDGW HA8 ... 173 P5
  HARP AL5 ... 102 B2
  PEND EN3 ... 156 C7
  RKW/CH/CXG WD3 ... 160 F7
Westwick Cl HHNE HP2 ... 118 B9
Westwick Pl GSTN WD25 ... 149 K4
Westwick Rw HHNE HP2 ... 134 F1
Westwood Av
  HTCHE/RSTV SG4 ... 49 M1
Westwood Cl AMS HP6 ... 146 A9
  POTB/CUF EN6 ... 139 K9
Westwood Dr AMS HP6 ... 146 A9
Wetheral Dr STAN HA7 ... 173 H5
Wetherby Cl STVG SG1 ... 51 M7
Wetherby Rd BORE WD6 ... 151 K9
  ENC/FH EN2 ... 155 K9
Wetherne Link
  LTNN/LEA LU4 ... 61 M1
Wexham Cl LTNN/LIM LU3 ... 45 P7
Weybourne Cl HARP AL5 ... 102 C2
Weybourne Dr LTNN/LIM LU3 ... 46 D8
Wey La CSHM HP5 ... 144 C2
Weymouth St HHS/BOV HP3 ... 133 N3
Weymouth Wk STAN HA7 ... 172 G3
Whaley Rd POTB/CUF EN6 ... 153 M3
Wharf Cl RAYLNE/WEN HP22 ... 112 C6
Wharfedale HHNE HP2 ... 117 P5
  LTNN/LEA LU4 ... 61 M1
Wharf La BERK HP4 ... 115 H2
  RKW/CH/CXG WD3 ... 161 J6
Wharf Rd BROX EN10 ... 142 E5
  BSF CM23 ... 74 A4
  HHW HP1 ... 2 A3
  RAYLNE/WEN HP22 ... 112 C6
Wharf Rw
  RAYLNE/WEN HP22 ... 95 J8
Wharley Hook HLWS CM18 ... 129 J6
Wheatbarn WGCE AL7 ... 105 L5
Wheat Cl STALW/RED AL4 ... 120 F4
Wheatcotes KNEB SG3 ... 85 M4
Wheat Cft BSF CM23 * ... 91 P1
Wheatcroft CHESW EN7 ... 142 A7
Wheatfield HAT AL10 ... 122 E5
  HHNE HP2 ... 117 N6
Wheatfield Rd HARP AL5 ... 101 P7
Wheatfield Crs ROY SG8 ... 20 D4
Wheatfields HARP AL5 ... 102 B1
  LTNN/LEA LU4 ... 61 H7
Wheatfields HLWE CM17 ... 111 N6
  PEND EN3 ... 156 D9
Wheathampstead Rd
  HARP AL5 ... 102 C4
Wheat La WLWT SG6 ... 36 B1
Wheatlands STVGE SG2 ... 51 M8
Wheatley Cl SBW CM21 ... 111 M3
  WGCE AL7 ... 105 K8
Wheatley Rd WGCE AL7 ... 105 J7
Wheatleys STALE/WH AL4 ... 121 H6
Wheatley Wy CFSP/GDCR SL9 ... 168 C3
Wheatlock Md
  STALW/RED AL3 ... 101 H7
Wheatsheaf Dr WARE SG12 ... 108 A1
Wheatsheaf Rd WARE SG12 ... 110 A2
Wheelers Cl WAB EN9 ... 143 K1
Wheelers Gn WAB EN9 ... 143 L1
Wheelers La HHNE HP2 ... 5 H6
  HHS/BOV HP3 ... 133 P1
Wheelers Orch
  CFSP/GDCR SL9 ... 168 C3
Wheelright Cl BUSH WD23 ... 163 K5
Wheelwrights
  RAYLNE/WEN HP22 ... 94 A9
Wheelwrights Cl BSF CM23 ... 91 M1
Whempstead La WARE SG12 ... 89 N4
Whempstead Rd STVGE SG2 ... 68 G3
Whetstone Cl
  TRDG/WHET N20 ... 167 H8
  WLYN AL6 ... 85 H5
Whielden Hts AMS HP7 ... 158 A2
Whielden La AMS HP7 ... 158 A2
Whielden St AMS HP7 ... 158 B2
Wheildon Gra HLWE CM17 ... 129 N5
Whinbush Gv
  HTCH/STOT SG5 ... 35 L8
Whinbush Rd
  HTCH/STOT SG5 ... 35 L8
Whippendell Rd WATW WD18 ... 12 A6
Whipperley Ring LTN LU1 ... 62 B9
Whipperley Wy LTN LU1 ... 62 C8
Whipsnade Rd
  DUN/WHIP LU6 ... 60 C7
Whisper Wd
  RKW/CH/CXG WD3 ... 160 F2
Whistler Gdns EDGW HA8 ... 173 M6
Whitby Gdns
  CDALE/KGS NW9 ... 173 N1
Whitby Rd LTNN/LIM LU3 ... 6 B1
Whitchurch Av EDGW HA8 ... 173 M4
Whitchurch Gdns EDGW HA8 ... 173 M4
Whitchurch La EDGW HA8 ... 173 J4
Whitchurch Pde EDGW HA8 * ... 173 N4
Whitebarns La BUNT SG9 ... 56 G6
Whitebeam Cl CHESW EN7 ... 141 M5
Whitebeams HAT AL10 ... 122 G9
White Bear STSD CM24 ... 58 F6

Whitebroom Rd HHW HP1 ... 117 H6
Whitechurch Cl LTNE LU2 ... 63 L4
Whitchurch Gdns LWTH SG6 ... 36 F5
White Craig Cl PIN HA5 ... 172 A2
White Crs RAYLNE/WEN HP22 ... 112 C5
Whitecroft STAL AL1 ... 122 A1
Whitecroft Rd LTNE LU2 ... 7 J3
White Crofts HTCH/STOT SG5 ... 25 J2
Whitefield Av LTNN/LIM LU3 ... 45 M8
Whitefields Rd
  CHES/WCR EN8 ... 142 B7
Whitefriars Av
  KTN/HRWW/WS HA3 ... 172 C6
Whitefriars Dr
  KTN/HRWW/WS HA3 ... 172 C6
Whitegate Cl
  HTCHE/RSTV SG4 ... 49 M1
White Gate Gdns
  KTN/HRWW/WS HA3 ... 172 C6
Whitegates
  RKW/CH/CXG WD3 ... 161 L3
Whitehall La WAB EN9 ... 143 K1
Whitehall La BSF CM23 ... 74 A1
Whitehall Rd BSF CM23 ... 73 P5
Whitehands Cl HOD EN11 ... 126 E5
White Hart Cl BUNT SG9 ... 40 C8
White Hart Ct
  CHESW EN7 ... 158 D9
White Hart Rd HHNE HP2 ... 118 B9
White Hill CHESW EN7 ... 141 M7
  LTNN/LIM LU3 ... 45 N4
Whitehaven Cl CHESW EN7 ... 141 N7
White Hedge Dr
  STALW/RED AL3 ... 120 B6
White Hern Ct
  CHES/WCR EN8 ... 142 B9
Whitehicks LWTH SG6 ... 25 L8
Whitehill BERK HP4 ... 116 A6
White Hi BERK HP4 ... 131 P5
  CSHM HP5 ... 145 H1
  DEN/HRF UB9 ... 170 C3
  HHW HP1 ... 117 J3
  STALW/RED AL3 ... 100 C4
  STVGE SG2 ... 52 D4
  WLYN AL6 ... 104 D2
Whitehill Av LTN LU1 ... 62 E9
White Hill Cl CSHM HP5 ... 131 H9
Whitehill Cl
  HTCHE/RSTV SG4 ... 49 M2
White Horse La KNEB SG3 ... 85 L4
Whitehorse La STVG SG1 ... 51 L4
Whitehorse St BLDK SG7 ... 26 A9
Whitehorse V LTNN/LIM LU3 ... 46 A6
Whitehouse Av BORE WD6 ... 165 H3
White House Cl
  CFSP/GDCR SL9 ... 168 C4
Whitehouse Dr
  DUN/HR/TOD LU5 ... 60 E2
Whitehouse La ABLGY WD5 ... 135 J5
White House La ENC/FH EN2 ... 155 K9
Whitehouse Wy
  STHGT/OAK N14 ... 167 M8
Whitehurst Av
  HTCH/STOT SG5 ... 35 L7
Whitelands Av
  RKW/CH/CXG WD3 ... 159 P2
White La HTCHE/RSTV SG4 ... 49 P9
Whiteleaf Rd HHS/BOV HP3 ... 133 M2
Whiteley Cl WARE SG12 ... 89 M1
Whitesmead Rd STVG SG1 ... 40 E1
White Lion Rd AMS HP7 ... 145 M9
White Lion Sq HAT AL10 ... 122 D5
White Lion St HHS/BOV HP3 ... 133 N3
White Lion Yd CSHM HP5 ... 145 G2
The White Ldg BAR EN5 * ... 166 C2
White Orchards STAN HA7 ... 172 G2
  TRDG/WHET N20 ... 166 D6
White Post Fld SBW CM21 ... 111 N2
White Shack La
  RKW/CH/CXG WD3 ... 148 A7
Whitesmead Rd STVG SG1 ... 51 H8
Whitestone Wk HHW HP1 ... 117 K5
White Stubbs La BROX EN10 ... 125 K7
Whitethorn WGCE AL7 ... 105 M3
Whitethorn Cl STVG SG1 ... 36 D5
Whitethorn Wy LTN LU1 ... 62 B8
Whitewaits HLW CM20 ... 3 H4
Whiteway
  HTCHE/RSTV SG4 ... 82 F1
  LTNE LU2 ... 64 E8
The White Wy STVGE SG2 ... 51 M8
Whitewebbs La ENC/FH EN2 ... 155 L5
Whitewebbs Pk
  ENC/FH EN2 ... 155 M5
Whitewebbs Rd ENC/FH EN2 ... 155 J5
Whitewood Rd BERK HP4 ... 115 M7
Whitfield Wy
  RKW/CH/CXG WD3 ... 160 D7
Whit Hern Ct
  CHES/WCR EN8 * ... 142 A9
Whitings Cl HARP AL5 ... 82 C9
Whitings Rd BAR EN5 ... 166 A4
Whitlars Dr KGLGY WD4 ... 134 A7
Whitley Cl ABLGY WD5 ... 149 H2
Whitley Rd HOD EN11 ... 126 E6
Whitmores Wd HHNE HP2 ... 118 C9
Whitney Dr STVG SG1 ... 50 F6
Whittingham Cl LTNE LU2 ... 63 N5
Whittingstall Rd HOD EN11 ... 126 D4
Whittington La STVG SG1 ... 91 P2
Whittington Wy BSF CM23 ... 171 N9
Whittle Cl GSTN WD25 ... 148 G4
Whittlesea Rd
  KTN/HRWW/WS HA3 ... 172 C4
Whittle Wy STVG SG1 ... 66 C2
Whitwell Cl LTNN/LIM LU3 ... 45 L5
Whitwell Rd GSTN WD25 ... 149 L5
Whitworth Crs PEND EN3 ... 156 F7
Whitworth Jones Av
  HNLW SG16 ... 24 A4

Whitworth Rd STVG SG1 ... 51 L4
Whomerley Rd STVG SG1 ... 11 F7
Whybrow Gdns BERK HP4 ... 20 D5
Whydale Rd ROY SG8 ... 20 D5
Whyke Av STALE/WH AL4 ... 103 J4
Whytingham Rd TRING HP23 ... 96 B8
Wick Av STALE/WH AL4 ... 103 J4
Wicken Flds LWTH SG6 ... 108 B1
Wickets End RAD WD7 ... 151 K5
The Wickets LTNE LU2 ... 85 K5
Wickfield KNEB SG3 ... 85 N4
Wickfield Cl KNEB SG3 ... 85 N4
Wickham Cl DEN/HRF UB9 ... 169 P5
Wickham Rd
  KTN/HRWW/WS HA3 ... 172 D6
Wickhams Whf WARE SG12 * ... 108 D3
Wickham St WARE SG12 ... 71 J3
Wick Hl DUN/WHIP LU6 ... 79 J5
Wicklands Rd WARE SG12 ... 110 A3
Wickmere Cl LTNE LU2 ... 63 N5
Wick Rd TRING HP23 ... 114 B3
Wickstead Av LTNN/LEA LU4 ... 61 P5
The Wick HERT/WAT SG14 ... 107 J3
Widbury Gdns WARE SG12 ... 108 E5
Widbury Hl WARE SG12 ... 108 F3
Widford Rd WARE SG12 ... 171 L9
Widewater Dr
  DEN/HRF UB9 * ... 169 N9
Widford Rd MHAD SG10 ... 90 B7
  WARE SG12 ... 110 A2
  WGCE AL7 ... 105 H6
Wicken Rd HTCHE/RSTV SG4 ... 49 L1
Widgeon Wy GSTN WD25 ... 149 M6
Widmore Cl CSHM HP5 ... 130 D5
Widmore Dr HHNE HP2 ... 118 B6
Wieland Rd HTCHE/RSTV SG4 ... 171 J4
Wiggenhall Rd WATW WD18 ... 13 C6
Wiggington Bottom
  TRING HP23 ... 114 C3
Wiggles La TRING HP23 ... 95 N5
Wigmore La TRING HP23 ... 95 N5
Wigmore Pl LTNE LU2 ... 63 M5
Wigmores North WGCW AL8 ... 104 C5
Wigram Wy STVGE SG2 ... 67 L2
Wigton Gdns STAN HA7 ... 173 L5
Wilbury Cl LWTH SG6 ... 61 H4
Wilbury Dr DUN/HR/TOD LU5 ... 61 H4
Wilbury Hills Rd LWTH SG6 ... 35 K2
Wilbury Rd LWTH SG6 ... 35 M5
Wilcon Wy GSTN WD25 ... 149 L4
Wilcot Av OXHEY WD19 ... 162 G6
Wilcot Cl OXHEY WD19 ... 162 G6
Wildacres NTHWD HA6 ... 161 P5
The Wilderness BERK HP4 ... 115 P7
Wildhill Rd BRKMPK AL9 ... 123 J9
Wild Oaks Cl NTHWD HA6 ... 161 P5
Wildwood NTHWD HA6 ... 170 D5
Wildwood Av
  LCOL/BKTW AL2 ... 135 N9
Wildwood La STVG SG1 ... 65 L1
Wilford Cl NTHWD HA6 ... 170 F4
Wilga Rd WLYN AL6 ... 86 A7
Wilkin's Green La HAT AL10 ... 121 P7
Wilkins Green Ter
  STALE/WH AL4 ... 121 N8
Wilkins Gv WGCW AL8 ... 104 C7
Wilkinson Cl CHESW EN7 ... 141 K5
Wilkinson Wy HHS/BOV HP3 ... 134 B5
Willenhall Av BAR EN5 ... 166 G5
Willenhall Cl LTNN/LIM LU3 ... 45 M4
Willetts Ms HOD EN11 ... 126 F4
William Burt Cl
  RAYLNE/WEN HP22 ... 112 A2
William Cl HHS/BOV HP3 ... 133 N3
William Covell Cl
  ENC/FH EN2 * ... 154 D5
William Dr STAN HA7 ... 172 G3
William Moulder Ct
  CSHM HP5 ... 130 G7
William Pl STVGE SG2 ... 67 K3
Williamson Wy
  RKW/CH/CXG WD3 ... 161 M4
William St BERK HP4 ... 116 A7
  BUSH WD23 ... 163 N1
  STAL AL1 ... 6 E1
  STALW/RED AL3 ... 79 P8
Williams Wy RAD WD7 ... 151 N9
Willian Church Rd LWTH SG6 ... 36 D5
Willian Rd HTCH/STOT SG5 ... 36 C4
Willian Wy LWTH SG6 ... 36 D5
Willinghall Cl WAB EN9 ... 157 J2
Williton Rd LTNE LU2 ... 63 N5
Willoughby Cl BROX EN10 ... 126 D9
Willoughby Rd HARP AL5 ... 82 A9
Willoughby Wy
  HTCHE/RSTV SG4 ... 49 M1
Willowbay Cl BAR EN5 ... 166 B5
Willowbrook
  RAYLNE/WEN HP22 ... 112 C4
Willow Cl LCOL/BKTW AL2 ... 137 J5
Willow Cha CSHM HP5 ... 130 D5
Willow Cl BSF CM23 ... 73 P6
  BUNT SG9 ... 41 M8
  CFSP/GDCR SL9 ... 168 C6
  CHESW EN7 ... 141 M5
  ROY SG8 * ... 20 B4
Willow Ct STAN HA7 * ... 173 K4
Willowcourt Av
  KTN/HRWW/WS HA3 ... 173 H9
Willow Crs DUN/HR/TOD LU5 ... 45 H5
Willow Dean PIN HA5 * ... 171 M1
Willow Dene BUSH WD23 ... 163 N6
Willowdene CHES/WCR EN8 ... 142 D5
  HERT/WAT SG14 ... 86 F2
Willow Edge KGLGY WD4 ... 134 B8
Willow End NTHWD HA6 ... 161 P6
Willowfield HLWS CM18 ... 128 G2
Willow Gv WGCW AL8 ... 104 G1
Willow La AMS HP7 ... 158 B7
  HTCH/STOT SG5 ... 49 H1
  WATW WD18 ... 12 D7
Willowmead HERT/WAT SG14 * ... 107 N6

Willow Md SBW CM21 ... 111 P3
Willow Rd EN EN1 ... 156 A5
Willow Rd EN EN1 ... 171 L6
Willowside LCOL/BKTW AL2 ... 137 K6
Willowside Wy ROY SG8 ... 20 B2
Willows La AMS HP7 ... 158 B7
Willows Link STVGE SG2 ... 67 K5
Willow Springs BSF CM23 ... 73 H6
Willows AMS HP6 ... 144 C5
  BORE WD6 * ... 151 M9
  EBAR EN4 ... 167 J5
  HHNE HP2 ... 118 C6
  HTCHE/RSTV SG4 ... 49 K2
  OXHEY WD19 ... 162 D6
  RKW/CH/CXG WD3 ... 160 E8
  STAL AL1 ... 123 J2
  STVGE SG2 ... 67 K6
  WGCE AL7 ... 108 G8
Willow Tree Wy
  HTCH/STOT SG5 ... 35 K6
Willow Vw WARE SG12 * ... 108 D4
Willow Vw WLYN AL6 ... 84 F5
Willow Wy DUN/WHIP LU6 ... 79 J7
  HARP AL5 ... 82 B9
  HAT AL10 ... 122 C9
  HHW HP1 ... 135 P6
  LCOL/BKTW AL2 ... 135 K6
  LTNN/LIM LU3 ... 153 L3
  POTB/CUF EN6 ... 143 J7
  RAD WD7 ... 150 D6
Willsden Av LTNN/LIM LU3 ... 6 A7
Wilshere Av STAL AL1 ... 136 B2
Wilshere Crs
  HTCHE/RSTV SG4 ... 35 P8
Wilshere Rd WLYN AL6 ... 84 D8
Wilsmere Dr
  KTN/HRWW/WS HA3 ... 172 E4
Wilson Cl BSF CM23 ... 74 A5
  STVG SG1 ... 50 G6
Wilson Cl STVG SG1 * ... 50 G6
Wilsons La BLDK SG7 ... 17 M6
Wilstone Br TRING HP23 ... 95 L3
Wilstone Dr STALE/WH AL4 ... 121 H3
Wilton Cl BSF CM23 ... 35 K7
Wilton Crs HERT/BAY SG13 ... 107 K9
Wilton Rd EBAR EN4 ... 167 K3
  HTCH/STOT SG5 ... 35 K7
Wilton Wy HERT/BAY SG13 ... 107 K8
Wiltshire La PIN HA5 ... 170 E1
Wiltshire Rd STVGE SG2 ... 11 K7
Wimbledon Cl SBW CM21 ... 111 N2
Wimborne Dr EDGW HA8 ... 173 N7
Wimborne Gv WAT WD17 ... 148 F7
Wimborne Rd LTN LU1 ... 62 C6
Winborne Rd LTNN/LEA LU4 ... 61 K4
Winch Cl HTCHE/RSTV SG4 ... 84 C5
Winchdells HHS/BOV HP3 ... 134 B2
Winchester Dr
  CDALE/KGS NW9 ... 173 M7
Winchester Cl AMSS HP22 ... 145 K9
  BSF CM23 ... 91 N1
  STVG SG1 ... 51 K5
Winchester Dr PIN HA5 ... 171 M9
Winchester Gdns
  LTNN/LIM LU3 ... 45 P6
Winchester Rd
  KTN/HRWW/WS HA3 ... 173 L8
Winchester Wy
  RKW/CH/CXG WD3 ... 161 M4
Winch St LTNE LU2 ... 79 P1
Winchfield Wy
  RKW/CH/CXG WD3 ... 160 G6
Winckley Cl
  KTN/HRWW/WS HA3 ... 173 M9
Windermere Av STAL AL1 ... 136 G1
Windermere Cl
  DUN/WHIP LU6 ... 60 D7
  HHS/BOV HP3 ... 118 D9
  RKW/CH/CXG WD3 ... 160 B4
  STVG SG1 ... 51 N5
Windermere Crs
  LTNN/LIM LU3 ... 62 A1
Windermere Hall
  EDGW HA8 * ... 173 M2
Winder Hall WGCE AL7 ... 73 P7
  WGCE AL7 ... 105 K5
Windhill Old Rd BSF CM23 ... 73 P7
Winding Hl MHAD SG10 ... 90 D1
Winding Shot HHW HP1 ... 117 K7
Winding Shot
  HERT/WAT SG14 ... 86 B6
Windmill Av STALE/WH AL4 ... 121 H4
Windmill Cl ROY SG8 ... 30 A4
  STSD CM24 ... 58 E5
  WAB EN9 ... 157 K4
Windmill Dr
  RKW/CH/CXG WD3 ... 161 K5
Windmill Fld WARE SG12 ... 108 D3
Windmill Hl BUNT SG9 ... 54 E1
  KGLGY WD4 ... 135 J9
Windmill La BAR EN5 ... 165 M5
  BUSH WD23 ... 163 N1
  CHES/WCR EN8 ... 156 F3
  HTCHE/RSTV SG4 ... 64 C4
  LTN LU1 ... 7 H6
  STALW/RED AL3 ... 80 B7
Windmills WARE SG12 ... 69 M6
Windmill St BUSH WD23 ... 164 B1
Windmill Wy MHAD SG10 ... 90 B4
  TRING HP23 ... 95 M3
Windmill Wd AMS HP6 ... 144 F7
Windmore
  POTB/CUF EN6 ... 152 F1
Windridge Cl STALW/RED AL3 ... 51 K4
Windrush Cl STVG SG1 ... 51 K4
Winds End Cl HHNE HP2 ... 118 B6
Windsor Av EDGW HA8 ... 173 P1
Windsor Cl HHNE HP2 ... 141 P9
  HHW HP1 ... 132 D7
  NTHWD HA6 ... 161 Q8
  STVGE SG2 ... 67 L7
  WLYN AL6 ... 104 E1
Windsor Crs HARP AL5 ... 171 M7
  PIN HA5 ... 171 N7
  STHGT/OAK N14 ... 167 N6

Windsor Dr
DUN/HR/TOD LU5 .... 60 G1
EBAR EN4 .... 167 K5
HERT/WAT SG14 .... 106 C5
Windsor Gdns BSF CM23 .... 73 M7
Windsor Pde
AMP/FLIT/BLC MK45 * 32 D4
Windsor Rd
AMP/FLIT/BLC MK45 .... 32 D4
BAR EN5 .... 166 B5
CSHM HP5 .... 130 C7
KTN/HRWW/WS HA3 .... 172 C5
LBUZ LU7 .... 96 B1
PEND EN3 .... 156 C6
ROY SG8 .... 20 D4
WATN WD24 .... 149 K8
WLYN AL6 .... 104 E1
Windsor St LTN LU1 .... 6 D6
Windsor Wk LTN LU1 .... 6 D6
Windsor Wy
RKW/CH/CXG WD3 .... 160 E7
Windward Ct PEND EN3 .... 156 C5
Windy Ri WAB SG12 .... 69 N7
Winfield St DUN/WHIP LU6 ..... 60 E5
Winford Dr BROX EN10 .... 142 E1
Wingate Gdns WLYN AL6 .... 84 E8
Wingate Rd
DUN/HR/TOD LU5 .... 61 H5
LTNW/LEA LU4 .... 61 P3
Wingate Wy STAL AL1 .... 118 F7
Wingfield Ct WATW WD18 * 161 P5
Wingrave Cross Roads
RAYLNE/WEN HP22 .... 76 A1
Wingrave Rd TRING SG4 .... 95 L2
Winifred Ct BAR EN5 .... 165 M5
Winifred Rd HHS/BOV HP3 ..... 153 N5
Winkers Cl CFSP/GDCR SL9 ... 168 D5
Winkers La CFSP/GDCR SL9 .. 168 D5
Winkfield Cl LTNW/LEA LU4 .... 61 L5
Winnington Rd PEND EN3 .... 156 B8
Winnipeg Wy BROX EN10 .... 142 D4
Winscombe Wy STAN HA7 ...... 172 C2
Winsdon Rd LTN LU1 .... 6 C6
Winslow Rd LTN LU1 .... 62 D2
Winslow Wy
RAYLNE/WEN HP22 .... 76 B1
Winston Churchill Wy
CHES/WCR EN8 .... 156 F8
Winston Cl HTCH/STOT SG5 ... 35 J9
KTN/HRWW/WS HA3 .... 172 F5
Winston Ct CE
KTN/HRWW/WS HA3 .... 172 B4
Winston Cl AMS HP6 .... 144 C4
Winstone Gdns BRKH HP4 ..... 115 L7
Winston Wy
POTB/CUF EN6 .... 153 K3
Winstre Rd BORE WD6 .... 151 M9
Winterscroft Rd HOD EN11 .... 126 E5
Winters La STVGE SG2 .... 57 L6
Winters Wy WAB EN9 .... 157 M3
Winthorpe Gdns
BORE WD6 .... 151 L9
Winton Ap
RKW/CH/CXG WD3 .... 161 N4
Winton Cl LTNE LU2 .... 46 E9
LWTH SG6 .... 25 N9
Winton Crs
RKW/CH/CXG WD3 .... 161 N4
Winton Dr CHES/WCR EN8 .... 142 D8
RKW/CH/CXG WD3 .... 161 N4
Winton Gdns EDGW HA8 .... 173 M4
Winton Rd WARE SG12 .... 108 E3
The Wintons BUSH WD23 * 163 M7
Winton Ter STAL AL1 * 9 H6
Wisden Rd STVG SG1 .... 51 J6
Wisdom Dr HERT/BAY SG13 .. 107 M6
Wiseman Cl LTNE LU2 .... 46 E8
Wisemans Gdns SBW CM21 ... 111 M3
Wistaria Dr LCOL/BKTW AL2 .. 136 C5
Wistlea Crs STALE/WH AL4 .... 137 N1
Wistow Rd LTNE LU2 .... 46 B9
Witchell RAYLNE/WEN HP22 .. 112 C7
Witchford WCCE AL7 .... 105 N6
Withy Cl LTNW/LEA LU4 .... 61 L1
Withy La RSLP HA4 .... 170 E9
Withy Pl LCOL/BKTW AL2 .... 136 A7
Witney Cl PIN HA5 .... 171 P3
Witter Av HTCH/STOT SG5 ...... 35 K4
Wiveton Cl LTNE LU2 .... 46 B8
Woburn Av BSF CM23 .... 73 M7
Woburn Cl BUSH WD23 .... 163 L5
STVGE SG2 .... 67 M7
Wodecroft Rd
LTNN/LIM LU3 .... 46 C9
Wolmer Cl EDGW HA8 .... 173 N1
Wolmer Gdns EDGW HA8 ...... 164 D9
Wolseley Rd
KTN/HRWW/WS HA3 .... 172 E7
Wolsey Av CHESW EN7 .... 141 N8
Wolsey Rd HHNE HP2 .... 4 E4
NTHWD HA6 .... 170 F1
Wolston Cl LTN LU1 .... 6 A5
Wolverton Rd STAN HA7 .... 173 H3
Wolverton Wy
STHGT/OAK N14 .... 167 N4
Wolvescroft KNEB SG3 * 85 K3
Wolves Mere KNEB SG3 .... 85 K3
Wonnacott PEND EN3 .... 156 C7
Woodacre Dr WLYN AL6 .... 85 K5
Woodbank
RKW/CH/CXG WD3 .... 160 G5
Woodbank Dr CSTG HP8 .... 159 K9
Woodberry Av
RYLN/HDSTN HA2 .... 172 C8
Woodbine Cl
HLWW/ROY CM19 .... 128 F5
Woodbine Gv ENC/FH EN2 .... 155 L8
Woodbridge Cl
LTNW/LEA LU4 .... 61 P2
Woodbrook Gdns WAB EN9 ... 157 K3
Woodbury Hi LTNE LU2 .... 62 F4
Woodbury Hill Pth LTNE LU2 .. 62 F4
Wood Cl DUN/WHIP LU6 .... 79 H5
HAT AL10 .... 122 E6
Woodcock Hi
RKW/CH/CXG WD3 .... 173 J9
RKW/CH/CXG WD3 .... 170 A2
Woodcockhill STALE/WH AL4 .. 121 J2
Woodcock Rd LTN LU1 .... 62 B7

Woodcote CI
CHES/WCR EN8 .... 142 B9
Wood Common HAT AL10 ...... 122 E3
Woodcote CI
CHES/WCR EN8 .... 142 B9
Woodcote Gv HHNE HP2 .... 5 F4
Woodcroft HLWS CM18 .... 128 F5
Woodcroft Av STAN HA7 .... 172 G5
WARE SG12 .... 109 J8
Woodcroft Rd CSHM HP5 ...... 131 J7
Woodcutter Pl
LCOL/BKTW AL2 .... 136 B6
Wood Dr STVGE SG2 .... 67 L4
Wood End LCOL/BKTW AL2 ... 136 B7
Wood End La HHNE HP2 .... 118 D7
Wood End Hl HARP AL5 .... 101 L1
Wood End La
STALW/RED AL3 .... 100 A4
Wood End Rd HARP AL5 .... 101 L1
Wood End Rd BAR EN5 .... 166 D4
Wood Farm Rd HHNE HP2 .... 5 H2
Woodfield Av NTHWD HA6 .... 170 D1
Woodfield Cl STAN SG4 .... 58 F5
Woodfield Dr EBAR EN4 .... 167 L7
Woodfield Gdns
HHS/BOV HP3 .... 134 D1
Woodfield La
DUN/HR/TOD LU5 .... 61 H8
Woodfield La BRKMPK AL9 .... 139 J2
Woodfield Pk AMS HP6 .... 144 C7
Woodfield Ri BUSH WD23 .... 163 M6
Woodfield Rd RAD WD7 .... 163 J6
STVG SG1 .... 50 F6
WGCE AL7 .... 105 J6
Woodfields STSD CM24 .... 58 F5
Woodfield STSD CM24 .... 58 F5
WATW WD18 * 13 G5
Woodfield Wy
STALE/WH AL4 .... 121 H5
Woodford Ct WAB EN9 .... 157 M3
Woodford Crs PIN HA5 .... 171 K6
Woodford Cl BLDK SG7 .... 17 K6
Woodford Rd
DUN/HR/TOD LU5 .... 61 H4
WAT WD17 .... 13 G1
Woodgate Cl NTHWD SG4 ...... 149 J3
Woodgate Av
POTB/CUF EN6 .... 154 C3
Woodgate Crs NTHWD HA6 ... 171 J3
Woodgate Ms WAT WD17 ...... 149 H9
Woodgrange Av
KTN/HRWW/WS HA3 .... 173 J9
Woodgrange CI
KTN/HRWW/WS HA3 .... 173 K9
Wood Green CI LTNE LU2 .... 63 J9
Wood Green Rd LTNE LU2 ...... 63 J1
Woodgreen Rd WAB EN9 .... 157 N3
Woodhall Av PIN HA5 .... 171 N5
Woodhall Ct HERT/WAT SG14 .. 107 K4
Woodhall Ct WCCE AL7 .... 105 M7
Woodhall Dr PIN HA5 .... 171 M5
Woodhall Ga PIN HA5 .... 171 M4
Woodhall Gv BSF CM23 .... 73 N8
Woodhall La HHNE HP2 .... 117 P7
OXHEY WD19 .... 162 F9
RAD WD7 .... 151 K5
WGCE AL7 .... 105 H8
Woodham Wy WARE SG12 ..... 109 H8
Woodhill HLWS CM18 .... 129 H6
Woodhouse Eaves
NTHWD HA6 .... 171 J2
Wood House La BROX EN10 ... 125 N9
Woodhurst LWTH SG6 .... 25 K9
Woodhurst Dr
DEN/HRF UB9 .... 169 K9
Woodhurst Dr
DEN/HRF UB9 .... 169 K9
Woodland Gv
HLWW/ROY CM19 .... 2 A5
Woodland Av HHW HP1 .... 4 A3
LTNN/LIM LU3 .... 62 C4
Woodland Ct HHW HP1 .... 4 A3
TRING HP23 .... 113 N1
Woodland Ct
STALW/RED AL3 * 120 E4
Woodland Dr STALE/WH AL4 .. 121 H7
WAT WD17 .... 12 C1
Woodland Mt
HERT/BAY SG13 .... 107 N6
Woodland Pl HHW HP1 .... 4 A3
WGCW AL8 .... 104 F4
Woodland Rd
HERT/BAY SG13 .... 108 B9
RKW/CH/CXG WD3 .... 169 H2
Woodlands BRKMPK AL9 .... 139 L6
BSF CM25 .... 74 D2
HARP AL5 .... 101 M1
LCOL/BKTW AL2 .... 136 B6
LTN LU1 .... 79 P3
RAD WD7 .... 150 F4
ROY SG8 .... 20 D4
RYLN/HDSTN HA2 .... 172 A8
Woodlands Av BERK HP4 .... 116 A8
DUN/HR/TOD LU5 .... 60 F2
Woodlands Dr HOD EN11 ...... 126 F6
HOD EN11 * 113 N1
TRING HP23 .... 113 N1
KGLGY WD4 .... 134 D7
STAN HA7 .... 172 F3
Woodlands Meade
HTCHE/RSTV SG4 .... 37 L8
Woodlands Rd BUSH WD23 ... 162 C3
ENC/FH EN2 .... 155 L8
HERT/BAY SG13 .... 107 N6
HHS/BOV HP3 .... 134 B6
HRW HA1 .... 172 E9
WARE SG12 .... 88 C7
The Woodlands AMS HP6 ...... 145 H5
STAN HA7 .... 173 H2
STHGT/OAK N14 .... 167 M7
Woodland Vw CSHM HP5 ...... 145 J3
Woodland Wy ABLGY WD5 .... 134 G6
BLDK SG7 .... 17 J2
CHESW EN7 .... 141 J7
STVGE SG2 .... 67 K5
WLYN AL6 .... 85 J6

Wood La BSF CM23 .... 58 F9
BUNT SG9 .... 42 D2
HHNE HP2 .... 4 A3
STAN HA7 .... 164 B9
Wood Lane End HHNE HP2 ... 118 C7
Woodlea LCOL/BKTW AL2 ...... 135 P4
Woodlea Gv NTHWD HA6 .... 170 E3
Woodley Ct HARP AL5 .... 118 E2
Woodley Cl AMSS HP7 * 145 J4
Woodley Hi CSHM HP5 .... 145 J4
Woodley Rd WARE SG12 .... 108 E2
Woodmans Yd WAT WD17 ...... 13 H5
Woodmere LTNN/LIM LU3 .... 46 B6
Woodmere Av WATN WD24 .... 149 L8
Woodmill Ms HOD EN11 * 126 F6
Woodpecker Cl BSF CM23 ...... 73 M8
BUSH WD23 .... 163 L7
HAT AL10 * 122 C9
KTN/HRWW/WS HA3 .... 172 F5
Woodredon CI
HLWW/ROY CM19 .... 127 N4
Wood Ride EBAR EN4 .... 153 N9
Woodridge Cl ENC/FH EN2 * .. 155 H9
Woodridge Wy
NTHWD HA6 .... 170 G3
Woodridings Av PIN HA5 .... 171 P5
Woodridings Cl PIN HA5 .... 171 P4
Wood Ri PIN HA5 .... 171 J9
Woods Av HAT AL10 .... 122 D7
Woodshots Meadow
WATW WD18 .... 161 P4
Woodside BORE WD6 .... 164 F3
BSF CM23 .... 74 E2
CHESW EN7 .... 155 P1
HERT/BAY SG13 .... 108 B9
WATN WD24 .... 149 H7
Woodside Av AMS HP6 .... 145 J6
Woodside Cl CFSP/GDCR SL9 .. 168 C5
STAN HA7 .... 172 G2
Woodside Gdns
HTCH/STOT SG5 .... 35 L9
Woodside Gv
HTCH/WDSPK N12 .... 166 G9
Woodside Hi
CFSP/GDCR SL9 .... 168 C6
Woodside La BRKMPK AL9 .... 123 J9
TRDG/WHET N20 .... 166 F9
Woodside Pk
DUN/HR/TOD LU5 .... 60 F3
Woodside Rd ABLGY WD5 ...... 149 J1
AMS HP6 .... 145 J7
LCOL/BKTW AL2 .... 135 N9
LTN LU1 .... 80 B4
NTHWD HA6 .... 171 H4
WLYN AL6 .... 104 E1
Woodside Wk AMS HP6 * 145 J7
Woods Pl
RAYLNE/WEN HP22 * 112 C7
TRING HP23 .... 95 P9
Woodstead Gv EDGW HA8 .... 173 L5
The Woods NTHWD HA6 .... 171 J2
RAD WD7 .... 150 G4
Woodstock KNEB SG3 .... 85 J2
Woodstock Cl
HERT/BAY SG13 .... 108 A4
STAN HA7 .... 173 L6
Woodstock Rd BROX EN10 .... 126 D7
BUSH WD23 .... 163 N6
Woodstock Rd North
STAL AL1 .... 120 G6
Woodstock Rd South
STAL AL1 .... 120 G8
Wood St BAR EN5 .... 166 A3
DUN/WHIP LU6 .... 60 F6
LTN LU1 .... 6 B6
Wood V HAT AL10 .... 122 E6
Woodvale Pk STAL AL1 .... 120 C8
Wood Vw HHW HP1 .... 117 L6
POTB/CUF EN6 .... 140 F6
Woodville Court Ms
WAT WD17 * 162 C1
Woodville Pl
HERT/WAT SG14 .... 107 J4
Woodville Rd BAR EN5 .... 166 F2
Woodward Gdns STAN HA7 .... 172 F4
Woodwards
RKW/CH/CXG WD3 .... 169 H2
Woodwaye OXHEY WD19 ...... 162 E6
Woodwicks
RKW/CH/CXG WD3 .... 169 H2
Woolacre STALW/RED AL3 * .. 101 H4
Woolgrove Rd
HTCHE/RSTV SG4 .... 35 M7
Woollam Crs
STALW/RED AL3 .... 120 B4
Woollams STALW/RED AL3 * .. 101 H8
Woollerton St WAB EN9 .... 157 H4
Woollerton Crs
RAYLNE/WEN HP22 .... 112 D6
Woolmans Cl BROX EN10 ...... 142 E1
Woolmer Cl BORE WD6 .... 151 M8
Woolmerdine Ct BUSH WD23 .. 13 K3
Woolmer Dr HHNE HP2 .... 118 D8
Woolmers La
HERT/WAT SG14 .... 124 C1
Woolners Wy STVG SG1 .... 50 A2
Woolpack Cl DUN/WHIP LU6 ... 60 F7
Woolston Av LWTH SG6 .... 36 D4
Wootton Cl LTNN/LIM LU3 ...... 46 C8
Wootton Dr HHNE HP2 .... 118 A3
Worboys Cn ROY SG8 .... 15 L6
Worcester Crs MLHL NW7 ...... 165 L9
Worcester Rd HAT AL10 .... 122 C5
Worcesters Av EN EN1 .... 155 P8
Wordsworth Cl HAT AL10 * 122 C7
Wordsworth Gdns
BORE WD6 .... 164 G4
Wordsworth Rd HARP AL5 ..... 101 P1
LTNN/LEA LU4 .... 61 K4
Works Rd LWTH SG6 .... 36 E1
World's End La
RAYLNE/WEN HP22 .... 112 A3
Worley Rd STALW/RED AL3 ..... 8 A4
Wormley Ct WAB EN9 .... 157 M3
Wormley Lodge Cl
BROX EN10 .... 142 E2
Wormyngford Ct WAB EN9 ..... 157 M3
Worsdell Wy
HTCHE/RSTV SG4 .... 35 N9

Worsted La BUNT SG9 .... 41 K9
Wortham Rd ROY SG8 .... 20 D5
Wortham Wy STVGE SG2 .... 67 L4
Worthington Rd
DUN/WHIP LU6 .... 60 C6
The Wraglins BSF CM23 .... 74 C5
Wrangley Ct WAB EN9 .... 157 M3
Wratten Cl HTCH/STOT SG5 ... 49 K1
Wratten Rd East
HTCH/STOT SG5 .... 49 K1
Wratten Rd West
HTCH/STOT SG5 .... 49 J1
Wrayfields HTCH/STOT SG5 ... 25 M2
Wraysbury Cl LTNW/LEA LU4 .. 61 K5
Wrenbrook Rd BSF CM23 .... 74 A5
Wren Cl HTCHE/RSTV SG4 ..... 82 G4
LTNE LU2 .... 47 K9
STVGE SG2 .... 51 L9
Wren Crs BUSH WD23 .... 163 L7
Wren Dr WAB EN9 .... 157 M4
Wrensfield HHW HP1 .... 117 K9
The Wrens HLWW/ROY CM19 .. 5 P4
Wren Wd WGCE AL7 .... 105 L5
Wrenwood Wy PIN HA5 .... 171 K8
Wright Cl STALE/WH AL4 .... 103 J5
Wright's Green La
RBSF CM22 .... 92 D2
Wrights Meadow STVGE SG2 .. 52 C7
Wrights Orch STVGE SG2 .... 67 P4
Wrotham Rd BAR EN5 .... 166 C1
Wroxham Av HHNE HP2 .... 5 F5
Wroxham Gdns
ENC/FH EN2 .... 155 H5
POTB/CUF EN6 .... 152 C1
Wroxham Wy HARP AL5 .... 118 A7
Wulstan Pk POTB/CUF EN6 .... 153 M2
Wulwards Cl LTN LU1 .... 62 C8
Wyatt Cl BUSH WD23 .... 163 N6
HTCH/STOT SG5 .... 35 J4
Wyatt's Cl
RKW/CH/CXG WD3 .... 160 E2
Wyatt's Rd
RKW/CH/CXG WD3 .... 160 D3
Wyburn Av BAR EN5 .... 166 D2
Wychdell STVGE SG2 .... 67 M6
Wych Elm HHW HP1 .... 2 D3
Wych Elm La WLYN AL6 .... 85 H2
Wych Elms LCOL/BKTW AL2 ... 136 A7
Wycherley Crs BAR EN5 .... 165 M5
Wychford Dr SBW CM21 .... 111 M3
Wychwood Av EDGW HA8 ...... 173 K3
LTNE LU2 .... 62 F2
Wychwood Rd EDGW HA8 ..... 173 K3
Wychwood Wy NTHWD HA6 ... 171 H4
Wycklond Cl
HTCH/STOT SG5 .... 25 J3
Wycliffe Cl CHES/WCR EN8 .... 142 C8
LTNN/LIM LU3 .... 46 D9
Wycombe Pl STAL AL1 .... 120 C5
Wycombe Wy LTNN/LIM LU3 ... 46 D7
STALE/WH AL4 .... 120 C5
Wyddial Gn WGCE AL7 .... 105 L6
Wyddial Rd BUNT SG9 .... 40 D8
Wyedale LCOL/BKTW AL2 .... 137 L6
The Wye HHNE HP2 .... 118 B3
Wyken Cl LTNN/LIM LU3 .... 46 B8
Wykeridge Cl CSHM HP5 .... 130 C6
Wylchin Cl PIN HA5 .... 170 G5
Wyldwood Cl HLWE CM17 ...... 111 M6
Wyllyotts Pl
POTB/CUF EN6 .... 153 J2
Wylo Dr BAR EN5 .... 165 M5
Wymondley Cl
HTCHE/RSTV SG4 .... 49 M1
Wymondley Rd
HTCHE/RSTV SG4 .... 49 M1
LWTH SG6 .... 36 C8
Wynches Farm Dr
STALE/WH AL4 .... 121 J7
Wynchgate
KTN/HRWW/WS HA3 .... 172 E4
Wynchlands Crs
STALE/WH AL4 .... 121 J8
Wyndham Rd EBAR EN4 .... 167 K7
LTNE LU2 .... 61 M4
Wyndhams End WCCE AL7 ..... 105 J3
Wynlie Gdns PIN HA5 .... 171 K6
Wynn Cl BLDK SG7 .... 26 C8
Wynn Gv EDGW HA8 .... 165 H9
Wyrley Dell LWTH SG6 .... 36 C8
Wyton WCCE AL7 .... 105 N6
Wyvern Cl LTNW/LEA LU4 .... 61 P3

Y

Yardley LWTH SG6 .... 36 E4
Yarmouth Rd STVG SG1 .... 50 D8
WATN WD24 .... 149 J8
Yarrowside AMSS HP7 .... 159 H1
Yately Cl LTNE LU2 .... 46 E8
Yearling Cl WARE SG12 .... 108 E5
Yeats Cl ROY SG8 .... 20 C1
Ye Cnr OXHEY WD19 .... 162 F5
Yeomanry Dr BLDK SG7 .... 26 C8
Yeomans Av HARP AL5 .... 101 K1
Yeomans Cl BSF CM23 .... 73 N9
Yeomans Ct HHNE HP2 .... 118 B2
Yeomans Dr STVGE SG2 .... 67 P4
Yeovil Rd LTNE LU2 .... 63 J4
Yew Cl CHESW EN7 .... 141 H6
Yew Gv WCCE AL7 .... 105 M7
Yewlands HOD EN11 .... 126 F6
SBW CM21 .... 111 P3
Yewlands Dr HOD EN11 .... 126 F6
Yews Av EN EN1 .... 156 A6
Yew St DUN/HR/TOD LU5 ...... 44 G8
Yew Tree Cl CSHM HP5 .... 131 M9
Yewtree Cl RYLN/HDSTN HA2 .. 172 B8
Yew Tree Ct BORE WD6 .... 164 D5
Yew Tree Dr HHS/BOV HP3 .... 132 E7
Yewtree End LCOL/BKTW AL2 .. 136 A6

Yew Tree Pl BSF CM23 .... 74 A2
Yew Wk HOD EN11 .... 126 F6
York Av STAN HA7 .... 173 H5
York Cl AMP/FLIT/BLC MK45 ... 32 D4
KGLGY WD4 .... 134 B8
York Crs BORE WD6 .... 165 K1
York La HTCH/STOT SG5 * 49 K2
Yorke Ga WAT WD17 .... 162 C1
Yorke Rd RKW/CH/CXG WD3 .. 161 K5
Yorkes HLWS CM18 .... 129 J5
York Rd BAR EN5 .... 166 G4
CHES/WCR EN8 .... 156 D4
HTCH/STOT SG5 .... 35 K8
STAL AL1 .... 9 J2
STVG SG1 .... 51 J5
WATW WD18 .... 13 H7
York St LTNE LU2 .... 7 G2
York Ter ENC/FH EN2 .... 155 L6
York Wy GSTN WD25 .... 149 L6
HHNE HP2 * 5 H4
ROY SG8 .... 20 A2
TRDG/WHET N20 .... 167 K9
STVG SG1 .... 51 J5
Youngfield Rd HHW HP1 .... 117 J7
Youngmans Cl ENC/FH EN2 ... 155 K9
Youngsbury La WARE SG12 .... 88 C5
Youngs Ms HERT/WAT SG14 .. 107 K6
Youngs Ri WGCW AL8 .... 104 B3
Yukon Rd BROX EN10 .... 142 D4
Yule Cl LCOL/BKTW AL2 .... 135 N9

Z

Zambesi Rd BSF CM23 .... 74 A5

Abbeygate Business Centre
LTNE LU2 ...... 7 G3
Abbey Gateway
STALW/RED AL3 ...... 8 D4
Abbey Mead
Industrial Park
WAB EN9 ...... 156 G4
Abbey Primary School
STAL AL1 ...... 8 D5
Abbey View Golf Club
STAL AL1 ...... 8 C6
Abbots Hill School
HHS/BOV HP3 ...... 134 C4
Abbots Langley
Primary School
ABLGY WD5 ...... 134 F8
Abbotsweld
Primary School
HLWS CM18 ...... 128 C5
Abbotswood
Medical Centre
ABLGY WD5 ...... 149 H2
Aboyne Lodge
Primary School
STALW/RED AL3 ...... 8 E2
Activity World
HAT AL10 ...... 122 E3
Adath Yisroel
Cemetery
EN EN1 ...... 155 N9
Adeyfield School
EN EN1 ...... 118 B3
Airport Executive
Industrial Park
LTNE LU2 ...... 63 L6
Akeman Business Park
TRING HP23 ...... 95 P9
Alban Arena Cinema
STAL AL1 ...... 9 F5
Alban Wood Primary School
GSTN WD25 ...... 149 J3
Albany School
(Grant Maintained)
PEND EN3 ...... 156 C8
Albury Primary School
STDN SG11 ...... 56 D9
Aldbury Primary School
TRING HP23 ...... 97 H6
Aldenham Country Park
BORE WD6 ...... 164 B4
Aldenham Golf &
Country Club
GSTN WD25 ...... 150 A8
Aldenham
Preparatory School
BORE WD6 ...... 163 P1
Aldwickbury Park Golf Club
HARP AL5 ...... 102 D3
Aldwickbury School
HARP AL5 ...... 102 D4
Algrey Trading Estate
HTCHE/RSTV SG4 ...... 35 M7
Allied Business Centre
HARP AL5 ...... 102 B1
All Nations Christian College
WARE SG12 ...... 108 C5
All Saints CE Primary School
BSF CM23 ...... 74 C2
TRDG/WHET N20 ...... 167 H8
Allum Lane Cemetery
BORE WD6 ...... 164 E4
Almond Hill School
STVG SG1 ...... 50 C7
Almond Lane Cemetery
STVG SG1 ...... 51 H7
Alpha Business Park
BRKMPK AL9 ...... 138 F2
Alpha Preparatory School
HRW HA1 ...... 172 E9
Alsa Business Park
STSD CM24 ...... 58 G2
Amersham & Chiltern RFC
AMS HP6 ...... 144 N4
Amersham General Hospital
AMSS HP7 ...... 158 A2
Amersham Hill CC
AMSS HP7 ...... 145 K8
The Amersham School
AMSS HP7 ...... 158 E1
Amersham Town FC
AMSS HP7 ...... 144 F9
Amersham & Wycombe
College
AMSS HP7 ...... 145 L4
CSHM HP5 ...... 131 J6
Amwell View Special School
WARE SG12 ...... 108 G8
Andrews Lane J & I School
CHESW EN7 ...... 142 N7
Anglian Business Park
ROY SG8 ...... 20 A3
Anstey First School
BUNT SG9 ...... 41 M2
Apex Business Centre
DUN/WHIP LU6 ...... 60 F4
Applecroft JMI School
WCCW AL8 ...... 104 E6
Apsley Mills Retail Park
HHS/BOV HP3 ...... 133 P3
The Arcade
LWTH SG6 ...... 36 C2
Ardeley Primary School
STVGE SG2 ...... 52 G4
Ardley Hill Lower School
DUN/WHIP LU6 ...... 60 E1
Ardmore House Hotel
STAL AL1 ...... 9 J1
Arianne Business Centre
LTNE LU2 ...... 60 E4
Arkley Golf Club
BAR EN5 ...... 165 M4
Arlesey FC
ARL/CHE SG15 ...... 24 E4
Arndale Shopping Centre
LTN LU1 ...... 6 E4
Arnett Hills
Primary School
RKW/CH/CXG WD3 ...... 160 E5
Arnold Middle School
AMP/FLIT/BLC MK45 ...... 32 E6

The Arthur Findlay
College
STSD CM24 ...... 59 H6
The Arts Educational School
TRING HP23 ...... 96 A9
Ascot Business Centre
LTN LU1 ...... 6 C5
Ascot Industrial Estate
LWTH SG6 ...... 36 E1
Ashcroft High School
LTNE LU2 ...... 63 K4
Asheridge Road
Industrial Estate
CSHM HP5 ...... 130 D7
Ashfield Junior School
BUSH WD23 ...... 163 K6
Ash Industrial Estate
HLWW/ROY CM19 ...... 128 C4
Ashley Business Centre
HTCH/STOT SG5 ...... 35 L8
Ashlyns School
BERK HP4 ...... 115 P9
Ashmole Centre
STHGT/OAK N14 ...... 167 N7
Ashmole School
STHGT/OAK N14 ...... 167 N7
Ashridge Estate (NT)
BERK HP4 ...... 97 K6
Ashridge Estate
Visitor Centre
BERK HP4 ...... 97 K6
Ashridge Golf Club
BERK HP4 ...... 97 N5
Ashridge
Management College
BERK HP4 ...... 97 P7
Ashton CE VA Middle School
DUN/WHIP LU6 ...... 60 E5
Ashton St Peters VA
Lower School
DUN/HR/TOD LU5 ...... 60 F5
Ashtree Primary School
STVGE SG2 ...... 67 M2
Ash Valley Golf Club
MHAD SG10 ...... 72 C8
Ashville Trading Estate
BLDK SG7 ...... 26 B8
Asquith Court School
HARP AL5 ...... 101 N1
Astley Cooper School
HHNE HP2 ...... 118 B3
Aston Clinton School
RAYLNE/WEN HP22 ...... 94 E7
Aston St Marys
Primary School
STVGE SG2 ...... 67 P3
Aycliffe Drive
Primary School
HHNE HP2 ...... 117 P4
Aylands School
PEND EN3 ...... 156 B6
Aylesbury RFC
RAYLNE/WEN HP22 ...... 94 B9
Aylward First & Middle
Schools
STAN HA7 ...... 173 K2
Baldock Cemetery
BLDK SG7 ...... 25 P9
Baldock Health Centre
BLDK SG7 ...... 37 J1
Baldock Industrial Estate
BLDK SG7 ...... 37 J1
Balloon Flights
RAYLNE/WEN HP22 ...... 94 F8
Bancroft Business Centre
HTCH/STOT SG5 ...... 35 L8
Bannister Stadium
KTN/HRWW/WS HA3 ...... 172 C3
Barbara Castle Health Centre
HLWW/ROY CM19 ...... 128 D7
Barclay School
STVG SG1 ...... 50 C7
Barkway CE First School
ROY SG8 ...... 30 A5
Barkway Park Golf Club
ROY SG8 ...... 30 C7
Barley VP First School
ROY SG8 ...... 21 M8
Barncroft JMI School
HHNE HP2 ...... 117 N3
Barnet College
BAR EN5 ...... 166 D3
EBAR EN4 ...... 167 K7
FBAR/BDGN N11 ...... 167 K9
Barnet FC (Underhill)
BAR EN5 ...... 166 D4
Barnet General Hospital
BAR EN5 ...... 166 B3
Barnet Health Centre
BAR EN5 ...... 166 E4
Barnet JMI School
BAR EN5 ...... 166 D4
Barnet Hospital Chest Clinic
BAR EN5 ...... 166 B3
Barnet Museum
BAR EN5 ...... 166 C3
Barnet Trading Estate
BAR EN5 ...... 166 D2
Barnfield College
LTN LU2 ...... 62 C9
LTNE LU2 ...... 62 E1
Barnfield College
Technology Centre
LTNN/LIM LU3 ...... 46 C7
Barn Theatre
WCCW AL8 ...... 104 F6
Barnwell School
STVGE SG2 ...... 67 L4
Barratt Industrial Park
LTNE LU2 ...... 63 K8
Barratt Way
Industrial Estate
RYLN/HDSTN HA2 ...... 172 D7
Barton Hills
National Nature Reserve
AMP/FLIT/BLC MK45 ...... 32 E6
Barton Industrial Estate
AMP/FLIT/BLC MK45 ...... 32 B4
Barton Rovers FC
AMP/FLIT/BLC MK45 ...... 32 D6

Batchwood Golf Club
STALW/RED AL3 ...... 120 A5
Batchwood School
STALW/RED AL3 ...... 120 C5
Bayford Primary School
HERT/BAY SG13 ...... 124 C6
Bayhurst Wood
Country Park
DEN/HRF UB9 ...... 170 B9
The Beacon School
AMS HP6 ...... 144 C5
Beales Hotel
HAT AL10 ...... 122 B5
Beaumont School
STALE/WH AL4 ...... 121 J7
The Bedford Arms Hotel
RKW/CH/CXG WD3 ...... 146 E8
Bedmond JMI School
ABLGY WD5 ...... 134 G7
Bedwell Community Centre
STVG SG1 ...... 11 H5
Bedwell Medical Centre
STVG SG1 ...... 11 J4
Bedwell Primary School
STVG SG1 ...... 11 J3
Beechfield JMI School
WATN WD24 ...... 149 H7
Beech Hill Community
Primary School
LTNW/LEA LU4 ...... 62 C5
Beech Hyde Primary School
STALW/RED AL3 ...... 103 J5
Beechwood Park School
STALW/RED AL3 ...... 99 J3
Beechwood Primary School
LTNW/LEA LU4 ...... 61 P2
Beechcroft Lower School
DUN/WHIP LU6 ...... 60 C5
Belcon Industrial Estate
HOD EN11 ...... 127 H5
Bellgate JMI School
HHNE HP2 ...... 117 P6
Bell Lane Combined School
AMS HP6 ...... 145 N8
Belmont First School
KTN/HRWW/WS HA3 ...... 172 F6
Belmont (Mill Hill
Preparatory School)
MLHL NW7 ...... 165 N9
Belswains Infant School
HHS/BOV HP3 ...... 134 A3
Bengeo Primary School
HERT/WAT SG14 ...... 107 K3
Benington Lordship
STVGE SG2 ...... 68 E2
Benington Primary School
STVGE SG2 ...... 68 E2
Bentfield Primary School
STSD CM24 ...... 58 E3
Bentley Wood Girls School
STAN HA7 ...... 172 F2
Berkeley Clinic
RKW/CH/CXG WD3 ...... 160 C1
Berkhamsted Castle
(Remains)
BERK HP4 ...... 116 A6
Berkhamsted Collegiate
Preparatory School
BERK HP4 ...... 115 N7
Berkhamsted Collegiate
School (Castle Campus)
BERK HP4 ...... 115 P7
Berkhamsted FC
BERK HP4 ...... 115 N5
Berkhamsted Golf Club
BERK HP4 ...... 116 B4
Berkhamsted Health Centre
BERK HP4 ...... 115 M6
Berkhamsted School House
BERK HP4 ...... 115 P7
Berkhamsted Tennis Club
BERK HP4 ...... 115 P6
Bernards Heath
Infant School
STAL AL1 ...... 120 E6
Bernards Heath
Junior School
STALW/RED AL3 ...... 120 D5
Berrygrove Primary School
GSTN WD25 ...... 149 L5
Best Western
Homestead Court Hotel
WCCE AL7 ...... 105 J8
Best Western
Stansted Manor Hotel
BSF CM23 ...... 74 E1
Best Western
the Roebuck Inn
BROX EN10 ...... 67 J5
Best Western
the Watermill Hotel
HHW HP1 ...... 132 F1
Best Western
White House Hotel
WATW WD18 ...... 12 E4
Beta Health Clinic
HHNE HP2 ...... 4 E1
Bigham's Park Farm
HHW HP1 ...... 117 H3
Birchanger CE
Primary School
BSF CM23 ...... 58 E8
Birchanger Industrial Estate
BSF CM23 ...... 58 B9
Bircherley Green
Shopping Centre
HERT/WAT SG14 ...... 107 L6
Birchwood Avenue
Primary School
HAT AL10 ...... 122 D4
Birchwood High School
BSF CM23 ...... 74 D2
Birchwood Industrial Area
BRKMPK AL9 ...... 122 F3
Birchwood Leisure Centre
HAT AL10 ...... 122 E3
Bishops Hatfield Girls School
HAT AL10 ...... 122 D6
Bishop's Park Health Centre
BSF CM23 ...... 74 A2

Bishops Stortford
Business Centre
BSF CM23 ...... 74 B4
Bishops Stortford College
BSF CM23 ...... 73 P7
Bishop's Stortford Golf Club
BSF CM23 ...... 74 E3
The Bishops Stortford
High School
BSF CM23 ...... 74 A6
Bishop's Stortford RFC
BSF CM23 ...... 73 N5
Bishops Wood Hospital
NTHWD HA6 ...... 170 D3
Bishop Wood School
EDGW HA8 ...... 95 P9
Blood Transfusion Centre
EDGW HA8 ...... 173 P4
Blue Gold Trading Centre
ARL/CHE SG15 ...... 24 E4
The Bobsleigh Hotel
HHS/BOV HP3 ...... 132 E5
Bondor Business Centre
BLDK SG7 ...... 37 H1
Bonny Grove SPLD Base
CHESW EN7 ...... 141 P9
Borehamwood FC
BORE WD6 ...... 165 H1
Borehamwood
Industrial Park
BORE WD6 ...... 165 K1
The Borough
Industrial Estate
LTNN/LIM LU3 ...... 62 B3
Botany Bay CC
ENC/FH EN2 ...... 154 E6
Boulevard 25 Retail Park
BORE WD6 ...... 164 C2
Bournehall J & I School
BUSH WD23 ...... 163 J4
Bovingdon Primary School
HHS/BOV HP3 ...... 132 B6
Bowmans Trading Estate
STVG SG1 ...... 66 E1
Bowman Trading Estate
CDALE/KGS NW9 ...... 173 N7
Boxmoor Golf Club
HHS/BOV HP3 ...... 133 H3
Boxmoor Primary School
HHW HP1 ...... 117 K9
Bramingham
Business Park
LTNN/LIM LU3 ...... 46 C7
Bramingham Park
Medical Centre
LTNN/LIM LU3 ...... 46 B7
Bramingham Park
Study Centre
LTNN/LIM LU3 ...... 46 C7
Bramingham
Primary School
LTNN/LIM LU3 ...... 46 C6
Brandles School
BLDK SG7 ...... 37 H1
Brays Grove School
HLWS CM18 ...... 129 L5
Breachwood Green
JMI School
HTCHE/RSTV SG4 ...... 64 D5
Breakspear Crematorium
RSLP HA4 ...... 170 E9
Breakspeare School
ABLGY WD5 ...... 148 F1
Brickendon Orange Golf Club
HERT/BAY SG13 ...... 125 J7
Bricket Wood Sports Centre
LCOL/BKTW AL2 ...... 150 A1
Brickfields Industrial Estate
HHNE HP2 ...... 118 C4
Bridgegate Business Centre
WGCE AL7 ...... 105 J5
Bridgewater Monument
BERK HP4 ...... 97 K5
Bridgewater School
BERK HP4 ...... 115 M5
Britannia Business Centre
CHES/WCR EN8 ...... 156 K9
Brittania Business Park
CHES/WCR EN8 ...... 156 E4
Broadfield JMI School
HHNE HP2 ...... 5 J1
Broadfields Primary School
EDGW HA8 ...... 164 G8
HLW CM20 ...... 3 H4
Broadmead School
LTN LU1 ...... 62 F9
Broadwalk
Shopping Centre
EDGW HA8 ...... 173 N3
Broadway Clinic
EDGW HA8 ...... 173 P5
Brockswood Primary School
HHNE HP2 ...... 118 D2
Bromet Primary School
OXHEY WD19 ...... 162 F6
Brookfield Retail Park
CHES/WCR EN8 ...... 142 C6
Brookland J & I School
CHES/WCR EN8 ...... 142 D7
Brookmans Park Golf Club
BRKMPK AL9 ...... 139 K4
Brookmans Park
Primary School
BRKMPK AL9 ...... 139 H5
Brookside Business Centre
BSF CM23 ...... 74 A9
Broom Barns JMI School
STVG SG1 ...... 11 F6
Broxbourne Business Centre
CHES/WCR EN8 ...... 142 C5
Broxbourne Primary School
BROX EN10 ...... 126 F9
Broxbourne Sailing Club
WAB EN9 ...... 127 J8
The Broxbourne School
BROX EN10 ...... 142 D1

Broxbourne Sports Club
BROX EN10 ...... 126 E9
Broxbourne Wood
National Nature Reserve
BROX EN10 ...... 125 L8
Brunswick Health Centre
FBAR/BDGN N11 ...... 167 L8
Brunswick Park JMI School
STHGT/OAK N14 ...... 167 L7
Brushwood Junior School
CSHM HP5 ...... 131 N8
Bucks Chilterns
University College
CSTG HP8 ...... 159 N8
The Bull Theatre
BAR EN5 ...... 166 D3
Buncefield Oil Refinery
HHNE HP2 ...... 118 E5
Burleigh Primary School
CHES/WCR EN8 ...... 142 C9
Burntmill Industrial Estate
HLW CM20 ...... 110 F9
Burnt Mill School
HLW CM20 ...... 3 H1
Bushey Golf & Country Club
BUSH WD23 ...... 163 J5
Bushey Grove Leisure Centre
BUSH WD23 ...... 163 H3
Bushey Hall Golf Club
BUSH WD23 ...... 162 G2
Bushey Hall School
BUSH WD23 ...... 163 H3
Bushey Health Centre
BUSH WD23 ...... 163 H4
Bushey Heath
Primary School
BUSH WD23 ...... 163 N1
Bushey Jewish Cemetery
BUSH WD23 ...... 163 K2
Bushey Manor
Junior School
BUSH WD23 ...... 163 H4
Bushey Meads School
BUSH WD23 ...... 163 L4
Bushey Museum &
Art Gallery
BUSH WD23 ...... 163 J5
Bushey & Oxhey
Infant School
BUSH WD23 ...... 162 G4
Bush Hall Hotel
BRKMPK AL9 ...... 122 G3
Bushmead Primary School
LTNE LU2 ...... 62 F1
Business Aviation Terminal
STSD CM24 ...... 59 J9
The Business Centre
LTNE LU2 ...... 7 H1
Business & Technology
Centre
STVG SG1 ...... 66 E1
Byfleet Industrial Estate
WATW WD18 ...... 161 N7
Caddington Sports Club
LTN LU1 ...... 80 A2
Calcot Medical Centre
CFSP/GDCR SL9 ...... 168 B5
Camp Industrial Estate
STAL AL1 ...... 120 C6
Camps Hill Community
Primary School
STVGE SG2 ...... 51 L9
Campus West Cinema
WGCW AL8 ...... 104 G5
Campus West Leisure Centre
WGCW AL8 ...... 104 F5
Canary Club FC
HTCH/STOT SG5 ...... 35 K8
Canons Brook Golf Club
HLWW/ROY CM19 ...... 128 D2
Canons High School
EDGW HA8 ...... 173 M6
Capel Manor College
EN EN1 ...... 156 A5
Capital Business Centre
WATN WD24 ...... 149 L6
Cardiff Road
Industrial Estate
WATW WD18 ...... 162 D5
Cardinal Newman Catholic
Secondary School
LTNN/LIM LU3 ...... 46 D6
Carpenders Park
Cemetery
OXHEY WD19 ...... 171 P1
Carterhatch Infant School
EN EN1 ...... 156 A9
Caryl Thomas Clinic
HRW HA1 ...... 172 E8
Cassiobury J & I Schools
WAT WD17 ...... 148 F9
Castle Hall Theatre &
Civic Centre
HERT/WAT SG14 ...... 107 K6
Castle Montessori School
BERK HP4 ...... 116 A7
Cathedral & Abbey Church
of St Alban
STAL AL1 ...... 8 D4
Cattle Market
TRING HP23 ...... 96 A8
The Causeway
Business Centre
BSF CM23 ...... 74 A3
The Cavendish School
HHW HP1 ...... 117 L7
Cecil Park Clinic
PIN HA5 ...... 171 N8
Cedars Manor School
KTN/HRWW/WS HA3 ...... 172 C5
Central Primary School
WAT WD17 ...... 13 H4
Chace Community School
EN EN1 ...... 155 M9
Chadwell Springs Golf Club
WARE SG12 ...... 108 B4
Chalfont Leisure Centre
CFSP/GDCR SL9 ...... 168 A5

Chalfont St Giles
Infant School
CSTG HP8 .... 159 H9
Chalfont St Giles
Junior School
CSTG HP8 .... 159 H9
Chalfont St Peter FC
CFSP/GDCR SL9 .... 168 B4
Chalfont St Peter
Infant School
CFSP/GDCR SL9 .... 168 A4
Chalfont St Peter
Junior School
CFSP/GDCR SL9 .... 168 B4
The Chalfonts
Community College
CFSP/GDCR SL9 .... 168 A4
Chalfonts & Gerrards Cross
Health Clinic
CFSP/GDCR SL9 .... 168 B5
Chalgrave Manor Golf Club
DUN/HR/TOD LU5 .... 44 D5
Challney High School for
Boys & Community College
LTNW/LEA LU4 .... 61 M3
Challney High School
for Girls
LTNW/LEA LU4 .... 61 M4
Chalton Lower School
LTNW/LEA LU4 .... 45 H6
Chambersbury JMI School
HHS/BOV HP3 .... 134 C2
Chancellors School
BRKMPK AL9 .... 139 K4
Chantry J & I School
LTNW/LEA LU4 .... 61 J2
Chartridge Combined School
CSHM HP5 .... 130 B6
Chartridge Park Golf Club
CSHM HP5 .... 130 C7
Chase Farm Hospital
ENC/FH EN2 .... 155 H6
Chater Infant School
WATW WD18 .... 12 C5
Chater Junior School
WATW WD18 .... 12 C5
Chaulden Infant School
HHW HP1 .... 117 H9
Chaulden Junior School
HHW HP1 .... 117 J9
The Chauncy School
WARE SG12 .... 108 A2
Cheddington
Combined School
LBUZ LU7 .... 77 P6
Chenies CC
RKW/CH/CXG WD3 ...... 146 F9
Chenies Combined School
RKW/CH/CXG WD3 ...... 146 F9
Chenies Manor House
RKW/CH/CXG WD3 ...... 146 E8
Cherry Tree Primary School
WATN WD24 .... 149 H6
Chesfield Downs Golf Club
HTCHE/RSTV SG4 .... 36 G9
Chesham Bois CE
Combined School
AMS HP6 .... 145 K5
Chesham Cemetery
CSHM HP5 .... 130 C9
Chesham
Community Hospital
CSHM HP5 .... 145 J1
Chesham Health Centre
CSHM HP5 .... 144 C2
Chesham High School
CSHM HP5 .... 131 J9
Chesham Leisure Centre
CSHM HP5 .... 145 J1
Chesham & Ley Hill Golf Club
CSHM HP5 .... 145 P1
Chesham Park
Community College
CSHM HP5 .... 130 F9
Chesham
Preparatory School
CSHM HP5 .... 131 M6
Chesham United FC
CSHM HP5 .... 144 G3
Cheshunt Cemetery
CHESW EN7 .... 155 P1
Cheshunt
Community Hospital
CHES/WCR EN8 .... 156 D1
Cheshunt FC
CHES/WCR EN8 .... 156 B2
Cheshunt Marriott Hotel
BROX EN10 .... 142 C5
Cheshunt Park Golf Club
CHESW EN7 .... 142 A6
Cheshunt School
CHESW EN7 .... 142 B9
Chesterfield Primary School
PEND EN3 .... 156 D7
Chestnut Lane First School
AMS HP6 .... 145 K6
Cheynes Infant School
LTNW/LEA LU4 .... 45 N7
Chiltern FM
DUN/WHIP LU6 .... 60 D5
Chiltern Forest Golf Club
RAYLNE/WEN HP22 ..... 112 G2
Chiltern Open Air Museum
CSTG HP8 .... 159 N8
Chiltern Park
Industrial Estate
DUN/HR/TOD LU5 .... 60 G4
The Chiltern Pools
CSHM HP5 .... 145 J8
Chishill Windmill
ROY SG8 .... 21 P8
Chorleywood Golf Club
RKW/CH/CXG WD3 ...... 160 B3
Chorleywood Health Centre
RKW/CH/CXG WD3 ...... 160 A3
Chorleywood Lawn
Cemetery
RKW/CH/CXG WD3 ...... 160 D2

Chorleywood
Primary School
RKW/CH/CXG WD3 ...... 160 A5
Chorleywood Road
Cemetery
RKW/CH/CXG WD3 ...... 161 H6
Chrishall Primary School
ROY SG8 .... 22 F7
Christ Church CE
Primary School
BAR EN5 .... 166 B1
RKW/CH/CXG WD3 ...... 160 D3
Christ Church
Primary School
WARE SG12 .... 108 D3
Christopher Place
Shopping Centre
STALW/RED AL3 .... 8 E3
Church Farm
Swimming Pool
STVG SG1 .... 167 K7
Churchgate CE
Primary School
HLWE CM17 .... 111 P9
Churchgate
Shopping Centre
HTCH/STOT SG5 .... 35 K9
Church Hill Infant School
EBAR EN4 .... 167 K6
Church Langley
Primary School
HLWE CM17 .... 129 M3
Church Street
Industrial Estate
WARE SG12 .... 108 C2
Cineworld
BSF CM23 .... 74 A4
HLW CM20 .... 111 J8
LTN LU1 .... 6 D3
STVG SG1 .... 10 B6
Circle Business Centre
DUN/HR/TOD LU5 .... 60 D3
Civic Hall Cinema
HOD EN11 .... 126 E6
Civic Medical Centre
HRW HA1 .... 172 E9
Claggy Road
Industrial Estate
HTCHE/RSTV SG4 .... 83 H3
Claremont High School
KTN/HRWW/WS HA3 ..... 173 L9
Clarklands Industrial Estate
SBW CM21 .... 91 N8
Clavering Primary School
SAFWS CB11 .... 43 M4
Clore Shalom School
RAD WD7 .... 137 K9
Coates Way JMI School
GSTN WD25 .... 149 M3
Cockernhoe Endowed
Primary School
LTNE LU2 .... 63 N2
Cockfosters Sports Ground
EBAR EN4 .... 167 K2
Codicote Primary School
HTCHE/RSTV SG4 .... 84 B4
Colehill CC
AMSS HP7 .... 158 A4
Coleman Business Centre
HTCHE/RSTV SG4 .... 83 H3
College Lake Wildlife Centre
TRING HP23 .... 96 B3
College of Osteopathy
BORE WD6 .... 165 H2
Collenswood School
STVGE SG2 .... 67 M2
Collett Special School
HHW HP1 .... 117 M7
The Collingwood Suite
Conference Centre
WCCW AL8 .... 104 F8
Colnbrook School
OXHEY WD19 .... 162 E8
Colne Bridge Retail Park
WAT WD17 .... 13 K7
Colne Valley Retail Park
WAT WD17 .... 13 K6
Colney Fields
Shopping Park
LCOL/BKTW AL2 .... 137 L7
Colney Heath JMI School
STALE/WH AL4 .... 137 P1
Colonial Business Park
WATN WD24 .... 149 K9
Commonswood School
HLWS CM18 .... 129 J7
Commonside School
WCCE AL7 .... 105 L9
Commonwealth College
LTN LU1 .... 104 B3
Community Care Centre
ENC/FH EN2 .... 155 L9
Community Leisure Centre
HLW CM20 .... 3 F5
Community Mental
Health Centre
GSTN WD25 .... 149 K4
Corinium Industrial Estate
AMS HP6 .... 145 L8
Corn Exchange
HERT/WAT SG14 .... 107 L3
Corus Hotel
BORE WD6 .... 164 E6
Coteford Infant School
PIN HA5 .... 171 J9
Cotswold Business Park
LTN LU1 .... 79 N3
Cotton Brown Park
LWTH SG6 .... 36 C1
Countess Anne
Primary School
HAT AL10 .... 122 H4
Courtland JMI School
MLHL NW7 .... 165 L4
Covered Market
STVG SG1 .... 10 D5
Cowley Hill Primary School
BORE WD6 .... 151 N9
CP House Business Centre
BUSH WD23 .... 149 N9

Crabtree Junior School
HARP AL5 .... 102 B3
Cranborne Industrial Estate
POTB/CUF EN6 .... 139 H9
Cranborne Primary School
POTB/CUF EN6 .... 153 H1
Cranbourne JMI School
HOD EN11 .... 126 C2
Crawley Green Infant School
LTNE LU2 .... 63 J6
Creswick Primary School
WGCE AL7 .... 104 C9
Crews Hill Golf Club
ENC/FH EN2 .... 154 C4
Cromer Road
Primary School
BAR EN5 .... 166 F2
Cromwell Hotel
STVG SG1 .... 50 F7
Cromwell Medical Centre
CHESW EN7 .... 142 A9
Crown Business Estate
AMS HP6 .... 131 H9
The Crown Hotel
AMS HP7 .... 158 B1
Crown Lane Clinic
STHGT/OAK N14 .... 167 N7
Crown Prosecution Service
STAL AL1 .... 9 F4
Cuffley School
POTB/CUF EN6 .... 140 C9
Cunningham Hill J & I School
STAL AL1 .... 136 F1
Dacorum Athletics Track
HHNE HP2 .... 5 J5
Dacorum Education
Support Centre
HHNE HP2 .... 118 B8
Dacre Industrial Estate
CHES/WCR EN8 .... 148 E8
Dallow Junior School
LTN LU1 .... 6 B3
Dallow Primary School
LTN LU1 .... 6 A3
Dalroad Industrial Estate
LTN LU1 .... 62 C6
Dame Alice Owens School
POTB/CUF EN6 .... 153 H3
Danegrove Primary School
EBAR EN4 .... 167 J5
Days Hotel
LTN LU1 .... 6 D5
MLHL NW7 .... 165 J8
Days Inn
BSF CM23 .... 74 F2
POTB/CUF EN6 .... 152 F4
De Bohun Primary School
STHGT/OAK N14 .... 167 M4
De Havilland Aircraft
Heritage Centre &
Mosquito Aircraft
Museum
LCOL/BKTW AL2 .... 137 N8
De Havilland Primary School
HAT AL10 .... 122 D8
Delrow School
GSTN WD25 .... 150 B9
Denbigh High School
LTNN/LIM LU3 .... 62 D4
Denbigh Junior School
LTNN/LIM LU3 .... 62 C4
Denham Aerodrome
DEN/HRF UB9 .... 169 J9
De Vere
Theobalds Park Hotel
CHESW EN7 .... 155 P3
Dewhurst St Mary
JMI School
CHES/WCR EN8 .... 142 A8
Diamond Industrial Centre
LWTH SG6 .... 36 F1
Divine Saviour RC
Primary School
ABLGY WD5 .... 148 E2
Downfield
Primary School
CHES/WCR EN8 .... 156 D1
Downside Junior School
LTNW/LEA LU4 .... 61 P5
Downside Lower School
DUN/HR/TOD LU5 .... 61 H7
The Downs Primary School
LTNW/LEA LU4 .... 3 F5
Dr Challoners
Grammar School
AMS HP6 .... 145 H8
Dr Challoners High School
AMS HP7 .... 159 H1
Driving School &
Road Safety Centre
KTN/HRWW/WS HA3 .... 172 C2
The Drizen School
EDGW HA8 .... 173 N4
Dukeminster
Trading Estate
DUN/HR/TOD LU5 .... 60 F5
Dunlmore School
HERF/WAT SG14 .... 107 K5
Dundale JM School
TRING HP23 .... 95 P7
Dundale Primary School
TRING HP23 .... 95 P7
Dunstable Cemetery
DUN/WHIP LU6 .... 60 D7
Dunstable Downs
Country Park
DUN/WHIP LU6 .... 78 C1
Dunstable Downs Golf Club
DUN/WHIP LU6 .... 60 C9
Dunstable FC
DUN/WHIP LU6 .... 60 C4
Dunstable Health Centre
DUN/WHIP LU6 .... 60 C4
Dunstable Icknield
Lower School
DUN/WHIP LU6 .... 60 E6
Dunstable Leisure Centre
DUN/WHIP LU6 .... 60 D6
Dunstable Road
Infant School
LTN LU1 .... 6 B3
Dunstable Town Bowls Club
DUN/WHIP LU6 .... 60 F7
Dunstablians RUFC
DUN/HR/TOD LU5 .... 44 D9
Durants School
PEND EN3 .... 156 B9
East Barnet Health Centre
EBAR EN4 .... 167 H4
East Barnet School
EBAR EN4 .... 167 K5
Eastbrook Primary School
HHNE HP2 .... 118 A3
Eastbury Farm JMI School
NTHWD HA6 .... 171 H1
Eastcote CC
PIN HA5 .... 171 K9
Eastern Avenue
Industrial Estate
DUN/HR/TOD LU5 .... 60 G6
Eastfield Primary School
CHES/WCR EN8 .... 156 C8
East Herts Golf Club
BUNT SG9 .... 70 G1
Edge Grove
GSTN WD25 .... 150 B7
Edgwarebury Cemetery
EDGW HA8 .... 164 G8
Edgware Clinic
EDGW HA8 .... 173 N3
Edgware Community
Hospital
EDGW HA8 .... 173 P4
Edgware & Kingsbury FC
EDGW HA8 .... 173 N4
Edgware Infant School
EDGW HA8 .... 173 N3
Edgware Junior School
EDGW HA8 .... 173 P3
Edwinstree School
BUNT SG9 .... 40 C8
Egerton Rothesay
Preparatory School
BERK HP4 .... 115 N7
Egerton Rothesay School
BERK HP4 .... 115 L7
Elangeni Junior School
AMS HP6 .... 145 K6
Eleanor Estate
CHES/WCR EN8 .... 156 E4
Ellen Mede School
TRDG/WHET N20 .... 166 B7
Elliswick Lawn Tennis Club
HARP AL5 .... 102 A2
Elmgrove Middle School
KTN/HRWW/WS HA3 .... 172 C8
The Elms Health Centre
POTB/CUF EN6 .... 153 M1
Elmtree Infant School
CSHM HP5 .... 130 C9
Elsenham Primary School
RBSF CM22 .... 59 L2
Elstree Aerodrome
BORE WD6 .... 163 P2
Elstree Golf & Country Club
BORE WD6 .... 164 D2
Elstree Studios
BORE WD6 .... 164 C2
Elstree Way Clinic
BORE WD6 .... 165 H1
Enfield Chace
Lower School
ENC/FH EN2 .... 155 M8
Enfield Crematorium
EN EN1 .... 156 A7
Epping Forest
Conservation Centre
LOU IC10 .... 157 P8
Epping Forest
District Museum
WAB EN9 .... 157 H3
Epping House School
HERT/BAY SG13 .... 124 D9
Ermine Point Business Park
WARE SG12 .... 88 A9
Essendon Primary School
BRKMPK AL9 .... 124 A5
Everest Sports Club
CHES/WCR EN8 .... 142 A8
Eversley School
SBW CM21 .... 111 N2
Executive Park
Industrial Estate
STAL AL1 .... 120 G8
Express by Holiday Inn
HHS/BOV HP3 .... 133 P4
STALW/RED AL3 .... 100 C2
Fairbrook Medical Centre
BORE WD6 .... 165 H1
Fairfield Hospital
HTCH/STOT SG5 .... 24 G7
Fair Field Junior School
RAD WD7 .... 150 D6
Fairlands Primary School
STVG SG1 .... 10 D1
Fairview Industrial Estate
AMS HP6 .... 145 L8
Fairway Primary School
MLHL NW7 .... 165 K8
Falconer Special School
BUSH WD23 .... 163 H4
Family Leisure Centre
LTN LU1 .... 6 D3
Farley Junior School
LTN LU1 .... 62 D9
Farnham CE Primary School
BSF CM23 .... 57 N9
Fawbert & Barnard
Infant School
SBW CM21 .... 111 P2
Fawbert & Barnards
(UNDL) Primary School
HLWE CM17 .... 111 M9

Fearnhill School
LWTH SG6 .... 35 P3
Fearnhill Sports Centre
LWTH SG6 .... 35 P3
Featherstone Wood
Primary School
STVGE SG2 .... 67 M3
Ferrars & I School
LTNW/LEA LU4 .... 61 L3
Fiddlebridge
Industrial Centre
HAT AL10 .... 122 D5
Field Infant School
WATW WD18 .... 13 H6
Field Junior School
WATW WD18 .... 13 H6
Finchley Catholic
High School
NFNCH/WDSPK N12 .... 166 G9
Firbank Industrial Estate
LTN LU1 .... 62 B6
Firs Hotel
HTCH/STOT SG5 .... 35 J8
First Garden City
Heritage Museum
LWTH SG6 .... 36 D3
Fisher Industrial Estate
WATW WD18 .... 13 G7
Five Oaks Middle School
LTN LU1 .... 80 A1
Flamstead End
Primary School
CHESW EN7 .... 141 P6
Flamstead JMI School
STALW/RED AL3 .... 100 C3
Fleetville Infant School
STAL AL1 .... 120 F8
Fleetville Junior School
STAL AL1 .... 120 F8
Florence Nightingale
Health Centre
HLWE CM17 .... 129 M3
Flowers Industrial Estate
LTN LU1 .... 7 G7
Forres CP School
HOD EN11 .... 126 G2
Forty Hall
ENC/FH EN2 .... 155 N7
Forty Hill CE Primary School
ENC/FH EN2 .... 155 P7
The Forum Retail Park
STVG SG1 .... 10 C4
The Forum
EDGW HA8 .... 173 N3
Forum Theatre
HAT AL10 .... 122 C5
Foulds School
BAR EN5 .... 166 B2
Four Swannes
Primary School
CHES/WCR EN8 .... 156 D3
Foxdell Infant School
LTN LU1 .... 62 B6
Foxdell Junior School
LTN LU1 .... 61 P6
Francis Bacon School
STAL AL1 .... 136 C2
Francis Combe School
GSTN WD25 .... 149 K2
Freezywater St Georges
CE Primary School
PEND EN3 .... 156 C6
Freman College
BUNT SG9 .... 40 C8
Frithsden Vineyard
HHW HP1 .... 116 E3
Frithwood Primary School
NTHWD HA6 .... 171 H3
Frogmore Road
Industrial Estate
HHS/BOV HP3 .... 133 N2
Furneux Pelham CE
JMI School
BUNT SG9 .... 56 D3
Furze Field Leisure Centre
POTB/CUF EN6 .... 153 H1
Furzehill School
BORE WD6 .... 164 G3
Gaddesden Row CP School
HHW HP1 .... 99 M5
Gade Valley JMI School
HHW HP1 .... 117 J2
Galaxy Leisure Centre
LTN LU1 .... 6 D3
Galleria Shopping Centre
HAT AL10 .... 122 C6
Garden Court
Business Centre
WCCE AL7 .... 105 J6
Garden Fields JMI School
STALW/RED AL3 .... 120 C5
Garden of Rest Cemetery
CFSP/GDCR SL9 .... 168 D4
Gardens of the Rose
(Royal National Rose)
LCOL/BKTW AL2 .... 135 N5
Garston Clinic
WATN WD24 .... 149 J3
Garston JMI School
GSTN WD25 .... 149 L3
Garston Manor
Special School
GSTN WD25 .... 149 K2
Garston Medical Centre
GSTN WD25 .... 149 K6
Gayhurst School
CFSP/GDCR SL9 .... 168 A8
Gazelda Industrial Estate
WAT WD17 .... 13 J6
George Street
Primary School
LTN LU1 .... 117 N7
Gerrards Cross Golf Club
CFSP/GDCR SL9 .... 168 D7
The Giles Infant School
STVG SG1 .... 51 J6
Glebe First & Middle School
KTN/HRWW/WS HA3 .... 173 K8
Glenwood School
DUN/WHIP LU6 .... 61 H9

Go Bowling
DUN/HR/TOD LU5 ....60 E5
Goffs Oak JMI School
CHESW EN7 ....141 J7
Goffs School
CHESW EN7 ....141 P8
Goldfield Infant School
TRING HP23 ....95 N9
Gooseberry Hill
Health Centre
LTNN/LIM LU3 ....46 C8
Gordon Craig Theatre
STVG SG1 ....10 B5
Gorhambury (Remains)
STALW/RED AL3 ....119 J7
Gosling Ski & Board Centre
WGCW AL8 ....104 F9
Gosling Sports Park
WGCW AL8 ....104 F9
Gothic Mede Lower School
ARL/CHE SG15 ....24 C3
Grange Junior School
LWTH SG6 ....25 K7
Grange Paddocks
Pool & Gym
BSF CM23 ....74 A1
Grangewood School
PIN HA5 ....171 J9
Grasvenor Avenue
Infant School
BAR EN5 ....166 E5
Graveley Primary School
HTCHE/RSTV SG4 ....50 E3
Great Gaddesden JMI School
HHW HP1 ....98 C9
Great Hadham Golf &
Country Club
MHAD SG10 ....90 G1
Greatham Road
Industrial Estate
BUSH WD23 ....162 G3
Great House Country Park
POTB/CUF EN6 ....140 B5
Grebe House Wildlife
Centre & Gardens
STALW/RED AL3 ....8 A4
Green End Business Centre
RKW/CH/CXG WD3 ....147 K7
Greenfield Primary School
OXHEY WD19 ....171 L2
Greenhill College
HRW HA1 ....172 F9
The Greenhouse
Health Centre
LTN LU1 ....6 C3
Green Lane Industrial Estate
LWTH SG6 ....36 E1
Green Lanes Primary School
HAT AL10 ....122 C2
The Green Man Hotel
HLWE CM17 ....111 N8
Greenside Special School
STVGE SG2 ....67 K4
Greenway First School
BERK HP4 ....115 L7
Greenwood Park
Leisure Centre
LCOL/BKTW AL2 ....136 A4
Greneway Middle School
ROY SG8 ....20 D3
Griffin Golf Club
LTN LU1 ....61 N8
Grimsdyke First &
Middle School
PIN HA5 ....171 P3
Grim's Dyke Golf Club
PIN HA5 ....172 A2
Grim's Dyke Hotel
KTN/HRWW/WS HA3 ....172 C1
Grovehill Medical Centre
HHNE HP2 ....118 A4
The Grove Hotel
RKW/CH/CXG WD3 ....148 D7
The Grove Infant School
HARP AL5 ....102 C4
The Grove Junior School
HARP AL5 ....102 C4
Grovelands
Business Centre
HHNE HP2 ....118 D6
Grove Road Primary School
TRING HP23 ....96 A7
Grove Theatre
DUN/WHIP LU6 ....60 E5
Grundy Park Leisure Centre
CHES/WCR EN8 ....142 D9
The Gryphon
Industrial Park
STALW/RED AL3 ....120 E4
Guardian Industrial Estate
LTN LU1 ....6 A3
Guilden Morden Cemetery
ROY SG8 ....15 M6
Guilden Morden CE
Primary School
ROY SG8 ....15 L6
Gunnels Wood
Industrial Estate
STVG SG1 ....66 F3
Gunpowder Park
WAB EN9 ....157 H6
Haberdasher Askes
Pre Preparatory School
LCOL/BKTW AL2 ....136 A7
The Haberdashers Askes
School
BORE WD6 ....164 B2
Haberdashers RUFC
BORE WD6 ....164 F1
Hadley Wood Golf Club
EBAR EN4 ....153 P9
Hadley Wood
Primary School
EBAR EN4 ....153 M8
Hadrian Lower School
DUN/HR/TOD LU5 ....61 H4
Haileybury College
HERT/BAY SG13 ....126 C1
Haileybury College Track
HERT/BAY SG13 ....126 C1

Hailey Hall Special School
HERT/BAY SG13 ....126 E1
The Hall Pre Preparatory
School
NTHWD HA6 ....170 F5
Halton Camp
RAYLNE/WEN HP22 ....112 F4
Halton Combined School
RAYLNE/WEN HP22 ....112 E4
Halyard High School
LTNW/LEA LU4 ....61 J3
The Hammond JMI School
HHNE HP2 ....118 A4
Haperbury Hospital
RAD WD7 ....151 H1
Happy Valley
Industrial Estate
KGLGY WD4 ....134 C7
The Harefield Academy
DEN/HRF UB9 ....169 P5
Harefield CC
DEN/HRF UB9 ....169 N6
Harefield Health Centre
DEN/HRF UB9 ....169 N5
Harefield Hospital
DEN/HRF UB9 ....169 N5
Harefield Infant School
DEN/HRF UB9 ....169 M6
Harefield Junior School
DEN/HRF UB9 ....169 N5
Harefield Road
Industrial Estate
RKW/CH/CXG WD3 ....170 A1
Haresfoot School
BERK HP4 ....131 N1
Haresfoot Senior School
BERK HP4 ....116 D5
Hare Street Primary School
HLWW/ROY CM19 ....2 C6
Harewood Down Golf Club
CSTG HP8 ....159 H5
Harkness Industrial Estate
BORE WD6 ....164 C3
The Harlequin
Shopping Centre
WAT WD17 ....13 G4
Harlowbury Primary School
HLWE CM17 ....111 N8
Harlow Business Park
HLWW/ROY CM19 ....128 B3
Harlow College
HLW CM20 ....2 E6
Harlow College
Recreation Centre
HLW CM20 ....3 C4
Harrow Museum
(Passmores House)
HLWS CM18 ....128 C4
Harlow RFC
HLW CM20 ....2 B1
Harlyn Primary School
PIN HA5 ....171 K7
Harpenden Common
Golf Club
HARP AL5 ....102 A6
Harpenden Golf Club
HARP AL5 ....101 N7
Harpenden Health Centre
HARP AL5 ....101 P7
Harpenden Hospital
HARP AL5 ....81 P9
Harpenden House Hotel
HARP AL5 ....102 A4
Harpenden Memorial
Hospital
HARP AL5 ....102 A2
Harpenden RUFC
HARP AL5 ....101 M6
Harpenden Sports Centre
HARP AL5 ....101 P5
Harpenden Swimming Pool
HARP AL5 ....101 P5
Harrow Arts Centre
PIN HA5 ....172 A4
Harrow College
KTN/HRWW/WS HA3 ....172 E3
Harrow Crown Courts
HRW HA1 ....172 D7
Harrow Heritage Museum
RPLN/HDSTN HA2 ....172 C7
Harrow Leisure Centre
KTN/HRWW/WS HA3 ....172 F7
Harrow RFC
HA7 HA7 ....164 B9
Harrow Weald Cemetery
KTN/HRWW/WS HA3 ....172 E3
Hartham Pool
HERT/WAT SG14 ....107 L5
Hart Hill Primary School
LTNE LU2 ....7 H7
Hartsbourne
Primary School
BUSH WD23 ....163 M8
Hartsfield Primary School
BLDK SG7 ....26 B3
Hartspring Industrial Park
BUSH WD23 ....163 J1
Hartspring Sports Centre
BUSH WD23 ....163 J1
Harvey Centre
HLW CM20 ....2 E5
Harvey Road
Primary School
RKW/CH/CXG WD3 ....161 L5
Harwood Hill JMI School
WGCE AL7 ....105 H2
Harwood Park
Crematorium
STVGE SG2 ....67 M8
Haslemere Industrial Estate
BSF CM23 ....74 B6
HLWW/ROY CM19 ....128 C3
WGCE AL7 ....105 J5
Haste Hill Golf Club
NTHWD HA6 ....170 G6
Hastingwood
Business Centre
HLWE CM17 ....129 M5

Hatch End High School
KTN/HRWW/WS HA3 ....172 B4
Hatch End Swimming Pool
PIN HA5 ....172 A4
Hatfield Business Park
ROY SG8 ....122 B6
Hatfield Forest (NT)
RBSF CM22 ....75 M5
Hatfield Forest National
Nature Reserve
RBSF CM22 ....75 L5
Hatfield Heath
Primary School
RBSF CM22 ....93 H6
Hatfield House, Park
& Gardens
BRKMPK AL9 ....122 G6
Hatfield Lawn Tennis Club
BRKMPK AL9 ....122 G6
Hatfield Leisure Centre
HAT AL10 ....122 E8
Hatfield London
Country Club
BRKMPK AL9 ....124 A7
Hatfield Road Cemetery
STAL AL1 ....120 F8
Hatfield Swim Centre
HAT AL10 ....122 D5
Hawridge & Cholesbury
CE Comb School
CSHM HP5 ....114 D9
Hawthorn Park
Lower School
DUN/HR/TOD LU5 ....44 G9
Haydon School
PIN HA5 ....171 H7
Haywood Grove School
HHNE HP2 ....118 B4
Heathcote School
STVGE SG2 ....67 K4
Heatherton House School
AMS HP6 ....145 H6
Heathfield Lower School
LTN LU1 ....79 P7
Heathlands Special School
STALW/RED AL3 ....120 D5
Heath Lane Cemetery
HHW HP1 ....4 C3
Heath Mount
Pre Preparatory School
HERT/WAT SG14 ....87 J3
Hemel Hempstead
(Camelot) RFC
HHW HP1 ....133 J1
Hemel Hempstead
General Hospital
HHNE HP2 ....5 F3
Hemel Hempstead RLFC
HHNE HP2 ....118 A5
Hemel Hempstead
Silver Blades Ice Rink
HHW HP1 ....5 K4
Hemel Hempstead
Sports Centre
HHW HP1 ....4 C5
Hemel Hempstead Town CC
HHW HP1 ....4 D6
Hemel Hempstead United FC
HHNE HP2 ....118 C3
Hemel Ski Centre
HHNE HP2 ....5 J5
Hemingrove School
TRING HP23 ....113 K7
Heritage Close
Shopping Centre
STALW/RED AL3 ....8 D4
Heritage House
Special School
CSHM HP5 ....131 J9
Heron Business Centre
LTNN/LIM LU3 ....45 M8
Hertford C&CC Site
HERT/BAY SG13 ....107 N8
Hertford Cemetery
HERT/WAT SG14 ....107 H5
Hertford County Hospital
HERT/WAT SG14 ....107 J6
Hertford Heath
Primary School
HERT/BAY SG13 ....108 A9
Hertford Museum
HERT/WAT SG14 ....107 L6
Hertford Regional College
BROX EN10 ....142 E4
WARE SG12 ....108 C4
Hertford Regional College
(Northgate Centre)
HERT/WAT SG14 ....74 A2
Hertford St Andrew
Primary School
HERT/WAT SG14 ....106 G5
Hertfordshire
Business Centre
LCOL/BKTW AL2 ....137 J5
Hertfordshire
Country Club
WGCE AL7 ....104 F9
Hertfordshire & Essex
Community Hospital
BSF CM23 ....74 D4
Hertford Town FC
HERT/BAY SG13 ....107 J7
Hertingfordbury Cowper
Primary School
HERT/WAT SG14 ....106 D8
Herts & Essex High School
BSF CM23 ....74 C3
Herts County Agricultural
Showground
STALW/RED AL3 ....100 F3
Hertsmere Jewish
Primary School
RAD WD7 ....151 N8
Hertswood School &
Sports Centre
BORE WD6 ....151 P9
Hester House
HLW CM20 ....2 C3

Hexton Primary School
HTCH/STOT SG5 ....33 H7
Heydon Grange Golf &
Country Club
ROY SG8 ....22 A1
High Beech CE
Primary School
LOU IG10 ....157 M9
High Beeches
Primary School
HARP AL5 ....102 C4
High Beech Golf Club
LOU IG10 ....157 N7
Highbridge Retail Park
WAB EN9 ....156 C4
Highbury Infant School
HTCHE/RSTV SG4 ....49 L1
Highfield School
LWTH SG6 ....36 A5
Highgate Montessori School
BAR EN5 ....166 C2
Highover JMI School
HTCHE/RSTV SG4 ....35 P7
High Street Business Park
CHES/WCR EN8 ....156 D2
Hightown
Recreation Centre
LTNE LU2 ....6 E2
Highwayman Hotel
DUN/WHIP LU6 ....60 G8
Highwood Primary School
BUSH WD23 ....149 M9
High Wych Primary School
SBW CM21 ....111 K3
Hillborough Infant School
LTN LU1 ....6 B7
Hillcrest Special School
DUN/HR/TOD LU5 ....61 H5
Hille Business Centre
WATN WD24 ....149 J9
Hill Farm Industrial Estate
GSTN WD25 ....148 C3
Hill Fort
STALE/WH AL4 ....103 L5
Hillgrove Business Park
WAB EN9 ....143 H1
Hillhouse CE
Primary School
WAB EN9 ....157 L3
Hillingdon Borough FC
RSLP HA4 ....170 D9
Hillmead JMI School
BSF CM23 ....74 D1
Hillmead Primary School
BSF CM23 ....73 M7
Hill Shott Infant School
HTCHE/RSTV SG4 ....36 D2
Hillside Infant School
NTHWD HA6 ....171 J4
Hillside Junior School
HHW HP1 ....4 C5
Hitchin Boys School
HTCH/STOT SG5 ....35 K8
The Hitchin Business Centre
HTCHE/RSTV SG4 ....35 M4
Hitchin Cemetery
HTCHE/RSTV SG4 ....49 L1
Hitchin CC
HTCH/STOT SG5 ....35 H9
Hitchin Girls School
HTCHE/RSTV SG4 ....35 L9
Hitchin Road Industrial &
Business Centre
ARL/CHE SG15 ....24 D6
Hitchin Swimming Pool
HTCH/STOT SG5 ....35 K8
HM Prison
HHS/BOV HP3 ....132 C5
Hobbs Hill Wood
Primary School
HHS/BOV HP3 ....134 C1
Hobletts Manor
Junior School
HHNE HP2 ....118 B7
Hockerill Anglo European
College
BSF CM23 ....74 B3
Hockerill Sports Club
BSF CM23 ....74 C5
Hoddesdon Health Centre
HOD EN11 ....126 F6
Hoddesdon
Industrial Estate
HOD EN11 ....127 H4
Hoddesdon
Lawn Tennis Club
HOD EN11 ....126 D5
Holdbrook Primary School
CHES/WCR EN8 ....156 C4
Holiday Inn
BORE WD6 ....165 L2
STALW/RED AL3 ....80 B9
Holland House School
EDGW HA8 ....173 N1
Hollies Way Industrial Estate
POTB/CUF EN6 ....153 L1
Hollybush Primary School
HERT/WAT SG14 ....107 H6
Holly Industrial Park
WATN WD24 ....149 K9
Holly Street Trading Estate
LTN LU1 ....6 E6
Hollywood Bowl
STVG SG1 ....10 A6
Holmshill School
BORE WD6 ....165 J1
Holtmere End
Junior School
HHNE HP2 ....118 C3
Holwell J & I School
WGCE AL7 ....105 H7
Holy Cross Catholic
Primary School
HLWS CM18 ....129 K5
Holy Rood Catholic
Primary School
WATN WD24 ....148 E6
Holy Trinity CE
Primary School
NTHWD HA6 ....170 E5
Holy Trinity Primary School
CHES/WCR EN8 ....156 C2

Holywell School
WATW WD18 ....162 B5
Home Farm
Industrial Estate
WARE SG12 ....109 L7
Home Park Industrial Estate
KGLGY WD4 ....148 C1
Homerswood J & I School
WGCW AL8 ....104 C2
Honeypot Business Centre
STAN HA7 ....173 L5
Honeypot Lane Centre
STAN HA7 ....173 K5
Honeypot Medical Centre
STAN HA7 ....173 L6
Honlands Primary School
EN EN1 ....156 A6
Hormead Primary School
BUNT SG9 ....41 L8
Horseshoe Business Park
LCOL/BKTW AL2 ....136 A9
Hotel Ibis
LTNE LU2 ....63 K7
STVG SG1 ....10 C4
Hotel St Lawrence
....6 E4
Hot Shots Ten Pin Bowling
HHNE HP2 ....5 K4
Houghton Regis
Health Centre
DUN/HR/TOD LU5 ....60 E1
Houghton Regis
Lower School
DUN/HR/TOD LU5 ....60 D2
Houghton Regis
Medical Centre
DUN/HR/TOD LU5 ....60 F1
Houghton Regis
Trading Centre
DUN/HR/TOD LU5 ....60 E2
House on the Hill Museum
Adventure
STSD SG24 ....58 G4
Howard Business Park
WAB EN9 ....157 J4
The Howard Centre
WGCW AL8 ....104 C4
Howard Industrial Estate
CSHM HP5 ....131 K4
Howe Dell Primary School
HAT AL10 ....122 C6
Howe Green House School
RBSF CM22 ....74 E8
How Wood Primary School
LCOL/BKTW AL2 ....136 B6
HSBC Group Management
Training College
LCOL/BKTW AL2 ....150 A1
Hunsdon Primary School
WARE SG12 ....110 A3
Hurst Drive Primary School
CHES/WCR EN8 ....156 B4
Hyatt Trading Estate
STVG SG1 ....66 D1
Hyde Heath Infant School
AMS HP6 ....144 B4
Icknield First School
ROY SG8 ....20 D3
Icknield High School
LTNN/LIM LU3 ....62 D1
Icknield Infant School
LWTH SG6 ....36 A2
Icknield Primary School
LTNN/LIM LU3 ....62 C1
Icknield Way
Industrial Estate
TRING HP23 ....95 M8
Immanuel College
BUSH WD23 ....163 N6
Innellan House School
PIN HA5 ....171 N7
Innkeeper's Lodge
BORE WD6 ....165 J1
LCOL/BKTW AL2 ....137 K6
RAYLNE/WEN HP22 ....112 A1
Innova Business Park
PEND EN3 ....156 E6
International University
BUSH WD23 ....163 H3
Ivinghoe Business Centre
DUN/HR/TOD LU5 ....60 E3
Jerounds Junior School
HLWW/ROY CM19 ....128 E6
John Colet School
WARE SG12 ....110 B1
John Dony Field Centre
LTNE LU2 ....46 F9
John F Kennedy RC School
HHW HP1 ....117 J7
The John Hampden
Wendover School
RAYLNE/WEN HP22 ....112 C4
John Henry Newman
RC School
STVG SG1 ....50 K6
John Penrose School
DEN/HRF UB9 ....169 P5
John Penrose
Sports Centre
DEN/HRF UB9 ....169 P5
The John Warner School
HOD EN11 ....126 G2
Jubilee Centre
STALW/RED AL3 ....9 F2
Jubilee Trading Estate
LWTH SG6 ....36 F1
The Junior School
BSF CM23 ....73 N7
Jupiter Drive JMI School
HHNE HP2 ....118 A4
Katherines Primary School
HLWW/ROY CM19 ....128 C5
Keats House Health Centre
HLWS CM18 ....129 J6
Kenilworth Primary School
BORE WD6 ....165 K2
Kenmore Park First School
KTN/HRWW/WS HA3 ....173 K3

Kensworth Lower School
DUN/WHIP LU6 .... 79 J5
Kenton CC
KTN/HRWW/WS HA3 ... 173 J8
Kenton Clinic
KTN/HRWW/WS HA3 ... 173 L9
Keys Meadow
Primary School
PEND EN3 .... 156 E6
Killigrew Infant School
LCOL/BKTW AL2 .... 136 A4
Kimpton JMI School
HTCHE/RSTV SG4 .... 83 H4
Kinetic Business Centre
BORE WD6 .... 164 F2
King Harold School
WAB EN9 .... 157 K3
Kingsbury Green
Primary School
CDALE/KGS NW9 .... 173 P9
Kingsbury High School
CDALE/KGS NW9 .... 173 P8
Kingsbury Junior School
CDALE/KGS NW9 .... 173 N8
Kingsbury Watermill
Museum & Waffle House
STALW/RED AL3 .... 8 A2
Kingscote
Pre Preparatory School
CFSP/GDCR SL9 .... 162 C7
Kingshill Primary School
WARE SG12 .... 108 C1
Kingshott School
HTCHE/RSTV SG4 .... 49 N2
Kings Houghton
Middle School
DUN/HR/TOD LU5 .... 44 G8
Kings Langley
Primary School
KGLGY WD4 .... 134 A7
Kings Langley School
KGLGY WD4 .... 133 P8
Kingsmoor Primary School
HLWW/ROY CM19 .... 128 F7
Kingsmoor
Recreation Centre
HLWW/ROY CM19 .... 128 E7
The Kings Oak
Private Hospital
ENC/FH EN2 .... 155 H8
Kings Park Industrial Estate
WATW WD4 .... 134 C8
The Kings School
HARP AL5 .... 81 N9
Kingsway Industrial Estate
LTN LU1 .... 62 B6
Kingsway Infant School
GSTN WD25 .... 149 H4
Kingsway Junior School
GSTN WD25 .... 149 H4
Knebworth Golf Club
KNEB SG3 .... 67 J8
Knebworth House,
Gardens & Country Park
KNEB SG3 .... 66 E8
Knebworth
Physiotherapy Clinic
STVGE SG2 .... 67 M7
Knightsfield School
WGCW AL8 .... 104 F1
Knights Templar School
BLDK SG7 .... 26 A3
Knutsford School
WATN WD24 .... 149 L8
Ladbrooke Primary School
POTB/CUF EN6 .... 153 L2
Lady Zia Werner School
LTNE LU2 .... 63 J3
Lahama Trading Estate
WATN WD24 .... 149 K8
Laings Sports Ground
BAR EN5 .... 165 L3
Lakeside Special School
WGCW AL8 .... 104 L8
Lancaster Road
Industrial Estate
EBAR EN4 .... 167 H4
Lancot Lower School
DUN/WHIP LU6 .... 60 B6
Langley Terrace
Industrial Park
LTN LU1 .... 7 F7
Lannock Primary School
LWTH SG6 .... 36 F4
Lark Rise Lower School
DUN/WHIP LU6 .... 60 E8
Larwood School
STVG SG1 .... 11 G1
Latton Bush
Business Centre
HLWS CM18 .... 129 J6
Laurance Haines School
WATW WD18 .... 162 C5
Lavender Primary School
ENC/FH EN2 .... 155 L8
Lawrence Industrial Estate
DUN/WHIP LU6 .... 60 C4
Layston First School
BUNT SG9 .... 40 E8
Leagrave Health Centre
LTNW/LEA LU4 .... 61 M2
Leagrave J & I School
LTNW/LEA LU4 .... 61 M2
Leah Manning Centre
HLW CM20 .... 3 F2
Lea Industrial Estate
HARP AL5 .... 82 B9
Lealands High School
LTNN/LIM LU3 .... 45 M7
Lea Manor
Recreation Centre
LTNN/LIM LU3 .... 46 A7
Lea Manor
Recreation Centre
LTNN/LIM LU3 .... 45 M7
The Lea Primary School
HARP AL5 .... 81 P9
Lea Road Industrial Park
CHES/WCR EN8 .... 156 F4
Lea Valley High School
EN EN1 .... 156 B5

Leavesden Green JMI School
GSTN WD25 .... 149 H4
Leavesden Hospital
ABLGY WD5 .... 149 H1
Lee Valley Caravan Park
HOD EN11 .... 127 H7
Lee Valley Park
WAB EN9 .... 142 C2
Lee Valley Park Farms
WAB EN9 .... 143 H7
Letchmore Infant School
STVG SG1 .... 50 C8
Letchworth Business Centre
LWTH SG6 .... 36 F2
Letchworth Garden City FC
LWTH SG6 .... 36 F3
Letchworth Golf Club
LWTH SG6 .... 36 C6
Letchworth Icknield
Cemetery
LWTH SG6 .... 35 P2
Letchworth Museum &
Art Gallery
LWTH SG6 .... 36 C3
Letchworth Swimming Pool
LWTH SG6 .... 36 D1
The Leventhorpe School
SBW CM21 .... 91 P9
Leverstock Green JMI School
HHNE HP2 .... 118 E3
Leverstock Green
Lawn Tennis Club
HHS/BOV HP3 .... 134 C1
The Leverton Infant School
WAB EN9 .... 157 L4
The Leverton Junior School
WAB EN9 .... 157 L4
Lewsey Farm Clinic
LTNW/LEA LU4 .... 61 J2
Ley Hill CC
CSHM HP5 .... 145 P1
Ley Hill School
CSHM HP5 .... 131 N9
Ley Park Primary School
BROX EN10 .... 142 E1
Leys Primary School
STVG SG1 .... 51 K5
The Library Theatre
LTN LU1 .... 6 D4
Lime Walk JMI School
HHNE HP2 .... 5 J5
Links Business Centre
BSF CM23 .... 74 D3
Lismarrine Industrial Park
BORE WD6 .... 164 B5
Lister Hospital
STVG SG1 .... 50 E5
Lister House Surgery
HAT AL10 .... 122 D5
Lister Medical Centre
HLWW/ROY CM19 .... 128 F6
Little Chalfont Golf Club
AMS HP6 .... 159 L1
Little Chalfont
Primary School
AMS HP6 .... 146 B9
Little Gaddesden CE
Primary School
BERK HP4 .... 97 P4
Little Green Junior School
RKW/CH/CXG WD3 ...... 161 L2
Little Hadham
Primary School
STDN SG11 .... 72 F4
Little Hallingbury CE
Primary School
RBSF CM22 .... 92 D1
Little Hay Golf Complex
HHS/BOV HP3 .... 132 F3
Little Heath Primary School
POTB/CUF EN6 .... 139 M9
Little Munden CE
Primary School
WARE SG12 .... 69 M6
Little Parndon
Primary School
HLW CM20 .... 2 B3
Little Reddings
Primary School
BUSH WD23 .... 163 K4
Little St Helens School
NTHWD HA6 .... 170 G3
Little Spring Primary School
CSHM HP5 .... 130 G7
Little Stanmore First &
Middle School
EDGW HA8 .... 173 L5
The Little Theatre
DUN/WHIP LU6 .... 60 F6
Liverpool Road
Health Centre
LTN LU1 .... 6 C4
Livingstone Primary School
EBAR EN4 .... 167 H2
Lochinver House School
POTB/CUF EN6 .... 139 L9
Lockers Park School
HHW HP1 .... 4 B1
Lodge Clinic
LTN LU1 .... 6 E5
Lodge Farm Primary School
STVG SG1 .... 51 M8
Lodge Sun Sports Club
WAT WD17 .... 148 F9
London Academy
EDGW HA8 .... 173 M1
London Colney JMI School
LCOL/BKTW AL2 .... 137 J4
London Colney
Nature Reserve
LCOL/BKTW AL2 .... 137 K7
London School
of Theology
NTHWD HA6 .... 170 F3
Longdean School
HHS/BOV HP3 .... 134 C2
Long Island Hotel
RKW/CH/CXG WD3 ...... 161 H6
Longlands Primary School
BROX EN10 .... 142 D4

Long Marston JMI School
TRING HP23 .... 77 J9
Longmeadow
Primary School
STVGE SG2 .... 67 L5
Longwood School
BUSH WD23 .... 162 G3
Lonsdale School
STVG SG1 .... 11 H1
Lordship Farm School
LWTH SG6 .... 36 D5
Loreto College
STAL AL1 .... 11 H3
Lovewood Museum
HOD EN11 .... 126 F6
Lowfield Sports Ground
HOD EN11 .... 126 E5
Luton Airport
LTNE LU2 .... 63 L7
Luton Church Cemetery
LTNE LU2 .... 7 J5
Luton Co-operative
Sports Club
LTNE LU2 .... 62 G4
Luton & Dunstable
Education Centre
LTNW/LEA LU4 .... 61 L4
Luton Hoo Hotel
LTN LU1 .... 81 H3
Luton Retail Park
LTN LU1 .... 7 J7
Luton Sixth Form College
LTNE LU2 .... 80 D2
Luton Town FC
(Kenilworth Road)
LTN LU1 .... 62 C6
Lyndhurst Middle School
LTNE LU2 .... 151 L9
Lyonsdown School
BAR EN5 .... 166 G4
Macintyre School
RAYLNE/WEN HP22 .... 76 D2
Madison Bowl
NTHWD HA6 .... 170 G4
Madrassa Islamic School
BAR EN5 .... 6 A1
Maidenhill Junior School
LTNW/LEA LU4 .... 62 B4
Maltings Arts Theatre
STAL AL1 .... 9 F4
The Maltings
Industrial Estate
SBW CM21 .... 92 A7
WARE SG12 .... 109 J8
The Maltings
Shopping Centre
STAL AL1 .... 8 E4
Maltmans Green School
CFSP/GDCR SL9 .... 168 A7
Malvern Way
Infant School
RKW/CH/CXG WD3 ...... 161 N4
Mandeville Health Centre
STAL AL1 .... 136 C2
Mandeville Primary School
SBW CM21 .... 111 N1
STAL AL1 .... 136 C2
Manland Primary School
HARP AL5 .... 102 A1
Manor Farm Business Park
HTCH/STOT SG5 .... 33 H2
Manor Fields
Primary School
BSF CM23 .... 73 N9
Manor Lodge School
RAD WD7 .... 137 P9
Manor of Groves Golf Club
SBW CM21 .... 111 J2
Manor of Groves Hotel
SBW CM21 .... 111 J2
Manor Place
Industrial Estate
BORE WD6 .... 165 J2
Manshead CE School
DUN/WHIP LU6 .... 61 J9
Manuden Primary School
BSF CM23 .... 58 B2
Maple Cross
Industrial Estate
RKW/CH/CXG WD3 ...... 169 J1
Maple Cross JMI School
RKW/CH/CXG WD3 ...... 169 H2
Maple Primary School
STAL AL1 .... 9 G2
Maple River
Industrial Estate
HLW CM20 .... 111 L6
Margaret Wix JMI School
STALW/RED AL3 .... 120 B4
Mark Hall Community
School & Sports College
HLWE CM17 .... 111 M9
Mark Hall Cycle Museum
HLW CM20 .... 111 L9
Markyate Village School
STALW/RED AL3 .... 79 N7
Marlborough First &
Middle School
HRW HA1 .... 172 E8
Marlborough School
STAL AL1 .... 136 B2
Marlin Montessori School
BERK HP4 .... 115 N7
Marlowes Health Centre
HHNE HP2 .... 4 D1
Marlowes Shopping Centre
HHNE HP2 .... 4 E3
Marquis Business Centre
BLDK SG7 .... 26 C8
Marriott Hanbury Manor
Hotel & Country Club
WARE SG12 .... 88 B3
Marriotts School
STVGE SG2 .... 11 K3
Marshgate Trading Estate
HERT/BAY SG13 .... 107 M5
Marsworth CE Infant School
TRING HP23 .... 95 P2

Martindale JMI School
HHW HP1 .... 117 J7
Martinfield Business Centre
WGCE AL7 .... 105 J5
Martins Wood
Primary School
STVG SG1 .... 51 L6
Mary Exton
Primary School
HTCHE/RSTV SG4 .... 35 P9
Marymead
Industrial Estate
STVGE SG2 .... 67 L6
Maunds Wood CP School
HLWS CM18 .... 128 C7
Mayfield Infant School
CHES/WCR EN8 .... 142 D6
Mayfield School
PIN HA5 .... 171 N7
The Mead Business Centre
HERT/BAY SG13 .... 107 M5
Mead Industrial Park
HLW CM20 .... 111 J8
Meadow Wood School
BUSH WD23 .... 163 L4
The Mead School
HLWS CM18 .... 129 H5
The Meads Primary School
LTNN/LIM LU3 .... 46 A9
Mentmore Golf &
Country Club
LBUZ LU7 .... 77 K3
Mercers College
WARE SG12 .... 108 D3
Merchant Taylors School
NTHWD HA6 .... 162 A7
The Meridian School
ROY SG8 .... 20 E2
Merry Hill Infant School
BUSH WD23 .... 163 K6
Meryfield Primary School
BORE WD6 .... 151 L9
Metropolis Centre
BORE WD6 .... 164 C2
Metropolitan Police
Bushey Sports Ground
BUSH WD23 .... 163 J2
Micklem JMI School
HHW HP1 .... 117 J7
Middlesex School of
Comp Medicine
STAN HA7 .... 173 L5
Middlesex University
EBAR EN4 .... 167 L5
STHGT/OAK N14 .... 167 N3
Middlesex University
(Trent Park Campus)
EBAR EN4 .... 167 N1
Middleton Special School
WARE SG12 .... 108 C5
Mid Herts Golf Club
STALE/WH AL4 .... 83 H9
Millbrook School
CHES/WCR EN8 .... 142 D8
Millfield First School
BUNT SG9 .... 40 D9
Mill Green Golf Club
WGCE AL7 .... 123 J2
Mill Green County High School
MLHL NW7 .... 165 L6
The Mill Hill CC
MLHL NW7 .... 166 A9
Mill Hill Golf Club
MLHL NW7 .... 165 L8
Mill Mead J & I School
HERT/WAT SG14 .... 107 K6
Mill Studio Business Centre
WARE SG12 .... 108 D3
Mill Vale Middle School
DUN/HR/TOD LU5 .... 61 H4
Milton's Cottage
CSTG HP8 .... 159 H9
Monkfrith Primary School
EBAR EN4 .... 167 L6
Monksmead School
BORE WD6 .... 165 J2
Monks Walk School
WGCW AL8 .... 104 F1
Monkswood Retail Park
STVG SG1 .... 66 G3
Monro Industrial Estate
CHES/WCR EN8 .... 156 D4
Moorlands School
LTNW/LEA LU4 .... 61 M3
Moor Park Golf Club
RKW/CH/CXG WD3 ...... 161 M9
Moor Park Industrial Estate
WATW WD18 .... 161 N6
Moreton Park
Industrial Estate
LTNE LU2 .... 63 H4
Morgans JMI School
HERT/BAY SG13 .... 107 L8
Moss Bury JMI School
STVG SG1 .... 51 K8
Mountfitchet Castle
Experience
STSD CM24 .... 58 G5
The Mountfitchet
High School
STSD CM24 .... 58 G7
Mount Grace School
POTB/CUF EN6 .... 139 L9
Mount Pleasant Lane
J & I School
BRKMPK AL9 .... 149 M8
Mount Vernon Hospital
NTHWD HA6 .... 170 D2
Mowat Industrial Estate
WATN WD24 .... 149 K8
MS Business Centre
PIN HA5 .... 171 N7
MSF Whitehall College
BSF CM23 .... 73 P5
Museum of Domestic
Design & Architecture
EBAR EN4 .... 167 L4

Nascot Wood Infant School
WAT WD17 .... 149 H8
Nash Mills Primary School
HHS/BOV HP3 .... 134 A4
Natural Art Gallery & Science
Pictures
HTCH/STOT SG5 .... 49 K1
The Natural History
Museum at Tring
TRING HP23 .... 95 P9
Nazeing CP School
WAB EN9 .... 143 K2
Nazeing Glass
Industrial Estate
BROX EN10 .... 127 H9
Nazeing Golf Club
WAB EN9 .... 143 P3
Nazeing Park School
WAB EN9 .... 143 P1
Newberries
Primary School
RAD WD7 .... 151 H5
New Cemetery
BSF CM23 .... 73 P8
New Elgiva Theatre
CSTG HP8 .... 144 C1
New England
Industrial Estate
HOD EN11 .... 127 H4
New River Trading Estate
CHES/WCR EN8 .... 142 C5
New Southgate Cemetery
FBAR/BDGN N11 .... 167 M9
New Southgate
Crematorium
FBAR/BDGN N11 .... 167 M9
Newtown School
CSHM HP5 .... 131 H9
New Town Trading Estate
LTNE LU2 .... 62 F9
Nicholas Breakspear
RC School
STALE/WH AL4 .... 121 K9
Nobel School
STVGE SG2 .... 51 M8
Norbury First &
Middle School
HRW HA1 .... 172 E9
Norman Booth
Leisure Centre
HLWE CM17 .... 111 N9
Northaw Primary School
POTB/CUF EN6 .... 140 B8
Northchurch CE
BERK HP4 .... 115 J4
Northfields Infant School
STVGE SG2 .... 25 K8
The Northfields
Technology College
DUN/HR/TOD LU5 .... 60 D3
Northgate Primary School
BSF CM23 .... 73 P5
North Hertfordshire College
LWTH SG6 .... 36 C2
STVG SG1 .... 10 D7
North Hertfordshire College
(Hitchin Centre)
HTCHE/RSTV SG4 .... 35 N8
North Hertfordshire College
(Stevenage Centre)
STVG SG1 .... 10 D7
North Hertfordshire
College for the Arts
HTCHE/RSTV SG4 .... 35 P7
North Hertfordshire
Leisure Centre
LWTH SG6 .... 36 F2
North Hertfordshire
Secondary Centre
LWTH SG6 .... 36 A5
North Herts Music School
HTCHE/RSTV SG4 .... 35 M9
North London
Collegiate School
EDGW HA8 .... 173 L3
The North London Hospice
NFNCH/WDSPK N12 ..... 166 F9
North Luton
Industrial Estate
LTNW/LEA LU4 .... 45 L8
North Middlesex Golf Club
NFNCH/WDSPK N12 ..... 167 H9
North Mymms CC
BRKMPK AL9 .... 138 D5
North Orbital
Trading Estate
STAL AL1 .... 136 F3
North Watford Cemetery
GSTN WD25 .... 149 H5
North Watford Health Clinic
GSTN WD25 .... 149 L4
Northway School
MLHL NW7 .... 165 K8
North & West Essex Adult
Community College
HLW CM20 .... 2 D2
Northwood Cemetery
NTHWD HA6 .... 171 H4
Northwood College
NTHWD HA6 .... 170 F4
Northwood FC
NTHWD HA6 .... 171 H6
Northwood Golf Club
NTHWD HA6 .... 170 F4
Northwood & Pinner
Community Hospital
NTHWD HA6 .... 171 J5
Northwood
Preparatory School
RKW/CH/CXG WD3 ...... 161 N8
Northwood School
NTHWD HA6 .... 171 K5
Northwood Sports Centre
NTHWD HA6 .... 171 K5
Norton Park
Primary School
LTNN/LIM LU3 .... 62 A2
Norton St Nicholas
Primary School
LWTH SG6 .... 25 N8

Novotel
STVG SG1 .... 66 F5
Nower Hill High School
PIN HA5 .... 172 A8
Nup End Industrial Estate
KNEB SG3 .... 84 E1
Oakfield Business Corner
LWTH SG6 .... 36 D1
Oakland CP School
EBAR EN4 .... 167 K5
Oaklands College
BORE WD6 .... 165 J1
HARP AL5 .... 102 A3
HAT AL10 .... 122 D6
STAL AL1 .... 9 H3
STALE/WH AL4 .... 121 K7
WGCW AL8 .... 104 C5
Oaklands JMI School
WLYN AL6 .... 85 H6
Oakleigh School
TRDG/WHET N20 .... 167 J9
Oak Lodge Medical Centre
EDGW HA8 .... 173 P4
Oakmere Primary School
POTB/CUF EN6 .... 153 N2
The Oaks Industrial Estate
HLW CM20 .... 111 J9
Oak View Primary School
HAT AL10 .... 122 E7
Oakwood Estate
HLW CM20 .... 111 K8
Oakwood JMI School
STALE/WH AL4 .... 121 H7
Oakwood Medical Centre
STHGT/OAK N14 .... 167 N4
Oasis Academy
PEND EN3 .... 156 E7
Oasis Academy Enfield
PEND EN3 .... 156 E6
Odeon Cinema
BAR EN5 .... 166 E4
CFSP/GDCR SL9 .... 168 C9
HAT AL10 .... 122 C5
.... 5 J4
Odhams Industrial Estate
WATN WD24 .... 149 K7
Odhams Trading Estate
WATN WD24 .... 149 H6
Officers Lawn Tennis Club
RAYLNE/WEN HP22 .... 112 C2
Offley Cross
HTCH/STOT SG5 .... 48 G2
Offley Endowed
Primary School
HTCH/STOT SG5 .... 48 B4
Old Airfield
Industrial Estate
TRING HP23 .... 77 L8
Old Boys School
STDN SG11 .... 55 L8
Old Flour Mill Golf Club
BAR EN5 .... 153 H9
Old Harlow Health Centre
HLWE CM17 .... 111 M8
Old Lyonian Sports Ground
RYLN/HDSTN HA2 .... 172 C9
Old Merchant Taylors
Sports Club
RKW/CH/CXG WD3 .... 161 M3
Old Millhillians
Sports Ground
RYLN/HDSTN HA2 .... 172 K1
Old Oak Close
Industrial Estate
ARL/CHE SG15 .... 24 E1
Old Owens Sports Ground
TRDG/WHET N20 .... 167 H1
Old Palace Lodge
DUN/HR/TOD LU5 .... 60 F6
Old Verulamians RFC
LCOL/BKTW AL2 .... 137 H4
Onslow St Audreys
School
HAT AL10 .... 122 E6
Optima Business Park
HOD EN11 .... 127 H4
Orchard House
Industrial Estate
CSHM HP5 .... 145 H2
Orchard Primary School
WATN WD24 .... 148 C6
Orchard School
AMP/FLIT/BLC MK45 .... 32 D7
Osidge JMI School
STHGT/OAK N14 .... 167 N7
Oughtonhead Common
Nature Reserve
HTCH/STOT SG5 .... 34 G7
Oughton Primary School
HTCH/STOT SG5 .... 35 H7
Our Ladys Catholic
Primary School
AMS HP6 .... 144 C5
Our Ladys RC
Primary School
HTCH/STOT SG5 .... 35 K6
WCCE AL7 .... 105 H8
Oxen Industrial Estate
LTNE LU2 .... 7 H1
Oxhey Park Golf Centre
OXHEY WD19 .... 162 F7
Oxhey Wood
Primary School
OXHEY WD19 .... 171 L1
Paines Lane Cemetery
PIN HA5 .... 171 N7
Palace Theatre
WAT WD17 .... 13 F3
Panshanger Aerodrome
WCCE AL7 .... 105 P6
Panshanger Golf &
Squash Complex
WCCE AL7 .... 105 M4
Panshanger JMI School
WCCE AL7 .... 105 K5
Paradise Wildlife Park
BROX EN10 .... 125 N9
Paramount
Industrial Estate
WATN WD24 .... 149 K8

Park Avenue Clinic
WAT WD17 .... 12 D1
Park Avenue
Industrial Estate
LTNN/LIM LU3 .... 45 L8
Park Farm Industrial Estate
BUNT SG9 .... 40 C7
Parkfield Medical Centre
POTB/CUF EN6 .... 153 L2
Parkgate Infant School
WATN WD24 .... 149 K7
Parkgate Junior School
WATN WD24 .... 149 K7
Park High School
STAN HA7 .... 173 K6
Park Industrial Estate
LCOL/BKTW AL2 .... 136 D6
Parkside Primary School
BORE WD6 .... 151 L8
Park Street CE
Primary School
LCOL/BKTW AL2 .... 149 L1
Parmiters School
WATN WD25 .... 149 K1
Parndon Wood
HLWS CM18 .... 128 G9
Parndon Wood Cemetery
HLWW/ROY CM19 .... 128 F9
Parndon Wood
Crematorium
HLWW/ROY CM19 .... 128 F9
Parsonage Farm
Industrial Estate
STSD CM24 .... 58 G8
Passmores School &
Technology College
HLWS CM18 .... 128 C5
Pear Tree Mead
Primary School
HLWS CM18 .... 129 K6
Peartree Spring
Junior School
STVGE SG2 .... 67 L3
Peerglow Industrial Estate
WATW WD18 .... 161 M6
Pendley Manor Hotel
TRING HP23 .... 96 D8
Peterborough &
St Margaret's School
STAN HA7 .... 163 N9
Petersword Infant School
HLWS CM18 .... 128 C7
Phoenix Business Centre
CSHM HP5 .... 130 C9
Phoenix Industrial Estate
HRW HA1 .... 172 F8
Pinehill Hospital
HTCHE/RSTV SG4 .... 35 M7
Pinewood Special School
WARE SG12 .... 108 C5
Pin Green Industrial Estate
STVG SG1 .... 51 L5
Pinner Hill Golf Club
PIN HA5 .... 171 K3
Pinner Medical Centre
PIN HA5 .... 171 N8
Pinner Park
Primary School
PIN HA5 .... 172 B7
Pinner View Medical Centre
HRW HA1 .... 172 C9
Pinner Wood School
PIN HA5 .... 171 L5
Pirton Cross
HTCH/STOT SG5 .... 34 F9
Pirton Hill Infant School
LTNW/LEA LU4 .... 45 L9
Pirton Primary School
HTCH/STOT SG5 .... 34 B4
Pitstone Green
Business Park
LBUZ LU7 .... 96 C2
Pixies Hill Primary School
HHW HP1 .... 117 J9
Pixmore Junior School
LWTH SG6 .... 36 D3
Playhouse Theatre
HLW CM20 .... 2 E5
Ponsbourne Park Hotel
HERT/BAY SG13 .... 140 F2
Ponsbourne St Marys
Primary School
HERT/BAY SG13 .... 140 F3
Ponsbourne Tunnel
HERT/BAY SG13 .... 125 H1
HERT/BAY SG13 .... 140 G3
Pope Paul RC
Primary School
POTB/CUF EN6 .... 153 J3
Porters Park Golf Club
RAD WD7 .... 151 H4
Portland Industrial Estate
ARL/CHE SG15 .... 24 D7
Potten End First School
BERK HP4 .... 116 E5
Potterells Medical Centre
BRKMPK AL9 .... 138 C4
Potters Bar CC
POTB/CUF EN6 .... 153 L2
Potters Bar FC
POTB/CUF EN6 .... 153 L2
Potters Bar Golf Club
POTB/CUF EN6 .... 153 K1
Potter Street
Primary School
HLWE CM17 .... 129 L5
Prae Wood Primary School
STALE/WH AL3 .... 119 P9
Premier Inn
BORE WD6 .... 165 K2
DUN/HR/TOD LU5 .... 61 K4
LTN LU1 .... 7 H1
STVG SG1 .... 50 E5
STVG SG1 .... 66 F3
Presdales School
WARE SG12 .... 108 C4
Preston Primary School
HTCHE/RSTV SG4 .... 49 J3
Priestmead Middle School
KTN/HRWW/WS HA3 .... 173 H7

Prince of Wales
Primary School
PEND EN3 .... 156 E7
Princess Alexandra Hospital
HLW CM20 .... 2 C4
The Princess Helena College
HTCHE/RSTV SG4 .... 49 K9
Priors Wood JMI School
WARE SG12 .... 108 F1
Priory Cinema
ROY SG8 .... 20 C4
Priory Middle School
DUN/WHIP LU6 .... 60 F6
Priory School
HTCH/STOT SG5 .... 35 K6
The Priory
HTCH/STOT SG5 .... 49 K1
Prospect Industrial Estate
CSHM HP5 .... 145 H2
Puller Memorial CE (VA)
Primary School
STDN SG11 .... 88 D3
Pump House Theatre
WAT WD17 .... 13 J6
Purford Green
Infant School
HLWS CM18 .... 129 K5
Purford Green
Junior School
HLWS CM18 .... 129 K4
Purwell Primary School
HTCHE/RSTV SG4 .... 35 P8
Putteridge High School
LTNE LU2 .... 63 K1
Putteridge J & I School
LTNE LU2 .... 63 K1
Putteridge
Recreation Centre
LTNE LU2 .... 63 K1
Quadrant Shopping Centre
DUN/WHIP LU6 .... 60 E5
Quality Hotel
STAL AL1 .... 136 E1
Queen Elizabeth II Hospital
WGCE AL7 .... 123 K1
Queen Elizabeth
Leisure Centre
BAR EN5 .... 166 D3
Queen Elizabeths
Boys School
BAR EN5 .... 166 B2
Queen Elizabeths
Girls School
BAR EN5 .... 166 D3
Queen Mother Theatre
HTCH/STOT SG5 .... 35 L9
Queensbury School
DUN/WHIP LU6 .... 60 D8
Queensgate Centre
HLW CM20 .... 111 H8
Queens School
HLW CM20 .... 163 H2
Queensway Health Centre
HAT AL10 .... 122 E5
Queenswell J & I School
TRDG/WHET N20 .... 167 H8
Queenswood School
BRKMPK AL9 .... 139 K7
Queen Victoria
Memorial Hospital
WLYN AL6 .... 84 D9
Rabia Boys School
LTNW/LEA LU4 .... 62 B5
Rabia Girls School
LTNW/LEA LU4 .... 62 B5
Radburn Primary School
LWTH SG6 .... 36 F3
Radisson SAS Hotel
STSD CM24 .... 59 P8
Radlett CC
RAD WD7 .... 150 G7
Radlett Lodge School
RAD WD7 .... 151 H2
Radlett
Preparatory School
RAD WD7 .... 151 H8
Ralph Sadleir
Middle School
STDN SG11 .... 71 K3
Ramada Hotel
GSTN WD25 .... 163 L2
HAT AL10 .... 122 B6
STALW/RED AL3 .... 101 N9
Ramridge Primary School
LTNE LU2 .... 63 J4
Ramsey Manor
Lower School
AMP/FLIT/BLC MK45 .... 32 E6
Rathbone School
LTN LU1 .... 6 D3
Ravensburgh Castle
HTCH/STOT SG5 .... 32 G8
Ravenscroft School
TRDG/WHET N20 .... 166 D6
Raynham Road
Industrial Estate
BSF CM23 .... 74 C2
Redbournbury Mill
STALW/RED AL3 .... 119 L1
Redbourn Golf Club
STALW/RED AL3 .... 101 J3
Redbourn Industrial Centre
STALW/RED AL3 .... 101 J7
Redbourn Infant School
STALW/RED AL3 .... 101 H6
Redbourn
Recreation Centre
STALW/RED AL3 .... 101 H5
Redcoats Farmhouse Hotel
HTCHE/RSTV SG4 .... 50 A5
Reddiford School
PIN HA5 .... 171 N8
Reddings Primary School
HHS/BOV HP3 .... 5 K6
Red Rose Trading Estate
EBAR EN4 .... 167 H4
Reed First School
ROY SG8 .... 29 L4
Reedings Junior School
SBW CM21 .... 111 P1

Richard Hale School
HERT/BAY SG13 .... 107 L7
Richard Whittington
Primary School
BSF CM23 .... 91 P1
Richmond Hill
Special School
LTNE LU2 .... 62 F4
Rickmansworth Park
RKW/CH/CXG WD3 .... 161 J6
Rickmansworth
PNEU School
RKW/CH/CXG WD3 .... 160 G5
Rickmansworth
Public Golf Club
RKW/CH/CXG WD3 .... 161 K8
Rickmansworth School
RKW/CH/CXG WD3 .... 161 K5
Rickmansworth
Sports Club
RKW/CH/CXG WD3 .... 161 J5
Ridlins Wood
Athletics Track
STVGE SG2 .... 67 N4
River Lee Country Park
WAB EN9 .... 142 G3
River Park Industrial Estate
BERK HP4 .... 115 M6
Riverside Business Park
STSD CM24 .... 58 F5
Riverside Industrial Estate
HARP AL5 .... 82 B9
LCOL/BKTW AL2 .... 137 K6
Riverside Shopping Centre
HHW HP1 .... 4 D4
Roaring Meg Retail Park
STVG SG1 .... 67 H3
Robertswood
Combined School
CFSP/GDCR SL9 .... 168 D4
Roebuck Hotel
WARE SG12 .... 108 B2
Roebuck Primary School
STVGE SG2 .... 67 J4
Roebuck Retail Park
STVG SG1 .... 67 H4
Roecroft Lower School
HTCH/STOT SG5 .... 25 L3
Roe Green Junior School
CDALE/KGS NW9 .... 173 P8
Roger Bannister
Sports Ground
KTN/HRWW/WS HA3 .... 172 C3
Roman Theatre of
Verulamium
STALW/RED AL3 .... 119 P8
Roman Way First School
ROY SG8 .... 20 B1
Rosary Priory High School
BUSH WD23 .... 163 N5
The Rose & Crown Hotel
TRING HP23 .... 96 A9
Rosedale Clinic
CHESW EN7 .... 141 P7
Roseland JMI School
HOD EN11 .... 126 E2
Rosh Pinah Primary School
EDGW HA8 .... 165 H8
Rossgate JMI School
HHW HP1 .... 117 K6
Rothesay Road Cemetery
LTN LU1 .... 6 B5
Round Diamond
Primary School
STVG SG1 .... 51 L4
Roundmoor Park School
HARP AL5 .... 101 M2
Roundwood
Primary School
HARP AL5 .... 101 M2
Rowans Primary School
WGCE AL7 .... 105 K3
Rowley Lane
Maccabi Sports Ground
BORE WD6 .... 165 L5
Royal Chace Hotel
ENC/FH EN2 .... 154 C8
Royal Gunpowder Mills
WAB EN9 .... 156 C2
Royal Masonic School
for Girls
RKW/CH/CXG WD3 .... 161 K4
Royal National
Orthopaedic Hospital
STAN HA7 .... 164 B7
Royal Veterinary College
BRKMPK AL9 .... 138 G7
Roydonbury
Industrial Estate
HLWW/ROY CM19 .... 128 C3
Roydon CP School
HLWW/ROY CM19 .... 127 N3
Royston Cemetery
ROY SG8 .... 20 C3
Royston & District Hospital
ROY SG8 .... 20 C5
Royston Golf Club
ROY SG8 .... 20 B4
Royston Health Centre
ROY SG8 .... 20 C4
Royston Museum
ROY SG8 .... 20 C4
Royston Swimming Pool
ROY SG8 .... 20 C4
Royston Town FC
ROY SG8 .... 20 D3
Rudolf Steiner School
KGLGY WD4 .... 133 P8
Ruislip Woods National
Nature Reserve
.... 170 E7
Russell Clinic
STALW/RED AL3 .... 8 E3
The Russell School
RKW/CH/CXG WD3 .... 159 P3
Russet House School
ENC/FH EN1 .... 156 A9
The Ryde Primary School
BRKMPK AL9 .... 122 F3

Rye House Stadium
HOD EN11 .... 127 J3
Rye Meads RSPB Reserve
HOD EN11 .... 127 J2
Rye Park Industrial Estate
HOD EN11 .... 127 H3
Sacred Heart
Language College
KTN/HRWW/WS HA3 .... 172 E6
Sacred Heart
Primary School
LTNE LU2 .... 63 H3
Sacred Heart RC JM School
TRDG/WHET N20 .... 167 J8
Sacred Heart RC
Primary School
OXHEY WD19 .... 163 H5
WARE SG12 .... 108 B3
Safari Cinema & Bingo
HRW HA1 .... 172 F9
Saffron Green
Primary School
BORE WD6 .... 165 K3
St Adrians RC
Primary School
STAL AL1 .... 136 B2
St Alban & St Stephen
Infant School
STAL AL1 .... 9 K5
St Alban & St Stephen
RC JM School
STAL AL1 .... 120 F8
St Albans City FC
STAL AL1 .... 9 J2
St Albans City Hospital
STALW/RED AL3 .... 120 B6
St Albans Girls School
STALW/RED AL3 .... 120 D4
St Albans High School
for Girls
STAL AL1 .... 9 C1
St Albans Lawn Tennis Club
STALE/WH AL4 .... 121 H6
St Albans Museum
STAL AL1 .... 9 C3
St Albans Musical Museum
LCOL/BKTW AL2 .... 136 A7
St Albans Music School
STALW/RED AL3 .... 120 C5
St Albans Organ Museum
STAL AL1 .... 120 C9
St Albans Primary School
.... 3 J1
St Albans Principal
Health Centre
STAL AL1 .... 9 G3
St Albans Retail Park
STAL AL1 .... 136 C1
St Albans School
STALW/RED AL3 .... 8 D4
St Albert the Great
RC Primary School
HHNE HP2 .... 118 B9
St Andrews CE JMI School
TRDG/WHET N20 .... 166 D8
St Andrews CE
Primary School
HTCHE/RSTV SG4 .... 35 M9
.... 90 C3
STHGT/OAK N14 .... 167 N6
St Andrews Primary School
WARE SG12 .... 109 J8
St Andrews School
RYLN/HDSTN HA2 .... 172 B9
St Anthonys RC
Primary School
WATW WD18 .... 162 A4
St Augustines RC
Primary School
HOD EN11 .... 126 C6
St Bartholomews
CE School
TRING HP23 .... 114 C2
St Bernadette RC
Primary School
LCOL/BKTW AL2 .... 137 J6
St Bernadettes RC Primary
KTN/HRWW/WS HA3 .... 173 M8
St Catherine of Sienna
RC Primary
GSTN WD25 .... 149 L2
St Catherines Hoddesdon
CE Primary School
HOD EN11 .... 126 C5
St Catherines
Primary School
WARE SG12 .... 108 A2
St Catherines RC School
BAR EN5 .... 166 D3
St Christopher School
LWTH SG6 .... 36 C5
St Christophers
Lower School
DUN/HR/TOD LU5 .... 61 J4
St Clement Danes School
RKW/CH/CXG WD3 .... 160 B1
St Clements Junior School
CHES/WCR EN8 .... 142 D6
St Columbas
Preparatory School
STALW/RED AL3 .... 8 B7
St Cross RC Primary School
HOD EN11 .... 126 F7
St Cuthbert Mayne
RC Primary School
HOD EN11 .... 117 L7
St Dominic RC
Primary School
HARP AL5 .... 102 A4
St Edmunds College &
St Hugh's Preparatory
School
STDN SG11 .... 70 F5
St Elizabeths Centre
MHAD SG10 .... 90 E7
St Francis College
LWTH SG6 .... 36 B3
St George of England
CP School
DUN/HR/TOD LU5 .... 44 C1

St Georges CE Infant School
AMSS HP7 .... 145 K8
St Georges Industrial Estate
AMSS HP7 .... 145 L8
St Georges School
DUN/HR/TOD LU5 .... 60 F6
St Georges School Technology College
BERK AL5 .... 102 A2
St Giles Primary School
POTB/CUF EN6 .... 152 D2
St Gregorys High School
KTN/HRWW/WS HA3 .... 173 K9
St Helens Primary School
STALE/WH AL4 .... 103 J4
St Helens School
NTHWD HA6 .... 170 C3
St Hildas School
BUSH WD23 .... 163 K6
St Ignatius College
ENC/FH EN2 .... 101 N2
St Ippolitts Cemetery
HTCHE/RSTV SG4 .... 49 N5
St Ippolyts Primary School
HTCHE/RSTV SG4 .... 49 N4
St James CE Primary School
HLWS CM18 .... 128 C7
St Joan of Arc RC School
RKW/CH/CXG WD3 .... 161 J6
St John Fisher RC First & Middle School
PIN HA5 .... 172 A8
St John Fisher RC Primary School
STALE/WH AL4 .... 121 H5
St Johns CE J & I (Mixed) School
WCCW AL8 .... 104 C7
St Johns CE Primary School
ENC/FH EN2 .... 155 J6
TRDG/WHET N20 .... 166 C8
WLYN AL6 .... 105 J2
St Johns Church of England School
STAN HA7 .... 172 G1
St Johns Infant School
RAD WD7 .... 150 E5
St Johns Preparatory School
POTB/CUF EN6 .... 153 P4
St Johns RC Primary School
BLDK SG7 .... 37 J1
RKW/CH/CXG WD3 .... 160 F7
St Johns School
NTHWD HA6 .... 171 K3
St Johns Senior School
ENC/FH EN2 .... 155 H9
St John the Baptist Primary School
WARE SG12 .... 108 F7
St Josephs CE Combined School
CFSP/GDCR SL9 .... 168 A7
St Josephs Infant School
HERT/WAT SG14 .... 62 B2
St Josephs in the Park
HERT/WAT SG14 .... 107 H8
St Joseph's Primary School
HERT/WAT SG14 .... 107 H5
St Josephs RC First & Middle School
KTN/HRWW/WS HA3 .... 172 G6
St Josephs RC JMI School
CHES/WCR EN8 .... 156 D3
St Josephs RC Primary School
BSF CM23 .... 73 N7
OXHEY WD19 .... 162 D9
St Lawrence CE School
WAB EN9 .... 157 L3
St Lukes Catholic Primary School
HLWW/ROY CM19 .... 128 F5
St Lukes Special School
STALW/RED AL3 .... 101 H6
St Margaret Clitherow RC Primary School
STVGE SG2 .... 67 J4
St Margaret of Scotland Infant School
LTN LU1 .... 62 C9
St Margaret of Scotland Junior School
LTN LU1 .... 62 B9
St Margarets School
BUSH WD23 .... 163 J6
St Marks West Essex Catholic School
HLWS CM18 .... 3 G7
St Marthas Junior School
BAR EN5 .... 166 C3
St Marthas Senior School
EBAR EN4 .... 153 K9
St Martin de Porres Primary School
LTNW/LEA LU4 .... 61 K2
St Marys Abbey
MLHL NW7 .... 165 N9
St Marys Catholic School
BSF CM23 .... 73 P7
St Marys CE Combined School
AMSS HP7 .... 144 G9
St Marys Cemetery
AMSS HP7 .... 158 B1
St Marys CE Primary School
EBAR EN4 .... 167 J5
RBSF CM22 .... 93 N3
STSD CM24 .... 58 F4
St Marys First School
BERK HP4 .... 115 K5
St Marys High School
EBAR EN4 .... 142 K9
St Marys Junior School
BLDK SG7 .... 37 K2
WARE SG12 .... 108 C1
St Marys Lower School
HTCH/STOT SG5 .... 25 L3
LTN LU1 .... 61 M1

St Marys Primary School
BRKMPK AL9 .... 138 E2
St Marys RC Primary School
ROY SG8 .... 20 C3
St Marys School
CFSP/GDCR SL9 .... 168 C8
St Matthews Infant School
LTNE LU2 .... 7 F1
St Meryl JMI School
OXHEY WD19 .... 162 G9
St Michaels CE Primary School
BSF CM23 .... 73 P7
ENC/FH EN2 .... 155 K9
St Michaels CE VA Primary School
STALW/RED AL3 .... 8 A3
St Michael's Manor Hotel
STALW/RED AL3 .... 8 B3
St Michaels Primary School
KNEB SG3 .... 85 K3
St Nicholas Health Centre
GSTN WD25 .... 149 K2
St Nicholas Primary School
HARP AL5 .... 101 P3
St Nicholas Recreation Centre
STVG SG1 .... 51 L4
St Nicholas School
BORE WD6 .... 164 E5
St Pauls CE Primary School
KGLGY WD4 .... 148 C4
St Pauls Primary School
KGLGY WD4 .... 147 K1
St Pauls RC Primary School
CHESW EN7 .... 142 A6
St Pauls Walden Primary School
HTCHE/RSTV SG4 .... 65 J7
St Peters JMI School
STAL AL1 .... 9 G6
St Peters Primary School
RKW/CH/CXG WD3 .... 160 F7
St Philip Howard Catholic Primary School
HAT AL10 .... 122 E6
St Roses RC Infant School
HHW HP1 .... 133 K1
St Teresa RC First & Middle School
KTN/HRWW/WS HA3 .... 172 C5
St Teresa's RC Primary School
BORE WD6 .... 165 H1
St Thomas More RC Primary School
BERK HP4 .... 115 M7
LWTH SG6 .... 36 A4
St Thomas of Canterbury RC Primary School
STDN SG11 .... 71 H3
St Vincent de Paul RC JMI School
STVG SG1 .... 11 J3
St Vincents Hospital
HARP AL5 .... 170 C7
St Vincents Lower School
DUN/HR/TOD LU5 .... 60 F1
Salcombe Preparatory School (Infants)
STHGT/OAK N14 .... 167 M5
Salcombe Preparatory School (Juniors)
STHGT/OAK N14 .... 167 N6
Salisbury Infant School
HAT AL10 .... 122 E4
Salisbury Lawn Tennis Club
STAL AL1 .... 120 C7
Salvatorian College
KTN/HRWW/WS HA3 .... 172 D6
Samuel Lucas Primary School
HTCH/STOT SG5 .... 35 J9
Sandon JMI School
BUNT SG9 .... 28 B8
Sandown Road Industrial Estate
WATN WD24 .... 149 K7
Sandridge Gate Business Centre
STALE/WH AL4 .... 120 E4
Sandridge School
STALE/WH AL4 .... 121 J1
Sandridge Youth Club & Sports Centre
STALW/RED AL3 .... 120 G2
Sandringham School
STALE/WH AL4 .... 120 G4
Sandy Lodge Golf Club
NTHWD HA6 .... 161 P8
Saracen Industrial Area
HHNE HP2 .... 118 B6
Sarbir Industrial Park
HLW CM20 .... 111 M7
Sarratt School
RKW/CH/CXG WD3 .... 147 K6
Sauncey Wood Primary School
HARP AL5 .... 82 C9
Sawbridge Health Clinic
SBW CM21 .... 111 P2
Sawexey Business Centre
CSHM HP5 .... 130 D7
Sceptre School
LTNW/LEA LU4 .... 45 L9
Scott's Grotto
WARE SG12 .... 78 N1
Sebright School
STALW/RED AL3 .... 79 N9
The Sele School
HERT/WAT SG14 .... 106 G6
Shaftesbury High School
KTN/HRWW/WS HA3 .... 172 B5
Shaftesbury Industrial Centre
LWTH SG6 .... 36 E1

Shakespeare Industrial Estate
WATN WD24 .... 149 H8
Sharp Sports Centre
EDGW HA8 .... 173 N3
Shaw's Corner (NT)
WLYN AL6 .... 83 M7
Sheepcot Medical Centre
GSTN WD25 .... 149 K4
Sheering CE Primary School
RBSF CM22 .... 92 E8
Shendish Manor Golf Club
HHS/BOV HP3 .... 133 N5
Shenley Primary School
RAD WD7 .... 151 L4
Shenval Industrial Estate
HLW CM20 .... 111 K8
Shephalbury Park Primary School
STVGE SG2 .... 67 L5
Shepherd Primary School
RKW/CH/CXG WD3 .... 160 F7
Sheredes School
HOD EN11 .... 126 E6
Sherrardswood School
WLYN AL6 .... 84 G8
Shire Horse Centre
CSTG HP8 .... 159 N9
The Shire London
BAR EN5 .... 152 F8
Silkmead Farm Industrial Estate
BUNT SG9 .... 41 J5
Silk Mill House Museum
STALW/RED AL3 .... 101 H7
Simon Balle School
HERT/BAY SG13 .... 107 M7
Sir Frederic Osborn School
WGCE AL7 .... 105 L5
Sir James Altham Swimming Pool
OXHEY WD19 .... 171 N2
Sir John Lawes School
HARP AL5 .... 102 B1
Sir John Newsom School
WGCE AL7 .... 105 H8
Sir Thomas Lipton Memorial Hospital
STHGT/OAK N14 .... 167 N4
Skidmore Clinic
RKW/CH/CXG WD3 .... 161 J7
Skyswood School
STALE/WH AL4 .... 121 N5
Sleep inn Baldock
BLDK SG7 .... 25 P3
Slip End Lower School
LTN LU1 .... 80 C4
Smug Oak Green Business Centre
LCOL/BKTW AL2 .... 136 A8
Snap Theatre
BSF CM23 .... 74 A3
Someries Castle
LTNE LU2 .... 63 M9
Someries J & I School
LTNE LU2 .... 63 K3
Sopwell House Hotel Country Club & Spa
STAL AL1 .... 136 E3
South Bedfordshire Golf Club
LTNE LU2 .... 46 E5
Southdown Industrial Estate
HARP AL5 .... 102 B4
Southfield Infant School
LTNW/LEA LU4 .... 61 J2
Southgate Cemetery
STHGT/OAK N14 .... 167 N8
Southgate College
STHGT/OAK N14 .... 167 N8
Southgate Compton CC
EBAR EN4 .... 167 K3
Southgate Health Centre
STVG SG1 .... 10 C6
Southgate Leisure Centre
STHGT/OAK N14 .... 167 P6
Southgate School
EBAR EN4 .... 167 N4
South Herts Golf Club
TRDG/WHET N20 .... 166 E7
South Hill JMI School
HHW HP1 .... 4 C3
South Luton High School
LTN LU1 .... 62 C9
Southmill Trading Centre
BSF CM23 .... 74 B4
Spellbrook Primary School
BSF CM23 .... 92 A2
Sphere Industrial Estate
STAL AL1 .... 120 F9
The Spinney Infant School
HLW CM20 .... 129 K2
The Spinney Junior School
HLW CM20 .... 129 K2
The Spires Shopping Centre
BAR EN5 .... 166 C2
Springmead JMI School
WGCE AL7 .... 105 M5
Stadium Industrial Estate
LTNW/LEA LU4 .... 61 L4
Stag Lane First School
EDGW HA8 .... 173 N6
Stags School
STALW/RED AL3 .... 120 D4
Stanborough Primary School
GSTN WD25 .... 149 K5
Stanborough School
GSTN WD25 .... 149 J5
WGCW AL8 .... 104 E8
Stanburn First School
STAN HA7 .... 173 J4
Standon Business Park
STDN SG11 .... 71 K5
Standon Health Centre
STDN SG11 .... 71 K4
Stanley Hill Cemetery
AMSS HP7 .... 158 E1

Stanmore College
STAN HA7 .... 173 H3
Stanmore Golf Club
STAN HA7 .... 173 H4
Stanmore Road Health Centre
STVG SG1 .... 50 F8
Stansted Airport
STSD CM24 .... 59 P8
Stansted Clinic
STSD CM24 .... 58 F4
Stansted Mountfitchet Windmill
STSD CM24 .... 58 E5
Stapleford Primary School
HERT/WAT SG14 .... 87 H6
Staple Tye Shopping Centre
HLWS CM18 .... 128 G6
Steeple Morden CE Primary School
ROY SG8 .... 15 M9
Stevenage Arts & Leisure Centre
STVG SG1 .... 10 C5
Stevenage Borough FC
STVGE SG2 .... 67 H4
Stevenage Business Park
STVG SG1 .... 51 M5
Stevenage CC
STVG SG1 .... 2 C3
Stevenage Golf Centre
STVGE SG2 .... 67 P5
Stevenage Leisure Park
STVG SG1 .... 10 A6
Stevenage Museum
STVG SG1 .... 10 C5
Stevenage Register Office
STVG SG1 .... 10 C5
Stevenage St Nicholas CE Primary School
STVG SG1 .... 11 G6
Stevenage Swimming Centre
STVG SG1 .... 10 D4
Stewards School
HLWS CM18 .... 128 F7
Stirling Industrial Centre
BORE WD6 .... 165 K4
Stirling Retail Park
BORE WD6 .... 165 K5
Stocks Golf & Country Club
TRING HP23 .... 97 H5
Stockwell Lodge Medical Centre
CHESW EN7 .... 141 P6
Stockwood Craft Museum & Gardens
LTN LU1 .... 80 E1
Stockwood Park Athletic Track
LTN LU1 .... 80 E2
Stockwood Park Country Park
LTN LU1 .... 80 E2
Stockwood Park Golf Club
LTN LU1 .... 80 E1
Stonehill Primary School
LWTH SG6 .... 25 J8
Stony Dean Special School
AMSS HP7 .... 145 L9
Stopsley High School
LTNE LU2 .... 62 G2
Stopsley Primary School
LTNE LU2 .... 63 H2
Stopsley Sports Centre & Sports Ground
LTNE LU2 .... 63 H1
Stormont School
POTB/CUF EN6 .... 153 M1
Stortford Hall Industrial Park
BSF CM23 .... 74 C3
Stort Valley Industrial Estate
BSF CM23 .... 58 C9
Stotfold Cemetery
HTCH/STOT SG5 .... 25 M2
Stotfold Health Centre
HTCH/STOT SG5 .... 25 J3
Strathmore Infant School
HTCH/STOT SG5 .... 35 K5
Streetfield Middle School
DUN/HR/TOD LU5 .... 61 H8
Stroud Wood Business Centre
LCOL/BKTW AL2 .... 136 D6
Studham Lower School
DUN/WHIP LU6 .... 78 E9
Studlands Rise First School
ROY SG8 .... 20 D5
Summercroft Junior School
BSF CM23 .... 74 D2
Summerswood Primary School
BORE WD6 .... 165 H3
Sumners Community Recreation Centre
HLWW/ROY CM19 .... 128 D7
Sunderland Estate
KGLGY WD4 .... 134 C8
Sundon Business Park
LTNN/LIM LU3 .... 45 L7
Sundon Hills Country Park
LTNN/LIM LU3 .... 45 M1
Sundon Industrial Estate
LTNN/LIM LU3 .... 45 L7
Sundon Lower School
LTNN/LIM LU3 .... 45 L3
Sundon Medical Centre
LTNN/LIM LU3 .... 45 M8
Sundon Park Junior School
LTNN/LIM LU3 .... 45 L3
Sun Hotel
HTCH/STOT SG5 .... 49 K1
Sunshine House School
NTHWD HA6 .... 170 D4
Surrey Street Primary School
LTN LU1 .... 7 F7

Susi Earnshaw Theatre School
BAR EN5 .... 166 D2
Swallow Dell Primary School
WCCE AL7 .... 105 K7
Swing Gate First School
BERK HP4 .... 116 A8
The Symonds Green Health Centre
STVG SG1 .... 50 D8
Tabard RFC
RAD WD7 .... 150 G7
TA Centre
HLW CM20 .... 173 P4
HRW HA1 .... 172 F9
Tanners Wood Primary School
ABLGY WD5 .... 148 F2
Tannery Drift First School
ROY SG8 .... 20 B4
Tanys Dell Primary School
HLW CM20 .... 111 K9
Taylor Trading Estate
HERT/BAY SG13 .... 108 A5
Telmere Industrial Estate
LTN LU1 .... 7 F7
Templewood Primary School
WGCW AL8 .... 104 F4
Tenby Road Clinic
EDGW HA8 .... 173 M6
Tennyson Road Primary School
LTN LU1 .... 62 E9
Tewin Bury Farm Hotel
WLYN AL6 .... 105 M3
Tewin Cowper Primary School
WLYN AL6 .... 105 P2
Tewin Road Business Centre
WGCE AL7 .... 105 N5
Tewin Water School
WLYN AL6 .... 105 K2
Thames Industrial Estate
DUN/WHIP LU6 .... 60 F6
The Elms Football & Tennis Club
STAN HA7 .... 173 H2
Theobald Business Centre
HTCHE/RSTV SG4 .... 35 L5
Theobalds Park C&CC Site
CHESW EN7 .... 155 P4
Therfield First School
ROY SG8 .... 28 F2
Therfield Heath Nature Reserve
ROY SG8 .... 19 P6
Thistle Hotel
LCOL/BKTW AL2 .... 135 N6
Thomas Alleyne School
STVG SG1 .... 50 F7
The Thomas Coram Middle School
BERK HP4 .... 116 A9
Thomas Harding Junior School
CSHM HP5 .... 144 G2
The Thomas Rivers Medical Centre
SBW CM21 .... 111 M3
Thomas Whitehead CE School
DUN/HR/TOD LU5 .... 60 E1
Thorley Hill Primary School
BSF CM23 .... 74 A6
Thorn Grove Primary School
BSF CM23 .... 74 C4
Thornhill Lower School
DUN/HR/TOD LU5 .... 44 G8
Thorpe House School
CFSP/GDCR SL9 .... 168 C8
Thundridge Business Park
WARE SG12 .... 88 C3
Thundridge CE Primary School
WARE SG12 .... 88 C6
Timbers Clinic
KTN/HRWW/WS HA3 .... 172 C5
Tithe Farm Lower School
DUN/HR/TOD LU5 .... 44 G9
Toddington Health Clinic
DUN/HR/TOD LU5 .... 44 C1
Toddington Medical Centre
DUN/HR/TOD LU5 .... 44 D1
Tonwell St Marys Primary School
WARE SG12 .... 87 M6
Totteridge CC
TRDG/WHET N20 .... 166 E8
Townsend CE School
STALW/RED AL3 .... 120 B3
Townsend Industrial Estate
DUN/HR/TOD LU5 .... 60 E2
Travellers Lane Industrial Estate
HAT AL10 .... 138 C1
Travelodge
BLDK SG7 .... 16 D3
CHES/WCR EN8 .... 156 B3
DUN/HR/TOD LU5 .... 45 H1
HAT AL10 .... 122 C5
HHNE HP2 .... 4 E1
HLW CM20 .... 110 G9
WATW WD18 .... 13 F4
Tree Cathedral (NT)
DUN/WHIP LU6 .... 78 C4
Trent CE Primary School
EBAR EN4 .... 167 K3
Trent Country Park
EBAR EN4 .... 167 L1
Trent Park Cemetery
EBAR EN4 .... 167 L2
Trent Park Golf Club
STHGT/OAK N14 .... 167 N3
Tricor Business Park
CHES/WCR EN8 .... 156 D4
Tricor Trading Estate
CHES/WCR EN8 .... 156 D4

Trident Industrial Estate
HOD EN11 .... 127 H4
Tring Business Centre
TRING HP23 .... 95 M8
Tring Cemetery
TRING HP23 .... 95 M9
Tring Health Centre
TRING HP23 .... 96 A8
Tring Reservoirs National
Nature Reserve
TRING HP23 .... 95 N4
Tring School
TRING HP23 .... 96 A8
Tring Sports Centre
TRING HP23 .... 96 A8
Trotts Hill Primary School
STVG SG1 .... 51 J6
Troy Industrial Estate
HRW HA1 .... 172 F9
Trust Industrial Estate
HTCHE/RSTV SC4 .... 35 M5
Tudor Enterprise Park
KTN/HRWW/WS HA3 ...... 172 D7
Tudor Primary School
HHNE HP2 .... 5 G5
Turnford School
CHES/WCR EN8 .... 142 D7
The Two Brewers Hotel
KGLGY WD4 .... 147 K1
Two Waters JMI School
HHS/BOV HP3 .... 133 N4
Twyford Business Centre
BSF CM23 .... 74 B5
Underhill Infant School
BAR EN5 .... 166 C4
University of Bedfordshire
LTN LU1 .... 7 F5
LTNE LU2 .... 47 L9
University of Hertfordshire
HAT AL10 .... 122 D5
HERT/BAY SG13 .... 125 J2
STAL AL1 .... 9 J6
University of Hertfordshire
(College Lane Campus)
HAT AL10 .... 122 C8
University of Hertfordshire
(de Havilland Campus)
HAT AL10 .... 122 A6
University of Hertfordshire
Faculty of Law
STAL AL1 .... 9 G2
University of Hertfordshire
(Fielder Centre)
HAT AL10 .... 122 A3
University of London
ENC/FH EN2 .... 155 P6
Upshire Primary School
WAB EN9 .... 157 N3
Uxendon Manor JMI School
KTN/HRWW/WS HA3 ...... 173 L9
The Vale Cemetery
LTNE LU2 .... 47 J9
The Vale Crematorium
LTNE LU2 .... 47 J9
Vale Industrial Estate
WATW WD18 .... 161 N7
The Van Straten Clinic
LBUZ LU7 .... 77 P4
Verulam Golf Club
STAL AL1 .... 136 E1
Verulam Industrial Estate
STAL AL1 .... 9 J7
Verulamium Museum
STALW/RED AL3 .... 8 A3
Verulam School
STAL AL1 .... 120 F7
Vicarage Road Cemetery
WATW WD18 .... 12 D5
Victoria CE First School
BERK HP4 .... 115 P7
Victoria Square
Business Area
STAL AL1 .... 9 J5
Vita et Pax School
STHGT/OAK N14 .... 167 M4
Vue Cinema
GSTN WD25 .... 149 K3
Walkern Primary School
STVGE SG2 .... 52 C7
Walker Primary School
STHGT/OAK N14 .... 167 P8

Waltham Abbey Gatehouse,
Bridge & Entrance
to Cloisters
WAB EN9 .... 157 H3
Waltham Abbey
Marriott Hotel
WAB EN9 .... 157 L4
Waltham Abbey
Swimming Pool
WAB EN9 .... 157 J5
Waltham Holy Cross
Infant School
WAB EN9 .... 157 J3
Warden Hill Infant School
LTNN/LIM LU3 .... 46 D8
Warden Hill Junior School
LTNN/LIM LU3 .... 46 D8
Wardown House
(Luton Museum & Gallery)
LTNN/LIM LU3 .... 62 E3
Wardown Swimming &
Leisure Centre
LTNN/LIM LU3 .... 62 E4
Ware Cemetery
WARE SG12 .... 108 A1
Wareside Primary School
WARE SG12 .... 109 K1
Warren Dell Primary School
OXHEY WD19 .... 162 E9
Warrenwood
Industrial Estate
HERT/WAT SG14 .... 86 G7
Watchlytes School
WGCE AL7 .... 105 L6
Water Gardens
Shopping Centre
HLW CM20 .... 2 E5
Water Lane Primary School
HLWW/ROY CM19 .... 128 D7
Watermill Industrial Estate
BUNT SG9 .... 54 D1
Waterside
Combined School
CSHM HP5 .... 145 J3
Waterside Industrial Estate
HOD EN11 .... 127 J6
Waterside School
CSTM CM23 .... 57 P8
Watersmeet Centre
RKW/CH/CXG WD3 .... 161 J6
Waterways Business Centre
PEND EN3 .... 156 E8
Waterways
Heritage Museum
RKW/CH/CXG WD3 .... 161 J7
Watford Arches Retail Park
WAT WD17 .... 13 J7
Watford Business Centre
WAT WD17 .... 12 E2
Watford FC & Saracens RFC
(Vicarage Road Stadium)
WATW WD18 .... 12 E6
Watford General Hospital
WATW WD18 .... 12 E7
Watford Grammar School
for Boys
WATW WD18 .... 12 A4
Watford Grammar School
for Girls
WATW WD18 .... 13 G6
Watford Museum
WATW WD18 .... 13 H6
Watford Sports &
Leisure Centre
GSTN WD25 .... 149 K3
Watling Boys' Club
EDGW HA8 .... 173 N4
Watling Lower School
DUN/WHIP LU6 .... 60 E7
Watling View
Special School
STAL AL1 .... 136 C3
Watton-at-Stone
Primary School
HERT/WAT SG14 .... 86 E2
Waulud Primary School
LTNN/LIM LU3 .... 45 P8
Waverley Industrial Estate
HRW HA1 .... 172 D7
Weald Middle School
KTN/HRWW/WS HA3 ...... 172 F4

Weatherfield
Special School
DUN/WHIP LU6 .... 60 B5
Wedgewood Gate
Industrial Estate
STVG SG1 .... 51 L5
Welwyn Garden City CC
WGCW AL8 .... 104 G2
Welwyn Garden City
Football & Social Club
WGCE AL7 .... 105 L4
Welwyn Garden City
Golf Club
WGCW AL8 .... 104 E6
Welwyn RFC
WGCW AL8 .... 104 F7
Welwyn Roman Baths
WLYN AL6 .... 84 C9
Welwyn St Marys
Primary School
WLYN AL6 .... 84 E7
Welwyn Tennis Club
WLYN AL6 .... 84 E9
Welwyn Viaduct
WLYN AL6 .... 105 H2
Wendover CE
Junior School
RAYLNE/WEN HP22 .... 112 C6
Wendover Health Centre
RAYLNE/WEN HP22 .... 112 C6
Wendover House
Special School
RAYLNE/WEN HP22 .... 112 D8
Wendover Middle School
RAYLNE/WEN HP22 .... 112 C5
Wendover Tennis &
Squash Club
RAYLNE/WEN HP22 .... 112 C7
Wenlock Junior School
LTNE LU2 .... 63 J6
The Wenta
Business Centre
WATN WD24 .... 149 L7
Westbrook Hay
Preparatory School
HHW HP1 .... 132 G2
Westbury Primary School
LWTH SG6 .... 36 B3
Western House Hospital
WARE SG12 .... 108 C2
Westfield Cemetery
HARP AL5 .... 81 P9
Westfield Community
Primary School
HOD EN11 .... 126 E4
Westfield Community
Technology College
WATW WD18 .... 12 A7
Westfield First School
BERK HP4 .... 115 L6
Westgate Centre
STVG SG1 .... 10 C4
Westgate Shopping Centre
STVG SG1 .... 10 D4
West Grove Primary School
STHGT/OAK N14 .... 167 P6
West Herts
Business Centre
BORE WD6 .... 165 H2
West Herts Cemetery
GSTN WD25 .... 149 L1
West Herts College
(Cassio Campus)
WAT WD17 .... 149 H8
West Herts College
(Dacorum Campus)
HHNE HP2 .... 117 M7
West Herts College
(Leggatts Campus)
WATN WD24 .... 149 H6
West Herts College
(Watford Campus)
WAT WD17 .... 12 C1
West Herts Crematorium
GSTN WD25 .... 149 L1
West Herts Golf Club
RKW/CH/CXG WD3 .... 161 P2
West Lodge Middle School
PIN HA5 .... 171 M8
West Lodge Park Hotel
EBAR EN4 .... 154 A8

Westminster Lodge
Athletic Track
STALW/RED AL3 .... 8 B6
Westminster Lodge
Leisure Centre & Pool
STAL AL1 .... 8 D7
Weston Primary School
HTCHE/RSTV SC4 .... 37 M7
Weston Road Cemetery
STVG SG1 .... 51 H6
Westwood School
BUSH WD23 .... 163 M8
Wheatcroft School
HERT/BAY SG13 .... 107 P5
Wheatfields Junior School
STALE/WH AL4 .... 120 C4
Whelpley Hill Park
CSHM HP5 .... 132 A5
Whipperley Infant School
LTN LU1 .... 62 B8
Whipsnade Park Golf Club
BERK HP4 .... 78 B8
Whipsnade Wild
Animal Park
DUN/WHIP LU6 .... 78 C6
Whitchurch Middle School
STAN HA7 .... 173 J4
Whitefield Junior School
LTNN/LIM LU3 .... 45 P7
Whitefriars First &
Middle School
KTN/HRWW/WS HA3 ...... 172 E6
Whitefriars
Trading Estate
KTN/HRWW/WS HA3 ...... 172 D6
Whitehall Estate
HLWW/ROY CM19 .... 128 B4
White Hill
Community Centre
CSHM HP5 .... 145 H1
Whitehill Golf Club
WARE SG12 .... 69 P8
Whitehill Junior School
HTCHE/RSTV SC4 .... 49 M2
White Lion
DUN/HR/TOD LU5 .... 78 A6
White Lion Retail Park
DUN/HR/TOD LU5 .... 60 F5
Whiterose Trading Estate
EBAR EN4 .... 167 J6
The Whitewebbs Museum
of Transport & Industry
ENC/FH EN2 .... 155 J5
Whitewebbs Park Golf Club
ENC/FH EN2 .... 155 L7
Whitings Hill
Primary School
BAR EN5 .... 166 A4
Whittal Industrial Estate
STVG SG1 .... 10 A5
Widewater
Business Centre
DEN/HRF UB9 .... 169 N9
Widford J & I School
WARE SG12 .... 90 A9
Wigmore Primary School
LTNE LU2 .... 63 M4
Wilbury Junior School
LWTH SG6 .... 36 B2
William Austin
Infant School
LTNN/LIM LU3 .... 62 D2
William Austin
Junior School
LTNN/LIM LU3 .... 62 D2
William Ellis
Sports Ground
ENC/FH EN2 .... 173 N5
William Penn
Leisure Centre
RKW/CH/CXG WD3 .... 160 D7
William Ransom
JMI School
HTCHE/RSTV SC4 .... 35 N9
Willowfield Lower School
LTN LU1 .... 80 A1
Willowgate Trading Estate
LTNN/LIM LU3 .... 45 L7
Wilshere Dacre
Junior School
HTCH/STOT SG5 .... 35 K8

Wilstone Reservoir
Nature Reserve
TRING HP23 .... 95 L5
Windermere JMI
Primary School
STAL AL1 .... 136 C1
Windhill Primary School
BSF CM23 .... 73 P9
Windmill Trading Estate
LTN LU1 .... 7 J5
Windsor Industrial Estate
HERT/BAY SG13 .... 108 A4
Wingrave CE
Combined School
RAYLNE/WEN HP22 .... 76 B2
Wisteria House Clinic
WLYN AL6 .... 84 E7
Wodson Park Sport &
Recreation Centre
WARE SG12 .... 88 C9
Wolfson Hillel
Primary School
STHGT/OAK N14 .... 167 P5
Wolsey Business Park
WATW WD18 .... 161 P6
Woodcock Hill Cemetery
RKW/CH/CXG WD3 .... 169 P1
Wood End School
HARP AL5 .... 101 L1
Woodfield Special School
HHS/BOV HP3 .... 134 D1
Wood Green Animal Shelter
ROY SG8 .... 22 D7
Woodhall School
OXHEY WD19 .... 171 N1
Woodlands First &
Middle School
KTN/HRWW/WS HA3 ...... 172 C4
Woodlands
Primary School
BORE WD6 .... 151 M9
Woodlands
Secondary School
LTNN/LIM LU3 .... 46 A8
Woodridge Primary School
NFNCH/WDSPK N12 .... 166 E9
Woodside Clinic
DUN/HR/TOD LU5 .... 60 G6
Woodside Farm &
Wildfowl Park
STALW/RED AL3 .... 80 A5
Woodside Industrial Estate
DUN/HR/TOD LU5 .... 60 C3
Woodside Industrial Park
LTN LU1 .... 36 E1
Woodside Junior School
AMS HP6 .... 145 K8
Woodside Park
Industrial Estate
DUN/HR/TOD LU5 .... 60 F3
Woodside Stadium
CHESW EN7 .... 141 K8
Woodside Stadium
GSTN WD25 .... 149 K3
Woodwell Cemetery
GSTN WD25 .... 118 E7
Woolenwick Junior School
STVG SG1 .... 50 F9
Woolgrove School
LWTH SG6 .... 36 G3
Worcesters Primary School
ENC/FH EN2 .... 155 N8
Wormley Primary School
BROX EN10 .... 142 D2
The Wroxham School
POTB/CUF EN6 .... 152 F1
The Wyllyotts
Centre Cinema
POTB/CUF EN6 .... 153 J2
Wymondley
Primary School
HTCHE/RSTV SC4 .... 50 B3
Yavneh College
BORE WD6 .... 165 H3
Ye Olde Fighting Cocks Inn
STALW/RED AL3 .... 8 C5
Yorke Mead Primary School
RKW/CH/CXG WD3 .... 161 L4
York House School
RKW/CH/CXG WD3 .... 161 K1

Acknowledgements

Schools address data provided by Education Direct.

Petrol station information supplied by Johnsons.

Garden centre information provided by:

Garden Centre Association  Britains best garden centres

Wyevale Garden Centres

The statement on the front cover of this atlas is sourced, selected and quoted
from a reader comment and feedback form received in 2004

Speed camera locations

Speed camera locations provided in association with RoadPilot Ltd

RoadPilot is the developer of one of the largest and most accurate databases of speed camera locations in the UK and Europe. It has provided the speed camera information in this atlas. RoadPilot is the UK's pioneer and market leader in GPS (Global Positioning System) road safety technologies.

microGo (pictured right) is RoadPilot's latest in-car speed camera location system. It improves road safety by alerting you to the location of accident black spots,

fixed and mobile camera sites. RoadPilot's microGo does not jam police lasers and is therefore completely legal.

RoadPilot's database of fixed camera locations has been compiled with the full co-operation of regional police forces and the Safety Camera Partnerships.

For more information on RoadPilot's GPS road safety products, please visit **www.roadpilot.com** or telephone 0870 240 1701

GPS Antenna
microGo is directional, it only alerts you to cameras on your side of the road

Visual Countdown
To camera location

Your Speed
The speed you are travelling when approaching camera

Camera Types Located
Gatso, Specs, Truvelo, TSS/DSS, Traffipax, mobile camera sites, accident black spots, congestion charges, tolls

Voice Warnings
Only if you are exceeding the speed limit at the camera

Plug and Go
Easy to move from vehicle to vehicle

64 Colour Options
To match vehicle's illumination

Speed Limit at Camera
Screen turns red as additional visual alert

Single Button Operation
For easy access to speed display, camera warning, rescue me location, trip computer, congestion charge, max speed alarm, date and time

ALARM MODE

RoadPilot

SPEED READING